Veröffentlichungen des
Instituts für Europäische Geschichte Mainz

Abteilung für Abendländische Religionsgeschichte
Herausgegeben von Irene Dingel

Beiheft 143

Orthodoxy in the Agora

Orthodox Christian Political Theologies
Across History

Edited by
Mihai-D. Grigore and Vasilios N. Makrides

Vandenhoeck & Ruprecht

This publication was printed with support of
The Leibniz Open Access Monograph Publishing Fund.

The gender-related formulations used in the chapters
correspond to the preference of the respective authors.

Bibliographic information published by the Deutsche Nationalbibliothek:
The Deutsche Nationalbibliothek lists this publication
in the Deutsche Nationalbibliografie; detailed
bibliographic data available online: https://dnb.de.

© 2024 by Vandenhoeck & Ruprecht, Robert-Bosch-Breite 10, 37079 Göttingen, Germany,
an imprint of the Brill-Group (Koninklijke Brill NV, Leiden, The Netherlands;
Brill USA Inc., Boston MA, USA; Brill Asia Pte Ltd, Singapore;
Brill Deutschland GmbH, Paderborn, Germany; Brill Österreich GmbH, Vienna, Austria)
Koninklijke Brill NV incorporates the imprints Brill, Brill Nijhoff, Brill Schöningh,
Brill Fink, Brill mentis, Brill Wageningen Academic, Vandenhoeck & Ruprecht,
Böhlau and V&R unipress.

This publication is licensed under a Creative Commons Attribution – Non Commercial –
No Derivatives 4.0 International license, at https://doi.org/10.13109/9783666302565.
For a copy of this license go to https://creativecommons.org/licenses/by-nc-nd/4.0/.
Any use in cases other than those permitted by this license requires the
prior written permission from the publisher.

Cover image: Vladimir Putin during the Christmas Liturgy on January 6, 2018
in the Church of Symeon the God-Receiver and Anna the Prophetess, St Petersburg
(background: Archpriest Oleg Skoblya).
The cover image was subjected to critical discussion by the editors.
Image source: Leibniz ScienceCampus – Byzantium
between Orient and Occident – Mainz/Frankfurt

Cover design: SchwabScantechnik, Göttingen
Typesetting: le-tex publishing services, Leipzig

Vandenhoeck & Ruprecht Verlage | www.vandenhoeck-ruprecht-verlage.com

ISSN 0170-365X (print)
ISSN 2197-1056 (digital)

ISBN 978-3-525-30256-9 (print)
ISBN 978-3-666-30256-5 (digital)

Table of Contents

Foreword 9

Mihai-D. Grigore, Vasilios N. Makrides
Mapping Orthodox Christian Political Theologies. An Introduction 11

Daniel Benga
»Political Theologies« from Constantine to Justinian – some Key
Aspects and Main Changes 23

Anthony Kaldellis
Three Byzantine Theories on the Origin of Political Communities 39

Boris A. Todorov
Relics and the Political. Late Mediaeval Bulgaria and Serbia 53

Mihai-D. Grigore
Politics, Theology, Political Theologies. Three Examples of
Practical Political Theology in the Danubian Principalities
(Fourteenth to Sixteenth Centuries) 69

Jan Kusber
Autocracy as a Form of Political Theology? Ruler and Church in
Early Modern Muscovy (1450s–1725) 83

Nikolas Pissis
Russian Tsars and Greek Hierarchs. Political Theology and
Legitimisation in the Seventeenth Century... 101

Dimitris Stamatopoulos
»Papism is a Centre without Periphery, Protestantism is a Periphery
without Centre«. Tanzimat as Re-Confessionalisation? The Political
Theology of Constitutionality in the Late Ottoman Empire 115

Daniela Kalkandjieva
The Political Theology of the Bulgarian Orthodox Church Between
Ecclesiology, Nationalism and Modernity (1870–1922).............................. 131

Evert van der Zweerde
Give to God's Kingdom What is God's Kingdom's.
Political Theologies in Late Nineteenth-Century Russia 151

Lora Gerd
Russian Political Theologies. Messianism, Mythologisation of
History, and Practical Policy in the Nineteenth and Early Twentieth Century .. 169

Stanislau Paulau
The *Kəbrä Nägäśt* (Glory of the Kings) Goes Global.
Transnational Entanglements of Ethiopian Orthodox
Political Theology in the Early Twentieth Century.. 181

Vladimir Cvetković
Saint-Savahood (*Svetosavlje*) between Political Theology and
Ideology of Nationalism in Serbia 203

Ioannis Zelepos
Orthodoxy as Political Theology – the Case of the Church of Cyprus............ 221

Marian Pătru
Religion, Politics, and Social Change. An Overview of the
Intellectual History of Orthodox Political Theology in Romania in
the Short Twentieth Century 237

Regula M. Zwahlen
Towards a Negative Orthodox Political Theology?
The Russian Orthodox Diaspora in Western Contexts 265

Kristina Stoeckl
The Origins, Development and Diffusion of »Political Hesychasm« 289

Sebastian Rimestad
In the Shadow of a »Big Brother«. Political Theology in the
Orthodox Minority Churches from Finland to Poland 307

Sophie Zviadadze
State, Church, and the Post-Soviet Political Theology of the
Georgian Orthodox Church 323

Alexander Ponomariov
Orthodox Theopolitical Philosophies in post-2014 Ukraine 353

Efstathios Kessareas
The »Gordian Knot« of Ethnocentrism and Universality.
Comparing the Political Theologies of the Church of Greece and
the Ecumenical Patriarchate of Constantinople... 375

Index 413

Notes on Contributors.. 425

Foreword

The present volume is the result of a successful collaboration between the Department of Religious History of the Leibniz Institute of European History in Mainz (IEG) and the Chair of Religious Studies (Orthodox Christianity) at the University of Erfurt. The volume goes back to an international conference held at the IEG from 24 to 26 April 2018, which was supported financially by the German Research Foundation (DFG) and institutionally by the IEG. Stefanie Mainz from the Department of Public Relations at the IEG came to our rescue in helping to organise this conference. In addition, the contribution of the Leibniz Science Campus Mainz *Byzantium between Orient and Occident* and of the research unit *Historical Cultural Sciences* at the University of Mainz for funding our project should not go unrecognised. We are deeply indebted to all of them.

This volume includes most of the papers presented during the conference. We also strove to include additional contributions to the broad and multifaceted topic of Orthodox Christian political theologies, covering various aspects that were not specifically addressed at the conference. We are grateful to those who were willing to contribute to our project and sent their contributions at a later stage. Despite our intention and concerted efforts, we regret that we were not able to cover some undoubtedly fascinating aspects of the topic, which could have rounded up the entire volume thematically. This is because some conference participants and other invited scholars, in spite of repeated reminders, for various reasons were unable to submit their contributions for inclusion in the volume: for example, on the political theologies of Eastern Orthodox and Oriental Churches in the Middle East (Karl Pinggéra), the Armenian Orthodox context (Sargis Melkonyan), or the Greek Orthodox milieu of the USA (Elizabeth Prodromou). Despite these limitations, we still think that the present anthology is quite representative of the broad scope and richness of Orthodox Christian political theologies, both historically and in the present.

Such an extensive and complex project was made possible thanks to generous institutional and personal support, for which the editors would like to express their sincere gratitude. First and foremost, our thanks go to the former director of the Leibniz Institute of European History in Mainz, Irene Dingel, who provided the institutional support for our project and approved the inclusion of this volume in the prestigious series *Veröffentlichungen des Instituts für Europäische Geschichte Mainz*. We also owe a special debt of gratitude to Benjamin Fourlas, the coordinator of the Leibniz Science Campus Mainz *Byzantium between Orient and Occident*, who spared no effort in guiding us through the thicket of various formal and bureaucratic challenges. Among other things, he kindly allowed us to use the image for the cover of this volume. It should also be mentioned here that additional financial support for this publication came from the Chair of Religious Studies (Orthodox Christianity) at the University of Erfurt. We would also like to thank Joe Paul Kroll for proofreading the entire volume, and Friederike Lierheimer, Vanessa Weber and Christiane Bacher of the IEG for their editorial support. Last but not least, all those who supported us and who are not mentioned here by name should know that they are not forgotten and that our thanks go to them as well.

Mainz and Erfurt, in January 2024

Mihai-D. Grigore and Vasilios N. Makrides

Mihai-D. Grigore, Vasilios N. Makrides

Mapping Orthodox Christian Political Theologies

An Introduction

Political Theology and its Orthodox Christian Versions

The expression or term »political theology« encompasses two basic meanings: one broader, one narrower. In its broader sense, it has a long historical background and relates to specific discourses (ideas, visions, verbal and non-verbal articulations, practices, etc.) about religion and political power and their multiple interferences; for example, concerning the political valence of religious life and activities and their role in maintaining specific political orders, the fusion between religion and politics, and the interference of political reason in the management of religious communities – all of which are dimensions of politico-theological relevance. The term »political theology« is not always used explicitly in past sources, in some cases being replaced by »political philosophy«[1], with varying conceptualisations in each specific case. Even so, it is still possible to locate related and sometimes well-formulated discourses about this connection already in Greek and Roman antiquity – consider, for example, the role of theology and religion in the political philosophy of Plato[2] or the »tripartite theology« of the Roman polymath Marcus Terentius Varro, which included, among other things, »civil theology«[3]. Later on, the new religion of Christianity, both in East and West, drew on this pre-existing rich background, yet it unavoidably introduced various changes due to the transition from polytheism to monotheism and the novel religious frame of reference. It comes as no surprise, then, that issues related to political theology were consequently deeply reflected upon and discussed in both Christian traditions, despite the unavoidable differences that arose as a result of the distinct development of each Christian world.

In fact, by its very claim to universality, Christianity facilitated the emergence and ordering of communal life. From the beginning, Christian instances saw themselves

---

1 Francis DVORNIK, Early Christian and Byzantine Political Philosophy: Origins and Background, vols. 1–2, Washington, D.C. 1966.
2 Carl Eugene YOUNG, Plato's Cretan Colony: Theology and Religion in the Political Philosophy of the Laws, PhD thesis, Duke University, Chapel Hill, NC 2016. See also Spyridon D. KYRIAZOPOULOS, Ἡ πολιτικὴ θρησκεία τῆς Ἑλλάδος, Ioannina 1970.
3 Jörg RÜPKE, Die Religion der Römer. Eine Einführung, Munich 2001, pp. 121–125.

as ecclesiastical, i. e., communal, dimensions of gathering believing church members, who were at the same time state citizens in different forms of political bodies. Their theology represented the civil relevance of the religious existence in the manner of a θεολογία πολιτική or *theologia civilis*. By its very nature, Christianity thus was and still remains political[4]. Accordingly, the point of departure for political theology are the universalist and communal accents of the Christian religion itself. Political theology informs the language of human plurality in relation to God the Creator, if we are to maintain Hannah Arendt's distinction between man, in the singular, as God's creation, and human beings, the plural form of socio-political community on earth and in history[5]. Political theology also means enacting this plurality with all its expectations, excuses, fears, convictions, justifications, reasons, attitudes, actions, and concepts in religious life.

The narrower sense of the term, on the other hand, concerns specific discourses that arose and were formulated in various constellations within the Western religious and broader intellectual realm during the 19th and 20th centuries. These were aimed at a deeper analysis of the complex interface between religion and politics, particularly within the modern frame, without definitively abandoning the historical projection. Given that they were seriously challenged by modern secular and liberal projects, this was most urgently felt by the Roman Catholic Church and the wider Protestant realm, as these had to struggle with modern politics in order to articulate their respective political visions and strategies anew, either in relation or in contrast to the past. However, it also pertained to other religions, such as Judaism, which also faced dramatic challenges from socio-political developments (e. g., totalitarian regimes)[6]. In these contexts, the concept of political theology also related to a specific (theological) trend that was critical of political authority, society, and even the church itself.

Aside from this, political theology also became an important part of modern political philosophy, examining the patent and latent influences of theological ideas and concepts upon political theory, practices, state structures and language – in other words, a »secularised theology of politics« or a »religionised politics«. In this respect, it is about a particular theory of state, society and law aimed at legitimising a related symbolic imaginary of the social – all in the wake of the ground-breaking, much-discussed and much-debated work of the controversial German jurist and

---

4 Leo KARRER, Wieviel Öffentlichkeit vertragen die Religionen?, in: Mariano DELGADO et al. (eds.), Religion und Öffentlichkeit. Probleme und Perspektiven, Stuttgart 2009, pp. 79–98, at pp. 80–82.

5 Hannah ARENDT, Der Liebesbegriff bei Augustin. Versuch einer philosophischen Interpretation, Hildesheim ²2006, pp. 77–79.

6 Miguel VATTER, Living Law: Jewish Political Theology from Hermann Cohen to Hannah Arendt, Oxford 2021.

political theorist Carl Schmitt (1888–1985)[7], whose relevance remains undiminished to this day[8]. The same applies to other important theorists (e. g., Eric Voegelin, 1901–1985[9]), who explored the religious dimensions underlying the apparently secular agenda of modern politics. As a result, political theology has often been transformed today into a distinct academic specialisation or even discipline, albeit in different contexts.

Needless to say, many scholars often use other expressions or terms to demarcate the two trajectories of political theology discussed above. They usually reserve the term »political theology« itself for the modern, narrower category, while preferring to designate related past cases by other terms (e. g., as theology of politics, theological politics, religious politics)[10]. It is more than obvious, however, that there are numerous connections and overlaps between these terms and expressions. Without denying or glossing over potential differences, political theology may thus include both the political consequences of theological principles and concepts (e. g., derived either from polytheistic or monotheistic visions and ideas), as well as those political agendas containing elements of theology.

The concept of political theology that informs this volume, aside from a few chapters, has, however, little to do with that of Carl Schmitt. We take it to mean neither a theological vindication of politics nor simply the task of social and political criticism that the churches sometimes level against what they perceive to be un-Christian about society and state, as suggested, albeit based on fundamentally different premises, by Johann Baptist Metz[11] and, in his work on Orthodox Christian anarchism, by the Orthodox theologian Davor Džalto[12]. Nor do we take political theology to be a mere aspect, a *particula*, of theology in general. On the contrary, it represents a distinct dimension of a complex and intertwined way of addressing politics, policy, and the polity from the perspective of revealed truth filtered through a community's faith. In this sense, our concept of political theology envisages all the mentioned dimensions as objects of study through the prism of critical analysis and historical contextualisation. Following Manfred Walther's definition, we understand »political theology« in terms of »[the relations] between religion and

---

7 Carl Schmitt, Politische Theologie. Vier Kapitel zur Lehre von der Souveränität, München 1922; id., Römischer Katholizismus und politische Form, Hellerau 1923.
8 Mitchell Dean et al. (eds.), Political Theology Today: 100 Years after Carl Schmitt, London 2023.
9 Eric Voegelin, Die politischen Religionen, ed. by Peter Opitz, Munich ³2007.
10 Carsten Bagge Laustsen, Studying Politics and Religion: How to Distinguish Religious Politics, Civil Religion, Political Religion, and Political Theology, in: Journal of Religion in Europe 6/4 (2013), pp. 428–446.
11 Johann Baptist Metz, Zum Begriff der neuen Politischen Theologie, 1967–1997, Mainz 1997.
12 Davor Džalto, Anarchy and the Kingdom of God. From Eschatology to Orthodox Political Theology and Back, New York 2021.

politics, church(es) and state, which derive from a theological interpretation and permeation of a religion or of its basic heuristics – rules, that is, in which religion is the *controlling* force and which hence are laid down by theologians«[13].

Turning our attention specifically to Orthodox Christianity, it is possible to realise from the outset a striking asymmetry, especially in relation to the wide and creative Western preoccupation with political theology, academic or not. In the past, this domain has been largely neglected in the Orthodox Christian realm, which did not sufficiently reflect upon it. In fact, the entire topic of political theology, historically speaking, has been much more comprehensively, systematically and theoretically elaborated in Western Christian discourse, theological and otherwise, and has been promoted by various actors in numerous constellations, both individually and institutionally. This holds true not only for the past, but especially for modern times and into the present.

There are several reasons for these differences between East and West[14]. Truth be told, reflection on the many entanglements between politics and theology is certainly not absent from the long and varied history of Eastern Orthodox Christianity. After all, it is exactly in this particular area where the first Christian political formations officially appeared in the context of the Roman Empire during the 4th century, starting with the radical changes and reforms implemented by Emperor Constantine I. These were especially praised by Eusebius, Bishop of Caesarea in Palestine, a most influential »political theologian« in his day and still a relevant figure[15]. However, despite its enormous influence, Eusebian political theology – with its emphasis on the close, God-sanctioned relation between the emperor and the church – was not the only approach even at the time. One may find a different trajectory, formulated by Ignatius, Bishop of Antiochia, in which the church remains the centre of attention and reference without any mundane preoccupations[16]; or more extensively, by Athanasius, Bishop of Alexandria[17], in which the focus

---

13 Manfred WALTHER, Luthers dualistische politische Theologie der zwei Reiche und zwei Regimente – Das Problem der Lokalisierung der sichtbaren Kirche, in: Id. (ed.), Religion und Politik, Baden-Baden 2004, pp. 105–112, at p. 106 (emphasis in original).

14 Vasilios N. MAKRIDES, Political Theology in Orthodox Christian Contexts: Specificities and Particularities in Comparison with Western Latin Christianity, in: Kristina STOECKL et al. (eds.), Political Theologies in Orthodox Christianity: Common Challenges – Divergent Positions, London/New York 2017, pp. 25–54.

15 Devin SINGH, Eusebius as Political Theologian: The Legend Continues, in: The Harvard Theological Review 108 (2015), pp. 129–154; Michael J. HOLLERICH, Making Christian History. Eusebius of Caesarea and his Readers, Oakland, CA 2021.

16 Andrew LOUTH, Ignatios or Eusebios: Two Models of Patristic Ecclesiology, in: International Journal for the Study of the Christian Church 10/1 (2010), pp. 46–56.

17 Sophie CARTWRIGHT, Athanasius' »Vita Antonii« as Political Theology: The Call of Heavenly Citizenship, in: The Journal of Ecclesiastical History 67/2 (2016), pp. 241–264.

is rather placed on a notion of the church as a »hermit in the desert«, strongly oriented towards the divine world and clearly detached from the worldly affairs of emperor and state. This notion owes its most striking modern elaboration to the Russian Orthodox theologian Georges Florovsky[18]. All this points to various conceptions of political theology among early Christian thinkers, who left their mark on later developments. Even so, the long-term differences between East and West in this very domain are still conspicuous and undeniable, as they principally reflect different relations between church and state/politics in their respective worlds.

This notwithstanding, a fresh Orthodox interest in this topic has been triggered by the radical socio-political changes at the end of the 20th century, especially in the wake of the fall of communism in many predominantly Orthodox countries of Eastern and Southeastern Europe. As a result, Orthodox theologians, intellectuals and other thinkers have started to reflect more thoroughly on issues pertaining to political theology while trying to articulate a specifically Orthodox one, not least in critical discussion with related Western discourses[19]. Aside from various older[20] or more recent sourcebooks[21] related to (Orthodox) Christian political theologies, recent years have also seen the publication of conference papers and other edited volumes, either specifically on this topic[22] or on related questions[23], which have gone a long way towards filling the gap. Relevant attempts to approach »typical« Orthodox political theologies in the historical perspective of Byzantium, the *Slavia*

---

18 Georges FLOROVSKY, Antinomies of Christian History: Empire and Desert, in: Id., Christianity and Culture, Belmont, MA 1974, pp. 67–100.
19 Pantelis KALAITZIDIS, Orthodoxy and Political Theology, Geneva 2012; Aristotle PAPANIKOLAOU, The Mystical as Political: Democracy and Non-Radical Orthodoxy, Notre Dame, IN 2012; see also Paul Nadim TARAZI, Land and Covenant, St Paul, MN 2009; Cyril HOVORUN, Political Orthodoxies: The Unorthodoxies of the Church Coerced, Minneapolis, MN 2018.
20 Ernest BARKER (ed.), Social and Political Thought in Byzantium: From Justinian I to the Last Palaeologus, Oxford 1957.
21 Oliver O'DONOVAN/Joan LOCKWOOD O'DONOVAN (eds.), From Irenaeus to Grotius: A Sourcebook in Christian Political Thought 100–1625, Grand Rapids, MI 1999; Adolf Martin RITTER, »Kirche und Staat« im Denken des frühen Christentums. Texte und Kommentare zum Thema Religion und Politik in der Antike, Bern 2005; Philip WOOD, »We Have No King But Christ«: Christian Political Thought in Greater Syria on the Eve of the Arab Conquest (c. 400–585), New York 2010.
22 George E. DEMACOPOULOS/Aristotle PAPANIKOLAOU (eds.), Christianity, Democracy, and the Shadow of Constantine, New York 2016; STOECKL et al. (eds.), Political Theologies in Orthodox Christianity.
23 Mihai-D. GRIGORE/Florian KÜHRER-WIELACH (eds.), Orthodoxa Confessio? Konfessionsbildung, Konfessionalisierung und ihre Folgen in der östlichen Christenheit Europas, Göttingen 2018 (VIEG Beiheft 114), URL: <https://doi.org/10.13109/9783666570780> (10-12-2023); Kostas SARRIS et al. (eds.), Confessionalization and/as Knowledge Transfer in the Greek Orthodox Church, Wiesbaden 2021; Hans-Peter GROSSHANS/Pantelis KALAITZIDIS (eds.), Politics, Society and Culture in Orthodox Theology in a Global Age, Paderborn 2023.

Orthodoxa or in post-Byzantine paraenetic literature have already been made and constitute noteworthy contributions[24]. All this signifies a welcome addition of Orthodox voices to a politico-theological discourse that has long been dominated by Roman Catholic and Protestant perspectives, with the purpose of enabling a more ecumenical discussion about politics and Christian theology[25].

However, there are still many research desiderata; for example, an examination of the politically relevant aspects of the theology of the Greek Fathers in the manner of the Western Latin analyses of Tertullian or Augustine. An important attempt was, for example, taken by a scholar who was neither Orthodox nor a theologian: the legal scholar, political philosopher, and diplomat Stephan Verosta (1909–1998), who in 1960 published an unequalled monograph on John Chrysostom's political theology of the state[26]. Furthermore, the *Bases of the Social Concept*, officially promulgated by the Russian Orthodox Church in 2000, a document which drew quite large international attention, also amounted to a political theology of Russian Orthodox provenance – one that, moreover, was thought to constitute some kind of »Political Hesychasm«[27]. Aside from this, numerous scholars of various backgrounds and disciplines have dealt with specific aspects of Orthodox political theology in its diverse manifestations (written, visual, practised), either in the Byzantine period[28], the

---

24 Dimiter ANGELOV, Imperial Ideology and Political Thought in Byzantium, 1204–1330, Cambridge, MA 2007; Ivan BILIARSKY et al. (eds.), Religious Rhetoric of Power in Byzantium and South-Eastern Europe, Brăila 2021; Mihai-D. GRIGORE, Neagoe Basarab – Princeps Christianus. The Semantics of Christianitas in Comparison with Erasmus, Luther and Machiavelli (1513–1523), Oxford 2021.

25 Jonathan COLE, The Addition of Orthodox Voices to (Western) Political Theology, in: Studies in Christian Ethics 33/4 (2020), pp. 549–564; Sotiris MITRALEXIS, On Recent Developments in Scholarly Engagement with (the Possibility of an) Orthodox Political Theology, in: Political Theology 19/3 (2018), pp. 247–260.

26 Stephan VEROSTA, Iohannes Chrysostomus. Staatsphilosoph und Geschichtstheologe, Graz 1960.

27 Vladimir V. PETRUNIN, Политический исихазм и его традиции в социальной концепции Московского Патриархата, St Petersburg 2009. See also Antoine LEVY, »Political Hesychasm« and the Foundational Structure of the Russian State, in: Analogia. The Pemptousia Journal for Theological Studies 5 (2018), pp. 57–81. See also Kristina Stoeckl's contribution on »Political Hesychasm« in this volume.

28 Gerhard PODSKALSKY, Politische Theologie in Byzanz zwischen Reichseschatologie und Reichsideologie, in: Cristianità d'Occidente e cristianità d'Oriente (Secoli VI–XI), 24–30 aprile 2003, vol. 2, Spoleto 2004, pp. 1421–1434; Petre GURAN, Eschatology and Political Theology in the Last Centuries of Byzantium, in: Revue des études sud-est européennes 45 (2007), pp. 73–87; Dan Ioan MUREŞAN, The Hesychasts: »Political Photianism« and the Public Sphere in the Fourteenth Century, in: Augustine CASIDAY (ed.), The Orthodox Christian World, London/New York 2012, pp. 294–302; Ioannis BEKOS, Nicholas Cabasilas' Political Theology in an Epoch of Economic Crisis: A Reading of a 14th-Century Political Discourse, in: Markus VINZENT (ed.), Studia Patristica, vol. 63: Papers Presented at the Sixteenth International Conference on Patristic Studies held in Oxford 2011, Leuven 2013, pp. 405–412; Ashley M. PURPURA, God, Hierarchy, and Power: Orthodox Theologies of Authority

post-Byzantine era[29] or the modern and contemporary world, and in a wide variety of contexts[30]; for example, focusing on the political theology of the well-known Greek theologian and philosopher Christos Yannaras (*1935)[31]. Comparisons were also frequently made between Eastern Orthodox and Western Latin[32] or Islamic political theologies[33]. In fact, it would not be inappropriate to speak here of diverse forms of Orthodox political theologies (in the plural), both historically and more recently. Hence, despite its overall underdevelopment in comparison to the West, the Orthodox case has its own merits and deserves scholarly attention, comparative examination, suitable contextualisation, and adequate evaluation.

The present volume attempts to contribute to this goal by examining this topic from a broader perspective that is both systematic and interdisciplinary. Given that most previous studies examined it from a perspective interested mainly in theology, dogmatics, and moral and socio-ethical questions, this volume focuses especially on the historical evolution of Orthodox Christian political theologies across time,

---

from Byzantium, New York 2017; Tristan SCHMIDT, Politische Tierbildlichkeit in Byzanz – Spätes 11. bis frühes 13. Jahrhundert, Wiesbaden 2020.

29 Nikolaos PANOU, How to Do Kings with Words: Byzantine Imperial Ideology and the Representation of Power in Pre-Phanariot Admonitory Literature, PhD thesis, Harvard University 2008; Petre GURAN, God Explains to Patriarch Athanasios the Fall of Constantinople: I.S. Peresvetov and the Impasse of Political Theology, in: Olivier DELOUIS et al. (eds.), Héritages de Byzance en Europe du Sud-Est à l' époque moderne et contemporaine, Athens 2013, pp. 63–78.

30 Nikolaos ASPROULIS, Pneumatology and Politics: The Role of the Holy Spirit in the Articulation of an Orthodox Political Theology, in: RES – Review of Ecumenical Studies Sibiu 7/2 (2015), pp. 184–197; Pantelis KALAITZIDIS, Eastern Orthodox Thought, in: William T. CAVANAUGH/Peter Manley SCOTT (eds.), The Wiley Blackwell Companion to Political Theology, Hoboken, NJ ²2019, pp. 97–110; Nathaniel WOOD/Aristotle PAPANIKOLAOU, Orthodox Christianity and Political Theology: Thinking Beyond Empire, in: Rubén Rosario RODRÍGUEZ (ed.), T&T Clark Handbook of Political Theology, London 2020, pp. 337–351; Alexandra MEDZIBRODSZKY, Orthodox Political Theologies: Clergy, Intelligentsia and Social Christianity in Revolutionary Russia, PhD thesis, Central European University, Budapest 2020.

31 See the special issue on »Christos Yannaras and Political Theology« of the journal Political Theology 20/4 (2019), which includes the following articles: Jonathan COLE, Personhood, Relational Ontology, and the Trinitarian Politics of Eastern Orthodox Thinker Christos Yannaras, pp. 297–310; Sotiris MITRALEXIS, The Eucharistic Community is Our Social Program: On the Early Development of Christos Yannaras' Political Theology, pp. 311–330; and Dionysios SKLIRIS, Aristotelian Marxism, Critical Metaphysics: The Political Theology of Christos Yannaras, pp. 331–348.

32 Aristotle PAPANIKOLAOU, Love, Life and Politics: Comparing Lutheran and Orthodox Political Theologies, in: RES – Review of Ecumenical Studies Sibiu 10/2 (2018), pp. 257–265.

33 Johannes NIEHOFF-PANAGIOTIDIS, Avoiding History's Teleology: Orthodox and Islamic Political Philosophy, in: Regula FORSTER/Neguin YAVARI (eds.), Global Medieval-Mirrors for Princes Reconsidered, Cambridge 2015, pp. 112–121; Vasileios SYROS, Ὁ Εὐστάθιος Θεσσαλονίκης γιὰ τὶς ἀπαρχὲς τοῦ κοινωνικοῦ βίου καὶ τὴν ἐξέλιξη τοῦ πολιτισμοῦ: Σημεῖα σύγκλισης μὲ τὸν πολιτικὸ στοχασμὸ τοῦ Δυτικοῦ Μεσαίωνα, in: Θεολογία 91/3 (2020), pp. 251–285.

following a chronological thread from early Byzantium until today – an ambitious task for sure, but, given the tremendous backlog in the field, a necessary one. However, even this volume is hardly exhaustive of the immense richness of the topic. It should instead be understood as providing encouragement for further studies.

As for the goals of this volume: First, the contributions it gathers examine and compare the historical background and numerous forms and articulations of Orthodox political theologies in various local contexts, both past and present. Second, they consider and analyse the specific parameters and factors that gave rise to these political theologies or have shaped them across time. Third, they try to locate and critically evaluate the reasons for the specificities and particularities of these political theologies across history. Finally, some contributions also try to contextualise the entire issue more broadly, especially by comparing Orthodox with Western Christian political theologies and at the same time looking for specific historical constellations and contingencies. Given that the topic of political theology enjoys significant popularity and currency among various scholarly disciplines today, it is hoped that the present volume will contribute to the rich literature in the field. It may also help widen the academic discourse on political theology – which, in the last two centuries, evolved on multiple levels primarily within Western scholarship – by including in it the until now mostly ignored Eastern Orthodox Christianity with its *modes* of thinking about man, time, history, humankind, political forms, and their *raison d'être* in terms of the divine.

A further important goal of this volume is to break some widespread clichés and stereotypes. For instance, scholarly concern with political theology from a historical point of view usually attends only to the late antique or Byzantine heritage before leaping to modernity, thereby ignoring the fertile political thought in various local Orthodox traditions after 1453. On the other hand, there is an irritating tendency to reduce all politico-theological traditions of Eastern Christianity to the so-called Byzantine »symphony« between church and state, a diagnosis which has lost value by having been made too often. Not everything was, or still is, arranged symphonically in the »body politic« of the entire and multiform Orthodox world. Important dissident discourses of political theology *against* the state and secular power, in the Byzantine and post-Byzantine era, are drowned out by such frequent and unnuanced references to Emperor Justinian's establishment of »symphony«. A mythology of symphony and its re-establishment persists among numerous Orthodox cultures today[34]. This makes it high time to counter such simplistic reductionism and show the different contexts of Orthodox political theologies in their multifaceted complexity.

---

34 Cyril Hovorun, Is the Byzantine »Symphony« Possible in Our Days?, in: Journal of Church and State 59/2 (2017), pp. 280–296.

Last but not least: Considering the ongoing war in Ukraine after the Russian invasion of February 2022, in which Orthodoxy is a factor to be reckoned with on both sides, political theology – to think of the Moscow Patriarch Cyril's rhetoric and statements in favour of the invasion and the war[35] – has taken on an unexpected relevance. Many analyses in this volume anticipate the potential for conflict latent in the problematic connection between state, politics, nation, and church in Orthodox Europe. As history rushes ahead in its most violent form and irrupts into the meta-history of the Christian ideal of peacefulness and the divine commandment of love, these diagnoses seem almost prophetic. In such troubled times, the need for the Orthodox Christian mind to make sense of death, bloodshed, and fratricide elevates political theology to a meaning-giving dimension that church and state alike cannot ignore. The question of legitimation is of more existential importance than ever, while in the context of the Ukrainian conflict political Orthodoxy almost assumes the character of a critical infrastructure of war.

The Contributions: A Short Overview

In order to do justice to the pluriform nature of the topic, the contributions to this volume have been written by scholars working in a variety of disciplines, thereby highlighting Orthodox political theologies from diverse, albeit often interconnected, angles. In this way, perspectives from religious studies, late antique, medieval, early modern or contemporary history, theology and church history, political philosophy, and political science combine to attest to the richness of political theologies during the centuries of evolution of the Orthodox Christian East. Because of the complexity of the interdisciplinary approaches, and because none of them remains in disciplinary isolation, the contributions can be arranged according to multiple overlapping patterns.

Different fields of inquiry preoccupied the respective authors, starting of course with the discussion of the basics, i. e., the Byzantine paradigm of symphony between the spiritual (*sacerdotium*) and the temporal power (*imperium*), its boundaries and deficiencies (Daniel Benga) as well as its persistence, and its unavoidable transformations within Russian political autocracy in early modern times (Jan Kusber). By affirming a *translatio imperii* from Jerusalem to Ethiopia and by employing narratives analogous to Russian political theology, Ethiopian political glorification theology, although non-Chalcedonian, was an equally indispensable topic for this

---

35 Alar Kɪʟᴘ, Patriarch Kirill and Metropolitan Hilarion on Religious Conflict and Secular War in Ukraine: A Diachronic Study of Religious Leaders' Messages, in: Sõjateadlane. Estonian Journal of Military Studies 20 (2022), pp. 141–174; Cyril Hovorun, Russian Church and Ukrainian War, in: The Expository Times 134/1 (2022), pp. 1–10.

volume (Stanislau Paulau). This contribution displays a continuity – grounded mainly in certain politico-theological arguments held in common – with other studies on the theocratically-founded Russian autocracy of the tsars, which has been strongly connected with messianic imperial and neo-imperial agendas from the sixteenth to the nineteenth century, such as »Moscow, the Third Rome«, »Pan-Slavism«, and »Pan-Orthodoxism« (Nikolas Pissis and Lora Gerd).

Theological speculation on the role of the Christian state and ruler at the apex of God's creation, or the reasons for the very existence of a political order analogous to that creation, continue to offer much material reflection, ranging from the Byzantine political theology of Photios I, Patriarch of Constantinople (Anthony Kaldellis) through the history of the Danubian Principalities (Mihai-D. Grigore) to the Russian monarchism, socialism, fascism, historiosophy, sophiology, and Messianism of the nineteenth and twentieth centuries (Regula M. Zwahlen and Evert van der Zweerde). The controversial concept of »Political Hesychasm« and its ideologically integrative function in earlier epochs or as an interface for contemporary anti-Western Russian philippics (Kristina Stoeckl) offers an indispensable case study in this regard.

Over the last centuries, the very principles and ideals of a Christian order in history and in the world led to perpetual bargaining over influence and power between secular and ecclesiastical instances, also considering the simple fact that state subjects were at the same time the flock of Christ under the care, supervision and control of the church. Such turmoil was experienced especially in the context of the late mediaeval or early modern Ecumenical Patriarchate of Constantinople's politics under Ottoman rule, but also in the context of the national revival, nationalist exclusivism, modernity, and state emancipation in Southeastern Europe from the eighteenth century to the present. Modern state institutions struggled bitterly for emancipation, both from foreign Ottoman rule and, internally, from the jurisdiction of the Ecumenical Patriarchate and its historical control of the Orthodox Rum *millet*. Local churches wrestled with Constantinople for autocephaly and identity, thereby feeding into strong nationalist and emancipative narratives (Dimitris Stamatopoulos on the Ecumenical Patriarchate in the late Ottoman period, Daniela Kalkandjieva on Bulgaria, Marian Pătru on Romania, Ioannis Zelepos on Cyprus). This tension is also masterfully explicated by Efstathios Kessareas with regard to the tenuous relations between the Patriarchate of Constantinople and the autocephalous Church of Greece and their respective universalist and ethnocentric discourses, despite the ethnic and historic closeness of the two churches.

Such emancipatory ideals often gained legitimacy by symbolic communication and reference to emblematic holy figures and their relics, whose perpetuation over centuries gave fundamental impulses to cultural identity, political independence, and national pre-eminence. The contributions of Boris Todorov and Vladimir Cvetković on Saint-Savahood testify to the durability of such motives, the former referring to the late Middle Ages and the latter to twentieth-century Serbia. A similar argument is pursued by Mihai-D. Grigore, who assesses the importance for emerging local Orthodoxies – like those of mediaeval and early modern Hungro-Wallachia and Moldavia – of »possessing« national saints in order to efficiently secure their political aspirations in the international context.

Finally, Alexander Ponomariov critically evaluates – in a welcome corrective to the idealising mainstream of our days – the Ukrainian way of theologically articulating the country's desire for a distinct political, religious, and cultural identity as a means of setting itself apart from the Moscow Patriarchate and its expansionism. This ties in with the broader topic of the specific situation of »smaller Orthodoxies«, such as the Baltic, Polish, or Georgian ones, whose desire for affirmation is often threatened with suffocation by »larger and stronger Orthodoxies« – in this case, the Russian Orthodox Church (Sebastian Rimestad and Sophie Zviadadze).

We hope that, in view of the renewed academic interest in political theology and its topical relevance today, this volume will be of interest to an international scholarly readership beyond the limits of Eastern Orthodox Christian studies. Any examination of the different political theologies in their respective historical environment ought always to bear in mind a point emphasised by Quentin Skinner:

> We shall do well to concentrate in particular on the concepts we employ to describe and appraise what Hobbes called our artificial world, the world of politics and morality. This in turn means that we shall need to focus on the various terms – the entire normative vocabulary – in which such concepts are habitually expressed. […] These terms, the paradigms of which are the names of the virtues and vices, are those which perform evaluative as well as descriptive functions in natural languages[36].

In sum, the conceptualisation of political theology in general unfolds in two main directions: On a systematic level, it may be understood as a dialectical positioning of the political as idea, politics as practice, and politicians as institutionally organised actors in God's relations with human beings in particular and in God's creation more broadly. On a historical level, political theology can also be regarded as the dialectical location of the political as idea, politics as practice, and politicians as institutionally organised actors in the history of humanity with reference to God. Political theology is thus a matter of approach and perspective, as well as of finality and telos. The case of Orthodox Christian political theologies, on its own merit and as evidenced in the various contributions of this volume, is of eminent relevance to the above conceptualisation.

---

36 Quentin SKINNER, Visions of Politics, vol. 1: Regarding Method, Cambridge ⁶2009, p. 175.

Daniel Benga

»Political Theologies« from Constantine to Justinian – some Key Aspects and Main Changes

The present contribution comes as a response to the invitation I received from the organisers of the conference to prepare a short article containing some central observations on the »political theologies« from Constantine I (306–337) to Justinian I (527–565). This topic requires some clarifications from the very beginning due to the fact that not only does the expression »political theology« have a multitude of meanings in contemporary research, but also the interpretation of the motivations behind Constantine's religious policy is until today a still highly debated issue[1]. Against the background of this complex reality and on the basis of contemporary research, I shall use the next few pages to briefly answer the following question by means of some concrete examples: What were the politico-ecclesiastical consequences of the religious convictions of the emperors Constantine I (r. 306–337), Theodosius I (r. 379–395) and Justinian I (r. 527–565) or, in other words, how did their religious convictions influence the agenda of their religious policy? In addition to these questions, I shall explore the manner in which the so-called »symphony« between the emperor and the Christian Church in Byzantium manifested itself.

---

1 In 2013, on the occasion of the 1700-year anniversary of the so-called *Edict of Milan*, I was a member of the organising committee for a large international conference in Bucharest attended by a large number of distinguished European historians (including church historians). In the debates that unfolded, I was able observe directly that there was hardly any consensus on the interpretation of Constantine the Great's actions. What exactly did Constantine see on the eve of the battle of the Milvian Bridge? The interpretations range from a solar eclipse to the sight of the Holy Cross in the sky. Can one talk about the emperor's conversion to Christianity? The answers differ greatly. Historians often discuss the vexing coexistence of and parallelism between Christianity and paganism, for instance on the coins issued by Constantine. Scholars approach these theological and historical debates from their various cultural and religious backgrounds, which, in turn, produce different modes of inquiry and analysis. In my view, a more precise definition and description of the terms and concepts with which we operate would bring about a better understanding and consensus with regard to the actions and decisions of world's first Christian emperor. The contributions of the above conference have been published in Emilian POPESCU/Viorel IONIȚĂ (eds.), Cruce și Misiune. Sfinții Împărați Constantin și Elena – promotori ai libertății religioase și apărători ai Bisericii, vol. 2, Bucharest 2013. On the difficulties and challanges of contemporary Constantine research see also the chapter »Drei Mauern: Wege und Abwege der Konstantinforschung« in Martin WALLRAFF, Sonnenkönig der Spätantike. Die Religionspolitik Konstantins des Großen, Freiburg im Breisgau 2013, pp. 7–33.

Constantine the Great – How the Christian God Influenced his Political Agenda

I have always been impressed by how Constantine is always portrayed as looking skyward[2]. Jacob Burckhardt's portrayal of Constantine as a great unreligious politician, who made use of the different ancient religions in order to support his own political power, influenced historical research for a century and a half[3]. Modern research has replaced this vision with a profoundly religious one, which has revealed the important role that the first Christian emperor's religious beliefs played in his political-religious decisions. Alexander Schmemann, the Russian Church historian, offers an accurate summary of Constantine's religiosity: »He always had mystical interests, a faith in dreams, visions, and illuminations. He firmly believed in his election, and his whole political career was marked by his personal contacts with heaven«[4].

Modern historiography has left behind the one-sided views generated by an over-emphasis on the political aspects of Constantine's personal ambitions in his religious policy and has come to acknowledge a religious evolution of the emperor in his sincere search for the true God. Volkmar Keil, an important editor of sources on Constantine's religious politics, has thus observed: »The gradual journey from the god of sun conceived monotheistically to Christianity is a lifelong conversion which came to its true end in the baptism performed on his deathbed«[5]. Considering the very limited space allotted to the presentation of the political-theological convictions of the first Christian emperor, I shall analyse, drawing upon the latest interpretations by Klaus Martin Girardet and Hans Christoph Brennecke, the manner in which Constantine's religious beliefs permeated some of his main political-religious decisions.

Freedom of Christian faith and worship was attained gradually and by different means across the Roman territories at the beginning of the fourth century. In 306, already under the rule of Constantine, the wave of liberty swept from Gaul, Britain and Spain to Italy, the Balkans, Asia Minor and the Orient. However, it was not until the summer of 313 that Christians were granted complete freedom throughout

---

2 See the coins reproduced in WALLRAFF, Sonnenkönig der Spätantike, p. 8 and in Klaus Martin GIRARDET, Der Kaiser und sein Gott. Das Christentum im Denken und in der Religionspolitik Konstantins des Großen, Berlin 2010, p. 57, 94.
3 Ibid., pp. 5–7.
4 Alexander SCHMEMANN, The Historical Road of Eastern Orthodoxy, New York 2003, p. 64.
5 Volkmar KEIL (ed.), Quellensammlung zur Religionspolitik Konstantins des Grossen, Darmstadt 1995, p. 19.

the entire Roman Empire⁶, while persecutions in the East continued for several more years.

The decisive point, which essentially influenced the Emperor Constantine's entire political outlook, was the famous and yet (as far as historians are concerned) vision he had at the Milvian Bridge on the eve of the battle against the usurper Maxentius on 28 October 312. After all, this battle was pivotal for his conversion to the Christian God. One fundamental element, though, has not been yet sufficiently stressed in historiography, namely the fact that Constantine converted to Christianity as emperor and not as an ordinary individual. The faith in the Christian God »had not come to him through the Church, but had been bestowed personally and directly for his victory over the enemy – in other words, as he was fulfilling his imperial duty«⁷. This fundamental element of being directly chosen by God without undergoing baptism determined Constantine to act independently of the Church, and the Church in its turn accepted and acknowledged him in loyalty.

Following his victory over Maxentius, Constantine became ruler of the entire Roman West, granting freedom to the Christians and taking direct, personal action in Africa Proconsularis for the restoration of goods confiscated during earlier persecutions, allotting a significant amount of money to the clergy and exempting it from public service. The emperor also wrote to his co-regents in the East urging them to grant the same freedom to Christians. Licinius agreed to do so, in the autumn of 312 or in February 313 issuing the so-called »Edict of Milan«, which he co-signed with Constantine⁸. Maximinus Daia, however, continued his persecutions up to the summer of 313, when, fleeing from Licinius, he committed suicide at the Cilician Gates. It was only at this moment that the edict granting freedom to the Christians of the Roman Empire was actually implemented in its Eastern part as well. In fact, the *libertas religionis* guaranteed to all represents the first formulation of this principle in history⁹.

Between November 312 and February 313, the new emperor composed a number of letters, two of which were addressed to Anulinus, proconsul of Africa, and one to Caecilian, bishop of Carthage¹⁰. From these, Constantine's political stance towards

---

6 For a detailed description, see Klaus Martin GIRARDET, Von der Verfolgung zur Anerkennung. Rom und die Christen in dioklezianisch-konstantinischer Zeit, in: POPESCU/IONIȚĂ (eds.), Cruce și Misiune, pp. 83–96, at pp. 85–87.
7 SCHMEMANN, The Historical Road, p. 66.
8 On the present state of research referring to the Edict of Milan, see Adrian MARINESCU, Edictul de la Milan. Scurtă schiță a stadiului actual al cercetărilor, in: Emilian POPESCU/Mihai Ovidiu CĂȚOI (eds.), Cruce și Misiune. Sfinții Împărați Constantin și Elena – promotori ai libertății religioase și apărători ai Bisericii, vol. 1, Bucharest 2013, pp. 87–150.
9 GIRARDET, Von der Verfolgung zur Anerkennung, pp. 90–92.
10 A new commentary on these letters is offered by GIRARDET, Der Kaiser, pp. 125–128; cf. Hermann DÖRRIES, Das Selbstzeugnis Kaiser Konstantin, Göttingen 1954, pp. 16–19.

the Christians may be deduced. Beside the general religious freedom, the emperor also adopted the following measures for Africa Proconsularis:

1. The restoration of goods confiscated in the course of previous persecutions (churches, gardens, houses);
2. The granting of considerable financial support to the clergy of the catholic (i. e., universal) church along with an offer of any further assistance required;
3. The exempoltion of the clergy from public duties and obligations (including taxes) in order that they may practice the cult of the »Christian God« unhindered[11].

Klaus Martin Girardet interprets Constantine's attitude and statements in his letter to Anulinus as follows:

> Likewise, the emperor did not present himself in the letter to the pagan proconsul as an advocate of the abstract (*summa*) *divinitas/mens divina* of the pagan-philosophical henotheism that had no cult, order and ministers for its exertion: He speaks very clearly about the monotheistic religion and its specific cult (as well as about its ministers). Therefore, the divinity worshipped in the Christian cult, which is to say the Christian God as »the holiest God«, called thus and otherwise by Christian writers, is to him not the head of a »hierarchy of the gods« or a defining concept of the divine lacking any cult, but rather the only true God, to be worshipped in precise forms[12].

The Emperor Constantine was preoccupied to the point of obsession with the unity of the Christian Church and its cult. Therefore, the cult was for Constantine the surest way to preserve the empire and its unity. Nevertheless, Constantine did not accept any cult, but trusted only that of the »catholic church«, to which he gave his whole support. This also explains why Constantine imposed uniformity in the celebration of Sundays and Christian feasts like Easter. Klaus Martin Girardet has recently proved that

> the establishment of the *dies solis* as a regular day of rest by Constantine is absolutely a novum in antiquity. The text of the law is not preserved, but two texts of the year 321 (*Codex Theodosianus* II,8,1 and *Codex Iustinianus* II 12,2 [3]) hint at the fact that Constantine established the *dies solis* in connection to the laws about the clergy and the building of churches in 312/313. It follows that the character of the *dies solis* cannot be

---

11 Daniel BENGA, Politica lui Constantin cel Mare față de creștini intre octombrie 312 și februarie 313, in: POPESCU/IONIȚĂ (eds.), Cruce și Misiune, pp. 237–247, at p. 243.
12 Klaus Martin GIRARDET, Die konstantinische Wende. Voraussetzungen und geistige Grundlagen der Religionspolitik Konstantins des Großen, Darmstadt 2006, p. 97 (my translation).

considered as pagan or syncretic, but as an early step towards the Christianisation of the Roman Empire. Even the Roman army had to observe the *dies solis* in a Christian manner [cf. Eusebius, *Vita Constantini*, IV], from 311/312 onwards. In this early time, of course, the new rules were only realised in the Western part of the Empire, only from 324 onwards did the Eastern part accept the new rhythm of time. Early Egyptian papyri show that the Christian name of the day (*dies dominicus, dominica*) is used even in documents written by pagan administrators from 325 onwards[13].

Thus, if one were to synthesise what has been discussed above from the perspective of the so-called »Byzantine symphony«, one might conclude with the words of the Church historian Cyril Hovorun: »Thus, symphony in its original Constantinian form had a decidedly ritual dimension. From his perspective, it strengthened the integrity of the empire and enhanced his own legitimacy«[14].

From another point of view, however, Constantine's decisions of 312–314 to intervene in the Donatist controversy by virtue of his imperial function – uncontested by any of the rival Christian groups[15] and in fact made at their request[16] – and the repeated interventions later in the Arian disputes established a model of state-church relations that had substantial effects on the subsequent history of the church and on what is labelled today as political theology. Rather than accepting the decision of the church to condemn Donatism, which was made independently of him, he accepted the request for a new investigation of the facts, thus – in the words of Alexander Schmemann – »inaugurating the tragic misunderstanding between the theocratic empire and the Church which was to last for many centuries«[17].

The institution of the synod, which up to this point had been an exclusively ecclesiastical one, now became an institution through which relations between church and emperor were mediated, and by means of which the latter maintained the unity of belief across the empire and the true cult due to the true God. The emperor was interested in harmony (ὁμόνοια, *concordia*) as a condition of public safety (*salus rei publica*) and was convinced that he had received directly from

---

13 Klaus Martin Girardet, Kaisertum, Religionspolitik und das Recht von Staat und Kirche in der Spätantike, Bonn 2009, pp. 214f. (my translation).
14 Cyril Hovorun, Is the Byzantine »Symphony« Possible in Our Days?, in: Journal of Church and State 59/2 (2016), pp. 280–296, at p. 284.
15 Constantine convoked two synods in Rom in 313 and Arelate in 314.
16 This is in fact no novelty, but rather a Christian attitude in evidence even during the persecutions, when the Christians never denied the role of imperial power: »For from the age of the apostles onwards, Christians had believed that Roman emperors were appointed by God to judge all disputes among their subjects«, Timothy D. Barnes, Emperors and Bishops of Constantinople (324–431), in: George E. Demacopoulos/Aristotle Papanikolaou (eds.), Christianity, Democracy, and the Shadow of Constantine, New York 2016, pp. 175–201, at p. 175.
17 Schmemann, The Historical Road, p. 68.

God the assignment to preserve ὁμόνοια in the Christian church or to enforce it by the means at his disposal as emperor[18]. The opening discourse at the Ecumenical Council of Nicaea (325), recorded by Eusebius (*Vita Constantini*, III, 12), reveals the emperor's most ardent desire in clear terms: the re-establishment of ὁμόνοια in the entire church[19].

A further relevant issue regarding Constantine's direct involvement in ecclesiastical affairs was his presiding over the Synod of Nicaea (325), which had fundamental politico-ecclesiastical consequences. In this respect, Girardet argues:

> The historical fact of Constantine's pontifical practice towards the church and its bishops under the form, among other things, of his presidency of the council, means that Christianity found a visible head for the first time in its history. Eusebius, bishop of Caesarea, accounted for this state of affairs through his conception about the Christian-theological ruler, attributing to Constantine a specifically Christian high priesthood based on the model of Christ, which spiritually placed the emperor, as the personification of the unity between imperium and sacerdotium, above the church and its ministerial priesthood. During the fourth century, it seems that this conception gained currency in both the East and the West[20].

Constantine's theological and political views as well as those of the succeeding emperors were marked by an element insufficiently considered up to now, namely the role played by various influential counsellors at the imperial court. This is why the models of political theology implemented by emperors can be deemed contextual and sometimes subjective. According to Eusebius, Constantine invited, right after his victory over Maxentius, many Christian priests to join his imperial suite, so that they might advise him on church politics and Christian practices. Thus, the quick assignment of Osius of Cordoba as his ambassador to Africa, mentioned in the letter to the bishop Caecilian of Carthage, attests to the presence of Christian ministers in his entourage and explains why the emperor was so well informed, for example, about the troubles caused by the Donatist disputes in Africa[21]. Moreover, it is obvious that Eusebius of Caesarea and Eusebius of Nicomedia, two semi-Arian hierarchs, were in favour with the emperor after 326–327. Their influence

---

18 Hans Christoph BRENNECKE, Constantin und die Kirche nach dem Konzil von Nicaea (325–337), in: POPESCU/IONIȚĂ (eds.), Cruce și Misiune, pp. 375–394, at p. 379.
19 Ibid., pp. 379–382.
20 GIRARDET, Kaisertum, p. 105 (my translation).
21 On the Emperor Constantine's implication in the Donatist controversy and the measures adopted by him in this context, see Daniel BENGA, Threskeia și coercitio. Gândirea religioasă constantiniană oglindită în scrisorile imperiale privitoare la controversa donatistă, in: Anuarul Facultății de Teologie Ortodoxă București, vol. 6 (2006), pp. 207–217.

can be seen in the fact that Arius was granted permission to return from exile, while Eustacius of Antioch and Marcellus of Ancyra, his fiercest adversaries, were banished, as was later Athanasius of Alexandria[22]. Hence, one encounters politico-religious decisions made under the influence of Christian hierarchs who enjoyed Constantine's trust over the years.

In the following, I wish to emphasise some elements related to the manner in which Constantine's »political theology« is described in the hymnography of the Orthodox Church[23]. A powerful influence over the people in Orthodox traditions is exerted today by the cult of the Church, while the Emperors Constantine, Theodosius and Justinian are acknowledged as saints in the Orthodox Church and are worshipped accordingly through divine services dedicated to them. The discovery of the Holy Cross in Constantine's time led to a high symbolic correlation between the first Christian emperor and the Christian sign of God's love for the world. This is clearly expressed in the Kontakion of his feast, on 21 May, which reads: »Today Constantine and his mother Helen / reveal the precious Cross, / the weapon of the faithful / against their enemies. / For our sakes, it has been shown to be a great sign, and fearsome in battle«[24].

This exceedingly strong symbolic link makes the memory of Constantine return in the living memory of the church each time a feast dedicated to the Holy Cross is celebrated during the liturgical year, i. e., the Exaltation of the Holy Cross on 14 September and the third Sunday of Lent. Constantin's veneration as a saint is first mentioned in texts by fifth-century Church historians and gradually became a generalised practice over the centuries. In the hymns dedicated to him, the church praises him for codifying the Creed and drawing the line between right belief and heresy, as well as for the discovery of the Holy Cross and the promotion of Christianity throughout the empire[25].

Elements of a political theology may also be found in the Troparion of the feast, which emphasises the fact that the imperial city was given by God into the hands of Constantine, who led it in peace:

---

22 BRENNECKE, Constantin und die Kirche, pp. 388f.
23 For a general presentation of the way in which the personalities of the Emperor Constantine and his mother Helen are reflected in the services of the Orthodox Church, see Ion VICOVAN, Sfinții Împărați Constantin și mama sa Elena reflectați în slujbele Bisericii Ortodoxe, in: POPESCU/CĂȚOI (eds.), Cruce și Misiune, pp. 487–505.
24 OCA.ORG, s.v., Kontakion tone 3, URL: <https://oca.org/saints/troparia/2014/05/21/101452-equal-of-the-apostles-and-emperor-constantine-with-his-mother-he> (08-31-2023).
25 On the worship of the Emperor Constantine and his mother Helen in the Orthodox Church, see Viorel IONIȚĂ, Die Verehrung der Heiligen Kaiser Konstantin und seiner Mutter Helena in der Orthodoxen Kirche, in: Martin ILLERT/Martin SCHINDEHÜTTE (eds.), Theologischer Dialog mit der Rumänischen Orthodoxen Kirche. Die Apostolizität der Kirche. Heiligung und Heiligkeit, Leipzig 2014, pp. 213–218.

> Having seen the figure of the Cross in the heavens, / and like Paul not having received his call from men, O Lord, / Your apostle among rulers, the Emperor Constantine, / has been set by Your hand as ruler over the Imperial City / that he preserved in peace for many years, / through the prayers of the Theotokos, O only lover of mankind[26].

This synthetic interpretation of his memory has remained in the cult of the Orthodox Church. However, Schmemann underscores »the radical distinction« between St Paul's conversion and that of St Constantine:

> What Paul experienced on the road to Damascus was a real and profound crisis, a »transvaluation of all values«. Between the old and the new lay an impenetrable line which changed everything in the apostle's life and psychology. This was not true of Constantine. However, it was not by chance that his conversion occurred at the most critical point in his political and imperial career. It was not a matter of political calculation or »Machiavellianism«, as some historians have asserted; yet neither was it a transformation of personality, as it had been for Paul. The explanation of Constantine's conversion must be sought in his psychology and religious and political ideology, which alone will furnish clues for an understanding of his place in Christian history[27].

Theodosius the Great – Bringing People to Christ by Law

The death of the Arian Emperor Valens in the war against the Goths in August 378 led his co-emperor Gratian to ask for the support of the Spanish General Theodosius, who became co-emperor of the East in 379. Choosing as his residence the city of Thessaloniki, where the anti-Arian bishop Acholius, a close friend of Pope Damasus, was in office, the Emperor Theodosius I (r. 379–395) became an advocate of Nicene orthodoxy like no one before him. The baptism that he received from Acholius in 380 after falling ill severely and his subsequent recovery obviously influenced his later politico-religious decisions. Whether the interpretation of Valens' death in the battle against the Goths as a punishment for the Arian heresy – as some Nicene groups claimed – really played a role in the decisions of Theodosius is difficult to prove[28]. The need to continue the war against the Goths, the fact that he was coming from the West, as well as that he was a man of action and stood under the

---

26 OCA.ORG, s.v., Troparion tone 8, <https://oca.org/saints/troparia/2014/05/21/101452-equal-of-the-apostles-and-emperor-constantine-with-his-mother-he> (08-31-2023).
27 SCHMEMANN, The Historical Road, p. 63.
28 For details, see Wilhelm ENSSLIN, Die Religionspolitik des Kaisers Theodosius des Großen, Munich 1955; Richard Malcolm ERRINGTON, Roman Imperial Policy from Julian to Theodosius, Chapel Hill, NC 2006, pp. 212–215.

influence of Bishop Acholius – all these motivated him to promote the Nicene faith through a first edict, *Cunctos populos*, issued on 28 February 380:

> We wish the citizens of all cities that the moderation of Our Clemency rules to practice that form of religion which, as the religious tradition introduced by himself and reaching out until the present day maintains, Holy Peter the Apostle brought to the Romans, and which it is evident that Bishop Damasus and Peter, bishop of Alexandria, a man of apostolic holiness, follow: that is, that we should believe, in accordance with apostolic teaching and the doctrine of the evangelists, in the single divine being of the Father, the Son, and the Holy Spirit, within an equal majesty and a Holy Trinity. We command persons accepting this rule to embrace the name of catholic Christians; but the rest, whom we judge to be out of their minds and insane, shall suffer the disgrace attached to heretical dogma, their meeting places shall not bear the name »church«, they are first to be stricken by punishment from God, but later by the vengeance of our passion, which we shall have assumed in accordance with the judgment of heaven (*quem ex caelesti arbitrio sumpserimus*)[29].

This edict, initially addressed to the people of Constantinople, is the first law introduced by a Byzantine emperor that contains in its preamble a definition of what Theodosius considered to be »religious orthodoxy«. This decree was obviously a confession of faith proclaimed by the emperor, but it is worth remembering that this decision was based only on a Nicene minority in Constantinople, while the overall majority was held by the Arians[30]. At the end of the edict, the emperor emphasises that his inner religious attitude towards God and his belief (*ex caelesti arbitrio*) led to the decision described above. Both Constantine's and Theodosius' decisions to favour and promote religious minorities at the moment of their accession to the throne debunks the idea of what one may call political opportunism, showing that it was above all their religious convictions that strongly influenced their political decisions.

---

29 »Cunctos populos, quos clementiae nostrae regit temperamentum, in tali volumus religione versari, quam divinum Petrum apostolum tradidisse Romanis religio usque ad nunc ab ipso insinuata declarat quamque pontificem Damasum sequi claret et Petrum Alexandriae episcopum virum apostolicae sanctitatis, hoc est, ut secundum apostolicam disciplinam euangelicamque doctrinam patris et filii et spiritus sancti unam deitatem sub parili maiestate et sub pia trinitate credamus. Hanc legem sequentes Christianorum catholicorum nomen iubemus amplecti, reliquos vero dementes vesanosque iudicantes haeretici dogmatis infamiam sustinere nec conciliabula eorum ecclesiarum nomen accipere, divina primum vindicta, post etiam motus nostri, quem ex caelesti arbitrio sumpserimus, ultione plectendos« (*Codex Theodosianus*, 16. 1. 2). The English translation is by ERRINGTON, Roman Imperial Policy, pp. 217f.

30 Ibid., p. 218.

In his recent analysis of the relations between the Byzantine emperors and the bishops of Constantinople between 324 and 431, Timothy Barnes proved the absolute power of emperors in the election or deposition of bishops, especially in the context of the dispute between Arianism and Nicene orthodoxy that erupted after the death of Constantine, albeit through the approval of the councils of bishops. Theodosius was the first emperor to violate a rule observed by Constantine when he »unceremoniously expelled Demophilus from Constantinople without waiting for him to be condemned by a council of bishops«[31].

Considering this Theodosian decision within the politico-religious development of the empire after Constantine the Great, one can state that already under his sons, between 337 and 361, the freedom of belief that he had upheld was gradually restricted through anti-pagan and anti-heretical legislation. The rule of Theodosius I definitely marks the end of *libertas religionis* for the people of Antiquity: Any sort of witchcraft was prohibited in 379 (*Codex Theodosianus*, 16. 5. 5.), Nicene Christianity was declared the state religion in 380 (*Codex Theodosianus*, 1. 2. and 25), and as of 391–392, performing pagan rites became punishable by law and even entering temples was forbidden (*Codex Theodosianus*, 10. 10 and 12). Only the Jews were exempted[32].

In his doctoral thesis on religious intolerance in the Byzantine Empire, Philip Tilden points out that Theodosian anti-pagan legislation was in fact milder than that against Christian heresies:

> The punishments for heretics were also worse than for pagans; consistently the legislation sought to place heretics beyond the bounds of society, either physically through expulsion or exile or more symbolically (though no less practically) through depriving them of testamentary power. Again, no such punishments were levelled against pagans. As such, it should be concluded that heretics were considered to be worse than pagans[33].

Schmemann construes the theologico-political resolutions of Emperor Theodosius in the following manner:

> It must be frankly admitted that the Church demanded of the state that it combat paganism and itself denied the principle of toleration. […] But the minds of Christians, in which the evangelical ideal of religious freedom had flared up briefly during the experience of martyrdom, were blinded for a long time by the vision of a Christian theocracy that would

---

31 BARNES, Emperors and Bishops, p. 187.
32 GIRARDET, Von der Verfolgung zur Anerkennung, pp. 93f.
33 Philip TILDEN, Religious Intolerance in the Later Roman Empire. The Evidence of the Theodosian Code, Ph.D. Dissertation, University of Exeter 2006, p. 281.

bring men to Christ not only by grace but by law as well. Much time passed before the pagan nature of this theocracy was recognized. State sanctions gave the Church unprecedented strength, and perhaps brought many to faith and new life, but after Theodosius the Great it was no longer only a community of believers; it was also a community of those obliged to believe[34].

By endorsing the Orthodox faith and proscribing anyone who believed otherwise, in his political agenda,

> Theodosius interpreted church-state symphony as the ὁμόνοια (like-mindedness) of his subjects on matters of faith. This was a reduction of the Eusebian vision of the empire and of the very notion of faith, which was downgraded to what one believed about the Trinity and the Incarnation. Under Theodosius, symphony became a doctrinal and ethical category and turned into a precondition for the salvation of the state and individuals[35].

This reality is not to be interpreted according to the norms of the present modern secular state. At the time, emperor and church alike sincerely believed in the truth they were defending, just as the »heretics« believed in the truth for which they were ready to die. The idea of a religiously neutral state was completely alien to the mentality of the age[36]. The concept of »political Orthodoxy«, understood as the adoption and propagation of the Nicene-Constantinopolitan dogma by political power as a means of defining cultural and political identity, which was recently proposed for the post-iconoclastic period by James Skedros, can be already identified in the time of the Emperor Theodosius I[37].

Justinian and the Concept of *Symphony*

Remembered in the history of humankind particularly for two extraordinary accomplishments – his legislation compiled in *Corpus Iuris Civilis* and the cathedral of Hagia Sophia in Constantinople – the Emperor Justinian I (r. 527–565) practiced a religious policy that could be reduced to the formula »One state, one law, and one church«[38]. His simultaneously political and religious programme was underpinned not by the dialectic between *religio licita* or *illicita*, as it had been at the time of

---

34 SCHMEMANN, The Historical Road, pp. 110f.
35 Cyril HOVORUN, Is the Byzantine »Symphony«, p. 285.
36 SCHMEMANN, The Historical Road, pp. 117f.
37 James C. SKEDROS, »You Cannot Have a Church Without an Empire. Political Orthodoxy in Byzantium«, in: DEMACOPOULOS/PAPANIKOLAOU (eds.), Christianity, pp. 219–231, at pp. 222f.
38 Alexander A. VASILIEV, History of the Byzantine Empire (324–1453), Madison, WI 1952, p. 148.

Constantine, but by a fundamental conviction about *religio vera* according to his understanding of the right faith[39]. Being certain, like other emperors before him, that the imperial office was entrusted to him by God, he relied on his faith in the Holy Trinity that created and ruled over the entire cosmos[40].

Just as Marcus Aurelius was seen as a philosopher on the throne, so Justinian can be regarded as a »theologian« on the throne. On the one hand, he involved himself in the theological controversies related to the Chalcedonian formula and its reception, in the debate over Origen's theology and in the well-known dispute over the »three chapters« trying to reconcile the miaphysite and dyophysite groups by promoting the famous neo-Chalcedonian theology, while on the other hand, he initiated the construction of many new churches and monasteries.

Justinian's politico-religious vision continued and deepened that of Theodosius. At the beginning of his long reign, he passed several edicts, in which the Orthodox faith proclaimed by the first four Ecumenical Councils was decreed as normative within the entire empire[41] and the canons of the Ecumenical Councils were declared »imperial laws«[42]. Novel 32 of 4 April 544, reveals his politico-religious views:

> We believe that the first and greatest good of all people is the right confession (ὀρθὴν ὁμολογίαν) of the true and immaculate faith of the Christians, such that it has to be strengthened in all respects, and all the holy priests of the inhabited world (τῆς οἰκουμένης) in unanimity (εἰς ὁμόνοιαν) must come together (συναφθῆναι) and in one voice (ὁμοφώνως) confess and preach the right faith of the Christians, and any reason invented by heretics must be removed, as is shown both in my various writings and in my edicts[43].

The famous sixth novel from his *Corpus Iuris Civilis* epitomised the concept of symphony as it had developed in the 530s:

> There are two greatest gifts which God, in his love for man, has granted from on high: the priesthood and the imperial authority – *hierosyne* and *basileia*, *sacerdotium* and *imperium*. The first serves divine things, while the latter directs and administers human affairs; both, however, proceed from the same source and adorn the life of mankind. Hence, nothing

---

39 For Justinian's religious legislation, see Hamilcar S. Alivisatos, Die kirchliche Gesetzgebung des Kaisers Justinian I., Aalen 1973.
40 Mischa Meier, Justinian. Herrschaft, Reich und Religion, Munich 2004, p. 7.
41 Teodor Tăbuș, The Orthodoxy of Emperor Justinian's Christian Faith as a Matter of Roman Law (CJ I, 1, 5–8), in: Studia Patristica 92/18 (2017), pp. 411–422, at p. 415.
42 John Meyendorff, The Byzantine Legacy in the Orthodox Church, New York 1982, p. 47.
43 Rudolf Schöll/Wilhelm Kroll (eds.), Corpus Juris Civilis: Novellae, vol. 3, Berlin 1895, pp. 665f.; Samuel P. Scott, The Civil Law, vol. 17, New York 1932, p. 132, quoted by Tăbuș, The Orthodoxy of Emperor, p. 411.

should be such a source of care to the emperors as the dignity of the priests, since it is for their imperial welfare that they constantly implore God. For if the priesthood is in every way free from blame and possesses access to God, and if the emperors administer equitably and judiciously the state entrusted to their care, general harmony (*symphonia tis agathi*) will result and whatever is beneficial will be bestowed upon the human race[44].

Although this preamble is often quoted, it has to be interpreted in the context of Novel 6 as a whole, the real aim of which is »to legislate on the marital status of the clergy, on church property, on episcopal residence, on clergy selection and education, on obstacles to ordination, and on the legal status of the clergy«[45]. In this context, the expression »human affairs« refers to all the legal aspects of the ecclesiastical structures that are within the emperor's power and jurisdiction. The »divine things« belonging to the jurisdiction of the priesthood included the liturgy and the administration of the sacraments. Through the importance given to divine worship, Justinian continued and developed the perspective of Constantine the Great. To the present day, the Orthodox Holy Liturgy shows Justinian's influence. During his time, essential doctrinal elements were introduced into its structure, including the Creed and the hymn »Only – Begotten Son«, which were meant to offer a correct expression of Chalcedonian theology in the context of the miaphysite disputes and to affirm the link between *lex orandi* and *lex credendi* necessary to its comprehension[46].

It is worth noting here that both powers, the temporal and the ecclesiastical, share the same origin and purpose. They are connected by their divine origin and their purpose, since for Justinian the well-being of humankind was related not only to earth, but also to heaven, having as ultimate goal the salvation of souls. This Novel does not, therefore, refer to distinct entities, *imperium* and *sacerdotium*, but, as Georges Florovsky has pointed out, to one society: »There was but *One* and comprehensive *Christian Society*, which was at once a Church and a State«[47]. Treitinger has also argued that this theory was not new, but was taken over from Ancient Israel, which had been »a Kingdom and a Church« at the same time, as well as from the pagan Roman Empire, which had always been »a politico-ecclesiastical institution« and remained so even after being »christened«[48]. The consequence

---

44 Quoted by MEYENDORFF, The Byzantine Legacy, p. 48.
45 Ibid., p. 49.
46 Cf. Karl Christian FELMY, Vom urchristlichen Herrenmahl zur Göttlichen Liturgie der orthodoxen Kirche. Ein historischer Kommentar, Erlangen 2000, pp. 85–93.
47 Georges FLOROVSKY, Antinomies of Christian History. Empire and Desert, in: Id., Christianity and Culture, Belmont, MA 1974, pp. 67–100, on p. 75.
48 Otto TREITINGER, Die oströmische Kaiser- und Reichsidee nach ihrer Gestaltung im höfischen Zeremoniell, Jena 1938, p. 44.

was quite simple: Only Christians could be citizens of the empire, and they were compelled to be orthodox in their faith and demeanour[49].

Although many aspects of the Byzantine *symphony* did undergo changes and adaptations in the course of history, this reality based on »the idea of a single theopolitical body in which the church and the state are inseparable from each other« remained a constant in the Byzantine political theology. Nevertheless, this understanding is missing in modern interpretations of the *symphony*,

> which presupposes that the church and the state are two entities that interact with one another. This presupposition, however, does not apply to Byzantium. After the conversion of the Roman Empire to Christianity, the church and the state merged for the majority of the Byzantines into a single theopolitical entity[50].

What has to be mentioned at this point is Schmemann's critique of Justinian and of any Byzantine theopolitical conception that, in his opinion, stifles the freedom of the church and leads to the fact that »religion itself has the state as the goal of its functions, and in this sense is subject to it as the final value, for the sake of which it exists«[51]. For the Christians of the first centuries, the church was not a reality of this world. They were a new people that was not bound to any human, earthly state. For them, the absolute values of history were God and human beings, while the state was constrained by its very nature, as it pertained solely to this world. Instead, as Schmemann puts it, »in Justinian's synthesis, the Church appears to dissolve, and the awareness that it is radically alien to the world and the empire disappears once and for all from state thinking«[52].

Some final Remarks

Since Byzantium did not possess a fully-fledged constitution to concretely describe the powers and competences of the emperors, the way the state related to the church differed from one emperor to the other. Systematic political treatises that defined the theoretical basis for political legitimisation did not exist in Byzantium, political power being always in the hands of the imperial office. The complex nature of the Byzantine political theology has been fittingly encapsulated by Hans-Georg Beck:

---

49 Ibid., p. 75.
50 Hovorun, Is the Byzantine »Sympony«, pp. 288f.
51 Schmemann, The Historical Road, p. 152.
52 Ibid., p. 153.

Because there was no written imperial constitution, but also because canonical law never provided a clear distinction between emperor and church [...], the problem can be reduced *per se* to a question of principles and person. With the former, one must consider that in theological and political thought, the Byzantine state and church are not separate or even separable institutions, but rather modes of appearance of one and the same Christianity, modes of appearance of which one would be unimaginable without the other. Hence, a two-power theory would have been inconceivable in Byzantium[53].

Therefore, the *libertas religionis* promoted by Constantine cannot be understood in today's sense of religious freedom and separation between church and state. Such a separation would have been inconceivable to a worldview in which the religious and political spheres were constantly intertwined. Although Constantine had intended freedom for all in his political-religious programme beginning in 312–313, the destruction of many temples by his orders as well as the de-paganisation of public life indicate his preference and support for Christianity and the Christian cult. From Constantine's decisions and documents, it can thus be inferred how his religious evolution influenced his political decisions in the last two decades of his rule. He traced the outlines of a vision that the Emperors Theodosius and Justinian transformed into the prohibition of any form of religious organisation outside Chalcedonian orthodoxy.

During the rule of Theodosius, the Byzantine state and church constituted not only the community of believers, but rather the community of those obliged to believe in a certain way, thus inaugurating what James Skedros called »political Orthodoxy«. This direction, set by the integration of the right faith into the political agenda of the emperors, was followed by numerous Byzantine autocrats, even though many of them failed to realise their religiously founded political vision. Interestingly enough, the new historical reality in which the Orthodox Churches in the states of the European Union find themselves today tends to conform to a paradigm that resembles the first Christian centuries rather than the paradigm supported by Theodosius and Justinian. I would argue that these churches would do well to search for inspiration in the first Christian centuries marked by confession of faith and martyrdom rather than in the Eastern Roman Empire of Late Antiquity with its established »political Orthodoxy«.

---

53 Hans-Georg BECK, Kirche und theologische Literatur im byzantinischen Reich, Munich 1977, p. 36 (my translation).

Anthony Kaldellis

Three Byzantine Theories on the Origin of Political Communities

Introduction

How did the first political communities at the dawn of human history come into being? What forces induced and enabled primitive people to build cities, lay down laws, and establish complex political regimes? These questions were a blind spot of Byzantine thought and received little attention, most of which was incidental to other intellectual problems. The Bible glosses over these questions in a manner so notorious that its account of human origins continues to elicit scepticism among the faithful. After Adam and Eve were expelled from Eden, they had two sons, Cain and Abel. Cain kills Abel, but Cain is then said to have a wife, who appears out of nowhere, and with her he has a son, Enoch. Cain then builds a city that he names after his son (Genesis 4). The text does not explain where these other people came from, why they came together to form a city, or by what mental, social, and intellectual resources they put this project into motion. Some Byzantine chronicles, relying on apocryphal sources, explained that Cain's wife was his sister Azoura, but this still left unanswered the question of where all the other people came from who populated the first cities, and what dynamics enabled them to create cities in the first place. The same was true of apocalyptic texts, such as Pseudo-Methodios (late seventh century), which sketches the early days of human history down to the establishment of the first kingdoms, but still does not explain how any of this took place: The people and the cities simply appear, and that text focuses instead on the sexual immorality of Adam's descendants[1].

It was possible to approach the problem from the opposite direction and trace back to its origins the history of the longest-lived state in world history, i. e., the Roman polity. This was done, for example, by the statesman and philosopher Theodoros Metochites (early fourteenth century), but it did not result in a general anthropological model that accounted for the whole of human development from

---

1 For chronicles, see Georgios the Monk, Chronicle, in: Carl Gotthard de Boor (ed.), Georgii Monachi Chronicon, rev. Peter Wirth, 2 vols., Stuttgart 1978, vol. 1, pp. 6f.; cf. Georgios Synkellos, Georgii Syncelli Ecloga chronographica, ed. by Alden A. Mosshammer, Leipzig 1984, pp. 8–10; Pseudo-Methodios, Die Apokalypse des Ps.-Methodios, in: Anastasios C. Lolos (ed.), Meisenheim am Glan 1976.

primitive times to advanced civilisation. In his essay on how Rome grew to such great power from so small a beginning, Metochites merely relied on the ancient historians to recount the tale of Aeneas and Romulus, and how the latter especially gathered his band of outcasts and laid the foundation of Rome's future greatness[2]. This was the tale of one city, not a leap in human development as such. The latter was neither explained by the Bible nor covered by the ancient historians. A number of ancient thinkers, for example Plato, had presented imaginative models to explain the origin of cities and civilisation in prehistory, yet it does not appear that Byzantine thinkers relied on them in developing their own[3].

In fact, Byzantine writers did not develop a coherent or self-conscious tradition of thought on this question, a consolidated anthropological discipline that dealt with the origins of civilisation. The focus here will be on a handful of thinkers of the middle and late Byzantine periods who happened, in the course of answering other questions, to veer into this territory. The survey will avoid the early period, as the lingering traces of classical anthropology complicate its intellectual scene. The focus will also be on Orthodox writers (not, therefore, on Psellos, Plethon, and the like), in order to understand how their analysis engaged with the broader issues of »political Orthodoxy«. Specifically, the thinkers who will be discussed here are Photios (ninth century), Eustathios of Thessalonike (twelfth century), and Manuel Moschopoulos (early fourteenth century). They wrote without knowledge of each other's works and in different genres. Responding to a different set of concerns, each touched on the question of how civilisation began and by what mechanisms or values it was originally and subsequently sustained. A number of them wrestled with the further question of whether those mechanisms were Christian or even compatible with Christianity. This created an intellectual space where the political sphere could be seen as essentially secular and all-too-human, in striking contrast to the way in which contemporary imperial panegyric depicted the Roman political order as a divine institution for propagating Christian values. Was the message of Christianity superimposed on a political world that had already been devised by mere mortals, or was it somehow baked in from the start?

If asked about the origin of political communities, most Byzantines would likely have said that God had something to do with it, that he instituted them for the good of mankind. St Paul had implied as much in Romans 13. These banal assumptions are expressed, for example, in a letter of Maximos the Confessor (d. 662), which he addressed before 642 to an official, Ioannes *koubikoularios*, who had posed the question: »Why has God judged it right that men be ruled by other men, given that

---

2 Theodoros METOCHITES, Kephalaia, in: Theophilus KIESSLING (ed.), Theodori Metochitae Miscellanea, Leipzig 1821, pp. 699–703.

3 For example, PLATO, The Laws. Cambridge Texts in the History of Political Thought, ed. by Malcolm SCHOFIELD/Tom GRIFFITH, Cambridge 2016, in book 3.

they all share the same nature?«. The Fall, Maximos responds, introduced disorder and immorality into the lives of men, who were mired in the material life. God accordingly instituted »the law of kingship among men« in order to prevent them from sinking to the level of animals and killing each other like the fishes in the sea. Kings are meant to restrain the abuses that the powerful visit upon the weak (a traditional refrain of Roman imperial propaganda). That is, kingship is meant to ensure justice. Righteous rulers are those who acknowledge their dependence on God and follow his commandments, whereas those who rule for their own benefit are tyrants. Maximos briefly raises the possibility of human self-governance, or kingship independent of God: When people separate themselves from God's kingdom, he still allows them to be governed by their own kings, lest the ensuing anarchy or polyarchy bring destruction to the whole of mankind. This is perhaps a necessary concession to history, as most monarchies in history were not Christian. But generally, Maximos can imagine good kings only as enforcers of God's decrees, probably having in mind the controversy over Monothelitism that he had stirred up. In sum, Maximos offers a theological and not anthropological account, inscribing it within a moral framework defined by the fall of man and an association of evil with materiality. Maximos claims that he received this account from wise men of the past, and will stick with it even though he knows of alternatives, which he does not divulge[4]. But later Byzantine thinkers would deviate greatly from this approach.

Photios

Like Maximos, Photios also fielded philosophical questions from correspondents who were court officials. One Christophoros *protospatharios* and *protasekretis* set Photios off by asking him about Luke 12:33: »Sell your possessions and give [the money] to the poor«. It is not clear what Christophoros' precise question was, but it reminded Photios of an anti-Christian argument made by the Emperor Julian the Apostate (r. 361–363) on precisely this point. If everyone did this, who would be left to buy? And how could any city, nation, or household continue to function? Jesus' commandment undermined the foundation of the social and political order. In a long letter that is also a mini-treatise and diatribe, Photios set out to refute the

---

4 MAXIMOS THE CONFESSOR, Letter 10, in: Patrologia Graeca 91: 449A–453A; for self-governance, see 452C. Concerning the date, see Marek JANKOWIAK/Phil BOOTH, A New Date-List of the Works of Maximus the Confessor, in: Pauline ALLEN/Bronwen NEIL (eds.), The Oxford Handbook of Maximus the Confessor, Oxford 2017, pp. 19–76, at p. 38; brief discussion in: Phil BOOTH, Crisis of Empire. Doctrine and Dissent at the End of Late Antiquity, Berkeley 2014, pp. 222f.

hated pagan emperor; in the process, he grappled with the dynamics that created and sustained political communities from the start[5].

Photios' response hurls many insults at Julian, which need not detain us. Neither should another problem with which he wrestles, namely the degree to which Jesus' commandments were meant to be universalised, or, in modern terms, whether they should be treated as Kantian categorical imperatives, which is what Julian seems to have been doing. Photios does not think that they were meant to be universalised. People being what they are, Jesus' commandments would likely be followed by only a few, making political orders »safe« from excessive compassion and philanthropy. Nevertheless, in Photios' view, their universal application would lead to a utopia that strongly resembles some twentieth-century communist ideals. Be that as it may, Photios expects that most human beings will choose to remain selfish, amassing their private fortunes by exploiting the labour of others[6]. In sum, Photios displays a rather negative estimation of human nature in its exercise of free will. In fact, he says that free will makes it extremely unlikely that all will follow Jesus' commandments, »no matter what threats he used, even if he were to have buttressed his words with thunder and lightning and cracks in the earth«. People are always going to be both good and bad. To be sure, it would have been absurd for Jesus not to impart his moral advice just because not everyone would follow it, but Photios essentially (if tacitly) concedes that a Christian moral order encompassing the majority of humanity is an impossibility[7].

It is only at the end of the letter that some hope appears: The Christian message has spread throughout the world and it is possible that more people will take it up. Photios points to monasteries as places where Jesus' commandments are literally applied to human communities as a whole. However, monasteries do not prove that Christian principles can underpin an entire political order, as they are small and situated within and sustained by surrounding political societies[8].

In order to respond to Julian, Photios dissociates Jesus' commandments from the (exploitative) modes and orders that have governed political societies essentially since the dawn of human history. Photios concedes those modes and orders to

---

5 PHOTIOS, Letter 187, in: Vasileios LAOURDAS/Leendert Gerrit WESTERINK (eds.), Photii Patriarchae Constantinopolitani Epistulae et Amphilochia, 3 vols., Leipzig 1983–1987, vol. 2, pp. 76–87; Christophoros also received Letter 129 on Matthew 6.17: »But thou, when thou fastest, anoint thine head, and wash thy face«. For the fragments of Julian's work to which Photios may have been responding, see Anthony KALDELLIS, The Byzantine Republic. People and Power at New Rome, Cambridge, MA 2015, pp. 183f.
6 For categorical imperative, see PHOTIOS, Letter 187, lines 105–165; for utopia, see lines 36–65; for labor of others, see lines 67f.
7 Ibid., lines 209–221.
8 Ibid., lines 275–325.

Julian and claims for Christianity the precepts that will improve human life. The latter include not only »Sell your possessions«, but a host of others too, such as »give and you shall receive«, »love your enemies«, and so on. The strong implication is that human societies were not originally founded on or subsequently sustained by Christian principles, which only made their appearance during Christ's ministry. Even eight hundred years later, in Photios' time, they had still not managed to create a political order that could override the all-too-human orders championed by »Julian«.

But we do not need to rely on implications only. Photios makes this radical disjunction explicit in lines 176–206. He accuses Julian of mistakenly assuming that the Saviour intended to impart anything of significance regarding »the political art«. Photios concedes, that the Saviour had nothing to say about strategy, armies, soldiers, supplies, market-controls, judges, and lawgivers:

> You idiot, do you not realise that our Saviour and God was not chiefly concerned about political forms (*politikoi typoi*) and their orders (*taxis*)? For he knew that human beings would make sufficient provision for all that through their experience, as need and necessity instructed them efficiently on a daily basis, and later generations would examine the mistakes of the previous ones and make all course-corrections.

The Saviour's primary concern was not with such »political conduct or bodily wellbeing«, but with »the salvation of souls and the introduction of a higher and more philosophical way of life«. This is not to say that the Saviour was indifferent toward politics or that he did not help human beings along the way, but that this was not his *primary* goal. The world of politics emerged from the bottom up, through human trial and error.

Have we uncovered a truth about Photios' political thought here? Can we say that this patriarch believed that political communities emerged through largely worldly efforts of human trial and error? Or that Christianity appeared only later to add a spiritual, salvific layer on top of them, but was not terribly concerned with how they operated on the ground? Not necessarily. In other works, for example in homilies before the emperor or in the legal text that scholars often attribute to him (the *Eisagoge*), Photios ascribes to God a much deeper role in the creation of the Roman political order, as well as in supporting, maintaining, and even regulating it on the more granular level of its laws[9]. Letter 187 should not be taken to override those texts, but it should caution us against taking them at face value at the letter's

---

9 See especially the proem of the *Eisagoge* in: Andreas SCHMINCK, Studien zu mittelbyzantinischen Rechtsbüchern, Frankfurt am Main 1986, pp. 4–11; see also Cyril A. MANGO, The Homilies of Photius, Patriarch of Constantinople, Cambridge, MA 1958.

expense. Each of Photios' pronouncements was stamped by its specific rhetorical circumstances. In Letter 187, Photios had to contend with the powerful claims made by Julian on behalf of pagan antiquity as the creator of the world's political institutions. In that context, it served the patriarch well to renounce Christian claims to them and stick to salvation as Jesus' goal. Political regimes thereby appear as secular, all-too-human, and basically un-Christian both by origin (in historical time) and by nature (at all times). Speaking before the emperors, by contrast, Photios could dispense with the claims of antiquity and could make grander ones on behalf of his faith.

Eustathios of Thessaloniki

Eustathios wore many hats during the course of his career, being at various times professor of rhetoric, classical scholar and commentator on Homer, court orator, and bishop of Thessaloniki. In addition to his orations, massive commentaries, letters, homilies, and his famous account of the capture of Thessaloniki by the Normans in 1185, he also wrote a number of what we can only call essays on a range of topics, though these have received little attention, in part because they are written in maddeningly obscure prose. One of the most interesting and least studied of these essays bears the title *On the Proper Obedience that is Owed to a Christian Government*[10]. If it is about that topic, however, it is only indirectly. The first half of it contains a long discussion of the emergence of civilisation in the period between Adam and Moses (sections 1–22), followed by briefer accounts of the irruption of Mosaic and then Christian law (sections 22–25 and 26–34 respectively) and a recapitulation of the story thus far (sections 35–44). The second half of the text (sections 45–89) is a rambling effort to persuade the audience to adopt civilised standards of behaviour, as Eustathios believed that his society had again become crude and immoral.

It is impossible to give a proper close reading of this text here, but (pending future studies) the main argument of its first part can be presented and analysed. The narrative that interests us takes place between Adam and Moses, which is why its protagonists are called *Adamiaioi*, but is not set in any specific location or culture.

---

10 Eustathios of THESSALONIKE, On the Proper Obedience that is Owed to a Christian Government, in: Gottlieb Lukas Friedrich TAFEL (ed.), Eustathii metropolitae Thessalonicensis opuscula, Frankfurt am Main 1832; reprinted Amsterdam 1964, pp. 13–29; reprinted (and easier to read) in: Patrologia Graeca 136, pp. 301–358; discussion by Paolo CESARETTI, The Exegete as a Storyteller. The Dawn of Humanity according to Eustathios of Thessalonike, in: Panagiotis ROILOS (ed.), Medieval Greek Storytelling. Fictionality and Narrative in Byzantium, Wiesbaden 2014, pp. 131–140. For Eustathios in general, see Filippomaria PONTANI et al. (eds.), Reading Eustathios of Thessalonike, Berlin 2017.

Jews as such are absent from the text, as are the Patriarchs of the Old Testament. The tale is set in the context of the Biblical narrative, but it is generically human.

There was a time before law and the proper shepherding of human affairs, before order, governance, assemblies, society, or civilisation itself (*hemerotes*), the distinctive mark of humanity (1). Unlike Photios, Eustathios sees human beings as rational and divine by nature, as second only to the angels, but in the evil days after Cain and Abel they became irrational and beastly by choice (2). But there were a few good seeds scattered among these violent beasts who wanted to improve the rest, because they realised that this beastly behaviour was a deviation from human nature, which was inherently divine (3–6). They prayed to God for assistance and God did indeed show them favour, facilitating the assembly of people into groups, »a populous *synodos* for the common good« (6–7). The good people, whom Eustathios emphatically and frequently calls »teachers«, reminded all the others of the punishments that God could visit upon them (»he left Paradise empty, what makes you think he won't do the same to the entire earth?«) (8). This stands in contrast to Photios' view that even Christ could not threaten mankind enough to change its ways for the better. Moreover, Eustathios alternates between attributing the success of these teachers to God and to their own efforts. In one place he calls them »self-taught wise teachers« (9), but then he ascribes their wisdom to the fear of God (10). These teachers were inspired both by looking to the heavens and by their own natural reasoning. They were aware of no communication by God since the days of Adam in Paradise; they had not met Abraham or knew about him.

To make a long story short, these wise teachers gathered the people and made them more truly human. They instituted feasts, assemblies, festivals, singing, and dancing, and even persuaded the »solitaries« to join these group activities (10–11); this may reflect Eustathios' general criticism of the monasticism of his period, especially of hermits and other exotic types, whom he attacked in other works[11]. The religion (*threskeia*) of this »archaic« society was »correct and learned« (13). It could not by definition have been Christian, which makes this an endorsement of »natural« religion by Eustathios. Aphrodite stopped being so indiscriminate and marriage was instituted in one-to-one relationships, with each family in its own tent; children were no longer of ambiguous parentage. »And so now man was truly man« (14). The »most God-loving chief counsellors and arch-teachers« and »self-made deacons of the Good« were now praised and made into rulers (*archons*) (15–16). Their societies grew and became more complex, and at some point, they also invented letters. This elicits a long panegyric of the written word by Eustathios, in part because letters enabled the laws to be written down, and thus

---

11 Anthony KALDELLIS, Hellenism in Byzantium. The Transformations of Greek Identity and the Reception of the Classical Tradition, Cambridge 2007, pp. 253f.

recently-formed custom gave way to fixed rules (17–18). Under these conditions, people returned to the original form of human nature, which was simple, peaceful, and calm (21). This way of life was founded on the »common counsel of the wise men« and gave rise to »a law that was natural (*physikos*) and common to all peoples (*ethnikos*)«, a translation of *ius naturalis* and *ius gentium*. This utopia was not Christian, for all that God lurked behind it somewhere.

All this, the account continues, happened a long time ago. At some point God decided to contribute a Second law on top of the first and Natural law, and this was Mosaic law (22). Eustathios is evasive about what Mosaic law actually prescribed and what good, if any, it did. He stresses that it was obscure and mysterious and only hinted at what was to come, namely the Incarnation, or Third law, which resolved the hazy mysteries of Mosaic law (22–25). We have by now entered historical time, though the tale does not become more concrete: It remains an abstract sequence of moral phases. After explaining, in frustratingly vague terms, the moral contributions of the Third law (25–34), Eustathios decides to recapitulate the achievement of the first men and especially of their wise teachers (35–44), thereby squeezing his brief survey of the Mosaic law and Christianity between two longer and more specific sections on Natural law. The latter thereby emerges as the true protagonist and focus of his account. Guided by their teachers, the first men developed pastoralism and stopped killing each other (35); they left the caves, built houses, and instituted marriage (36); developed agriculture, as »Mother Earth provided honeyed milk for men, her children«, a fitting image for a natural system (37); and their daring gave rise to overseas trade, hunting, and fishing (37–40). Many other arts were also invented that »gave a political organisation to men who had previously been artless and unable to live politically« (42). Eventually, this resulted in the making of cities (43).

It should be noted that Eustathios' recapitulation of life under Natural law omits the religious dimension: Human evolution becomes a purely secular process. Neither does God himself intervene nor are these feats accomplished out of respect for him and his Creation. The Patriarchs of the Mosaic law improved upon those foundations and then Christianity filled the world with churches and the correct form of worship (43). It does not seem, from Eustathios' recapitulation here, that the Second and Third laws added much to the fundamental components or basis of human civilisation. They added organized religion, but civilization was prior to that.

The remainder of the treatise excoriates Eustathios' contemporaries for sliding back into the savage and uncivilised ways that preceded the making of the Natural law, and exhorts them to rise back up to the standard that it had set. Eustathios also accuses his contemporaries of falling short of Christian morality, but it seems that the focus of his critique is elsewhere:

The cause of the current *pathos* is as follows: we love the arts that were invented after the first taming – the one that took place according to human standards. We love those arts as if it were impossible to live without them. But we are reluctant to obey the good orders and laws that went with them (51).

Eustathios is judging the Roman Empire of the twelfth century by the standards of humanity during the period of Natural law. And this perhaps explains the emphasis that this work as a whole places on that first period of human development, especially on the fact that its accomplishments were pioneered by teachers (or *didaskaloi*, as he calls them repeatedly). Eustathios, a professional *didaskalos* in both the Church and the secular schools, is about to set himself up as a teacher for a new age of evil. He hopes, through »pedagogical reproaches« (*didaskalikoi oneidismoi*), to reinstate the natural order and »incite mankind to seek higher things« (56). He is doing exactly what the original »noble *Adamiaioi*« had done in the original environment. It is likely that Eustathios' entire presentation of the accomplishments of the primal teachers was designed to create a model for his own pedagogical goals in the second half of the treatise and in his career as a whole. In a later section (59), he compares God to a supreme instructor who assigns subordinate teaching roles to his assistants. Eustathios thus implicitly casts himself as a teaching assistant of God, who will replicate the achievement of the *Adamiaioi*.

There are two more reasons why Eustathios chose to emphasise the First law in his moral history of mankind and to separate it from explicit connection with both Jews and Christians. The first is that he wanted to talk about teachers who could function as a template for himself within the logic of the text and it would have been presumptuous, and possibly blasphemous, to compare himself to the introducers of the Second and Third laws. The second is that Eustathios may well have been a proponent of Natural law. He certainly was a Christian proponent of it, but one who was willing to recognise a system of ethics and civilisation that had predated direct divine interventions in the laws that governed men. Let us also not forget that Eustathios was, above all, a classical scholar with a deep love for the literature of Greek antiquity and an appreciation for all that could still be learnt from it. The Greeks for him were paragons of natural virtue, just as ignorant of divine revelation as his *Adamiaioi*, and Homer in particular was for him the one great teacher of mankind, a »teacher of every theorised art of learning, from whose Ocean all rivers and all methods of knowledge flow«[12]. Someone who believed that

---

12 Eustathios of THESSALONIKE, Commentary on the Odyssey, in: Gottfried STALLBAUM (ed.), Eustathii archiepiscopi Thessalonicensis commentarii ad Homeri Odysseam, 2 vols., Leipzig 1825–1826; reprinted Hildesheim 1970, vol. 1, 2; for discussions, see KALDELLIS, Hellenism in Byzantium, pp. 314f.; id., Classical Scholarship in Twelfth-Century Byzantium, in: Charles BARBER/David JENKINS (eds.), Medieval Greek Commentaries on the Nicomachean Ethics, Leiden/Boston 2009, pp. 1–43,

would structure his model for the evolution of human culture around the advances made by unaided natural wisdom, whose knowledge of God was limited to what it could infer from looking at the cosmos.

Manuel Moschopoulos

Late Byzantium produced a wild profusion of political discourse and theory, as the increasingly complicated history of the beleaguered empire elicited an ever greater diversity of responses by its intellectuals. Eventually, Byzantium even produced a pagan-Platonic theorist of society and the state in the person of Georgios Gemistos Plethon (d. 1452). Less radical thinkers drew attention to various elements of society that, in their view, provided *the* formative principles of the state and political sphere. Each of course was writing with an eye on specific interests. For example, shortly before he ascended to the throne, the Emperor Theodoros II Laskaris (r. 1254–1258) wrote a brief work identifying and extoling *friendship* as the main bond holding societies together, with the more specific interest of promoting personal loyalty to himself. The fourteenth-century theologian Nikolaos Kabasilas wrote what amounted to a paean to *private property* as the foundation of society, though his proximate goal was to attack those who were appropriating monastic lands (possibly imperial officials)[13]. Both of those writers could have constructed a narrative that showed how friendship or private property was the driving force that led to the emergence of complex political societies from a less structured original environment – some of their arguments point in that direction –, but they chose not to go there. However, one scholar who did, at the beginning of the fourteenth century, take his argument right back to the dawn of human civilisation was Manuel Moschopoulos, and he made *oaths* his foundational principle.

Specifically, Moschopoulos' work on the topic begins precisely by saying that »in the beginning, man was forced to come together into partnership and to live in groups for this reason, namely that he was not self-sufficient in providing for his

---

on pp. 34–36; and Baukje van den BERG, The Wise Homer and His Erudite Commentator. Eustathios' Imagery in the Proem of the Parekbolai on the Iliad, in: Byzantine and Modern Greek Studies 41 (2017), pp. 30–44.

13 For Georgios Gemistos Plethon, see Niketas SINIOSSOGLOU, Radical Platonism in Byzantium. Illumination and Utopia in Gemistos Plethon, Cambridge 2011; Theodoros II LASKARIS, To Georgios Mouzalon who asked how servants ought to behave toward their masters and the reverse, in: Aloysius TARTAGLIA (ed.), Theodorus II Ducas Lascaris. Opuscula rhetorica, München/Leipzig 2000, pp. 120–140; discussion by Dimiter ANGELOV, Imperial Ideology and Political Thought in Byzantium, 1204–1330, Cambridge 2007, in chapter 7; for a specific view on Kabasilas, see Ihor ŠEVČENKO, »Nicolas Cabasilas' ›Anti-Zealot‹ Discourse. A Reinterpretation«, in: Dumbarton Oaks Papers 11 (1957), pp. 79–171.

needs«. For how could he be a farmer, bronzesmith, potter, builder, cook, shepherd, baker, worker, and generally make all the things that people need?

Therefore many people came together out of necessity, so that each could offer up his own product and receive those of the others. But they had different opinions and they disagreed about their transactions, which led to battles, and this was inappropriate for an intelligent animal such as man. It was therefore necessary to find one man who surpassed the others in wisdom and experience and make him the judge over all, indeed a ruler, or to find many such men. The first would be monarchy and the second aristocracy, but monarchy is vastly superior to aristocracy, for where there is more than one there is always suspicion of a plot. However, a further problem appeared in resolving disputes. Those things that are done openly are known to all, but those that are invisible, which are hidden in the mind of each man, are known only to God. Thus, for such matters it was decided that each man would swear an oath to God that he was dealing properly with others, so that all might get along together in confidence. Moreover, plots against the common good or against the ruler himself also occurred in monarchies, so the oath countered this problem too in the name of security (*asphaleia*): And I call this the »political oath«[14].

Moschopoulos does not link these developments to any time or place and wishes to present them as situated at the origin of political communities. But he did have an eye on contemporary realities. For example, those who swear the political oath do not receive a salary for so doing. They are permitted to emigrate and join other polities, even to enlist in foreign armies that wage war against their original homeland, but they are not permitted to reveal the secrets of their original polity, such as where the hidden water sources are. When a foreign ruler wants to employ such men as his soldiers, to have friends and enemies in common, he cannot force them to join his side, but must pay them, and the oath that they swear to him is the »imperial oath« (or »royal oath«)[15]. The difference might be understood as that between an oath of loyalty to the nation and a feudal oath of service.

Having established his theory of oaths, Moschopoulos now turns to address the religious objections that someone might bring against it, and his tone becomes polemical. Specifically, »someone« might object that God prohibited the swearing

---

14 Manuel MOSCHOPOULOS, Letter 5, in: Lionello LEVI (ed.), Cinque lettere inedite di Emanuele Moscopulo (Cod. Marc. Cl.XI, 15), in: Studi italiani di filologia classica 10 (1902), pp. 55–72, at pp. 64f. (my translation); discussions by Ihor ŠEVČENKO, The Imprisonment of Manuel Moschopoulos in the Year 1305 or 1306, in: Speculum 27 (1952), pp. 133–157; ANGELOV, Imperial Ideology, in chapter 10; Petre GURAN, Une théorie politique du serment au XVIe siècle. Manuel Moschopoulos, in: Marie-France AUZÉPY/Guillaume SAINT-GUILLAIN (eds.), Oralité et lien social au Moyen Âge (Occident, Byzance, Islam). Parole, donnée, foi jurée, serment, Paris 2008, pp. 169–185.
15 LEVI (ed.), »Cinque lettere«, p. 65.

of oaths (Matthew 5:33–37), and indeed many Byzantine churchmen disapproved of the practice. Moschopoulos considers such objections »irresponsible«. He goes on to argue that the constitution of political communities was essentially a secular business that did not and should not heed such religious scruples. This is a radical argument for a Byzantine to make. After all, he says, Jesus also enjoined keeping the peace (Mark 9:50), not casting the first stone (John 8:7), and not judging lest you be judged (Matthew 7:1). Yet even so men make war and sinful judges pass judgment on others. No one accuses soldiers of killing others or judges for passing sentence on criminals. Thus, religious scruples should not get in the way of oaths, for »they hold polities together and sustain the peace (for who would trust a man who will not swear?)«. The Church itself requires oaths in certain context, so if it is permitted in such »minor« cases how can it not be in this »major« case, on which everything else depends[16]? Moschopoulos essentially articulates a concept of »reason of state« overriding and transcending particular religious commandments, even those stated in explicit terms by the mouth of Jesus himself. Whereas Photios viewed the original environment as a state of sin and exploitation that could be escaped if only people accepted Jesus' commandments, Moschopoulos argued that people had raised themselves out of savagery through their own institutions and that they were duty-bound to maintain those institutions even in the face of Jesus' commandments to the contrary. If the latter were enforced absolutely, as some seemed to want, they would undermine social stability and political survival.

As with Laskaris and Kabasilas, Moschopoulos' immediate context shapes the formulation of his theory. Moschopoulos was an expert classical scholar, who in ca. 1305–1306 was imprisoned by the government of Andronikos II Palaiologos (r. 1282–1328) on suspicion of treasonous activity. We do not know which plot he was implicated in, but those years were turbulent for the regime, including both domestic challengers and foreign enemies on all sides. In 1305, the emperor had sought to buttress his rule by requiring the population of Constantinople to swear an oath of loyalty to him, with his officials going door-to-door with copies of Gospel to extract it. Loyalty oaths were a staple of imperial politics in Byzantium, used in both routine contexts (e. g., in the army) and in extraordinary moments of political instability[17]. Moschopoulos' work was therefore not taking a subversive position by emphasising the priority of political stability over religious scruples. Instead, he was advocating on behalf of the emperor's legitimacy in a fraught context, clearly in order to find favour and pardon. Andronikos himself and the Palaiologan dynasty

---

16 Ibid., pp. 65f.; for ecclesiastical disapproval, see ANGELOV, Imperial Ideology, p. 318.
17 Georgios PACHYMERES, History, in: Albert FAILLER (ed.), Georges Pachymérès. Relations historiques, 5 vols., Paris 1984–2000, vol. 4, pp. 597–599; for oaths, see KALDELLIS, Byzantine Republic, pp. 40f. (and the notes there); Claudia RAPP, Brother-Making in Late Antiquity and Byzantium. Monks, Laymen, and Christian Ritual, Oxford 2016, pp. 27f.

generally had numerous critics on the religious side, so this approach would have endeared Moschopoulos to the regime. In fact, it appears that the work in question was addressed to Moschopoulos' disciple Matarangides, who refused to swear on precisely such grounds, and Moschopoulos prepared another version of the work that he addressed directly to the emperor with all the requisite flattery:

> I say that it is necessary and advantageous for all of your subjects to swear loyalty to your regime. How might cities and villages hold together, containing so many countless different opinions as they do, if they are not constrained by a bond securing their loyalty to the republic and to its protector[18]?

Conclusions

It was not easy for Byzantine scholars to talk about the dynamics that gave rise to the first human societies. The Bible was supposed to be authoritative about the Creation, but offered little to clarify, and much to confuse, this particular point. Byzantine scholars also knew from their historical education that civilisations had emerged outside the Bible's limited geographical horizon and, more importantly, also outside the narrative of salvation and election that it contained. But beyond those parameters lay only the swampy terrain of pagan myth. To be sure, there were more anthropological and less mythological theories to be found among the ancient writers, but there is no evidence that the Byzantines formed a coherent tradition for their study and analysis. The three thinkers examined here – Photios, Eustathios, and Moschopoulos – were not part of a common discussion that stretched across the centuries. Each took up the question along quite divergent interpretive lines in order to achieve different rhetorical goals. Photios was called upon to refute a powerful challenge from the long-dead emperor Julian the Apostate. Eustathios devised a myth to bolster his efforts at moral reform in Thessaloniki. And Moschopoulos was under pressure to prove his loyalty not just by swearing an oath, but by arguing that the oath being demanded by the emperor was the very cornerstone of civilisation and the political order. These texts aimed, therefore, not so much at answering timeless questions for posterity than at addressing an immediate concern, a specific rhetorical situation that has been called the »hidden face« of the Byzantine text[19].

Even so, a perennial question does emerge to form a thread that links all three texts. Do human societies form on the basis of religious principles, possibly even

---

18 Moschopoulos, Letter 5 annex, in: Levi (ed.), Cinque lettere, pp. 66f.
19 Paolo Odorico (ed.), La face caché de la littérature byzantine. Le texte en tant que message immédiat, Paris 2012.

Christian ones, or are they instead the product of secular forces and impulses? Contrary to a misconception that is common among scholars, the Byzantines were perfectly capable of thinking in secular terms and frequently distinguished between »worldly« (or »profane«) and »religious« (or »sacred«) matters. These categories often overlapped, were blurry, or changed depending on perspective and rhetorical moment, but they do that in all periods, including our own, so this is no argument against their very existence in the Byzantine intellectual landscape[20]. They form, in fact, a prominent driving anxiety or focus of the texts examined here. Were the operations that gave rise to the first societies in accordance with the precepts of the Gospels, at variance with them, or neutral with regard them? Did the first societies form in secular ways, that is without divine intervention or without much human regard for God's will? Did Christianity come along to perfect a trajectory that had been leading towards it all along (Eustathios)? To censure and correct the worldly vices that underpinned the first states in a way that might lead to their abolition as states (Photios)? Or were nations founded on institutions that flouted Jesus' commandments, and did they need to continue to flout them in order to survive (Moschopoulos)? We need to distinguish between the secular and the religious in order to understand what is going on in their texts because their authors did too, and did so in explicit terms.

One final observation: The question about the emergence of civilisation in prehistorical times took our authors outside the comfort zone of the banalities of »Byzantine political ideology«, the name that scholars give to court propaganda about God favouring the emperor and the emperor imitating God. It was, in part, precisely because they had to step outside that space and think about the issues anew and on a fundamental level that Photios, Eustathios, and Moschopoulos produced such interesting and original theories[21].

---

20 KALDELLIS, Byzantine Republic, pp. 185–194.
21 For Byzantine originality, see now Apostolos SPANOS, Was Innovation Unwanted in Byzantium?, in: Ingela NILSSON/Paul STEPHENSON (eds.), Byzantium Wanted. The Desire for a Lost Empire, Uppsala 2014, pp. 43–56.

Boris A. Todorov

Relics and the Political

Late Mediaeval Bulgaria and Serbia

I.

St Sava, the first archbishop and spiritual patron of the thirteenth-century Serbian Church, son of the canonised Serbian Prince Stefan-Simeon Nemanja, spent the last few weeks of his earthly life in the capital of the Second Bulgarian Empire, Trnovo. In 1235–36 the Bulgarian Tsar Ivan Asen II (r. 1218–1241) was at the height of his power, dominating much of the peninsula. The head of the Bulgarian Church had just been granted the title of Patriarch at the Eastern Orthodox Council of Lampsakos (1235) and Sava's visit may very well have been a show of respect and good will at a time when dynamic developments in the Bulgarian, Serbian and post-conquest Byzantine ecclesiastical hierarchies opened the ground for disputes over dioceses. Sava died on 14 January 1236, and his body was quickly buried with all due honours in the church of the Forty Holy Martyrs of Sebasteia on the banks of the Yantra, between the twin fortified citadels of Trnovo. The site had only recently been chosen as a royal burial ground and built, or substantially renovated, by Ivan Asen, who used it to commemorate his victory over Theodore Komnenos Doukas, the Emperor of Thessaloniki (Klokotnitsa, 1230). In the words of Domentijan, one of two hagiographers writing only a few years after the events: »The Tsar, upon hearing of the holy man's demise, sang the praises of God, who had sent this saintly man as a gift to him: to bless him, to bless his house and to bless his city too«[1].

Soon after, however, the Serbian King Vladislav, a nephew of Sava's, decided otherwise and, »steeling himself with the help of the Holy Spirit, he took the long road from the West (Serbia) to the East (Bulgaria), because he could not suffer the sight of his true shepherd in a foreign land« arriving in Trnovo to petition for the dead body of Sava[2]. Since the locals expected various benefits from the presence of such worthy relics, the tsar was reluctant to give them up but eventually succumbed to Vladislav's entreaties. Sava's relics were raised (*elevatio*) from his

---

1 Djura DANIČIĆ (ed.), Život svetoga Simeuna i svetoga Save. Napisao Domentijan, Belgrade 1865, p. 333: »Car' že slyšav' o prěstavljenii svetaago, i proslavi boga pos'lav'šaago jemou sveta mouža na blagoslovenije jego i domou i grada jego«.
2 Ibid., p. 334: »sam' s' nimi opl'čiv' se doukhom' svetyim' načeše š'stvije tvoriti ot' zapada v' v'stokou«.

grave and carried (*translatio*) to the monastery of Mileševa, where Vladislav himself would later choose to be buried[3].

This episode in Bulgarian-Serbian political and ecclesiastical exchanges is significant first for being quite certainly a true event rather than a later hagiographical fabrication, since the hagiographer who reported it wrote only a few years after the events and the audience he addressed would have consisted largely of direct or indirect witnesses to the solemn procession of Sava's body from Trnovo to Mileševa[4]. Second, it connects in a single narrative long-term practice, observable in ample alternative evidence, that Bulgaria and Serbia followed over the thirteenth and fourteenth centuries (and in the Serbian case, even much later) and that built up concurrent (and contrasting) views regarding the significance of holy relics in perpetuating a vision of the political.

The Nemanjići dynasty, which ruled and indeed built Serbia, from the 1180s (the ascent of Stefan Nemanja) to 1359 (the death of the Stefan Uroš V, the last of the line), consistently pursued the tradition of venerating their deceased royalty as saints and establishing local cults in different monastic foundations that became the focus of pilgrimage and the accumulation of pious donations[5]. The Bulgarian tsars of various dynasties were no less consistent in upholding the tradition of collecting relics of various saints for the many churches of the royal city of Trnovo[6]. Just as Ivan Asen regarded Sava as one more case of a saint adorning the religious institutions of his city, Vladislav regarded the translation of Sava's remains to the *zadužbina* (pious foundation) of Mileševa as one more case of a Nemanjić being incorporated into the growing network of such foundations in the territorial nucleus of the expanding Serbian Kingdom. Vladislav immodestly had himself buried even closer to the altar of the same church, but this may also be a reason why he was of the few Nemanjići to be excluded from posthumous veneration.

Serbs and Bulgarians constructed their political and ecclesiastical institutions within roughly the same cultural and theological framework – Eastern Orthodox Christianity in the Slavonic language. Both countries produced relatively little of their own theological and less still legal or political scholarship that could testify to theoretical approaches, intellectual debates and traditions, or clearly conceived visions of the political in terms both of prescribing norms for and of justifying

---

3 Sima ĆIRKOVIĆ, The Serbs, Malden, MA 2004, pp. 45f.; on Sava's and Vladislav's graves, see Danica POPOVIĆ, Srpski vladarski grob u srednjem veku, Belgrade 1992, pp. 46–49.

4 Radoslava STANKOVA, »Zhitiiata na hilendarskite monasi Domentiian i Teodosii vuv vienskite rukopisi i vuprosut za poiavata na stila ›pletenie sloves‹ v srubskata agiografiia ot XIII vek«, in: Wiener slavistisches Jahrbuch 50 (2004), pp. 153–170, at p. 154.

5 ĆIRKOVIĆ, The Serbs, pp. 34–76.

6 Boris A. TODOROV, »Trnovo«, in: David WALLACE (ed.), Europe: A Literary History, 1348–1418, vol. 2, Oxford 2016, pp. 405f.

governmental action. It is disputable whether the very concept of political theorising would have been accessible to monarchical or ecclesiastical decision-makers in the medieval period. This is what makes the adopted traditions of contextualising holy relics into the framework of political decision-making a useful marker and reference: It made possible the formulation and communication of alternative and complementary visions of earthly and abstract hierarchies, including constructed identities and acceptable policymaking. Their use and treatment of relics is what set Bulgarians and Serbs apart from one another in the thirteenth and fourteenth centuries. The policy-building implications of the essentially theological framework of the cult of saints and the veneration of relics were fundamentally different and reflected the territorial and institutional expansion or decline of the Bulgarian and Serbian medieval polities.

At the same time, medieval Serbs and Bulgarians shared a common trend in their adoption of Christian practices – they both looked for surreptitious ways to avoid supervision and interference in their internal affairs, including the ecclesiastical organisation and the related control of tax collecting, endowments, appointments, and spiritual control over political affairs. Holy relics, most importantly the bodily remains of new, or newly *invented* saints, gave freedom that other religious practices blocked. For complex reasons, the veneration of relics was among the least debated and least strictly regulated aspects of Christian theology. Relics were a central concept in the view of the world adopted by all churches before the Reformation in the West and they continue to be an integral part of the Christian experience in the Eastern Orthodox world. The incorruptibility of the holy man's (or woman's) body was evidently related to the belief in the Christ's resurrection and his victory over death as celebrated in the Christian liturgy as well as a sign of the godly life of the venerated saint. Just as martyrs of the faith that fell to persecution in late antiquity emulated Jesus Christ's suffering on the Cross and testified to His victory over death, both the miracles performed by the saints in their lifetime and the mysterious power of their mortal remains to perform miracles and affect the living, reconfirmed the Christ's promise of salvation and eternal life.

II.

Not until relatively late did it occur to the Orthodox Church to turn relics into one more instrument of integration and control: Only at the Second Nicaean Council in 787, when the veneration of the icons was re-established for the first time, did the synod stipulate (in Canon VII) that new churches required holy relics to be enshrined somewhere in the altar[7]. This was an obvious move to prevent the indiscriminate foundation of new Christian churches, and gave the existing Byzantine eparchies important leverage over Christian missions in newly converted countries. A new church needed not only the word and blessing of the previously established hierarchy, but the actual granting of a material token. The expanding Christian areas in Eastern and Northern Europe depended on several important sources of legitimacy: catechetical instruction that could be brought only by learned and ordained priesthood, canonical discipline that had to comply with the decisions of the councils, and ordination of the local priesthood by a bishop. Yet in time all these might escape the control of the metropolis, since over the generations the local priesthood could instruct and co-opt more and more locals, ordaining them more or less independently.

Relics provided a means of slowing down this emancipation of local churches, since regardless of local resources and the demographic situation in the newly converted lands, the ultimate decision to build new foundations and to turn them into instruments of social cohesion, along with control over the circulation of goods and the accumulation of resources, remained dependent on the good will of Constantinople (in the Serbian and Bulgarian case) to provide new and new relics for the churches. There was one more, and seemingly formidable, check on the autonomy of young churches – the holy chrism used for the sacraments of confirmation and ordination. One of the important questions addressed by Boris-Michael, the Bulgarian King, to Pope Nicholas II was in fact whether the Greeks were correct in claiming the chrism could come only from them[8]. Five hundred years later, in the 1360s, the issue of the proper chrism used in Bulgaria came once more to the fore with renewed urgency. The Bulgarian hesychast Teodosii (Theodosios) made a public display of loyalty to Constantinople by willingly receiving a second confirmation in the city, thereby pointedly defying the usages of the Bulgarian Patriarch of Trnovo[9]. The problem, however, from the point of view of the missionary centres like Constantinople, was precisely that there was never a clear and permanent definition of relics. It would be inconceivable for the Christian mindset to presume that sainthood and miracle-performing relics could be restricted to just the early

---

7 Erich LAMBERTZ (ed.), Concilium Universale Nicaenum Secundum. Concilii Actiones VI–VII, Berlin 2016, pp. 908f.
8 Responsa Nicolai I papae ad consulta Bulgarorum, chapter 94, in: Ernst PERELS (ed.), Monumenta Germaniae Historica. Epistolae VI. Karolini aevi IV, Berlin 1925, p. 597: »Graecos dicere perhibetis, quod in illorum patria chrisma oriatur et ab illis per totum mundum tribuatur«.
9 Vasil N. ZLATARSKI (ed.), 'Zhitie i zhizn' prepodobnago ottsa nashego Theodosia... izhe v Tr"nove postnich'stvovavshago s"pisano sveteishim' patriarkhom' Konstantina grada kyr' Kalistom, in: Sbornik za narodni umotvoreniia i kultura 20 (1904), pp. 1–41, at p. 32; Konstantin RADCHENKO, Religioznoe i literaturnoe dvizhenie v Bolgarii v epokhu pered turetskim zavoevaniem, Kyiv 1898, pp. 179–184.

centuries of the church. Divine Grace continued to operate through time and there was a growing number of saints who were beyond the effective control of the older churches. Moreover, some of these relics might well ooze myrrh (it was believed) and break the monopoly over it claimed by the Eastern Patriarchs.

The cult of relics has prompted a lot of interesting and thought-provoking research when it comes to late antiquity and the Middle Ages in Latin Christendom. The miraculous intervention in the worldly affairs of the living by saints whose relics were preserved, or believed to be preserved, in particular religious foundations have been of interest first for researchers intrigued by the fundaments of medieval mentalities and popular culture. Since the 1970s, however, a number of Western medievalists have discussed, and hotly debated, the place of rituals in marking identity, building social networks, conflict management, property disputes and property consolidation, and as substitutes or support for political institutions. Relics were often the focal point in ritualised acts: sometimes dramatic events, like their theft (attempted or successful), their public humiliation through removal from altars or reliquaries, or their solemn and victorious procession, which could serve to confirm spatial boundaries or threaten feuding parties with calamity and destruction[10]. Relics proved important in providing social cohesion and functional public exchange in times of weak or non-existent governmental institutions. They enabled the consolidation of the territorial domains of the reformed monastic communities of the tenth and eleventh centuries and allowed ecclesiastical foundations to exert pressure on lay transgressors and royal and feudal power holders. Anthropological approaches focusing on the ceremonial, visual, or textual aspects of the veneration of saints and their relics provide ample evidence for the gestation of social order and balance, and the growth and expansion of ecclesiastical foundations in the feudal age.

III.

Much less research has been done on possible relic-centred ritualised acts in the South Slavic area, yet the hagiographic evidence hints at a possible anthropological

---

10 Most importantly: Patrick J. GEARY, Thefts of Relics in the Central Middle Ages, Princeton, NJ 1978; id., Humiliation of Saints, in: Id., Living with the Dead in the Middle Ages, Ithaca, NY 1994, pp. 95–115, initially published in French in: Annales: Économies, Sociétés, Civilisations 34 (1979), pp. 27–42; Geoffrey KOZIOL, Monks, Feuds, and the Making of Peace in Eleventh-Century Flanders, in: Thomas HEAD/Richard LANDES (eds.), The Peace of God. Social Violence and Religious Response, Ithaca, NY 1992, pp. 239–259; Steven D. WHITE, Custom, Kinship, and Gifts to Saints. The Laudatio Parentum in Western France, 1050–1150, Chapel Hill, NC 1988.

analysis of the veneration of saints. A key source on the Serbian tradition of venerating the relics of royal saints and building a politically meaningful tradition over the decades is Archbishop Danilo II's *Lives of Serbian Kings and Archbishops*[11]. The work is intended as a continuation of the earlier *Lives* of the three great early royal saints: Stefan-Symeon Nemanja and his sons, Archbishop Sava and King Stefan the First-Crowned. As will be reiterated below, the work testifies to a crystallised intellectual interpretation of the dynastic continuity as the expression of Divine Will, focused on the concept of the *vineyard bearing holy fruit* (*svetorodna loza*). Danilo's project to write extensive hagiographical or quasi-hagiographical accounts of the reigns of the less significant members of the dynasty may be interpreted within a purely literary context: He knew of no other narrative genre and constructed the history of Serbian Kings as lives of saints for lack of a better model[12].

The work contains little historical content – a few selected events of significance are mentioned, yet they are sufficient to suggest a historical context that Danilo can hardly have constructed from scratch. An interesting case is the emphatic if somewhat redundant story of the elevation of the body of King Stefan Uroš I's spouse, Helen of Anjou, from the sarcophagus in which she had been buried in for several years, in the narthex of her own pious foundation at Gradac. The ceremony served as the background for the reconciliation between her two sons, Dragutin and Milutin. Although Dragutin was the elder, he had been forced to relinquish the kingdom to his younger brother and move to a large principality as a vassal of the Hungarian King. The *elevatio* of Queen Helen had been preceded by preliminary shows of respect to the deceased by her daughters-in-law, Queens Katalina and Simonida, and since Danilo most probably orchestrated the ceremony himself, we can discern the real crucible of political decision-making through the hagiographical discourse[13].

The theological implications of attributing to a deceased queen's remains the power to produce social cohesion are somewhat disputable since the queen's claims for sainthood were weak. She had not performed miracles when alive or dead, she had been no martyr, hermit or recluse, nor could she could boast of any deed that would have gained her a place among God's chosen. It is the response of the church to her death that placed her in the centre of hagiographical discourse and liturgical practices. Queen Helen died a nun in 1314, in the nunnery of St Nicholas near Scutari and close to the Adriatic, but was buried in her *zadužbina* at Gradac, at the end of a long and solemn procession that Danilo consciously likens to that of a holy woman. The same meagre dossier of sainthood proofs applied to her late husband

---

11 Djura DANIČIĆ (ed.), Životi kraljeva i arhiepiskopa srpskih, Zagreb 1866.
12 On Danilo most importantly: Francis J. THOMSON, Archbishop Daniel II of Serbia: Hierarch, Hagiographer, Saint, in: Analecta Bollandiana 111 (1993), pp. 103–134.
13 DANIČIĆ (ed.), Životi kraljeva i arhiepiskopa srpskih, pp. 98–100.

Stefan Uroš I, who had similarly died as a monk somewhere in Hum (modern Herzegovina), yet was loyally taken to Sopoćani, the monastery he founded in the Nemanjić heartland in 1277[14]. Dragutin, the couple's eldest son, was laid to rest in his personal pious foundation, Đurđevi stupovi, in the city of Ras, the dynasty's ancestral home[15].

All these were consistent imitations of the example of Stefan Nemanja, the forefather who had spent several years in the monastic community of Hilandar on Mount Athos and whose myrrh-oozing relics were taken to Studenica at the insistence of King Stefan the First-Crowned. As a scholar of Danilo's work, Stanislaus Hafner, remarked half a century ago, the Nemanjići consistently mixed *Heiligenverehrung* and *Ahnenverehrung* – the veneration of saints with that of ancestors[16]. There was nothing unusual about the practice, since it was the common-sense decision of any generous *ktitor* to choose for his final resting place an institution they had founded or supported in their lifetime.

The peculiar coincidence confirmed by the case of Sava's demise in Trnovo was that all these sanctified members of the royal dynasty seem to have chosen to die far from their foundations, thereby necessitating a procession over several days to their final resting place. In the absence of written treatises on the nature of royal authority, dynastic continuity and territorial cohesion, the procession carrying the relics of the deceased merged the theological concepts of sainthood and divine grace with the developing ideas of statehood based on bloodline. It also emphasised filial piety, the conciliation of brothers whose rights on the succession were never clearly defined, and the consolidation of family property across territorially dispersed foundations, which eventually blurred the distinction between private and ecclesiastical domains and the kingdom proper. It is therefore striking that the practice of associating royalty with holiness and with a specific pious foundation was broken by the self-proclaimed Tsar Stefan Dušan, whose empire had extended to such a degree that he expected to gain nothing from such an association.

The veneration of relics and – for lack of true martyrs' or miracle-performing saints' relics – the mortal remains of kings and queens gradually expanded into a consistent ideological framework focused on the concept of *svetorodna loza*. It is referred to in the iconography of the cathedral church of Peć, where the hagiographer Danilo was Archbishop. Danilo commissioned a building and an iconic programme in which the images of the canonised descendants of Stefan Nemanja were connected in an intricate web of vines[17]. Imagery and text in Danilo and his

---

14 Ibid., p. 19.
15 Ibid., p. 52.
16 Stanislaus HAFNER, Studien zur altserbischen dynastischen Historiographie, München 1964, p. 37.
17 Dragan VOJVODIĆ, Ot horizontalne ka vertikalnoj genealoškoj slici Nemanjića, in: Zbornik radova vizantološkog instituta 44/1 (2007), pp. 295–312.

continuators and emulators built up a consistent ideological framework that served a number of mutually complementary purposes: legitimation of the ruling dynasty, sanctification of the Serbian Church as both part and recreation of the Orthodox canonical and institutional tradition, affirmation of the symphony between church and state[18]. There is rich and comprehensive scholarly work on the ideological dimensions of Serbian literature and iconography of the fourteenth century that tends to emphasise the Byzantine, Orthodox and intellectual dimensions of the phenomenon[19] and to overshadow or practically neglect the gradually expanding practice of worshiping the royal relics in the darker thirteenth century. They also tend to overlook the all-important practical aspect of Nemanja's myrrh-oozing graves, both at Hilandar and Studenica: Although the Serbian Church, until the short imperial period of Dušan, typically stayed loyal to Constantinople and hence was never in need of its own supply, to draw its holy unction drawn from the relics of its own holy King Nemanja was a trump card worth having in case relations should be strained or severed.

IV.

This is the proper place to turn our attention to the Bulgarian approach to relics and myrrh. Bulgarian rulers adopted and continuously repeated the old practice of discovering (*inventio*) and moving to their capital city (*translatio*) the relics of various saints from lands they conquered and held for longer or shorter periods. On at least one occasion, they pressured another power – the Latin Empire of Constantinople – to let them have the relics of a particular saint. The practice of bringing precious relics to the city was very Byzantine, but from an earlier period – in the tenth century successive emperors brought to the City important relics related to Christ, such as the *Mandylion* or the Holy Lance[20]. The accumulation of relics proved to be one of the major incentives for the Latin conquest of the city, but even after the sack of 1204 enough remained to capture the admiration of travellers, many of them Russian, visiting in the course of the fourteenth century[21].

---

18 Boško BOJOVIĆ, L'idéologie monarchique dans les hagio-biographies dynastiques dans le Moyen Âge serbe, Rome 1995, p. 9.
19 Radmila MARINKOVIĆ, Svetorodna gospoda srpska. Istraživanja srpske književnosti srednjeg veka, Belgrade 1998.
20 Sysse G. ENGBERG, Romanos Lekapenos and the Mandilion of Edessa, in: Jannic DURAND/Bernard FLUSIN (eds.), Byzance et les reliques du Christ, Paris 2004, pp. 123–142.
21 George P. MAJESKA, The Relics of Constantinople after 1204, in: DURAND/FLUSIN (eds.), Byzance, pp. 183–190.

The first Bulgarian tsar attested to have captured and moved a saint's relics was Samuel who, in the early eleventh century, punished the citizens of Larissa in Thessaly by claiming for his royal residence the remnants of St Achilles[22]. Yet it is questionable whether tsars of the Second Bulgarian Empire knew anything of that story; more likely, they renewed the practice because they saw similar profits in it. Ivan Asen I (r. 1185–1196), the founder of the second empire, brought the relics of the tenth-century anchorite John of Rila from Sredets (present-day Sofia)[23]. This is the clearest case of the relics of a previously well-attested and venerated saint being captured by the rulers of Trnovo: John lived in the tenth century, became the model of anchoretic life in the southwestern Bulgarian lands and founded the opulent and influential Rila monastery. His body had been translated to Sredets in the eleventh century by the Byzantine governor George Skylitzes, brother of the famous historian, who had been personally convinced of the healing powers of the holy hermit[24]. In an interesting episode, the relics were stolen by the invading Hungarians but then returned because Hungarian clergy refused to acknowledge John as a true saint.

Asen's younger brother Kaloyan obtained the relics of Hilarion, Archbishop of Moglena, somewhere in Macedonia[25]. In the prolonged vita (*prostrannoe žitie*) Evtimii (Euthymios) of Trnovo dedicated to him in the last quarter of the fourteenth century, he is presented as a defender of the faith and a strict judge of heretics, whom he relentlessly brought back to the Orthodox flock. The *vita* proved a relative success in Russian lands and it was a frequently included in *menologia*[26]. Yet, going back in time, there is no alternative source on Hilarion's historicity, or even any clear idea when approximately he might have lived. Kaloyan reportedly carried a few other relics to Trnovo in the booty of his successful raids in Thrace in the years 1204–1207: the late antique female hermit Philothea (Evtimii names her origin as Molyvotos but it seems this is an invented location); of John, an eighth-century bishop of Polyvotos, in Phrygia, who had struggled against the iconoclasts, from the city of Mosynopolis on the Thracian Aegean coast; and Michael, a mysterious military saint from the unidentified location of Potuka[27]. The remains of St Paraskevi (Petka

---

22 Klimentina IVANOVA, »Vuzpiavam te, otche Ahilie, na arhiereite ukrasa« (izdanie na teksta na srubskata sluzhba za sv. Ahil), in: Arheografski prilozi 24 (2002), pp. 143–176, at p. 145.
23 Emil KAŁUŻNIACKI (ed.), Werke des Patriarchen von Bulgarien Euthymius (1375–1393), Wien 1901, pp. 23–25.
24 Vasil N. ZLATARSKI, Georgi Skilitsa i napisanoto nego zhitie na sv. Ivana Rilski, in: Izvestiia na Istoricheskoto druzhestvo v Sofiia 13 (1933), pp. 49–80.
25 KAŁUŻNIACKI, Werke des Euthymius, pp. 56f.
26 Klimentina IVANOVA, Bibliotheca hagiographica balcano-slavica, Sofia 2008, pp. 260f.
27 Survey of the hagiographical tradition of the listed saints, in: Ibid.: 19 October (John of Rila), 21 October (Hilarion), 22 November (Michael the Soldier), 4 December (John of Polybotos), 28 May (Philothea).

in South Slavic), a holy woman whose local cult in the town of Epivatos, on the Marmara Sea close to Constantinople, had developed more than a century earlier, were the fruit of diplomacy: Ivan Asen II obtained them as a gift on behalf of the Latins and had the miraculously preserved body encased in the Patriarchal church of the Ascension of God in Trnovo[28]. Her cult grew most impressively over the centuries, as attested by seven different redactions of liturgical texts dedicated to her between the thirteenth and fifteenth centuries. Unlike most of her peers, her journey continued long after the fall of Trnovo to the Ottomans: in western Bulgaria (Vidin)[29], then in the late Serbian Principality under the Hrebeljanović dynasty, then in Iași, in Moldavia.

We owe this detailed sequence of holy men and women brought to the Bulgarian imperial residence of Trnovo to the existing list of Patriarch Evtimii's hagiographical and homiletical works. Evtimii carefully composed a short account of the invention and translation of each saint's relics, quite probably because his works were intended for reading at the location where each particular saint reposed. That he included all in the same contextual, historical and topographical framework is evident from his address to the audience in the *Homily of St John of Polyvotos*:

> But come forth ye, Christian tribe, and rejoice today! [...] Stir up for prayer the father whom we commemorate today, and let him call upon his neighbours lying around. Entreat the saint whom we are celebrating today to pray, so that he, on his part, entreats to pray all his neighbours and close ones: the blessed Hilarion, once shepherd of Moglena [...] and John the dweller in the Rila desert, the venerable Paraskevi and Theophano the queen who reigned here and still reigns in the kingdom to come, and the anchorite Philothea, etc. [...] some being his co-citizens, others members of his community, others his peers in [godly] life, others, finally, his friends[30].

Some of these commemorations and celebrations of saints may have been complete innovations on Evtimii's part. This is hinted at by the account of the translation of John of Polyvotos, where Evtimii confuses locations within the wider Byzantine sphere: Amorion in Phrygia (where the historical John may well have died) with the region of Morea (the last remaining Byzantine enclave in the Peloponnesus at the time of Evtimii), and Mosynopolis in Byzantine Thrace (where Tsar Kaloyan plausibly *invented* the relics) with Messina in Morea. Still, most of the other listed saints had been included in the liturgical calendar of the Bulgarian Church much earlier, as shown in the short (*prolog*) *vitae* or in the *troparia* in the liturgical canons

---

28 Kałużniacki, Werke des Euthymius, pp. 70f.
29 Ibid., pp. 432f.
30 Ibid., pp. 201.

for particular feast days. In this sense, the cult of the relics of the Trnovo saints was much older than Evtimii's literary programme and reflects the mentalities, ideological frameworks and urban traditions of the darker thirteenth century, just as we have seen it to be the case with the canonised Serbian Kings and queens.

The recurrent theme in the hagiographical texts related to Trnovo, whether by Evtimii or his predecessors or continuators, was that the saints provided the city with divine protection against enemies and confirmed the supremacy of Bulgarian tsars over their neighbours. Evtimii emphatically called upon the greatness of Kaloyan, who proudly captured and plundered Greek cities before *inventing* and *translating* to his city the miraculous relics of the saints. The practice of obtaining relics by force from the Byzantines dated back to the very first years of the Second Bulgarian Empire, when Kaloyan's elder brother Asen I defeated Emperor Isaac Angelos and captured his treasury including reliquaries containing pieces of the True Cross and drops of the Virgin's milk. These sacred objects became the focus of processions on the feast of Epiphany observed by the Nicaean diplomat and historian George Akropolites in 1261. The captured relics had thus become proof of political power and imperial sovereignty[31]. Furthermore, the very topography of Trnovo consistently emulated Constantinople and provided a tangible framework to a vision of divinely ordained world where the empire on earth reflected the transcendent celestial powers.

One of these miracle-performing saints was missing from Evtimii's work: the myrrh-oozing saint Varvar (*Barbaros*) Mirotochets, also known as Varvaros the Brigand, a holy man whose cult was attested first in the region of Dyrrhachion, or even further south in continental Greece. A practical explanation for this omission is that a *long life* of the saint had been already composed in Trnovo a little before Evtimii; still, this does not explain he is not mentioned together with the other local saints in the passage cited above. Evtimii had more important serious theological reasons to overlook Varvar: According to an official encyclical by Patriarch Kallistos I of Constantinople, the relics of Varvar, together with a myrrh-oozing icon of St Demetrios that Bulgarians claimed had miraculously chosen to leave Thessaloniki for Trnovo back in 1185, had been used for decades by the Patriarch of Trnovo for sacraments[32]. This was a practice that Evtimii and his teacher Teodosii of Trnovo may have objected to, since they both made clear their loyalty to the Ecumenical Church in Constantinople and had spent years in the city[33]; for the sake of Orthodox unity and the observance of the canons, the cult of Varvar could be ignored at least for a while. From the perspective of the pragmatic claims of the

---

31 August HEISENBERG/Paul WIRTH (eds.), Georgii Acropolitae opera, vol. 1, Stuttgart 1978, p. 20.
32 Klimentina IVANOVA, Zhitieto na Varvar Mirotochets Pelagoniiski (Bitolski), in: Palaeobulgarica 24/2 (2000), pp. 40–60, at p. 47.
33 See footnote 9 above.

Bulgarian Church for autonomy set out above, Varvar's miracle-performing relics were in fact the most valuable: They made possible the observance of Christian rites even during prolonged periods in which relations with the Patriarchs of Constantinople, who had consistently downplayed the autocephaly claims of Trnovo, were virtually severed.

V.

To sum up this essay's argument so far: Both Serbs and Bulgarians each developed rather different strategies for the use of holy relics – whether of their own royal personages or saints captured from the enemy – to make ecclesiastical institutions independent in their administration of the divine mysteries and in the accumulation of domains and resources. These practices thrived, regulating the liturgical calendar and political processes even without a canonical theological justification: Serbs simply knew that their kings were all saints, just as Bulgarians knew that their capital city was the true seat of divinely ordained authority. Over time, however, Danilo and his disciples in Serbia, Evtimii, in Bulgaria, constructed sophisticated ideological edifices that enshrined the local traditions in a universal Christian theological discourse and associated power with Orthodoxy.

In the Serbian case, the unbreakable chain of royal sainthood made visual in the iconographic composition of the *svetorodna loza* was reconsidered as the proof of harmonious existence over the centuries of authority and Orthodoxy. Serbian Kings were guarantors of Orthodoxy, just as the divine miracle associated with their incorruptible bodies were proofs of supreme guarantees of their legitimate power. The monastery reflected the kingdom, the kingdom extended the monastery[34]. At the same time, this monastery-kingdom fitted into the framework of Byzantine Orthodoxy perfectly and without any palpable friction, since the forefather Stefan Nemanja had strictly observed Orthodox practices, had chosen Mount Athos as the proper location for his hermitic retirement, and had placed the monasteries of Hilandar and Studenica under well-balanced and theologically sound regulations (*typika*) in the Byzantine fashion. Gradually the monasteries grew to become episcopal sees and thus the Serbian Kingdom developed its own ecclesiastical organisation – not through contesting or taking over older dioceses but by building new ones. The harmony between local and universal church was further confirmed by the principle of *symphony* between *imperium* and *sacerdotium* enshrined in St Sava's *Nomokanon*: the relics of Sava and all his kin merely confirmed the divinity

---

34 Léonis MAVROMATIS, Le monastère reflet du royaume, in: Branislav CVETKOVIĆ (ed.), Huit siècles du monastère de Chilandar au Mont Athos, Belgrade 2002, pp. 5–8.

of his canon law treatise³⁵. The Serbian diocese extended the area administered by Constantinople rather than diminishing it: Clergy and royalty co-operated and were mutually useful.

This was not obviously the case for the Second Bulgarian Empire. The collection of relics was the least offensive aspect of the Bulgarian political expansion under Asen I and Kaloyan into the Orthodox dioceses in the Central Balkans, in Macedonia and Thrace. The Bulgarian tsars not only chased the Greek bishops from the north of the country where they initially ruled, but continued the process of displacing the bishops in the provinces conquered later. This created long-term frictions that canon law was unable to smooth: Some texts written in the 1220s Demetrios Chomatenos, Archbishop of Achrida, make it explicit that with every change of sovereignty over the disputed areas entailed a change of bishops³⁶. With the exception of the Lampsakos Synod of 1235, which bestowed the venerable title of Patriarchate on the see of Trnovo, the Bulgarian Church was more often than not at odds with Constantinople, which may help explain why the Bulgarian intellectual revival of the second half of the fourteenth century did not produce clear ideological tenets for the legitimacy of Bulgarian imperial institutions and the symphony between divine and worldly authority. In fact, the hagiographical programme of Evtimii harked back, consciously or not, to late antique models of associating sainthood with the political, that completely ignored, even resisted, the imperial principle.

The practice of inventing, elevating and solemnly translating holy relics to their imperial cities (e. g., Constantinople, Trnovo or Kyiv) may have been appropriated by emperors and tsars in the middle and later Byzantine period, but its roots go back to late antiquity, when it was used to bolster the civic unity of the *polis* as a strategy for defence and survival in a period of upheaval, change and catastrophe³⁷. The issue was raised by Claudia Rapp in relation to her study of late antique bishops. The Syriac *Life of St Symeon the Stylite* explains why the holy man's body was carried to the city of Antioch: »Because our city has no wall as it fell in anger, we brought him to be for us a fortified wall that we may be protected by his prayers«³⁸. There are explicit connotations to the same effect in late medieval Bulgarian hagiography. How was it possible that the invaders had broken through the protection granted to Trnovo by the relics of St Petka? Because God wanted it so. Grigorii (Gregory) Tsamblak puts it in his account of the translation of Petka from Trnovo to Vidin.

---

35 Bojović, L'idéologie monarchique, p. 319.
36 Günter Prinzing (ed.), Demetrii Chomateni Ponemata diaphora, Berlin 2002, pp. 423–428.
37 Petre Guran, Invention et translation des reliques – un cérémonial monarchique?, in: Revue des études sud-est européennes 36/1–4 (1998), pp. 195–229.
38 Claudia Rapp, City and Citizenship as Christian Concepts of Community in Late Antiquity, in: Ead./Harold E. Drake (eds.), The City in the Classical and Post-Classical World: Changing Contexts of Power and Identity, New York 2014, pp. 153–166, at p. 158.

»›Leave this city‹, God ordered Petka, ›because your prayers are like bronze walls defending it against my wrath‹«[39].

This invocation of the saint's power may be clearly understood both in the physical sense of protecting the city from invasion and plunder, and in the spiritual sense of instilling fortitude and virtue among the faithful, but the overall message is clear: The saint's body comes in where civic and imperial institutions fail. Rapp points out to three characteristics which were typical for the ancient city: the delineation of its territory by walls, the observance of a common set of rules, and the community's shared participation in religious cults. These were expressed through three concepts of the same derivation: *polis*, *politeuma* and *politeia*[40]. Gradually, late antique cities managed to re-contextualise all three within the discourse and practices of the Christian communities – more specifically, the growing monastic communities. At the same time, as Rapp puts it with reference to the *Life of St Anthony*, »the desert was made a *polis* because it housed a community of good men and women who followed their conscience and the call to asceticism and thus were inevitably led to the observance of the same way of life, a shared ascetic *politeia*«[41].

In his hagiographical and homiletic programme, dedicating works to most of the saints housed in the churches of his city, Evtimii was refurnishing with meaning the three late antique concepts of the city: The body of the saint (martyr, anchorite or defender of the faith) gave walls to the city, turning it into a *polis*. The life of the saint – the Greek concept of *politeia* was translated into Slavic as *žitie* – provided the unshakeable ethical foundations of the Christian community of the city. Finally, the miracles that God allowed to be performed in defence of the city were the divine sanction of the spiritual fortitude of the faithful – the *politeuma*. The invocation of John of Polyvotos, urging the other saints to pray with him, thus receives a much deeper meaning. It is not a simple rhetorical device, but a conscious development of the concepts describing the citizens' community: The saints are *edinogradniky* because they dwell in the same city and build the same city walls as in the *polis*; they are *sobeštniky* because they share the same ethical and community values and experiences as in the *politeia*; they are *ravnožiteli* because they build up the same spiritual community of God's elect and are equally able to perform God-granted miracles, as in the *politeuma*. Instead of adding to a traditional ideological framework in which the tsar figured as guarantor of order and hierarchy, Evtimii was turning back to late antique concepts joining together the desert and the city. In so doing, he was contributing to a novel theological vision of Orthodoxy and staunch

---

39 KALUŽNIACKI, Werke des Euthymius, p. 433.
40 Claudia RAPP, The Christianization of the Idea of the Polis in Early Byzantium, in: Iliia G. ILIEV et al. (eds.), Proceedings of the 22nd International Congress of Byzantine Studies (Sofia, 22–27 August 2011), vol. 1: Plenary Papers, Sofia 2011, pp. 263–284, at pp. 267–269.
41 RAPP, The Christianization, p. 283.

monasticism, maintained by the miraculous power of the city's relics, to provide the new foundations of a community that, in the last quarter of the fourteenth century, faced the grim peril of conquest and destruction by the »infidel«. From expressions of the growing imperial power of the Bulgarian tsars in the thirteenth century, the relics in Trnovo grew to become the hope of the city's survival.

This essay thus concludes with the observation that relics remained central to both Serbian and Bulgarian medieval polities because they allowed for flexible interpretation and for constructing and contextualising different ideological frameworks. In the case of Serbia, relics provided instruments for political conciliation and dynastic continuity, for smooth adaptation of new ecclesiastical hierarchies to the body of Orthodox Christianity, and for the conceptualisation of a permanent cooperation (symphony) between worldly and spiritual authority. In that of Bulgaria, they stood for imperial claims, ecclesiastical independence and defence of the Christian community as such. The lack of strict canonical regulations in the conception and use of those powerful assets of divine authority – the miracle-performing holy relics – made possible a rich and mutually complementary local theology that suited local churches and alternative sources of power and goes a long way towards explaining the inherent paradox of Eastern Orthodox Christianity: How a common faith can produce independent and even hostile religious and political communities.

Mihai-D. Grigore

Politics, Theology, Political Theologies

Three Examples of Practical Political Theology in the
Danubian Principalities (Fourteenth to Sixteenth Centuries)

Introduction

This chapter will deal with the close entanglement of theological discourse and political action in pre-modern Wallachia – in other words, the focus is on practical political theology. On the one hand, political theology is the dialectical anchoring of the political as an idea, of policies and politics as practice, and of politicians as institutionally organised individuals, in man's history with God. On the other, it is the way observers discuss and describe it. Political theology takes always place concurrently *in*, and with regard *to*, both church and state. Political theology cannot be independent of institutional symbolisation.

Institutions are concrete symbols mediating and imparting cultural meaning – *kulturelle Sinnproduktion*, in Karl-Siegbert Rehberg's phrase –, which are effective by imposing binding values and norms, offering a »synthesis of ideal and practical orientations«[1]. Because some (though by no means all) Christian Churches are at the same time confessions, such institutions are concerned with and combine both the secular and the religious dimensions of institutionally symbolised (i. e., embodied) orders[2]. In pre-modern and early modern history, they exist in permanent interdependence with the body politic. In this sense, all political theology must be practice; it cannot remain mere dialectical speculation and idealism.

Taking mediaeval Wallachia as a case study, and based on three examples of well-known personalities in the Orthodox Commonwealth – Nikodemos of Tismana (c. 1320–1406), Nephon II of Constantinople (c. 1440–1508), and Neagoe Basarab (c. 1480–1521) – I here suggest a related if less familiar perspective on the concept of »political theology«. In order to do so, I will begin with the theological-systematic discourse, which will reveal the discrepancies between the (Christian moral) ideal and political and historical reality.

---

1 Karl-Siegbert Rehberg, Symbolische Ordnungen. Beiträge zu einer soziologischen Theorie der Institutionen, Baden-Baden 2014, p. 54.
2 Ibid., p. 55: »Institutionen erbringen symbolische Ordnungen, genauer gesagt: Das Institutionelle an einer Ordnung ist die symbolische Verkörperung ihrer Geltungsansprüche«; see also ibid., pp. 152f.

As the title of this contribution suggests, I describe political and historical circumstances in order to see which politico-theological discourses – ideas, policies, actors and media – were deployed for the legitimation and explanation of political action. My starting point is the process of state formation in Wallachia, beginning in the fourteenth century, consolidating during the fifteenth century, and coming to completion at the beginning of the sixteenth century. On this basis, I shall examine how theological discourses determined or followed political transformations.

What I am trying to reach is therefore less an ethical theology of politics than a perspective on practical political theology and communication. The temporal power elites, the lords of Wallachia, were led in their political action primarily by political reason (not uncoupled, to be sure, from religious considerations), while the ecclesiastical actors involved in the political process were guided by a theological and moral value system. That is why the collaboration sometimes succeeded flawlessly and sometimes erupted in conflict between *politeia* (πολιτεία) and *basileia* (βασιλεία). My analysis considers three important parameters of what I call politico-theological practice: first, the historical and political context, second, religious policy in the ecclesiastical and secular spheres, and, third, the theological dialectics concerning political power.

The goal of this study is to reveal the three most important functions assumed by political theology in relation to temporal power in the pre-modern Orthodox world: first, to discursively reinforce and support it; second, to actively complement and symphonically cooperate with it; and, finally, to critically observe, admonish and amend it. What kind of political theology is activated by the different political-historical constellations is interesting and instructive to observe.

To this end, I will follow four steps: After a discussion of the three personalities mentioned above, I conclude with brief theoretical considerations. I argue that political theological discourse, which is strictly connected *with* and even dependently *on* political practice, takes on the unmistakable characteristics of a theology of history when trying to understand, explain and amend historical events in the light of revelation and theological argument. In conclusion, I argue that political theology is nothing, but a historical approach to practices concerned with the ahistorical finality of man's salvation in eternity.

Nikodemos of Tismana on the Eve of the Wallachian Principality

The area between the Lower Danube, the Carpathians and the Dniester is increasingly mentioned in the sources after the sack of Constantinople by Latin crusaders in 1204. An entangled religious and political situation in the region emerge from the textual evidence, testifying to the importance of this area occupied at the junction of the Assenid Bulgarian Empire, the Cuman dominion, the later Golden Horde, the Hungarian Crown and, of course, the successor Byzantine states of Nicaea and Epirus[3].

A predominance of the Byzantine-Orthodox rite may be assumed in the territories north of the Danube. This troubled the Latin missionaries sent by the Curia and was a stubborn obstacle to the Hungarian Kingdom's territorial expansion, which used Latin religious propaganda in order to promote the confessional incorporation of these territories[4]. The strong attraction exerted by the Byzantine rite through dioceses along the Danube in the imperial province *Paradounavon* (*Παραδούναβον* or *Παρίστριον*), all of them under Constantinople's jurisdiction[5], was evident in the presence of numerous *schismatici*, *eretici* or *infideles* – to use the terminology of Papal, Hospitaller, Teutonic, Minorite or Dominican sources[6] – north of the Danube. These »schismatics« were presumably under the pastoral care of itinerant bishops (*χωρεπίσκοποι*, *chorepiscopi*) or priests and frustrated both the missionary policy of the Curia as well as the expansionist policy of the Hungarian Crown. This relied on Latin centres such as the Cistercian monasteries in Cârța (*monasterium beatae Mariae virginis in Candelis de Kerch*) in Transylvania and its mother-house Egreș (*monasterium de Egres*) in Făgăraș – other centres were in Banat, and those of the Dominicans in Siret (east of the Carpathians) and in the

---

3 Angeliki LAIOU (ed.), Urbs capta. The Fourth Crusade and Its Consequences, Paris 2005. On the geopolitical situation in the region: Șerban PAPACOSTEA, »Prima unire românească«. Voievodatul de Argeș și Țara Severin, in: Studii și materiale de istorie medie 28 (2010), pp. 9–24; Alexandru SIMON, Între coroanele Arpadienilor și Asăneștilor. Implicațiile unui document de la Bela III, in: Studii și materiale de istorie medie 28 (2010), pp. 127–136.
4 Krista ZACH, Konfessionelle Diversität und Dynamik im donaukarpatischen Raum und die Rumänen 11.–14. Jahrhundert, in: Mihai-D. GRIGORE/Florian KÜHRER-WIELACH (eds.), Orthodoxa Confessio? Konfessionsbildung, Konfessionalisierung und ihre Folgen in der östlichen Christenheit Europas, Göttingen 2018 (VIEG Beiheft 114), pp. 205–245, URL: <https://doi.org/10.13109/9783666570780.205> (09-05-2023).
5 Emilian POPESCU, Configurația religioasă la Dunărea de Jos în ajunul și după cruciada a IV-a, in: Id./Mihai Ovidiu CĂȚOI (eds.), Istorie bisericească, misiune creștină și viață culturală. Creștinismul românesc și organizarea bisericească în secolele XIII–XIV. Știri și interpretări noi, Galați 2010, pp. 139–165, at pp. 144–146, 151, 153.
6 Harald ZIMMERMANN, Der Deutsche Orden im Siebenbürgen. Eine diplomatische Untersuchung, Köln ²2011.

Banate of Severin (*terra Ceurin*)⁷ – in order to spread the Latin faith south of the Carpathians⁸.

We hear, for instance, Pope Gregory IX complaining in his letter from Perugia of 14 November 1234 about the Latin Church's difficult situation in the territories east of the Carpathian Mountains, where the Dominicans had just created a new bishopric for the newly Christianised Cumans⁹. In the Bishopric of the Cumans, the pope wrote, lived a people called Wallachians (*Walat[h]i*), who committed many injuries to the true faith, although they called themselves Christians. They had they own rite, the Greek (*Graecorum ritus*), and did not turn to the Latin bishop for liturgical services. Moreover, they had their own »false bishops« (*pseudoepiscopi*), who provided them with pastoral care. To make matters even worse, the Latin believers in the area – the Hungarian, German and Cuman subjects of the Hungarian Crown, who were nominally of the Latin faith (*orthodoxi*) – despised the Latin bishop and had joined the *schismatici*. They were adopting the customs, religious practices and the liturgies of these *schismatici* with their false bishops, thereby forming a single people (*populus unus facti*)¹⁰.

The deed of donation – to give another example – issued in 1247 by the Hungarian King Bela IV (r. 1235–1270) to the Knights Hospitaller¹¹, who were to be settled in southern Transylvania for purposes of defence, conquest and mission, referred to *archiepiscopi* and *episcopi* in the Wallachian territories south of the Carpathians. Since they are not mentioned in the Byzantine sources of Nikaia, these dioceses

---

7 Géza ENTZ, Le chantier cistercien de Kerc (Cîrța), in: Acta Historiae Artium 9/1–2 (1963), pp. 3–38; Ivan S. DUJCEV, Il francescanesimo in Bulgaria nei secoli XIII e XIV, in: Id., Medioevo Bizantino-Slavo I, Rome 1965, pp. 395–425, at pp. 413–415; Kristó GYULA et al., Korai Magyar Történeti Lexicon (9–14 század), Budapest 1994, p. 219; Viorel ACHIM, Ordinul franciscan în Țările Române în secolele XIV-XV. Aspecte teritoriale, in: Revista Istorică 7/5–6 (1996), pp. 391–410, at pp. 399f.; Christopher MIELKE, No Country for Old Women. Burial Practices of Hungarian Queens (975–1301), College Park, MD 2010, pp. 28–30; Emil DUMEA, Catolicismul în Moldova în secolul al XVIII-lea, Iași 2003, pp. 35–38.
8 Șerban TURCUȘ, Sfântul Scaun și românii în secolul al XIII-lea, Bucharest 2001, pp. 251–276.
9 Viorel ACHIM, Politica sud-estică a regatului ungar sub ultimii arpadieni, Bucharest 2008, pp. 56–60.
10 »In Cumanorum episcopatu, sicut accepimus, quidam populi, qui Walati vocantur, existunt, qui etsi censeantur nomine christiano, sub una tamen fide varios ritus habentes et mores, illa committunt, que huic sunt nomini inimica. Nam Romanam ecclesiam contempnentes, non a venerabili fratre nostro [...], episcopo Cumanorum, qui loci diocesanus existit, sed a quibusdam pseudoepiscopis, Grecorum ritum tenentibus, universa recipiunt ecclesiastica sacramenta, et nonnulli de regno Ungarie, tam Ungari, quam Theutonici et alii orthodoxi morandi causa cum ipsis transeunt ad eosdem et sic cum eis, quia populus unus facti cum eisdem Walathis eo contempto, premissa recipiunt sacramenta, in grave orthodoxorum scandalum et derogationem non modicam fidei christiane«, Academia Republicii Socialiste România (ed.), Documenta Romaniae Historica. D. Relațiile între Țările Române I (1222–1456), Bucharest 1977, No. 9, p. 20.
11 Ibid., No. 10, p. 22.

must have been under the jurisdiction neither of Rome nor of Constantinople. Liturgically they were, however, presumably of the Greek rite.

Beginning with 1351, we can observe an intensification of Latin missionary efforts. Wallachia's Princes had to react. Nicholas Alexander strengthened the close familial and dynastic ties with the Orthodox countries of Bulgaria and Serbia, giving his daughters in marriage to the rulers of these countries[12]. The Wallachian Prince also wrote to Patriarch Kallistos I of Constantinople (1350–1353, 1354–1363) to ask him for permission to move the important metropolitan centre of Vicina to the Wallachian capital of Curtea de Argeş. This move led, in 1359, to the foundation of the Metropolis of Hungro-Wallachia. It immediately enjoyed the official recognition of the Ecumenical Patriarchate, which also sent the first Greek hierarchs to Wallachia[13]. Wallachia's decision to opt for Constantinople was the princes' first step in their religious policy of building a strong Orthodox identity for their country in order to ensure its political autonomy.

The second step was the creation of an efficient institutional infrastructure. The princes created new bishoprics within their metropolis to enhance the episcopal coverage of the territory, but – and this is important – also revived and organised the monkish tradition by a stringent programme of founding monastic centres throughout their territories[14]. The main figure of this monastic reform as instrument of political stabilisation was the monk Nikodemos (c. 1320–1406).

We have no contemporary sources concerning Nikodemos (Nicodim) of Tismana, who was probably Serbian by birth. There is the travelogue of the Syrian deacon Paul of Aleppo (post-1657), the *synaxarion* on Nicodemos' feast day on

---

12 Ştefan ANDREESCU, Alliances dynastiques des princes de Valachie (XIVe–XVIe siècles), in: Revue des études sud-est européennes 23/4 (1985), pp. 359–368; Mihai Florin HASAN, Aspecte ale relaţiilor matrimoniale dinastice munteano-maghiare din secolele XIV–XV, in: Revista Bistriţei 27 (2013), pp. 128–159, at pp. 148f.

13 Academia Republicii Populare Române (ed.), Documente privind Istoria României. Veacul XIII, XIV şi XV. B. Ţara Românească (1247–1500), Bucharest 1953, No. 9, pp. 13f.; No. 10, pp. 14–16; Franz MIKLOSICH/Joseph MÜLLER (eds.), Acta et diplomatica Graeca medii aevi. 1: Acta patriarchatus Constantinopolitani 1315–1402, vol. 1, Aalen 1968, No. 171/1, pp. 383–386; No. 171/2, pp. 386–388. See Alexandru MORARU, Întemeierea Mitropoliei Ungrovlahiei (1359) receptată în istoriografia românească, in: POPESCU/CĂŢOI (eds.), Istorie bisericească, misiune creştină şi viaţă culturală, pp. 306–334, at pp. 309–314; Matei CAZACU/Dan Ioan MUREŞAN, Ioan Basarab. Un domn român la începuturile Ţării Româneşti, Chisinau 2013, pp. 162–167; Lidia COTOVANU, Deux cas parallèles d'oikonomia byzantine. Appliquée aux métropolites Anthime Kritopoulos de Séverin et Cyprien de Kiev de Petite-Russie et des Lituaniens (Deuxième moitié du XIVe siècle), in: Revue roumaine d'histoire 42 (2003), pp. 19–60; HASAN, Aspecte, pp. 128–148.

14 Mihai-D. GRIGORE, Ein Glaubensgutachten für Neagoe Basarab (1512–1521). Jurisdiktion und Glaube in der Walachei bis Anfang des 16. Jahrhunderts, in: GRIGORE/KÜHRER-WIELACH (eds.), Orthodoxa Confessio?, pp. 247–263, at pp. 256–258, URL: <https://doi.org/10.13109/9783666570780.247> (09-05-2023).

26 December (post-1767), and the saint's *vita*, composed in 1839 by the monk Stefan from Tismana Monastery[15]. Nikodemos was monk for a time on Mount Athos, in the hesychastic centre of Chilandar, which also produced Chariton, the Metropolitan of Hungro-Wallachia. After that, Nikodemos spent a short time in the Kingdom of Vidin, where he founded a number of Orthodox monasteries. Vidin was across the Danube from the Banate of Severin, a fief of the Hungarian Crown. From here started the Hungarian offensive south of the Danube in 1366.

Nikodemos fled to Wallachia in the retinue of the Metropolitan Daniel of Vidin, who was held in high esteem there and had almost been appointed metropolitan of Severin[16]. Here, Nikodemos acted on the basis of his experience in founding monasteries on behalf of the country's ruler, Prince Vladislav Vlaicu I (r. 1364–1377), for the development of a monastic infrastructure, since the governing elite had decided in 1359 in favour of the Eastern Rite and against the Latin faith. In 1372 and 1376, Nicodemus founded as coenobitical *samovlastia* (gr. αὐτοδεσποτεία, σταυροπήγιον) – which means they were exempt of local obligations and stood under direct patriarchal authority – the monasteries of Vodița and Tismana, on the border of the Kingdom of Hungary and the aforementioned Banat of Severin. In the foundation of these two centres, we encounter a fascinating entanglement of religious practice and political finality: The monasteries were built in the wildness of the Carpathians, isolated from human habitations, in keeping with the principle of monastic seclusion. On the other hand, they were built on problematic borders and along routes frequented by Latin missionaries. Maintaining and radiating Orthodoxy, with their fortified walls the monasteries served as border citadels as well religious centres.

The monastic infrastructure begun by Nikodemos was expanded by the Princes Radu I (r. 1377–1385), Dan I (r. 1385–1386) and Mircea I (r. 1386–1418) with further monasteries: Nucet, Cozia (pre-1383) and Snagov (1408). These and later similar monasteries in Wallachia enjoyed the princes' full economic support, including rich estates, donations of money and jewellery, permission to collect taxes, and tax exemptions. Of 38 deeds of donation issued by the voivode's chancellery between 1372 (the founding year of Vodița) and 1418 (the year of Mircea I's death), 22 are in favour of the five monastic centres named above[17].

In 1375, Nikodemos took part in a delegation aiming to effect a reconciliation between Orthodox Churches of Serbia and Constantinople, which had been divided

---

15 Emil Lăzărescu, Nicodim de la Tismana și rolul său în cultura veche românească I (până la 1385), in: Romanoslavica 11 (1958), pp. 237–285, at pp. 238–253.
16 Cotovanu, Deux cas, pp. 50–52.
17 Documente B. Țara Românească, pp. viii–x.

since 1346[18]. This dispute had been triggered in 1346 by the Serbian Tsar Stefan Uroš IV Dušan (r. 1331-1355) who, in order to emphasise his imperial ambitions, had decided to declare the Serbian Church a Patriarchate, thereby violating the Ecumenical Patriarchate's jurisdiction[19]. The delegation, which included among others Nikodemos of Tismana, Isaiah of Chilandar and Theophanos Protos, the head (πρῶτος) of the monastic community of Athos, was sent to Constantinople by Lazar Hrebeljanović (r. 1371-1389) of Serbia[20].

The delegation's internationality shows how monastic and ecclesiastical as well as political factors were interwoven, leading to a complex entanglement of strategies, goals and reasons. For the Serbian ruler came under pressure from the Ottomans and urgently needed the support of all Orthodox rulers in the region. This, however, was prevented by his schismatic status, the Serbs being anathematised by the Ecumenical Patriarch. Hence the urgency to settle the dispute with the Patriarchate. The Patriarchate and the Princes of Wallachia had an interest, on the other hand, in promoting a strong Orthodoxy against the Latins, the former for jurisdictional reasons, the latter for political reasons, in their conflict with the Hungarian Crown.

The establishment of a monastic infrastructure went hand in hand with the reinforcement of Orthodox dogma and with moral reform of clergy and laymen. Two recently discovered letters from Patriarch Euthymios of Tarnovo (1375-1393) to Nikodemos – who was in charge of the religious integration of the country into the Orthodox Commonwealth – confirm this. In these letters, the patriarch clarified some dogmatic points against the Bogomil heresy, which seems to have spread among the people. On this anti-heretical basis, Euthymios proclaimed the urgent necessity of reforming the Wallachian clergy in accordance with a high standard of pure Orthodox doctrine, morality and liturgical life. In response to Nikodemos, the patriarch pleads for strict hierarchical structures in the church, reflecting the strict hierarchy of angels discussed by Pseudo-Dionysius the Areopagite. In this hierarchical thinking, the authority of the patriarchs of Constantinople as spiritual and ecclesiastical guide and as administrator of the Seven Ecumenical Councils' Orthodox normativity is strongly accentuated. In another letter to the Metropolitan of Wallachia, Antimos Critopoulos, Euthymios explains his opposition to second

---

18 Nicolae Chifăr, Contextul politico-religios sud-est european privind întemeierea Mitropoliei Țării Românești, in: Popescu/Câțoi (eds.), Istorie bisericească, misiune creștină și viață culturală, pp. 286–305, at p. 293.

19 Constantin Rezachevici, Istoria popoarelor vecine și neamul românesc în Evul Mediu, Bucharest 1998, p. 368; Günter Prinzing, Längeschnitt – Kirchengeschichte, in: Konrad Clewing/Oliver Jens Schmitt (eds.), Geschichte Südosteuropas. Vom frühen Mittelalter bis zur Gegenwart, Regensburg 2011, pp. 61–65, at p. 65; Stefan Rohdewald, Götter der Nationen. Religiöse Erinnerungsfiguren in Serbien, Bulgarien und Makedonien bis 1944, Köln 2014, pp. 126–128.

20 Lăzărescu, Nicodim, pp. 267–270.

and third marriages[21]. While this was not of much concern for the common people, problems occurred when princes or other political magnates married several times, thereby giving rise to internal and international succession and dynastic disputes.

In Nikodemos of Tismana's example, we see transregional hesychastic networks at work, exerting influence on apparently unpolitical issues like monastic life, the Bogomil heresy and moral reform – issues which, however, turn out to be political when we consider the wider geopolitical situation[22].

Nephon II, Patriarch of Constantinople and Metropolitan of Wallachia

The main source for the life of Nephon II of Constantinople is his Vita, written by Gabriel, the *protos* of Mount Athos between 1517 and 1519[23], approximately ten years after Nephon's death[24]. According to the Vita, Gabriel met Nephon personally and had seen him in a number situations, and may therefore be said to have known him well enough[25]. Of course, the Vita is always a difficult literary genre[26], with its required panegyric tone always at risk of sacrificing historical reality for hagiographical enthusiasm. Still, the *Vita Nephonis*, as I shall call it here, grants significant insights into the history and religious policies of Southeastern Europe under Ottoman rule, especially those of Wallachia under the reign of four rulers[27]. Furthermore, other Ottoman or Christian sources confirm the historical informa-

---

21 Gheorghiță CIOCIOI (ed.), Sfântul Eftimie Patriarh de Târnovo. Corespondența cu Sfântul Nicodim de la Tismana, Mitropolitul Antim al Ungrovlahiei, Monahul Ciprian viitorul mitropolit al Kievului și al întregii Rusii, Bucharest 2014.
22 Flavius SOLOMON, Politică și confesiune la început de Ev Mediu moldovenesc, Iași 2004, pp. 148f.; Mihai-D. GRIGORE, Neagoe Basarab – Princeps Christianus. The Semantics of Christianitas in Comparison with Erasmus, Luther and Machiavelli (1513–1523), Frankfurt am Main 2015, pp. 152–156.
23 On Gabriel Protos, see Nicolae M. POPESCU, Nifon II Patriarhul Constantinopolului, in: Analele Academiei Române. Memoriile secțiunii istorice 36 (1914), pp. 731–798, at pp. 748–751.
24 The edition of the Old Romanian redaction is: Tit SIMEDREA (ed.), Gavriil Protul, Viața și traiul Sfântului Nifon patriarhul Constantinopolului, Bucharest 1937 (cited here as »Protul [TS], Nifon«). This redaction is more comprehensive on the history of Wallachia than the Greek redaction edited by Vasile Grecu: Vasile GRECU (ed.), Gavriil Protul, Viața Sfântului Nifon. O redacțiune grecească inedita, Bucharest 1944 (cited here as »Protul [VG], Nifon«).
25 PROTUL (VG), Nifon, p. 32.
26 Stephanie HAARLÄNDER, Vitae episcoporum. Eine Quellengattung zwischen Hagiographie und Historiographie, untersucht an Lebensbeschreibungen von Bischöfen des Regnum Teutonicum im Zeitalter der Ottonen und Salier, Stuttgart 2010, pp. 1f.
27 Dumitru MAZILU, Contribuțiuni cu privire la studiul vieții Sf. Nifon, Patriarhul Constantinopolului, in: Dumitru SIMONESCU/id. (eds.), Contribuții privitoare la istoria literaturii române, Bucharest 1928, pp. 21–36.

tion contained in the *Vita*. In fact, the *Vita Nephonis* is the first historiographical work on Wallachia[28]. For all these reasons, it merits consideration here.

Nephon, whose baptismal name was Nicholas, was born in the Peloponnese in 1440. Nicholas received the tonsure and the associated monastic name Nephon quite early, after completing his novitiate in a variety of monastic settings (monastery schools, private lessons with monks, or even as pupil of a hermit)[29]. Before going to Mount Athos, he had to earn his living with calligraphy, as a copyist of books[30]. He drew attention to himself with his intransigent propaganda against the so-called *latinofrones*, the adepts of the church union signed at the council of Ferarra and Florence, which took place in 1438 and 1439[31]. Nephon became Metropolitan of Thessaloniki in 1483 and participated at the Constantinople Council from 1484, signing the *tomos* against the union of Florence[32]. In 1486, he was elected Ecumenical Patriarch of Constantinople – with the aid, as Steven Runciman supposes, of the Lord of Wallachia, Vlad the Monk (r. 1481–1495, with interruptions), who used his influence at the Ottoman Court[33].

Nephon's first term of office as patriarch lasted only until 1488, when Sultan Bayezid II (r. 1481–1512) deposed and exiled him for interfering in inheritance disputes between the Patriarchate and the Ottoman administration of Constantinople[34]. Recalled from exile on the initiative of the Prince of Wallachia, Radu the Great (r. 1495–1508), he returned as Patriarch of Constantinople in 1497, but again only for a short time. In 1498 he was once more sent into exile, this time to Adrianople, where he was placed under house arrest[35]. It was here in 1502 that the Prince asked him to come to Wallachia as the country's metropolitan, which he accepted after turning down a final appointment as Ecumenical Patriarch. Prince Radu therefore obtained permission from the Sublime Porte and Nephon became the Metropolitan of Hungro-Wallachia[36].

Nephon's biographer, Gabriel Protos, cites the words of Prince Radu inviting the holy man to become metropolitan: »From now on, dear Father, we possess in you our very mentor and shepherd. I will reign over external affairs (τὰ ἐσωτερικά),

---

28 Ibid., p. 21.
29 PROTUL (TS), Nifon, pp. 2f.
30 PROTUL (VG), Nifon, p. 43.
31 Ibid., p. 47.
32 POPESCU, Nifon II, pp. 738, 771.
33 Steven RUNCIMAN, The Great Church in Captivity. A Study of the Patriarchate of Constantinople from the Eve of the Turkish Conquest to the Greek War of Independence, Cambridge 1968, p. 195.
34 POPESCU, Nifon II, pp. 774f.
35 PROTUL (VG), Nifon, p. 75.
36 Ibid., pp. 77–79; POPESCU, Nifon II, pp. 780f.

while your Holiness will take care of the church's internal affairs«[37]. This functional division is not new in Christian political theology. It begins with Eusebius, occurs in a well-known letter of Charlemagne to Pope Leo III, and is also mentioned by Emperor John Tzismiskes in the tenth century[38].

Radu's goal was to bring Wallachia under ecclesiastical authority in order to implement Orthodox conformity. For Radu, this meant first of all the stabilisation of his own princely power in the country in attempting to counteract the centrifugal tendencies of the high boyars. Nephon's first act was to organise a local council of the Wallachian Church, which implemented the decisions of the Holy Synod of Constantinople in matters of canonical law, liturgical services, monastic rule and the moral life of the faithful. The synod created new bishoprics as well in order to improve the territory's ecclesiastical administration and pastoral coverage. What is important is that this local synod not only regulated ecclesiastic internal matters, but also clarified political structures. It included in its canonical ordinances that the prince was the country's only legislative authority and highest administrator of justice[39]. This way the synod interfered in public life in order to support the prince in his centralisation policy.

The supposition that Radu had problems with the local aristocracy is strengthened by the observation that he tried to rely on foreign boyars. One of them was Bogdan, a Moldavian who, promoted by Prince Radu, occupied at one time or another most prominent functions in Wallachia. Bogdan was a fugitive from Moldavia, where he left his wife. His asylum in Wallachia added to political tensions between the two Danubian Principalities. Maybe in order to keep him in Wallachia and also maybe because Bogdan himself wanted to put down roots in his adoptive country, Radu organised a new marriage for the foreign boyar, this time to his own sister, Caplea. Nephon opposed this strongly because – as mentioned – Bogdan was already married in Moldavia, making the marriage with Caplea bigamous. This caused a harsh quarrel between Radu and Nephon, culminating in the latter's exile[40]. The symbiosis between temporal and spiritual power was, because of Bogdan, destroyed.

This example demonstrates that the political intentions of the temporal power could collide with the theological and moral framework of ecclesiastical institutions

---

37 PROTUL (VG), Nifon, pp. 79–81.
38 Mihai-D. GRIGORE, Der Mensch zwischen Gott und Staat. Überlegungen zu politischen Formen im Christentum, in: Studii Teologice. Revista Facultăților de teologie din Patriarhia Română 6/1 (2010), pp. 105–175, at pp. 164f.
39 Nikos PANOU, Greek-Romanian Symbiotic Patterns in the Early Modern Period. History, Mentalities, Institutions. Part I, in: The Historical Review/La Revue Historique 3 (2006), pp. 71–110, on pp. 62–83.
40 PROTUL (VG), Nifon, pp. 81–93; POPESCU, Nifon II, pp. 783f.

and persons. Underneath the argument for Christian moral renewal and reform, Radu's ostensible reason for bringing Nephon into the country, lay the prince's desire to check centrifugal tendencies in the high nobility and to discipline his subjects both low- and high-born. However, this moral reform – which implied, among other things, patriarchal canons against bigamy – became a weapon against the voivode's policy.

Furthermore, the Ecumenical Patriarchate had no interest in the political dispute between Moldavia and Wallachia, intensified by Radu's patronage of the fugitive boyar Bogdan, because both Danubian Principalities were important pillars of the Orthodox Commonwealth. Late Byzantium experienced a growth of ecclesiastical power and the political influence of the patriarchs, inverting the classical division of roles: The emperor was only the symbolic head of the church, while the patriarch assumed the active role of guarantor of the emperor's secular power[41]. Like his predecessors, Nephon expected unconditional obedience from secular magnates in both religious and secular matters. This may also explain Nephon's short periods of office as patriarch as a result of clashes with the Ottoman authorities.

Interestingly, the first decision of Neagoe Basarab (r. 1512–1521), Lord of Wallachia after Radu the Great, was – as Gabriel Protos informs us – to execute Bogdan. This comes as little surprise if we consider that, on the one hand, Neagoe Basarab was rooted in the local Wallachian high nobility and that, on the other, he was an apprentice of Nephon and cultivated close relations with the Ecumenical Patriarchate. Gabriel Protos demonises Bogdan, presenting him as a factor of satanic dissent and the disturbance of social and political harmony, as an instrument of the devil because of his immoral life and as a foreign body in the socio-political organism of Wallachia. As far as Neagoe Basarab was concerned, Bogdan's execution was fully legitimate and an act of pastoral care for the integrity of the Christian flock[42].

Neagoe Basarab and the Usurper's Legitimation Trouble

Historians have long debated whether the twenty-fifth ruler of Wallachia, Neagoe Basarab, was a dynastic successor from the old Basarab lineage or a usurper who acceded to the throne from the Wallachian aristocracy. The body of evidence shows, as I have discussed at length elsewhere[43], that he was not descended from the princely dynasty and occupied the throne by usurpation. Neagoe Basarab removed

---

41 Petre Guran, L'origine et la fonction théologico-politique de la couronne patriarcale, in: Dossiers byzantins 7. Le Patriarcat Œcuménique de Constantinople aux XIVe–XVIe siècles. Rupture et continuité, Paris 2007, pp. 407–427, at pp. 409f., 415.
42 Grigore, Neagoe Basarab – Princeps Christianus, pp. 46f.
43 Ibid., pp. 32–50.

his predecessor from the throne using Ottoman troops and executed him. However, his contemporaries knew that he had no claim on the throne, and this is evident in the fate of his son, Theodosius, who was removed from throne after only a few months.

Neagoe Basarab is the author of a unique mirror for princes (*speculum principis*). This lengthy moral and political treatise, the so-called *Teachings of Neagoe Basarab to his Son Theodosius*[44], written around 1519-1520, is a work of great theological, political, military and diplomatic erudition. It was first printed in Bucharest in 1843, having previously existed only in manuscript form. The Slavonic original is preserved in fragments, and we possess nine complete or partial manuscripts of the Old Romanian translation as well as a Greek translation from about 1525-1530. This testifies to a broad reception, not only in the Greek and Wallachian area, but also in the Grand Duchy of Moscow. The work is in two parts. The first is a theological and theoretical deliberation on the political order in the cosmos, the likeness of the prince to God and the illumination of the ruler in a hesychastic manner. The second is the practical part, which deals with the selection of counsellors, diplomatic affairs, military strategy, philanthropy and the protocol at official occasions[45].

The interesting point for the present analysis of applied political theology is that Neagoe Basarab, conscious of his precarious claim to the Wallachian throne and anticipating difficulties for his successor, tries to offer Theodosius a manual of rulership. We should note that in Wallachia, dynastic continuity and affiliation were much more important than, for instance, in the Byzantine Empire, where some authors have seen the imperial dignity as »open« on merit[46]. To go back to the *Teachings*, the human coordinates of rulership – such as dynastic succession or elective procedures – are minimised as far as possible, whereas the transcendental aspects of God's absolute will and providence are maximised.

Throughout the treatise, Neagoe Basarab emphasises that only God makes rulers and that no human criteria – whether dynastic lineage, election or personal merit – are legitimate qualifications for the supreme duty of leadership. The only legitimation comes from God himself as an act of pure will and benevolence. In this anti-meritorious acceptance of leadership, Neagoe Basarab seems almost to anticipate Lutheran ideas[47]. For him, the ruler is neither a representative of God on Earth nor his substitute. The relation of the Christian ruler to God was one

---

44 Neagoe BASARAB, Învățăturile lui Neagoe Basarab către fiul său Theodosie, ed. by Florica MOISIL/ Dan ZAMFIRESCU, Bucharest ³1984.
45 GRIGORE, Neagoe Basarab – Princeps Christianus, pp. 69–130.
46 Alexandru I. BUZESCU, Domnia în Țările Române până la 1866, Bucharest 1943, p. 67; Karen PIEPENBRINK, Konstantin der Große und seine Zeit, Darmstadt ³2010, p. 62.
47 Mihai-D. GRIGORE, Reformatorische Ideen in der Walachei und der Moldau zwischen 1519 und 1521? Mögliche Transferwege von reformatorischem Gedankengut südlich und östlich der Karpaten,

of likeness (ὁμοίωσις): »You are [as ruler] exactly like Him«, declares Basarab in his *Teachings*⁴⁸.

In a manner similar to Martin Luther, Basarab believes that the ruler does not need to justify his position by philanthropy or good works. His leadership is the exclusive favour of God's grace, *gratia Dei*. Moreover, exactly like Luther, Basarab stipulates that any meritorious works performed by the Christian ruler are not what makes a ruler, but only the fruits of the effective operating grace of God. Good deeds are neither cause nor reason, but *consequences* of divine favour⁴⁹. Basarab thus advises his son Theodosius: »That is why you shall praise Him who raised you from the ground and made you His son; He made you emperor of heaven and of the peoples, He made you vanquisher and great commander of men, He instituted you as *dominus* on earth [...]«⁵⁰.

Neagoe Basarab was especially concerned to create a theoretical and theological framework for the ruler's autonomy from any human instances. The Christian ruler's authority is *immediately* connected to God; he is God's *Synbasileus* or co-ruler⁵¹. Not even the church is needed in this argumentative framework: Basarab makes no reference at all to any intercession on the part of the clergy, granting it only the function of officiating at liturgical services. The sovereign is responsible only to God, because only God makes rulers on earth⁵². In spite of his personal piety, Basarab was not prepared to concede any political prerogatives to the church.

In short, the *Teachings to Theodosius* are an example of what is widely understood by the term »political theology«: a scholarly text citing traditional arguments from the Holy Scriptures and the Fathers and interpreting them in its own historical context. I have tried to show the interconnection with the concrete situation of Neagoe Basarab which reveals the *Teachings* as an instance of applied political theology. It is not pure political expediency and propaganda, because of the deep and ardent faith of the author who is honestly convinced that he rules because, despite all human logic, God wants him to. On the other hand, it is not just a politico-theological speculation of a high scholarly standard. It is also deeply rooted in immediate historical reality, which is seen as the manifestation of God's will on earth through specific historical agents.

---

in: Jahrbuch des Bundesinstituts für Kultur und Geschichte der Deutschen im Östlichen Europa 22 (2015), pp. 189–212, at pp. 193–202.

48 »(C)ând ai cap pre Hristos, cându din trupul lui te pricestuiesti, cându esti frate lui si mostean si întocmai cu dânsul«, Basarab, Învățăturile, 13 (emphasis added).
49 Grigore, Reformatorische Ideen, p. 202.
50 Basarab, Învățăturile, 9.
51 Grigore, Neagoe Basarab – Princeps Christianus, p. 145, fn. 591.
52 Ibid., p. 75.

Conclusion

In this chapter, I gave three samples of politico-theological practice. In so doing, I attempted to throw new light on political theology beyond the common understanding of it as a scholarly discourse and speculative exercise. In the interpretation I suggest here, political theology is a framing category, one that includes agency and communication between the temporal and ecclesiastical dimensions of pre-modern human socialisation. Postulating political theology as a communication process, I had to relate it closely to persons, to human agency and to constellations of power, all of which are constantly shifting. This liveliness of political transformation, with all its changes, circumstances, negotiations and reversals, makes politico-theological communication a process simultaneously of action, reaction, and synergy. In this process, political reasons are interwoven with theological significance in a complex web of factors determining human agency.

Moreover, all this makes applied political theology – understood as communication and practice – not historically contingent, but historically *relative*, by relating transcendental ahistorical truth to historical existence in the world.

Jan Kusber

Autocracy as a Form of Political Theology?

Ruler and Church in Early Modern Muscovy (1450s-1725)

I.

My intention in this chapter is to discuss a period crucial for the religiously grounded idea of *Autocracy* in Muscovy and Russia after the fall of Byzantium in 1453. The question concerning the respective realms of church and ruler had already been the subject of negotiations in 1448, after Iona, the Metropolitan of Muscovy, claimed to be the head of a *de facto* »autocephalous« church[1]. These more or less open and ongoing discourses on political theology in pre-modern Russia will be discussed for crucial moments of the relationship between church and autocrats up to the dissolution of the Moscow Patriarchate under Peter I in 1721. The actors and the facts are, of course, not new to historians. There is a long and ongoing debate on church-state-relations in mediaeval and early modern Russia, on the theological traditions from Byzantine and autochthonous sources, and on whether the church became a handmaiden of the state or not. One thing is certain: The whole development cannot be understood without the state and the rule of the Tsar. This necessitates reiterating some turning points in the development of a Muscovite Orthodox political theology. Although these are quite widely known, they are mostly discussed by theologians or historians with regard to their specific research interests. This chapter aims at bringing together the disciplinary viewpoints of political history and the history of ideas with the help of the concept of political theology, which is at the centre of this volume.

Of course, if one had asked a contemporary actor whether there existed a political theology in fifteenth- or sixteenth-century Muscovy, he or she would not have understood the question. The chronicles and other depictions of the most Orthodox ruler, who was carrying out his duties in defending his subjects and the right faith against the infidels in East and South (mostly the Tatars) and those in the West (the Latin Church and the Latin powers) defined the whole topic[2]. This is not surprising for the chronicles of the sixteenth and seventeenth century – the famous and in

---

1 Polnoe Sobranie Russkikh Letopisei (henceforth PSRL), vol. 25: Moskovskii letopisnyi svod kontsa XV veka, Moscow/Leningrad 1949, pp. 248-270.
2 On the example of the conquest of Kazan 1552, see Michael KHODARKOVSKY, The Non-Christian Peoples on the Muscovite Frontiers, in: Maureen PERRIE (ed.), The Cambridge History of Russia, vol. 1: From Early Rus to 1689, Cambridge 2006, pp. 317-337, at pp. 319f.; Richard WORTMAN, Scenarios

many ways unreliable *Nikon Chronicle*[3], but also the *Muscovite Chronicle* from the last third of the fifteenth century, edited and translated by Peter Nitsche brilliantly some fifty years ago[4] – are full of such characterisations of the Grand Dukes of Muscovy. The authors, learned clergyman of course, left only the slightest hints whether each ruler, beginning with Vladimir the Saint, fulfilled his duty before God and the Orthodox faith[5]. Instead, they justified the *translatio imperii* from Kiev via Vladimir in the thirteenth century, after the sack of Kiev in 1241 by the Mongols and the migration of the metropolitan of the Rus from Kiev to Vladimir, and then in the fourteenth century to Moscow[6].

The founding of the Sergei-Troitsky-Lavra near Moscow as a spiritual centre nearly as important as the Monastery of the Caves in Kiev was a visible sign for this. The famous Sergei of Radonezh blessed Grand Duke Dmitrii Donskoi before fighting the Tatars led by Emir Mamai in the well-known battle of 1380[7]. Thus, the protection and well-being of the Christian (Orthodox) state and protection of the church in his branches created a win-win-situation. This symbiosis – or *symphonia*, to use a more controversial term – was not described in terms of political theology or policy, but was conceived as ongoing discourse on the right and true Christian faith. Contemporaries – those, for example, who prepared Ivan Groznyi for his famous debate with Antonio Possevino – thought and wrote of religiosity and

---

of Power. Myth and Ceremony in Russian Monarchy, vol. 1: From Peter the Great to the Death of Nicholas I, Princeton, NJ 1995, pp. 29f.

3   Russkaia letopis' po Nikonovu spiku. Izdannaia pod smotreniem imperatorskoi Akademii Nauk (St Petersburg 1767–1792), URL: <https://dlib.rsl.ru/viewer/01004095257#?page=1> (09-14-2023). The chronicle contains a large number of facts not found in earlier sources. Some of these interpolations are thought to reflect a political ideology of the nascent Tsardom of Russia, see: Donald OSTROWSKI, Muscovy and the Mongols. Cross-Cultural Influences on the Steppe Frontier 1304–1589, Cambridge 2002, pp. 147–149.

4   PSRL, vol. 25: Moskovskii letopisnyi svod kontsa XV veka; Peter NITSCHE, Der Aufstieg Moskaus. Auszüge aus einer russischen Chronik, vols. 1–2, Graz et al. 1966–1967.

5   The authors of the Moscow chronicle, for example, quite openly criticised Dmitrii Donskoi for leaving Moscow in 1382, when the Tatar horsemen were advancing in revenge for the defeat of 1380. Dmitrii, they argued, was not acting as a Christian ruler, cf. PSRL, vol. 25: Moskovskii letopisnyi svod kontsa XV veka.

6   Ekkehard KLUG, Wie entstand und was war die Moskauer Autokratie?, in: Eckhard HÜBNER et al. (eds.), Zwischen Christianisierung und Europäisierung. Beiträge zur Geschichte Osteuropas in Mittelalter und Früher Neuzeit. Festschrift für Peter Nitsche zum 65. Geburtstag, Stuttgart 1998, pp. 91–113.

7   The legend of the saint, written around 1400, also deploys a crusading rhetoric. Of the battle, it says: »God helped the great, victorious champion Dmitrii, and the pagan Tatar sons were defeated and put to final destruction. The damned saw that God's anger was against them and turned to flee; the flag of the cross chased the enemies for a long time«, quoted in Legende vom Heiligen Sergij von Radonesch, in: Ernst BENZ (ed.), Russische Heiligenlegenden, Zurich ³1989, pp. 292–362, at p. 353.

power[8]. Although they used scholarly concepts, the texts they produced were filled less with theories than with what we might call »practices of political theology«.

The core problem that must briefly be discussed here is that of autocracy[9]. In its practical manifestations, grand ducal and then Tsarist autocracy (*tsarskoe samoderzhavie*) may be understood as a form of autocracy specific to the Grand Duchy of Moscow, which later became the Tsardom of Russia and the Russian Empire. In it, all power and wealth were controlled (and distributed) by the Tsar, who performed his duties with divine assistance. The Tsar's rule was given by God, which made the Tsar only responsible only to God[10]. Tsars had more power than other monarchs, who were usually constrained by law and counterbalanced by a legislative authority, as was the case in England, Sweden or the Holy Roman Empire. They even had more authority on religious issues than Western monarchs. In Russia, this phenomenon originated during the times of Ivan III (r. 1462–1505)[11], Vasilii III (r. 505–1533)[12] and Ivan IV (r. 1533–1582). Ideologically, autocracy in early modern Russia was rested on a religious foundation, and Alexander Dvorkin has referred to the free autocracy of the Russian Rulers as a »religious type«. We know that the practical features of rule, including the title of Tsar, derived not only from religious sources, but also from non-Christian, Tatar practices, or from texts well-known in mediaeval and early modern Russia, such as the Byzantine Emperor Constantine VII's *De administrando imperii* (Πρὸς τὸν ἴδιον υἱὸν Ρωμανόν) from the tenth century[13].

---

8 For a useful selection in English translation, see Hugh F. GRAHAM (ed.), The Moscovia of Antonio Possevino, S.J., Pittsburgh 1977. For the context of this debate, see Walter DELIUS, Antonio Possevino S.J. und Ivan Groznyj. Ein Beitrag zur Geschichte der kirchlichen Union und der Gegenreformation des 16. Jahrhunderts, Stuttgart 1962; and, recently, Maike SACH, »Griechischen« Glaubens und »Erbe von Byzanz«? Fehleinschätzungen, kulturelle Missverständnisse und konfligierende Konzepte über das Selbstverständnis in den Gesprächen zwischen Zar Ivan IV. und dem päpstlichen Legaten Antonio Possevino im Jahre 1582, in: Ludger KÖRNTGEN et al. (eds.), Byzanz und seine europäischen Nachbarn. Politische Interdependenzen und kulturelle Missverständnisse, Mainz 2020, pp. 151–178.

9 Apart from the literature already mentioned, see Werner PHILIPP, Die gedankliche Begründung der Moskauer Autokratie bei ihrer Entstehung (1458–1522), in: Forschungen zur Osteuropäischen Geschichte 15 (1970), pp. 59–118.

10 Ivan IV feared God as judge, which did not, however, alter his politics as an autocrat: Ludwig STEINDORFF, Mehr als eine Frage der Ehre. Zum Stifterverhalten Zar Ivans des Schrecklichen, in: Jahrbücher für Geschichte Osteuropas 51 (2003), pp. 342–366.

11 John L.I. FENNELL, Ivan the Great of Moscow, Cambridge 1961.

12 Jan KUSBER, Vasilij III. Ivanović, Großfürst von Moskau, Herrscher der ganzen Rus' (1502/1505-33) (1479–1533), in: Lexikon des Mittelalters, vol. 8, Munich 1997, pp. 1422f.; Aleksandr I. FILJUSHKIN, Vasilii III, Moscow 2010.

13 Michael CHERNIAVSKY, Khan or Basileus. An Aspect of Russian Mediaeval Political Theory, in: Journal of the History of Ideas 20/4 (1959), pp. 459–476.

By around 1480, it seemed as if the position of the Grand Prince of Muscovy, Ivan III, was unassailable. He had demonstrated his ability to cope with the declining Tatar states, he sacked the wealthy republic of Novgorod in 1478 with its lands and connections to the West, he »collected a good part of the Russian Soil« when he compelled his co-princes from other branches of house of Rurik to bequeath their realms to him, including the once mighty Grand Duchy of Tver[14]. His first wife having died in 1467, he then married Zoe Sophia Palaiologina (d. 1503), the niece of the last Byzantine Emperor and, in the words of Hildegard Schaeder, the most honourable Princess of Europe[15]. She arrived in Moscow with an entourage of some one hundred Greeks and Italians, among them translators, artists and architects. These people had an enormous impact on the cultural life at the court and served Ivan's ambitions well[16]. The rebuilding of Kremlin in Moscow, with its ensemble of cathedrals at the core and walled with red stone, a silhouette that endures to this day, bears witness to these ambitions. Both Sophia's impact on politics exists and the question of how prestigious this marriage really was for Ivan III remain the subject of a long and ongoing debate[17].

By the end of fifteenth century, the situation of the Russian Orthodox Church had become rather complicated. After the Ottoman conquest of Constantinople in 1453, the Russian Church finally became *de facto* independent and nothing could now influence its relations with the temporal power. Some of the hierarchs of the Orthodox Church aspired to strengthening the power of the Grand Prince and the state, thereby laying the ground for autocracy as a religious type of rule. Among these hierarchs was, of course, Iona, who had already been elected without the approval of Byzantium in 1448. Letters soliciting such approval have survived, but there seems to have been no answer[18]. The *symphonia* between the Grand Prince of Moscow and the church was already full in swing, and the metropolitans made sure always to side with the winning faction. That was the case in the dynastic crisis of the mid-fifteenth century, in which Vasilii (II) Temnyi triumphed, and with Ivan III, the less belligerent Grand Prince of Muscovy[19].

---

14 Ekkehard KLUG, Das Fürstentum Tver' (1247–1485). Aufstieg, Selbstbehauptung und Niedergang, Wiesbaden 1985.
15 Hildegard SCHAEDER, Moskau das Dritte Rom. Studien zur Geschichte der politischen Theorien in der slavischen Welt, Darmstadt 1957; Manfred HELLMANN, Moskau und Byzanz, in: Jahrbuch für Geschichte Osteuropa 17 (1969), pp. 321–344, at pp. 323–328.
16 Gustave ALEF, The Origins of Muscovite Autocracy. The Age of Ivan III, Wiesbaden 1986.
17 Isolde THYRET, Paleologue, Sophia, in: Encyclopedia of Russian History, vol. 3, New York 2004, pp. 1131f.
18 Sergej V. TROICKIJ, »O tserkovnoi avtokefalii«, in: Zhurnal Moskovskoi Partiarchii 7 (1948), pp. 33–54.
19 »Stand at the River«, quoted in the second Chronicle of Sophia in PSRL, vol. 6, St Petersburg 1853, pp. 225–227. For a thorough discussion on this, see Jakov S. LUR'E, Dve istorii Rusi XV veka. Rannie

At the same time, the authority of the church inside the country was strongly shaken by deepening social contradictions. Protest among the lower strata of the society tended to be expressed in a religious form, with several so-called heretics appearing in the largest Russian cities in the last third of the fifteenth century. Their activity was perceived as especially dangerous for the church. The hierarchs were alarmed around 1492, the year 7000 of the Byzantine calendar[20] approached. It was in this context that the idea of a *translatio imperii* was articulated. In 1492, when recalculating the Easter tables, which had become necessary at the end of the seventh millennium of the Byzantine world era, and under the impression of widespread near-end expectations, the Moscow Metropolitan Zosima declared Grand Duke Ivan III (1440–1505) the new Constantine and Moscow as Constantine's City. This was not mere flattery but an appeal to the Grand Duke to protect his faithful Christian subjects[21].

A new upsurge of heretical movement took place towards the end of the fifteenth century in Novgorod. That was due to the activity of one Skarii, a Jew, who arrived from Lithuania in 1471. His doctrine, of which the surviving texts give only a vague idea, was perceived as similar to Judaism. This heresy became widespread among the lower clergy of Novgorod. The most irreconcilable persecutors of heretics were the Archbishop of Novgorod Gennadii and an outstanding church figure, the hegumen and founder of the Iosifo-Volokolamskii Monastery, Joseph Volotskii (Ivan Sanin)[22], who gave his name to a religious movement – »the Josephians«.

The Moscow circle of heretics was formed of clerks and merchants headed by Ivan Kuritsyn, who was Ivan III's councillor and assistant as well as being a Duma clerk. The heretics stood for strengthening of the Grand Prince's power and the restriction of the church's landownership. They declared that every man was able to address God without the mediation of the church. Even the heir to the throne showed sympathy for this movement. A church council condemned and cursed the heretics in 1490. Supporters of heresy were banned from Moscow; heretics in Novgorod were strictly punished. There was no unity in the attitude towards heretics among church circles. The opposition to the Josephians was headed by

---

i pozdnie, nezavisimye i ofitsial'nye letopisi ob obrazovanii Moskovskogo gosudarstva, St Petersburg 1994, pp. 168–179.
20 The Byzantine calendar counts the years beginning with the creation of the world, supposed to have taken place in 5509 BC.
21 See Mitropolita Zosimy Izveshchenie o paschalii na os'muiu tysiachu let i predislovie k samoi paschalii, in: Russkaia istoricheskaia biblioteka 118/6 (1880), pp. 795–802.
22 See the classic article by George Vernadsky, The Heresy of the Judaizers and the Policies of Ivan III of Moscow, in: Speculum 8/4 (1933), pp. 436–454; Andrei Pliguzov, Archbishop Gennadii and the Heresy of the »Judaizers«, in: Harvard Ukrainian Studies 16/3–4 (1992), pp. 269–288.

Nil Sorskii (d. 1508), the elder of the Kirillo-Belozersk Monastery[23], and challenged such an intolerant approach to the heretics. They proposed instead to concentrate on polemics and maintained that the true service of the church lay in an ascetic way of life and the eschewal of mundane riches and possessions. Ivan III was inclined to support »the non-possessors« for some time, although we have evidence that he was also heavily interested in the revenues of church lands or in the land itself.

But at the church council of 1503, militant Josephians put up stubborn resistance in the question of ecclesiastical landholdings. The following year, the council sentenced heretics to death[24] and Kuritsyn's circle in Moscow was broken up. These were the very first steps in the development of an alliance between the temporal power and the most Orthodox part of the clergy led by Joseph Volotskii[25], who proclaimed the priority of the church over the state and the principles of Orthodoxy as the basis of autocracy. Ivan III did not accept any supremacy of the church over his *samoderzhavie*, but left the it in peace to enjoy its wealth.

It was not an uncommon opinion in sixteenth-century Moscow that, after the fall of Constantinople (1453) and the aforementioned marriage of the Ivan III with Zoe Sophia about 20 years later, Moscow had become the heir to the Byzantine Empire: the »Third Rome«, after the city of Constantine on the Bosporus, the »Second Rome« (even if the Byzantines always referred their capital as the »New Rome«). The Byzantinist Herbert Hunger came to the following assessment, following that of his colleague Georg Ostrogorsky:

> When Tsar Ivan married Zoe, the niece of the last Byzantine emperor Constantine, who had died in the siege for Constantinople in 1453, it was a deliberate act of diplomatic policy, which included the adoption of the imperial double-headed eagle of the Palaiologoi and the external form of court ceremonial. The purpose was to declare Moscow the official successor of Constantinople, or in other words the Third Rome and successor to the Second Rome on the Bosporus. With the Byzantine eagle, the Russian Tsars also adopted the idea

---

23 Fairy von Lilienfeld, Nil Sorskij und seine Schriften. Die Krise der Tradition im Russland Ivans III, Berlin 1963; Hans-Dieter Döpmann, Der Einfluß der Kirche auf die moskowitische Staatsidee. Staats- und Gesellschaftsdenken bei Josif Volockij, Nil Sorskij und Vassian Patrikeev, Berlin 1967; David M. Goldfrank, Recentering Nil Sorskii. The Evidence from the Sources, in: Russian Review 66/3 (2007), pp. 359–376.
24 Jurij K. Begunov, »Slovo inoe«. Novonaidennoe proizvedenie russkoi publitsistiki XVI v. o bor'be Ivana III s zemlevladenien tserkvi, in: Trudy Otdela Drevnerussko Literatury, vol. 20, Moscow/Leningrad 1964, pp. 251–264.
25 David M. Goldfrank, Old and New Perspectives on Iosif Volotsky's Monastic Rules, in: Slavic Review 34/2 (1975), pp. 279–301; T. Allan Smith, Divine Economy and Repentance in Discourse 4 of the Enlightener by Iosif Volotskii, in: Canadian Slavonic Papers 60/1–2 (2018), pp. 7–25.

of empire described above, its universal claim and imperial mysticism. Throughout the centuries, the Byzantine emperors appeared as patrons of the Orthodox Church[26].

Those who followed the tradition of seeing Moscow as »Third Rome« cited the famous epistle of the monk Filofei of Pskov, written in the early decades of the sixteenth century[27]. Fearing, as many in the Byzantine world did at the time, the impending end of the world, Filofei tried to formulate a history of salvation based on the notion of *translatio imperii*. He had, however, no political *translatio imperii* in mind[28], drawing instead on the prophet Daniel. If heresy took hold in the Moscow Empire, he warned, not only the »Third Rome«, in which true Christianity had found its home, would perish, but Christianity as a whole. Two Romes had already fallen, and the third had to follow true Christianity if it was to save itself. When examining the reasons for autocracy in the sixteenth century, it should be remembered that the narrative of Moscow as the »Third Rome« was not thought of as a political legacy[29].

Soon after his death, in the first decade of his son Vasilii III's reign, the same Filofei wrote a letter to his provincial authorities that was *de facto* targeted at the Grand Prince and his duties as an autocratic ruler. In this letter, Filofei laid ground for an ongoing discussion, not only in theology, but in historical ideas and geopolitics from the sixteenth century to the present. I quote the relevant passages:

> Now I beg you and beg you again, please remember what I have said. For God's sake, please also remember that now all [Orthodox] Christian kingdoms have merged into your tsardom. Henceforth we can expect only one kingdom to come. That kingdom is eternal. I have written this because, admiring you as I do, I have appealed and have prayed to God that He may bless you. Change your parsimony to generosity and your inclemency to kindness. Comfort those who cry and wail day and night. Protect the innocent from their

---

26 Herbert HUNGER, Das Reich der neuen Mitte. Der christliche Geist in der byzantinischen Kultur, Graz et al. 1965, p. 377 (my translation).
27 V.N. MALININ, Starets Eleazarova monastyria Filofei i ego poslanie, Kiev 1901; Nikolay ANDREYEV, Filofey and His Epistle to Ivan Vasilyevich, in: Slavonic and East European Review 38 (1959), pp. 1–31; Frank KÄMPFER, Beobachtungen zu den Sendeschreiben Filofejs, in: Jahrbücher für Geschichte Osteuropas 18 (1970), pp. 1–46; Nina V. SINITSYNA, Tretii Rim. Istoki i evolutsiia russkoi srednevekovoi kontseptsii (XV–XVI vv.), Moscow 1998.
28 Peter NITSCHE, Translatio imperii? Beobachtungen zum historischen Selbstverständnis im Moskauer Zartum um die Mitte des 16. Jahrhunderts, in: Jahrbücher für Geschichte Osteuropas 35 (1987), pp. 321–338; Edgar HÖSCH, Die Idee der Translatio Imperii im Moskauer Russland, in: Europäische Geschichte Online, Mainz 2010, 12-03-2010, URL: <http://www.ieg-ego.eu/hoesche-2010-de> (09-12-2023).
29 Daniel B. ROWLAND, Moscow – The Third Rome or the New Israel?, in: The Russian Review 55/4 (1996), pp. 591–614, at p. 594.

tormentors. I repeat here what I have written above. Pious tsar! Hearken and remember that all Christian kingdoms have now merged into one, your [tsardom]. Two Romes have fallen. The third stands [firm]. And there will not be a fourth. No one will replace your Christian tsardom [...][30].

This was not the first time that such an idea was articulated. Hints at and variations on the idea can already be found in documents from Tver and Novgorod, Moscow's defeated rivals. But this is the first instance of the ruler of Moscow being portrayed as heir of the first and the second Rome. The fall of Constantinople in 1453 had left the Grand Prince and Tsar as the only rightful Christian ruler, able to defend the Orthodox faith. It was an invocation of his might and his responsibilities in a panegyric form[31]. The fact that Moscow had defeated the Tatars added weight to its claims. By being tolerant towards the Orthodox Church and granting the Dukes of Moscow the *yarlyk* (the grand ducal honour) and the *baskak* (the right to collect tributes) in one person, the Muscovites were able to profit from Tatar rule after 1241. It was not until the times of Grand Duke Dmitrii (Donskoi) that defending the Christian faith and fighting the Tatars became the foremost task of the Grand Dukes and their clerical advisers[32]. Before the famous stand at the Ugra, when Ivan III hesitated to fight the Tatars, Bishop Vassian of Rostov urged the Grand Duke to fulfil his duty as a Christian ruler[33].

At this time, Russian sources begin to refer to the Russian people as the »New Israel«, an idea which became subsumed into that of the »Third Rome« without ever fading away. Even long time after, Moscow was sometimes called »New Jerusalem«. It was not by chance that Patriarch Nikon built a monastery bearing that very name in the mid-seventeenth century. The New Jerusalem Monastery was founded in 1656 as a Patriarchal residence on the outskirts of Moscow. This site was chosen for its resemblance to the Holy Land, with the River Istra standing for the Jordan and the buildings for the »sacral space« or holy places of Jerusalem. Patriarch Nikon

---

30 Alar LAATS, The Concept of the Third Rome and its Political Implications, in: Alar KILP/Andres SAUMETS (eds.), Religion and Politics in Multicultural Europe. Perspectives and Challenges, Tartu 2009, pp. 98–113, at p. 98. For a Russian edition with comments and further references, see Poslaniia Startsa Filofeia. Podgotovka teksta pereovo i kommentariii V.V. Kolesova, URL: <http://lib.pushkinskijdom.ru/Default.aspx?tabid=5105> (09-14-2023).
31 Wil van den BERCKEN, Holy Russia and Christian Europe. East and West in the Religious Ideology of Russia. London 1999, pp. 141–144.
32 Irene NEANDER, Die Bedeutung der Mongolenherrschaft in Rußland, in: Geschichte in Wissenschaft und Unterricht 5 (1954), pp. 257–270; Peter NITSCHE, Mongolensturm und Mongolenherrschaft in Rußland, in: Stephan CONERMANN/Jan KUSBER (eds.), Die Mongolen in Asien und Europa, Frankfurt a. M. 1997, pp. 65–79.
33 Quoted in the second Chronicle of Sophia, in PSRL, vol. 6, pp. 225–227. For a discussion of the sources, see LUR'E, Dve istorii, pp. 168–179.

recruited a number of monks of non-Russian origin to inhabit the monastery, a symbolic representation of the multi-ethnic Orthodoxy of the Heavenly Jerusalem[34]. The architectural ensemble of the monastery included the Resurrection Cathedral (1656–1685) – modelled on the cathedral of the same name in Jerusalem – Nikon's residence (1658), a stone wall with towers (1690–1694) and the Church of Holy Trinity (1686–1698).

II.

In what regard did ideas about Moscow as the »Third Rome«[35] or the »New Jerusalem« have relevance for political and/or theological contexts? For one thing, they supported the claims of the Princes of Moscow to legitimacy. His marriage to Zoe Sophia Palaiologina provided Ivan III with a pretext for adopting the Byzantine title of »autocrat« ($αὐτοκράτωρ$) and informally also that of »emperor«. Both the envoy of Habsburg, Jörg Schnitzenpaumer, and the Nordic Kings recognised these titles, although the Habsburg (Holy Roman) Emperors would later withdraw their recognition. Vasilii III used this title in a treaty with Emperor Maximilian[36].

The first Grand Prince to be crowned Tsar was Ivan IV, who had acceded to power in 1533, aged three. Under the influence of the powerful Metropolitan Makarii, he was crowned with Monomakh's Cap at the Cathedral of the Dormition at the age of sixteen, on 16 January 1547[37]. As the first person to be crowned as »Tsar of All the Russias«, the title offered him a claim to the succession of Kievan Rus[38]. By being crowned a Tsar in a new ceremonial, Ivan sent a message to the world and to Russia: He was now the one and only supreme ruler of the country, and his will was not to be questioned. As Donald Ostrowski put it: »The new title symbolised an assumption of powers equivalent and parallel to those held by the former Byzantine

---

34 Aleksandr BALATOV/Tatiana VIATCHANINA, Ob ideinom znachenii i interpretatsii ierusalimskogo obroaza v russkoi arkhitekture XVI–XVII vekov, in: Arkhitekturnoe nasledstvo 36 (1988), pp. 22–42.
35 See the analyses in Peter NITSCHE, Moskau – das Dritte Rom?, in: Geschichte in Wissenschaft und Unterricht 42 (1991), pp. 341–354.
36 Aleksandr I. FILIUSHKIN, Titul russkikh gosudarei, Moscow/St Petersburg 2006, pp. 200f.
37 On his coronation and its implications, see David MILLER, The Coronation of Ivan IV of Moscow, in: Jahrbücher für Geschichte Osteuropas 15 (1967), pp. 559–584; Peter NITSCHE, Großfürst und Thronfolger. Die Nachfolgepolitik der Moskauer Herrscher bis zum Ende des Rjurikidenhauses, Cologne/Vienna 1972, pp. 259–268.
38 Hans HECKER, Propagierte Geschichte. Die »stepennaja kniga« (Stufenbuch) und die Herrschaftsideologie in der Moskauer Rus' (16. Jahrhundert), in: Johannes LAUDAGE (ed.), Von Fakten und Fiktionen, Cologne et al. 2003, pp. 371–388; Aleksei S. USHACHEV, Stepennaia kniga i drevnerusskaia knizhnost' vremeni metropolita Makariia, Moscow 2009.

emperor and the Tatar khan, both known in Russian sources as Tsar. The political effect was to elevate Ivan's position«.

The new title not only secured the throne but also granted Ivan a new dimension of power, one intimately tied to religion. He was now a »divine« ruler appointed to enact God's will; »church texts described Old Testament kings as ›tsars‹ and Christ as the Heavenly Tsar«. The new title was then passed on from generation to generation, as »succeeding Muscovite rulers […] benefited from the divine nature of the power of the Russian monarch […] crystallized during Ivan's reign«, to quote the Russian historian Sergei Bogatyrev[39]. For the Tsar, the text of the coronation became the grounds on which he justified his actions. As Alexander Dvorkin explains: »The general policy of Ivan's rule, in the years immediately following, indicates that the coronation provided Russia with its most important source for claiming to be the continuator of the Roman Empire and for establishing the new ecumenical role of the Muscovite state, church, and tsar«[40]. But does it follow from this observation that for Ivan IV, the religious concept of the »Third Rome« became an ideology that directed his policy, both in internal affairs and in foreign policy?

What is certain is that he felt himself to be the ruler appointed and sent by God. In 1552, the *History of the Tsardom of Kazan* and other chronicles use a crusading rhetoric to justify the conquest[41]. Whether he succeeded in fulfilling this theocratic ideal is of course another question. Internally, Ivan was a real autocrat, an absolutist ruler like the Byzantine Emperors. In the sixteenth century, Russia was the last independent Orthodox country; all other Orthodox peoples were by that time subjects of »infidel« rulers. This singular position made the Grand Prince of Moscow the most eminent and perhaps the strongest defender of the Orthodox faith. Nor was it a mere title. A large part of the political biography of Ivan IV is covered by wars against the last Eastern dominions and the eternal Western enemy, the Khanate of Kazan and the »heretical« Kingdoms of Poland-Lithuania and Sweden. But the title of the Emperor of »Third Rome« was useful for Russia in diplomatic contacts with European powers, allowing Moscow to meet them on equal terms. The doctrine of the »Third Rome« could be interpreted as raising Ivan IV above the Western Kings and may have given confidence to Moscow in its interaction with the »First Rome«, the Pope, and the Roman Emperor, the Habsburg

---

39 Both quotations in Sergei BOGATYREV, Ivan IV, 1533–1584, in: Maureen PERRIE (ed.), The Cambridge History of Russia, vol. 1, Cambridge 2006, pp. 240–263, at p. 263.
40 Alexander DVORKIN, Ivan the Terrible as a Religious Type. A Study of the Background, Genesis and Development of the Theocratic Idea of the First Russian Tsar, and his Attempts to Establish »Free Autocracy« in Russia, Erlangen 1992, p. 39.
41 Frank KÄMPFER (ed.), Historie vom Zartum Kasan (Kasaner Chronist), Graz et al. 1969, pp. 173f. For the history of the text, see id., Die Eroberung von Kasan 1552 als Gegenstand der zeitgenössischen Historiographie, Wiesbaden 1969; KHODARKOVSKY, The Non-Christian Peoples, at pp. 319f.

monarch. However, he refused to use such an argumentation openly, especially after the death of Metropolitan Makarii.

The doctrine of the »Third Rome« influenced church affairs as well. If it emboldened the state of Moscow to claim a privileged political status, then it is not surprising that the church and especially the metropolitan should have had similarly high pretentions. In the middle of the sixteenth century, a wave of canonisations of Russian saints occurred. As one Russian ecclesiastical writer explained: »It was needful to prove that although the Russian Church came forth only at the eleventh hour of history, by her diligence she has nevertheless surpassed the workers even of the first hour«[42]. Thus, the Russian Church asserted its high status above other churches, including the Church of Constantinople. There was a Pope in the »First Rome«, and there was a Patriarch in the »Second Rome«. However, there was a metropolitan only in the Third Rome. Therefore, the Muscovite state and its church made attempts at changing Moscow's status from a metropolis to a Patriarchate. The decision about the Patriarchate of Moscow had to be made by the other Patriarchs, who were in no hurry to do so. When the title was finally obtained *de jure* in 1589, it was by bribery: The Patriarch of Constantinople had become financially dependent on Russia, and he would continue to receive financial support only in exchange for the elevation of the autocephalous Russian Church to a Patriarchate[43].

»This was not only an ecclesiastical but also an ideological victory for Moscow over Constantinople, since the doctrine of the Third Rome is explicitly mentioned in the document«[44], thereby recognising Russia as the political heir of Byzantium. Later, the new position of the Russian Church was canonically approved by all Eastern Orthodox Patriarchs. However, not all Moscow's expectations were fulfilled. As Moscow had claimed the symbolic position of the Byzantine Empire and the Tsar had become the new Christian Emperor, there were expectations that the new Patriarch would be at least the third Patriarch in the order of precedence. But in 1589 he only became the fifth, after the Patriarchs of Constantinople, Alexandria, Antioch and Jerusalem. At least, however, the Tsar of Russia was recognised outside Russia as the guardian of the whole Orthodox world. It was thus with a certain pride and self-confidence that Ivan IV told the Jesuit ambassador Antonio Possevino during the aforementioned dispute: »I do not believe in the Greeks,

---

42 Anton V. Kartashev, Ocherki po istorii Russkoi Tserkvi, vol. 1, Moscow 1993, p. 433.
43 Jan Kusber, Die »byzantinische Autokratie« als »Travelling Concept«. Das Beispiel Russland, in: Ludger Körntgen et al. (eds.), Byzanz und seine europäischen Nachbarn. Politische Interdependenzen und kulturelle Missverständnisse, Mainz 2020, pp. 139–149, at pp. 143f.
44 Bercken, Holy Russia, p. 160.

I believe in Christ«[45]. Ivan IV was clearly trying to emphasise the independence of the autocratic traditions of rule grounded in the right faith in Russia in the diplomatic correspondence with Western potentates[46]. He avoided any reference to the imperial court in Constantinople. The story of the Princes of Vladimir (*Skazanie o knyazyakh Vladimirskikh*), which also originated at the turn to the sixteenth century, and the similar writing of Spiridon-Savva on the genealogy of the Russian Princes provided the appropriate arguments. Both sources traced the ancestral line of the Russian rulers via the legendary imperial brother Prus directly to the Roman Emperor Augustus (63 BC–14 AD)[47] and described the alleged handover of the Roman rulers' insignia (including the wooden cervical cross from the life-giving Wood of the Cross of Christ, the Tsar's crown, the purple coat, the silver cup of the Emperor Augustus, the golden breast chain) by emissaries of the Byzantine Emperor Constantine IX Monomachos to Grand Prince Vladimir Monomakh (1053–1125) and his coronation as Tsar of Orthodox Christianity[48]. The individual sets of such anachronistic legends had found their way into contemporary literature and the official chronicles of the court[49].

Bearing all this in mind, there was a set of theological sources from which the Muscovite Grand Duke and Tsar could draw support for their cause. The line of argument every ruler chose depended on the concrete historical context. Ivan III and Vasilii III did not use the »Third Rome« doctrine as an argument; Makarii, on the contrary, did so in the context of the coronation of Ivan IV. In his later years, for example in his talks with Antonio Possevino, Ivan IV cited other genealogical myths and reiterated his pride in Moscow's own Orthodox tradition[50].

The story of Moscow as the »Third Rome«, with its serious implications for the autocratic Tsar as a ruler with a universal claim and its ongoing discourse, has been foregrounded by, for example, Alexander Dvorkin, Frank Kämpfer and Alar

---

45 Peter NITSCHE, »Nicht an die Griechen glaube ich, sondern an Christus«. Russen und Griechen im Selbstverständnis des Moskauer Staates an der Schwelle zur Neuzeit, Düsseldorf 1991; cf. SACH, »Griechischen« Glaubens, pp. 169f.

46 John MEYENDORFF, Rome, Constantinople, Moscow. Historical and Theological Studies, New York 1996, p. 136.

47 Hans HECKER, Dynastische Abstammungslegende und Geschichtsmythos im Russland des 16. Jahrhunderts, in: Peter WUNDERLI (ed.), Herkunft und Ursprung. Historische und mythische Formen der Legitimation. Akten des Gerda Henkel Kolloquiums. Veranstaltet vom Forschungsinstitut für Mittelalter und Renaissance der Heinrich-Heine-Universität Düsseldorf 13. bis 15. Oktober 1991, Sigmaringen 1994, pp. 119–132.

48 Maria V. PLIUCHANOVA, Suzhety i simvoly moskovkogo tsarstva, St Petersburg 1995.

49 A.A. ZIMIN, Antichnye motivy v russkoi publitsistike kontsa XV v., in: Vladimir T. PASHUTO (ed.), Feodal'naia Rossiia vo vsemirno-istoricheskom protsesse. Sbornik statei, posviashchennyi L'vu Vladimirovichu Cherepninu, Moscow 1972, pp. 128–138.

50 Priscilla HUNT, Ivan IV's Personal Mythology of Kingship, in: Slavic Review 2/4 (1993), pp. 769–809.

Laats. There is another group which argues that Moscow's claims to the legacy of Constantinople should by no means be overestimated, for example Peter Nitsche, Christine Roll, Donald Ostrowski[51] and especially Marshall T. Poe. In the sixteenth and seventeenth centuries, he pointed out, the »Third Rome« doctrine circulated only among churchmen, but was not popular even in clerical circles and received no substantial development. The idea seemed to have had no official status and was probably not well-known to the secular elite that ruled the Muscovite state. Daniel Rowland has highlighted the scarcity of evidence for the notion of the »Third Rome« in sixteenth-century sources[52], yet this changed in the second half of the seventeenth century, when it was adopted by the »Old Believers«[53]. This major sectarian movement believed that the Russian Orthodox Church had abandoned the true faith and its obligation to act as the »Third Rome«. They separated from Russian Orthodoxy in the times of the aforementioned Patriarch Nikon and claimed that their community alone embodied the »Third Rome«.

Be this as it may, the »Third Rome« and the associated idea of »Russian Messianism« have not gone away. Western commentators continue to invoke them when explaining Soviet and contemporary Russian foreign policy. More significantly, many Russians, bewildered by the rapid demise of the Soviet Empire, have turned to the »Third Rome« for an understanding of Russia's place in world history[54]. Patriarch Kirill and his hierarchs echo these views. Daniel Rowland, one of the historians who has questioned the centrality of the »Third Rome« doctrine, has highlighted the plentiful references to the Old Testament in the letters of *starets* Filofei, drawing a line to the coronation of Ivan IV in 1547:

> At the most solemn moment of the service, after Ivan had asked to be crowned as his father had wished, the metropolitan intoned a prayer which explicitly invoked the Old Testament kingship of David as the model for Ivan's rule, followed by bestowing the regalia upon the young prince: King of Kings and Lord of Lords, Who by Samuel the Prophet didst choose Thy servant David and anoint him to be king (tsar) over Thy people Israel, [...] look down from Thy sanctuary upon Thy faithful servant the Great Prince Ivan Vasilievich whom

---

51 Donald OSTROWSKI, »Moscow the Third Rome« as Historical Ghost, in: Sarah T. BROOKS (ed.), Byzantium: Faith and Power (1261–1557). Perspectives on Late Byzantine Art and Culture, New York 2006, pp. 170–179.
52 ROWLAND, Moscow, pp. 188–234.
53 Christine ROLL, Drittes Rom, in: Heinz DUCHHARDT et al. (eds.), Europäische Erinnerungsorte, vol. 2, Munich 2012, pp. 291–298.
54 See, for example, the Russian documentaries The Fall of an Empire – The Lesson of Byzantium (2008) and The Slavic Nations' Search for God. Moscow: Third Rome (2014).

Thou hast deigned to raise up as tsar over Thy people (*v iazytse tvoem*), whom Thou hast redeemed with the precious blood of Thine only-begotten Son[55].

At the very heart of the coronation, Ivan was declared to be the heir of David, and Muscovy to be God's new chosen people. Indeed, each side of this equation deserves attention. David was appointed King directly by God via Samuel, just as Ivan was divinely appointed by the doing of Metropolitan Makarii. The dominant and powerful message was clearly that Ivan ruled by God's will.

One of the most important and certainly the most compendious official ideological collections in Moscow is Metropolitan Makarii's *Velikoe Poslanie* or *Great Menology*[56]. In this enormous trove of materials, we find the aforementioned letters of Filofei and texts replete with references to the concept of Muscovy as the »New Israel«. Some make a claim to universal rule, others do not. In contrast to Marshall T. Poe and Daniel Rowland, I would insist on the point that the compendium was available not only in monasteries, but also at court. Therefore, the autocratic ruler could choose which concept was useful and which was not depending on context. In the times of Nikon and Aleksei, this was still ambivalent. Styling Muscovy the »New Jerusalem« or the »New Israel« did not imply that the Patriarch and the Tsars did not at the same time regard themselves as heirs of Byzantium and took pride in the Orthodox tradition[57].

III.

The theological conceptualisation of autocracy and the imperial claims, as they have been seen by historians since the nineteenth century, are only one part of the story. The other is the idea of harmony and *symphonia* between church and ruler. What is the realm of ruler, what is that of the church[58]? Both were convinced – and we have written evidence from Ivan IV, Aleksei and Peter I to that effect – that they saw their power as derived from God and believed themselves to be accountable only him. When it came to church land, Ivan III failed to invoke the idea of symphonia

---

55 Quoted in ROWLAND, Moscow, pp. 596f.
56 David B. MILLER, The Velikie Minei Chetii and the Stepennaja Kniga of Metropolitan Makarii and the Origins of Russian National Consciousness, in: Forschungen zur osteuropäischen Geschichte 26 (1979), pp. 263–382.
57 Ekkehard KRAFT, Moskaus griechisches Jahrhundert. Russisch-griechische Beziehungen und metabyzantinischer Einfluss 1619–1694, Stuttgart 1995.
58 See the discussion from the independence of the Russian Orthodox Church up to now in Regina ELSNER, Die Russische Orthodoxe Kirche vor der Herausforderung Moderne. Historische Wegmarken und theologische Optionen im Spannungsfeld von Einheit und Vielfalt, Würzburg 2018.

in his favour and gave in; in the other three cases, there was open conflict, and the outcome was that the autocratic ruler defeated or – as ecclesiastical writers sometimes put it – harmed the church. I would like to end this chapter by touching very briefly on these three well-known cases.

The first example is the famous clash between Ivan Groznyi and Metropolitan Filip[59]. Filip was born Feodor Stepanovich Kolychev into one of the noblest families of Muscovy. It was said that he had been on friendly terms with Ivan IV of Russia since his childhood. According to other accounts, he was involved in the conspiracy of Prince Andrei of Staritsa against the Grand Princess Elena Glinskaia, the *de facto* regent of Russia between 1533 and 1538[60]. When their plans were discovered, he escaped to the Solovetskii Monastery on the White Sea. However, he entered the Solovetskii Monastery at the age of 30, and a year and a half later he was tonsured under the monastic name of Filip. In 1566, Ivan called Filip back to Moscow. Filip agreed on condition that Ivan would abolish the *Oprichnina*, the notorious regime of terror the Tsar had established in his vast territories. On 25 June 1566, Filip was consecrated a bishop and enthroned as Metropolitan of Moscow and all Russia. After only two years, however, Ivan the Terrible resumed the murderous regime of *Oprichnina*. When, during Great Lent, on the Sunday of the Veneration of the Cross, 2 March 1568, the Tsar came to the cathedral to attend the divine liturgy, Filip refused to bless him and publicly rebuked him for the ongoing bloodshed. Ivan took his revenge by causing Filip to be removed from office on trumped-up charges of sorcery and dissolute life. The metropolitan was arrested while officiating liturgy at the Cathedral of Dormition, put in chains with a heavy collar around the neck, and was deprived of food for few days. Two days before Christmas, on 23 December 1569, Filip was strangled by a minion of the Tsar named Malyuta Skuratov[61]. As if aware of his approaching death, Filip had asked to receive Holy Communion three days earlier. It was not by chance that in 1652, Patriarch Nikon persuaded Tsar Aleksei to bring Filip's relics to Moscow, where he was glorified (proclaimed a saint) later that same year.

Nikon and Aleksei are the central characters of the second example: Nikon was the seventh Patriarch of the Russian Orthodox Church, serving officially from

---

59 For the following, see Dmitrii M. VOLODICHIN, Mitropolit Filip, Moscow 2009; Aleksandr A. ZIMIN, Mitropolit Filip i Oprichnina, in: Voprosy istorii, religii i ateizma 11 (1963), pp. 269–292.
60 On this conspiracy, see Hartmut Rüss, Elena Vasil'evna Glinskaya, in: Jahrbücher für Geschichte Osteuropas (New Series) 19/4 (1971), pp. 481–498.
61 A. M. KURBSKIJ, Istoriia o velikom kniaze Moskovskom. Glava VIII. O stradaniiakh sviashchen-nomuchennika Filipa mitropolita Moskovskogo, Moscow 2001, URL: <http://www.sedmitza.ru/lib/text/438716/> (09-14-2023); Isabel de MADARIAGA, Ivan the Terrible. First Tsar of Russia, New Haven, CT 2006, pp. 225–239.

1652 to 1666⁶². He was renowned for his eloquence, energy, piety, and close ties to Tsar Aleksei. For many years he was a dominant political figure, often equalling or even overshadowing the Tsar. His liturgical reforms were unpopular among conservatives and led into the schism between the Russian Orthodoxy and the *raskol* or »Old Believers«⁶³. From 1652 to 1658, Nikon was not so much the minister of the Tsar as his co-regent. In both public documents and private letters, he was permitted to use the sovereign title. This was especially the case during the wars with the Polish-Lithuanian Commonwealth 1654–1667, when the Tsar was away from Moscow with his armies for long time periods. In 1654, when embarking on his great military campaign, the Tsar left Nikon at home as regent. Nikon aimed at decoupling the church from secular authority, indeed, permanently separating church and state. Yet he also believed that the church and state should work in harmony while remaining separate from each other. He also sought to organise the church with a hierarchy similar to the state's apparatus – with the Patriarch in complete control. Nikon was hence especially keen to annul *Sobornoe Ulozhenie*, the Russian legal code of 1649, which reduced the powers of the clergy and made the Church in effect subservient to the state. His actions roused numerous enemies against him. By the summer of 1658, they convinced Aleksei that the Patriarch was eclipsing the sovereign Tsar. Aleksei suddenly cooled towards his »bosom friend«, as he once had called him. Nikon left Moscow that year for the New Jerusalem Monastery, never to return. In December 1666, Nikon was tried by a synod of church officials, deprived of all his sacerdotal functions, and reduced to the status of a simple monk. He had failed to free the church of the Tsar's supremacy. This was because Aleksei, perhaps the most Orthodox ruler in his conceptions of power, insisted on the supremacy of autocratic rule⁶⁴.

Third, it was Peter the Great, Aleksei's son, who completed the subjugation of the church. Although Peter was deeply religious, growing up in the Orthodox faith, he had little regard for the church hierarchy, which he kept under tight governmental control. In 1700, when the office of the Patriarch fell vacant after the death of Adrian, Peter refused to name a replacement, allowing the Patriarch's coadjutor (or deputy), Stefan Javorskii, to undertake the duties of the office. Peter could not tolerate the Patriarch exercising a power superior to the Tsar, as in the cases of Filaret (1619–1633)⁶⁵ and Nikon (1652–1666). He therefore abolished the Patriar-

---

62 For a biographical overview, see Aleksandr P. BOGDANOV, Patriarch Nikon, in: Voprosy istorii 1 (2004), pp. 51–117.
63 Paul BUSHKOVITCH, Religion and Society in Russia. The Sixteenth and Seventeenth Centuries, New York/Oxford 1992, pp. 63–75.
64 Hans-Heinrich NOLTE, Religiöse Toleranz in Russland 1600–1725, Göttingen 1966, pp. 122–127.
65 Filaret, of course, acted as the regent and father of Tsar Mikhail. See John L.H. KEEP, The Régime of Filaret 1619–1633, in: The Slavonic and East European Review 38/91 (1960), pp. 334–360.

chate, replacing it with a Holy Synod controlled by a senior bureaucrat. The Tsar appointed all bishops. In 1721, Peter followed the advice of Feofan Prokopovich, archbishop of Novgorod and an enlightened reformer who had studied in Leipzig[66], in building up the Holy Synod as a council of ten clergymen with a secular official as chairman. For leadership in the church, Peter turned increasingly to the Ukrainians, who were more open to reform and better educated[67], thereby fostering a tendency already in full swing. Peter, who felt that too many men were being wasted on clerical duties when they could be joining his new and reformed army, implemented a law stipulating that no Russian man could enter a monastery before the age of 50[68]. Some Soviet historians wanted to see in Peter an atheist[69], which he of course was not. He was, however, a strong pragmatist, and was not alone in his convictions. A considerable part of the clergy, including Feofan Prokopovich, supported his plans.

IV.

To sum up: In the Russian context, political theology may be conceptualised as an arena for negotiating relations between the church and the autocratic ruler. The church claimed to represent the right Christian faith and accordingly made an appeal to the Tsars, the rulers of the »Third Rome«, in a spiritual sense. The autocrats saw themselves, on the contrary, as heads of the church. They sought advice and were theologically interested, if not all as comprehensively and openly as Ivan IV, who was preoccupied with theological questions and probably suffered from mental illness. But they also exhibited an internal religiosity, like the barely governable Tsar Fedor I (r. 1584–1598) or Tsar Aleksei, who faced the challenge of the *raskol*. The church rarely attempted to assert its primacy; open resistance against the background of differing theological views was rare.

It is requiring no further elaboration that, in the complex relations that obtained between state and church in Russia, it was the state that had physically stronger, leaving the weaker to seize its advantages opportunistically. The church had no argument weightier than the transience of earthly things set against the eternal

---

66 Lorenz ERREN, Orthodoxer Aufklärer oder zynischer Protestant? Feofan Prokopovič im Urteil der deutschen und russischen Geschichtsschreibung, in: Jahrbuch des Bundesinstituts für Kultur und Geschichte der Deutschen im östlichen Europa. Erinnerung und Religion 23 (2015), pp. 59–72.
67 Max J. OKENFUSS, The Rise and the Fall of Latin Humanism in Early-Modern Russia. Pagan Authors, Ukrainians, and the Resiliency of Muscovy, Leiden 1995.
68 James CRACRAFT, The Church Reform of Peter the Great, Oxford 1971.
69 For example, V.V. MAVRODIN, Pëtr I, Moscow 1949; V.I. BUGANOV, Pëtr Velikii i ego Vremya, Moscow 1989.

Kingdom of God. Metropolitan Filip had said to Tsar Ivan Groznyi's face: »You are mortal too«[70] – and became a martyr for his boldness. Although there was room for different formats of autocracy, no political power was possible outside Orthodoxy. Although all rulers built their legitimacy on the claim to defend the true faith, in terms of personal religiosity, there was a wide spectrum from Ivan III to Peter the Great. Despite these varying forms and degrees of piety, they all acted harshly when the church challenged the pre-eminence of the Tsar as head of Russian Orthodoxy. In that respect, they employed various doctrines and concepts in a very functional and pragmatic way in order to justify their expansionist plans and geopolitics in early modern Europe.

---

70 Quoted in Georgiï P. FEDOTOV, Sviatoi Filipp, mitropolit Moskovskii, Paris 1928, p. 143; see also Günther STÖKL, Staat und Kirche im Moskauer Rußland. Die vier Moskauer Wundertäter, in: Jahrbücher für Geschichte Osteuropas 29/4 (1981), pp. 481–493, at pp. 491–493.

Nikolas Pissis

Russian Tsars and Greek Hierarchs

Political Theology and Legitimisation in the Seventeenth Century

I.

Political theology in the broader and the narrower sense alike – both of which inform the concept of this volume[1] – figures prominently in recent philosophical, theological, and historical studies. One the one hand, the whole complex of questions regarding monotheism and monarchy, or the secularisation thesis that is centred on the Schmitt-Peterson-Blumenberg debate, has recently (if somewhat belatedly) attracted considerable interest beyond the German-speaking academic community[2]. On the other hand, in the historiographical wake of the cultural history of politics, issues of religious legitimisation of power through rituals and ceremonies, images, and discourses have attracted the attention of scholars who have largely abandoned strict dichotomies of »real« and »rhetorical«. Especially historians of the early modern age have stressed the various links between sacral languages and the constitution of political power in an attempt to refresh debates on an old but still paramount question, that of the relationship between religion and politics in the age of Reformation, confessionalisation, and religious wars[3]. To

---

1 Robert Hepp, Theologie, politische, in: Historisches Wörterbuch der Philosophie, vol. 10, Berlin 1998, pp. 1106–1111; Jan Assmann, Herrschaft und Heil. Politische Theologie in Altägypten, Israel und Europa, Frankfurt am Main 2002, pp. 15–31.
2 See, for instance, Graham Hammill/Julia Reinhard Lupton (eds.), Political Theology and Early Modernity, Chicago/London 2012; Celina María Bragagnolo, Secularization, History, and Political Theology. The Hans Blumenberg and Carl Schmitt Debate, in: Journal of the Philosophy of History 5/1 (2011), pp. 84–104; Nathan Gibbs, Modern Constitutional Legitimacy and Political Theology. Schmitt, Peterson and Blumenberg, in: Law and Critique 30 (2019), pp. 67–89; György Geréby, Political Theology versus Theological Politics. Erik Peterson and Carl Schmitt, in: New German Critique 105 (2008), pp. 7–33.
3 Luise Schorn-Schütte, Gottes Wort und Menschenherrschaft. Politisch-theologische Sprachen im Europa der Frühen Neuzeit, Munich 2015; Bernhard Jussen, Diskutieren über Könige im vormodernen Europa. Einleitung, in: Id. (ed.), Die Macht des Königs. Herrschaft in Europa vom Frühmittelalter bis in die Neuzeit, Munich 2005, pp. xi–xxiv, at pp. xiv–xvi; Achim Landwehr, Einleitung, in: Id. (ed.), Aspekte der politischen Kommunikation im Europa des 16. und 17. Jahrhunderts. Politische Theologie – Res Publica-Verständnis – konsensgestützte Herrschaft, Munich 2004, pp. 1–12; Barbara Stollberg-Rilinger, Was heißt Kulturgeschichte des Politischen? Einleitung, in: Ead. (ed.), Was heißt Kulturgeschichte des Politischen?, Berlin 2005, pp. 9–24; Montserat Herrero et al. (eds.),

highlight a particularly instructive case: Biblicism – understood as such a sacral language – constitutes a paramount component of early modern political theologies[4]. Although a clear-cut distinction between the two notions of political theology is not thoroughly workable, reference will be made here only to the second and more specific. Political theology will thus be primarily understood as a political language which performs a sacral legitimisation of political power responding to certain needs and exigencies. This entails a stress on the functional character of such a language and on the interests, it may serve on either side[5].

The objective of this chapter is to demonstrate this functional quality of politico-theological discourses with reference to the role played by Greek ecclesiastics, patriarchs, and metropolitans of the Eastern Church, and to a lesser extent its priests and monks, in the legitimisation of the upcoming Muscovite Tsardom as the leading power of the Orthodox world in the seventeenth century. The century's second half was a period of particularly intense relations between Russians and Greeks in the early modern, pre-national age, a period in which concerted attempts were made – with mixed results – to imagine and design a common Orthodox identity, an Orthodox unity, modelled after the Western confessional blocks in the context of inter-confessional struggles and the confessionalisation of Christian Churches and denominations.

The common tradition of Christian Monarchy was initiated with Emperor Constantine's conversion and with what Francis Oakley has called the »Eusebian Accommodation«[6]. Whether this implied a departure from the New Testament and thus the theological poverty of political theology is, as already noted, a question that cannot be addressed here[7]. In any case it was the Old Testament to which Gilbert Dagron has famously attributed »constitutional value« in Byzantine history

---

Political Theology in Medieval and Early Modern Europe. Discourses, Rites, and Representations, Turnhout 2017.

4 Andreas Pečar/Kai Trampedach, Der »Biblizismus« – eine politische Sprache der Vormoderne?, in: Iid. (eds.), Die Bibel als politisches Argument. Voraussetzungen und Folgen biblizistischer Argumentation in der Vormoderne, Munich 2007, pp. 1–18.
5 Graham Hammill/Julia Reinhard Lupton, Introduction, in: Iid. (eds.), Political Theology, pp. 1–20, at p. 1: »We take the phrase ›political theology‹ to identify the exchanges, pacts, and contests that obtain between religious and political life, especially the use of sacred narratives, motifs, and liturgical forms to establish, legitimate, and reflect upon the sovereignty of monarchs, corporations and parliaments«.
6 Francis Oakley, Kingship. The Politics of Enchantment, Oxford 2006, pp. 68–76.
7 Nevertheless, it is ironic enough that Eusebius' Christian legitimisation of imperial rule should have been closely linked to his not quite »Orthodox« Christological views. See Per Beskow, Rex Gloriae. The Kingship of Christ in the Early Church, Stockholm 1962, pp. 259–268; Hans-Georg Beck, Das byzantinische Jahrtausend, Munich 1978, pp. 96f.

from the time of Constantine onwards[8]. The Constantinian model, by providing models rather than a normative theory, constituted the obvious frame of reference for every conceptualisation of monarchical power and its imagery in the Orthodox world, as well as for the complex and ambivalent relationship between the emperor and the church. This ambivalence is captured in Hans-Georg Beck's term »political Orthodoxy«[9]. This was the case during the Byzantine millennium but can also be observed in Byzantium's long afterlife.

And yet, this imperial legacy need not be perceived in terms of a long endurance, a »permanence of cultural forms«, as Nicolae Iorga has put it in his *Byzance après Byzance*[10]. The excessive but nevertheless selective uses of Byzantium in the »post-Byzantine« Orthodox world testify rather to an »invention of tradition«, an imagined Byzantium that was the product of cultural strategies, of recontextualisation according to contemporary needs and interests. This was a creative rather than a preserving process – even or indeed all the more so when stability was proclaimed[11].

Moreover, this did not represent an Orthodox or Eastern European peculiarity. Before Byzantium came up against the severe judgement of Enlightenment thinkers, it provided a source for monarchical legitimisation across both Catholic and Protestant Europe[12]. The most prominent case of this Byzantine trend is France

---

8 Gilbert DAGRON, Emperor and Priest. The Imperial Office in Byzantium, transl. by J. BIRRELL, Cambridge 2003, p. 50: »No event was wholly true nor any emperor wholly authentic until they had been recognized and labeled by reference to an Old Testament model. In Byzantium, the Old Testament had a constitutional value; it had the same normative role in the political sphere as the New Testament in the moral sphere«.

9 BECK, Jahrtausend, pp. 87–108; id., Geschichte der orthodoxen Kirche im byzantinischen Reich, Göttingen 1980, pp. 5f.; see also Marie Theres FÖGEN, Das politische Denken der Byzantiner, in: Iring FETSCHER/Herfried MÜNKLER (eds.), Pipers Handbuch der politischen Ideen, Munich/Zurich 1993, vol. 2, pp. 41–85, at pp. 59–67; ead., Um 1262: Warum Canossa in Byzanz nur zur Parodie taugte, in: JUSSEN (ed.), Die Macht des Königs, pp. 205–215; Dimiter ANGELOV, Imperial Ideology and Political Thought in Byzantium 1204–1330, Cambridge 2007, pp. 360–365.

10 Nicolae IORGA, Byzance après Byzance. Continuation de »l'Histoire de la vie byzantine«, Bucharest 1935; see also Paschalis M. KITROMILIDES, Introduction, in: Id., An Orthodox Commonwealth. Symbolic Legacies and Cultural Encounters in Southeastern Europe, Aldershot 2007; Johann P. ARNASON, Approaching Byzantium. Identity, Predicament and Afterlife, in: Thesis Eleven 62 (2000), pp. 39–69.

11 Eva CANCIK-KIRSCHBAUM/Anita TRANINGER, Institution – Iteration – Transfer. Zur Einführung in: Eaed. (eds.), Wissen in Bewegung. Institution – Iteration – Transfer, Wiesbaden 2015, pp. 1–13; for an understanding of »tradition« as a cultural strategy, see Aleida ASSMANN, Zeit und Tradition. Kulturelle Strategien der Dauer, Cologne et al. 1999; for imagined Byzantium constructs, see Alena ALSHANSKAYA et al. (eds.), Imagining Byzantium. Perceptions, Patterns, Problems, Mainz 2018.

12 Thomas James DANDELET, The Renaissance of Empire in Early Modern Europe, Cambridge 2014, pp. 168–174; id., Creating a Protestant Constantine. Martin Bucer's De Regno Christi and the Foundation of English Imperial Political Theology, in: Christopher OCKER et al. (eds.), Politics and

under the Sun King, Louis XIV[13], but Byzantine references, not only to Emperors Constantine and Theodosius, abounded in contemporary political discourses and imagery. Catholic and Protestant court ideologues alike drew from Byzantine models, not least from Byzantine parenetical writings. The »Chapters« of Agapetos Diakonos, for instance, were repeatedly translated and printed in the sixteenth and seventeenth centuries[14] and furnished not only a politico-theological legitimisation for absolute monarchy but more specifically supported the primacy of the king *vis-à-vis* the church. Still, the wider context of these uses can be described as the re-sacralisation of European monarchies in the wake of confessionalisation and increased need for legitimisation. As Heinz Schilling has put it: »The state became more sacral, before it became more secular«[15].

II.

In the seventeenth century Muscovy faced its own exigencies in terms of royal legitimisation – both domestically, as far as the new Romanov dynasty was concerned, and abroad, concerning Muscovy's place in the emerging European state system[16]. This last exigency was painfully manifested in the Peace of Westphalia 1648, when the tsar, an ally of the Swedes, was still referred to as »magnus dux Moscoviae«[17].

Reformation. Communities, Polities, Nations and Empires. Essays in Honor of Thomas A. Brady Jr., Leiden/Boston 2007, pp. 539–550.

13 Anne-Marie CHENY, Une bibliothèque byzantine. Nicolas-Claude Fabri de Peiresc et la fabrique du savoir, Ceyzérieu 2015, pp. 232–240; ead., Humanisme, esprit scientifique et études byzantines La bibliothèque de Nicolas-Claude Fabri de Peiresc, in: XVIIe siècle 62/249 (2010), pp. 689–709; ead., L'Empire romain d'Orient, nouvel objet de recherche dans la première moitié du XVIIe siècle, in: XVIIe siècle 67/268 (2015), pp. 427–441; Marie-France AUZEPY/Jean-Pierre GRÉLOIS, Byzance retrouvée. Érudits et voyageurs Françaises (XVIe–XVIIIe siècles), Paris 2001.

14 Ihor ŠEVČENKO, Agapetus East and West. The Fate of a Byzantine Mirror of Princes, in: Revue des études sud-est européennes 16 (1978), pp. 3–44. See also Ševčenko's comment on the Kiev Slavonic edition of 1628: »To be sure, the print of 1628 was a sign of a Byzantine revival; but it also was an echo of what was going on in contemporary European publishing«, id., Ljubomudrějši; Kÿr' Agapit Diakon. On a Kiev Edition of a Byzantine Mirror of Princes, in: Id., Byzantium and the Slavs in Letters and Culture, Cambridge, MA 1991, Study XXIX, pp. 499–529, at p. 525.

15 Heinz SCHILLING, Confessional Europe, in: Thomas A. BRADY Jr. et al. (eds.), Handbook of European History 1400–1600. Late Middle Ages, Renaissance and Reformation, vol. 2, Leiden/New York 1995, pp. 641–681, at p. 644; see also Paul KLÉBER MONOD, The Power of Kings. Monarchy and Religion in Europe, 1589–1715, New Haven, CT 1999.

16 Philip LONGWORTH, Alexis. Tsar of all the Russias, New York 1984, pp. 229–231.

17 Klaus ZERNACK, Die Expansion des Moskauer Reiches nach Westen, Süden und Osten von 1648 bis 1689, in: Id. (ed.), Handbuch der Geschichte Russlands, vol. 2/1, Stuttgart 1986, pp. 123–152, at p. 145; Günther BARUDIO, Moskau und der Dreißigjährige Krieg, in: Ibid., pp. 87–96, at p. 95.

The tsar's image as an Orthodox ruler and its Byzantine underpinnings form a constant theme, a thread throughout early modern Russian history[18]. Donald Ostrowski has demonstrated how the Russian church leaders gradually managed, during the sixteenth century, to »fashion the Khan into Basileus«, i. e., to remodel the tsar's image from a Mongol to a Byzantine frame of reference[19]. But this process was continued in the seventeenth century, »Muscovy's Greek Century« according to Ekkehard Kraft[20]. It reached its peak during the reign of Aleksei Mikhailovich, the second Romanov Tsar from 1645 through 1676, with unforeseen implications[21].

Greek hierarchs were already familiarised with the role of the trustees of the Orthodox, Byzantine imperial legacy and the divine sanctioning of Orthodox rule in their intense relationship with the Princes (Hospodars) of the Danubian Principalities, Moldavia und Wallachia[22]. The models emerging from what may be described, in somewhat simplified terms, as an exchange of symbolic in return for material capital, proved useful for the distinct context of Muscovy and for the legitimisation of the tsar as the Orthodox emperor, head of an Orthodox community. They were particularly appealing to those keen to imagine an Orthodox confessional-political unity.

The turn to Constantinople and the Greeks on the part of the Muscovite Tsars was not simply based on their supposed symbolic capital or on the tsars' own increased legitimisation needs, which called for external confirmation. It also helped circumvent the Russian Church and avoid pertinent risks of readjusting the balance in Muscovy. This was a pattern that had already been applied by Ivan IV the Terrible with regard to the confirmation of his title of tsar by the Patriarch of Constantinople

---

18 As described in Jan Kusber's contribution to the present volume.
19 Donald Ostrowski, Muscovy and the Mongols. Cross-cultural Influences on the Steppe Frontier, 1304–1589, Cambridge, MA 1998, pp. 164–218.
20 Ekkehard Kraft, Moskaus griechisches Jahrhundert. Russisch-griechische Beziehungen und metabyzantinischer Einfluß 1619–1694, Stuttgart 1995.
21 Ibid., p. 80, 96f.; Longworth, Alexis, pp. 230f.; Nadezhda P. Chesnokova, Khristianskii Vostok i Rossiia. Politicheskoe i kul'turnoe vzaimodeistvie v seredine XVII veka, Moscow 2011, pp. 159–198; Richard S. Wortman, Scenarios of Power. Myth and Ceremony in Russian Monarchy, vol. 1, Princeton, NJ 1995, pp. 132–139; Igor Andreev, Zeremoniell als Sinnbild der Macht. Die ersten Romanovs und ihre kirchlichen und höfischen Zeremonien, in: Otto Gerhard Oexle/Michael A. Bojcov (eds.), Bilder der Macht im Mittelalter und Neuzeit. Byzanz – Okzident – Rußland, Göttingen 2007, pp. 517–537, at p. 520.
22 Andrei Pippidi, À la recherche d'une tradition politique byzantine dans les pays roumains, in: Nouvelles Études d'Histoire, vol. 6, 1, Bucharest 1980, pp. 121–130; id., Entre héritage et imitation. La tradition byzantine dans les pays roumains. Nouvelles réflexions vingt ans après, in: Paschalis M. Kitromilides/Anna Tabaki (eds.), Relations Gréco-Roumaines. Interculturalité et identité nationale, Athens 2004, pp. 23–37; Daniel Ursprung, Herrschaftslegitimation zwischen Tradition und Innovation. Repräsentation und Inszenierung von Herrschaft in der rumänischen Geschichte, Heidelberg/Kronstadt 2007.

in 1557. It would be re-applied several times in the seventeenth century, the most prominent case being the church council of 1667 under the guidance of Greek hierarchs, which resolved the conflict between Tsar Aleksei and Patriarch Nikon[23]. If the tsar took advantage of the symbolic capital of the Greek ecclesiastics to sanction certain decisions of his own, they could in turn invoke the Constantinian model – that is, an emperor gifted by God to his church as protector and benefactor – to promote their own interests.

The context of this rapprochement was marked by several overlapping and interconnected projects and developments in the 1650s: church reform in Russia, which was designed to bring the Russian Church into line with the supposedly Byzantine model of the Eastern Church as a precondition for securing Muscovy's destiny as the leading Orthodox power; then a complex of intense conspiratorial political activity on behalf of part of the Greek hierarchy and its networks, inspired by the Cossack rebellion, the Muscovite-Polish war and the Cretan war, and aiming to influence the tsar's foreign policy; finally, and as a result of these developments, an increase in the sheer number and the frequency of Greek ecclesiastics visiting Moscow and seeking alms[24] as well as political support for their projects. The symbolic forms in which this upgrade of relations was articulated encompassed not only verbal discourses, but also material transfers: holy objects, relics and icons with imperial connotations; a *translatio sanctorum* that explicitly supported a *translatio imperii*[25].

Still, the most obvious sources to which this politico-theological legitimisation can be traced are the writings of Greek ecclesiastics addressed to the tsar. They involved a careful reapplication of the Byzantine imperial titles and attributes to the tsar[26] as well as a catalogue of the imperial virtues he combined in his person: imperial metaphors such as the sun par excellence, or the safe haven; the obligatory Old Testament *exempla*, in some cases applied in the typological sense of prefiguration and fulfilment; the tsar as the new Moses, Joshua, Gideon, or Solomon, but also as the new Constantine, Justinian, Alexander the Great, or in the case of Tsar Aleksei, the new Alexios Komnenos. They also involved historical

---

23 Wolfram von SCHELIHA, Russland und die orthodoxe Kirche in der Patriarchatsperiode 1589–1721, Wiesbaden 2004, pp. 235–311; David A. FRICK, Sailing to Byzantium. Greek Texts and the Establishment of Authority in Early Modern Muscovy, in: Harvard Ukrainian Studies 19 (1995), pp. 138–157, at p. 143.
24 On this at the time widespread phenomenon, see Iannis CARRAS, Orthodoxe Kirche, Wohltätigkeit und Handelsaustausch. Kaufleute und Almosensammler entlang der osmanisch-russischen Grenze im 18. Jahrhundert, Erfurt 2020.
25 For the overall context, see Nikolas PISSIS, Russland in den politischen Vorstellungen der griechischen Kulturwelt 1645–1725, Göttingen 2020; Vera G. TCHENTSOVA, Ikona Iverskoi Bogomateri (Ocherki istorii otnoshenii Grecheskoi Tserkvi s Rossiei v seredine XVII v. po dokumentam RGADA), Moscow 2010; KRAFT, Moskaus griechisches Jahrhundert, pp. 56–83.
26 KRAFT, Moskaus griechisches Jahrhundert, pp. 92–96.

elaborations of the tsars' imperial legacy, invoking the marriages of Vladimir to Anna Porphyrogennita (989) or of Ivan III to Zoe Sophia Palaiologina (1472).

Particularly illustrative in this context is a letter of Gavriil Vlasios, Metropolitan of Nafpaktos and Arta (1647–1660), professor of the Patriarchal Academy and one of the »ideologues of the Eastern Church«[27], to Tsar Mikhail Fedorovich in February 1644: »Whether [the Empire] stands in Moscow or in Constantinople, it makes no difference. Only the seat changes, but the Empire remains identical. In the same manner that the Empire moved from Rome to Constantinople, it moved from there to Moscow«[28]. Along similar lines, Paisios Ligarides, the learned yet scandalous Metropolitan of Gaza[29] who may have been the most sophisticated among the Greek panegyrists of the Tsar Aleksei, addressed the latter as

[…] Augustus, genuine heir to the Empire of the Palaiologoi, to which you are linked as if by a golden lineage of origin, since you stem from the Empress Sofia Palaiologina. Therefore, be strong and courageous [Deuteronomy 31:6] in order to reclaim the throne which has long been owed to you […][30].

We expect the freedom of the Hellenic Empire and its reclaiming by you, the mighty Russians, who nowadays possess the Greek [Roman] monarchy and Orthodoxy[31].

---

27 On Vlasios see Boris L. FONKICH, Greko-slavianskie shkoly v Moskve v VII veke, Moscow 2009, pp. 49–63; TCHENTSOVA, Ikona Iversko Bogomateri, pp. 79–85; Boris N. FLORIA, Dva poslaniia G. Vlas'eva cariu Mikhailu Fedorovichu, in: Grecheskii i slavianskii mir v srednie veka i rannee novoe vremia, Moscow 1996, pp. 216–227.

28 Rossiiskii Gosudarstvennyi Arkhiv Drevnikh Aktov, Moscow [hereafter: RGADA]. Fond 52: Snosheniia Rossii s Gretsiei, Opis' 2, No. 209, 2 February 1644: »[…] καὶ τόσον νὰ εἶναι εἰς τὴν Μοσχοβίαν, καθὼς νὰ ἦτον καὶ εἰς τὴν Κωνσταντινούπολιν, δὲν εἶναι καμία διαφορά, μόνον ὁ τόπος ἀλλάζει, ἀμὴ ἡ αὐτὴ βασιλεία εἶναι. Καὶ καθὼς ἀλλάχθη ἀπὸ τὴν Ῥώμην, καὶ ἐπῆγε τὸ βασίλειον εἰς τὴν Κωνσταντινούπολιν, ὁμοίως καὶ ἀπὸ ἐκεῖ πάλιν εἰς τὴν Μοσχοβίαν« (my translation).

29 Philip LONGWORTH, The Strange Career of Paisios Ligarides, in: History Today 45 (1995), pp. 39–45; Gerhard PODSKALSKY, Griechische Theologie in der Zeit der Türkenherrschaft (1453–1821). Die Orthodoxie im Spannungsfeld der nachreformatorischen Konfessionen des Westens, Munich 1988, pp. 251–258; Ovidiu OLAR, Prophecy and History. Notes on Manuscripts in Circulation in the Romanian Principalities (Matthew of Myra and Paisios Ligaridis), in: Byzantine Manuscripts in Bucharest's Collections, Bucharest 2009, pp. 84–95; Harry T. HIONIDES, Paisius Ligarides, New York 1972; Fedor B. POLJAKOV, Paisios Ligarides und die ostslavische Barockliteratur in Moskau, in: Wiener Slavistisches Jahrbuch 49 (2003), pp. 143–156.

30 Gosudarstvennyi Istoricheskii Muzei [hereafter GIM] 409 (469), fol. 279v: »[…] Αὔγουστον, γνήσιον διάδοχον τῆς βασιλείας τῶν Παλαιολόγων, ἐξ ἧς ὡς ἀπὸ χρυσῆς τινος σειρᾶς διατελεῖς καταγόμενος ἀπὸ τῆς Παλαιολογίνας δηλαδὴ βασιλίσσης Σοφίας. Διὰ τοῦτο ἀνδρίζου καὶ ἴσχυε, τοῦ ἐπανακτήσασθαι τὸν ἐποφειλόμενόν σοι ἐκ πολλοῦ θρόνον« (my translation).

31 GIM 409 (469), fol. 287v: »[…] καραδοκοῦντες καὶ τὴν ἐλευθερίαν τῆς ἑλληνικῆς βασιλείας καὶ τὴν ἀνάκτησιν ἀφ' ὑμῶν τῶν ἰσχυρῶν Ῥώσων, τῶν νῦν βασιλευόντων καὶ κατεχόντων τὴν τῶν Ῥωμαίων μοναρχίαν τε καὶ ὀρθοδοξίαν« (my translation).

Their rhetoric as well as the vocabulary employed – especially as far as a certain group or network of persons around the Patriarch of Jerusalem Paisios Lampardis (1645–1660), including Vlasios and Ligaridis, is concerned – seem to have been to a degree orchestrated[32]. It is not just the choice from the broad available arsenal of topoi and rhetorical tools that is telling, but the stress on the tsar's quality and mission as the protector and saviour of the Eastern Church, the champion of Orthodoxy, and especially on a providential mission assigned to him by God as a stage in the history of salvation: the tsar as head of the entire Orthodox community. Following a decrease in the late 1660s and 1670s, these discourses were reinforced in the latter part of the seventeenth century in the letters to Tsar Fedor and especially to Peter the Great composed by the leading figure among the Greek hierarchs, Dositheos, Patriarch of Jerusalem (1669–1707)[33]. More explicitly than his predecessors, Dositheos articulated the imagined order of an Orthodox world as a kind of condominium under the secular leadership of the Russian Tsar and the spiritual guidance of the Greek hierarchs – in terms, to be sure, of the Byzantine *symphonia*, but more or less openly excluding the Russian Church[34].

Perhaps most telling in this regard is the missive Dositheos sent to Peter in January 1705 advising him that instead of seeking domestic solutions to ecclesiastical matters, he should as a rule circumvent the Muscovite hierarchy and appeal to the Eastern Patriarchs to get matters resolved without »quarrels, doubts, and headache«[35]. Dositheos repeatedly described in his letters his services as those of a political mentor to the young tsars. Once he offered Peter an indulgence of sorts for breaking oaths towards Augustus II (the Strong) of Poland, a move that he had suggested to the tsar himself:

---

32 TCHENTSOVA, Ikona Iversko Bogomateri.
33 PODSKALSKY, Griechische Theologie, pp. 282–295; Klaus-Peter TODT, Dositheos II. von Jerusalem, in: Carmelo Giuseppe CONTICELLO/Vassa CONTICELLO (eds.), La théologie byzantine et sa tradition, vol. 2, Turnhout 2002, pp. 659–720; Athanasios E. KARATHANASIS, Οἱ Ἕλληνες λόγιοι στὴ Βλαχία (1670–1714). Συμβολὴ στὴ μελέτη τῆς ἑλληνικῆς πνευματικῆς κίνησης στὶς Παραδουνάβιες Ἡγεμονίες κατὰ τὴν προφαναριωτικὴ περίοδο, Thessaloniki ²2000, pp. 109–114; Chrysostomos PAPADOPOULOS, Δοσίθεος Πατριάρχης Ἱεροσολύμων (1641–1707), Jerusalem 1907.
34 Cf. KRAFT, Moskaus griechisches Jahrhundert, p. 100; Helmut NEUBAUER, Car und Selbstherrscher. Beiträge zur Geschichte der Autokratie in Rußland, Wiesbaden 1964, p. 105.
35 RGADA, Fond 52, Opis' 1, 1705, No. 1, fol. 6v: »Διὰ νὰ ἔχῃ ἡ μεγάλη σου βασιλεία τὴν φροντίδα μόνης τῆς πολιτείας, καὶ ἡ ἐκκλησία πάντοτε νὰ εἶναι εἰρηνικὴ καὶ ἀστασίαστη, νὰ προστάξῃ γενναίως καὶ σταθερῶς, ὅτι ἂν τύχῃ τι ζήτημα ἐκκλησιαστικόν, νὰ μὴν γίνεται ἡ λύσις εἰς τὰ αὐτόθι, διὰ νὰ μὴν προξενοῦνται ἔριδες καὶ ἀμφιβολίαι καὶ πονοκεφαλίσματα τῶν βασιλέων, ἀλλὰ νὰ γράφεται γράμμα εἰς τοὺς τέσσαρας ἁγιωτάτους πατριάρχας καὶ ἀπ' ἐκεῖ νὰ ζητεῖται ἡ λύσις«; see also SCHELIHA, Russland und die orthodoxe Universalkirche, pp. 143f.

The divine emperor should consider the interest of his own state and not be afraid to break oaths towards heretics and perjurers. Nor should he enquire about this any barbarians, churchmen with no experience in such matters. Because the papists and the other heretics are many rulers and they are helping each other. However, the Orthodox monarch is one and only-begotten. [...] If the divine emperor wishes to ask something in such great matters, here he should ask those who have spiritual knowledge and political praxis, and principally those who understand the symphony between the state and the church[36].

This brief sketch may suffice to highlight the functional character of political theology. For the Muscovite Tsars, the ideological offer of the Greeks had symbolic as well as pragmatic benefits. One can point, for example, to the fact, that some of the holy objects with a powerful symbolic function that were transferred, like the so-called »Cross of Constantine« or the Icon of Blachernitissa, were received in Moscow in meticulously and lavishly organised processions and celebrations. More specifically, this icon was supposed to be the same that, according to tradition, had saved Constantinople from Persian and Arab conquest, thereby symbolising the invincibility of the faithful Orthodox against all odds. In Moscow, the Blachernitissa stood in the Dormition Cathedral opposite to another powerful symbol of Russian Orthodox Tsardom, namely the Theotokos of Vladimir (the *Vladimirskaia*). It is obvious that such symbols were employed in »scenarios of power« designed to promote the tsar's image as the »New Constantine«. They were also adopted as *palladia* to accompany the army on the tsar's campaign against the Poles and the Swedes 1654 and 1656, campaigns that were staged as religious wars, a kind of an Orthodox crusade[37]. A few years later, in 1660, the tsar ordered new regalia or imperial insignia, including an orb, and a collar, from Constantinople, supposedly after the model of Emperor Constantine's insignia, via the same Greek networks[38].

---

36 Letter of Dositheos to Chancellor Fedor Alekseevich Golovin, June 1706, RGADA, Fond 52, Opis' 1, 1706, No. 1, fol. 28v: »Πρέπει ὁ θειότατος νὰ ἀποβλέψῃ εἰς τὸ συμφέρον τῆς ἰδίας πολιτείας καὶ τὴν ἀθέτησιν τῶν αἱρετικῶν καὶ ἐπιόρκων νὰ μὴ φοβηθῇ, μήτε περὶ αὐτοῦ νὰ ἐρωτήσῃ βαρβάρους καὶ περὶ τὰ τοιαῦτα ἀπράκτους πνευματικούς [...] καὶ οἱ παπισταὶ καὶ οἱ ἄλλοι αἱρετικοὶ εἶναι πολλοὶ ἡγεμόνες, ὁ νας τὸν ἄλλον βοηθεῖ, ἀμὴ ὁ ὀρθόδοξος μονάρχης εἶναι μόνος καὶ μονογενὴς [...] ὁ θειότατος εἰς τοιαῦτα μεγάλα πράγματα ἂν ἔχῃ νὰ ἐρωτήσῃ τίποτες, ἐδῶ ἂς ἐρωτᾷ, ἐκείνους ὁποῦ ἔχουν πνευματικὴν γνῶσιν καὶ πολιτικὴν πρᾶξιν, καὶ μάλιστα ἐκείνους ὁποῦ γιγνώσκουσι τὴν συμφωνίαν τῆς πολιτείας καὶ ἐκκλησίας« (my translation).
37 Kevin M. KAIN, Before New Jerusalem: Patriarch Nikon's Iverskii and Krestnyi Monasteries, in: Russian History 39 (2012), pp. 173–231; LONGWORTH, Alexis, pp. 94–96; Sergej V. LOBAČEV, Patriarkh Nikon, St Petersburg 2003, pp. 139–145; TCHENTSOVA, Ikona Iverskoi Bogomateri, p. 242.
38 M. V. MARTYNOVA, Barmy Caria Alekseia Mikhailovicha, in: Rossiia i Khristianskii Vostok 2–3 (2004), pp. 363–376; O.A. CICINOVA et al., Tema grecheskogo naslediia v tserkovnoi i gosudarstvennoi ideologii XVII veka, in: I. A. BOBROVNICKAIA/M. V. MARTYNOVA (eds.), Tsar' Aleksei Mikhailovich i Patriarkh Nikon, Moscow 2005, pp. 104–128.

But it is the »constitutional« conflict between Tsar Aleksei and Patriarch Nikon that provides the most manifest illustration[39]. The authority of Greek hierarchs was drawn upon in order to resolve the conflict in accordance, so it was claimed, with the tradition of the Byzantine emperors and the Eastern Church. It was the metropolitan of Gaza, Paisios Ligaridis from the island of Chios, an expert on canon law and Byzantine history, who virtually directed the council, formulating and justifying its decisions. He raised the constitutional issue (emperor vs. patriarch or empire vs. priesthood) in order to trap, provoke, and isolate Nikon. This tactic proved quite successful and the eventual resolution served the interests of both the tsar and Greek hierarchy[40].

The employment of political theology was functional for the Greek hierarchs in more than one way. Indeed, to read the encomia addressed to the tsars as mere conventional flattery would be to miss the point. However conventional and predictable, they represented moral admonitions and constant reminders of the duties the imperial office involved – duties that were redefined by the very flatterers who thereby underlined and secured their role. Moreover, the symbols and images invoked were not simply interchangeable. If, for example, a Patriarch of Jerusalem or an archimandrite of the Holy Sepulchre called the tsar »a new Solomon, founder of the temple«, this pointed to his special obligation to support the holy sites, or Orthodox claims to their possession[41]. This functional quality reveals itself not only in the promotion of certain particular interests but also in the self-legitimisation performed by politico-theological discourses. It was through the articulation of such language that the Greek prelates' claim to the symbolic capital of the spiritual leadership of the Orthodox world was made, a claim, in short, to indispensability. As has been aptly observed, »even after 1589, the Greeks who came to Moscow for alms remained convinced that the Greek ›mother church‹ was still the ultimate arbiter of Eastern Orthodox belief and practice«[42].

---

39 Paul MEYENDORFF, Russia, Ritual and Reform. The Liturgical Reforms of Nikon in the 17th Century, Crestwood, NY 1991; Robert O. CRUMMEY, The Orthodox Church and the Schism, in: Maureen PERRIE (ed.), The Cambridge History of Russia, vol. 1: From Early Rus' to 1689, Cambridge 2015, pp. 618–639.

40 Ihor ŠEVČENKO, A New Greek Source concerning the Nikon Affair. The Sixty-One Answers by Paisios Ligarides given to Tsar Aleksej Mixajlovič, in: ΓΕΝΝΑΔΙΟΣ. К 70-letiiu akademika G. G. Litavrina, Moscow 1999, pp. 237–263; Charalampos K. PAPASTATHIS, Paisios Ligaridis et la formation des relations entre l'église et l'état en Russie au XVIIe siècle, in: Cyrillomethodianum 2 (1972/73), pp. 77–85; Dimitrios A. PETRAKAKOS, Ὁ Γάζης Παΐσιος ὡς κανονολόγος, in: Θεολογία 15 (1937), pp. 193–207; NEUBAUER, Car und Selbstherrscher, pp. 149–181.

41 Paisios Lampardis to Tsar Aleksei Michailovich, RGADA, Fond 52, Opis' 2, No. 264, 21 September 1646: »[…] καὶ μάλιστα ἡμεῖς ὁ ἀποστολικὸς καὶ ἁγιώτατός μας θρόνος τῆς ἁγίας πόλεως Ἰερουσαλήμ […] ἀπὸ ἐσένα τὸν δεύτερον Σολομῶντα, τὸν μέγα βασιλέα Ἀλέξιο Μιχαηλοβίτζη«.

42 CRUMMEY, The Orthodox Church and the Schism, p. 618.

This claim was clothed in the classic discourse of the two divine gifts, *sacerdotium* and *imperium* (βασιλεία καὶ ἱερωσύνη). The customary emphasis on their interdependence helped gloss over questions about the primacy of one over the other. Dionysios Mouselimis, the most eminent Patriarch of Constantinople in the last third of the seventeenth century (1671–1673, 1676–1679, 1682–1684, 1686–1687, 1693–1694)[43] and an antagonist of Dositheos – not least concerning their competition over access to and influence over the Muscovite authorities – suggested an analogy between this discourse and the traditional dualism of body and soul:

> God thereby gifted certain gifts – that is, the Empire and the priesthood – so that through them both states and churches are guarded. Through the Empire the political matters are governed, through the priesthood the spiritual ones. As the body is animated with the soul, so is the Empire strengthened with the priesthood and it rules[44].

A curious instance might help illustrate this claim and its effectiveness. Although their actual substance is doubtful, rumours circulating in the middle of the seventeenth century about Greek Patriarchs aiming to crown and anoint Orthodox rulers in the imperial manner are telling with regard to the expectations of contemporaries. In 1645, in the context of anti-Ottoman »crusade« conspiracies, the Patriarchs of Constantinople Parthenios II and Athanasios Patellaros supposedly planned to crown the Hospodar of Moldavia Vasile Lupu as emperor[45], while Paisios Lampardis, »le grand ordonnateur des relations dites ›gréco-russes‹ dans les années 1650«[46], was believed to be preparing a crown

---

43 KARATHANASIS, Οἱ Ἕλληνες λόγιοι στὴ Βλαχία, pp. 104–108.
44 Dionysios Mouselimis to the Tsars Ivan and Peter, RGADA, Fond 52, Opis' 2, No. 679, 11 June 1688: »[…] χαρίζοντας [ὁ Θεός, N.P.] χαρίσματα διάφορα, βασιλεία φημὶ καὶ ἱερωσύνη, ἵνα δι' αὐτῶν καὶ πολιτεῖαι καὶ ἐκκλησίαι φυλαττέτωσαν, διὰ μὲν τῇ βασιλείᾳ διοικήτωσαν τὰ πολιτικά, διὰ δὲ τῇ ἱερωσύνῃ τὰ πνευματικά, καὶ ὥσπερ ψυχὴ σὺν τῷ σώματι ζωογονεῖται, οὕτω καὶ ἡ βασιλεία σὺν τῇ ἱερωσύνῃ κρατύνεται καὶ ἐξουσιάζῃ« (my translation).
45 Eudoxiu de HURMUZAKI, Documente privitoare la Istoria Românilor, vol. IV/2, Bucharest 1894, p. 535, vol. XIV/1, p. 180; id., Fragmente zur Geschichte der Rumänen, vol. 3, Bucharest 1884, p. 144; Francisc PALL, Les relations de Basile Lupu avec l'Orient orthodoxe et particulièrement avec le Patriarcat de Constantinople, in: Balcania 8 (1945), pp. 66–140, at pp. 85–89, 98f., 117–133; Nicolae IORGA, Basile Lupu, prince de Moldavie, comme successeur des empereurs d'Orient dans la tutelle du Patriarcat de Constantinople et de l'église orthodoxe (1640-1653), in: Académie Roumaine. Bulletin de la section historique 2/1 (1914), pp. 88–123, at pp. 115f.
46 Vera G. TCHENTSOVA, Le patriarche d'Antioche Macaire III Ibn al-Za'im et la chrétienté latine, in: Marie-Hélène BLANCHET/Frédéric GABRIEL (eds.), Réduire le schisme? Ecclésiologies et politiques de l'Union entre Orient et Occident (XIIIᵉ–XVIIIᵉ siècle), Paris 2013, pp. 313–335, at p. 335.

for the Cossack Hetman Bohdan Khmelnytsky (1648)[47] or for Tsar Aleksei himself (1657)[48].

At this point, a comment on the ambivalence inherent in these discourses is in order. On the one hand, it concerns the difference or gap between the status accorded to the tsar and to the Russian Church, respectively. On various occasions before and after the council of 1667, Greek ecclesiastics displayed contempt for their Russian colleagues and their theological competence, leaving no doubt that in their understanding of Orthodoxy there was no place for an equal and influential Russian Church. This went so far as implicitly to question the legitimacy of the Moscow Patriarchate as a member of the established community of the Eastern Orthodox Patriarchates[49].

On the other hand, ambivalence permeated the entire complex of notions of *translatio imperii*. It was never clarified whether this was a *translatio* or an expected *restitutio* imperii. After all, the tsar was repeatedly exhorted to capture Constantinople at once to obtain – only then, in the imperial capital – his legitimate imperial inheritance and dignity. In such imagery, he was assigned the role of the divine instrument sent by God for the salvation of his enslaved people. If the Old Testament provided the suitable imagery, there was no unanimity on *who* the »New Israel«, the Chosen People, was to be[50].

Such ambivalences could, as a rule, be rhetorically accommodated without ever being resolved. They emerged in several instances, and it seems that this formed an underlying tension in the case of Patriarch Nikon's relations with the Greek hierarchs and their evolution from close alliance to antagonism and eventually to his condemnation[51]. It certainly emerged as a collision of interpretation in the *translatio sanctorum*. Was the transfer of holy relics to Moscow temporal or eternal? Was Moscow the new capital of Orthodoxy or a stop-gap, a *provisorium*? These

---

47 Vossoedinenye Ukrainy s Rossiei. Dokumenty i materialy, vol. 2, Moscow 1953–1954, pp. 118–120.
48 Vera G. Tchentsova, Mitra Paisiia Ierusalimskogo – ne prislannyi russkomu gosudariu venets caria Konstantina', in: E. M. Jukhimenko (ed.), Patriarkh Nikon i ego vremia, Moscow 2004, pp. 11–39.
49 Nikolas Pissis, The Image of the Moscow Patriarchate in the Eastern Church. Status and Legitimacy, in: Kevin M. Kain/David Goldfrank (eds.), Russia's Early Modern Orthodox Patriarchate, vol. 1: Foundations and Mitred Royalty, 1589–1647, Washington, DC 2020, pp. 49–69.
50 On early modern »New Israels«, see Alois Mosser (ed.), Gottes auserwählte Völker. Erwählungsvorstellungen und kollektive Selbstfindung in der Geschichte, Frankfurt am Main 2001; Philip S. Gorski, The Mosaic Moment. An Early Modernist Critique of Modernist Theories of Nationalism, in: American Journal of Sociology 105 (2000), pp. 1428–1468; Diana Muir Appelbaum, Biblical Nationalism and the Sixteenth-century States, in: National Identities 15 (2013), pp. 317–332; on the Muscovites as the »New Israel«, see Daniel B. Rowland, Moscow – The Third Rome or the New Israel?, in: Russian Review 55 (1996), pp. 591–614; on the Byzantine background, see Shay Eshel, The Concept of the Elect Nation in Byzantium, Leiden/Boston 2018.
51 Kain, Before New Jerusalem.

were not theoretical issues, since, for example, Athonite monks who clamoured for the return of the relics found themselves exiled to the White Sea[52]. In this particular case (Vatopedi Monastery), the tension is further illustrated by the fact that the two relics in question (the heads of John Chrysostom and Gregory of Nazianzus) are today simultaneously kept in Moscow as well as in the Athos. Whether the Athonite monks had prudently sent duplicates to Moscow in the first place or, what is more probable, they silently replaced the relics in the late seventeenth century when they were certain that they would not be returned, is of minor importance.

III.

If the examination of the role played by Greek hierarchs in the legitimisation of the Russian Tsars as leaders of all Orthodox peoples has brought to light tensions and cleavages that crossed a hardly coherent Orthodox world, this should not overshadow the fact that the same political language was employed by Russians and Greeks alike[53]. Again, to address the comparative dimension, this common inheritance does not really represent an Orthodox exceptionalism. After all, typical ecclesiastical discourses addressed to Christian Princes and Kings as *defensores ecclesiae* and champions of the true faith – whether Catholic, Lutheran, Calvinist, Anglican, or Orthodox – resembled one another throughout Europe, drawing on Biblicism, especially the Old Testament, and the Constantinian model. The most experienced among the Greek ecclesiastics of the seventeenth century referred to had enjoyed a Western (specifically Italian) education and saw no contradiction between their Latin and Greek erudition or between classical and biblical images. There are good reasons to categorise a great part of their discourses on Russia as belonging to a common type of an early modern Christian or, if one prefers the term, Baroque politico-theological language.

---

52 Nikolai KAPTEREV, Kharakter otnoshenii Rossii k pravoslavnomu vostoku v XVI i XVII stoletiiakh, Sergiev Posad 1914 [reprint: The Hague/Paris 1968], pp. 60–71; Boris L. FONKIČ, Chudotvornye ikoni i sviashchennye relikvii Khristianskogo Vostoka v Moskve v seredine XVII v., in: Ocherki feodalnoi Rossii 5 (2001), pp. 70-97, at pp. 95-97; Vera G. TCHENTSOVA, Pisets Nikolai Armiriot i Krest caria Konstantina. K istorii sviazei Vatopedskogo monastyria s Rossie v XVII veke, in: Palaeoslavica 19/ 12 (2011), pp. 60-109, at pp. 64-66, 97; ead., Ierusalimskii protosinkell Gavriil i ego okruzhenie. Materialy k izucheniiu grecheskikh gramot ob ikone Vlakhernskoi Bogomateri, in: Palaeoslavica 15/ 1 (2007) pp. 57–136, at pp. 108f.
53 See, for example, Valerie KIVELSON et al. (eds.), The New Muscovite Cultural History. A Collection in Honor of Daniel B. Rowland, Bloomington, IN 2009; along with the list of pertinent publications by Daniel B. Rowland included in the volume.

Dimitris Stamatopoulos

»Papism is a Centre without Periphery, Protestantism is a Periphery without Centre«

Tanzimat as Re-Confessionalisation? The Political Theology of Constitutionality in the Late Ottoman Empire

Introduction

The publication of the February 1870 firman, by which Grand Vizier Mehmed Âli Paşa recognised the founding of an autonomous Bulgarian Church (i. e., the Bulgarian Exarchate), was a double scandal for the Ecumenical Patriarchate. First, because never before had representatives of a state – moreover, one of a different religion – extracted ecclesiastical eparchies from the Ecumenical Patriarchate's jurisdiction and created a new church without this having been preceded by the secession and statehood of these areas, as has been the case with Serbia and Greece several decades earlier. The new ecclesiastical entity rested on national foundations despite being an Exarchate, i. e., despite the fact that it should have recognised its jurisdictional dependence on the Patriarchate. As we know, two years later, in 1872, this would lead to its denunciation as schismatic by a local synod convened in Constantinople[1].

But there was another reason that the Patriarchate viewed this text as dangerous: This was the infamous Article 10, according to which an ecclesiastical eparchy would be considered Patriarchal or Exarchial if two-thirds of its population supported one or the other side. The Patriarchate did have serious reservations about this provision because it could foresee that this article would trigger a four-decade clash between Greeks and Bulgarians for the control of Macedonia and Thrace[2]. It viewed the article as scandalous because it accepted the position that the Bulgarians had formulated back at the Grand »National« Assembly[3] of 1858–1860 when they spoke

---

1 Dimitris STAMATOPOULOS, The Bulgarian Schism Revisited, in: Modern Greek Studies Yearbook 24/25 (2008–2009), pp. 105–125.
2 See chapters 11 and 12 of Paschalis KITROMILIDES, Enlightenment, Nationalism, Orthodoxy. Studies in the Culture and Political Thought of South-Eastern Europe, Aldershot/Brookfield, VT 1994; ²2008.
3 We should be cautious about calling the assembly of the representatives of the *millet* in 1858–1860 a »National Assembly« or »National Provisional Council« *stricto sensu*. The Ottoman text refers to a »commission« (*komisyon*), which undertook the task of formulating the General Regulations. The term »national« became established in Greek texts of the late nineteenth century, when the developments described in this article as »splitting of the *millet*« were re-interpreted as the »rise of

for the principle of proportionality in the representation of national groups, both in the Assembly itself and in the procedures for electing the Patriarch. Indeed, in 1864, they would take it a step further by requesting that the Patriarchate's collective bodies – the Holy Synod and the Mixed Council – be comprised equally of Greeks and Bulgarians[4].

The Church as State

The Patriarchate would see this invocation of the principle of majority – that is, the invocation of the »democratic principle« in a society that had yet to experience free parliamentary elections – repeated by the Ottoman state itself in subsequent decades. The state aimed to absorb some of what were considered the church's privileges (e. g., its right to adjudicate cases involving clergy, the control of the Patriarchate's schools, its jurisdiction over cases involving family law, the issue of the conscription waiver in exchange for payment of a military tax). Thus, an even bigger problem emerged along with the national problem related to the Bulgarians: the new role that Ottoman power had in mind for the Patriarchate in the context of Tanzimat modernisation. The most important intellectuals of the Patriarchate's environment (chiefly Manuel Gedeon, the most notable figure of an »organic intellectual« in the sense developed by Antonio Gramsci[5]) tried to respond to this attack by placing emphasis on two points: first, the seniority of the privileges (in order to legitimise the privileges as well as the Patriarchate's *status in statu* within the Ottoman Empire); and second, the Ottoman Empire's continuity with the Byzantine Empire, arguing

---

the nation«, i. e., the Greek nation, within the framework of the Ottoman Empire. However, this is an anachronism and a projection of national stereotypes onto a more complex reality. This is why I put the adjective »National« in this specific case in quotation marks. For the Assembly of 1858–1860, one may also employ the term *Millet-i Assembly*, i. e., Assembly of the Orthodox *millet* (although the great majority of representatives were Greek Orthodox, particularly after the withdrawal of two of the four Bulgarian representatives); or the Patriarchate's Assembly, in order to distinguish it from the Assembly of the Bulgarian Exarchate.

4 For details, see Dimitris STAMATOPOULOS, Μεταρρύθμιση και Εκκοσμίκευση: Προς μια ανασύνθεση της Ιστορίας του Οικουμενικού Πατριαρχείου τον 19° αιώνα [Reform and Secularisation: Towards a Reconstruction of the History of the Ecumenical Patriarchate in the Nineteenth Century], Athens 2003.

5 In his *Prison Notebooks*, Antonio Gramsci speaks of »organic intellectuals« as social agents from an underprivileged social class, as opposed to »traditional intellectuals«, who adhere to no specific social class or discourse. Such »organic intellectuals« are not interested in their own personal career, upward mobility and success, but remain strongly connected with the interests of their own social class and try to ameliorate its overall condition.

that Mehmed the Conqueror essentially reproduced the model of the state-religion relationship typical of Byzantium and especially of late Byzantium[6].

At the end of the nineteenth century and the start of the twentieth, the Patriarchate's intelligentsia rejected the issue of invoking the »democratic principle«. Nonetheless, they knew that this was not sparked solely by some Bulgarian initiative, but was a structural element of the 1858–1860 »National« Assembly, so they had to position themselves against that event and the ideological tension it carried. Convening the Assembly was perhaps the most salient moment of the nineteenth century in terms of how the Patriarchate perceived its relationship to the Ottoman state: It was at this moment that a political theology of constitutionality was cemented.

This process reached its height in the mid-nineteenth century with the Tanzimat reforms. To be precise, it occurred within those provisions of the imperial decree of 1856 that foresaw the re-organisation of the Empire's Orthodox *millet* (and others as well), introducing into its administration lay elements through the convocation of mixed (clergy-laity) *millet* Assemblies. The constitutional text, which was derived from the Great Mixed Assembly of the Orthodox *millet* in Istanbul between 1858 and 1860, namely *The General Regulations* (*Γενικοὶ Κανονισμοί*) determined the history of the Patriarchate up to the end of the Ottoman Empire in 1923[7]. However, this move caused a long-lasting opposition within the Patriarchate among those supporting the reforms and those (chiefly high-ranking clerics) who supported the primacy of the Orthodox clergy on the basis of the priority of the Holy Canons in opposition to the new »constitution« imposed by the Tanzimat.

The following scheme arose from this confrontation as a commonplace in the argumentation of various »organic intellectuals« on both sides. The Patriarchate was likened to a space in which, apart from spiritual and political »rights«, the Patriarch combined the highest spiritual with political leadership. Here unfolds

---

6 I have described how deeply this model of approaching the Ottoman Empire's history influenced the historiographical works of this period in another paper: Dimitris STAMATOPOULOS, The Western Byzantium of Konstantinos Paparrigopoulos, in: Alena ALSHANSKAYA et al. (eds.), Imagining Byzantium. Perceptions, Patterns, Problems, Mainz 2019, pp. 39–46.

7 Γενικοὶ Κανονισμοὶ περὶ διευθετήσεως τῶν ἐκκλησιαστικῶν καὶ ἐθνικῶν πραγμάτων τῶν ὑπὸ τὸν Οἰκουμενικὸν θρόνον διατελούντων Ὀρθοδόξων Χριστιανῶν ὑπηκόων τῆς Α. Μεγαλειότητος τοῦ Σουλτάνου [General Regulations Concerning the Arrangement of Ecclesiastical and National Affairs of the Orthodox Christians Subjects of His Majesty the Sultan under the Ecumenical Throne], Constantinople 1862. The text has been published in French by Louis PETIT, Règlements Généraux de l'Église Orthodoxe en Turquie, in: Revue de L'Orient Chrétien 3 (1898), pp. 227–246. For the text in its Ottoman version, see Düstur (Ottoman Code of Public Laws), vol. 2, Istanbul 1873–1874, pp. 902–937. For a translation into modern Turkish, see Yorgo BENLİSOY/Elçin MACAR, Fener Patrikhanesi [Patriarchate of Fener, viz Ecumenical Patriarchate], Ankara 1996, pp. 71–107; on this topic, see STAMATOPOULOS, Μεταρρύθμιση καὶ Εκκοσμίκευση.

a new confrontation, that of the constitutional vs. the absolute. The two bodies convened in the Ecumenical Patriarchate, namely the Holy Synod and the Mixed Council, enjoyed a position corresponding to the representative bodies in the Orthodox *millet* – the small »parliaments«. Finally, the faithful and the subjects of the Ottoman realm constituted the body from which the above-named institutional organs drew their power.

It is obvious that the representation of the Patriarchate as a civil body[8] arose within the framework of increased expectations emerging from the declaration of *Hatt-i Hümayûn*, but here two details should be noted: first, that it owes a great deal to the discussion during the preceding decades with regard to the autocephalous Greek Church[9]; and second, that it created a new dynamic which preceded the constitutional change of the year 1864 in Greece by four years[10] and the concession of the 1876 constitution by Grand Vizier Midhat Paşa (under Sultan Murat V) by twelve years. In other words, it was connected to the hope for reforms that would establish a type of parliamentary representation without undoing the regime's imperial character.

The likening of the church to the state in the Ottoman Empire – both cases involving a section of the clergy – and its formation as representation catalytically shaped the subsequent relations between church and state. It is typical that, whenever necessary, the representatives of the clergy supported the authenticity of the Holy Canons alongside the constitutionality of the *General Regulations*, in order to

---

8 For details, see Dimitris STAMATOPOULOS, Η Εκκλησία ως Πολιτεία. Αναπαραστάσεις του Ορθόδοξου Μιλλέτ και το μοντέλο της συνταγματικής μοναρχίας (δεύτερο μισό 19ου αι.) [Church as State: Representations of the Orthodox *millet* and the Model of Constitutional Monarchy (Second Half of the 19th c.)], in: Μνήμων 23 (2002), pp. 40–76.

9 Charles A. FRAZEE, The Orthodox Church and Independent Greece. 1821–1852, Cambridge 1969; Dimitris STAMATOPOULOS, The Orthodox Church of Greece, in: Lucian LEUSTEAN (ed.), Eastern Christianity and Nationalism in Nineteenth-Century Europe, New York 2014, pp. 34–64. From the perspective of the post-Ottoman Balkans, we might say that the model of subjugation of the church to the state through autocephaly was dominant: The autocephalous ecclesiastical organisations were turned into mechanisms for legitimising the newly founded states ideologically and played a decisive role in creating national identity. We might also say unreservedly that this model came to dominance through Russia: The eighteenth-century reforms of Peter the Great had already presaged that the ruler would be the »head« of the church, vesting the ecclesiastical power in a »Permanent Holy Synod«. The purpose of this was to weaken the official head of the Russian Church, the Patriarch (the Metropolitan of Moscow) – who, as demonstrated in the past, had the capacity to develop into a power figure out of the Tsar's control. All this was repeated in the Greek Autocephalous Church, as well as in other Balkan Churches.

10 After the expulsion of the Bavarian royal couple of Otto and Amalia in 1862, the new pro-English King George I (of the house of Glücksburg) was forced to proclaim a new constitution in 1864, which introduced universal suffrage for the first time in the political history of Greece and was in the same time a pioneering project in the wider European context.

adapt it to theories of the nation-state. When the Holy Canons were invoked, their legislative element was not theological authenticity, but the fact that they represented that version of the Christian religion best suited to the nation-state model of constitutional monarchy. In contrast, the *General Regulations* as the most important expression of the reformation (»secularism«) movement within the Orthodox *millet* should have been invoked only to the degree that they did not provoke imbalances in the model of the »innate« constitutionality of Orthodoxy.

It seems then as if the »reformation« in the Orthodox *millet*, considered as a process of secularisation, joined the state and the church in a relation not of classification, but of reflection. The state did not classify religion – we could further argue that it undermined the traditional ruling force. On the other hand, however, of interest here is also the religious attempt to be part of the political field through the adoption of state models. In order to settle the issues of social and political hegemony within the *millet*, the representatives of the opposed wing invoked a superior ideology – a symbolic reality – of the organic relation between Orthodoxy and the constitutional model, precisely to legitimise the defence of their proportional interests. This invocation, however, would contribute to the blurring of boundaries between the two spheres – religious and political – one of the most important peculiarities of the Balkan region.

This return to Augustine, however, namely the likening of the religious and the political, might be considered common to both the Roman Catholic and the Orthodox Churches at the end of the nineteenth century. This return did not simply recall the distinction between the City of God and the City of Man[11], but the organisation of the latter according to the principles of the former. Did this return have the wider aim of settling intra-communal clashes? In my opinion, the problem is connected to the emergence of what we would call »civil society«[12].

The Reform Paradoxes

The »National« Assembly was convened with two major aims: to give the laity a role in the Patriarchal election process and in church administration (which was seen as a form of Protestant influence), and to distinguish the »material« (financial)

---

11 AUGUSTINE, De Civitate Dei [Bibliotheca scriptorum Graecorum et Romanorum Teubneriana], Leipzig 1928–1929, XIV.28; XV.1 & 21.
12 Şerif MARDİN, Civil Society and Islam, in: John A. HALL (ed.), Civil Society. Theory, History, Comparison, Cambridge 1995, pp. 278–300, at pp. 292f.; see also id., Ideology and Religion in the Turkish Revolution, in: International Journal of Middle East Studies 2 (1971), pp. 197–211; for further details, see Dimitris STAMATOPOULOS, Orthodox Church and Civil Society in the Ottoman Balkans. The Model of Annexation and the Control of the Private Sphere, Erfurt 2019.

jurisdictions from the »spiritual«. Material jurisdictions would now be exercised by the Mixed Council, while the Holy Synod would have jurisdiction over the spiritual, with both bodies under Patriarchal oversight. But this arrangement led to a paradox.

Stephanos Karatheodoris, the leader of the reformist wing in the »National« Assembly and personal physician of the last Sultan, Abdul Mecid II (r. 1922–1924), sought to legitimise the laity's institutionalisation in the election process by pointing out that the Patriarchal institution combined political and spiritual elements. Consequently, if the Holy Synod's senior clergy legitimately participated in the election because of the institution's spiritual nature, then the laity had the same rights because of the Patriarch's political authority. Therefore, he defended the laity's participation in church administration by linking it to the legitimacy the Patriarchal institution derived from its political authority – that is, the Patriarch as a mediator between the Sublime Porte and the Orthodox subjects. This expanded the problem at its base: It was not simply about lay participation, but rather about the participation of Ottoman subjects.

This brings us to the issue of Gerontism, in which the Ottomans officially granted senior Hierarchs (»elders«) the right to administer the affairs of the Patriarchate together with the Patriarch. Gerontism, whose supporters recognised the same unity of the spiritual and political elements in the Patriarchal institution, had been prevalent in the Patriarchate's administration since the mid-eighteenth century and was directly challenged by the reform movement. As a result, the establishment of the Gerontist regime weakened the Patriarch's power. The Patriarchal seal was split in four and divided among members of the Holy Synod, who thereby acquired a »standing« status. The Gerontist Holy Synod in fact brought to Constantinople the model of the Russian Standing Holy Synod of Tsar Peter the Great. The system seems to have been weighted towards the clerical elite rather than bolstering the Phanariots. This is evident from the fact that the imposition of this administrative system was based mainly on a stringent financial monitoring of the provincial metropolitans by the Gerontes, that is, the permanent senior metropolitans on the Holy Synod. And here lies the first paradox: The »democratisation« process of the Tanzimat reforms, namely the participation of laymen in Patriarchal administration, was coming to doubt the limitation of the Patriarch's competencies as it was expressed in eighteenth-century Gerontism. Long before the nationalised autocephalous Orthodox Churches used the synodal system as expression of the supposed »democratic« spirit of the Orthodoxy in the nineteenth century, the Patriarchate of Constantinople followed the Russian model of the restriction of its »absolute monarchism« by the »aristocrat« metropolitans of the Gerontist Holy Synod.

However, the latter, seeking to defend the Patriarchal institution's »ethnarchic«[13] character in order to safeguard the elder metropolitans' rights to exercise their political and spiritual duties, placed special emphasis on its spiritual dimension. According to them, a prerequisite for the »ethnarchic« tradition was not only an identification with the religious element, but the latter's predominance over the former.

If such arguments were logical in the case of the clericalist wing as long as they were not in danger of shattering its unity, it was different in the case of Stephanos Karatheodoris and the reformist wing in general, which was dissolved the moment the issue of the Mixed Council's composition was put to discussion. And this is because the reformist idea was thought to lead to a separation of the spiritual authorities from the political: The former would be exercised by the Patriarch in cooperation with the Holy Synod, while the so-called material jurisdiction (which concerned mainly the Patriarchate's finances and, by extension, its political representation before the Ottoman state) would be exercised by the Mixed Council. Thus, while Karatheodoris was forced to legitimise the laity's admission into the election process based on the unity of the political and spiritual elements, he simultaneously demanded their separation so that jurisdiction over the material would pass into lay control. This meant that in order to legitimise lay participation, the Patriarchate's »ethnarchic« dimension had to be contested; that is, the unity of the spiritual and political authority supposedly exercised by the Patriarch. And herein lies another contradiction: The lay element that was the source of the legality and the body over which the Patriarchate had political control would, according to the reformers' argument, also mark the restriction of the Patriarch's authority in the spiritual sphere.

This »paradox« can and must at least be interpreted within the framework of the Ottoman reformers' objectives. The separation of political and spiritual authority, which Karatheodoris was forced to support, can only be understood on the part of the Ottoman reformers as an intermediate phase for attaining their ultimate aim. This was not just to separate the political from the religious sphere at the *millet* level and the subsequent formation of mixed (clergy-laity) administrative bodies, but on another level to absorb the political authority exercised by the clergy, which would now be assumed by the lay subjects in the Ottoman Empire. This direction did not become sufficiently clear in the »National« Assembly's immediate aftermath because the Ottoman reformers Âli Paşa and Fuad Paşa had to deal with a backlash

---

13 The term is as problematic as the translation of *Millet-i Assembly* as »National Assembly« (see above fn. 3) since it appeared when the Orthodox Church in the Ottoman Empire was about to become nationalised. Similarly, »ethnarch« was the translation of the term *millet-başı*, which proclaimed the political status of the Patriarch as mediator between the Christian Orthodox subjects and the Ottoman authorities.

from the conservatives in the Ottoman government as well as the reaction of their spiritual mentor, Reşid Mehmed Paşa, who disagreed with the *Hatt-i Hümayûn* reforms in general.

From this perspective, it is interesting to see how the issue was approached in a diatribe published in instalments in Ὁμόνοια (*Concord*), the clericalists' organ and the Patriarchate's official newspaper during the first term of office of Joachim II (1860–1863)[14]. The author disputed the capacity of a secular legislative body (the »National« Assembly) to address issues of spiritual nature (e. g., the election of Patriarchs). The article was signed »K.«, which may well have stood for the newspaper's publisher G. Katselidis, son-in-law of the Metropolitan Gerasimos of Chalcedon, who was one of Gerontism's most prominent advocates in the mid-nineteenth century. It is thus not impossible that these views may have also reflected those of Patriarch Joachim II, who shared Gerasimos' views.

»K.« raised a simple question: If lay participation in the election of a Patriarch at the head of the ecclesiastical structure was institutionalised, what possibility would a cleric, in any community within the Empire, have to resist the intervention of the local, usually omnipotent, *kotzambasis* (or προεστοί, influential lay notables in local Orthodox Greek communities) in ecclesiastic issues such as weddings or baptisms? Despite the seemingly exaggerated example of the *kotzambasis*, the question raised the issue of the clergy's new role in the community and what type of relationships would develop between clerics and local archons under the new regime arising from the reforms.

The metaphorical likening of church and state can only be understood in the political framework set by the Patriarchal centralist concentration of power and in the broader framework of the Tanzimat reform. Raising the issue of equality, egalitarianism, and equity in the Patriarchate's jurisdiction would only mean the end of the »aristocracy of the elders«. The dispute between Konstantinos Adosidis and Nikolaos Aristarchis, two prominent neo-Phanariots, during the 1858–1860 »National« Assembly is widely known. To Aristarchis' statement that »the holy High Priests are considered equal in the eyes of religion, but the laity is not in the eyes of the king«, Adosidis replied: »Here, in Turkey, there is no aristocracy, our government is not aristocratic, our religion teaches us equality. Therefore, since there is no aristocracy either by faith or by government, why should we create one?«[15] Here the constitutionality of the Holy Synod is directly linked to the rejection of the »aristocracy of elders« and the imposition of egalitarian rules between archpriests and the Ecumenical see. If »religion teaches equality«, then the passage

---

14 See Newspaper Ὁμόνοια 56, 17 November 1862.
15 Chrysanthos PHILIPPIDIS (Archbishop of Athens), Οἱ Γενικοὶ Κανονισμοὶ τοῦ Οἰκουμενικοῦ Πατριαρχείου ἐπὶ τῇ βάσει τοῦ κώδικος ΤΕ ΄ τοῦ Πατριαρχικοῦ Ἀρχειοφυλακείου (Πρακτικὰ Ἐθνοσυνελεύσεως, 1858–1860), Athens 1946, pp. 9f.

of the *General Regulations* stipulating a new type of Holy Synod is tantamount to the adoption of a constitution that organises the Patriarchate's internal affairs.

The image of the Patriarch as a state ruler was, however, not destined to be perceived uniformly by the opposing parties within the Patriarchate. Let us examine the development of this model in the works of some of the intellectuals of the period, starting with a representative of the reformist faction, Grigorios Pavlidis, the Holy Synod's head secretary during the 1858–1860 »National« Assembly. Pavlidis had composed the response to the reforms outlined in the Διαμαρτύρησις (*Protest*), issued by the elders after their forced eviction from Constantinople in the spring of 1859. He was later elected metropolitan of Chios where, inspired by ethnocentric ideas, he distinguished himself through his hostile treatment of the island's Roman Catholics. This resulted in the rejection of his candidacy by the Sublime Porte in the Patriarchal handover from 1871, since he did not meet the terms set by the *General Regulations* regarding Ottoman legality.

In a polemic against »heresies« – i. e., Protestantism and (especially) Roman Catholicism – Grigorios Pavlidis outlines the main criteria distinguishing them from Orthodoxy. The issue addresses a deeper order between faith and language that is preserved in Orthodoxy, but is disrupted in Protestantism and Roman Catholicism. He thus concludes his thought:

> So Papism is spiritual tyranny and waiving of logic and scientific enquiry, Protestantism is spiritual anarchy and disavowal of ecclesiastic authority and patristic tradition, while Orthodoxy is a harmony of authority and rational research, that is, faith and word […]. Papism is a centre without periphery, Protestantism is periphery without centre, while Orthodoxy is simultaneously centre and periphery[16].

In Pavlidis' view, such a disruption of the balance between faith and speech was exactly what fomented the rise of corresponding state models from the religious mould. In this case, the simulation of ecclesiastic administration with a state regime legalised the confrontation with opposing dogmas, whose influence was expanding dangerously among the Empire's peoples. But if the adoption of the constitutional model as a framework for the Ecumenical Patriarchate's future status by a representative of the reform faction seems consistent and logical, we need to explain why this view was also shared by some representatives of the clericalist faction.

In the *Omonoia* diatribe cited earlier, the author »K.« – who, as we noted, was most likely the newspaper's publisher, G. Katselidis – in attempting to legitimise positions favouring the strengthening of Patriarchal power and the restriction of

---

16 Grigorios Pavlidis (Metropolitan of Chios), Ἡ Φωνὴ τῆς Ὀρθοδοξίας, Chios 1863.

de jure lay authority, also drew a parallel between the three major Christian dogmas and corresponding state regimes.

> Mistakes ultimately become lessons, and between unfettered democracy and absolute tyranny, a new excellent type of amalgamated government was devised, that of constitutional monarchy. We have written before in *Omonoia* that of the Christian Churches' three main branches, the Protestant often leaned towards unfettered democracy, the Roman Catholic towards absolutist tyranny, while only the Orthodox Church, which maintains Christ's robe seamless and whole, desires and preserves an organisation that is constitutional and parliamentary[17].

His argument impressively resembles that made by Grigorios Pavlidis, although »K.« goes a step further by attempting an outline of constitutional government. Thus, it is not constitutionality in general that is sought, but rather an ecclesiastical regime that simulates constitutional monarchy. Naturally, the role of the constitutional archon would be filled by the Patriarch. If the Patriarchate had to quietly accept reform, this is because it held the possibility of the return to a regime wherein the Patriarch would reacquire the autonomy lost as a result of the elders' interventions, yet without turning the Patriarch into an absolute monarch.

The operationalisation of the constitutionality model is not the same in the arguments of the two rival factions. In any case, it served different political agendas. Whereas, in the case of Grigorios Pavlidis, the reference to the constitutionality of Orthodoxy aimed at legitimising the imposition of the *General Regulations* in pursuit of national identity, as we shall see later, in »K.'s« case, the reference aimed at constructing the Patriarch's image as a constitutional monarch, who had to meet the prerequisites set by the constitution, but at the same time be in a position to rule the church without being a pawn of either the Holy Synod or the Mixed Council. In »K.'s« case, the condemnation of »unfettered democracy« that corresponded to the Protestant version of Christianity aimed precisely at the participation of the laity, which was threatening to limit the clergy's authority in spiritual matters.

However, not the entire clericalist faction accepted the model. There was a current, represented at that time chiefly by Patriarch Gregory VI, which drew attention to the model's dangers. In early 1867, just before Gregory's election as Patriarch, Efstathios Kleovoulos – an archimandrite and later deputy (*protosyncellus*) of the Patriarch – sent a letter to the newspaper *Βυζαντίς* (*Byzantium*), published by Dimitrios Xenis, who was known for his pro-Russian stance.

---

17 »K.« (G. Katselidis), [no title], in: Newspaper Ὁμόνοια 57, 21 November 1862.

Kleovoulos' letter effectively supported Grigorios' rise to the Patriarchal throne and opposed Joachim, another candidate. Kleovoulos agreed with the view expressed by Xenis regarding the life tenure of the Patriarch. In his opinion, however, the most important issue concerned the authority that the Patriarch exercised (»what and how much authority does the Ecumenical Patriarch hold?«); in other words, what was his relationship to the Holy Synod and the Mixed Council? In an article brimming with sarcasm, he took aim at the pretensions of constitutionalism:

> [...] But since 1858, minds have changed and those who were considered the pillars of the people on account of their wealth, education or profession did not hesitate to project and declare the Son of God and Saviour of the World as the constitutional president of the twelve fishermen and that the majority opinion of them could raise or eject him according to the parliamentary ethic [...]; in other words, like a mere clerk of twelve high priests or eight parish elders of random abilities [...]; and the Patriarchal Synod [...] as equal and equivalent to the parish representatives[18].

It is, however, interesting that this bloc of clericalists, which did not accept the separation of spiritual and material authority and thus defended a classic »ethnarchic« model of Patriarchal authority and demanded that the *General Regulations* be adapted to canon law and not the other way around, would more easily and with greater honesty attach itself to the positions of Constantinople's radical ethnocentric circles than the circle of bankers and Patriarchs (Joachim II and Joachim III) that these radical ethnocentric circles supported.

The identification of clericalists and ethnocentrists resulted from shared attitudes – attitudes regarding the Orthodox *millet* rather than Patriarchal authority. As mentioned earlier, when the issue of the Bulgarian Exarchate emerged, both sides supported the view that the problem was ecclesiastical, not political. Thus, the only authority competent to resolve it was the Patriarchate, not the Sublime Porte. Conversely, supporters of Patriarchal consolidation after the pattern of constitutional monarchy appeared to better accommodate the ideals of the Ottoman establishment (and consequently the Ottoman state's absorption of »political« jurisdiction »privileges«) than those who rejected the constitutional simulation.

---

18 As the newspaper *Βυζαντίς* did not publish the letter, Kleovoulos sent it to another newspaper of Constantinople, whose publisher, Vasilios Kalliphron, was a supporter of the reforms within the Patriarchate. See Efstathios KLEOVOULOS, Letter, in: Newspaper Ἀνατολικὸς Ἀστήρ 436, 28–29 February 1867.

»Europeanism«: Orthodoxy versus Nationalism?

Instituting and reproducing the model of constitutionality was catalytic, it seems, for the entire spectrum of political forces around the Patriarchate at that time, and not only for the various blocs within the clericalist movement. But if the issue of adopting the constitutional monarchy model ushered in (or translated at a symbolic level) the fragmenting of the clericalist wing, as described earlier, the issue of handling the national ideology had the same results in terms of the reformist wing's cohesion. Let us look at some of the views of the »organic intellectuals«, who supported the reforms on this issue.

A diatribe published in instalments in the newspaper Ἀνατολικὸς Ἀστήρ (*Eastern Star*) a few years earlier made use of the method we saw above – that is, Orthodoxy's contrast to Roman Catholicism (»Papism«) and Protestantism, – but not in order to elevate the former in terms of its supposed privileged relation to the institution of constitutionality. This time the criterion was the relationship of each of the three major Christian Churches/confessions with nationalism.

The unsigned diatribe was titled »European ideas, that is, Europeanism«. Based on the writing style and the author's description by the publication's editor as »one of the distinguished writers and theologians of our nation«, the author was likely the aforementioned supporter of reforms Stephanos Karatheodoris. The author understood »Europeanism« as the historical outcome of the struggle between »Papism and reform, formation and transformation, façade and post-façade«. Europeanism is compared with the meaning of Orthodoxy, to the degree that the latter shows a hostile disposition to »universal domination« and to the reverence characteristic of Papism as well as to the sense of »anarchism« typical for Protestantism[19]. The distinction between Orthodoxy and Papism/Protestantism is that, while the former sacrifices the ego to God, in the latter case »the divine things are sacrificed to the person, to the ego«[20]. But other than censuring Europeanism's secular character, the diatribe makes another important observation that mainly concerns the nature of Papism: Papism is nothing but the transformation of the ancient despotism of Rome. As such, according to the author, »Papism has nationalism as its principle […] it is the same as nationalism, [but] in the guise of Christianity, and this is why Papism is more destructive and devastating than nationalism«[21]. The author offers as an example the Romans, who had merely instrumentalised Christianity to survive as a nation.

---

19 [N.N.], European ideas, that is, Europeanism, in: Newspaper Ἀνατολικὸς Ἀστήρ 35, 29 May1862.
20 See Newspaper Ἀνατολικὸς Ἀστήρ 36, 5 June 1862 and 38, 19 June 1862.
21 See Newspaper Ἀνατολικὸς Ἀστήρ 39, 26 June 1862.

Equating Papism with nationalism was especially efficient. The arguments used struck at both supporters of the national ideology, which appeared as a particularly strong option for the reform of the *millet*, as well as – and mainly – for the supporters of the Patriarchal centralist consolidation of authority. (Earlier we also saw how Katselidis flirted with the Papal model on this point.) Thus, the author's target was Patriarch Joachim II's attempt to divert the reform effort towards the construction of a »Papal« model of Patriarchal power. On the other hand, the simultaneous condemnation of Papism and nationalism served to recall the then-intense problem of the Uniatism's expansion to the Bulgarians – a problem that the reformers blamed on Joachim II.

Conversely, the author's criticism of Protestantism was milder. He believed the Reformation was the work of the Teutonic and Germanic peoples suffering under the despotism of Ancient Rome and Papism. Yet the Reformation had gone to the opposite extreme, namely to »anarchy«, in an exaggerated reaction to Papism. The diatribe, nonetheless, linked Protestantism to nationalism only to the degree that it also used the »weapons« of Papism[22]. Here the more favourable treatment of Protestantism certainly derived from the special role of the laity in the Protestant-style church administration.

We can also observe a similar treatment of the Anglican Church by Grigorios Pavlidis. Accusing the Western »sects«, Roman Catholicism and Protestantism, of abandoning the authority of the Holy Synod, he excludes the Anglican Church from this accusation. In his view, after fierce clashes with hard-line Calvinists, Anglicanism had defended the »synodal stature and tradition of the ancient church«. He also recalls the efforts for a convergence between Orthodoxy and Protestantism by Patriarch of Constantinople Jeremias III in 1723 (although not the analogous efforts of the controversial Patriarch Cyril Loucaris, which led to his notorious and ill-fated »Calvinist Confession«).

In Pavlidis' case, the means he chose to splice together the transcendent (or spiritual) with the rational – which we discussed earlier – did not imply only the reference to a different type of statehood, but also the need for people to choose one of these national identities. What interested him was the case of the Greeks. For Grigorios Pavlidis,

> the Greek, in such a display of disgust, above all opposed the two divergences of the polity […]. It was obvious that it was impossible for him to recognise in his spiritual homeland […]) either the sovereignty and the absolute dominance of a mortal man [the

---

22 See Newspaper Ἀνατολικὸς Ἀστήρ 41, 10 July 1862.

model of Roman Catholicism] [...] or polyarchy and anarchy [the model of Protestantism], which as in political so and in religious society, is the most formidable of tyrannies[23].

Conversely, the Greek »was obliged to remain a faithful and dedicated worshipper of Orthodoxy's God-like and synodal constitution«. Pavlidis' argument does not just leave open the possibility of linking reform to national ideology; it sees this as necessary.

If constitutional monarchy is the state model that corresponds to the nature of Orthodoxy, it is open to question whether the direct correlation of the religious with the state refers to a type of national identity – in our case, the Greek. For the reformist cleric Grigorios Pavlidis, the answer is yes. For Stephanos Karatheodoris, one of the lay representatives of the reformist wing, the answer is no. This fissure in the reformist wing regarding the national idea will not become as visible as that within the clergy-laity wing over the imposition of the Patriarchal concentration-of-power model. This is because the problem was handled appropriately by the ruling group of bankers.

»K.«, who wrote the above-mentioned diatribe in Ὁμόνοια, fully understood the »nationalisation« of laity as a process to make it more menacing to the Empire's social cohesion and thus by extension also to the traditional ecumenical model of the Orthodox world. Attacking the supporters of reform, and especially the rival newspaper Ἀνατολικὸς Ἀστήρ, he will denounce them as defenders of »nationalism«:

> And [the editors of Ἀνατολικὸς Ἀστήρ] who, on the one hand abet and for their own interest coddle this misconduct, have dubbed themselves »Nationalists« (by worthy of their pay!), on the other hand, after consideration, try through peaceful means to smooth over any objections raised by dubbing these [supporters of reform] »anti-national«; they, thus, dance to the tune of their paymaster, for in truth these words »national« and »antinational« have no meaning, as the infamous Populism reaches its extreme! (There is no charge more severe than that of Populism)[24].

For »K.«, the defence of the constitutional model did not necessarily mean the defence of Greek national identity, as was the case with Grigorios Pavlidis. Conversely, for the latter, the term »national« was negatively connoted, and it is hardly certain that the model of Patriarchal centralism that he defended should be translated into the ethnarchic *millet-başı* model.

---

23 Pavlidis, Ἡ Φωνὴ τῆς Ὀρθοδοξίας.
24 »K.« (G. Katselidis), [no title], in: Newspaper Ὁμόνοια 56 (17 November 1862).

Conclusions

If someone was searching in the history of the Ottoman Empire for a culmination of a process of confessionalisation, namely the formation or consolidation of religious identities as constituents of a state building, along the lines suggested by the German historians Wolfgang Reinhard and Heinz Schilling, it would have to be during the so-called second phase of the Tanzimat reforms. The imperial decree of 1856 began a process of reconstruction of non-Muslim religious communities (*millets*). Some historians even speak of a fundamental reinvention of religious communities in the sense that for the first time they were engaged in developing a discourse on defending their »ancient privileges« in front of the Sublime Porte. Though these »privileges« were real, their »antiquity« was often fabricated or exaggerated. But what was the logic of this reconstruction of the *millet* system?

Most importantly, it institutionalised the participation of the laity in the administration of religious mechanisms; something that was perceived by contemporary observers of the time as the direct influence of a Protestant conception of the association of clergy and laity – and this idea was in fact promoted by Stratford Canning, the British ambassador in Istanbul, himself. In fact, the *millet* assemblies convened in the following years were characterised by intense clashes between the high clergy, which wished to maintain its privileges, and the reformers, who had aligned themselves with the basic political directions of the Ottoman government.

The Armenian *millet* experienced the most intense of these clashes, but as early as the 1830s, two more *millets* had sprung from it, the Roman Catholic and the Protestant. In fact, in the case of the Armenians, we have the only successful process of conversion to Western doctrines, and this happened because the questioning of the supreme clergy begun very early by powerful members of the Armenian bourgeoisie. In the case of the Jews, there were also conflicts, but mainly at a regional level, which can be explained by the non-centralised character of the *millet* (the great dispersion of Sephardi, Askenazi, and Romaniote Jews and their synagogues throughout the Empire).

In the case of *Rum millet*, namely the Greek Orthodox religious community, which was also the most numerous in the Empire, the clergy not only managed to resist the questioning of its privileges, but also to reproduce its dominant social status, at least until the catastrophe of 1922 in Asia Minor. The reformists managed to impose the participation of laity in the administration of the Patriarchate, but the election of the Patriarch depended in the end on the clergy: The laymen would have to choose three candidates, but the final election of the Patriarch was made by the Holy Synod. By preserving the right to control the office of the Patriarch, who was considered not only a religious but also a political leader, the high clergy confirmed its strong position at the top of the *millet* hierarchy.

These were the reasons that 15 years ago, when I published my dissertation, I called what happened in the late 1850s in Constantinople a »failed secularisation«. However, this failed secularisation created the conditions for a »failed confessionalisation« as well. For the Ottomans, of course, the problem of the reorganisation of religious communities had nothing to do with doctrinal issues, but with some basic aims: first, to detach the political, economic and judicial powers from the Orthodox clergy (which would only have spiritual competencies), and second, to absorb them into Ottoman mechanisms of administration.

Through the creation of small parliaments within the *millets*, the Ottomans sought to avoid the creation of a regular parliament. However, the failure of the 1876 experiment with the rise of Sultan Abdul Hamid II to the throne and the prevalence of Pan-Islamism as a sovereign state ideology, renewed the religious legitimacy of the Empire's institutions, with the consequence that the »absorption« of the material background of the *millets* could not take place. At the same time, the modernisation of the Empire would once more be postponed, which means – to put it another way – till the Greek calends. In fact, failed confessionalisation meant the transformation of the Ottoman Empire's populations into national bodies while old religious communities became »ethnic minorities«.

The perception of the church as a body analogous to the state on the part both the reformists and some within the clergy-laity wing as well as its repetition and construction described above had a catalytic effect in shaping the relationship between the religious and the political. It is characteristic that even when the representatives of the clergy-laity wing were forced to defend the authority of canon law versus the constitutionality of the *General Regulations*, they were forced to do so through theories of state. When canon law was invoked, the element of their legitimation was not theological authority, but the fact that at that time they represented the branch of the Christian faith that was most compatible with the state model of constitutional monarchy. Accordingly, the *General Regulations*, as the most important expression of the reformist (»secularising«) movement within the Orthodox *millet*, had to exist, but only to the degree that they did not cause imbalances in the model of Orthodoxy's »intrinsic« constitutionality.

It thus seems as if reforms in the Orthodox *millet*, seen as a process of secularising it, put the political and the religious in a relationship not quite of subjection, but of reflexes and refractions. On the one hand, the political sphere did not dominate the religious; rather, we might say it undermined its traditional canonical power. On the other hand, the religious sphere tried to reproduce itself by adopting state models. This process preserved a blurred boundary between the two. As a consequence, most critically, it obstructed the construction of a society of citizens, even though this discussion itself could be considered as the cornerstone of the latter's emergence.

Daniela Kalkandjieva

The Political Theology of the Bulgarian Orthodox Church Between Ecclesiology, Nationalism and Modernity (1870–1922)

Introduction

Contemporary scholars employ »political theology« as an umbrella term that covers a broad set of visions developed by different religious traditions regarding their relationship with the realm of politics. According to Annika Thiem, its origins were to be found in Stoic teaching about the division of theology into *theologia mythikē, physikē*, and *politikē*. Within this philosophical framework, political theology was associated with »cultic practices as a means of public governance«[1]. At the beginning of the fifth century, however, Christian thinkers launched a bitter criticism of pagan political theology. As a result, this wording disappeared until the seventeenth century, when it re-emerged in philosophical treatises as a reference to the deification of leaders in antiquity[2]. At the same time, its use as a conceptual framework for the study of the relationship between religion, society, and politics is a modern development linked to the process of secularisation[3]. Although the last rediscovery of the term occurs in Mikhail Bakunin's *The Political Theology of Mazzini and the International* (1886), its contemporary meaning is widely associated with Carl Schmitt's *Political Theology* (1922), which popularised the idea of the religious roots of modern political theory[4].

Over the last century, the study of political theology has made considerable progress, especially in the cases of Catholicism, Lutheranism, Anglicanism, and Calvinism. Yet Eastern Orthodoxy has only recently attracted the attention of researchers[5], who have highlighted the failure of this religious tradition to create a

---

1 Annika THIEM, Political Theology, in: Michael GIBBONS (ed.), Encyclopedia of Political Thought, Chichester 2015, pp. 1–15, at p. 1.
2 Ibid., p. 4.
3 Kristina STOECKL, Modernity and Political Theologies, in: Ead. et al. (eds.), Political Theologies in Orthodox Christianity, London 2017, pp. 15–24, at p. 15.
4 THIEM, Political Theology, p. 7; see also Pantelis KALAITZIDIS, Orthodoxy and Political Theology, Geneva 2012, pp. 15–44.
5 Aristotle PAPANIKOLAOU, The Mystical as Political. Democracy and Non-radical Orthodoxy, Notre Dame, IN 2012; KALAITZIDIS, Orthodoxy; STOECKL et al. (eds.), Political Theologies.

political theology that is simultaneously consistent with its theology and practice while being adequate to the norms of liberal democracy[6]. In the view of these scholars, this weakness has historical roots[7], specifically in the subordinate status of most Orthodox Churches under the Ottoman sultans and, later, communist regimes, as well as in the restraining effect of ethno-religious nationalism on these churches[8]. At the same time, it is worth mentioning that the pre-1917 Russian Orthodox Church, which operated in a polity dominated by Orthodoxy, also failed to produce an original political theology. Instead, it was strongly influenced by Western Christianity »in terms of its language, its presuppositions, and its thinking«[9]. In short, all these developments did not allow the Orthodox Churches to take an active part in major twentieth-century theological discussions[10].

At present, the study of Orthodox political theology concentrates predominantly on the Byzantine era and the works of the early Church Fathers. Meanwhile, modern developments are analysed mostly with reference to the works of Russian religious thinkers. This leaves the contribution of the other Orthodox Churches critically underexplored. Furthermore, despite the two-way relationship between theology and politics, most analysts do not go beyond the responses of Orthodox Churches to the challenge of politics. Therefore, they fail to reveal how »varying political orientations and practices influence the consequent theological reformulations of the understanding of central notions, such as authority, the human condition, and history and the human tasks in it«[11].

From the perspective of this state of affairs in the study of Orthodox political theology, this chapter pursues a twofold goal: to provide information about the lesser-known case of the Bulgarian Orthodox Church and to demonstrate the impact of secular politics on its political theology. In particular, it examines the impact of nationalism and Bulgaria's defeat in World War I on the church's vision of its mission, autonomy, and authority. In this regard, it also discloses the different roles played by the episcopate, clergy, and laity in the invention and reconsideration of Bulgarian political theology. For this purpose, I have employed multiple archival

---

6 PAPANIKOLAOU, The Mystical as Political, p. 5, 195.
7 PAPANIKOLAOU, The Mystical as Political; Alfred STEPAN, Religion, Democracy, and the »Twin Tolerations«, in: Journal of Democracy, 11/4 (2000), pp. 37–57, at p. 52; Peter L. BERGER, Orthodoxy and Global, Pluralism, in: Wallace L. DANIEL et al. (eds.), Perspectives on Church-State Relations in Russia, Waco, TX 2008, pp. 7–17, at p. 12.
8 KALAITZIDIS, Orthodoxy, pp. 68f.; Vasilios N. MAKRIDES, Political Theology in Orthodox Christian Contexts. Specificities and Particularities in Comparison with Western Latin Christianity, in: STOECKL et al. (eds.), Political Theologies, pp. 25–54, at p. 42.
9 KALAITZIDIS, Orthodoxy, p. 75.
10 Ibid., p. 76.
11 THIEM, Political Theology, p. 3.

and published documents that reveal the church's attempts to cope with changed political realities at home and abroad.

Bulgarian Political Theology in the Age of Nationalism

The advent of nationalism in Southeastern Europe coincided with the disintegration of the Ottoman Empire. Both processes brought about radical change, not only on the political map of the region, but also on the religious one. More specifically, they stimulated the creation of national Orthodox Churches, which tended to associate their mission with the salvation of a particular nation. Since the nation came to be perceived as an eternal ethno-religious body, this idea seriously undermined the universalist ethos of Christianity[12]. Established in 1870 under the name »Bulgarian Exarchate«, the modern Bulgarian Orthodox Church was no exception. Correspondingly, its modern political theology took shape under the influence of »the emerging ethno-religious nationalisms in the Balkans«[13]. In contrast with the churches in Greece, Serbia, and Romania, however, the Bulgarian one was not set up by an Orthodox authority, but by the Ottoman ruler – i. e., in agreement not with canon law, but with the laws of a non-Christian polity.

More specifically, being created by a sultan's decree, the Bulgarian Exarchate found itself in a bizarre situation: It enjoyed legal recognition within the Ottoman Empire, but its canonical legitimacy was questioned by other Orthodox Churches. In 1872, these tensions were further aggravated by the decision of the Patriarchate of Constantinople to declare the young Bulgarian Church schismatic, thereby blocking it from canonical communication with the other Orthodox Churches[14]. At the time, the Exarchate was not able to rely on the support of its own nation-state, unlike the Orthodox Churches of Greece, Serbia, Romania, and Albania. As a result, the main factor in shaping its early political theology turned out not to be the state, but the laity, whose moral and material support was decisive for the establishment and the survival of the Bulgarian Orthodox Church. In this regard, it is essential to stress that 80 per cent of the deputies in the First Popular Church Council (1871), who adopted the first statute of the modern Bulgarian Orthodox Church and elected its first

---

12 KALAITZIDIS, Orthodoxy, pp. 68–70.
13 MAKRIDES, Political Theology, p. 42.
14 This issue is discussed in detail in Daniela KALKANDJIEVA, The Bulgarian Orthodox Church, in: Lucian N. LEUSTEAN (ed.), Orthodox Christianity and Nationalism in Nineteenth Century Southeastern Europe Century, New York 2014, pp. 164–201.

Exarch, were laymen[15]. This peculiarity determined the young Bulgarian Church's vision of its role in society and its relations with the political and ecclesiastical authorities in the Balkans for decades to come.

Besides, the sultan's decree established not only a new religious institution, but also a new »millet«, that of Bulgaria. Taking into account the changes introduced in the Ottoman legislation after the Crimean War (1853–1856), this act meant that the Exarchate's members were recognised as a separate nation[16]. Correspondingly, the Bulgarian Exarch was not merely a religious leader, but a representative of the civil, linguistic, and ethnic rights of his Orthodox compatriots before the Sublime Porte. In addition, the 1870 decree guaranteed broad institutional autonomy to the Exarchate. More specifically, it imposed a ban on the Patriarchal See of Constantinople from intervening in the affairs of the new church (Article 3) while obliging the Bulgarian Exarch to seek the advice of the former in the sphere of theological matters (Article 6) and to receive the Holy Myron from it (Article 7).

No less important is that the sultan's decree outlined the Exarchate's territory. It listed the dioceses of the new Orthodox Church and envisioned a mechanism through which new ones might join it in the future (Article 10). It also allowed for the transfer of a diocese from the Patriarchate to the Exarchate by a majority of two thirds of the faithful in a referendum. Over the subsequent years, the Exarchate successfully used this mechanism to spread its jurisdiction over new dioceses[17]. In this regard, it is necessary to underline that some referenda took place before the Liberation of Bulgaria (1878), i. e., the Bulgarian Orthodox Church's initial territorial growth occurred without the assistance of a nation-state. This is another feature that distinguishes the Bulgarian case from those of the other national Orthodox Churches in Southeastern Europe, those of Greece, Serbia, Romania, Albania, and more recently North Macedonia. This also means that, despite the entanglement of religion with Bulgarian nationalism, the early formation of Bulgarian political theology was free of state influence. Furthermore, the fact that the Bulgarian Orthodox Church was constituted before the corresponding nation-state conditioned the development of a political theology that emphasised the Exarchate's role as a guardian of the national identity of Bulgarians against the neighbouring Orthodox

---

15 The First Church Popular Council consisted of five hierarchs, one archimandrite, four priests, and 40 laymen, see Hristo TEMELSKI (ed.), Tsarkovno-narodniyat sabor, 1871 g. [The Church-Popular Council 1871], Sofia 2001, pp. 60–62.

16 Simeon EVSTATIEV, Milletic Secularism in the Balkans. Christianity, Islam, and Identity in Bulgaria, in: Nationalities Papers 47/1 (2019), pp. 87–103.

17 The dioceses of Skopje and Ohrid joined the Bulgarian Exarchate in 1873, while those of Debar, Bitola, and Strumica (now in North Macedonia), and that of Nevrokop (the present city of Gotse Delchev in Bulgaria) did the same after the liberation of Bulgaria (1878), see Zina MARKOVA, Balgarskata Ekzarkhiya, 1870–1879 [The Bulgarian Exarchate, 1870–1879], Sofia 1989, p. 31.

Churches and especially against the Patriarchate of Constantinople. As a result, Bulgarian political theology tended initially to employ motives related to nationhood and history rather than specifically religious concepts such as the eucharist and eschatology.

While the establishment of the Principality of Bulgaria (1878) did not bring about serious changes to this paradigm, it did affect the church's organisation. To a great degree, this specific development is determined by the fact that only a part of the Exarchate's dioceses and communities of believers were included in the new Bulgarian state, while the others remained under Ottoman rule. Meanwhile, the Exarchate not only survived the political changes, but preserved its territorial jurisdiction over the dioceses situated on both sides of the Bulgarian-Ottoman border. In this way, it became the only national institution able to preserve the unity of the Bulgarian people, whether they lived in the liberated lands or those remaining under Ottoman rule. In an attempt to guarantee this function of the Bulgarian Orthodox Church, the Constitutive Assembly of the Principality included a special text in the first *Bulgarian Constitution* (1879). It reads:

> *Constituting an integral part of the Bulgarian church territory, the Bulgarian Principality, in ecclesiastical terms, is subjected to the Holy Synod* – the Supreme spiritual authority of the Bulgarian Church, *wherever this authority has been situated*. By means of this authority, the principality is kept united with the Ecumenical Eastern Church in everything that relates to the dogmas of [Orthodox] faith[18].

Having dioceses on both sides of the Bulgarian-Ottoman border, the Bulgarian Orthodox Church changed the mode of its governance. One the one hand, its Exarch chose to preserve his Ottoman citizenship and his office in Istanbul – a location that allowed him to continue to run the religious, cultural, and civil affairs of his flock in the Ottoman Empire. In contrast with pre-1878 practice, however, he was not able to secure the functioning of a Holy Synod at his office. Instead, his work was assisted only by the so-called Mixed Council – a body that consisted of laymen and clerics, elected by believers living in the Bulgarian dioceses in the Ottoman Empire.

On the other hand, a new Holy Synod was established in Sofia, the capital city of Bulgaria. It consisted of four metropolitans, who were Bulgarian citizens and whose dioceses were situated in the principality. As a result, the Synod's duties also suffered serious changes, being restricted to purely religious issues while the Bulgarian state took care of civil ones (e. g., the management of schools, municipal

---

18 See Article 39 (my emphasis). The text of the 1879 *Constitution* is available in Bulgarian on the website of the Bulgarian National Assembly: Konstitucija na Blgarskoto knjazhestvo, 1879, published by Parliament.bg, URL: <https://www.parliament.bg/bg/17> (09-12-2023).

affairs). Finally, the different political and societal conditions in the two sections of the Bulgarian Orthodox Church provoked changes in the Exarchate Statute of 1871. The Exarch's administration in the Ottoman Empire continued to observe this act, while the Holy Synod in Sofia adopted its amended version under the pressure of the Bulgarian government in 1883. The Holy Synod made a series of attempts for its revision over the following years and in 1895 succeeded in persuading the state authorities to introduce new changes. As a result, bishops obtained full control over the finances and properties of the Orthodox Church within Bulgarian territory, while the role of laity and clergy in the management of ecclesiastical affairs was drastically reduced.

To a high degree, this duality in the church's governance was facilitated by Bulgaria's status as a tributary principality of the Ottoman Empire. In 1908, however, the Young Turk Revolution allowed the political elite of Bulgaria to break free from its dependence on the Ottoman Empire and to become a sovereign kingdom. Its international recognition changed the geopolitical situation in the Balkans. Under the new conditions, the Bulgarian government continued to treat the Exarchate as a national-political institution, but gave preference to diplomacy and war as more effective tools for joining the Bulgarian population in the Ottoman provinces to its state. Neither the Balkan Wars (1912–1913) nor World War I (1914–1918), however, brought the expected results. Under the Treaty of Bucharest (28 June 1913), Bulgaria had to transfer southern Dobrudja to Romania[19]. This entailed a loss to the Bulgarian Orthodox Church of its administrative structures there as well as 300,000 believers, who were placed under the jurisdiction of the Romanian Patriarchate[20].

Meanwhile, World War I caused new losses. Under the Treaty of Neuilly (27 November 1919), 91,888 Bulgarian inhabitants of the regions of the cities of Bosilegrad and Dimitrovgrad (Serbia) as well as of Strumica (North Macedonia) became subjects of the new Kingdom of Serbs, Croats, and Slovenes, widely known as Yugoslavia. Correspondingly, the local Bulgarian parishes were placed under the jurisdiction of the Serbian Orthodox Church. Besides, the Bulgarian Exarchate's structures in the Ottoman provinces disappeared after the division of Macedonia between Greece and Serbia. As a result, 617,077 of its members came under the jurisdiction of the Kingdom of Serbs, Croats, and Slovenians and its Orthodox Church. The same happened with the 183,530 Orthodox Bulgarians who lived in the post-1913 territory of Greece[21]. In its turn, the Sublime Porte

---

19 In 1940, the Treaty of Craiova returned southern Dobrudja to Bulgaria, and the Bulgarian Orthodox Church restored its jurisdiction there.
20 Nikola STANEV, Nay-nova istoriya na Balgariya, 1912–1920 [The Newest History of Bulgaria, 1912–1920], vol. 2: Voyni za obedinenie [Unification Wars], Sofia 1925, p. 146.
21 Ibid., p. 138.

forced 51,127 Bulgarians from Asia Minor and other Turkish provinces to abandon their homes and to move to Bulgaria, thus making space for the Turkish refugees from Macedonia and Thrace[22]. Since, under these circumstances, the Bulgarian Exarch had no more flock to administrate in Macedonia and Aegean Thrace, he left Istanbul and settled in Sofia. After his death in 1915, the Bulgarian Holy Synod began to elect one of its members as temporary vicar-chair (*Namestnik Predsedatel*), a practice that ended with the election of the next Exarch of Bulgaria in 1945.

Furthermore, during the peace negotiations, the schismatic status of the Bulgarian Orthodox Church did not allow its hierarchy to refer to canon law as a means of preserving its administration over these areas. Therefore, the Sofia-based Holy Synod used secular rather than religious arguments in its memorandum addressed to the representatives of the victorious states who had gathered in Paris to draw the post-war map of Europe[23]. Taking advantage of Woodrow Wilson's principle of the self-determination of nations, the Bulgarian hierarchs built their motives on the studies of Western scholars about the Bulgarian nation and historical sources as well as on relevant decisions taken by the Istanbul Conference of the Great Powers (1876) and the Treaty of San Stefano (1878). They also stressed that the Bulgarian Orthodox Church was the »gatherer and guardian of the Bulgarian people« throughout the centuries. The Synodal memorandum also outlined the imaginary boundaries of the Bulgarian Orthodox Church by specifying the areas inhabited by the Orthodox Bulgarians, which included Bulgaria proper and the regions of Macedonia, Thrace, Doburdja, and Pomoravlje (today in eastern Serbia). In this regard, the only theological reference made was an allusion to the crucifixion of Jesus Christ in the appeal for the Bulgarian nation, described as bearing a crown of thorns, to be shown Christian mercy.

The memorandum had no effect. The Treaty of Neuilly (27 November 1919) buried the Holy Synod's hopes of preserving the church's jurisdiction outside the post-war borders of Bulgaria. For the first time since 1878, the Exarchate's territory overlapped with that of the state, and the Bulgarian Orthodox Church became a truly domestic institution, i. e., the Bulgarian state became the only party with which the Bulgarian Orthodox hierarchs had to negotiate the legal status and public activities of their church. The previous duality in the church's governance also disappeared. All this called for a paradigm shift.

---

22 Ibid., p. 147.
23 TsDA [Tsentralen Darzhaven Arhiv – Central State Archive], f. [fonds] 791k, op. [inventory] 1, a.e. [archival unit] 32, Proceedings of the Holy Synod, No. 17 from 8 April 1919, § 36.

Towards a New Paradigm

The Treaty of Neuilly shifted the focus of the Bulgarian Orthodox Church from the issue of national unity to its inner ecclesiastical affairs. In this regard, the most burning question was that of the Exarchate Statute. On the one hand, the loss of the dioceses in the former Ottoman provinces meant that its original version of 1871 has ceased to apply. The Bulgarian ecclesiastical and secular authorities, however, abstained from its official suspension, since such an act would have cast doubt on the very foundations of their church. On the other hand, the 1895 Exarchate Statute stirred up bitter disappointment among laity and clergy who perceived the new regulations as a betrayal of the principles of conciliarity on which the Exarchate had been originally built. In their view, this act identified the church with the Holy Synod rather than the community of believers[24]. In particular, laymen and priests opposed the new texts that diminished their role in the governance of church affairs, while empowering the episcopate to introduce changes in the Statute without the approval of the Church Popular Council. On these grounds, the dissidents called for a restoration of their previous rights, namely to participate in the governance of church affairs on an equal footing with bishops[25]. In the meantime, the post-Neuilly shrinking of the church's territorial jurisdiction to the state borders and the approaching fiftieth anniversary of the first Church Popular Council (1871) gave a new impetus to their campaign for transforming the Bulgarian Orthodox Church into a »public institution«[26].

Facing these challenges, on 6 November 1919 the Holy Synod set up a special Ecclesiastical Commission tasked with analysing the Exarchate Statute(s) and other church-related legislation in Bulgaria in the light of the post-war situation and with drafting amendments[27]. Under the chairmanship of Metropolitan Simeon of Varna, its members – Archimandrite Stefan (Bishop Markiyanopolski of 1921, Metropolitan of Sofia of 1922, and Exarch of Bulgaria of 1945), Archimandrite Pavel (Bishop Dragovitiyski of 1921 and Metropolitan of Stara Zagora of 1923), and Protopresbyter Stefan Zankow – held a series of sessions between 22 February and 19 July 1920[28]. According to some contemporaries, the initial idea of the Holy

---

24 Hristo VARGOV, Konstitutsiyata na Balgarskata pravoslavna tsarkva. Istroiya i razvoy na Ekzarhiyskiya ustav [The Constitution of the Bulgarian Orthodox Church. The History and Development of the Exarchate Statute], Sofia 1920, p. 541.
25 Ibid., p. 509.
26 Ibid., p. 487.
27 TsDA, f. 166k, op. 1, a.e. 53, Letter from the Synod's Vicar-Chair Metropolitan Vasilii of Dorostol and Cherven to the Minister of Foreign and Religious Affairs, 6 December 1919, pp. 2f.
28 Protokoli na Duhovnata Komisiya za preglezhdane na Ekzarhiyskiya ustav i vsichki deystvuvashti dnes vav vedomstvoto na Bylgarskata pravoslavna tsarkva tsarkovni naredbi [Proceedings of the

Synod was to introduce changes in the Exarchate Statute without seeking their approval by a church popular council, as had been the rule since 1895[29].

When the Synod informed the Ministry of Foreign and Religious Affairs about the Commission's work, however, the government instigated steps towards the convocation of a church popular council[30]. In response, on 28 September 1920 the hierarchs sent a letter of protest to the Minister of Foreign and Religious Affairs, invoking the constitutional status of the Holy Synod as the supreme spiritual power of the Bulgarian Orthodox Church as an argument that this institution alone was entitled to pass decisions on all church-related issues[31]. According to the church's leadership, the state legislative authorities were allowed to give consent for certain religious initiatives, but *only upon the issuance of the corresponding decision and its blessing by the Holy Synod*. In this regard, the Orthodox hierarchy declared its readiness to organise a church popular council with the participation of the episcopate, clergy, and laity to discuss and adopt the future Exarchate Statute.

The state, however, went on with its plan. On 6 October 1920 the National Assembly voted a law on the convocation of a church popular council[32]. One of its paragraphs abolished the Holy Synod's privilege to approve or disapprove any state initiatives concerning the local Orthodox Church, which had been established by the 1895 Adapted Exarchate Statute (Article 180). At the same time, it restored the principle of state consent in the case of convoking church popular councils, as required by the Exarchate Statute of 1871 (Article 134) and the adapted one of 1883 (Article 105)[33]. Furthermore, the same legal act guaranteed equal rights to bishops, priests, and laymen in the decision-making process. It also secured a numerical preponderance of lay participants over churchmen (bishops, archimandrites, priests, monks). The attempts of the Orthodox hierarchs to object the bill were in vain and on 20 October Tsar Boris III signed it into law[34].

Under these circumstances, the Holy Synod resorted to passive resistance. The Ministry of Foreign and Religious Affairs, however, took countermeasures. On 30 November 1920, it appointed a special working group to prepare the rules for

---

Ecclesiastical Commission in Charge of the Reviewing the Exarchate Statute and all Currently Active Regulations on the Church's Affairs in the Kingdom of Bulgaria], Sofia 1920.

29 Vargov, Konstitutsiyata, p. 467.
30 TsDA, f. 166k, op. 1, a.e. 53, Letter from the Synod's Vicar-Chair, Metropolitan Vasilii of Dorostol and Cherven, to the Minister of Foreign and Religious Affairs, 2 July 1920, p. 8.
31 TsDA, f. 166к, op. 1, a.e. 47, Letter from the Holy Synod to the Minister of Foreign and Religious Affairs, 28 September 1920, pp. 4f.
32 Vargov, Konstitutsiyata, pp. 507f.
33 TsDA, f. 791k, op. 1, a.e., 32, Proceedings of the Episcopal Conference No. 2, 4 December 1920, pp. 15f.
34 TsDA, f. 166k, op. 1, a.e. 53, Decree No. 355 for the approval of the Law on the amendment of the Exarchate Statute, 20 October 1920, p. 20.

the convocation of the Church Popular Council as well as the Council's agenda. It included three officials of the Ministry (two laymen and a priest), a schoolteacher, and a member of the National Assembly[35]. This time the Synod did not waste time and convened the Episcopal Conference on 2 December[36]. The Ministry's Working Group and the Episcopal Conference spent the next two months discussing the issue of church autonomy.

Debates on Church Autonomy

The Orthodox hierarchs and the state officials agreed about the disparate nature of church and state, but approached it differently: The former gave preference to theology, the latter to secular law. Their visions of church autonomy accordingly differed. More specifically, the Episcopal Conference stressed that the church was a divine institution set up by Jesus Christ himself. In contrast to the state, whose foundations were laid down by the Constitution, the church was established by Christ himself, by a divine will expressed in the Holy Scriptures and the Holy Tradition (*sveto predanie*)[37]. On these grounds, the Episcopal Conference concluded that the church was something distinct and separate from the state and indeed any merely human society. The church had its own autonomous sphere of activities, which was determined by its duty to serve the religious and moral needs of its flock. Therefore, any state intrusion into this sphere presented an attack against the church's exclusive rights, its inner essence, and its original purpose[38]. The main fallacy in this reasoning stems from its asymmetrical approach, in which the theological notion of the church as God's body is conflated with the Bulgarian Orthodox Church as a historically constructed institution. It also fails to address the difference between a divine will that is not restricted in time and space and the constitution of a modern state, confined by borders.

Furthermore, although the Holy Synod and the Episcopal Conference recognised the need for a church popular council, they disagreed with the state's initiative and raised the question: *Who has the right to convoke such a forum?* The Bulgarian hierarchs admitted that the Ecumenical Councils had been convoked by the Byzantine

---

35 Vargov, Konstitutsiyata, p. 512.
36 The Holy Synod in Sofia consisted of four metropolitans elected for a four-year period by all bishops (1895 Adapted Exarchate Statute, Article 27): Ekzarhiyski ustav prisposoben v Knyazhestvoto, in: Darzhaven Vestnik [State Gazette], No. 23, 30 January 1895. In parallel, in 1920, the Episcopal Conference consisted of twelve metropolitans and four non-diocesan bishops: TsDA, f. 791k, op. 1, a.e. 32, Proceedings of the Episcopal Conference No. 1, 2 December 1920, p. 2.
37 Kristina Stoeckl et al., Introduction, in: Ead. et al. (eds.), Political Theologies, pp. 1–12, at p. 5.
38 TsDA, f. 791k, op. 1, a.e. 32, Proceedings of the Episcopal Conference No. 1, 2 December 1920, p. 5.

Emperor, but argued this happened only at the request of the bishops themselves. They also held that the convocation of these forums, as well as all issues about the church's organisation and governance, fell into its own exclusive sphere and therefore concluded that the law on the Convocation of the Church Popular Council had infringed the authority of the Bulgarian Orthodox Church[39]. The Episcopal Conference also disagreed with another of the law's provisions, which organised the elections of the deputies for the Church Popular Council in accordance with the civil territorial administrative structures and entrusted them to civil judges[40]. An intriguing aspect of the defence of the church's rights was the reference to the experience of the Russian Orthodox Church, many of whose clerics and laypeople had found asylum in Bulgaria after the Bolshevik revolution. Accordingly, the Holy Synod stressed the long and thorough preparation of the Local Russian Church Council (1917–1918)[41].

In an attempt to defend the church's rights, the Episcopal Conference elaborated an alternative draft law and asked the government to assist its adoption by the National Assembly. This time, the hierarchs looked for a compromise. In contrast to their original decision to exclude state representatives from the future Church Popular Council, their draft law envisioned three such deputies[42]. Similarly, the plan for reduced lay participation in the forum was abandoned and the hierarchs accepted a slight lay preponderance of 15 to 20 over the bishops, priests, and monks[43]. At the same time, the draft obliged the state to endorse the future Church Statute without any objection. In parallel, in their correspondence with the secular authorities, the Orthodox hierarchs continuously repeated that the state had no right to introduce changes to the Exarchate Statute without the church's agreement[44]. In their view, the constitution not only had distinguished the Orthodox Church from the state, but also had explicitly guaranteed the former the right of autonomous self-government. On these grounds, the episcopate claimed exclusive authority to resolve all religious matters, including the amendments to the Exarchate Statute. The only concession the church was prepared to make was to realise these changes in collaboration with the state, that is to say, the Orthodox hierarchy did not accept the abolition of Article 180 in the Adapted Exarchate Statute of 1895[45].

---

39 TsDA, f. 791k, op. 1, a.e. 32. Proceedings of the Episcopal Conference No. 2, 3 December 1920, pp. 24–27.
40 Ibid., Proceedings of the Episcopal Conference No. 4, 6 December 1920, pp. 40f.
41 Ibid., Proceedings of the Episcopal Conference No. 1, 2 December 1920, p. 10; Proceedings No. 2, 3 December 1920, p. 27.
42 Ibid., Proceedings of the Episcopal Conference No. 5, 7 December 1920, pp. 55–57.
43 Ibid., Proceedings of the Episcopal Conference No. 4, 6 December 1920, pp. 47f.
44 Ibid., Proceedings of the Episcopal Conference No. 1, 3 December 1920, p. 5.
45 Ibid., Proceedings of the Episcopal Conference No. 7, 9 December 1920, pp. 79–81.

In its turn, the working group at the Ministry of Foreign and Religious Affairs regarded the church's inner autonomy as a condition that would allow this body to observe its specific religious principles. At the same time, it distinguished this autonomy from the separation of church and state. According to the working group, the second model required the church to cover the priestly salaries. As the Bulgarian Orthodox Church had not enough financial resources for this purpose, the group recommended the church-state separation as an ideal whose realisation had to be postponed until the church became strong enough economically. Furthermore, the debates on church-state relations revealed differences in the views of the working group's members. The majority believed that the church was simply a judicial entity and thus enjoyed the same autonomy as the other judicial entities. According to the minority opinion, the church was obliged to assist the state by offering sacred sanction to its acts and by teaching people to obey the ruling powers as divinely ordained[46].

Meanwhile, the conflict between the episcopate and the state escalated. When the hierarchs failed to secure the adoption of their draft law by negotiation, they decided to boycott the Church Popular Council. Finally, this crisis was overcome through the mediation of priests who appealed the government to find a peaceful solution. In particular, they welcomed the state position on the composition of the Council and the principle of equality of its members. In their view, this framework would allow the Council to function as an *ecclesiastical chamber* fully equipped for the role it had to play in the life of the Bulgarian Orthodox Church. At the same time, clergy invited the state authorities to accept all requirements of the Episcopal Conference except the bishops' veto over the Council's decisions, which would transform the Council into a purely consultative body subjected to the episcopate[47].

Finally, the compromise reached between the episcopate and the state allowed the opening of the Second Church Popular Council. Its sessions took place between 6 February 1921 and 6 February 1922. In its turn, the Episcopal Conference continued to function as an upper chamber in an attempt to influence the Council's decision-making process. Now, church-state relations became a secondary issue and the debate was concentrated on inner ecclesiastical matters. The discussions on them deserve special attention as they outlined a new political theology that redefined the roles of hierarchy, clergy, and laity in the management of ecclesiastical affairs in post-Neuilly Bulgaria.

---

46 TsDA, f. 166k, op. 1, a.e. 54, The Working Group's Proceedings No. 41, 1 February 1921, p. 55.
47 Ibid., pp. 90f. Letter from the editorial board of *Bratstvo* [The newspaper of the Union of Bulgarian Orthodox Priests] to the Prime Minister and the Minister of Foreign and Religious Affairs, 6 January 1921.

Tab. 1: Timeline Table

1920												1921												1922							
Feb	Mar	Apr	May	Jun	Jul	Aug	Sep	Oct	Nov	Dec		Jan	Feb	Mar	Apr	May	Jun	Jul	Aug	Sep	Oct	Nov	Dec	Jan	Feb	Mar	Apr	May	Jun	Jul	
Ecclesiastical Commission																															
								Working Group																							
										Episcopal Conference																					
												Church Popular Council																			

New Visions of the Institution of the Exarchate

Under the Treaty of Neuilly, the Sofia-based Holy Synod had no chance of realising its claims over the Exarchate's structures that had remained outside the Bulgarian borders. There were also serious doubts whether the Exarchate's vicariate (*Ekzarhiysko zamestnichestvo*) established in Istanbul upon the death of Exarch Josif (1915) would survive in the new political situation. On 26 August 1918 the sultan decreed its transformation into an Archbishopric for the Orthodox Bulgarians in Turkey[48]. Soon afterwards, however, the Treaty of Sèvres (10 August 1920) abolished all wartime Ottoman legislative acts concerning religious institutions[49]. Therefore, the Bulgarian state had to seek a new agreement with Turkey for the recognition of the former Exarchate's headquarters in Istanbul. Due to the Greco-Turkish War (1919–1922) and the subsequent peace negotiations, Bulgaria did not settle relations with Turkey until 1925[50].

Meanwhile, the Ecclesiastical Commission, the Episcopal Conference, and the Church Popular Council had to decide how to proceed with the former Exarch's office in Istanbul. In this regard, the Ecclesiastical Commission suggested that, given the new circumstances, the term »Exarchate« ought to be associated with former Exarch's office in Istanbul rather than with the notion of the church as a whole. Therefore, it proposed renaming the »Exarchate Statute« the »Statute of the Orthodox Bulgarian Church«. As it is seen, the Church's name was also modified from »Bulgarian Orthodox Church« into »Orthodox Bulgarian Church«. By emphasising the Orthodox character of this religious body, the Commission argued

---

48 TsDA, f. 791k, op. 1, a.e. 37, Proceedings of the Holy Synod No. 72, 21 July 1921, § 23.
49 Ibid., a.e. 38, Proceedings of the Holy Synod No. 12, 22 February 1922, § 4.
50 Treaty of Friendship between Bulgaria and Turkey. Singed at Angora on 18 October 1925, available in English at: Treaty of Friendship between Bulgaria and Turkey. Singed at Angora on 18 October 1925, published by Ungarisches Institut München, URL: <http://www.forost.ungarisches-institut.de/pdf/19251018-1.pdf> (09-12-2023).

that it was refuting accusations of ethnophyletism, thus facilitating its canonical recognition by the other Orthodox Churches. On this subject, the Commission also commented that »all local Orthodox Churches have well defined geographic borders« and explained that »the Bulgarian Church has its own geographic borders, which overlap with those of the Bulgarian Kingdom«, as was the case with the Russian, Serbian, or Romanian Churches[51]. From this perspective, the new name was synonymous with »the Orthodox Church in the Kingdom of Bulgaria«[52]. Correspondingly, the Commission proposed that the future Church Statute should encompass only the dioceses situated within the post-war territory of Bulgaria.

At the same time, considering the Exarchate's unsettled canonical status, the Commission did not want categorically to exclude a future expansion of the jurisdiction of its church beyond the Bulgarian state territory. According to its members, the exclusion of such an opportunity would constitute an act of betrayal of the Orthodox Bulgarians who remained outside the post-1919 Bulgarian borders and accepting the denationalisation of those Bulgarians who »would become subjects not only of foreign political and linguistic, but also of religious influences«[53]. For this reason, the Commission decided:

> While the Bulgarian Church, even within the borders of the Bulgarian Kingdom, lacks international recognition, and until there is a chance for the Bulgarians in neighbouring states, under certain circumstance, to be in touch with their native church, it does not make sense for the Bulgarian Church prematurely to give up its jurisdiction outside the Kingdom's borders without expecting reciprocal gestures on the part of [the Patriarchate of] Constantinople and the other neighbouring Orthodox Churches. When the Bulgarian Church's international status has been finally settled and the Bulgarian communities that have remained outside the borders of the Bulgarian Kingdom have received the guarantees necessary for their normal development, then the proper jurisdiction of the Bulgarian Church could be finally arranged[54].

At the same time, the working group established by the Ministry of Foreign and Religious Affairs for the convocation of the Church Popular Council adopted a different approach. It argued that the elimination of the reference to the Exarchate in the name of the future Church Statute would disappoint the Bulgarians who had remained outside the borders of post-Neuilly Bulgaria. Such a change, it claimed,

---

51 Protokoli na Duhovnata Komisiya (henceforth Proceedings of the Ecclesiastical Commission), pp. 9f.
52 Ibid., pp. 9f.
53 Ibid., p. 9.
54 Ibid.

also harboured threats to the implementation of a forthcoming international convention on minority rights, which would hopefully allow the Orthodox Bulgarians in the neighbouring Balkan states to remain under the Exarchate's jurisdiction[55]. On these grounds, the Working Group proposed that the future Exarchate Statute start with the following article: »The self-governing Bulgarian Orthodox Church is an inseparable member of the One Holy Ecumenical and Apostolic Church and consists of all Bulgarians wherever they may live«[56].

Between 6 February 1921 and 6 February 1922, the Church Popular Council and the Episcopal Conference also discussed the issue of the Exarchate. In this regard, they agreed that the new Church Statute should not contain a reference to the Istanbul location of the former Exarch's office. In their view, such a paragraph would mean that the Bulgarian Church had deserved its schismatic status. Besides, neither the sultan's decree of 1870 nor the Exarchate Statutes (1871, 1883, 1895) had mentioned this location[57].

Authority in the Church

The Treaty of Neuilly opened a new chapter in the development of Bulgarian political theology. Under the new conditions, the Bulgarian Orthodox Church lost its capacity to unify the Bulgarian nation across the borders. Besides, its previous duality made no more sense after the loss of the Bulgarian dioceses abroad. As a result, post-war Bulgarian political theology gave priority to the issue of authority in the church over that of national unity. In addition, the political changes gave new strength to the lay call for church reforms. Therefore, the role of the laity in church affairs became a central theme in the debates of the Ecclesiastical Commission. Its members admitted the contradiction in the ways in which the laity was treated in the different versions of the Exarchate Statute (1871, 1883, 1895). They also recognised that the 1895 Statute *de facto* excluded laity from the management of church affairs. In an attempt to find a solution, the Commission referred to the Holy Scriptures and the historical experience of the Christian Church. In particular, it cited passages from the Acts of Apostles (4:32; 11:1–18; 6:2–5; 15:22–23) that provided arguments in favour of the involvement of laymen and priests in the management of church affairs. In a similar manner, it reviewed the corresponding

---

55 TsDA, f. 166k. op. 1, a.e. 54, Working Group's Proceeding No. 23, 10 January 1921, p. 35.
56 TsDA, f. 166k, op. 1, a.e. 54, Working Group's Proceeding No. 25, 12 January 1921, p. 37.
57 The location of the Patriarch of Constantinople is guaranteed by canon law. In addition, the canons do not allow the establishment of a second episcopal throne in a city where there is already such a throne.

past and contemporary practices of the other Orthodox Churches. According to the Ecclesiastical Commission,

> the partaking of clergy and laity in the supreme church governance is sufficiently attested in historical terms and once it has been placed within canonically defined clear boundaries, it would enhance the influence of church authority and assist church welfare[58].

At the same time, the Ecclesiastical Commission stressed that such participation had always been supervised by the Apostles. According to it, the episcopate had exclusive rights over all matters related to the religious doctrine, dogmas, canons, and liturgy. This monopoly was justified by the method of apostolic succession, granted to bishops by God Himself. It was also supported by references to the Bible (Matthew 28:19–20; Mark 16:15; John 20:22–23) as well as to the practice of the Apostles (Acts 6:1–6; Canon XIX of the Sixth Ecumenical Council in Constantinople of 680–681, Canon VI of the Council of Carthage of 419)[59]. In final terms, the Ecclesiastical Commission concluded that lay involvement was »desirable and canonically justifiable for the Orthodox Bulgarian Church«[60]. It also recommended the establishment of a local church council to include not only bishops, but also clerics and laymen, to be convoked periodically and to function as a church legislative authority.

Furthermore, the Ecclesiastical Commission discussed the intermingling of the administrative and the judiciary power in the church. Its members agreed that these two powers were separated neither in the ancient church nor in the then-existing polities, but acknowledged that the separation of powers in the modern state began to be regarded as a sign of its political and legal progress[61]. They also concluded that, although the rules of the state were not binding on the church, life itself had demonstrated the advantage of the principle of separation of powers. On these grounds, the Commission suggested that it was inappropriate for the same church authority simultaneously to act as a law-maker, prosecutor, and judge. It recommended that the Holy Synod, as the supreme power of the Bulgarian Church, set up new auxiliary bodies with lay participation which to exercise specific types of power (legislative, judiciary, and executive-administrative) under episcopal supervision[62]. In support of this model, the Commission argued that the first seven deacons had been appointed as assistants of the apostles (Acts 6:1–6) and pointed

---

58 Proceedings of the Ecclesiastical Commission, p. 13.
59 Ibid., p. 16; TsDA, f. 791k, op. 1, a.e. 32, Episcopal Conference Proceedings No. 27, 2 February 1922, pp. 238f.
60 Proceedings of the Ecclesiastical Commission, p. 13.
61 Ibid., p. 14.
62 Ibid., p. 15.

to the decisions of the ecumenical councils that bishops should run economic affairs with the assistantship of lay stewards and treasurers (Canon XXXVIII of the Apostles, Canon XXVI of the Fourth Ecumenical Council in Chalcedon of 451, Canon XI of the Seventh Ecumenical Council in Nicea of 787, Canon VIII of Gangra of 340–341, Canon XXIV of Antioch of 341). In addition, the Commission commented on modern developments, especially the customs adopted by the Ecumenical Patriarchate of Constantinople and the Russian émigré churches, which economic activities were entrusted to lay or mixed bodies whose work was supervised by the corresponding supreme church authority[63]. Later on, the Church Popular Council also came up with a similar proposal[64]. The introduction of this practice in the Bulgarian Orthodox Church was expected to allow its hierarchy to pay more attention to the theological questions that formed their competence and to increase the commitment of the laity to the church cause.

Quite different was the approach of the working group appointed by the Ministry of Foreign and Religious Affairs. According to its draft church statute, the supreme power in the Bulgarian Orthodox Church was presented by the Church Popular Council (Article 2)[65], with the Holy Synod as the executive (Article 6)[66]. The same document also envisioned a new format for the Holy Synod, consisting of bishops, priests, and laymen in equal numbers (the Exarch, one bishop, two priests, and two laymen)[67]. The Episcopal Conference, however, immediately attacked this project as anticanonical. Moreover, the hierarchs threatened that none of them would attend the forthcoming ecclesiastical forum. To placate the bishops, the working group made a step back and edited its draft statute. According to its new version, the Holy Synod was a laity-free body that included the Exarch, one metropolitan, two bishops, and two priests (Article 7)[68]. Under this second draft, the Synod had canonical jurisdiction and supervision over all diocesan hierarchs (Article 9), but did not represent the executive power in the church, which was now transferred to the so-called Lay Council (Article 8)[69]. Under the chairmanship of the Exarch, this council had to take care of the church's administrative and judicial affairs, i. e., of issues beyond the sphere of theology, dogma, and canon law (Article 10)[70].

---

63 Ibid., p. 17.
64 TsDA, f. 791k, op. 1, a.e. 32, Proceedings of the Episcopal Conference No. 27, 2 February 1922, p. 240.
65 TsDA, f. 166k. op. 1, a.e. 54, Working Group's Proceeding No. 26, 13 January 1921, p. 38.
66 Ibid., Working Group's Proceeding No. 28, 15 January 1921, p. 40.
67 Ibid., Working Group's Proceeding No. 30, 18 January 1921, p. 42.
68 Ibid., Working Group's Proceeding No. 34, 24 January 1921, p. 47.
69 Ibid.
70 TsDA, f. 166k. op. 1, a.e. 54, Working Group's Proceeding No. 36, 26 January 1921, p. 49.

Nor did the working group's second draft did not receive the approval of the Episcopal Conference. At the same time, the approaching Church Popular Council urged the hierarchs to place emphasis on issues linked with its tasks. In general, their attitude to this forum built on St Paul's definition of the church as an organism, with every member, however eminent or humble, contributing to the welfare of the whole[71]. Nevertheless, taking into account its legislative nature and its commitment to church reforms, the episcopate distinguished between the contribution of its participants and their roles in the decision-making process[72]. In particular, the Episcopal Conference adopted the principle that the Church Popular Council's decisions on dogmatic, canonical, and liturgical issues should have no force without the approval of two thirds of the Orthodox bishops[73]. The same majority was required for votes of disapproval[74]. This right of veto was justified by the church's teaching on bishops as supreme guardians of the Christian faith and by the canons of ecumenical councils on the sacramental authority of bishops as successors of the Apostles[75].

Furthermore, the Episcopal Conference preserved the supreme authority of the Holy Synod, but envisioned changes in its format. The future Synod had to include all diocesan and non-diocesan bishops, i. e., it planned to transform the old Episcopal Conference into a Synod[76]. For this purpose, the Church Popular Council was invited to vote the following formula:

> The supreme judicial and executive power in the Orthodox Bulgarian Church is executed by the Holy Synod as well as by the two other bodies established at the same Synod, namely the Supreme Church Court and the Church Council, which shall function within limits defined by the present Statute[77].

Finally, the question of the supreme authority in the church was raised once more during the Church Popular Council. About two-thirds of its deputies, mostly laymen and priests, maintained that this power had to be represented by the Council and

---

71 TsDA, f. 791k, op. 1, a.e. 32, Proceedings of the Episcopal Conference No. 27, 2 February 1922, p. 239.
72 Ibid., Proceedings of the Episcopal Conference No. 6, 8 December 1920, p. 74.
73 Ibid., Proceedings of the Episcopal Conference No 27, 2 February 1922, p. 239; TsDA, f. 166k, op. 1, a.e. 54, Motives of the Episcopal Conference for its own Draft Law for the Amendment of the State adopted Law on the amendment of the Exarchate Statute, 5 December 1921, pp. 5f.
74 TsDA, f. 791k, op. 1, a.e. 32, Proceedings of the Episcopal Conference No. 24, 28 May 1921, p. 228.
75 Ibid., Proceedings of the Episcopal Conference No. 6, 8 December 1920, p. 75; Proceedings of the Episcopal Conference No. 16, 4 February 1921, p. 186.
76 Ibid., Proceedings of the Episcopal Conference No. 21, 18 May 1921, p. 218.
77 Ibid., Proceedings of the Episcopal Conference No. 27, 2 February 1922, p. 240.

not by the Synod. For this reason, the Episcopal Conference, which held its sessions in parallel with those of the Church Popular Council, returned to this issue. This time, the majority supported the view that the »the supreme judicial power belongs to both the Holy Synod and the Church Popular Council«. After heated debates, the Episcopal Conference unanimously adopted the formula: »The supreme judicial power *belongs* to the Holy Synod and is *exercised* by the Church Popular Council«[78].

These compromises made by hierarchs and lay deputies in the Church Popular Council allowed the successful accomplishment of the work on the new Church Statute by February 1922. The government, however, postponed its adoption while elections to the National Assembly took place. The new political formations that took power in the country in a *coup d'état* on 9 June 1923 also refused to endorse it. One reason lays in the hope of the Bulgarian political elite for a revision of the Treaty of Neuilly. Therefore, the Church Statute adopted by a Church Popular Council without the participation of representatives of the Exarchate's dioceses that had been come under the Romanian, Serbian, and Greek Orthodox Churches was regarded as a potential threat for the restoration of the pre-1913 territorial jurisdiction of the Bulgarian Orthodox Church. As a result, this church continued to be administered under the Adapted Exarchate Statute of 1895. At the same time, the Bulgarian episcopate became more sensitive to the lay wish for broader participation in church affairs. In the 1920s, the Holy Synod developed a new policy that allowed priests and ordinary believers to take an active part in the church's life by establishing a wide network of by priestly and lay brotherhoods, who were involved in social, charity, and religious education projects.

Conclusions

The political theology developed by the modern Bulgarian Orthodox Church during the first five decades of its existence was an incredibly dynamic process determined by the problems which this religious institution had to resolve. Created before the Bulgarian nation-state, however, this particular church relied on the laity to secure its normal functioning. Therefore, its initial political theology was suffused with the spirit of ethno-nationalism while being less preoccupied with Orthodox dogmas and canons. In 1878, the establishment of the Principality of Bulgaria opened a new stage in the development of Bulgarian political theology. This event allowed the episcopate to take the upper hand in formulating the political theology of the Bulgarian Orthodox Church, but only within the liberated state territory.

---

78 Ibid., Proceedings of the Episcopal Conference No. 23, 27 May 1921, pp. 226–228.

Meanwhile, the laity continued to play a decisive role in the Bulgarian dioceses that had remained under Ottoman rule. This duality caused uncertainty in Bulgarian political theology. It was additionally aggravated by tensions between the different »stakeholders« in the Bulgarian Orthodox Church, namely bishops, priests, and ordinary believers. While the episcopate worked for a return to the ancient norms of Orthodox ecclesiology, laymen called for reforms that would align the church's organisation with the modern world. In this regard, the influx of several hundreds of thousands of Bulgarian refugees from the former Ottoman provinces after Bulgaria's defeat in the Second Balkan War and World War I gave additional strength to the lay movement for church reforms. No less important a factor were the increasing number of Bulgarian graduates of Western European universities who called into question the church's relations with the state and its model of church governance. In this way, the themes of church autonomy and the division of powers in the Bulgarian Orthodox Church appeared in its political theology for the first time.

In their turn, priests underwent an intriguing evolution. While under Ottoman rule, they were paid by the laity and usually took their side when conflicts erupted with the bishops of Patriarchate of Constantinople and even those of the Bulgarian Exarchate[79]. In free Bulgaria, however, the incomes of priests depended on the episcopate. As a result, clerics began to support the position of their diocesan hierarchs. This trend became a rule after the Treaty of Neuilly, as a result of which the territories of the Bulgarian Church and state overlapped. In conclusion, early Bulgarian political theology reflected the interests of the church's principal actors (episcopate, clergy, and laity) and evolved under the influence of domestic and international political developments. It also demonstrates the tensions between Orthodox ecclesiology and the modern concepts of ethno-nationalism, church autonomy, and authority.

---

79 Daniela KALKANDJIEVA, The Bulgarian Orthodox Church and the »Ethic of Capitalism«, in: Social Compass 57/1 (2010), pp. 83–99, at pp. 86f.

Evert van der Zweerde

Give to God's Kingdom What is God's Kingdom's

Political Theologies in Late Nineteenth-Century Russia[1]

> Historicized eschatology is inevitably Promethean,
> courting disaster in overreaching itself.
>
> Richard Bauckham, *Eschatology* (2000)[2]

> The Great Being [*Grand Être*] is not an empty form but an all-embracing divinely-human fullness of the spiritual and material, divine and created life, revealed to us in Christianity. Comte's conception of the true Great Being was incomplete [...], but he implicitly believed in its completeness and bore witness to it in spite of himself. But how many believing Christians, both past and present, have never known, or wanted to know, this very essence of Christianity which, though only half understood by him, inspired wholehearted devotion in the godless infidel – Comte!
>
> Vl. Solov'ëv, *The Idea of Humanity in Auguste Comte* (1898)[3]

---

[1] The topic of this contribution is also addressed, with small overlaps, in my publications: Evert van der ZWEERDE, Theocracy, Sobornost' and Democracy – Reflections on Vladimir Putin's Philosophers, in: Christoph SCHNEIDER (ed.), Theology and Philosophy in Eastern Orthodoxy, Cambridge 2019, pp. 11–31; id., Between Mysticism and Politics. The Continuous Pattern of Vladimir Solov'ëv's Thought, in: Interdisciplinary Journal for Religion and Transformation in Contemporary Society 5/1 (2019), pp. 136–164; id., Vladimir Solov'yov on Terror, Love & Violence, in: Mahmoud MASAELI/Rico SNELLER (eds.), Responses of Mysticism to Religious Terrorism. Sufism and Beyond, Oud-Turnhout 2020, pp. 177–198; id., Russian Political Philosophy: Anarchy, Authority, Autocracy, Edinburgh 2022.
[2] Richard BAUCKHAM, Eschatology, in: Adrian HASTINGS et al. (eds.), Oxford Companion to Christian Thought, Oxford 2000, pp. 206–209, at p. 208.
[3] Quoted in S.L. FRANK (ed.), A Solovyov Anthology, London ²2001 [first published in 1950], p. 59; original: Id., Ideia chelovechestva u Avgusta Konta, in: Cosmopolis, April & December issues (1898); also, in: Vladimir SOLOV'ËV, Sochineniia v dvukh tomakh, vol. 2, Moscow 1988, pp. 562–581.

Introduction

Political theology may be the least definable concept in human intellectual history. Is it an applied branch of theology? Has it been a core element of a Christian political tradition ever since St Paul? Is it perhaps God's own discourse in matters political? Is it a precursor of modern political theory, as Carl Schmitt claimed? Is it an academic discourse? A political one? A religious one? Is it a thing of the past or is it permanent? All these possibilities entail a core of truth, which makes definition a difficult task.

In the case of nineteenth-century Russia, we encounter further complications: the direct subordination of the Russian Orthodox Church to the tsarist government from 1721 until 1917, which led to an extra-ecclesiastical flourishing of theology; the exceptionally rapid processes of social, cultural, economic, and political change that Russia underwent, especially towards the end of the nineteenth century; the fact that, intellectually, Russia has been under the impact of »Western« theological, scientific, and philosophical theories, while also having access to a more specifically Orthodox Christian tradition that reached back to the Greek church fathers. Here, as in other fields, Russian thinkers always had reasons to identify (but also not to identify) with either »the West« or with »one's own« tradition, or to seek a balance between or beyond the two. Generally being well familiar with Western currents and positions, Russian thinkers have addressed these issues consciously and explicitly, leading to such labels as Westernisers (*западники*) and Slavophiles (*славянофилы*), but also to repeated attempts to return to ancient Christian roots, especially the Graeco-Byzantine church fathers.

In this chapter, I use a broad definition of political theology. »Theology« refers to any discourse that explicitly refers to God or the Divine: This includes theories that take their departure from positive religion, whether Orthodox Christianity or »universal« religion (as in Vladimir Solovëv), as well as theories that explicitly deny the existence of anything Divine, such as the anarchism of Mikhail Bakunin. It includes academic theology as well as the official theologies of political regimes. From this angle, we can distinguish positive and negative, monotheist and polytheist, pantheist and atheist, militant and quietist, protesting and conciliatory, esoteric and popular, and many other forms of political theologies. »Political« refers to »the political« (broader than, but including what we habitually call »politics«, »state«, or »political system«), understood as the ubiquitous dimension of possible conflict and concord in society. »Politics« is any form of dealing with »the political« and comes in four basic forms: denial/negation, suppression/control, canalisation/giving form, and »unchaining«, including Walter Benjamin's »divine violence«[4]. It also includes revolutionary, reformist, progressive, conservative, and reactionary visions of a future society as well as visions of a lost past.

The first part of this chapter addresses political theology as a phenomenon of all societies, and then zooms in on Orthodox Christianity with some assistance by Merab Mamardashvili. The second part briefly discusses some creationist and abolitionist political theologies of the nineteenth century in Russia before moving to the existential political theology of Fëdor Dostoevsky. In the third part of the chapter, I address the sophiological political theology of Vladimir Solovëv, and discussion of the »fate« of his sophiological impulse leads up to a general conclusion.

Political Theology as a Universal Phenomenon

If we make the barely hypothetical assumption that in all parts of the world, in all civilisations and cultures, we find both »politics« and »religion« – because, first, »the political« is indeed ubiquitous and thus has to be »dealt with« everywhere, and, second, because humans everywhere generate a symbolic order that somehow relates them to something supra-natural, whether in the form of spirits, ancestors, or in one form of divinity or another – we can venture the hypothesis that *political theology is a phenomenon of all civilisations and cultures*. Abrahamic monotheism was a *polemical* reaction to polytheism, just as atheism is a polemical reaction against theism. Christian political theology did not come out of the blue, but was a position occupied in an already existing battlefield. Indeed, Jan Assmann retraces political theology to Ancient Egypt, while Marin Terpstra has shown the pre-Christian roots in Greek and Latin Antiquity[5]. Ancient Greek θεολογία πολιτική, later transformed into *theologia civilis*, would now be called *civil religion*, and even if early Christian writers like St Augustine rejected »political theology«, the nexus between political theology and civil religion, clearly distinct in our days, never left the scene completely: Any justification of a particular political reality in theological terms, from a regime to a revolution to a new regime, can be linked to both political theology and to civil religion. It is in that latter sense that it reappears in a text like Jean-Jacques Rousseau's *Du contrat social*: as a concluding chapter which *sits oddly*

---

[4] See Jan Assmann, Of God and Gods. Egypt, Israel, and the Rise of Monotheism, Madison 2008, pp. 142f.

[5] See, among others Jan Assmann, Herrschaft und Heil. Politische Theologie in Altägypten, Israel und Europa, Munich 2000; Marin Terpstra, Fortdauer der theologia politikè? Varro, Spinoza, Lefort. Drei Etappen in der Geschichte der Politischen Theologie, in: Manfred Walther (ed.), Religion und Politik. Zu Theorie und Praxis des theologisch-politischen Komplexes, Baden-Baden 2004, pp. 179–198; Elizabeth Philips, Political Theology. A Guide for the Perplexed, London 2012.

with the rest of the text, and this »oddity« is, I venture, crucial for understanding the specificity of *Christian* political theology.

Christian political theology, arguably different from all other kinds of political theology on this point, is specifically Christian in its reference to the figure of Jesus Christ as God-Man, i. e., as both divine and human. (NB: I completely abstain here from the question whether the Gospel is a human *myth* or a divine *truth*; that is a matter of faith, not philosophy.) Because the Kingdom of God, *my* Kingdom in Jesus Christ's words, is not *of* or *from* this world (John 18:36), while His claim *that* it is, did take place *in* this world, thus generating a vision *from this world*, we obtain three perspectives on Christian political theology: a perspective »from above« or »from a transcendent position« – in other words, from the perspective of that Kingdom itself; a perspective »from below« or »from within the immanent frame« (Charles Taylor) – in other words, a perspective of *this* »here-world« in which Christian political theology must appear as one form (among many) of »continuing the political struggle by other means«; a perspective *from the very oddness itself*, from the »between« (what Sergej Bulgakov and William Desmond call the »between« [μεταξύ][6]), from what we might call the space of indeterminacy, of non-identity, and (arguably) agnosticism.

Zooming in on Orthodoxy, and following the Georgian philosopher Merab Mamardashvili (1930–1990) in his diagnosis that »European culture is based on […] the idea of giving form to everything, to political life, to spiritual life, *giving form*«, we could argue that Orthodox (including Russian) civilisation has struggled to find a middle ground between suppressing and unchaining the political – between, as it were, autocracy and anarchy. It found a third way in *idealisation*. To quote Mamardashvili once more: »Orthodox culture is obsessed by ideality. The thing or the concrete form is never the ideal. Hence, if it is not the ideal, it is nothing at all. What is wanted is all or nothing«[7]. I would take this beyond any »idealisation« (!) of the West and argue that »the West« or Europe has also found it hard to find a middle ground. The hypothesis then would be that the organising opposition is that between suppression and unchaining, with two possible third ways, one being idealisation (a denial of the real), the other channelling (Mamardashvili's *giving*

---

6 See, among others William DESMOND, God and the Between, Hoboken 2007; Sergei BULGAKOV, Svet Nevechernii, Moscow 1994, p. 189; cf. Josephien van KESSEL, Sophiology and Modern Society. Sergei Bulgakov's Conceptualization of an Alternative Modern Society, Nijmegen 2020.

7 Merab MAMARDACHVILI, La pensée empêchée. Entretiens avec Annie Epelboin, La Tour d'Aigues 1991, p. 61: »La culture européenne est basée sur […] l'idée de donner forme à tout, à la vie politique, à la vie spirituelle, *donner forme*«; and »La culture orthodoxe est obsédée par l'idéalité. La chose ou la forme concrète n'est jamais l'idéal. Alors, ci ce n'est pas l'idéal, ce n'est rien du tout. On veut tout, ou rien«.

form), while a third, far-reaching hypothesis holds that the theory of democracy developed by Claude Lefort, author of the article *Permanence du théologico-politique? (Permanence of the Theologico-Political?* – a title in which the question mark is the key element!) turns exactly around the idea of *donner forme*. That the latter should also be a critical position in political philosophy hardly seems accidental.

If theology is »discourse about God«, then atheist denials of God's existence are cases of theology too, and if these denials connect the non-existence or »Death« of God to politics, then they are cases of *political* theology. Taken together, political theology is any type of discourse that deals with the political through an explicit reference, positive or negative, to God or the Divine, and in doing so can be both an inspirational worldview or an ideal vision – as well as a legitimising ideology or, more modestly, a source of motivating and justifying ideologemes[8].

Clearly, then, political theology neither implies nor suggests theocracy – nor, however, does it necessarily reject any such implication. It does not necessarily imply a »negative« attitude towards politics or the political, nor does it imply or prohibit a »civil religion«. All these variants depend on how political theology is understood and by whom. Not only can political theology be militant or belligerent, it can also be exclusionary or divisive as well as inclusive or irenic, and it can, in a variety of ways, imply active engagement in this »here-world«: mediaeval crusades, Latin American liberation theology, Russian »Christian politics« (Vladimir Solovëv, Sergei Bulgakov), Christian democracy in Western European history, American »civil religion«, and John Milbank's »radical Orthodoxy« all rely on positions in political theology, as do the Islamic State or the Jewish state of Israel.

There is, from the political-theological perspective, *more* than just this »here-world« *and* this »more« is politically relevant in or for »this world«. The »other« world is identified, at least in the Abrahamic religious traditions, with eternity, infinity, omnipotence, truth, justice, unity, and peace; by implication, their opposites, i. e., transiency, finitude, struggle, opinion, injustice, partition, and war, typically belong to *this* world. This contrasts most clearly with the polytheistic political theology of antiquity, which, if anything, extends human plurality and difference to the divine domain while at the same time importing the gods directly into *this* world. From the perspective of Abrahamic political theology generally, and of Christian political theology in particular, the political and politics are things of *this*, not of *the* world. Consequently, politics can both be a positive task and thus a good (*bonum*), or a necessary evil (*malum*), but in both cases it relates to our earthly existence in historical time, an existence which does not exhaust our human reality. In both

---

8 Typical examples include the discourse of traditional Christian political parties in a pluralist context, for example a Dutch party like the SGP (Staatkundig Gereformeerde Partij, »Polity-aware Reformed Party«), which adheres to the idea of theocracy as its ultimate ideal, while at the same time accepting, in this fallen world, the powers that be.

cases, the ultimate goal of politics is to overcome itself, and as a necessary evil it is bound to »secular« time. So far, political theology in Russia does not seem to differ from political theology generally. Paradoxically, all this equally holds for explicitly atheist political theologies as we find them in Marx or Bakunin, as well as for those forms of humanism that »deify« humankind, e. g., Comtean positivism or, in fact, any form of »God-building« (*богостроительство*).

Thus, by understanding political theology broadly as an intrinsically political discourse organised by concepts like Omnipotence, Creation, Divine Humanity, Prophecy, Kingdom of God, *Katechon*, and Apocalypse, we can highlight a number of issues, the relevance of which goes well beyond Russian contexts. This includes the initially »innocent« but increasingly influential introduction by Ivan Kireevskii of the notion of *soborny/sobornost'*, the search for a historical task or role of Russia as part of a Divine Plan from Pëtr Chaadaev up to Nikolai Berdyaev, the political atheism of Mikhail Bakunin, rightly seen by Carl Schmitt as his most principled opponent, the creationist notion of the Russian Idea, »i. e., what God thinks about the nation in eternity«[9], debates about the »Jewish question«, which generated both anti-Semitism and philo-Semitism, attempts to incorporate social progress while preventing a shift from Christian »Divine humanity God-Manhood/Theanthropy « (*богочеловечество*)[10] to »Promethean« »Man-Godhood« (*человекобожество*), and utopian and dystopian apocalyptic visions of the »end« of history; in much of this, the works of Vladimir Solovëv play a central role[11]. Key to nineteenth-century Russian political theology is its resistance against both the *solely* human construction of God's Kingdom on Earth (the Marxist project) and against the murder of God (the Nietzschean vision of fate) that clears the ground for human construction of any number of »gods« (*богостроительство*) which, from a Christian point of view, appears as idolatry. The most important »positive« political theologies – the existential political theology of Dostoevsky, the sophiological political theology of Solovëv and others, and the mostly twentieth-century neo-patristic, neo-Palamitic (hesychast) political theologies, e. g., of Georges Florovsky[12] – were articulated first and foremost *in reaction* to nineteenth-century Russian anti-religious and atheist political theologies.

---

9 See Vladimir SOLOVIEV [Solovëv], L'idée russe, in: François ROULEAU (ed.), Vladimir Soloviev. La Sophia et les autres écrits français, Lausanne 1978, p. 83.

10 The rendering of *bogochelovechestvo* as theanthropy was suggested by Oliver SMITH, Vladimir Soloviev and the Spiritualization of Matter, Boston 2011, p. 93.

11 Cf. Nel GRILLAERT, What the God-seekers found in Nietzsche. The Reception of Nietzsche's Übermensch by the Philosophers of the Russian Religious Renaissance, Amsterdam 2008.

12 Vladimir PETRUNIN, Politicheskii isikhazm i ego traditsiia v sotsial'noi kontseptsii Moskovskogo Patriarkhata, St Petersburg 2009; Daniel P. PAYNE, The Revival of Political Hesychasm in Contemporary Orthodox Thought, Lanham, MD 2011, esp. chapter IV.

Creation, Abolition, Love

If humans generally desire to make sense of the social and political reality that surrounds them, and if they also have, though not necessarily, the urge to give direction to their own societal and political life, then political theology is one of the types of discourse that perform this function. We can discuss and understand this discourse irrespective of the »truth« of the elements of that discourse, and also irrespective of the »existence« of the God or Divinity they refer to. I thus approach nineteenth-century Russian political theology from an agnostic point of view. One important consequence of this approach is that *both* explicitly theistic political theologies (e. g., those of Vladimir Solovëv or Nikolai Fëdorov) *and* explicitly atheistic political theologies (e. g., those of Mikhail Bakunin or Anatolii Vasilevich Lunacharskii) come into view.

The idolatrous »man-made Divinity« did not pass Russia by. In the late nineteenth century, various forms of »Enlightenment optimism« gained prominence among Russian scientists and intellectuals. The earlier opposition between giving form/shape and idealisation, introduced with the help of Mamardashvili, allows us to place all of these positions in the »idealisation« camp: A future society would have to be just, rational, and well-organised, but it would have to come about not as a result of re-forming what already existed, or of channelling the existing forces in society, but rather as a result of replacing existing society and creating something new. This creationism included the replacement of the traditional God of Russian Orthodox Christianity by a new »God«: Reason, Progress, and Nature. Typical examples include Russian Positivism (e. g., Pëtr Lavrov, 1823–1900), which aimed at the construction of a rational and socialist society, Russian Marxism (e. g., Aleksandr Bogdanov, 1873–1928), which aimed to put science at the service of social engineering, and Russian Cosmism (e. g., Nikolai Fëdorov, 1828–1903), which strove to merge science and religion into a »common cause« (*общее дело*). What all these positions share is that they aim at »total transformation« and that traditional religion and theology do not sufficiently serve their purpose; what they also share is a strong sense of historical progress. As a result, they all tend towards political theologies that merge the Divine and the human, that transfer the Kingdom of God largely or wholly to this here world, and that connect philosophy, science, and religion rather than opposing them: Consequently, they also aim at some transformation of political theology in the direction of a positive idealisation of humankind and society.

Contrasting with these *positive* forms of idealisation is the *negative* idealisation that we encounter in Mikhail Bakunin (1814–1876). For Bakunin, the human being is intrinsically good, and all evil comes from oppressive structures that can be captured under the joint labels of »State« and »God«, of which the first refers to something existing in the world and the second to one of humankind's »phantasmagorical creations and [the] dreams of our drunken imagination«[13]. These two seem to be more important for Bakunin than social classes or Capital: For Marxists, political structures and religious »ideology« are part of the »reproductive« mechanism of a given mode of production, while for Bakunin, they are projections and imaginations that we can rid ourselves of:

> We finally realized that by playing, just like children, at peopling with dreams that immense Void, that God, that Nothingness created out of our own power of abstraction or negation [...], we were abandoning society and putting all our real existence at the mercy of the prophets, tyrants and religious, political and economic exploiters of the divine idea on earth, and that by seeking out an ideal liberty isolated from the conditions of the real world we were condemning ourselves to the most dismal, shameful slavery[14].

Bakunin, author of *La théologie politique de Mazzini et l'Internationale* (1871), in all likelihood was the source of Carl Schmitt's reintroduction of the concept of »political theology«. In Bakunin, Schmitt rightly perceived the most radical opponent of theism: »Clearly influenced by Auguste Comte, Proudhon has engaged in the battle against God. Bakunin has continued it with a Scythian rage«[15]. In line with Schmitt's principle »that the decision whether something is *non-political*, always implies a *political* decision, irrespective of who takes it or in what arguments [*Beweisgründe*] it is clothed«[16], and emphasising that »political theology« would be one type of *Beweisgrund* among others, we understand why »in the greatest anarchist of the nineteenth century, Bakunin, we run into the peculiar paradox, that he theoretically had to become the theologian of the anti-theological«[17].

In politico-theological terms, Bakunin's position is that of a fragmentised pantheism, a multitude of human beings that can connect and cooperate in concord, but are kept from doing so by hierarchical structures framed in terms of State and/or God, *both of which therefore must be destroyed* – the first as a reality, the second as an idea, hence his well-known reversal of Voltaire's dictum »If God did not exist, it

---

13 Michael BAKUNIN, The Political Theology of Mazzini, quoted from: Id., Selected Writings, ed. by Arthur LEHNING, New York 1973, pp. 229f.
14 Ibid., p. 230.
15 Carl SCHMITT, Politische Theologie. Vier Kapitel zur Lehre von der Souveränität, Berlin 1996, p. 54: »Unter dem deutlichen Einfluss von Auguste Comte hat Proudhon den Kampf gegen Gott aufgenommen. Bakunin hat ihn mit einer skythischen Wucht fortgesetzt«.
16 Ibid., p. 7; Vorbemerkung zur zweiten Ausgabe, November 1933: »dass die Entscheidung darüber, ob etwas *unpolitisch* ist, immer eine *politische* Entscheidung bedeutet, gleichgültig wer sie trifft und mit welchen Beweisgründen sie sich umkleidet«.
17 Ibid., p. 70: »bei dem größten Anarchisten des 19. Jahrhunderts, Bakunin, ergibt sich die seltsame Paradoxie, dass er theoretisch der Theologe des Anti-Theologischen [...] werden musste«.

would be necessary to invent him«: »A jealous lover of human liberty, and deeming it the absolute condition of all that we admire and respect in humanity, I reverse the phrase of Voltaire, and say that, *if God really existed, it would be necessary to abolish him*«[18].

Bakunin is a prime example of the nihilism that the existential political theology of Fëdor Dostoevsky (1821–1881) was oriented against. Whether God exists or not, and what are the consequences of his existence or non-existence for humans and their freedom, is one of the questions that torment many protagonists in his works. Having himself discovered Christianity while in prison, he was personally familiar with the positivistic, nihilistic, and atheistic positions of his contemporaries. Contrary to their science-based projects of creating a new society and/or new man as a result either of co-creation with God or of creation in God's stead, Dostoevsky's perspective is existential and, in a way, individualistic – »in a way«, because the modality of becoming a true human being is through overcoming oneself in the direction of a »Christ-like love in individual existence«, inspired by the God-Man who alone is capable of replacing the man-God of the revolutionaries and the nihilists[19]. A »true inner transformation in the image of Christ«[20] – which, by default, takes place at the level of the tormented individual who struggles with the abyss of freedom – is the basis of a »politics of humility« that is the opposite of any grand humanitarian project, liberal, socialist, or Catholic, including that exemplified by the »Grand Inquisitor«. »Dostoevsky's political message is clear: A politics of humility is required for Russia's [and, by extension, the world's] salvation. A paradoxical ›monk in the world‹ will be necessary. This, of course, is the role of the novel's hero, Alyosha [Alësha] Karamazov«[21].

It is disputable whether Alyosha Karamazov really is the novel's hero. Given the polyphonic nature of Dostoevsky's work highlighted by Mikhail Bakhtin, it can be argued that there cannot be a single hero and that at least Ivan, whose mind is a battlefield of positions, is another hero of the book. It has often been suggested that the model for Alyosha was Dostoevsky's humble younger friend Vladimir Solovëv, who accompanied him to Optina Pustyn' in 1878 after the death of Dostoevsky's three-year-old son, Alyosha; also, Marina Kostalevsky has convincingly argued that

---

18 Quoted in Michael Bakunin, God and the State, New York 1970, p. 17, 28; Russian version: М.А. Бакунин, Государственность и анархия, Moscow 2014, pp. 277, 287: »если бы Бог дейсвительно существовал, следовало бы уничтожить его«.
19 David Walsh, Dostoevsky's Discovery of the Christian Foundation of Politics, in Richard Avramenko/Lee Trepanier (eds.), Dostoevsky's Political Thought, Lanham 2013, p. 11, 17.
20 Ibid., p. 21.
21 John P. Moran, This Star Will Shine Forth from the East. Dostoevsky and the Politics of Humility, in: Avramenko/Trepanier (eds.), Dostoevsky's Political Thought, p. 53.

Dostoevsky saw in Solov̈ev at least as much the other brother, Ivan[22]. As Kostalevsky states, »one should not expect a literal reproduction of Soloviev's personality in the characters of the novel: Dostoevsky did not copy his characters. Nevertheless, it is easy to see in the young philosopher that synthesis of ›head and heart‹ without which Alesha is naïve while Ivan is cruel«[23]. Whether we are entitled to speak of a »synthesis« here remains an open question, but Kostalevsky's analysis offers an interesting perspective on Solov̈ev.

The Political Sophiology of Vladimir Solov'ëv

In *Political Theologies in Orthodox Christianity*, Davor Džalto refers to a »popular, laconic phrase ›One God in Heaven, one King on Earth‹«, which supposedly expresses the core of the concept of *symphonia* and can serve as a key to understanding why »Orthodox theologians have been developing political theologies that were mostly defending monarchy and autocracy as *the* Orthodox Christian model of government«[24]. However, while this phrase is obviously monotheistic and monarchic, it does explain, but rather overtly contradicts, the existence of a plurality of kings as heads of empires or national governments, and this is at odds, at least potentially, with the tendency of Orthodox Churches to align themselves with the nation(-state) of which they are the national church. We see this tension return in the *two* models elaborated by Vladimir Solov̈ev in the second half of the nineteenth century: the utopian idea of a universal free theocracy and the more realistic idea of a truly Christian Russian Empire.

While *both* models are examples of »ideal theory«, they are so at different levels of ideality. Solov̈ev's ultimate ideal of a free theocracy is a tripartite model of One King (the Russian Tsar having become ruler of the entire world), One Priest (the Roman Pope having [re]united all Christians), and one Prophetic Society (the religious intelligentsia having becoming a global community beyond national division and linguistic limitation), all under One God. His second-best ideal, that of a Christian constitutional monarchy-cum-welfare-state with a free public sphere, as he elaborates it in *Opravdanie dobra* and other texts, is a more »realistic« version of the same model, this time on a national scale and hence still marked by the »sin« of *particularity* or *particularisation* (обособление).

We can look at the political theology of Solov̈ev from three perspectives: that of the rapidly changing social and political situation in Russia during his lifetime;

---

22 Marina Kostalevsky, Dostoevsky and Soloviev. The Art of Integral Vision, New Haven 1997, p. 66.
23 Ibid., p. 67.
24 Davor Džalto, Orthodox Political Theology. An Anarchist Perspective, in: Kristina Stoeckl et al. (eds.), Political Theologies in Orthodox Christianity, London 2017, pp. 111–134, at pp. 112f.

that of the Orthodox Christian tradition of relating religion to politics, and, more narrowly, church to state; and that of the inner logic and structure of his thought as a whole. If we start with the latter, we should first of all emphasise that Solov̌ev is rightly regarded as the most systematic of all nineteenth-century Russian philosophers. If, in line with this evaluation as a systematic thinker, we abstract from the development and changes in his lifelong project of *integral life* (цельная жизнь), it is perhaps most adequate to state that this project took shape in permanent interaction with a large, indeed huge number of authors and currents that Solov̌ev acquainted himself with, as well as with the circumstances of the day, both in Russia and beyond it. Yet it should equally be emphasised that this project received its drive and coherence from his repeated encounters, as recounted by himself in dialogue form between Sophia, understood simultaneously as Divine Wisdom and World Soul, and »the philosopher«.

As I have argued elsewhere, Solov̌ev's vision of a just Christian society can equally be derived from the truth revealed to him by Sophia[25]. The text *La Sophia* (1875–1876, but published only in 1978), in which he presents his encounter, contains the key elements of his thought, as he himself confirmed in letters written as late as 1890. Even his last writings, such as *The Meaning of Love* (Смысл любви) (1892–1894), elaborate elements articulated in his mystical vision. While Solov̌ev certainly aimed to give his vision a rationally convincing systematic form and not present it as esoteric »wisdom for the initiated«, it should also be emphasised that the very structure of his project makes its cornerstone and key source inaccessible to others than those who somehow share the encounter with Sophia.

From the perspective of tradition, one striking point of difference is the replacement of the traditional Byzantine dyadic scheme of worldly and ecclesiastical powers, tsar and patriarch, state and church, ideally existing in a relationship of symphony (συμφωνία, симфония), by a triadic scheme of *three* instances that Solov̌ev traces back to Old Testament times: King, Priest, and Prophet. Their relationship should still be *harmonious*, as Solov̌ev states in *L'idée russe* (1888):

> So, the three ends of social existence are *simultaneously* represented in the true life of the universal church led by these three main agents at one and the same time: the spiritual authority of the universal Pontifex (infallible leader of priesthood), representing the true lasting history of humanity; the secular power of the national sovereign (legitimate head of state), uniting and personifying the interests, the rights, and the obligations of the present; and, finally, the free ministry of the prophet (inspired head of human society

---

25 This perception of Solov̌ev's thought and life as a single »project« is not universally accepted in Solov̌ev scholarship; in line with, and inspired by, the works of George L. Kline, Oliver Smith and, recently, Henrieke Stahl, this perception does not deny development, though it does reject the hypothesis of major shifts or stages.

as a whole), inaugurating the realisation of humanity's ideal future. The concord and harmonious action of these three main agents [*facteurs principaux*] is the first condition of genuine progress[26].

Solověv explicitly draws a parallel with the Holy Trinity:

> Just like, in the Trinity, each of the three hypostases is God perfectly, and yet, *due to their consubstantiality*, there is only one God [...], in the same way each of the three main dignities of theocratic society possesses true sovereignty without there being three different powers [...], because the three representatives of divine-human sovereignty must be *absolutely solidary* among themselves, merely forming three main organs *of one and the same social body*, exercising three fundamental functions of one and the same collective life [emphasis added][27].

Despite this explicit organicism, the third of the three offices or »services« (*служения*) is, first of all, intrinsically connected to freedom, and, secondly, to the idea of a moral *check* on the other two:

> However, priestly authority as well as state power, both inextricably connected with external advantages, are exposed to temptations that are too powerful. [...] All external obligatory restrictions are [...], in terms of an ideal, incompatible with the supreme dignity of both the high priest's authority and royal power. However, a purely moral control [чисто нравственный контроль] *by the free forces of the nation and by* society on them is not just possible but desirable to the highest degree. In Ancient Israel, there was a third supreme calling, namely, that of the prophet. *De jure* eliminated by Christianity, it, *in fact*, virtually disappeared from the historical scene [...]. Hence, we have all the anomalies of medieval and modern history. [...] The true prophet is a social figure who is

---

26 Vladimir SOLOVIEV, L'idée russe, Paris 1888, pp. 99f.: »Ainsi les trois termes de l'existence sociale se trouvent représentés simultanément dans la vraie vie de l'Église universelle dirigée à la fois par ces trois agents principaux: l'autorité spirituelle du Pontife universel (chef infaillible du sacerdoce), représentant le vrai passé permanent de l'humanité; le pouvoir séculier du souverain national (chef légitime de l'État), concentrant en lui et personnifiant les intérêts, les droits et les devoirs du présent; enfin le ministère libre du prophète (chef inspiré de la société humaine dans sa totalité), inaugurant la réalisation de l'avenir idéal de l'humanité. La concorde et l'action harmonique de ces trois facteurs principaux sont la première condition du véritable progrès«.

27 Ibid., p. 100: »Comme, dans la Trinité, chacune des trois hypostases est Dieu parfait et cependant, *en vertu de leur consubstantialité*, il n'y a qu'un seul Dieu [...], de même chacune des trois dignités principales de la société théocratique possède une véritable souveraineté sans qu'il y ait pour cela trois pouvoirs différents [...], car les trois représentants de la souveraineté divino-humaine doivent être *absolument solidaires* entre eux, ne formant que trois organes principaux *d'un seul et même corps social*, exerçant trois fonctions fondamentales d'une seule et même vie collective«.

unconditionally independent, fearless in the face of anything external and subordinate to nothing external. Along with the bearers of unconditional authority and power, there must be bearers of unconditional freedom in society. [...] *The right to be free* is based in the human essence itself and must be protected externally by the state [emphasis added][28].

This »control« of state and church by prophetic society is to be not only *totally free*, but also *purely moral*: It does *not* have any »power« or »authority« that could challenge either of the other »services«; moreover, it does *not* point to democracy, parliament, or anything of the kind:

> This freedom cannot belong to the masses; it cannot be an attribute of democracy. [...] Only those who are internally unconnected to anything external have real [польный, i. e., full] freedom, both inner and outer. Only they, in the final analysis [в последнем основании], know no other standard of judgment and behaviour than the good will and a pure conscience[29].

Significantly, Solovëv does not address the question *who* or *what* will decide who has this »real freedom« – on the one hand, one would expect this decision to be God's, but on the other hand, in actually existing society it can hardly be anyone but the public and/or the »prophetic person(s)« themselves. State and church, though they do have the power to limit externally the freedom of those who dare to speak, may be wrong, and Solovëv no doubt held them both of them have often been wrong in his own day, including in his own case. We also have every reason to believe that he considered himself to be such an »internally unconnected and fully free« person that the censorship that forced him to publish several of his writings abroad was an entirely unjustified »anomaly«. To be fair, it should be added that this was an injustice of the tsarist state rather than of the decapitated and subordinated

---

28 Vladimir Solov'ëv, Justification of the Moral Good, ed. by Thomas Nemeth, Cham 2015, pp. 415f. I follow this new translation of *Opravdanie dobra* by Thomas Nemeth instead of the translation by Nathalie Duddington that was re-edited by Boris Jakim [Vladimir Solovyov, The Justification of the Good, Grand Rapids, MI 2004, pp. 401f.], not only because Nemeth stays much closer to the Russian original, but also because his translation systematically indicates the differences between the first edition of 1897 (the one translated by Duddington) and the second one of 1899. A similar critical edition has, to my knowledge, not yet appeared in Russia. In the citation given here, bold printing indicates the 1899 additions; the Russian original (of 1899) can be found in Vladimir Solov'ëv, Opravdaniie dobra, in: Id., Sochineniia v dvukh tomakh, vol. 1, Moscow 1988, pp. 541f.

29 Ibid. Duddington and Jakim translate »в последнем основании« with »in the last resort« (p. 402) – in this case, their translation is closer to the original than Nemeth's. A purely literal translation would be »in the last/final foundation«.

church itself – a situation of which Solovëv himself proved highly critical on many occasions[30].

Finally, from the perspective of rapidly changing Russian reality, we may presume that, had he lived longer, Solovëv would have perceived the development of Russian society in the early twentieth century as both partly realising his ideas and as deeply betraying them. Born in 1853, he would have been 69 when the USSR was established in 1922, and he would have witnessed the transformation of his beloved Russia into the home of one of the most horrible regimes in human history. Here was a regime that *certainly* would not have let him speak or publish, and that likely would have liquidated him as it did Pavel Florenskii (d. 1937) and Gustav Shpet (d. 1937). His only chance for survival would have been o shift to purely academic work, as he had partly done when he started working on a translation of Plato and on entries for the Russian Brokgauz-Efron encyclopaedia.

In a way, we can compare Solovëv's »second best« vision with the Leninist (and later specifically Stalinist) idea of the »construction of socialism in one country«[31]. Solovëv's »truly Christian Russian Empire« is the »construction of free theocracy in one country«. Importantly, in such a Christian Russia, not only would the church be liberated and have regained its independent position as authority (which would be a return to the symphonic model), but the public sphere, »society« (общество) as Solovëv usually calls it, with its prophetic role, would also be a specifically *Russian* public sphere. In the event, Soviet reality took Russia in a different direction, one about which Mikhail Ryklin aptly wrote: »The postulate ›to Caesar what is Caesar's, to God what is God's‹ no longer holds, insofar as the two realms merge in the new order«[32].

Both realisation and disappointment were part of the reality of thinkers who, though none of them his pupil, all were deeply influenced by his thought. Among them, Semën Frank (1877–1950), Nikolai Berdyaev (1874–1948) and Sergei Bulgakov (1871–1944) tried to elaborate theoretically, underpin empirically, and (partly) apply practically, ideas and concepts that have their roots in the Solovëvian notions of *all-unity* (всеединство), God-Manhood/Divine Humanity/Theantropy (богочеловечество), and human co-creation leading to the improvement of humankind, the *spiritualisation* (одухотворение) of matter, and the preparation

---

30 See, e. g., SOLOVIEV, L'idée russe, p. 91, 101.
31 See Erik van REE, The Political Thought of Joseph Stalin, London 2006.
32 Michail RYKLIN, Kommunismus als Religion. Die Intellektuellen und die Oktoberrevolution, Frankfurt am Main 2008, p. 33: »Das Postulat ›dem Kaiser, was des Kaisers ist, und Gott, was Gottes ist‹ funktioniert nicht mehr, insofern beide Bereiche in der neuen Ordnung zusammenfließen«.

for the Kingdom of God in close cooperation with Sophia[33]. In this respect, this »sophiological« strand in Russian Orthodox Christian political theology was broadly progressive and activist, while also being consistently anti-pluralistic, essentially anti-democratic (as democratic systems enhance rather than supersede the dividedness of society through political *parties*), remarkably anti-positivistic (Solovëv was critical of Fëdorov's claim that the creation of God-Manhood was a *scientific* project)[34]. Yet it was also clearly anti-revolutionary and indeed cautiously liberal, claiming freedom of speech for itself, and by implication, for everyone, but wary of setting free society's economic and political forces. In the second respect, it contrasts with both conservative monarchism and socialism/communism, and certainly with bolshevism, and often comes close to liberal and Christian-democratic positions, while in the first respect, it contrasts with the other main strand, neo-patristic political theology which is much less oriented towards »changing the course of the created world«. In fact, it distances itself from such »hubristic« projects, holding that the sophiological progressives are always at risk of lapsing into millenarianism/chiliasm, »Prometheism«, and the divinisation of man (человековожество). Arguably, the most consistent sophiological political theology, turned into a theory of society and politics, is the 1930 *The Spiritual Foundations of Society* (Духовные основы общества) by Semën (Semyon) Frank[35]. As I have tried to show elsewhere, main positions in the so-called Russian religious philosophy of the twentieth century oscillate, when it comes to their political theology, between the notion of theocracy with its mundane translation of the sovereign state and the concept *sobornost'* as a variant of communitarian thinking: Ivan Il'in represents the first line of thought, Nikolai Berdyaev and Semën Frank the second[36].

Conclusion: Back to Political Theology

The field of position in political philosophy is often dominated by the opposition between monistic and dualistic understandings of reality: The first understanding, which can be found among Marxists, positivists, Jacobins, and many others, holds that there is only a single, by definition historical, reality with which we as humans

---

33 For further discussion, see Evert van der ZWEERDE, The Rise of the People. The Political Philosophy of the Vekhovtsy, in: Ruth COATES/Robin AIZLEWOOD (eds.), Landmarks Revisited. The Vekhi Symposium One Hundred Years On, Boston 2013, pp. 104–127.
34 KOSTALEVSKY, Dostoevsky and Soloviev, pp. 64f.
35 See Evert van der ZWEERDE, Gesellschaft, Gemeinschaft, Politik. Zur Aktualität der Sozialphilosophie Semën Franks, in: Holger KUßE (ed.), Kultur als Dialog und Meinung, Munich 2008, pp. 113–139.
36 Cf. van der ZWEERDE, Theocracy, Sobornost' and Democracy.

have to deal, opening the possibility of constructing a perfect society; the second understanding, which is typical of conservatives of different feathers, holds that there are two cities, and that, as long as the time for the second, Divine City, has not yet come, the main task of political order is to prevent a turn to chaos of the earthly city. The opposition is stated with maximum clarity by Carl Schmitt when, in his *Politische Theologie*, he depicts Bakunin as the prototypical enemy of his own, conservative-dualistic view. What both Bakunin and Schmitt, in their substitution of simplicity for clarity, fail to acknowledge is that there is a third possibility, namely to situate the political (among others) in the »between« of the world as it is and the world as it ought to be.

The central distinction in Christian political theology between what is God's and what is Caesar's raises three questions: Apart from the question of *what* is God's and *what* is Caesar's, and the question of how the »two kingdoms« are, can, or should be related, there is a third, political question: *Who* or *what* answers these questions? The Eastern-Roman, Byzantine, and Russian Orthodox traditions have predominantly answered both questions by establishing the duality of a Caesar-led state and a patriarch-led church, which jointly divide and symphonically administer Caesar's and God's affairs. This division of labour neutralises the fundamental tension and political potential that is generated by the key claim that God's – the God-Man's »my« – Kingdom is not of *this* world by creating a symmetrical duality of two realms, that of the church and that of the state. If this ruling duality can be understood as St Paul's τὸ κατέχον or ὁ κατέχων (2 Thessalonians 2:6–7; *удерживающий* in Russian), we should note that it not only keeps out the Antichrist, but also neutralises the revolutionary potential of the asymmetrical message that this kingdom here on earth is not God's. This complex issue has certainly led Christian-inspired thinkers in many different directions: from attempts to realise God's Kingdom in this world to the position that any *katechon* is better than none at all. If Schmitt was right that »all significant concepts of the modern theory of the state are secularised theological concepts«[37], then we should take this position to imply that the whole spectrum of positions in the field of theology finds its parallel in the field of political theory.

The Russian political theologies of the late nineteenth century discussed in this chapter revived, against the backdrop of the reduction of symphonic *Doppelherrschaft* to monistic autocracy, the potential of Christian political theology, readdressing the two questions indicated above and toying with the lid of Pandora's box. Bakunin not only aimed at the destruction of both κατεχωντες, his Deicide also paves the way, ideally, for a »flat« and godless »Kingdom of God« after the apocalyptic revolution, populated by a multitude that has left evil behind. Nothing

---

37 SCHMITT, Politische Theologie, p. 43: »Alle prägnanten Begriffe der modernen Staatslehre sind säkularisierte theologische Begriffe«.

is Caesar's, nothing is God's, man – humanity – is free at last. Dostoevsky's political theology appears as torn between the demonic polyphony facilitated by anarchic freedom and the κατέχων *par excellence* who, at the same time, is the Antichrist incarnate: the Grand Inquisitor who no longer needs Jesus Christ and laughingly sends him away. Solovëv's triune sophiology reactivates the third, prophetic »office« in opposition not only to tsarist subordination of the church to the state and its consequent erection of one instead of two heads, but also in opposition to the dyadic division of labour between patriarch and caesar; from Solovëv's perspective, the prophet's role to voice divine truth independently from the king and/or priest, not only underpins the critical role of public debate and opinion, but also blocks any claim by the powers and authorities to alone represent God's Kingdom in this world. The Prophet is a mouthpiece of Sophia in this »here-world«, which implies that there is no relation of hierarchy between king, priest, and prophet. Solovëv thus replaces a dyadic symphony with a triadic and triune one. As Pamela Davidson has shown in detail, Solovëv stylised himself as a prophet by placing himself implicitly in the sequence Pushkin – Dostoevsky – Solovëv[38].

If Christian political theology articulates the non-identity and non-coincidence of *this* world and *the* world, this implies an asymmetrical dividing line »between« what exists in space and time and what truly is. This »between« is, simultaneously, the expression of a duality – heavens and earth, divine and human, Augustine's *Civitas Dei* and *civitas terrena*, Bulgakov's Два града, but also, potentially, the opening up of a triad. Arguably, then, political order (including, but not limited to, constellations of state and religion/church) will always try to close the gap by reducing the triad to a duality, whereas political activity (protest, reform movements) will always try to open up and expand the »between« for its own purposes. Yet it risks identifying the two opposed realms and collapsing into a unitary vision of this »here-world«, a vision that eventually becomes totalitarian whatever its starting point may have been. Hypothetically, the reintroduction of a third element always and everywhere opens up the space of the political, allowing different forms of politics to deal with it: denial and escape, suppression and idealisation, channelling and giving shape/form, and unchaining as revolution and violent destruction, all of them at, given the perceived limitations of *this* world, the *maximum* realisation of *the* world. The unchaining of negative-theologically legitimised destructive forces in the case of Bakunin, the denial of politics in the name of universal love in the case of Dostoevsky, the suppression-plus-realisation in the case of the tsarist state-plus-church regime which understood itself as κατέχων and was theologically underpinned by Constantine Pobedonostsev and others. The formation of a triune

---

38 See Pamela DAVIDSON, Vladimir Solovyov and the Ideal of Prophecy, in: The Slavonic and East European Review 78/4 (2000), pp. 643–700.

regime, allowing for limited channelling in the case of Solovëv, illustrated the spectrum of possibilities – interestingly, when we recall Merab Mamardashvili, the latter's attempt to *give form* to political reality explains his perception as a Westerniser, *zapadnik*.

If we have reason to expect the world to remain »as furiously religious at it ever was«[39], we should also expect politico-theological discourse to be as permanent as it has ever been – and we can delete the question mark from Lefort's famous essay: The theologico-political *is* permanent. The basis of all forms of political theology is that both the political and the religious dimension of society are inevitable – even if both of them can of course be denied. Any »regime«, which settles the relationship of the religious and the political, of religion and politics, or, at an organisational level, of state and church, is itself a form of politics that deals with precisely the dimension of possible conflict entailed in the relation between those pairs, and in that sense *must* itself rely, implicitly or explicitly, on a political theology. This may appear, for longer or shorter periods, to not be the case, but as recent shifts and rifts in many parts of the world show, any such regime can fall victim to changing circumstances, including a different demographic, class, or denominational composition of society. Its symbolic dimension will, in all cases, be organised along monolithic, dualistic, and triadic lines, and the questions *what* is Caesar's and *what* is God's (however »God« may be understood), *how* the two realms do or should relate to each other – and *who* decides – are likely to remain with us forever. Of the authors discussed in this chapter, Vladimir Solovëv stands out, not as a thinker who offered a final answer to these questions, but as one who articulated the underlying problems in greater clarity than any of his contemporaries.

---

39 Peter L. BERGER, The Desecularization of the World. A Global Overview, in: Id. (ed.), The Desecularization of the World. Resurgent Religion and World Politics, Grand Rapids, MI 1999, pp. 1–18, at p. 2.

Lora Gerd

Russian Political Theologies

Messianism, Mythologisation of History, and Practical Policy in the Nineteenth and Early Twentieth Century

> Μῶρε Τοῦρκοι, Τουρκαλάδες,
> νὰ προσέχετε καλά,
> Γιατὶ ὁ Ροῦσσος κατεβαίνει
> μὲ τὰ ἄρματα πολλά,
> Ὡς τε καὶ μικρὰ Ρουσσόπουλα,
> γιὰ νὰ πάρουνε τὴν Πόλη καὶ
> τὴν Ἅγια Σοφιά[1].

I.

Modern Russian political theologies take us back to the sixteenth century, when the idea of Moscow as the Third Rome was first formulated by Filofei, the hegumen of the Pskov Eleazar Monastery. During more than 150 years, this theory was related more to Christian apocalypticism than to practical policy. According to Filofei, the First (i. e., Ancient) Rome and the Second (»New«) Rome (Constantinople) had fallen because of their heresies (i. e., the Union of Ferrara-Florence of 1439). Moscow was thus the capital of the only true Orthodox Christian Tsar, the keeper of the true faith, and therefore the third and last Rome[2]. At the same time, parallel ideas of Moscow as the New Jerusalem were being elaborated; they found their realisation in the foundation of the New Jerusalem Monastery near Moscow by Patriarch Nikon in 1656. The universalist idea of unification of the Eastern Christian world under the protection of the Russian Tsar, was rooted in the ancient notion of the *oikumene*, the inhabited, civilised world. In this view, the Russian Tsardom was the

---

1 A Greek folk poem from the First World War, written down in 2003 after Olympia Ntalakmanova, who was born on the Bosporus and at that time was living in Sozopolis (Bulgaria). It warned Turks of Russian military power and referred to traditional Greek dreams about the Russians capturing Constantinople and taking control over the church of Hagia Sophia, its most distinctive Orthodox monument in the city with great symbolic power.
2 Hildegard Schaeder, Moskau das Dritte Rom, Hamburg 1929; Dimitri Stremoukhoff, Moscow the Third Rome. Sources of the Doctrine, in: Speculum 28/1 (1953), pp. 84–101; Nina V. Sinitsyna, Tretii Rim. Istoki i evolutsiia russkoi srednevekovoi kontseptsii (XV–XVI vv.), Moscow 1998.

heir of the Greek Christian Empire, which had been conquered by the Ottomans, and Moscow thus inherited the dignity of Constantinople. Relics and venerated icons were brought to Moscow during the sixteenth and especially the seventeenth century, supposedly transmitting the sacred status of Eastern Christianity to Russia. This ideology was supported by the numerous Eastern abbots, monks and bishops, who arrived in Russia, gathering donations for their churches[3]. Yet the idea of *translatio imperii* was not unique, and many parallels can be found in the West European, »Roman« Empires of the Middle Ages and later.

At the end of the seventeenth century, Tsar Peter I undertook the first serious campaigns against the Ottomans. After that, Russian Messianic ideas of the liberation of Eastern Christianity and its two sacred towns, Jerusalem and Constantinople, from the Muslims converged with similar expectations on the side of the Greeks and Southern Slavs. The old oral prophesies about the liberation of Constantinople were transformed into a literary work named »Agathangel's prophesies«. It was first composed in the German territories by the Greek hieromonk Theoklitos Polyeidis around 1750 and enjoyed wide circulation in manuscript form before appearing in print. This text went through many editions until the 1840s; the central idea was that the »blond nation« would liberate Constantinople and the church of Hagia Sophia from the Ottomans[4].

After the failure of Peter's plans to conquer Ottoman territories, the eastward gaze of Russian political and military activities was replaced by Westernisation, which formed the main stream of Russian policy during the whole eighteenth century. The strict limitations placed on donations and the prohibition of open fundraising in Russia brought about a severance of contacts with the churches of the East. A new wave came in the 1760s, with the start of Catherine II's campaigns against Ottoman Turkey. After the treaty of Kuchuk-Kainarji (1774) Russia became the *de facto* protector of the Orthodox populations in the Ottoman Empire, which

---

3 N. F. Kapterev, Kharakter otnoshenii Rossii k Pravoslavnomu Vostoku v XVI I XVII stoletiiakh, Sergiev Posad ²1914; id., Snosheniia Ierusalimskogo Patriarkha Dosifeia s russkim pravitel'stvom (1667–1707 gg.), Moscow 1891; id., Snosheniia Ierusalimskikh Patriarkhov s russkim pravitel'stvom s poloviny XVI do konca XVIII stoletiia, St Petersburg 1895; Sergei M. Kashtanov, Rossiia i grecheskii mir v XVI veke, Moscow 2004; Vera G. Tchentsova, Ikona Iverskoi Bogomateri. Ocherki istorii otnoshenii grecheskoi tserkvi s Rossiiei v seredine XVII veka po dokumentam RGADA, Moscow 2010; Nadezhda P. Chesnokova, Khristianskii Vostok i Rossiia. Politicheskoe i kul'turnoe vzaimodeistvie v seredine XVII veka, Moscow 2011; Constantin A. Panchenko, Arab Orthodox Christians under the Ottomans, 1516–1831, Jordanville, NY 2016.

4 John Nicolopoulos, From Agathaggelos to the Megale Idea. Russia and the Emergency of Modern Greek Nationalism, in: Balkan Studies 26/1 (1985), pp. 41–56; Damianos Doikos, Ὁ Ἀγαθάγγελος ὡς προφητικὸν ἀποκαλυπτικὸν ἔργον καὶ τὸ μήνυμά του, Thessaloniki 1971; O. Misiurevich, Russkaia partiia i razvitie natsional'noi idei v Gretsii. Prorochestva o vosstanovlenii Vizantiiskoi Imperii v 1840 godu, in: Vestnik Moskovskogo Universiteta, Istoriia (1997), p. 6.

became the basis of all claims and representations of the Russian embassies to the Ottomans until the First World War. Documents usually referred to the Russian Tsar as »the natural protector« of the Orthodox in Turkey. Between 1774 and 1792, projects of further infiltration into the Ottoman Empire and the creation of a Greek Christian Empire were elaborated. During expeditions to the Aegean Islands, Count Nikita Panin (1718–1783) planned to establish a state that would be similar to the seventeenth-century Netherlands, but under Russian control. The most famous of these plans was the so-called »Greek Project« of Catherine the Great. The idea was hatched by her secretary Alexander Bezborodko and the famous courtier and commander-in-chief Grigorii Potëmkin (Pot'omkin); it was first expressed in a letter from the Empress, dated 10 (22) September 1782 to the Austrian Emperor Joseph II. Catherine proposed that, in case of a successful war against Turkey, the Balkans should be divided into spheres of influence, with Russia controlling the eastern part and Austria the western. The Danubian Principalities would be united into a buffer state named »Dakia«. A Greek kingdom in the Southern Balkans would be created as part of the restored Byzantine Empire. But the main target of Catherine's geopolitical aspirations was of course Constantinople as the future capital of the Greek kingdom[5]. After the annexation of Crimea in 1783, a golden medal was minted with Hagia Sophia and a rising star above it.

Catherine's »Greek Projects« were to a great extent inspired by a romantic view of antiquity and Ancient Greece of a kind very popular all over Europe in the eighteenth century. Unlike Western Philhellenes, Russian politicians always kept in mind the Byzantine past and Russo-Byzantine ties. For them, the history of the Greek nation and spirit did not end with antiquity. In the case of Russia, the intellectual was combined with romantic interest, as well as the stated aim of restoring the Christian Byzantine Empire. Catherine's grandson Constantine (born in 1779) was certainly named after the last Byzantine Emperor, Constantine XI Dragases (r. 1449–1453), and was supposed to become king of Greece after the »Reconquista«. Greek wet-nurses tended to him in his early childhood. The events of Catherine's second campaign against the Ottoman Empire and the death of Emperor Joseph, however, postponed the realisation of the »Greek Project«.

---

5 Edgar Hösch, Das sogenannte »Griechische Project« Katharinas II, in: Jahrbücher für Geschichte Osteuropas 12 (1964), pp. 168–206; O. P. Markova, O razvitii tak nazyvaemogo »Grecheskogo proekta« (80-e gody XVIII veka), in: Voprosy metodologii i izucheniia istochnikov po istorii vneshnei politiki Rossii, Moscow 1989, pp. 5–46; Grigorii L. Arsh, Predystoriia grecheskogo proekta, in: Vek Ekateriny. Dela balkanskie, Moscow 2000, pp. 209–213; P. V. Stegnii, Eshcho raz o grecheskom proekte Ekateriny II. Novye dokumenty iz AVPRI MID Rossii, in: Novaia i Noveishaia Istoriia 4 (2002), pp. 100–118.

II.

After the series of Russo-Ottoman wars at the beginning of the nineteenth century, Russia became an active competitor in the struggle between the Great Powers over the so-called »Eastern Question«. After the treaty of Adrianople (1829), Russia's policy towards the Eastern Christians took a new direction. In the 1830s, attention began to be paid to the Orthodox Arabs in Syria and Palestine for the first time. In 1847, a Russian mission was established in Jerusalem to improve organisation of pilgrimages, support Orthodoxy in the country, and control the use of Russian donations to the Holy Sepulchre[6]. The mission was followed by other organisations established after the Crimean War – the »Palestine Committee« (1859) and the *Imperial Orthodox Palestine Society* (1882). The Russian pilgrims, whose number gradually increased (by the beginning of the twentieth century they were 6,000 per year), created a passive background for Russian political ambitions in the Middle East. At the same time, these people, mainly illiterate peasants, were the mouthpiece of Messianic dreams of the Russian people, who regarded Jerusalem as their »spiritual Motherland«[7].

The nineteenth century is the age of Romanticism. The romantic idea of nation, adopted from Germany, found a fertile soil in Russia and flourished in Slavophile theory. The state ideology of Nicholas I's reign was based on the triad »Orthodoxy, Autocracy, National Consciousness« (*Pravoslavie, Samoderzhavie, Narodnost'*). In foreign policy, this meant the »discovery« and the instrumentalisation of different nations in the Orthodox East for the sake of Russian plans and visions[8]. Students from Slavic countries came to study at Russian universities and Orthodox Arabs first appeared in the account of his travels to Syria and Palestine by archimandrite Porfirii Uspenskii, who was sent there by the Russian government in the early 1840s. Dreams about the future liberation of Constantinople and the unification of the

---

6 Aleksei Afanas'evich DMITRIEVSKII, Episkop Porfirii Uspenskii kak initsiator i organizator pervoi russkoi dukhovnoi missii v Ierusalime, St Petersburg 1906; id., Uchrezhdenie i pervyi period deiatel'nosti Russkoi Dukhovnoi missii pod nachal'stvom Arkhimandrita Porfiriia (1842–1855), in: Nikolai N. LISOVOI (ed.), Rossiia v Sviatoi Zemle. Documenty i materialy, vol. 2, Moscow 2000.

7 Theophanis G. STAVROU, Russian Interests in Palestine, 1882–1914. A Study on Religious and Educational Enterprise, Thessaloniki 1963; Derek HOPWOOD, The Russian Presence in Syria and Palestine, 1843–1914. Church and Politics in the Near East, Oxford 1969; Elena ASTAFIEVA, La Russie en Terre Sainte. Le cas de la Société Impériale Orthodoxe de Palestine (1882–1917), in: Christianesimo nella istoria 1 (2003), pp. 121–134.

8 N. I. TSIMBAEV, Slavianofil'stvo. Iz istorii russkoi obshestvenno-politicheskoi mysli XIX veka, Moscow 1986.

Orthodox world can be found throughout the pages of Porfirii's journals[9]. Such ideas were shared by many of his contemporaries. The poet and diplomat Theodor T'utchev expressed the dream about Constantinople and the universal Russian Empire in his poem *Russian Geography* (1848):

> Moscow and Peter's city as well as Constantine's city,
> These are the cherished capitals of the Russian kingdom.
> But where are their borders, and where their boundaries?
> To the North, East, South, and Sunset?
> The fate of times to come will reveal them.
> Seven domestic oceans, and seven great rivers
> From the Nile to the Neva River
> From the Elbe River to China
> From the Volga to the Euphrates, from the Ganges to the Danube
> There lies the Russian kingdom and shall never pass away
> As the Spirit saw and Daniel prophesied.

The Crimean War brought new strategies in Russian Middle Eastern policy. Between 1856 and 1878, theoretical Slavophilism was replaced by practical Pan-Slavism. The policies of Alexander II supported the Bulgarians and other Balkan Slavs in their struggle against the Ottoman authorities and Greek Church primacy[10]. Inside Russia, the interests of the educated public were focused on Russian history and its Byzantine background. The expeditions of Pëtr Sevast'ianov to Mount Athos in 1857–1859 received support from Grand Duchess Maria Nikolaevna, and the artefacts he acquired there were exhibited at the Winter Palace in Petersburg. Sevast'ianov was the first to photograph the frescoes and manuscripts of Athos,

---

9 Porfirii Uspenskii, Kniga bytiia moego. Dnevniki i avtobiograficheskie zapiski episkopa Porfiriia Uspenskogo, vol. 2, St Petersburg 1895; Pavel V. Bezobrazov (ed.), Materialy dlia biografii episkopa Porfiriia Uspenskogo, 2 vols., St Petersburg 1910.

10 S.S. Tatishchev, Imperator Aleksandr II, ego zhizn' i carstvoanie, St Petersburg 1903; S.A. Nikitin, Slavianskie komitety v Rossii v 1858–1876 godakh, Moscow 1960; K.S. Liluashvili, Natsional'no-osvoboditel'naia bor'ba bolgarskogo naroda protiv fanariotskogo iga i Rossiia, Tbilisi 1978; A.N. Pypin, Panslavism v proshlom i nastoiashchem, St Petersburg 1913; Hans Kohn, Panslavism. Its History and Ideology, Notre Dame, IN 1953; Alfred Fischel, Der Panslavismus bis zum Weltkrieg, Stuttgart 1919; B.H. Sumner, Russia and the Balkans. 1870–1880, Oxford 1937; Michael B. Petrovich, The Emergency of Russian Panslavism, 1856–1870, New York 1956; Frank Fadner, Seventy Years of Panslavism in Russia. From Karamzin to Danilevsky 1800–1870, Washington, DC 1962; Andrzej Walicki, The Slavophile Controversy. History of the Conservative Utopia in Nineteenth-Century Russian Thought, Oxford 1975; Jelena Milojković-Djurić, Panslavism and National Identity in Russia and in the Balkans, 1930-1880. Images of the Self and Others, Ann Arbor, MI, 1994.

and his passion for Eastern Christian art led to further serious research into the Slavonic and Greek monuments of Athos[11].

The political events following the Russo-Ottoman war of 1877–1878 and its disappointing outcome, together with the assassination of Alexander II in 1881, brought a new turn to Russian Middle East policy and in the political ideology related to it. During the reign of Alexander III (r. 1881–1894) and with Constantine Pobedonostsev acting as Ober-Procurator (Chief Procurator) of the Holy Synod (1880–1905), Pan-Slavism was replaced by imperial nationalism[12]. Middle Eastern policy was now built on a revival of the Third Rome ideology, with St Petersburg as the centre of Orthodoxy and the Russian Tsar as protector of the Orthodox all over the world. The Russian school of Byzantine Studies was rapidly developing during the 1880es and 1890es. By the beginning of the twentieth century, it reached the level of the leading research centres of Germany or France. In 1894, the Russian Archaeological Institute in Constantinople (RAIK) was founded[13]. This institution contributed – along with the Palestine research carried out by the *Palestine Society* – to so-called »cultural diplomacy« in the Middle East. The scholars involved did not pursue overtly political ends, and most of them kept their distance from Messianic political romanticism. The Director of the RAIK, Feodor Uspenskii, carefully avoided giving rise to any suspicion on the part of rival powers. Yet at the same time, Byzantine Studies were strongly promoted by the Russian state. The *Palestine Society*, for instance, was under the direct patronage of the imperial family. Directly or indirectly, Byzantine Studies served imperial geopolitical ambitions.

Meanwhile, a small group of politicians and philosophers kept up a philhellenic line of political romanticism, staying close to the Greek »Megali Idea«. The state controller Tertii Filippov started an open polemic with Ivan Troitskii, professor at the St Petersburg Theological Academy, over the question of the one-thousand-year anniversary of Patriarch Photios I (858–867 and 878–886). The Russian Church, according to Filippov, ought to remain aware of its subordination to its Mother Church in Constantinople. Filippov's friend, the well-known diplomat, writer,

---

11 Lora GERD, Russian Research Work in the Archives of Mount Athos, in: Olivier DELOUIS/Kostis SMYRLIS (eds.), Lire les Archives de l'Athos, Paris 2019, pp. 535–538; ead., Petr Sevast'anov and his Expeditions to Mount Athos (1850s). Two Cartons from the French Photographic Society, in: Scrinium 16 (2020), pp. 105–123.
12 Lora GERD, Russian Policy in the Orthodox East. The Patriarchate of Constantinople (1878–1914), Warsaw 2014; Denis VOVCHENKO, Containing Balkan Nationalism. Imperial Russia and the Ottoman Christians, 1856–1914, New York 2016.
13 Konstantinos K. PAPOULIDIS, Τὸ Ρωσικὸ Ἀρχαιολογικὸ Ἰνστιτοῦτο Κωνσταντινουπόλεως (1894–1914). Συμβολὴ στὴν πνευματικὴ δραστηριότητα τῆς Ρωσίας στὴ χριστιανικὴ Ἀνατολὴ στὰ τέλη τοῦ 19ου μὲ ἀρχὲς τοῦ 20οῦ αἰώνα, Thessaloniki 1987; E.J. BASARGINA, Russkii Arkheologicheskii Institut v Konstantinopole, St Petersburg 1994; Pinar ÜRE, Reclaiming Byzantium. Russia, Turkey and the Archaeological Claim to the Middle East in the 19th Century, London 2020.

and philosopher Konstantin Leont'ev adopted a similar view and created his own vision of »Byzantinism« in the political, ecclesiastical, and ethnic mosaic of the Ottoman Empire[14].

At the beginning of the twentieth century, the national ambitions of the Balkan peoples reached their highest peak, as did the competition of the Great Powers in the »Eastern Question«. The collapse of the Ottoman Empire seemed likely in the nearest future, and the ecclesiastical struggle between Greeks on one side and Bulgarians or Arabs on the other intensified. Political romanticism and practical diplomacy continued to guide Russian policy-makers and diplomats in the early twentieth century. The idea of neo-Byzantine national imperialism was still dominant. Meanwhile, Pan-Slavic aspirations returned. Between 1906 and 1911, the Balkan League was established. The Western Powers, first of all Britain, were looking forward to the creation of a union with Greece at its head, while Russia aimed at uniting the Slavic peoples. In fact, the unification of all Southern Slavs had been the aim of Russian policy in the Balkans since 1856, but only in the first decades of the twentieth century there was real hope that it could be also realised. This political dream was partly fulfilled after the First World War by the creation of the Kingdom of Yugoslavia. However, the October Revolution prevented Russia from drawing any political profit from this.

All these tendencies converged in the first years of the First World War. The religious romanticism of Russian policy culminated between 1914 and 1916. Images of the glorious mediaeval past were dusted off. Alexander Nevsky (1236–1263), the canonised national hero from the Rurik dynasty, became the symbol of the struggle against the (German) Teutonic Order. The religious character of the war was constantly stressed: Posters depicted Emperor Wilhelm II as the devil. The dreams about Constantinople, »the spiritual capital« of Russia, and of Jerusalem, »the spiritual motherland« of Orthodoxy, were given new interpretations.

From the outset, Russian journalists declared the war to be the »Great War«, the crusade for the liberation of the Christian peoples of the East. When Turkey entered the war in October 1914, the Russian press went into a frenzy of political romanticism. For conservative church politicians, the capture of Constantinople represented the fulfilment of the old Messianic dream of restoring the Orthodox *basileia*. Constantinople was regarded as »the key of our home«, with the Bosporus and Dardanelles guarding the Black Sea against hostile invasions. Moreover, in order to ensure a land connection with both straits, one article argued that Russia

---

14 Dimitris STAMATOPOULOS, Το Βυζάντιο Μετά το έθνος. Το πρόβλημα της συνέχειας στις Βαλκανικές ιστοριογραφίες, Athens 2009, pp. 211–252; Konstantin LEONT'EV, Pro et contra, 2 vols., St Petersburg 1995; GERD, Russian Policy, pp. 20–39.

should annex the southern coast of the Black Sea as well[15]. The political side of the future ideal symphony of powers was logically (according to the Byzantine model) completed by the spiritual side. The discussions envisaged the restoration of the Patriarchate in Russia, a question which had been projected since the first Russian revolution from 1905 to 1907. What should be the position and the power of the patriarch? Should he really become an Ecumenical one? How would the dualism of power (tsar-patriarch) function in the new world after the war? Articles pretending to practical realism were followed by decidedly phantasmagorical ones. One author wrote that because Russia was larger than Ancient Byzantium, it ought to possess not only one, but several Patriarchs. Moscow, Kiev, Petrograd, Vil'na, Kazan', Tiflis, and Irkutsk should all, in his vision, be Patriarchal sees. Questions concerning all churches would be resolved at councils of Eastern bishops, where the Russian bishops would take the pre-eminent place[16]. Liberated Constantinople would become the cradle of the Kingdom of Christ on earth. After erecting the cross on Hagia Sophia, the division of the Christian world would cease, prophesied another author[17]. In some Russian provinces, people already started to collect money for the cross on the dome of Hagia Sophia, so that everything was ready for the happy moment when the Russian troops would enter Constantinople.

The dream of reconquering Constantinople seemed within reach, not only to those swept along by nationalist hysteria, but to the very heads of the Russian foreign policy establishment. In the first months of 1915, during the Dardanelles campaign, the Allies needed Russian aid. Britain and France proposed a plan to divide Turkey. In case of success, Russia was promised Constantinople and the straits with their adjacent territories. Two secret treaties were signed in March 1915[18]. On this occasion, a number of specialists were asked to write drafts about the future integration of those territories supposed to be incorporated by the Russian state. The opinion of experts in ecclesiastical matters was also solicited. Memoranda for the Holy Synod were written by Ivan Sokolov, Professor at St Petersburg Theological Academy, and by Archbishop Antonii Khrapovitskii, an influential theologian. Sokolov wrote a long exposition with plenty of references to Byzantine history. The present state of

---

15 G.F. CHIRKIN, Kolonial'nye interesy v sovremennoi voine i nashi zadachi na Blizhnem Vostoke, St Petersburg 1915; see also N.A. ZACHAROV, Nashe stremlenie k Bosphoru i Dardanellam i protivodeistvie emu zapadno-evropeiskikh derzhav. Doklad, chitannyi v petrogradskom klube obshestvennykh deiatelei 23 ianvaria 1915 g., St Petersburg 1916.

16 M.L., K chemu tserkovnym sferam nuzhno gotovit'sia? (K voprosu o budushchei organizatsii otnoshenii mezhdu vostochnymi tserkvami), in: Kolokol 2630 (11 February 1915).

17 Budushchaia kolybel' Tsarstva Khristova, in: Kolokol 2660 (18 March 1915).

18 See the edition of these documents in E.A. ADAMOV (ed.), Konstantinopol' i prolivy. Po sekretnym documentam byvshego ministerstva inostrannyh del, Moscow 1925, pp. 221–304; see also Prolivy (Sbornik), with an introduction by F. ROTHSTEIN and an essay by E. ADAMOV, Moscow 1924, pp. 88–93.

affairs was held to be a restoration of the Byzantine Empire under the rule of the Russian Tsars. The position of the Russian Patriarch would be restored as well, with the second place in the Patriarchal hierarchy after the Ecumenical Patriarch, and the tsar would make Constantinople one of his residences[19]. Archbishop Antonii, who was well known for his philhellenic views, suggested offering Constantinople to the Greeks as token of gratitude for the Christianisation of Russia in the Middle Ages.

The director of the Russian Archaeological Institute in Constantinople, Feodor Uspenskii, himself wrote a note on this subject on 23 March 1915. He stressed the importance of the main historical monument of the city, Hagia Sophia, which was to be the centre of the Greek liturgy, while the church of Blachernae was to be the focus for Slavonic worship. Its significance to Russian history lay in the icon of the Theotokos Blachernitissa that was sent to Moscow by Athonite monks in 1653 as a gift to Tsar Aleksei Mikhailovich. As for the patriarch, Uspenskii rejected all plans to unite the Ecumenical Patriarchate with the Russian Church, and called for a strict application of Orthodox canon law. At the same time, he did not exclude the possibility that the Patriarch of Constantinople, who was also a Turkish official, might follow the Sultan's government and retreat to the interior of Asia Minor[20]. Some authors thought that a Russian bishop should be permanent member of the Holy Synod of the Ecumenical Patriarchate; others suggested a complete Russification of the town, which would have meant placing the Patriarch alongside other Russian diocesan bishops[21].

All these discussions ceased after the summer of 1915, when it became clear that Dardanelles campaign had failed. In 1916 Pavel Mil'iukov, a deputy in the Duma, discovered the texts of the secret treaty of March 1915 and made them public. In light of the victories of the Russian army at the front in Caucasus, this revived dreams of a Reconquista: Some authors were already looking forward to a possible incorporation into Russia of half the Middle East: Mesopotamia, Cilicia, and the gulf of Alexandretta[22].

Palestine, the spiritual dream of the Russians, would not be so easily conquered. Journalists and politicians therefore focused on the role Russia would play in the European protectorate over the Holy Land. A French protectorate struck most of them as less favourable to Russian interests than the British one, because the

---

19 Nikolai N. LISOVOI, Russkaia Tserkov' i Patriarkhaty Vostoka. Tri tserkovno-politicheskie utopii XX veka, in: Religii mira. Istoriia i sovremennost' (2002), pp. 143–219, at pp. 156–196.
20 Lora GERD, Eshe odin projekt »Russkogo Konstantinopol'a«. Zapiska F.I. Uspenskogo 1915 g., in: Vspomogatel'nye Istoricheskie Discipliny 30 (2007), pp. 424–433.
21 [Aleksei A. DMITRIEVSKII], Konstantinopol'skia Tserkov' i russkaia vlast', typewritten with notes by Aleksei A. DMITRIEVSKII, Russian National Library, Manuscript Department, Fond 253, op. 1, d. 41, ff. 20–47; id., Vselenskii Patriarkh i russkaia grazhdanskaia vlast' v Konstantinopole, ff. 48–50.
22 A. IASHCHENKO, Russkie interesy v Maloi Asii, Moscow 1916.

Catholics had been working for several centuries to push the Orthodox into a church union and were thus in open confrontation with the Eastern Christians. The British had shown, at least in the last decades before the First World War, more tolerance towards the Orthodox and were ready to cooperate with them. Finally, there was a group of dreamers who even believed in the success of a Russian crusade to the Holy Land. Public discussions started at the beginning of 1915. The first extensive publication was an interview made by the journal *Birzhevye Vedomosti* under the title *Liberation of the Holy Sepulchre*[23]. The rector of St Petersburg Theological Academy, Bishop Anastasii Gribanovskii, fully advocated an exclusive Russian protectorate.

> A neutral status of the Holy Land is of course a fine thing but is unlikely to be realised. The Greeks will never give up their domination of the Holy Places. It would be much better to declare a Russian protectorate over Palestine, and all Christian nations would have the right of free access to the Holy Places. […] Russia is a »kind« state and will manage to defend the just spiritual interests of all believers[24].

Most respondents were in favour of neutrality for the Holy Land: This was, for instance, the opinion of the Greek Church's parish priest in St Petersburg, of the chair of the Lutheran consistory, and of the Roman Catholic collegium. A patriotic journalist, however, supported the extreme position of Bishop Anastasii: »The direct brave words of Bishop Anastasii come closer and warmer to the heart of the Orthodox. Indeed, it is Russia, the heir of the great Byzantine legacy, that should guard the most Holy Place of the world«[25].

The question of Palestine's future became a subject in a session of the St Petersburg Slavonic Benevolent Society on 9 February 1915. The deputy of the Duma and member of the Oktiabrist party Evgenii Kovalevskii gave a speech called »The Holy Land: The Promised and Lost Land«. The speaker focused on the well-known problems of the Russian presence in Jerusalem and the Holy Land, i. e., the rivalry with Greek clergy, the situation of the Russian pilgrims, and the introduction of the Slavonic liturgy. At the same time, he went further and proposed that the head of the Russian mission should be ordained bishop[26]. One of his main tasks was to be the organisation of extended Russian worship at all the Holy Places. Answering

---

23 Lora GERD, Russkie proekty budushchego Palestiny posle okonchaniia Pervoi Mirovoi voiny, in: Religii mira. Istoriia i sovremennost' (2006–2010) (2012), pp. 551–578.
24 Ibid., pp. 553f.
25 Ibid.
26 In fact, this proposal was discussed many times during the nineteenth century and constantly rejected as anti-canonical, especially after the failure of Bishop Cyril Naumov, chief of the Russian mission between 1858 and 1863.

to this speech, another expert on Palestine, Nikolai Riazhskii, claimed that control over the Holy Places should be given to a committee of representatives of the Slavic Orthodox nations. Such a demand, raised in the spirit of neo-Pan-Slavism, may come as a surprise given that Riazhskii had for a long time been inspector of the Russian schools in Syria and Palestine and author of an extended report on the ecclesiastical situation in Jerusalem. In his report to the vice chair of the *Palestine Society*, Aleksei Shirinskii-Shikhmatov, of 28 February 1915, Riazhskii stressed that Russia should obtain the official honour of protector of Orthodoxy in the Middle East. Catholic Europe would be opposed not by a weak Orthodox congregation, as it was before, but by a strong union of all Orthodox states led by Russia[27]. In fact, at the beginning of the First World War, the *Palestine Society* left aside the policy of supporting the Arabs against the Greeks in the Middle East and defended a transnational universalist model of the neo-Byzantine imperial type. A contrast to these debates was the phantasmagorical claim of the student of Petersburg theological academy, Archimandrite Mardarii Uskokovich, who demanded the capture of the Holy Land by Russia at any price.

III.

The Great War was the last, the Fifth Crusade, affirmed professor Aleksei A. Dmitrievskii at the next session of the Slavonic Society on 2 March 1915[28]. According to him, the liberation of Constantinople was the target of the practically minded part of his contemporaries. The real spiritual goal of the war was, however, the liberation of the Holy Land with its Jerusalem at its centre. Palestine would be liberated by Russian troops, and »our allies, the French and the English, probably will not prevent us in the fulfilment of this sacred deed. Thus, we will reach what each of us desires so much«, he said. After this moving statement, Dmitrievskii started a discussion about the future status of the Holy Places. He was quite sceptical about an international protectorate of Russia, Britain, and France. »The idea of an exclusive protectorate of our Holy Orthodox Russia over the Holy Places is the dearest to Russian Orthodox hearts« – as well, he continued, »as the desire to appear at the Holy Sepulchre as a legitimate and natural master«. This dream was, however, far from reality, as shown by the rest of Dmitrievskii's speech on the possibility of a French or British protectorate in Palestine. In his opinion, in case a

---

27 Cf. Nikolai N. Lɪsovoɪ, Russkoe dukhovnoe i politicheskoe prisutstvie v Sv'atoi Zemle i na Blizhnem Vostoke v XIX–nachale XX veka, Moscow 2006, pp. 369–381.
28 Russian National Library, Manuscript Department, Fond 253, f. 37.

protectorate of the three powers should not be possible, that of Britain would be less harmful to the interests of Orthodoxy.

Some specialists on the Middle East did not share Dmitrievskii's optimism about a British protectorate. They expressed their opinion in the official journal *Tserkovnye vedomosti*[29]. Professor Ivan Sokolov, in his article *The future fate of Palestine*, criticised the Anglophiles and stressed that only Russian domination could secure the interests of all Orthodox nations at the Holy Places in equal measure[30]. These political dreams were partly balanced by the more modest and realistic opinions of experts on the Middle East, like Nikolai Bobrovnikov, who foresaw the future revival of the Arabs and their creation of independent states[31]. However, the collapse of the Russian Empire in 1917 put an end to the political theologies and Messianic dreams in Russian foreign policy. Orthodoxy as an ideological basis for policy and politics was replaced by communism for the next 70 years.

---

29 Pribavleniia k Tserkovnym Vedomost'am 22 (1901), pp. 781–786.
30 Lisovoi, Russkaia Tserkov' i Patriarkhaty Vostoka, pp. 187–192.
31 See the publication of his note Nikolai Bobrovnikov, Russian Interests in Palestine (9 March 1914), in: Gerd, Russkie proekty budushchego Palestiny posle okonchaniia Pervoi Mirovoi voiny, pp. 564–576.

Stanislau Paulau

The Kəbrä Nägäśt (Glory of the Kings) Goes Global

Transnational Entanglements of Ethiopian Orthodox
Political Theology in the Early Twentieth Century

Introduction: Solomonic Political Theology and its »Neo-Solomonid« Reconfigurations

Unlike in the Greco-Roman world, where Christianity spread from the lower classes to the ruling elite, in the Horn of Africa Christianity was introduced as a court religion. It is therefore not surprising that both the Aksumite Kingdom – one of the first polities to proclaim Christianity as its state religion, doing so as early as around 340 AD – and the Ethiopian Empire, its political successor, have heavily relied upon theology as a means both of self-fashioning and of self-legitimation[1].

The central theme of Ethiopian Orthodox political theology is undoubtedly the *translatio imperii* from Ancient Israel to Ethiopia, an idea manifesting itself in a vast number of texts, but reaching its most profound articulation in the highly influential mediaeval treatise *Kəbrä nägäśt* (»Glory [or Nobility] of the Kings«)[2]. The *Kəbrä nägäśt* substantiated this claim in a twofold way. Firstly, by creating a genealogical link, tracing the Ethiopian monarchy back to Solomon, King of Israel, and the Queen of Sheba, referred to in the text as Makkəda and the »Queen of the South« (*Nəgəśtä Azeb*)[3]. And secondly, by putting forward an elaborate narrative

---

1 See, for example, two studies that are widely regarded as classics of their kind Taddesse TAMRAT, Church and State in Ethiopia, 1270–1527, Oxford 1972; Eike HABERLAND, Untersuchungen zum äthiopischen Königtum, Wiesbaden 1965.
2 The Gəʿəz text has been critically edited and translated into German by Carl BEZOLD, Kebra Nagast. Die Herrlichkeit der Könige. Nach den Handschriften in Berlin, London, Oxford und Paris zum ersten Mal im äthiopischen Urtext herausgegeben und mit deutscher Übersetzung versehen, Munich 1905. The much-reprinted English translation by Ernest Budge is to be used with caution, since it has a number of notorious flaws: Ernest Alfred Thompson Wallis BUDGE, The Queen of Sheba and Her only Son Menyelek. Being the History of the Departure of God & His Ark of the Covenant from Jerusalem to Ethiopia, and the Establishment of the Religion of the Hebrews & the Solomonic Line of Kings in That Country: A Complete Translation of the Kebra Nagast with Introduction, London 1922.
3 This narrative develops the biblical story related in 1 Kings 10:1–13 and 2 Chronicles 9:1–12. For a detailed discussion of the figures of the Queen of Saba and Solomon in Ethiopian tradition, see Alessandro BAUSI, La leggenda della Regina di Saba nella tradizione etiopica, in: Fabio BATTIATO et al. (eds.), La Regina di Saba. Un Mito fra Oriente e Occidente, Naples 2016, pp. 91–162; Witold WITAKOWSKI/ Ewa BALICKA-WITAKOWSKA, Solomon in Ethiopian Tradition, in: Joseph VERHEYDEN (ed.), The

about the transfer of the Ark of the Covenant from Jerusalem to Aksum, which in its turn was interpreted as a visible sign of the divine election of Ethiopians as God's new chosen people. The legendary Mənilək I, the supposed son of Solomon and the Queen of the South[4], would have been the first in a line of Ethiopian rulers, which stretched to the reign of Emperor Ḥaylä Śəllase (1930–1974).

The rise of the Solomonic political theology is generally associated with the reign of Yəkunno Amlak (1270–1285), who had interrupted the rule of the non-Israelite Zagʷe dynasty and claimed to »restore« the legitimate Solomonic lineage[5]. The compilation of the *Kəbrä nägäśt* in its present form around 1314–1322 is generally believed to be part of this legitimisation process, even though some parts of the text may be of a much earlier origin[6]. Certainly, the ideas of Israelite descent and the claim to possess the Ark of the Covenant both predate the *Kəbrä nägäśt*, as can be seen from the famous Arabic text by the Coptic priest Abū l-Makārim Saʿdallāh

---

Figure of Solomon in Jewish, Christian and Islamic Tradition. King, Sage and Architect, Leiden 2013, pp. 219–240.

4 According to well-established later Ethiopian tradition, the son of Solomon and the Queen of Sheba was called Mənilək. However, in the *Kəbrä nägäśt* itself, he is called Bäynä Ləḥkəm (from Arabic Ibn al-Ḥakīm, »son of the wise man«).

5 In a most prominent way, the story of the restoration of the Solomonic dynasty by Yəkunno Amlak is recounted in the treatise *Bəʾəlä nägäśt* (»Riches of the Kings«), composed in the seventeenth century. See Sevir CHERENTSOV, Bəʿəlä nägäśt, in: Siegbert UHLIG (ed.), Encyclopaedia Aethiopica, vol. 1, Wiesbaden 2003, pp. 514f.; George Wynn Brereton HUNTINGFORD, »The Wealth of Kings« and the End of the Zagwe Dynasty, in: Bulletin of the School of Oriental and African Studies 28/1 (1965), pp. 1–23. Remarkably, it is often transmitted within the same manuscripts as the *Kəbrä nägäśt*. Cf. Marie-Laure DERAT, L'énigme d'une dynastie sainte et usurpatrice dans le royaume chrétien d'Éthiopie du XIe au XIIIe siècle, Turnhout 2018, pp. 157–160.

6 Some scholars argue that the core of the text can be traced back to the sixth century. See Muriel DEBIÉ, Le Kebra Nagast éthiopien. Une réponse apocryphe aux événements de Najran?, in: Joëlle BEAUCAMP et al. (eds.), Le massacre de Najrân. Religion et politique en Arabie du sud au VIe siècle, II: Juifs et chrétiens en Arabie aux Ve et VIe siècles: regards croisés sur les sources, Paris 2010, pp. 255–278; Glen BOWERSOCK, Helen's Bridle, Ethiopian Christianity, and Syriac Apocalyptic, in: Jane BAUN et al. (eds.), Studia Patristica XLV: Ascetica. Liturgica, Orientalia, Critica et Philologica, First Two Centuries. Papers Presented at the Fifteenth International Conference on Patristic Studies Held in Oxford 2007, Leuven 2010, pp. 211–220; George BEVAN, Ethiopian Apocalyptic and the End of Roman Rule. The Reception of Chalcedon in Aksum and the Kebra Nagast, in: Jitse Harm Fokke DIJKSTRA/Greg FISHER (eds.), Inside and Out. Interactions between Rome and the Peoples on the Arabian and Egyptian Frontiers in Late Antiquity, Leuven 2014, pp. 371–390. The *Kəbrä nägäśt*'s relation to earlier traditions circulating throughout the Eastern Mediterranean and the context of its translation into Gəʿəz are also still being debated. For an introduction to the discussion and further bibliography, see Paolo MARRASSINI, Kəbrä nägäśt, in: Siegbert UHLIG (ed.), Encyclopaedia Aethiopica, vol. 3, Wiesbaden 2007, pp. 364–368; Pierluigi PIOVANELLI, The Apocryphal Legitimation of a »Solomonic« Dynasty in the Kəbrä nägäśt – A Reappraisal, in: Aethiopica 16 (2013), pp. 7–44.

b. Ǧirǧīs (died after 1208), *The Churches and Monasteries of Egypt and some Neighbouring Countries*, dating back to the early thirteenth century[7]. Consequently, the idea of the superiority of the Christian Kingship of Ethiopia was already bound to the monarch's claim to Zion – i. e., the Ark of the Covenant preserved in, and ultimately identified with, Aksum – at quite an early date[8]. The head of the Solomonic state was honoured first and foremost as *Nəguśä Ṣəyon* (»King of Zion«).

The idea of Solomonic descent was part of a wider set of associations which played a decisive role in Ethiopian political theology. First of all, the direct lineage from Israel and the notion of the purity of faith were closely interconnected. Since the *Kəbrä nägäśt* argued that the Ethiopians had already converted to monotheism and adopted the Old Testament in the time of the Queen of Sheba, the Ethiopian theologians could claim to be safeguarding the purest version of Scripture. This idea harked back to the popular polemical *topos* of the Jews who had deliberately changed a certain number of key passages or excluded whole books of the Old Testament. In the *Mäṣḥafä məsṭir* (»Book of the Mystery«), written in 1423–1424, the renowned Ethiopian Orthodox theologian Giyorgis of Sägla (ca. 1365–1425) made this claim in the following terms:

> Concerning the books of the Old [Testament], they have been translated from Hebrew into Gəʿəz in the days of the Queen of the South who visited Solomon. Therefore, the interpretation of the prophetic books found in the land of the Agʿazi [i. e., Ethiopia] was faithful, because they had adopted the Jewish Law before the birth of Christ. If they had translated them after the birth of Christ, the crucifiers would have changed the true word into a testimony of falseness[9].

While the whole Ethiopian nation was imagined as *verus Israel*, members of the Solomonic dynasty were seen as keepers and defenders of the true faith. To express

---

[7] The author not only mentions that the Ethiopian rulers are »of the family of Moses and Aaron«, but states that the Ethiopians possess »the Ark of the Covenant, in which are the two tables of stone, inscribed by the finger of God with the commandments which he ordained for the children of Israel«, Basil Thomas Alfred EVETTS (ed.), The Churches and Monasteries of Egypt and Some Neighbouring Countries Attributed to Abu Salih, the Armenian, Oxford ²1969, pp. 287f. Note that this famous description was for a long time wrongly ascribed to Abū Ṣāliḥ, a Christian Arab author from the thirteenth century. However, the work was compiled by Abū l-Makārim Saʿdallāh b. Ǧirǧīs. Cf. Franz-Christoph MUTH, Abū Ṣāliḥ, in: UHLIG (ed.), Encyclopaedia Aethiopica, vol. 1, pp. 54f.

[8] See Amsalu TEFERA, Traditions on Zion and Axum, in: Id., The Ethiopian Homily on the Ark of the Covenant, Leiden 2015, pp. 39–80.

[9] The English translation follows PIOVANELLI, The Apocryphal Legitimation, p. 11, note 19; for a critical edition see Yaqob BEYENE, Giyorgis di Sagla. Il libro del Mistero (Maṣḥafa Mesṭir), vol. 1 [textus], Leuven 1990, pp. 124f. and ibid., vol. 2 [versio], pp. 75f.

the unique relationship with biblical Israel, Ethiopian rulers have often depicted themselves as ʾƏsraʾelawiyan (»Israelites«), Däqqä ʾƏsraʾel (»Children of Israel«), or even Betä ʾƏsraʾel (»House of Israel«)[10].

This set of ideas was also instrumental for the »Neo-Solomonids«, Ethiopian rulers who ascended the throne from the 1850s onward, following a period of monarchical weakness and decentralisation known as Zämänä mäsafənt (»Era of the Judges [or Lords]«)[11]. The »Neo-Solomonic« political theology that drew on the mediaeval tradition of the Kəbrä nägäśt, but also modified it, adapting it to the challenges of modernity, remained the decisive ideological force of imperial Ethiopia until its fall in 1974.

But what precisely was new about »Neo-Solomonic« political theology? Donald Crummey has suggested that the »Neo-Solomonids« introduced three main innovations introduced into traditional political ideology: Firstly, they formulated a new principle of legitimate descent, not linked to direct succession through the male line only. Secondly, as active warlords, they abandoned the historic Solomonic practice of ritual seclusion. And thirdly, whereas mediaeval Solomonids had practiced structured polygamy, the »Neo-Solomonids« have revolutionised royal marriage customs by adopting the marital customs of the clergy: a strict monogamy sanctioned by the sacrament of marriage[12]. Some further studies have demonstrated how Ethiopian Emperors of the late nineteenth century re-invented the coronation rite in order to strengthen their claim to Solomonic descent and use it as a means of legitimisation in the internal political struggle[13]. Without diminishing the high value of the findings made in this field over the last decades, one notable limitation of previous research must be pointed out. »Neo-Solomonic« political theology (or ideology, as some authors prefer to refer to it) has been

---

10 Steven KAPLAN, Solomonic Dynasty, in: Siegbert UHLIG (ed.), Encyclopaedia Aethiopica, vol. 4, Wiesbaden 2010, pp. 688–690. In keeping with this royal ideology, several of the outstanding rulers of this period had names with strong biblical Israelite connotations including Amdä Ṣəyon (lit. »Pillar of Zion«) and Zärʾa Yaʿəqob (lit. »Seed of Jacob«). Emperor Dawit II, counted second after Dawit (David), the father of Solomon.

11 The name of this period that was marked by conflicts among regional rulers and warlords over the control of the emperor refers to Judges 21: 25. It is conventionally dated between 1769 and 1855. The end of this period is associated with the reign of Tewodros II (1855–1868). For a short historical overview, see Sophia DEGE, Zämänä mäsafənt, in: Alessandro BAUSI (ed.), Encyclopaedia Aethiopica, vol. 5, Wiesbaden 2014, pp. 122–129.

12 Donald CRUMMEY, Imperial Legitimacy and the Creation of Neo-Solomonic Ideology in 19th-Century Ethiopia, in: Cahiers d'Études Africaines 28/109 (1988), pp. 13–43, at p. 15.

13 The most prominent instance is that of Yoḥannəs IV (1871–1889), who organised his coronation in Ancient Aksum, see Izabela ORLOWSKA, The Legitimising Project. The Coronation Rite and the Written Word, in: Aethiopica 16 (2013), pp. 74–101; ead., Re-Imagining Empire. Ethiopian Political Culture under Yohannis IV, 1872-92, PhD Thesis, School of Oriental and African Studies, London 2006.

analysed exclusively within the Ethiopian national context and its internal dynamics, thereby neglecting the increasing importance of international relations for Ethiopia and its high impact upon all spheres of life in the Horn of Africa in the age of New Imperialism.

While Western historiography often tends to exoticise Ethiopian Orthodoxy by highlighting its absolute uniqueness (usually explained by a reference to its supposedly continuous isolation from the rest of Christendom), this chapter seeks to question this assumption by employing a distinctly transnational perspective. Even though the Solomonic narrative of the *Kəbrä nägäśt* ought indeed to be considered a distinctive and highly remarkable form of political theology, neither its emergence nor its development can be understood without considering Ethiopia's entanglements with the wider world. The same applies to »Neo-Solomonic« theology. In the following, I will argue that the transformations of Ethiopian political theology can only be comprehended in connection with the novel conditions in the field of international relations which the Ethiopian Empire had to face in the late nineteenth and early twentieth centuries, not least with the threat of European colonialism. Consequently, »Neo-Solomonic« political theology can be seen as a product of complex transnational entanglements. In order to substantiate this assertion, I am going to demonstrate how the transformations of Ethiopian political theology performed by three »Neo-Solomonid« rulers of the early twentieth century – Mənilək II (1889–1913), Zäwditu (1917–1930), and Haylä Śəllase – were influenced by their intellectual and/or political engagement with the wider world. By doing so, I shall analyse the influence of Ethio-German, Ethio-British, and Ethio-Japanese entanglements upon reconfigurations and new articulations of Solomonic theology.

Emperor Mənilək II: Ethio-German Entanglements, Theology of Colonisation, and the Quest for Historicity of the Solomonic Narrative

Even though by the end of the nineteenth century the Ethiopian Empire was virtually the only state on the entire African continent to retain its independence, it was surrounded by European colonial territories: Eritrea and Italian Somaliland (the southern and central parts of present-day Somalia) belonged to Italy; Sudan, British East Africa (present-day Kenya), and British Somaliland (the northern of present-day Somalia) belonged to Great Britain; French Somaliland (present-day Djibouti) belonged to France. In this context, relations with European powers were of immense importance for Ethiopian politics. The German Empire as a state that had no discernible colonial ambitions towards Ethiopia was perceived as a potential ally, which contributed to a dynamic development of contacts between both countries[14]. Ethio-German diplomacy unveiled some reconfigurations of »Neo-Solomonic« political theology that otherwise would not have been observable. In the following, two such aspects should be discussed: the Ethiopian attitude towards European colonisation and the quest for new historical evidence for the Solomonic narrative.

Already in the early 1870s Ethiopian Emperor Yoḥannǝs IV had succeeded in establishing contacts with German Emperor Wilhelm I (1871–1888). In the absence of alternative diplomatic channels through which political communication between Ethiopia and Germany could have taken place, in the initial stage correspondence turned out to be the principal instrument of exchange[15]. From the very beginning, the idea of a shared Christian identity became the main feature of the Ethio-German diplomatic discourse. Thus, Wilhelm I expressed the conviction that Ethiopia and Germany were fundamentally connected to each other by belonging to »the same precious Christian faith« (»*demselben theuern christlichen Glauben*«)[16]. In their turn, Ethiopian monarchs, in order to create a sense of a Christian communion often began their letters with a doxological Trinitarian formula and explicitly referred to their letter recipients as fellow-Christians. For example, Yoḥannǝs IV spoke of Wilhelm I as a »firm Christian« (*ṭǝnnu krǝstiyan*)[17] and of the chancellor of the

---

14 About early relations between Germany and Ethiopia, see Ursula GEHRING-MÜNZEL, 100 Jahre deutsch-äthiopische diplomatische Beziehungen, in: Walter RAUNIG/Asfa-Wossen ASSERATE (eds.), Orbis Aethiopicus. Ethiopian Art – A Unique Cultural Heritage and Modern Challenge, Lublin 2007, pp. 67–101; Adelheid ZELLEKE, 100 Jahre Deutsch-Äthiopischer Freundschafts- und Handelsvertrag 1905–2005, Bonn 2004; Dag ZIMEN, Rosen für den Negus. Die Aufnahme diplomatischer Beziehungen zwischen Deutschland und Äthiopien 1905, Göttingen 2005; Wolbert G.C. SMIDT, Five Centuries of Ethio-German Relations, in: Language Department of the German Foreign Office (ed.), Ethio-German Relations, Addis Abeba 2004, pp. 6–14; id., Photos as Historical Witnesses. The First Ethiopians in Germany and the First Germans in Ethiopia. The History of a Complex Relationship, Münster 2015; Rudolf FECHTER, History of German Ethiopian Diplomatic Relations, in: Zeitschrift für Kultur-Austausch. Sonderausgabe Äthiopien (1973), pp. 149–156; Bairu TAFLA, Ethiopia and Germany. Cultural, Political and Economic Relations 1871–1936, Wiesbaden 1981, pp. 73–144.
15 So far, the correspondence has only been partially edited. See TAFLA, Ethiopia and Germany, pp. 188–303; Wolbert G.C. SMIDT, »Annäherung Deutschlands und Aethiopiens«. Unbekannte Briefe des Kaisers Menelik II. und seines Gesandten 1907–08, in: Stefan BRÜNE/Heinrich SCHOLLER (eds.), Auf dem Weg zum modernen Äthiopien. Festschrift für Bairu Tafla, Münster 2005, pp. 197–224. A number of not yet edited letters are to be found in the Political Archive of the German Foreign Office (*Politisches Archiv des Auswärtigen Amts*) in Berlin.
16 Political Archive of the Foreign Office [henceforth PA AA], Allg. A 3900, Letter of Wilhelm I to Yoḥannǝs IV, 9 July 1880; cf. TAFLA, Ethiopia and Germany, pp. 195–199.
17 PA AA, Allg. A 23/197, Letter of Yoḥannǝs IV to Wilhelm I, 8 Nähase 1864 Ethiopian calendar [= 13 August 1872]; cf. TAFLA, Ethiopia and Germany, pp. 188f.

German Empire, Otto von Bismarck (in office 1871–1890) as a »kind man [and] perfect Christian« (*dägg säw faṣum krəstiyan*)[18].

The Ethiopian Emperor Mənilək II[19], who succeeded Yoḥannəs IV in 1889, followed the same rhetorical pattern in his correspondence with German Emperor Wilhelm II (1888–1918), highlighting the common Christian identity of both nations. However, more importantly, he formulated a theological reflection on the European colonisation of Africa. One of the most notable passages addressed to the German Emperor on this subject reads as follows:

> The Ethiopian Empire was for many centuries located between Moslems and heathens; today, the European powers have, by the will of God and by the effort of Europe, become neighbours of Ethiopia in all directions. The way is open for knowledge and commerce. […] Even though the territories of Germany are far away from our country, it is likely that the subjects of both will meet[20].

This statement has important implications not least in terms of political theology. Firstly, Mənilək II portrays European colonisation in the Horn of Africa not primarily as a change of political order, but rather as a shift within the religious landscape of the region. Secondly, he accentuates the Christian and, from his point of view, »God-willed« (*bäəgziʾabḥer fäqad*) nature of the new political regimes in Ethiopia's vicinity, and welcomes them as a long-awaited disruption of the religious isolation of Christian Ethiopia. As far as the causes of this isolation are concerned, Mənilək II points to »the desert and the followers of Islam« (*bärähäna yäʾəslam wägännoččə*) who, he claims, had prevented contact with the »Kings of the Christians« (*yäkrəstiyan nägäśtat*)[21].

Such favourable attitude towards the ongoing process of European colonisation of Africa and its interpretation primarily in terms of Christian domination over the »heathens« was rooted in Mənilək's II political theology and was at the same time related to the recent developments in Ethiopia itself. The end of the nineteenth century was marked by an enormous territorial expansion, in which the Ethiopian

---

18 PA AA, Allg. A 3233, Letter of Yoḥannəs IV to Bismarck, 11 Yäkatit 1873 Ethiopian calendar [= 17 February 1881]; cf. Tafla, Ethiopia and Germany, pp. 204f.

19 On Mənilək II, see Christopher Clapham, Mənilək II, in: Uhlig (ed.), Encyclopaedia Aethiopica, vol. 3, pp. 922–927; Harold G. Marcus, The Life and Times of Menelik II. Ethiopia 1844–1913, Lawrenceville, NJ, 1995; Chris Prouty, Empress Taytu and Menelik II. Ethiopia 1883–1910, London 1986.

20 PA AA, A 14623, Letter of Mənilək II to Wilhelm II, 7 Ḥamle 1893 Ethiopian calendar [= 14 July 1901]; cf. Tafla, Ethiopia and Germany, pp. 230–233.

21 PA AA, A 2829, Letter of Mənilək II to Wilhelm II, 6 Taḥśaś 1882 Ethiopian calendar [= 15 December 1889]; cf. Tafla, Ethiopia and Germany, pp. 208–221.

Empire more than doubled its territory, a process that ran in parallel to European colonisation. Since the areas conquered in the course of Ethiopia's expansion, like the parts of Africa dominated by European colonial powers, were predominantly inhabited by non-Christian populations, both processes were interpreted as a triumph of the Christian faith. Thus, in his letters to the German monarch, Mənilək II situated the incorporation of new territories into the Ethiopian Empire on the one hand and European colonisation on the other in an unambiguous relationship, with Christianity as the main reason for the success of both these endeavours[22]. The theological foundation of such an understanding may lie in the *Kəbrä nägäśt* and related texts of Solomonic tradition that contain the important *topos* of the eschatological religious war, in which Christian forces united under the leadership of the Kings of Ethiopia and of »Rom« (a toponym initially related to Constantinople, which later received a larger set of associations connected to powerful Christian polities outside of Ethiopia) win the final battle against the »enemies of the Christian faith«[23].

The progress of Ethio-German encounters at the end of the nineteenth and early twentieth century culminated in the plan to establish official diplomatic relations in 1905. By that time, the Ethiopian Empire had already entered into diplomatic relations with France (since 1897), Great Britain (since 1897), Russia (since 1898), Italy (since 1889), and the United States of America (since 1904). In March 1905, Wilhelm II sent a special imperial legation under the leadership of the Orientalist and diplomat Friedrich Rosen (1856–1935)[24] to Ethiopia with the aim of signing an official »Friendship and Trade Treaty«[25]. Two initially secret agreements made in the context of these negotiations reveal how Solomonic political theology had been reconfigured under the conditions of the early twentieth century.

---

22 PA AA, A 6118, Letter of Mənilək II to Wilhelm II, 14 Miyazya 1883 Ethiopian calendar [= 21 April 1891]; cf. TAFLA, Ethiopia and Germany, pp. 214–217.

23 On Ethiopian eschatology and in particular on the figure of the Ethiopian King therein, see André CAQUOT, La royauté sacrale en Éthiopie, in: Annales d'Ethiopie 2 (1957), pp. 205–218; HABERLAND, Untersuchungen, pp. 149–172; Robert BEYLOT, Le millénarisme, article de foi dans l'Église Éthiopienne, in: Rassegna di Studi Etiopici 25 (1971–1972), pp. 31–43; Merid Wolde AREGAY, Literary Origins of Ethiopian Millenarianism, in: Anatoly GROMYKO (ed.), Proceedings of the Ninth International Congress of Ethiopian Studies, Moscow, 26–29 August 1986, vol. 5, Moscow 1988, pp. 166–169.

24 On Friedrich Rosen, see Werner DAUM, Gelehrter und Diplomat. Friedrich Rosen und die Begründung der diplomatischen Beziehungen zwischen Deutschland und Äthiopien, in: Walter RAUNIG/ Steffen WENIG (eds.), Afrikas Horn. Akten der Ersten Internationalen Littmann-Konferenz, Wiesbaden 2005, pp. 265–281.

25 The itinerary of the trip as well as the diplomatic negotiations are documented in Felix ROSEN, Eine deutsche Gesandtschaft in Abessinien, Leipzig 1907; Hans VOLLBRECHT, Im Reiche des Negus Negesti Menelik II, Stuttgart 1906; Carl BOSCH, Karawanen-Reisen. Erlebnisse eines deutschen Kaufmanns in Ägypten, Mesopotamien, Persien und Abessinien, Berlin 1928, pp. 141–239.

The Germans arrived in the Ethiopian capital Addis Ababa on 12 February 1905, and were granted several audiences by the Ethiopian Emperor during the first weeks of their stay. However, initial negotiations produced no results. An extraordinary opportunity to change this course of things appeared on 27 February, when Mənilək II paid his first visit to the premises of the German legation. It was at this meeting that contentious issues that still stood in the way of signing the bilateral agreement between Ethiopia and Germany were resolved. The factor lay in Friedrich Rosen's accounts of his travels to the Near East and the latest successes of German archaeologists in the field of biblical archaeology. The Ethiopian Emperor displayed considerable interest in the German excavations in Babylon, »which have shed a good deal of new light on the events dealt with in the Bible«[26]. Evidently, the news that certain biblical accounts could be validated with the help of modern science had deeply impressed Mənilək II. He therefore granted – quite to the surprise of the German diplomats – to Germany the right to undertake archaeological excavations in Aksum, the ancient Ethiopian capital. Felix Rosen, a member of the imperial legation and brother of its leader, Friedrich Rosen, commented on this decision: »The great understanding which the Negus showed here for a purely scientific question, already led us to assume that the wise ruler, by the standards of his country, would be a promoter of art and science«[27].

However, for Mənilək II the decision to undertake archaeological excavations in Aksum was by no means a »purely scientific question«. Rather, the Ethiopian Emperor aimed at establishing a continuity of modern Ethiopia with the ancient Aksumite Kingdom and its supposedly »biblical« roots, as they were depicted in the Kəbrä nägäśt. Archaeological excavations were supposed to reveal Aksum's splendour at the time of the Queen of Sheba and provide historical evidence supporting the Solomonic narrative. In other words, the archaeologists were expected to prove the historicity of the Solomonic narrative and thus maintain its credibility under the conditions of modernity.

Wilhelm II, who was himself very much interested in archaeology, welcomed this news[28]. However, the information about planned archaeological excavations

---

26 »[…] die so manches neue Licht auf die in der Bibel behandelten Ereignisse geworfen haben«, ROSEN, Eine deutsche Gesandtschaft, p. 266.
27 »Das große Verständnis, das der Negus hier einer rein wissenschaftlichen Frage entgegenbrachte, ließ uns schon vermuten, daß der kluge Fürst, nach den Verhältnissen seines Landes, ein Förderer von Kunst und Wissenschaft sein würde«, ibid., pp. 266f. (my translation).
28 On Wilhelm II's enthusiasm for archaeology, see the articles in Thorsten BEIGEL/Sabine MANGOLD-WILL (eds.), Wilhelm II. Archäologie und Politik um 1900, Stuttgart 2017. Unfortunately, the excavations in Aksum are not considered in this volume, which nevertheless offers a good introduction to the political and scientific context of such undertakings and demonstrates the importance of archaeology in the reign of Wilhelm II.

in Aksum was supposed to be kept hidden from German academic circles for the time being. The German Emperor left the following handwritten marginal note on a telegram sent to him by the head of the German imperial legation to Ethiopia: »Bravo, Rosen! He did a splendid job! Shall receive high decoration! [...] Better not inform scholars yet, they gossip just like old wives«[29]. Apparently, Wilhelm II feared a possible continuation of the only recently settled »Babel-Bible controversy«[30], not least because excavations in Aksum might raise the question of the authenticity of the Ark of the Covenant supposedly located there.

Using archaeology as a means of historical legitimisation was indeed a major innovation in Ethiopian Orthodox political theology on the part of Mənilək II. In the same year, 1905, without waiting for the arrival of the German specialists, he initiated excavations in Aksum and announced the discovery of the grave of his legendary predecessor, Mənilək I, son of Solomon and the Queen of Sheba. Thereby, the most immediate »evidence« of the authenticity of the Solomonic narrative was provided and the relicts of the first Ethiopian King were solemnly transferred to the church of Aksum Ṣəyon, the place where the Ark of the Covenant was believed to be kept. Remarkably, the German archaeological expedition that arrived at Aksum in spring 1906 under the leadership of Enno Littmann (1875–1958) did not categorically dispel this mystification. Their survey of the archaeological site showed that the so-called »grave of Mənilək« was in fact of more ancient origin than most other structures to be found in Aksum[31].

There was yet another secret agreement made in the context of negotiations over the »Friendship and Trade Treaty« that aimed at the validation of Ethiopian Orthodox political theology. Germany was supposed to intervene in favour of Ethiopia in the question of the ownership of the Dayr as-Sulṭān (Arabic: دير السلطان; Gəʿəz: *Der Sə̄lṭan*) monastery in Jerusalem[32], which had become a bone of contention between

---

29 »Bravo Rosen! Hat seine Sache ganz vortrefflich gemacht! Soll hohe Dekoration erhalten! [...] Gelehrte lieber noch nicht informieren, die plaudern ebenso wie die alten Weiber«, PA AA, R 14914 and R 131418, Marginal note on the telegramme from Friedrich Rosen to the Foreign Office, 10 March 1905.
30 On this controversy, see Suzanne L. MARCHAND, German Orientalism in the Age of Empire. Religion, Race and Scholarship, New York 2009, pp. 244–249; Klaus JOHANNING, Der Bibel-Babel-Streit. Eine forschungsgeschichtliche Studie, Frankfurt am Main 1988; Reinhard G. LEHMANN, Friedrich Delitzsch und der Babel-Bibel-Streit, Göttingen 1994.
31 Cf. ROSEN, Eine deutsche Gesandtschaft, p. 475; Enno LITTMANN/Daniel KRENCKER, Vorbericht der deutschen Aksumexpedition, Berlin 1906, p. 30.
32 The Ethiopian Orthodox community had been established in Jerusalem since the Middle Ages. In the fourteenth and fifteenth centuries, it had owned four chapels within the church of the Holy Sepulchre and a monastery on Mount Zion. However, since the sixteenth century, only the monastery of Dayr as-Sulṭān, located on the roof of the chapel of Helena in the church of the Holy Sepulchre, remained in its possession. And by the eighteenth century at the latest, the Coptic Church disputed

the Ethiopian and Coptic Churches[33]. Thus, Wilhelm II, who himself was Protestant, was to become the advocate of the Ethiopian Church in an inner-Orthodox conflict[34]. This at the first glance unexpected role was assigned to the German Emperor because he maintained close connections with the Ottoman Empire and had a powerful diplomatic network in the region.

The monastic settlement in Jerusalem was of considerable importance for Mənilək II, not only as a spiritual and intellectual centre of the Ethiopian Orthodox Church, but also as vivid proof of the Solomonic narrative. According to Ethiopian tradition, the name of the monastery – Dayr as-Sulṭān means »Monastery of the Sovereign« – indicated that the site of the monastery had been given to the Queen of Sheba by the ruler of Jerusalem, King Solomon[35].

Both these agreements deeply connected with Ethiopian Orthodox political theology paved the way for the signing of the German-Ethiopian »Friendship and Trade Treaty« and made the establishment of diplomatic relations between both countries possible[36]. The entanglement of political theology and diplomatic relations found its symbolic expression in a special celebration in Aksum on Easter Sunday, 30 April 1905. On this day, the German legation reached the city on the way back to Europe and was welcomed with a service held in its honour in the front of the famous church of Aksum Ṣəyon. As representatives of an allied Christian Empire, the mem-

---

the Ethiopian property rights to the monastery and were only prepared to grant rights to its use. A new level of escalation was reached in 1890, when the Copts closed two chapels and the Ethiopian community was forced to celebrate its services in the open air, near these chapels. For the history of the Ethiopians in Jerusalem, see Enrico CERULLI, Etiopi in Palestina. Storia della communità etiopica di Gerusalemme, vols. 1–2, Rome 1943–1947; Salvatore TEDESCHI, Profilo storico di Dayr as-Sultan, in: Journal of Ethiopian Studies 2 (1964), pp. 92–160; Kirsten STOFFREGEN-PEDERSEN, The History of the Ethiopian Community in the Holy Land from the Time of Emperor Tewodros II till 1974, Jerusalem 1983.

33 On the history of the dispute over the monastery, see Tigab BEZIE, Ethiopia's Claim on Deir es-Sultan Monastery in Jerusalem, 1850s–1994. Roots, Litigation, Current Status, Saarbrücken 2011; Kirsten STOFFREGEN-PEDERSEN, Deir es-Sultan. The Ethiopian Monastery in Jerusalem, in: Quaderni di studi Etiopici 8–9 (1987–1988), pp. 33–47.

34 For this purpose, an Amharic document in French translation was given to Friedrich Rosen. It contained numerous earlier judicial decisions concerning the property rights on the monastery: PA AA, A 14563, Rosen to the Foreign Office, 16 August 1905. The documents were later published, Abba FILƎPPOS, The Rights of the Abyssinian Orthodox Church in the Holy Places, Jerusalem 1962.

35 Kirsten STOFFREGEN-PEDERSEN, Dayr as-Sulṭān, in: Siegbert UHLIG (ed.), Encyclopaedia Aethiopica, vol. 2, Wiesbaden 2005, p. 117. According to Ethiopian tradition, it was the Empress Helena (ca. 250–330), mother of Constantine the Great (r. 306–337), who herself assigned the Ethiopians the specific location on which to build their chapel. Cf. Maurice de COPPET (ed.), Chronique du règne de Ménélik II roi des rois d'Éthiopie, vol. 2, Paris 1930, pp. 489f.

36 PA AA, Vertragsarchiv. Deutsch-Äthiopischer Freundschafts- und Handelsvertrag; cf. ZIMEN, Rosen, pp. 47–50.

bers of the German imperial legation were included in the liturgical practice of the Ethiopian Orthodox Church at a particularly sacred place[37]. The special status that Mənilək II attributed to the visit of the German imperial legation was emphasised by $Aq^w aq^w am$, the liturgical dance of the Ethiopian clergy[38].

Empress Zäwditu: Ethio-British Entanglements and the Quest for a Female Role Model

After Mənilək's II death in 1913, Ethiopia entered a period of deep political crisis. At first, Mənilək's grandson Iyasu (1913–1916) became the designated emperor[39]. However, his reign proved to be short. In 1916, before he had even been officially crowned, Iyasu was charged with apostasy, alleging that he had converted to Islam and thus lost his right of succession within the Solomonic dynasty.

After some hesitation, the head of the Ethiopian Orthodox Church, *abunä* Matewos (1843–1926)[40], supported the *coup d'état* and released the nobility from its oath of loyalty to Iyasu, who was declared deposed from the throne and excommunicated from the church[41]. The assembly of nobles asked Zäwditu, Mənilək II's youngest daughter, to ascend the throne and become Empress of Ethiopia. At the same time, Täfäri Mak^wännən (the future Emperor Ḥaylä Śəllase) was elevated to the title of *Ras* and made heir to the throne[42]. Zäwditu was to become the first female sovereign in Ethiopian history ruling in her own right rather than as the

---

37 ROSEN, Eine deutsche Gesandtschaft, p. 467.
38 This dance – accompanied both by singing and by the traditional church musical instruments, the prayer stick (*mäqq^wamiya*), the sistron (*ṣänaṣəl*) and the drum (*käbäro*) – served as expression of a special spiritual joy and was prohibited in Lent; see Kay KAUFMAN-SHELEMAY, Aq^waq^wam, in: UHLIG (ed.), Encyclopaedia Aethiopica, vol. 1, p. 293; Donald Nathan LEVINE, Wax and Gold. Tradition and Innovation in Ethiopian Culture, Chicago 1986, p. 26.
39 On Iyasu and his period, see Ficquet ÉLOI/Wolbert SMIDT (eds.), The Life and Times of Lïj Iyasu of Ethiopia. New Insights, Münster 2014; Bahru ZEWDE, Iyasu, in: UHLIG (ed.), Encyclopaedia Aethiopica, vol. 3, pp. 253–256.
40 Initially, Matewos was a monk in the Coptic monastery of St Pachomius. In 1881, following a request of Emperor Yoḥannəs IV, he was ordained together with three other Coptic monks as bishop for Ethiopia. At first, he was bishop of the province of Šäwa, but when Mənilək II, with whom he maintained a close relationship, became emperor in 1889, he replaced then the head of the Ethiopian Church, *abunä* Peṭros IV (1881–1917) by permission of the Coptic Pope Kirellos V (1831–1927). On *abunä* Matewos, see Steven KAPLAN, Matewos, in: UHLIG (ed.), Encyclopaedia Aethiopica, vol. 3, pp. 867f.
41 Cf. Ahmed Hassen OMER, The Coup d'État of September 26, 1916. Different Perceptions, in: Journal of Ethiopian Studies 46 (2013), pp. 99–120.
42 *Ras* was the second highest rank and title (after *nəguś*, the emperor) in the hierarchy of the Ethiopian Empire; cf. Denis NOSNITSIN, Ras, in: UHLIG (ed.), Encyclopaedia Aethiopica, vol. 4, pp. 330f.

crowned spouse of an emperor. As a consequence, Ethiopian Orthodox political theology faced a previously unknown challenge.

The new accentuations of Solomonic theology manifested themselves during the coronation that took place on 11 February 1917 (= 4 Yäkkatit 1909 in the Ethiopian calendar). The traditional symbolism of the ceremony reflected continuity and emphasised deep respect for the long history of the Empire. At the same time, given the lack of precedent for a female sovereign in Ethiopian history, the tradition required creative adaptation. A new royal title was created, with the empress to be called *Nəgəśtä nägäśtat* (»Queen of Kings«), by analogy with the traditional imperial title of male monarchs, *Nəguśä nägäśt* (»King of Kings«)[43].

The ceremony of Zäwditu's coronation was marked by a combination of traditional patterns and innovative elements. It was the first coronation to which a high number of foreign guests and diplomats were invited. There were two main purposes behind this strategy. First, the coronation aimed to demonstrate the power of Ethiopia as an independent African country and to secure its diplomatic recognition as an equal of the European countries. Second, the presence of foreign guests was to attest the international support of the new regime and prove its commitment to modernisation[44]. Since the coronation took place when World War I was at its height, representatives of the British, Italian, French, and Russian legations were present, while the representatives of Germany and Ottoman Empire decided not to attend.

During the ceremony, before reciting the coronation prayer, *abunä* Matewos addressed the gathering. As a theological justification of the unusual fact that the monarch to be crowned was female, the archbishop mentioned the example of the Queen of Sheba, stressing that it was from her, and not from his father, Salomon, that Mənilək I had inherited the Ethiopian crown[45]. This motive was, however, intertwined with a modern European practice. *Abunä* Matewos referred to the example of the British Queen Victoria (1837–1901) and her successful reign[46]. The choice of Queen Victoria as a role model also had a clear political dimension, demonstrating to the foreign representatives at the ceremony that the new political

---

43 Gianfranco FIACCADORI, Nəguś, in: UHLIG (ed.), Encyclopaedia Aethiopica, vol. 3, p. 1164. The Ethiopian title of empress as the coronated spouse of an emperor was *Ǝtege*; cf. Hanna RUBINKOWSKA, Ǝtege, in: UHLIG (ed.), Encyclopaedia Aethiopica, vol. 2, p. 392.
44 Cf. Hanna RUBINOWSKA, A New Structure of Power: The Message revealed by the Coronation of Zawditu (1917), in: Annales d'Éthiopie 28 (2013), pp. 19–44, at p. 38.
45 Ibid., p. 31.
46 See also the recollections of a British eyewitness to the coronation, Leland Buxton (1884–1967): »A long proclamation was read out, which, by way of apologising for the sex of the monarch, referred to the great success achieved by Queen Victoria«, quoted in Arnold Weinholt HODSON, Seven Years in Southern Abyssinia, London 1927, p. 135.

elites saw themselves on the side of the Allies in the ongoing World War I, rather the Central Powers with which the disposed Iyasu had sympathised.

These two female figures, the Queen of Sheba and Queen Victoria, symbolised the political programme of the new Ethiopian Empress. Similarly, as Victoria's reign marked a long period of economic, cultural, and political growth, it was hoped that this would also be the case under Ethiopia's first empress. The reconfigurations of Ethiopian Orthodox political theology introduced by Zäwditu can be described as a »Sabean turn«. As underscored by the coronation, the Ethiopian royal dynasty was to be perceived not primarily as »Solomonic«, but rather as »Sabean«, since it was from the Queen of Sheba that Mənilək I had inherited the Ethiopian throne.

In her quest to normalise the idea of female leadership in Ethiopia, Zäwditu endeavoured to bring the Queen of Sheba out of the shadow of the figure of Solomon. An important step in this direction, was the institution of the »Order of the Queen of Sheba« in 1922[47]. As such, the use of orders following the European pattern was a fairly recent practice introduced in the Ethiopian Empire only in the second half of the nineteenth century[48]. Yoḥannəs IV had instituted the »Order of Solomon« as the highest imperial honour in the 1870s[49]. It was against this background that Zäwditu articulated her message. The insignia of the »Order of the Queen of Sheba« symbolically referred to the idea of *translatio imperii* from Ancient Israel to Ethiopia, thereby highlighting the central role of the Queen of Sheba in this process. It depicted a golden Star of David; at its centre was placed the right-facing profile of the Queen of Sheba superimposed over a three-pointed star, the symbol of the Trinity. Since orders were bestowed upon the highest nobility of the Ethiopian Empire as well as upon members of royal families of foreign states, they were an effective means of propagating the new ideology among the elites.

---

47 The »Order of the Queen of Sheba« was presented in six classes: Collar (only for members of the royal family); Grand Cordon (limited to 25); Grand Officer (limited to 45); Commander (limited to 55); Officer (unlimited); Member or Chevalier (i. e., »Knight«; also unlimited); cf. Gregory R. COPLEY, Ethiopia Reaches Her Hand unto God. Imperial Ethiopia's Unique Symbols, Structures and Role in the Modern World, Alexandria, VA, 1998, p. 151; cf. also Guntram FUHRMANN, Orden erzählen Geschichte. Von den Anfängen bis zur Zeit Friedrichs des Großen, Norderstedt 2015, pp. 16f.; Borna BARAC, Reference Catalogue – Orders, Medals and Decorations of the World Institutes until 1945, vol. 2, Zagreb 2010, pp. 41f.; Mario VOLPE, Signs of Honour – Compendium of Orders of Knighthood and Honours of Italy, Europe and the Rest of the World, vol. 2, Rome 2009, p. 410.

48 On the history of orders in Ethiopia, see Asfa-Wossen ASSERATE, Orders and Decorations, in: UHLIG (ed.), Encyclopaedia Aethiopica, vol. 4, pp. 44–46; Gregor GATSCHER-RIEDL, Die Orden des äthiopischen Kaiserreichs und der salomonidischen Dynastie, in Zeitschrift der Österreichischen Gesellschaft für Ordenskunde 91 (2013), pp. 1–22.

49 On the »Order of Solomon«, see COPEY, Ethiopia, p. 149; FUHRMANN, Orden, pp. 20f.; BARAC, Reference Catalogue, p. 21; VOLPE, Signs, pp. 408f.

At the same time, Zäwditu continued the quest for historical legitimatisation of the history of Solomon and the Queen of Sheba begun by Mənilək II. However, also in this endeavour, the Empress aimed to highlight the role of the Queen of Sheba. For this purpose, she commissioned an official of German-Ethiopian descent, Jakoub Adol Mar (1881-1952)[50], to collect »all legends, tales, songs and oral traditions about the history of the Queen of Sheba« and to write her biography with the greatest possible degree of historical truth[51]. Due to his family background and professional experience – he had spent 17 years in Germany, where he attended school and university, and later held several important administrative positions under Mənilək II – Jakoub Adol Mar was familiar with both worlds. Zäwditu held, therefore, the justified hope that he would confirm the Ethiopian traditional narrative with help of modern Western scholarship and sent him to Europe for this purpose. Although the diplomatic career of Jakoub Adol Mar, who was appointed Ethiopian consul in Belgium in 1922, cannot be described as successful[52], he fulfilled his assignment and wrote a treatise of over 2,000 pages in the Amharic language. The book about the Queen of Sheba was handed to Empress Zäwditu in handwritten form together with ten copies. While the Amharic treatise subsequently disappeared, in 1940 Jakoub Adol Mar published a novelistic account in French, *Makéda, Reine vierge. Roman de la Reine de Saba*, which was based upon his original research conducted for Zäwditu[53]. Even though the book had a distinctively

---

50 Jakoub Adol Mar was the last of the ten children of Johannes Mayer, a German Lutheran missionary, and an Ethiopian, Sara Nəguśe. His German name was Adolf Jakob Mayer; in the Ethiopian version, Mayer became »Mar« and Adolf became »Adol«. In Ethiopia, he was known mainly as »Ya'əqob Mar«. On Mar, see Wolbert G.C. SMIDT, Mayer, Adolf Jakob, in: UHLIG (ed.), Encyclopaedia Aethiopica, vol. 3, pp. 889f.
51 Prince JACOUB, Makéda, Reine vierge. Roman de la Reine de Saba, Paris 1940, p. 5.
52 Little is known of his direct consular activities in Belgium, but he was allowed to cooperate very closely with the German government following Hitler's seizure of power. He spent the years 1933 and 1934 in Ethiopia, where he was commissioned by the German ambassador to draw up an unrealised plan for the settlement of 20,000 Germans in Ethiopia. Cf. Bruce G. STRANG, Collision of Empires. Italy's Invasion of Ethiopia and its International Impact, Farnham 2013, p. 240. In 1937, he moved to France with his wife, the Belgian actress Hélène Smet (1888-1972), whom he had married in 1923. After the outbreak of World War II, as a German citizen, he was interned in France, but soon after the German occupation of France he was released. From then on, Jakoub Adol Mar worked for the German Propaganda Department in France under the *Dienststelle Ribbentrop*, where he ran his own radio programme, *Le quart d'heure colonial*. Later he was also responsible for the Arabic-language programme on the *Paris Mondial* station. After the war, Jakoub Adol Mar was held responsible for this activity and was sentenced to five years imprisonment. Cf. Ras Mar Jacob – honigsüß, in: Der Spiegel. Das deutsche Nachrichten-Magazin 1 (1947), p. 9.
53 JACOUB, Makéda. In 1997 the book was reissued: Jakoub Adol MAR, Makéda, ou, La fabuleuse histoire de la reine de Saba, Paris 1997; German translation: Id., Makeda, Königin von Saba, Munich 1998.

novel-like character, Jakoub Adol Mar was presented by the editors as a trustworthy scholar and »un érudit pour qui les mystères du monde oriental antique n'ont pas de secrets«[54]. The book was nothing more than a glorification of the Queen of Sheba, based upon various assumptions regarding ethnography and archaeology of the Ancient Orient and padded out with elements of Ethiopian everyday life projected onto the past.

All in all, the »Sabean turn« initiated by Empress Zäwditu can be described as a remarkable attempt to shift emphases within the traditional understanding of the Solomonic narrative. Whereas the Queen of Sheba provided a model of justification of a female rule within the Ethiopian tradition, the figure of Queen Victoria was undoubtedly an important contemporary point of reference. In the instruments she employed to reconfigure Ethiopian Orthodox political theology, Zäwditu followed the example of her father, Mənilək II. Both of them made use of modern Western scholarship in their attempts to provide historical evidence for the Ethiopian founding myth.

Emperor Haylä Śəllase: Ethio-Japanese Entanglements and the Quest for a Juridical Legitimation of the Solomonic Narrative

On 2 November 1930, *Ras* Täfäri Mak^wännən, who was to become the last Solomonic monarch, ascended to the throne and assumed the royal name Haylä Śəllase (Haile Selassie). In the course of his long reign, which lasted until 1974, Haylä Śəllase largely shaped »Neo-Solomonic« political theology. While his contribution to the Ethiopian Orthodox political thought certainly deserves a comprehensive study, in the following I would like to focus on one particular episode that arguably was formative for the further development of political theology in Ethiopia – the promulgation of the first modern constitution in Ethiopian history[55].

---

54 JACOUB, Makéda, p. 4.
55 Some scholars regard the ensemble of mediaeval writings – including the already often mentioned *Kəbrä nägäśt*, the *Śər'atä mängəśt* (»Order of the Reign«), and the *Fətḥa nägäśt* (»The Law of the Kings«) as the first written constitution that provided the ideological and legislative foundations of the Ethiopian monarchy; see Bairu TAFLA/Heinrich SCHOLLER, Ser'ata Mangest. An Early Ethiopian Constitution, in: Verfassung und Recht in Übersee 9 (1976), pp. 487–499; James C.N. PAUL/ Christopher CLAPHAM, Ethiopian Constitutional Development, 2 vols., Addis Ababa 1969–1971; Heinrich SCHOLLER, Constitutional law: From Tradition to the 20th Century, in: Id., Ethiopian Constitutional and Legal Development, vol. 1, Cologne 2005, pp. 79–86; cf. id., Constitutions, in: UHLIG (ed.), Encyclopaedia Aethiopica, vol. 1, pp. 788–791.

Ḥaylä Śəllase promulgated the constitution (*Ḥəggä mängəśt*) less than a year after his coronation, on 16 July 1931. It was drafted by a Russian-educated intellectual, Täklä Ḥawaryat Täklä Maryam (1884–1977)[56], and modified by the emperor and his advisers. It has to be stressed that the Ethiopian constitution to a certain extent followed and even copied the Japanese Meiji Constitution of 1889[57]. Whereas the Meiji Constitution in its turn was largely modelled on the Prussian constitution of 1850 and that of the German Empire of 1871, it had certain unique features that were missing in other modern constitutions. The feature of the Japanese constitution that doubtlessly appealed to Ḥaylä Śəllase, who sought to provide a juridical foundation to Ethiopian Orthodox political theology, was the idea of the emperor's sacral nature and the religiously connotated notion of royal succession. Accordingly, the Ethiopian constitution declared in its first chapter that »the imperial dignity shall remain perpetually attached to the line of His Majesty Haile Selassie I, descendant of King Sahle Selassie, whose line descends without interruption from the dynasty of Menelik I, son of King Solomon of Jerusalem and the Queen of Ethiopia, known as the Queen of Sheba«[58].

Thus, the descent of the Ethiopian royal dynasty from King Solomon and the Queen of Sheba (here called »the Queen of Ethiopia«) was not perceived as a matter of religious belief or historical inquiry, but was rather determined as a fundamental juridical principle. The formulation of this article has obvious parallels with that of the Meiji Constitution which referred to the »sacred imperial ancestors« as well as with the idea of »the throne of a lineal succession unbroken for ages eternal« expressed in its preamble[59]. An important innovation introduced by Ḥaylä Śəllase concerned the principle of legitimate succession to the throne. It stipulated that imperial power had to be transmitted exclusively within his own line rather than – as had previously been the case – within the Solomonic dynasty as a whole.

---

56 See Maxim ZABOLOTSKIH, Täklä Ḥawaryat Täklä Maryam, in: UHLIG (ed.), Encyclopaedia Aethiopica, vol. 4, pp. 829f.; Bahru ZEWDE, Pioneers of Change in Ethiopia. The Reformist Intellectuals of the Early Twentieth Century, Oxford 2002.
57 Cf. Joseph Calvitt CLARKE III, Alliance of the Colored Peoples. Ethiopia and Japan Before World War II, Rochester, NY 2011, pp. 37f.; PAUL/CLAPHAM, Ethiopian Constitutional Development, vol. 1, p. 370; Aberra JEMBERE, An Introduction to the Legal History of Ethiopia, 1434–1974, London 2000, pp. 167–172.
58 The Constitution of Ethiopia. Established in the Reign of His Majesty Haile Selassie I, July 16, 1931, Chapter I, Article 3, published by: WorldStatesmen.org, URL: <https://www.worldstatesmen.org/Ethiopia_1931.txt> (09-28-2023).
59 The Constitution of the Empire of Japan (1889), published by: Hanover Historical Texts Project, URL: <https://history.hanover.edu/texts/1889con.html> (09-20-2023) [abbreviated form of Hirobumi ITO, Commentaries on the Constitution of the Empire of Japan, trans. by Miyoji ITO, Tokyo 22nd year of Meiji 1889].

Another central feature borrowed from the Meiji Constitution was the proclamation of the idea of the sacral kingship[60]. Whereas the Japanese constitution stated in a concise manner, »the emperor is sacred and inviolable«[61], the Ethiopian constitution elaborated this formulation, deriving the sacrality of the emperor from his membership of the Solomonic dynasty and the sanction of the church expressed through anointment. The relevant passage of the Ethiopian constitution reads as follows:

> By virtue of his imperial blood, as well as by the anointing which he has received, the person of the emperor is sacred, his dignity is inviolable and his power indisputable. He is consequently entitled to all the honours due to him in accordance with tradition and the present Constitution. The law decrees that anyone so bold as to seek to injure His Majesty the emperor will be punished[62].

In effect, the Meiji Constitution provided an excellent foundation for Ḥaylä Śəllase's constitutional design that allowed him to enshrine central features of Ethiopian Orthodox political theology in the main legal document. Despite its remoteness in geographical as well as cultural and religious terms, in the 1930s Japan became a significant role model for Ethiopian intellectuals by offering an alternative paradigm of modernisation that differed markedly from Western models[63]. Even though, during the early period of Ḥaylä Śəllase's reign, Ethiopia cultivated a closer bilateral relationship with Japan[64], the most profound outcome of the Ethio-Japanese entanglements was certainly the promulgation of the Ethiopian constitution that adopted the Japanese idea of the sacral kingship and restated it in accordance with Ethiopian Orthodox political theology.

---

60 On the Japanese notion of the sacral kingship, see Yukata HIBINO, Learning the Sacred Way of the Emperor. The National Ideals of the Japanese People, New York 2010; Ben-Ami SHILLONY, Enigma of the Emperors. Sacred Subservience in Japanese History, Kent 2005; Emiko OHNUKI-TIERNEY, The Emperor of Japan as Deity (Kami), in: Ethnology 30/3 (1991), pp. 199–215.
61 The Constitution of the Empire of Japan, Chapter I, Article 3.
62 The Constitution of Ethiopia, Chapter I, Article 5.
63 See Bahru ZEWDE, The Concept of Japanization in the Intellectual History of Modern Ethiopia, in: Id. (ed.), Proceedings of Fifth Seminar of the Department of History, Addis Ababa 1990, pp. 1–17; CLARKE III, Alliance, pp. 7–21; Sara MARZAGORA, »We Proceed following Japan«. The Role of the Japanese Model in Early 20th Century Ethiopian Political Philosophy, in: Arno SONDEREGGER (ed.), African Thoughts on Colonial and Neo-colonial Worlds. Facets of an Intellectual History of Africa, Berlin 2015, pp. 17–32.
64 See Hideko FAËRBER-ISHIHARA, Japan, relations with, in: UHLIG (ed.), Encyclopaedia Aethiopica, vol. 3, pp. 267–269; CLARKE III, Alliance, pp. 31–61; Hideko FAËRBER-ISHIHARA, Heruy, le Japon et les »japonisants«, in: Alain ROUAUD (ed.), Les orientalistes sont des aventuriers, Paris 1999, pp. 143–149.

Conclusion

The *Kəbrä nägäśt* can indeed be regarded as a remarkable example of transnational entanglements within the Christian oriental world. This text was in all probability composed in Arabic language within a Coptic Christian context, was largely shaped by imagery of the Hebrew Bible as well as theological ideas originating from the Syrian milieu, was translated in the fourteenth century into Gəʿəz, and on the Ethiopian soil gave rise to a very particular Orthodox political theology. However, the history of its reception and re-interpretation in the modern times cannot be comprehended without also considering the numerous transnational entanglements involved.

The *Kəbrä nägäśt* provided the Ethiopian Empire with a strong and lasting Israelite identity and laid the foundation of Ethiopian Orthodox political theology built upon the Solomonic narrative. However, the »Neo-Solomonids« had to find new ways to articulate this narrative in the face of two major challenges. On the one hand, after the enduring period of decay of the monarchy known in Ethiopia as *Zämänä mäsafənt* (1769–1855), the position of the emperor needed reinforcement in order to be able to consolidate the state. On the other hand, the Ethiopian Empire had to assert its position as a powerful and sovereign state in view of the threat posed by European colonisation. The new expressions of the Solomonic narrative advanced in the early twentieth century functioned as a means to establish a political order that would be able to meet these challenges.

The paradox of the situation that the Ethiopian rulers found themselves in during the early twentieth century was that the Solomonic narrative that used to be regarded as indisputable and could therefore serve as the source of legitimation itself required a historical authentication. The Solomonic narrative was contested. Therefore, the Ethiopian rulers attempted to make use of European science, as in the cases of Mənilək II and Zäwditu, to provide (or rather to construct) historical evidence for the Ethiopian founding myth. Moreover, transnational entanglements made reconfigurations of Ethiopian Orthodox political theology and its embedding into new forms possible, as exemplified by the case of the »Sabean turn«. The incorporation of the Solomonic narrative into the first Ethiopian Constitution, largely inspired by the Japanese constitutional design, was a logical consequence of the process that Pierluigi Piovanelli has described as the »Solomonic reconstruction of Ethiopian reality«[65]. As demonstrated in this chapter, this Solomonic reconstruction was made possible not least by transnational entanglements of intellectual, diplomatic, and religious kinds.

---

65 Piovanelli, The Apocryphal Legitimation, p. 21.

Intensive exchange with the wider world not only contributed to the transformation of Ethiopian Orthodox political theology but also drew the attention of European scholars to the Solomonic narrative in general and to the *Kəbrä nägäśt* in particular. The rumour that the Ethiopian Christians have a book under the title *Gloria regum*, containing a story of the Queen of Sheba that deviates from the biblical account and enjoying an extraordinary authority »like another gospel« (*alterum quasi Evangelium*), was circulating in Europe since the Early modern period[66]. However, the text of the *Kəbrä nägäśt* remained virtually unknown in the West until the early twentieth century, when Carl Bezold published a critical edition of the *Kəbrä nägäśt*'s Gəʿəz text accompanied by a German translation[67]. Thus, the formative text of Ethiopian Orthodox political theology, previously known to European readers mainly through contradictory paraphrases, was for the first time made available in its entirety.

Numerous enthusiastic reviews of Bezold's edition bear witness to considerable interest in the *Kəbrä nägäśt*[68]. An interest in the Solomonic narrative evolved amid fascination for the Queen of Sheba that could be observed among early twentieth-century scholars. Remarkably, debates around her figure were held across disciplinary and national borders and involved not only theologians and historians

---

66 Hiob LUDOLF, Historia Æthiopica, sive brevis & succincta descriptio Regni Habessinorvm, Quod vulgo male Presbyteri Iohannis vocatur, Frankfurt am Main 1681, Cap. IV.II.I.

67 BEZOLD, Kebra Nagast. Previously, Franz Praetorius had edited a relatively small portion of the *Kəbrä nägäśt* (chapters 19–32 out of total 117 chapters) and provided it with a Latin translation: Franz PRAETORIUS, Fabula de Regina Sabaea apud Aethiopes, Halle 1870.

68 [book review] Theodore NÖLDEKE, Kebra Nagast. Die Herrlichkeit der Könige. Nach den Handschriften in Berlin, London, Oxford und Paris zum ersten Mal im äthiopischen Urtext herausgegeben und mit deutscher Übersetzung versehen, in: Wiener Zeitschrift für die Kunde des Morgenlandes 19 (1905), pp. 397–411; [book review] Hugo GREßMANN, Kebra Nagast. Die Herrlichkeit der Könige. Nach den Handschriften in Berlin, London, Oxford und Paris zum ersten Mal im äthiopischen Urtext herausgegeben und mit deutscher Übersetzung versehen, in: Zeitschrift der Deutschen Morgenländischen Gesellschaft 60 (1906), pp. 666–674; [book review] Johannes FLEMMING, Kebra Nagast. Die Herrlichkeit der Könige. Nach den Handschriften in Berlin, London, Oxford und Paris zum ersten Mal im äthiopischen Urtext herausgegeben und mit deutscher Übersetzung versehen, in: Göttingische Gelehrte Anzeigen 11/171 (1909), pp. 903–912; [book review] James CRICHTON, Kebra Nagast. Die Herrlichkeit der Könige. Nach den Handschriften in Berlin, London, Oxford und Paris zum ersten Mal im äthiopischen Urtext herausgegeben und mit deutscher Übersetzung versehen, in: Review of Theology and Philosophy 1 (1906), pp. 225–229.

but also Byzantinists[69], Germanists[70], and even Sinologists[71]. Thus, the *Kəbrä nägäśt* and the Solomonic narrative themselves became part of an increasingly globalised intellectual discourse.

---

69 Just to give an example, in the years 1902–1904 a notable debate took place in the pages of *Byzantinische Zeitschrift* on the identification of the Queen of Sheba with Sibyl in Byzantine historiography. The disputants were Samuel Krauss (1866–1948), professor of Hebrew at the Jewish Teachers' Seminary in Budapest, and the prominent New Testament scholar Eberhard Nestle (1851–1913); see Samuel KRAUSS, Die Königin von Saba in den byzantinischen Chroniken, in: Byzantinische Zeitschrift 11 (1902), pp. 120–131; Eberhard NESTLE, Zur Königin von Saba als Sibylle, in: Byzantinische Zeitschrift 13 (1904), pp. 492f.
70 Thus, in 1905 Wilhelm Hertz (1835–1902) published a revised version of the study in which he carefully examined the transfer of the legend of the Queen of Sheba and Solomon into German literature and art of the Middle Ages and early modern times: Wilhelm HERTZ, Die Rätsel der Königin von Saba, in: Friedrich von der LEYEN (ed.), Gesammelte Abhandlungen von Wilhelm Hertz, Stuttgart 1905, pp. 413–455.
71 For instance, the sinologist Alfred Forke (1867–1944) tried to show the influence of the Queen of Sheba, who in his view had been a historical figure ruling over a political entity in the Horn of Africa, upon Chinese mythology. In the Chinese goddess Si Wang Mu (literally: »the Queen Mother of the West«) and the mythical mountain of the gods Kunlun, the professor at the Seminar for Oriental Languages in Berlin saw nothing but a poetic reflection of the Queen of Sheba and the Ethiopian highlands. See Alfred FORKE, Mu Wang und die Königin von Saba, in: Mitteilungen des Seminars für Orientalische Sprachen an der Königlichen Friedrich-Wilhelms-Universität zu Berlin 7 (1904), pp. 117–172.

Vladimir Cvetković

Saint-Savahood (*Svetosavlje*) between Political Theology and Ideology of Nationalism in Serbia

Introduction

Nikolaj Velimirović's definition of *Svetosavlje* or Saint-Savahood from 1953 as Orthodox Christianity of Serbian style and experience is one of the most famous definitions of this term[1]. The term *Svetosavlje* was coined in early 1930s by students of the Faculty of Theology at University of Belgrade who launched a journal of that name[2]. *Svetosavlje* or Saint-Savahood refers to a medieval Serbian nobleman and the first archbishop of the Serbian Orthodox Church, Saint Sava Nemanjić (1175–1236). By linking *Svetosavlje* to Orthodox Christianity, Velimirović's definition implies its universal character while also, by restricting it to national history, particularising the universal Christian experience. While a number of Serbian authors such as Dimitrije Bogdanović[3], Žarko Vidović[4], and Atanasije Jevtić[5] emphasise the universal Christian character of *Svetosavlje*, a number of international scholars such as Thomas Bremer[6], Basilius Groen[7], Klaus Buchenau[8], Maria Falina[9],

---

1 Nikolaj VELIMIROVIĆ, Predgovor delu Svetosavlje kao filozofija života, in: Justin POPOVIĆ (ed.), Sabrana dela oca Justina u 30 knjiga [Collected Works of Father Justin in 30 Volumes], vol. 4, Belgrade 2001, p. 176.
2 Jelena GRBIĆ, Svetosavlje – omen za numen pravoslavlja, in: Sabornost 7 (2013), pp. 145–158, at p. 149.
3 Dimitrije BOGDANOVIĆ, Sveti Sava – predgovor delu, in: Id. (ed.), Sveti Sava. Sabrani Spisi, Belgrade 1986, pp. 9–28.
4 Žarko VIDOVIĆ, Njegoš i kosovski zavjet u novom vijeku, Belgrade 1989.
5 Atanasije JEVTIĆ, Sveti Sava i kosovski zavet, Belgrade 1992.
6 Thomas BREMER, Ekklesiale Struktur und Ekklesiologie in der Serbischen Orthodoxen Kirche im 19. und 20. Jahrhundert, Würzburg 1992.
7 Basilius J. GROEN, Nationalism and Reconciliation. Orthodoxy in the Balkans, in: Religion, State & Society 26/2 (1998), pp. 111–128.
8 Klaus BUCHENAU, Svetosavlje und Pravoslavlje. Nationales und Universales in der serbischen Orthodoxie, in: Martin SCHULZE WESSEL (ed.), Nationalisierung der Religion und Säkularisierung der Nation im östlichen Europa, Stuttgart 2006, pp. 203–232.
9 Maria FALINA, Svetosavlje. A Case Study in the Nationalization of Religion, in: Schweizerische Zeitschrift für Religion und Kulturgeschichte 101 (2007), pp. 505–527.

Stefan Rodewald[10], and Julia Anna Lis[11] refer to *Svetosavlje* exclusively in the context of interwar and contemporary Serbian nationalism.

One way to approach *Svetosavlje* is to consider it neither a universal Christian programme nor an ideology of Serbian nationalism, but a form of political theology. *Svetosavlje* as political theology, however, cannot be subsumed under the theological legacy of Carl Schmitt[12] or Johann Baptist Metz[13]. Nor can it be reduced to theologically-informed politics. *Svetosavlje* is a form of political theology understood as critical inquiry into the connections between religion and politics broadly understood, including ideas, practices, affects, and histories[14]. In this broad understanding, *Svetosavlje* is not a single political theology, but rather multiple political theologies with explicit connections to Orthodox Christianity and, generally, but not exclusively, the Serbian nation.

This chapter analyses how Nikolaj Velimirović, Justin Popović, and Atanasije Jevtić perceived *Svetosavlje*. They represent three successive generations of Serbian theologians who are also spiritually connected because Nikolaj Velimirović may be considered as a spiritual guide of Justin Popović, and Justin Popović a spiritual mentor of Atanasije Jevtić. Although one may notice a certain continuity in their views on *Svetosavlje*, the differences in their theological focus also led to differences in their understanding of the concept. All three authors express a need for a new theological paradigm, criticise Europe and European identity in the context of their ecclesiological project, and formulate *Svetosavlje* as a form of ecclesial identity. However, they do so in different periods: Velimirović during World War I and the creation of the Kingdom of Serbs, Croats, and Slovenes; Popović in the interwar period and during World War II; and Jevtić in the 1980s, during the dissolution of Socialist Yugoslavia. Thus, I will deal first with Velimirović, arguing that he employs Slavophile ideas and political Pan-Slavism for establishing *Svetosavlje* as a new ecclesial identity of the Yugoslav peoples. I will then turn to Popović, demonstrating that his synthesis between Russian religious philosophy and patristic thought is crucial for his understanding of *Svetosavlje*, which he then uses to fight

---

10 Stefan ROHDEWALD, Götter der Nationen. Religiöse Erinnerungsfiguren in Serbien, Bulgarien und Makedonien bis 1944, Cologne 2014.

11 Julia Anna LIS, Antiwestliche Diskurse in der serbischen und griechischen Theologie. Zur Konstruktion des »Westens« in den Schriften von Nikolaj Velimirović, Justin Popović, Christos Yannaras und John S. Romanides, Berlin 2019.

12 Carl SCHMITT, Political Theology. Four Chapters on the Concept of Sovereignty, Chicago 2006.

13 Johann Baptist METZ, Theology in the New Paradigm, in: William T. CAVANAUGH et al. (eds.), An Eerdmans Reader in Contemporary Political Theology, Grand Rapids, MI, 2012, pp. 316–326; id., Two-fold Political Theology, in: Francis SCHÜSSLER FIORENZA et al. (eds.), Political Theology. Contemporary Challenges and Future Directions, Louisville, KY 2013, pp. 13–22.

14 Vincent LLOYD/David TRUE, What Political Theology Could Be, in: Political Theology 17/6 (2016), pp. 505f., at p. 505.

communism, fascism, and capitalism of interwar Yugoslavia. Finally, I will explore Jevtić's understanding of *Svetosavlje* in the context of the so-called neo-Palamitic revival of Orthodox theology during the 1960s and of the dissolution of Yugoslavia.

Nikolaj Velimirović's *Svetosavlje*: European Nationalisms, Pan-Slavism, and Slavophiles

Nikolaj Velimirović (1881–1956) was a leading figure of the Serbian Church in the first half of the twentieth century. He held two PhDs from University of Bern, one in theology and another in history, as well as an honorary doctorate from Columbia University. He was the Bishop of Ohrid (now in North Macedonia) from 1920 till 1936, and the Bishop of Žiča (in Western Serbia) from 1936 until his detention by the Nazis during World War II, when he was deported to the Dachau concentration camp in Germany. After the end of the war, he did not return to communist Yugoslavia but emigrated to the United States, where he was dean of St Tikhon Russian Orthodox Seminary in Canaan, Pennsylvania, till the end of his life. He was canonised as a saint of the Orthodox Church by the Holy Synod of the Serbian Orthodox Church in 2003.

In order to understand Velimirović's idea of *Svetosavlje*, it is important to examine the historical context in which his ideas were developed. Prior to the establishment of the Kingdom of Serbs, Croats, and Slovenes in 1918 and the Serbian Patriarchate in 1920, the Serbian Church was divided among several foreign powers imposing different ecclesial jurisdictions[15]. And before to the establishment of the Principality of Serbia in 1815, Serbia had been under Ottoman rule and the Serbian Church under the jurisdiction of the Patriarchate of Constantinople. The political independence of the principality from the Sublime Porte led to the partial ecclesial independence of the Serbian Church in 1832, but the election of the metropolitan of Belgrade had still to be confirmed by the Patriarch of Constantinople. The Serbs in Hungary fell under the jurisdiction of the Metropolis of Sremski Karlovci, founded in 1690, which after 1868 enjoyed wider religious and cultural autonomy. After the abolition of the Patriarchate of Peć in 1766, the Serbian Church in Montenegro could escape falling under the jurisdiction of Constantinople. It remained autonomous until its integration into the Serbian Patriarchate. The Serbians in Bosnia and Herzegovina, however, remained under the ecclesial jurisdiction of the Ecumenical Patriarchate, because both countries were still within the territory of the Ottoman Empire. After the Austrian occupation in 1878, elections of the

---

15 BREMER, Ekklesiale Struktur, pp. 15f.

Metropolitan of Dabar-Bosnia had to be confirmed by the Austrian Emperor instead of the Patriarch of Constantinople. After 1828, Serbs in Dalmatia had gathered around the diocese of Zadar, which was controlled by the Austrian authorities, who constantly infringed on its autonomy.

The Serbian people experienced its division into several different states and even more ecclesiastical jurisdictions in different ways. Under the leadership of their intellectual elite, they began building their ethnic identity not on the basis of a common history and tradition, but on that of a common language[16]. Additionally, the ideas of the Enlightenment and the achievements of the French Revolution and of American republicanism, which propagated a transfer of political power from the monarch to the people, began to inspire a series of Serbian uprisings against foreign rule. Serbian ecclesial institutions began to adapt to new opportunities by ceasing to align themselves with the existing political authorities, but instead with the new factors on the political scene – the people or the nation[17]. During the nineteenth century, power within the church, which according to the medieval model belonged to the hierarchy or the episcopate, was transferred to the people – or, to be more precise, to the people's representatives at the synods. However, the resulting changes in the organisation of ecclesiastical authorities, and therefore the change in the church's self-understanding, led to deeper changes in perceived ecclesial identity. *The Encyclical of Eastern Patriarchs* of 1848, which claimed that the unmistakable truth of Christian dogma does not depend on church hierarchy, but is guarded by all people of the church as the Body of Christ, pointed to this renewed perception of the traditional model[18].

This turn to tradition had two consequences. The first consisted in positive changes in the process of decision-making regarding ecclesial and national issues. The decision-making process ceased to be a matter of a narrowly confined clerical elite, which, especially in the period under the Ottoman and Austro-Hungarian rule, had protected ecclesial interests by concessions to foreign authorities. Now, authority came to reside in a wider consensus of the representative bodies, which sought to protect the interests of both laypeople and the clergy. The second consequence pertains to the identification of ecclesial and national identity and the assimilation of church's interests with those of the nation.

The construction of ecclesial identity on the basis of national belonging was not only a feature of the Serbian Church and other Orthodox Churches in the Balkans, but a common phenomenon throughout Europe. In a series of lectures held in

---

16 Miloš Ković, Znamenja pobede, uzroci poraza. Kontinuiteti i diskontinuiteti u srpskoj istoriji, in: Svetlana Kurćubić Ružić (ed.), Ka srpskom stanovištu, Belgrade 2014, pp. 149–170, at p. 160.
17 Cyril Hovorun, Meta-Ecclesiology. Chronicles on Church Awareness, New York 2015, p. 21.
18 Kallistos Ware, Sobornost and Eucharistic Ecclesiology. Aleksei Khomiakov and his Successors, in: International Journal for the Study of the Christian Church 11/2-3 (2011), pp. 216–235, at p. 221.

London during World War I, the priest-monk Nikolaj Velimirović pointed to the danger European nationalism presented for Christian integrity. He claimed that the Early Church had triumphed over its worst enemies, Jewish patriotism and Roman imperialism, whereas Christianity in Europe had come to obediently serve the cause of European nationalism and imperialism[19]. Rendering themselves subservient to national or imperial aims, the churches in Europe were divided and particularised. This contradicted the universal nature of the church[20]. According to Velimirović, just as salvation for individual human beings depended on loving God and one's neighbour, so the salvation of any individual Christian community depended on its love of God and other churches[21]. The true identity of the church, unlike the identity of a nation, is seen by Velimirović as residing in the Nicene-Constantinopolitan Creed, which defines the church as »one, holy, catholic, and apostolic«. Thus, the attribute »one« refers not only to the numerical oneness of the church, but also to its unity[22]. The other characteristic of the church that Velimirović emphasises is holiness[23]. Holiness corresponds as qualitative pillar of the church's identity to the oneness or unity of the church as its quantitative characteristic. Holiness as the core of ecclesial identity, which derives from Christ's holiness, differentiates the church from any other institution or social group[24]. Velimirović feels a deep urge to identify nationalism as a danger to ecclesial identity and to establish the identity of the church on the traditional formulas introduced by the ecumenical councils. His critique of nationalism in the church was very broad, and was based on a comparison between the early church and the modern churches in Europe.

In his lecture »The Spiritual Rebirth of Europe«, delivered at King's College London in 1920, Bishop Nikolaj Velimirović argues that European civilisation would not endure unless it returned to the Christian religion, which for nineteen centuries had been the centre and principal guide of European civilisation[25]. In a short reconstruction of European identity, Velimirović ponders three reasons for Europe's decline: individualism, rationalism, and humanism. Individualism is problematic for Velimirović because it no longer treats salvation as an effort of the entire Christian community, but as an individual undertaking[26]. Rationalism, or the faculty of reasoning, is an uncertain foundation for building a civilisation, because it reduces

---

19 Nicholai VELIMIROVIC, The Agony of the Church, London 2017, p. 77.
20 Ibid., p. 88.
21 Ibid., pp. 94f.
22 HOVORUN, Meta-Ecclesiology, p. 11.
23 VELIMIROVIC, The Agony, p. 125.
24 HOVORUN, Meta-Ecclesiology, p. 12.
25 Nikolaj VELIMIROVIĆ, The Spiritual Rebirth of Europe, in: Bishop Nikolaj VELIMIROVIĆ, Sabrana dela [Collected Works], vol. 3, Šabac 2014, pp. 657–696, at p. 667.
26 VELIMIROVIC, The Agony, pp. 92-93.

humans to only one of their faculties rather considering them as a whole[27]. According to Velimirović, the third chief pillar of modern Europe is humanism, which by rejecting Christianity has opened the door to various European ideologies, whether political, scientific, or economic[28]. Against image of Europe, Velimirović sets the projected image of the church in Europe. He replaces individualism with *sobornost'* or catholicity as the permanent and immutable feature of the universal Church. In contrast to Alexei Khomyakov and Russian Slavophiles who constructed the notion of *sobornost'* in opposition Roman Catholic legalism and Protestant rationalism, Velimirović opposes *sobornost'* to individualism – not only of the personal kind, but also to sectarian and national individualism[29]. In his critique of rationalism, Velimirović argues that logic or reason should not precede love, but follow it[30]. Drawing on Dostoevsky and Solovyev, and in response to the European humanistic project, which according to Velimirović finds its deepest expression in Nietzsche's idea of *Übermensch*, he develops the idea of the pan-human and pan-humanism.

Velimirović recognises the image of secular Europe, conceived in terms of humanism, rationalism, and individualism as basic elements of its identity, as a counter-image to that of the church. He combines his criticism of Europe with Slavophile and Pan-Slavic ideas in an attempt to build a new national and ecclesial identity of Yugoslav people. For Velimirović, the new Yugoslav national identity has already been achieved through the political Pan-Slavism that existed in the Austro-Hungarian monarchy. With the Slavophil idea of *sobornost'*, he intends to fight the confessional individualism of Orthodox Serbs and Catholic Croats and Slovenes. However, Velimirović does not remain within a restrictive Slavophilism in regard to social unity. Similar to Dostoevsky, he expands this unity into universal pan-humanism. Velimirović's idea of the pan-human (*Svečovek*) stands in opposition to Nietzsche's idea of *Übermensch*, which he sees as the final expression of European humanistic and rationalistic project.

Velimirović constructs a new ecclesiology of the Yugoslav people, relying on Serbian sacred history and its *lieux de mémoire*[31]. According to Velimirović, Serbian sacred history begins with St Sava, St Simeon the Myrrh-Gusher, and continues with St Prince Lazar, the Battle of Kosovo, the Kosovo Testament, and the martyrdom under the Ottomans. While the Kosovo narrative played a crucial role in the decades

---

27 Id., The Spiritual Rebirth, p. 677.
28 Ibid., pp. 686f.
29 Nikolaj VELIMIROVIĆ, San o slovenskoj religiji, in: Bishop Nikolaj VELIMIROVIĆ, Sabrana dela [Collected Works], vol. 4, Šabac 2014, pp. 315–325, at p. 319.
30 Nikolaj VELIMIROVIĆ, Duša Srbije, in: Id., Sabrana dela [Collected Works], vol. 3, pp. 373–378, at p. 401.
31 Pierre NORA, Between Memory and History. Les Lieux de Mémoire, in: Representations 26 (1989), pp. 7–24.

of Serbian liberation from foreign rule throughout the nineteenth century, the references to St Sava predominated during World War I and the interwar period. St Sava is perceived as both a mediator for Serbian people before God on the eschatological level and, on the historical level, the founder of the Serbian Church as well as a consolidator of Serbia's medieval state and dynasty.

In the early works of Velimirović, references to St Sava served not only the purpose of unifying all Orthodox Serbs who lived in the newly founded Kingdom of Serbs, Croats, and Slovenes[32], they also provided a platform for creating a common Yugoslav identity as well as political and ecclesial unity. In the context of the Yugoslav project, Velimirović particularly emphasised the historical role of St Sava in linking the medieval Serbian state and nation with the church. According to Velimirović, the common national struggle and suffering of the Yugoslav people was inspired by the same Christian spirit, which animated both the Orthodox and the Roman Catholic faith[33]. The cause of World War I was the de-Christianisation of Europe's church, which failed to act in accordance with holiness as its basic principle[34]. Velimirović claimed that the national ideal of liberation and unification was best expressed through the idea of Yugoslavism, while the ecclesial ideal should be realised through the idea of holiness. Velimirović places St Sava at the very beginning of the common Serbo-Croatian-Slovenian history, as continued by Patriarch Arsenije Čarnojević, Karadjordje Petrović, Ljudevit Gaj, Valentin Vodnik, Ban Jelačić, Njegoš, and Štrosmajer[35]. According to Velimirović, St Sava reconciles Yugoslavism and holiness, the two ideals for which the new Yugoslav Kingdom, as well as the Yugoslav Church, should strive. His selective approach to history and construction of historical memory was to promote the ideal of holiness, once accomplished in the national Yugoslav history. He opposed this ideal to the secular and pro-European aspirations of the new state.

During the mid-1930's, Velimirović insisted that *Svetosavlje* or Savian nationalism should serve as evangelical platform for founding a Yugoslav national church. St Savian nationalism, unlike the nationalism that emerged from the Enlightenment and the secular tradition Velimirović severely criticised, is based on faith as its basic principle. While St Savian nationalism protects the integrity of the human person on its path to perfection, it also protects the organic uniqueness of nations, not allowing them to slip into imperialism or to vanish in internationalism[36]. According

---

32 Radmila RADIĆ, Serbian Christianity, in: Ken PARRY (ed.), The Blackwell Companion to Eastern Christianity, Oxford 2007, pp. 231–248, at p. 238.
33 Nikolaj VELIMIROVIĆ, Two Churches and One Nation, New York 1915, p. 14.
34 Id., The Agony, pp. 124f.
35 Id., Two Churches and One Nation, pp. 5–8.
36 Id., Nacionalizam Svetog Save, in: Bishop Nikolaj VELIMIROVIĆ, Sabrana dela [Collected Works], vol. 9, Šabac 2014, pp. 309f.

to this nationalism, all people on earth, regardless of blood, language, and religion, are one people of God and, as such, brothers. Although this might seem odd, especially considering subsequent crises over the Concordat, for Velimirović, *Svetosavlje* and St Savian nationalism signified the foundation of the Yugoslav national and ecumenical project. Velimirović opposed the Pope's power over Catholics in Yugoslavia, because he perceived it – similarly to the ecclesial rule of the Constantinopolitan Patriarchate over the Orthodox Serbs in the Balkans – as an expression of imperial policy in the form of ecclesial imperialism. For Velimirović, *Svetosavlje* was therefore both a political and an ecumenical project. As a political project it began as an anti-imperialist struggle for the political liberation and unification of the Yugoslav peoples, while as an ecumenical project it was meant to enable liberation from the sees of Rome and Constantinople, the dominant ecclesial powers of the time, and to establish a common Yugoslav Church.

Justin Popović's *Svetosavlje*: Russian Religious Renaissance, Asceticism and Church Fathers

Justin Popović (1894–1979) took his monastic vows as soldier of the Serbian army during World War I. He studied later for a BLitt degree in Oxford (the highest supervised degree at that time) and received his doctorate in theology from the University of Athens. He taught at the Orthodox seminaries of Sremski Karlovci, Prizren, and Bitolj and became a professor at the Faculty of Orthodox Theology (University of Belgrade) in 1934. After the end of World War II and the communist party coming to power, he was expelled from the university together with two hundred other professors. He lived till the end of his life in the monastery of Ćelije, near Valjevo in western Serbia. He was introduced into the diptych of the Orthodox saints by the Holy Synod of the Serbian Church in 2010.

Similarly to Velimirović, Justin Popović criticised nationalism in the church. He argued that the church is the God-human organism, not a human organisation, and as such it cannot be divided along national lines[37]. He claimed that on their path through history, many local churches, including the Serbian Church, were reduced to agents of nationalism, and he urged church representatives to cease to be servants of nationalism, and to become high priests of the one, holy, catholic, and Apostolic Church[38]. According to Popović, the goal of the church is »supra-national, universal, panhuman: to unite all people in Christ, regardless of nationality, race,

---

37 Justin Popović, Unutrašnja misija naše Crkve (realizacija Pravoslavlja), in: Hrišćanski život 9 (1923), pp. 285–290, at p. 287.
38 Ibid.

and class«[39]. Popović rejected the nationalism and national emancipation on which the Balkan churches built their ecclesial identity. He replaced such distortions by emphasis on ascetic practice as the chief element of ecclesial identity. According to Popović, asceticism abolishes divisions and leads to catholicity or *sabornost*.

Popović considers, as Velimirović also once did, nationalism as a danger to ecclesial identity. But unlike Velimirović, who criticised the nationalism of all European churches, Popović's critique was restricted to the Orthodox Church and focused on its ascetic tradition. A number of Velimirović's ideas, formulated as a counter-narrative to the secular image of Europe and directly inspired by the Russian religious renaissance, were more thoroughly developed in the works of Justin Popović. In addition to Dostoevsky's critique of the Enlightenment, Popović appropriates other ideas from Russian religious philosophy, such as the ideas of integral or »living« knowledge, all-unity, and Theo-humanism. Linking these ideas with the teachings of the Church Fathers, he opposes them to European rationalism, individualism, and humanism. Popović borrows the idea of integral knowledge from Russian religious thought, but unlike both the Russian religious thinkers and Velimirović, Popović attempts to prove its continuity with the monastic and ascetic tradition of the Christian East, particularly with authors such as Macarius of Egypt (in the fourth century) and Isaac the Syrian (in the seventh century). Another Russian idea that Popović »baptises« in the patristic tradition is the idea of all-unity, which he connects with *sobornost'* as »organic unity« in the church. In contrast to Vladimir Solovyev and in accord to Aleksey Khomiakov, Popović develops the idea of all-unity not as metaphysical ideal, but as concrete liturgical and catholic churchhood. The main idea of Popović's thought is the concept of the God-Man[40], which he formulates on the basis of the Chalcedonian dogma of the indivisible unity of Christ's two natures and partly in opposition to modern European humanism. Popović argues that European humanism stands for a revolt against the recognition of godliness in the human being, while God-Man liberates the forces of godliness in that same human being, imprisoned by the tyranny of humanism, empowering them to realise themselves in their immortal fullness[41]. According to Popović, the realisation of all human potential and the true unification of God and human beings is possible only in the person of the God-Man because he is a personal unity of two natures, divine and human.

From the mid-1930s and especially during World War II, St Sava and *Svetosavlje* also occupied Justin Popović's scholarly interest. Unlike Velimirović's writings from

---

39 Ibid., p. 286.
40 On the concept of God-man/Theanthropos in the Russian school, especially in the thinking of Vladimir Solovyev, see Evert van der Zweerde's contribution in this volume.
41 Justin Popović, Highest Value and Last Criterion in Orthodoxy, in: Justin Popovic, Orthodox Faith and Life in Christ, Belmond, MA 1994, pp. 70f.

the mid-1910s to the mid-1930s, which mostly refer to the St Savian ideal as the basis for building the Yugoslav social and religious unity, Popović's references to St Sava are not limited to the cause of Yugoslav unity, but aspire to proper ecclesial identity. He maintains that only the St Savian determination to engage in ascetic struggle could save the Serbian episcopate and priesthood from being immersed in nationalism and materialism. He solves the dilemma of whether the new Yugoslav society should be oriented towards West or East by offering the example of St Sava, who had directed the Serbian national soul, divided between the two worlds, towards the God-Man Christ. Like Velimirović before him, Popović identifies the Christian orientation of Yugoslav society with a *tertium quid* or a *dritter Raum*, a third realm between East and West[42]. Unlike Velimirović, for whom in a wider cultural sense the East was Asia and the West was Europe, and for whom in a narrower ecclesiastical sense the East was identified with the Constantinople Patriarchate and the West with the see of Rome, Popović remains indeterminate on this issue. He opposes the St Savian God-Man to European man, but he does not mention anything in the East that would stand in obvious contrast to the European man of the West.

In the late 1920s and early 1930s, Marxist ideas spread throughout the University of Belgrade, and in 1932 a group of students from the faculty of theology launched the journal *Svetosavlje* in order to counter the dissemination of revolutionary ideas among the students[43]. Popović, who had been assistant professor since 1934, reacted to the emergence and spread of these ideas in his article *Rastko and Contemporary Serbian Youth*[44]. As he had once contrasted the St Savian God-Man to the European man, he now opposed the St Savian God-Man to the new Soviet revolutionary man. Justin refers to Rastko, or St Sava, as the greatest revolutionary among Serbian or Yugoslav people because he rebelled not against social and political injustice but, in the name of eternity and immortality, against death.

At the end of the 1930s, in his sermon »A Fight for the Serbian Soul«, Justin Popović emphasised that only by following St Sava and his faith in Christ could the Serbs defeat the communist (red) international, i. e., the capitalist-fascist (yellow) international. He stood against Dimitrje Ljotić's fascist movement »Zbor«, for recruiting some of the Orthodox clergy. He warned those clergymen that if as priests of the Savian Church use violence to achieve their goals, they would

---

42 Tanja ZIMMERMANN, Der Balkan zwischen Ost und West. Mediale Bilder und kulturpolitische Prägungen, Cologne 2014, pp. 8–13.

43 Jelena GRBIĆ, Svetosavlje – omen za numen pravoslavlja, in: Sabornost 7 (2013), pp. 145–158, at p. 149.

44 Justin POPOVIĆ, Rastko i savremena srpska omladina, in: Svetosavlje 12 (1935), pp. 58–61.

immediately become inquisitors and, like the medieval Roman Catholic Church, convert Christianity to inquisition[45].

In the structure, at least, of his book *St Savian Philosophy of Life*, published in 1953, Popović relies on Velimirović's vision, revealed in several articles written during the 1930s. Velimirović pointed out that anyone referring to St Sava should also refer to his visions of church, state, education, army, family, art, culture, and monasticism[46]. The chapters of Popović's book are dedicated to St Savian philosophies of the world, progress, culture, society, values, norms, and education[47]. According to Popović, the St Savian philosophy of the world is based on two principles: 1) the world is an epiphany; 2) man is called to serve God[48]. In his treatment of St Savian philosophy of progress, Popović claims that man is truly human only through the God-Man, the only one to have linked progress with human immortality[49]. According to Popović, St Sava founded St Savian culture by leading medieval Serbia not towards the East or West, but towards the God-Man[50], who is the perfect unity and *sabor* of God and man[51]. In monastic fashion, Popović identifies the evangelical virtues by which humans attain the likeness of Christ – such as faith, love, hope, prayer, fasting, and meekness – with the instruments of St Savian philosophy of culture. According to St Savian philosophy of society, society should adapt itself to the church as its eternal ideal. In fact, the church should be the godly-human Person of Christ, extended through space and time. In the chapter »St Savian philosophy of values and criteria«, Popović argues that the God-Man is the highest value, since he was the only one who solved the problem of life and death, showing in his personality »the embodied and hypostasised immortality and life eternal«. Finally, in the last chapter of his work, Popović displays the St Savian philosophy of education, based on the principle that the God-Man as perfect God and a perfect man should be the goal and purpose of education. Finally, he concludes that St Sava, as a saint gaining perfection in the partaking to the God-Man, is the greatest enlightener of the Serbian people, because for Popović education is essentially devoted to the facilitation of holiness.

---

45 Id., Svetosavsko sveštenstvo i političke partije, in: Žički blagovesnik 12 (1940), pp. 20–24; 13 (1941), pp. 16–21.
46 Nikolaj VELIMIROVIĆ, Veliki jubilej naroda srpskog – Proslava sedamstogodišnjice smrti Svetog Save, in: Kalendar Srpske pravoslavne Patrijaršije, Belgrade 1935, pp. 74–77; id., Nacionalizam Svetog Save, pp. 308f.
47 Justin POPOVIĆ, Svetosavlje kao filozofija života [Saint-Savahood as Philosophy of Life], in: Id., Sabrana dela oca Justina u 30 knjiga, vol. 4, Belgrade 2001, pp. 175–266.
48 Ibid., p. 191.
49 Ibid., p. 207.
50 Ibid., pp. 211–213.
51 Ibid., p. 219.

The *Svetosavlje* exposed in *St Savian Philosophy of Life* is cleansed of all ideological elements. When pointing to Serbian national history, he omits all events that are not evangelical or connected to Christ. Like St Sava himself, who wrote the *Vita* of his father Simeon the Myrrh-Gusher in order to demonstrate that the ideal of holiness is achievable by members of his nation, Popović refers to St Sava and his work as the historical realisation of universal Christian principles under conditions of national particularity, and he commends that work as worthy of emulation in pursuit of holiness. For Popović, pursuing any national or ideological goal other than St Savian holiness means failure to achieve one's divine-human vocation.

Atanasije Jevtić's *Svetosavlje*: Byzantine Tradition, Bishop-centric Ecclesiology and Athonite Monasticism

Atanasije Jevtić (1938–2021) held a PhD in theology from the University of Athens. He pursued an academic career, at first as a lecturer at the Orthodox Institute of St Sergius in Paris, then professor of patristics and dean of the theological faculty in Belgrade. He was elected Bishop of Vršac in 1991, after which he was translated to the see of Zahumlje and Hercegovina, which he occupied from 1992 until his retirement in 1999.

Jevtić's writings on St Sava have a completely different orientation from comparison to the works of his predecessors and spiritual fathers, Velimirović and Popović. As a result of the historical-critical method applied to St Sava's literary work, Jevtić's writings not only reveal St Sava as a Chilandar monk, an abbot of Studenica monastery[52], the first Serbian archbishop[53], a capable ecclesiastical diplomat, and a theologian[54]. They also shed light on the theological milieu and spiritual practices of St Sava's time[55]. Therefore, Jevtić refers first of all to St Sava, the historical figure, and then to the term *Svetosavlje*. The focus of Jevtić's writings, however, is not only historical, for they propagate a certain theological programme. Jevtić adopted the theological ideas that emerged in the 1960s in the so-called Athenian school, whose most famous representatives are John N. Zizioulas, Christos Yannaras, Panagiotis Nellas, and Nikos Nissiotis. The Serbian monks and theologians who studied at that time in Athens, such as Atanasije Jevtić, Amfilohije Radović, Artemije Radosavljević, and Irinej Bulović, also belong to this school. This school or the movement of the restoration of Orthodox theology was deeply inspired by

---

52 Atanasije Jevtić, Dve studeničke besede Svetog Save, in: Id. (ed.), Bog Otaca naših, Hilandar 2009, pp. 121–141.
53 Atanasije Jevtić, Žička beseda Svetog Save o pravoj veri, in: Id. (ed.), Bog Otaca naših, pp. 89–120.
54 Id., Eklisiologija Svetog Save, in: Id. (ed.), Bog Otaca naših, pp. 224–239.
55 Id., Sveti Sava u tokovima Kirilo-metodijevskog predanja, in: Id. (ed.), Bog Otaca naših, pp. 147–154.

Russian émigré theology, characterised by the return to the tradition of the Church Fathers. As Pantelis Kalaitzidis argues, its theological interests included eucharistic ecclesiology, Christocentric anthropology, theological anti-Westernism, personalism, and the theology of personhood, theocentric humanism, mystical theology, and apophaticism, Hellenocentrism and Byzantinism, as well as the insistence on the restoration of monasticism and the existence of the ontological character of the Orthodox ethos[56]. By the beginning of the 1990s, however, when most of Jevtić's articles on St Sava were appearing, the movement's focus was shifting towards eschatology and its dynamic interpretation, towards ecclesiological themes, such as the place of the episcopal office in the church, the role of monasticism (especially Athonite) in the restoration of church life, and liturgical renewal and revalorisation of the mission[57]. Jevtić was not a passive recipient of these theological trends, but an active participant in their emergence and promotion.

In his early work *On Following the Holy Fathers* (1962), Jevtić perceives the works of the Fathers as a continuation of the mystery of Christ[58]. Similarly, in his inaugural lecture at the Institute of St Sergius in 1969, Jevtić identifies the Holy Fathers with »the teachers of the path that leads to life« in agreement with the troparion to St Sava[59]. Adherence to the Fathers and to the Holy Tradition was a constant in the works of Jevtić, including his those on St Sava. The Holy Tradition is the main theme of three of Jevtić's articles, written between 1985 and 1986 »St Sava in the Currents of Cyrillo-Methodian tradition«, »The Ecclesiology of St Sava« and »Two Sermons of St Sava from Studenica Monastery«. The tradition in his articles has a twofold meaning. On the one hand, Jevtić emphasises the ontological and soteriological character of tradition as handing down one and the same eternal Truth and Life[60]. Jevtić links the mystery of Christ (as mystery of Truth and Life) to the idea of the divine economy of salvation, which appears in the forefront in the *Lives of Saint Cyril and Methodius* and in the two St Sava's sermons delivered at Studenica monastery[61]. Jevtić considers the economy of salvation as the basis of St Sava's ecclesiology. According to Jevtić, the divine economy of salvation consists, for St Sava, in the coming of the Son of God into the world, an event that was »prophesied by the Prophets, proclaimed by the Apostles and confirmed by the Fathers«[62]. This aspect

---

56 Pantelis KALAITZIDIS, New Trends in Greek Orthodox Theology. Challenges in the Movement Towards a Genuine Renewal and Christian Unity, in: Scottish Journal of Theology 67 (2014), pp. 127–164, at pp. 130f.
57 Ibid., p. 128.
58 Atanasije JEVTIĆ, O sledovanju Svetim Ocima, in: Id. (ed.), Bog Otaca naših, pp. 30–52, at p. 38.
59 Id., Bog Otaca naših, in: Id. (ed.), Bog Otaca naših, pp. 11–29, at p. 28.
60 Id., Sveti Sava, pp. 148–150.
61 Id., Dve studeničke, p. 129, 136.
62 Id., Eklisiologija Svetog Save, p. 229.

of tradition, handed down as the truth of the divine economy, bears dogmatic and universal character.

On the other hand, Jevtić highlights the significance of the Cyrillo-Methodian and St Savian tradition for the historical and spiritual memory of the Serbian people and for their identity. According to Jevtić, Saint Cyril and Methodius and St Sava connected Slavs and Serbs with the existing tradition of the church, i. e., with Christ, the Apostles, and the Holy Fathers, and they introduced them into the existing church-canonical and political milieu of the Byzantine world[63]. At the same time, Jevtić considers these saints to have been apostles because they propagated not national or religious particularism, but ecclesial and catholic pleroma[64]. In the footsteps of his predecessors Velimirović and Popović, Jevtić argues that St Sava proved by his apostolic mission that the Church of Christ was the property neither of Rome nor of Constantinople[65]. Jevtić emphasises that true identity of the Serbian people is manifested only in the church[66]. Jevtić stressed this in the context of awakened nationalisms in Yugoslav society, which led to the collapse of a common state only a few years later.

Jevtić connects the idea of St Sava's apostolicity among Serbian people with St Sava's episcopal office. Jevtić pursues his investigation of St Sava's episcopacy through the lens of the episcopocentric (bishop-centric) ecclesiology promoted by Metropolitan John N. Zizioulas[67]. Jevtić links St Sava to the Apostles not only as founder of the Serbian Church, but also as a bishop because, according to the patristic ecclesiology promulgated by Jevtić, each bishop is successor to all the apostles and the living image of Christ among priests and people[68]. Jevtić adds a new and significant element to the bishop-centric ecclesiology of Zizioulas, one that is also emphasised by Velimirović and Popović: St Sava's sainthood. In his sermon delivered at Žiča Monastery on Ascension Day, 1221, St Sava referred to his episcopacy as holiness, because every bishop had been consecrated into his office by the Holy Spirit[69].

Finally, Jevtić emphasises the ascetic aspect as one of the main features of St Sava's legacy, claiming that St Sava's theology and ecclesiology originate from his Athonite spiritual experience[70]. The tendency to underline the special role of Athonite monasticism in the restoration of modern church life is another feature of the Athenian

---

63 Ibid., p. 238.
64 Ibid., p. 236.
65 Ibid., p. 238.
66 JEVTIĆ, Sveti Sava, p. 151.
67 Id., Eklisiologija Svetog Save, p. 226.
68 Ibid., p. 236.
69 JEVTIĆ, Žička beseda, p. 107.
70 Id., Dve studeničke, p. 138.

theological school, especially of Christos Yannaras and John Romanides. Jevtić fits into this trend because he also emphasises the significance of Athonite monastic practices for reviving monastic life in post-Communist Serbia. Jevtić points to the observation of Domentijan, a biographer of St Sava, that St Sava »wanted to transfer every spiritual pattern of the Holy Mountain into his fatherland [Serbia]«[71]. Jevtić perceives St Sava as a successor of the Cappadocian, Sinaitic, Studite ascetic and monastic tradition, and as the forerunner of Athonite Hesychasm[72].

In his work on St Sava, Jevtić to a certain extent follows Velimirović's counsel that a proper way of writing about St Sava must always include discussion of Sava's teachings on church, state, education, army, family, art, and monasticism, and therefore he is also following Popović, who writes about St Savian philosophy of the world, of progress, of culture, of society, of values, norms, and of education. Velimirović's focus on the state, society, education, and family is absent in Jevtić's works, because the latter's emphasis is on St Savian thinking on church and monastery. However, Jevtić's interest in other St Savian philosophies, to use Popović's term, is revealed through these categories. Jevtić portrays the St Savian world as Jesus Christ's economy of salvation, St Savian progress as an eschatological orientation of history, St Savian culture and education as a sacred tradition and »adherence to the Fathers«, St Savian values as holiness and likeness to Christ, which are a product of spiritual life and ascetical practice, and St Savian society as the church, which is a model and ideal for all human communities and institutions, whether state, society, or family.

Conclusion

It can be concluded that the three Serbian theologians reflect differently on the role of St Sava in Serbian history, depending on their theological focus and orientation as well as their historical context. Velimirović thinks of St Sava and *Svetosavlje* in terms of political pan-Slavism and Slavophile theological ideas, attempting to project the characteristics of the church defined by the Nicene-Constantinopolitan Creed – oneness, holiness, catholicity, and apostolicity – to all spheres of social life. Popović relies on the ideas springing from the Slavophile movement and the Russian religious renaissance, such as God-Manhood, integral knowledge, and *sobornost'*. Like the Slavophiles, he employs them in his critique of European humanism, rationalism, and individualism. Popović, however, »baptises« these Russian ideas in the ascetic thought of the early Church Fathers. Belonging to the

---

71 Ibid.; see also DOMENTIJAN, Žitije Svetog Save, Belgrade 1865, p. 205.
72 JEVTIĆ, Dve studeničke, p. 139.

so-called Athenian theological school of the 1960s, Jevtić, like the other members of this school, develops his theological discourse in accordance with the neo-patristic synthesis, episcopocentric ecclesiology, and Athonite ascetic and monastic practices.

The historical context of Velimirović's, Popović's, and Jevtić's reception of St Sava is as important as their affiliation to the theological trends of their time. Velimirović writes in the midst of the creation of the common state of the southern Slavs and the first years of its existence. He perceives St Sava as the forerunner of Yugoslav political and ecclesial unity and as an opponent to every kind of ecclesial imperialism. Velimirović attempts to incorporate *Svetosavlje* into the foundations of the new Yugoslav state and the new Yugoslav Church. Therefore, Velimirović employed *Svetosavlje* both for the restoration of the church's identity and for the transformation of a community based on a common language into a community sharing the same faith and historical memory. Yet Velimirović also acknowledges the importance of lower forms of social engagement on the way to holiness, such as national heroism or the ingenuity of church leaders in linking church and state in all spheres of public life.

Popović writes about St Sava immediately before, during, and after World War II, when Yugoslav society was at an ideological turning point and when the communist model of the state and its aggressive atheism had prevailed. Popović's model of *Svetosavlje* as political theology, therefore, is still within the framework of the Yugoslav state, but it also opposes the dominant socio-ideological paradigms of the time: Western, humanist, and capitalist ideology as well as Soviet atheist and communist ideology. In his works, *Svetosavlje* is presented both as the idealised model of the Christian past and the future and universally desired image of a Yugoslav society. Although St Sava is a historical figure and a national leader, *Svetosavlje* has been kept clear of any national element that deviating from or contradicting evangelical principles. National history is oriented towards places of historical memory exhibiting an exclusively Christian ethos. It thus becomes a type of sacred history, in which holiness is the basic principle and the measure of all things. Popović insists on ascetic struggle and the virtuous life as sole criteria of personal and communal progress. By placing St Sava and *Svetosavlje* in the perspective of national history, but in an eschatological perspective transcending history, Popović separates *Svetosavlje* from the national principle. Its relationship to national history remains limited to the extent to which the eschatological element dominated history.

Jevtić writes about St Sava and *Svetosavlje* in the years preceding the breakup of Yugoslavia as well as during the Yugoslav wars of the 1990s. Therefore, Jevtić frees *Svetosavlje* from any political agenda and any state framework. For Jevtić, the church is the only existing reality. By following Bishop Sava, who established the independent Serbian Church in order to strengthen Christianity in the medieval

Serbian state, Bishop Atanasije Jevtić rebuilt the church in Zahumlje and Herzegovina during the war in order to strengthen Serbian ecclesial identity in post-Dayton Bosnia and Herzegovina.

Regardless of the differences between them, all three authors underline the importance of the ideals of holiness and sainthood epitomised by St Sava. They also praise St Sava's role in founding an independent Serbian Church, regardless of whether they see this role as an expression of ecclesiastical anti-imperialism, a Theo-humanist orientation over the dominant social and ecclesial models, or an episcopocentric ecclesiology. Irrespective of the theological agenda applied to it, *Svetosavlje* remained an inspiration for some of the most impressive political theologies in twentieth-century Europe.

Ioannis Zelepos

Orthodoxy as Political Theology – the Case of the Church of Cyprus

Introduction

As a contribution to Orthodox Christian political theologies, the present chapter examines the Church of Cyprus, which at first glance seems to provide an excellent case study in view of its political role during a crucial period of the island's recent history. This period was closely connected with the tenure of Archbishop Makarios III (1950–1977), who became internationally known as one of the most prominent »political clerics« of the twentieth century. However, a second glance reveals that the topic is not that simple and requires a basic clarification in advance. This particularly concerns the term »political theology«, which, inasmuch as it is applicable at all for Orthodox Christianity in general[1], seems questionable with regard to a specific Cypriot context, at least in the narrow sense of »theology« as a theoretically elaborated and logically more or less consistent system of thought[2]. As a matter of fact, even the assumption of a specific »Cypriot Orthodox« theology as distinct from other Orthodox theologies may be misleading, considering that the Church of Cyprus, notwithstanding its historical autocephaly, had been an integral part of trans-regional Orthodox discourses since the time of the ecumenical councils of the first eight centuries[3].

---

1 For further discussion of this topic, see Vasilios N. MAKRIDES, Political Theology in Orthodox Christian Contexts. Specificities and Particularities in Comparison with Western Latin Christianity, in: Kristina STOECKL et al. (eds.), Political Theologies in Orthodox Christianity. Common Challenges – Divergent Positions, London 2017, pp. 25–54.
2 The main point of reference here is Carl Schmitt's conceptualising work *Politische Theologie* (1922), although it should be noted that the term was already coined in first century B.C. by Marcus Terentius Varro as »theologia civilis« (in distinction from »theologia naturalis« and »theologia mythica«) in a functionalist sense with respect to its state-oriented and its power-legitimising character. This meaning seems more compatible with the phenomena under examination here.
3 See John HACKETT, A History of the Orthodox Church of Cyprus. From the Coming of the Apostles Paul and Barnabas to the Commencement of the British Occupation (A.D. 45–A.D. 1878) together with some Account of the Latin and other Churches existing in the Island, London 1901, pp. 7–58; cf. Andreas MITSIDIS, Ἡ Ἐκκλησία τῆς Κύπρου, Nicosia 1972, pp. 6–13; Georghios THEODOULOU, The Origins and Evolution of Church-State Relations in Cyprus with special Reference to the Modern Era, Nicosia 2005, pp. 7–16.

In order to make the hermeneutical paradigm of political theology operable, it seems better therefore not to speak about »theology« *stricto sensu* but rather, less restrictively, about mechanisms of the utilisation of religion for political purposes. There is indeed no question that religion functioned for many centuries as essential reference point for the claim to political authority by the Orthodox Church of Cyprus, something which indeed applies to virtually every religious institution, but from late antiquity until the twentieth century took a very specific shape there, making Cyprus a unique case in modern Orthodoxy. The purpose of this study is therefore to point out central aspects of this development in a historical outline that focuses on the emergence and transformation of the so-called »ethnarchic« tradition in changing political contexts from imperial to colonial rule and, finally, Cypriot independence after 1960. The conclusion will discuss how these observations can be integrated into the theoretical framework of political theology.

The Historical Roots of Cypriot-Orthodox Ethnarchy Between Continuity and Disruption

Older scholarship on the Orthodox Church of Cyprus perceived its ethnarchic role – that is, its leadership both spiritual and political of its flock respectively its people – since early Byzantine times largely unquestioned as a historical reality. This coincides with the self-image of the Church, which emphasises its ancient origins and unbroken historical continuity, deriving from that an even »natural« ethnarchic leadership over the Orthodox Cypriot community[4]. By contrast, more recent critical scholarship has shown the empirical shortfalls and ideological bias of such a static perception, replacing it with a more dynamic methodological approach which considers the evolutionary character of the phenomenon and locates the formation of the ethnarchic authority of the Orthodox Church of Cyprus essentially in the period of Ottoman rule (1571–1878)[5].

This is does not mean, however, to completely deny institutional continuities going back beyond the early modern period and to ignore previous developments which, as a matter of fact, provided important historical references for later narratives of diachronic ethnarchic authority. One of these reference points was the

---

[4] The claim to »natural« leadership was, for instance, part of the political rhetoric of Archbishop Makarios III (1913–1977) since 1950. See footnote 35, below.

[5] For a ground-breaking discussion, see Michalis MICHAIL, Η Εκκλησία της Κύπρου κατά την οθωμανική περίοδο, 1571–1878. Η διαδικασία διαμόρφωσης ενός θεσμού εξουσίας, Nicosia 2005; cf. id., An Orthodox Institution of Ottoman Political Authority. The Church of Cyprus, in: Michalis MICHAEL et al. (eds.), Ottoman Cyprus. A Collection of Studies on History and Culture, Wiesbaden 2009, pp. 209–230.

autocephaly already officially granted to the Church of Cyprus at the Third Ecumenical Council of Ephesus (431) against the pretentions of the Patriarchate of Antioch and in practice seems to have been fully developed already a century earlier[6]. The autocephaly of the Church of Cyprus was confirmed in 478 by Emperor Zeno (r. 474–491), who, according to common opinion, endowed the Archbishop also with a number of special privileges which were clearly beyond the scope of clerical dignity and normally restricted to bearers of secular imperial authority: the right to sign in red ink, wear purple cloaks during ceremonies, and to carry an imperial sceptre (crowned with a golden globus cruciger) instead of a common pastoral staff. As far as this corresponds to historical facts – because positive source evidence regarding those privileges seems to date back only to the seventeenth century and thus to Ottoman rule[7] – it must probably be interpreted in the context of the church's internal dogmatic controversies of that time, namely, as politically motivated action on the part of the emperor in order to get Cyprus out of the sphere of the Church of Antioch, which supported monophysitism, and thereby to limit the growing influence of this dogma in the eastern parts of the Empire for the sake of stability[8]. Close ties between the Church of Cyprus and the political leadership of the Byzantine Empire are also in evidence about two centuries later, when, in 690, due to the Arab incursions on the island, the Archbishop, together with the Cypriot clergy and part of the Christian population were resettled to Nova Justinianopolis, near Kyzikos on the Sea of Marmara, where he was endowed with the same privileges of autocephaly he had enjoyed in Cyprus. This was enacted by the Council of Trullo in 691, but there are many uncertainties about the actual meaning of the source text, particularly whether the privileges were granted permanently or only temporarily, whether they continued or ceased to be valid after the return to

---

6 Evidence for the *de facto* independence of the Church of Cyprus in the fourth century is provided in the canons of the first two Ecumenical Councils of Nicaea (325) and Constantinople (381), see THEODOULOU, Origins, p. 8 (with quotations). As well as by the fact that, at Ephesus in 431, Antioch's claim of power over the Cypriot dioceses is explicitly characterised as an (implicitly unlawful) »innovation« (πρᾶγμα καινοτομούμενον), see HACKETT, A History, p. 19 (with quotation).
7 According to Venediktos ENGLEZAKIS, Τὸ μελανοδοχεῖον τοῦ Ἀρχιεπισκόπου Κυπριανοῦ, in: Κυπριακαὶ Σπουδαί 45 (1981), pp. 143–160, at p. 150 (quoted after Michalis MICHAEL, Kyprianos 1810–1821. An Orthodox Cleric »Administering Politics« in an Ottoman Island, in: Andrekos VARNAVA/id. (eds.), The Archbishops of Cyprus in Modern Age, Cambridge 2013, pp. 41–68, at p. 50, footnote 33), there is no mention of such privileges in Byzantine sources. According to Michael, the first written record regarding the privileges from Emperor Zeno dates from 1676, but the related source reference is unfortunately not to be found at the specified place (Kallinikos DELIKANIS, Τὰ ἐν τοῖς Κώδιξι [...] τοῦ Οἰκουμενικοῦ Πατριαρχείου πρὸς τὰς Ἐκκλησίας Ἀλεξανδρείας, Ἀντιοχείας, Ἱεροσολύμων καὶ Κύπρου, 1574–1863, Constantinople 1904, p. 633) nor elsewhere in the quoted collection of documents. The right to sign in red ink, however, is mentioned in 1679 by Paul RYCAUT, The Present State of the Greek and Armenian Churches, London 1679, p. 90.
8 Cf. THEODOULOU, Origins, p. 14.

Cyprus in 698 etc.⁹ What seems quite clear, however, is that the granting of these privileges, which came at the expense of the territorial jurisdiction of the Patriarchate of Constantinople, took place on the initiative of the Byzantine Emperor and thus must be interpreted in the context of imperial rather than ecclesiastical politics.

The historical reference points mentioned here give plausibility to the assumption that the Church of Cyprus took on an ethnarchic role in the early Middle Ages. However, in order to understand its character, it is important to note that this role did not emerge autonomously and much less »naturally«, but was highly dependent on, and closely connected with, an imperial centre of power that deliberately fostered it for reasons, which most probably were related to the geographical position of Cyprus at the periphery of the Orthodox Byzantine world. Consequently, the decline of Byzantine imperial power inevitably had analogous repercussions on this role, as well as on the position of the Church of Cyprus in general.

This decline became obvious when in 1192, in the aftermath of the Third Crusade, the French dynasty of Lusignan took control of the island and exercised it for longer than the Byzantine Empire was still to exist, being superseded only in 1489 by Venice, which held the island until 1571. Under Latin rule, which lasted for almost four centuries in total, the Orthodox Church of Cyprus was institutionally and, as a matter of fact, even spatially marginalised, deprived of its property and revenues, and formally subjugated to the jurisdiction of the Roman Catholic Church[10]. Under these circumstances, the Orthodox Church may have been able to maintain some moral authority, especially among the rural population, but it is hardly plausible to describe this in terms of an ethnarchic role in the sense of an unbroken historical tradition deriving from Byzantium or even from Late Antiquity. On the contrary, where the institutional ethnarchy of the Orthodox Church is concerned, the centuries-long Latin rule over Cyprus marks a period much less of continuity than of disruption.

The term »disruption« is used here with respect to the re-establishment of Orthodox Church authority by the Ottomans, who conquered the island in 1570–1571 and soon began integrating the church into their ruling apparatus, a policy they applied also in other dominions with predominantly Orthodox population. This included the restitution of most church buildings and other property previously taken over by the Latin Church, the restoration of privileges concerning judicial competencies and the levying of church taxes, as well as the primacy of the Orthodox Church, which became formally reunited with Constantinople under Patriarch

---

9 For a detailed account, see HACKETT, A History, pp. 36–45.
10 This was formalised by official decrees in 1220 and 1222 and confirmed with slight alterations by the *Bulla Cypria* issued by Pope Alexander IV in 1260, which was accepted by Archbishop Germanos and the higher Orthodox clergy of Cyprus. See HACKETT, A History, pp. 82–126.

Jeremias II, over all other Christian confessional groups (Maronites, Armenians, Catholics) on the island[11]. The specific framework of Ottoman rule enabled the Orthodox Church of Cyprus and its Archbishops to gain considerable political influence on the island and thereby eventually to take on an ethnarchic role. This process took place essentially in the seventeenth and eighteenth centuries, and thus coincided with the analogous emergence, though on a larger scale, of the Patriarchate of Constantinople as the leading institution of Ottoman Orthodoxy[12]. In both cases, the term »ethnarch« was understood as equivalent to the Turkish *millet başı* (»head of the nation«), which was related to the Ottoman concept of religiously defined *millets* (»nations«)[13] – and obviously not to its various meanings in ancient and mediaeval times, where the title »ethnarch« was used sometimes for rulers of foreign tribes, sometimes for commanders of mercenary troops, but never for bearers of religious authority[14].

As in the Byzantine past, however, the cornerstone of ethnarchic authority in Ottoman terms was recognition by the centre of imperial power and the concomitant possibility of communicating directly with its representatives in the capital. In Cyprus, this began around 1660 and was finally achieved around the middle of the eighteenth century, during the tenure of Archbishop Filotheos (1734–1759), a reform cleric who emphasised the autonomy of the Church of Cyprus and in 1740 even wrote an essay in which he claimed its equality in status with the Orthodox Patriarchates of the ancient »Pentarchy«[15]. Filotheos personally led an embassy to Constantinople in 1743, and in 1754 succeeded in obtaining a *firman* (sultan's decree) by which the Cypriot bishops were officially acknowledged as the political

---

11 See Theodoulou, Origins, pp. 27f.
12 In contrast to the foundation myths of the Orthodox *Millet-i-Rum*, which projected such a role back into the times of Mehmed the Conqueror in the fifteenth century. See extensive information in Paraskevas Konortas, Οθωμανικές θεωρήσεις για το Οικουμενικό Πατριαρχείο. Βεράτια για τους προκαθήμενους της Μεγάλης Εκκλησίας (17ος – αρχές 20ού αιώνα), Athens 1998. This development culminated in the eighteenth century with the abolition of the autocephalous Patriarchates/Archbishoprics of Ohrid and Peć (1766/1767) and the subordination of their dioceses under direct jurisdiction of Constantinople.
13 On the *millet* system and related research problems, see Benjamin Braude/Bernard Lewis (eds.), Christians and Jews in the Ottoman Empire, 2 vols. (New York 1982); Michael Ursinus, Zur Diskussion um »millet« im Osmanischen Reich, in: Südost-Forschungen 48 (1989), pp. 195–207; Konortas, Οθωμανικές θεωρήσεις; Tom Papademetriou, Render unto the Sultans. Power, Authority, and the Greek Orthodox Church on the Early Ottoman Centuries, Oxford 2015.
14 S.v. »ἐθνάρχης« in: Dimitrios Dimitrakos, Μέγα Λεξικόν ὅλης τῆς Ἑλληνικῆς Γλώσσης, 15 vols., Athens 1933–1953, here in vol. 5, p. 2250. Such a use would in any case have been inappropriate for a cleric, since the words ἔθνος, ἔθνη, ἐθνικός, and the similar in Greek Christian terminology were synonymous with »Heathen/Heathenism« (like *gentilis/gentiles* in Latin).
15 The text was edited in [Archimandrite] Kyprianos, Ἱστορία Χρονολογικὴ τῆς Νήσου Κύπρου [...] ἀπὸ τοῦ Κατακλυσμοῦ μέχρι τοῦ Παρόντος [...], Venice 1788, pp. 370–390.

representatives of the Christian population with full responsibility in taxation issues and the right to turn directly to the central government without the mediation of its local Muslim representatives on the island[16]. The peak of the church's political dominance in Cyprus can be localised in the long-lasting tenure of Archbishop Chrysanthos (1767–1810), something that is corroborated also by in contemporary accounts by European travellers[17]. This was, however, not a monopoly position but rather a sensitive power-triangle between the Archbishop, the *muhassıl* (Ottoman governor) and the *Dragoman* (literally »interpreter«) of the Seraglio, an office created for Cyprus in the early seventeenth century and occupied from 1780 to 1809 by the very influential Chatzigeorgakis Kornesios (mid-18th c.–1809) who, being married to a niece of Chrysanthos, had close family ties with the Archbishop[18].

The outbreak of the Greek war of independence in 1821 had severe consequences for the Orthodox Church of Cyprus. In July of that year, Archbishop Kyprianos (1756–1821) was executed in retaliation, together with the high clergy and many local Orthodox community leaders[19]. This was a major setback which, however, turned out to be only temporary, since the Ottomans continued to rely on the church as a central pillar of their rule in Cyprus. During the following reform era of Tanzimat, which began in the late 1830s, it was even strengthened institutionally, though at the expense of the personal authority of the prelates, in a process that has been described as »a particular secularization of the functioning of the Church itself«[20]. The last decades of Ottoman rule in Cyprus thus were a period of dynamic transition – in contrast to the image of static backwardness prevalent in contemporary Western European travelogues and in older scholarship – whereby the Orthodox Church became a state authority in modern terms. Consequently, this role was also the central reference point of its self-image at the beginning of British colonial rule in 1878, which meant a radical turning point in the history of the church as well as of the whole island.

---

16 See Michail, Η Εκκλησία, pp. 137–147.
17 See, for example, Domenico Sestini, Voyage de Constantinople a Bassora, en 1781 [...] et rétour à Constantinople, en 1782 [...], Paris 1798, p. 291: »Le clergé grec est l'auxiliaire des pachas, pour pressure le peuple; sans son secours ils ne viendraient pas à bout de lever les impôts et les contributions extraordinaires. *Les pachas font part du gâteau au clergé*. Et le peuple paie« (emphasis added).
18 See Michalis N. Michail, Ο Μουχασίλης, ο Δραγομάνος, ο Αρχιεπίσκοπος και η Διεκδίκηση της Πολιτικής Εξουσίας στην Κύπρο της Οθωμανικής Περιφέρειας, 1789–1810, in: Επετηρίδα Κέντρου Επιστημονικών Ερευνών 32, Nicosia 2006, pp. 229–237; cf. Theoharis Stavrides, Chrysanthos 1767–1810. Grappling with the Vicissitudes of Ottoman Power, in: Varnava/Michael (eds.), The Archbishops, pp. 17–40.
19 See analytically Michail, Η Εκκλησία, pp. 215–243.
20 See Michael, An Orthodox Institution, pp. 227f.

Cypriot-Orthodox Ethnarchy under Conditions of British Colonial Rule

Soon after the takeover of power in July 1878 it became obvious that the British were determined to break with established Ottoman ruling practices, which they mistakenly perceived as »traditional«, and to introduce principles of modern administration – at least as long they didn't contradict the prerogatives of colonial domination[21]. Accordingly, they were unwilling to acknowledge the church as the local political actor it had been under the Ottomans, and as Archbishop Sofronios III (1825–1900) and his metropolitans had formally requested in February 1879 in a memorandum to the first High Commissioner, Sir Garnet Wolseley (1833–1913)[22]. Wolseley met the Orthodox hierarchs, whom he described as »cunning and deceitful«, with personal hostility which undoubtedly had a cultural background in Anglican secularism. In order to minimise the church's influence, he denied recognition of its former competencies and privileges, including legal immunity, exception from land taxes, the validity of Orthodox canon law where it had hitherto been applicable, and so on. Not least, he refused to provide civil assistance to the clergy in collecting liturgical fees and other levies, as the Ottomans had done, something that dried out important revenue sources and soon reduced the church's income to one third[23].

This confrontative policy, initiated by the first High Commissioner and continued more or less unchanged by his successors, could only be understood as oppression on the part of the Orthodox clergy and placed its members in a position of structural antagonism to the British regime. The church thereby entered a period of deep institutional as well as ideological crisis which lasted until the middle of the twentieth century, covering the greater part of the colonial period. Clerical opposition to the British was conservative by nature, since it was essentially grounded in the reminiscence of the Ottoman past. In this respect, its outlook was much more an »imperial« than a »national«, even more as the Orthodox population was in its vast majority not yet affected by Greek nationalism except of parts of the small intellectual elite, who soon after the British takeover began to demand *Enosis*

---

21 See George HILL, A History of Cyprus, 4 vols. (London 1949–1952), here in vol. 4, pp. 417–419 on the Legislative Council established as an advisory board in September 1878 and partly consisting of elected representatives of the island's population (since 1881 nine Orthodox Greeks and three Muslim Turks, 18 members in total). The separation of the local population along religious criteria was the only Ottoman legacy the British were ready to accept, because it eased their policy of »divide and rule« based on the instrumentalisation of the Muslim minority as a counterweight in order to neutralise political demands of the island's Orthodox majority.
22 See Andrekos VARNAVA, Sophronios III 1865–1900. The Last of the »Old« and the First of the »New« Archbishop-Ethnarchs?, in: VARNAVA/MICHAEL (eds.), The Archbishops, pp. 106–147, at p. 125.
23 See THEODOULOU, Origins, p. 52.

(Ἕνωσις), that is, union of the island with Greece. It is questionable whether and to what extent this demand was shared also by Orthodox clerics at that time, but if so, it is at least clear that the church did not yet play a leading role in it[24].

Its initial indifference towards nationalism under the slogan of *Enosis* began to change, however, in the following decades, and eventually turned into the opposite when, after Sofronios' death in 1900, a lasting internal conflict broke out in the matter of his succession between conservatives and nationalists, the latter finally prevailing in 1909[25]. With the election of Kyrillos II (1845–1916) in the same year, a staunch supporter of *Enosis* ascended to the archiepiscopal throne. After entering the Legislative Council (the local parliament) in 1889, Kyrillos had already been a vigorous political activist for decades. With him the demand for *Enosis* was firmly integrated into the political agenda of the Orthodox Church of Cyprus. In order to understand this ideological shift, however, it is not sufficient merely to ascribe it to personal national sentiments Kyrillos and his like-minded fellows undoubtedly shared. One also has to consider the general situation of the Orthodox Church of Cyprus since the establishment of British rule. Notwithstanding its colonial character, British rule went along with a secular modernising impetus, which not only destroyed the institutional power of the Cypriot Church, but also threatened to dismantle its moral authority in the long term. Positioning itself as protagonist of the national cause was therefore an excellent means for the church to regain lost terrain and to secure its claim to leadership over the Orthodox Cypriot community by translating it into a modern political grammar. The demand for *Enosis* in this context functioned primarily as a lever to maintain or re-establish traditional power structures and only second, if at all, as a political goal in itself, all the more since it was not a realistic perspective then and, for the time being, *Enosis* remained anyway an elite project.

Only after the end of World War I, which led to the breakdown of the multi-ethnic empires in Europe and the Near East and to a temporary boom of the idea of the self-determination of peoples, this constellation began to change noticeably. In the early 1920s, there were first articulations of an *Enosis* movement carried by broader strata of Orthodox Cypriot society, in particular by younger people in the towns, with a considerable portion of high school students and boy scouts among them. It

---

24 See Varnava, Sophronios III, pp. 118–124 with an extensive discussion on example of the widespread assumption, although unsubstantiated by source evidence, that the Cypriot high clergy already demanded *Enosis* in their welcome address to Wolseley in 1878.

25 On the Archiepiscopal dispute, see Hill, A History, pp. 577–603; cf. Andrekos Varnava/Irene Pophiades, Kyrillos II 1909–1916. The First Greek Nationalist and Enosist Archbishop-Ethnarch, in: Varnava/Michael (eds.), The Archbishops, pp. 148–176, at pp. 154–161; see also the contemporary Georgios Frangoudis, Ἱστορία τοῦ Ἀρχιεπισκοπικοῦ Ζητήματος Κύπρου, 1900–1910, Athens ²2002 [first published in 1910].

speaks for the autonomous character of this movement that it gathered momentum just when the surrounding political constellation was at its least favourable. After defeat in Asia Minor (1919–1922) and the Lausanne Treaty (1923), Greece had definitely turned away from national expansionism and accordingly showed little interest in the Cypriot movement for *Enosis*, all the more so given that the island had never played a prominent role in the goals of Greek irredentism throughout the nineteenth century[26]. At the same time, Great Britain was determined to hold on its colonial possession. In 1925, it raised Cyprus, which hitherto had only been a protectorate, to the status of crown colony, a significant upgrade accompanied by some serious attempts to improve the social and economic situation of the population[27]. This policy, however, did not lead to a weakening of the *Enosis* movement, as the British had obviously hoped. On the contrary, it became stronger and increasingly radicalised towards the end of the 1920s, culminating in the October riots of 1931, which broke out in the aftermath of the collective resignation of the Orthodox Cypriot members from the Legislative Council[28]. Among the main promoters of the escalation was an organisation called »National Radical Union of Cyprus« (EREK), as well as high-ranking clerics of the Orthodox Church, in particular the Bishop of Kition, Nikodimos (1889–1937), who played a key role in heating up the atmosphere on the eve of the riots. As member of the Legislative Council, he declared his resignation in a public letter in which he denied fundamentally the legitimacy of British rule over Cyprus and announced that, in his capacity »as an ecclesiastical and national leader«, he would recommend his compatriots to exercise civil disobedience against it[29]. He actually did so in the second part of the letter, which was addressed to his »Greek brethren« in religiously heavily-charged rhetoric.

This letter deserves a closer look not only for the light it sheds on the ideological background of its author but also due to the fact that very similar rhetoric was used some twenty years later by Archbishop Makarios III, who was to become a key figure of Cypriot history in the second half of the twentieth century. The

---

26 See, for example, Harry PSOMIADES, Greek Nationalism in the Nineteenth Century. A Focus on Cyprus, in: Journal of Modern Hellenism 2 (1985), pp. 75–89.
27 See George GEORGHALLIDES, A Political and Administrative History of Cyprus, 1918–1926, Nicosia 1979; id., Cyprus under the Governorship of Sir Ronald Storrs, Nicosia 1985.
28 In that month, a demonstration for *Enosis* in the capital Nicosia got out of hand when several thousand participants moved to the residence of the British governor and burned it down. Nobody was killed, but riots followed in the larger towns of the island over the next days. For a detailed depiction of the events, see Heinz RICHTER, Geschichte der Insel Zypern. Part 1: 1878–1949, Mannheim 2004, pp. 285–308.
29 GEORGHALLIDES, Cyprus under the Governorship, pp. 688–690, [Nikodimos of Kition to Sir Ronald Storrs, 17 October 1931]: »[A]s an ecclesiastical and national leader I am now obliged to recommend to the Cypriots […] an unlawful opposition to unlawful authorities and unlawful laws«.

core elements of Nikodimos' letter were the invocation of divine justice[30] and, accordingly, the presentation of *Enosis* in terms of »salvation«, a term repeatedly used by Nikodimos:

> Our only *salvation* from all perspectives is our national liberation. [...] Looking, therefore, steadily at the bright star of Bethlehem and of our national *salvation* we have one and only one way to walk, the way which is narrow and full of sorrows but leads to *salvation*. [...] Let us be obedient to the voice-law, voice-order which comes down from the Mount Sinai of the National Edicts [...], a voice ascending from the graves of those who, for seven centuries, had sown their bones in the bosom of the land of Cyprus without the realization of their aspirations and dreams for a national *salvation*[31].

One can imagine what an emotionalising effect such words may have had on their addressees. However, it is no less important to observe here that by identifying *Enosis* with future salvation (»from all points of view«!), it became elevated into a kind of national eschatology far beyond the frames of *Realpolitik*.

The latter proved long lasting, but had also a tangible relation to the actual situation on Cyprus, which left no space for whatsoever discussions about a change of the island's political status. On the contrary, in response to the October riots of 1931, the British turned to a very repressive policy by imposing martial law, press censorship, and assembly prohibitions. They abolished also the Legislative Council, which, although quite limited in administrative competencies, had been nonetheless the central representative body of the Cypriot population, functioning simultaneously as main institution of the political integration of the Orthodox-Greek and the Muslim-Turkish communities. Furthermore, in an attempt to politically decapitate the Orthodox Greek community, many of its prominent representatives were arrested and deported to other colonies of the Empire. Among them were Nikodimos of Kition and Makarios, Bishop of Keryneia (1870–1950), who were both held responsible for instigating the riots. Their deportation had a serious impact on the Church of Cyprus, which became acute two years later. After the death of the elderly and sick Kyrillos III (1859–1933), the archiepiscopal throne remained vacant because, due to the exile of the two bishops, which the British refused to lift, it was impossible to set up a local synod in order to elect a successor according to

---

30   Ibid.: »[We] proclaim the union of Cyprus with Mother Greece [...] with the certainty that the God of Justice and Morality will assist in this struggle of Justice against vulgar force«.
31   Ibid. (emphasis added). The reference to »seven centuries« suggests that Cyprus had been fighting for national salvation since the beginning of Latin rule. The motif of ancestral bones »sown« in the soil was obviously inspired by the canon of Greek national allegories. See, for example, the first stanza of the national anthem, based on Dionysios Solomos' »Hymn to Liberty« of 1823, where liberty is depicted as a woman arising from the bones of the Ancient Hellenes.

canon law. This placed the church in an institutional limbo that continued for more than a decade until 1947, when a successor of Kyrillos was canonically elected in the person of Leontios (1896–1947), who since 1933 had acted as *locum tenens*, while his official tenure as Archbishop was to last only a matter of weeks[32].

The election was possible because the British had meanwhile become aware of the legitimacy deficit caused by their policy of harsh repression. Hesitantly, they began to loosen it in favour of a policy aimed at the political re-integration of the Cypriot population, by allowing a limited degree of self-determination[33]. This attempt, however, met with only limited success, not least because the deliberate exclusion of the island's population, both Orthodox Greek and Muslim Turkish, from any kind of political participation had favoured the strengthening of informal power structures in both communities, which were distant and, in the case of the former, even hostile to the official state. The Church of Cyprus can also be characterised as such a power structure, although »informal« only insofar as the colonial rulers never had accepted it as an official political actor. A side effect of institutional weakness is, however, always that it leaves even more space for personal based allegiances and charismatic leadership.

The Post-colonial Transformation of Cypriot-Orthodox Ethnarchy

Since 1950, this space was filled by Makarios III (1913–1977), undoubtedly one of the most charismatic clerical personalities in modern Orthodoxy. Even before his election as Archbishop in October of that year, he achieved a major political coup by organising a plebiscite on *Enosis*, which turned the Cypriot Question into an international issue, while simultaneously establishing himself as the unchallenged political champion of the island's Orthodox Greek community. This plebiscite, with which Makarios pre-empted a similar venture planned by the communist AKEL party, produced an overwhelming majority of 96 per cent votes in favour of *Enosis*,

---

32 On Kyrillos III and Leontios, see the related chapters of Irene POPHIADES and Alexis RAPPAS in: VARNAVA/MICHAEL (eds.), The Archbishops, pp. 177–239.
33 Since the abolition of the Legislative Council, which was not restored until the very end of British rule in 1960, the island was ruled exclusively by decree. In the early 1940s, however, the British began encouraging the foundation of political parties and even held elections, though only on a communal level, in 1943. Such a change in policy has to be understood against the background of World War II, when remote Cyprus suddenly became an area of high strategic importance close to the battlefronts of North Africa and the Aegean, while thousands of (Orthodox Greek as well as Muslim Turkish) volunteers were fighting under the Union Jack in the »Cyprus Regiment«. Cf. Jan ASMUSSEN, »Dark-skinned Cypriots will not be accepted!« Cypriots in the British Army (1939–1945), in: Hubert FAUSTMANN/Nicos PERISTIANIS (eds.), Britain in Cyprus. Colonialism and Post-Colonialism 1878–2006, Wiesbaden 2009, pp. 167–185.

but was not acknowledged by the British because of its more than dubious legal basis[34]. However, that was not important since Makarios' real goal was not to get his plebiscite officially acknowledged by the British, but rather to draw the attention of the international media towards Cyprus. To them he declared in a press conference held some weeks later:

> On the 15th of the preceding January 1950, the Ethnarchy of Cyprus, the natural national leader of this unredeemed Greek island, called the Cypriot people to express its will. [...] The plebiscite, under the supervision of the Ethnarchy, was carried out peacefully, without compulsion and freely. [...] [It] was a collective expression of the will of the Cypriots for union of their island with Greece, to which it ethnologically belongs[35].

He repeated his claim to natural leadership of ethnarchy when he was asked whether the mission of the church was not purely religious:

> The church in the subjugated Hellenism has not only religious but also political competencies. It is an ancient tradition that the church substitutes the Free Motherland. Nor should you forget that in Cyprus the church leaders are elected by the people whose natural leaders they are.

To the question, whether the institution of ethnarchy had any historical or legal basis, Makarios answered:

> Certainly. Since the times of Mehmed the Conqueror and even earlier, the Turkish government acknowledged the ethnarchic rights of the Church by *berats* and the British government since the occupation of Cyprus has respected and never questioned them.

The reference to Ottoman rule and sultan's decrees may have seemed quite anachronistic and picturesque to the international reporters, but it exactly denoted the actual historical source of Cypriot-Orthodox ethnarchy, although it is difficult to say whether Makarios himself was really aware of it or just used it as a reference point for a more or less »invented tradition« which had emerged in reaction to British

---

34 Cf. Stanley MAYES, Makarios. A Biography, London 1981, pp. 36–40. The polling lasted from 15 to 22 January 1950 and was carried out in churches, usually after worship and without sufficient secrecy. Such conditions provided every possibility to exert social and/or spiritual pressure on the voters, and of course excluded entirely the Muslim Turkish population.

35 See IDRYMA ARCHIEPISKOPOU MAKARIOU III, Ἅπαντα Ἀρχιεπισκόπου Μακαρίου Γ', 18 vols., Nicosia 1991–2008, here in vol. 1, pp. 275–280, also for the following quotations.

rule[36]. What seems clear, however, is that according to his argumentation, decrees issued by the sultans centuries ago continued to be legally valid, even if the Ottoman Empire meanwhile had ceased to exist, as long as they were not officially repealed by the British. British rule, moreover, was characterised as an »occupation«, an implication of deficient legitimacy that had been affirmed more explicitly already in the 1930s by Bishop Nikodimos.

Another important element of Makarios' understanding of ethnarchy was the complete autonomy of his own political leadership, something that he was eager to emphasise on many occasions and especially in relation to the Greek state. When asked at the same press conference whether he had had any previous consultations with the Greek government, he (truthfully) answered in the negative and declared that he was seeking assistance from »a friendly state« in order to bring the Cyprus issue before the UN General Assembly having in mind not Greece but Syria[37]. This can be explained, at first glance, by the actual political circumstances, namely by the reluctance of Athens to get involved in the Cyprus matter and to strain diplomatic relations with Great Britain and the Western Allies on whom Greece was highly dependent at that time. It was, however, also characteristic of the general attitude of Makarios towards the Greek state. As a matter of fact, while vigorously promoting the Cyprus issue internationally under the slogan of *Enosis* in the 1950s, Makarios at no time sought concrete cooperation with the government of the state to which he ostensibly wanted to attach his homeland[38]. This seems paradoxical, but provides a further indication that *Enosis* was much less a real diplomatic goal than an element – and even the core element – of a political eschatology whose essential purpose was to sustain the ethnarchic authority of the church and its Archbishop over the Orthodox Cypriot community. This may also explain why *Enosis*, although not really pursued practically in the 1950s and less still in the 1960s, after Cypriot independence[39], was never explicitly revoked by Makarios[40], at least

---

36 Cf. Sia ANAGNOSTOPOULOU, Makarios III. 1950–77: Creating the *Ethnarchic State*, in: VARNAVA/ MICHAEL (eds.), The Archbishops, pp. 239–292, who, in this context, even speaks of »the reinvention of Ethnarchism« (at p. 248).
37 See IDRYMA ARCHIEPISKOPOU MAKARIOU III, Άπαντα, p. 276, footnote 1.
38 See Ioannis ZELEPOS, The Historical Background of the Cyprus Problem – just a Conflict of Ethnic Nationalism?, in: Austrian Review of International and European Law 19 (2014), pp. 13–27.
39 See, for example, Makarios' fierce rejection of the Acheson Plan, a first version of which was presented in July 1964 and provided union of Cyprus with Greece against territorial compensations for Turkey, as »betrayal of Hellenism«; cf. ZELEPOS, Historical Background, pp. 24f., and ANAGNOSTOPOULOU, Makarios III, pp. 270f.
40 This is also true of the interview Makarios gave on 22 September 1958 to the British MP Barbara Castle (published two days later in the *London Times*), which became famous for opening the way for Cypriot independence. In contrast to a widespread misinterpretation, he actually did not abandon *Enosis* for the future but declared: »I would be prepared to accept the status of independence of

until the Turkish invasion of 1974. For to have done so would have undermined his whole construct of ethnarchy.

Holding on to *Enosis* as the ultimate goal while not practically pursuing it was a means of fostering the personal political authority of Makarios as Archbishop, but it was also embedded in a broader ideological background. The perception of the Orthodox Cypriots as an integral but nevertheless autonomous part of »greater Hellenism« referred to elder notions of Greek identity which can be found also in pre-World War I nationalists such as Ion Dragoumis (1878–1920), who distanced himself from the Greek state and stressed the polycentric character of the nation[41].

The main handicap for the functioning of the Republic of Cyprus, founded in 1960 on the principle of cooperation between the Orthodox Greek and Muslim Turkish communities, was therefore not *Enosis* as such, but rather the specific concept of ethnarchy, which by virtue of its premises was completely unsuitable to integrating the Muslim Turkish part of the island's population. This problem was underscored by the fact that Makarios, who never made a clear-cut differentiation between his offices as Archbishop and as president, cultivated a paternalistic style of governance much closer to traditional patterns of personal rule than to modern mechanisms of professional administration[42]. The failure of the early Republic of Cyprus, which eventually led to the partition of the island in 1974, was, however, not only caused by domestic politics. Apart from the role played by the so-called »mother countries«, Greece and Turkey, a significant factor was also the foreign policy of the President-Archbishop. From the very beginning of his *Enosis* campaign in 1950, Makarios had tried to get support mainly from the non-aligned countries and accordingly tried to succeed within the institutional framework of the United Nations rather than of the Western alliance. He continued his fixation on the UN and the non-aligned world in the 1960s, although this brought no tangible benefits for independent Cyprus. On the contrary, it soon turned out hazardous since it left the island without effective international protection which, in the extraordinary sensitive geopolitical setting

---

Cyprus on the condition that this status shall not be changed, either by union with Greece, by partition, or by any other way, *unless the UN approves such a change*« (emphasis added).

41 See for example his novel Ὅσοι ζωντανοί (*Those alive*), published in 1911, where he stated: »The political restoration of the nation can be achieved in the form of one or more than one Greek states [...]«, which would serve as intermediate stages until the creation of a »great state« (or empire). On the ideological context of such thoughts, see Gerasimos AUGUSTINOS, Consciousness and History. Nationalist Critics of Greek Society, 1897–1914, Boulder, CO 1977.

42 See Kyriacos MARKIDES, The Rise and Fall of the Cyprus Republic, New Haven, CT 1977, pp. 44–46, with a vivid contemporary description; for example, that he personally baptised more than a thousand children. This style of governance of course included also clientelist patronage, especially in favour of EOKA veterans, whose numbers, by the way, were continuously growing after the end of the fighting in 1959 (on this, see ZELEPOS, Historical Background, p. 22), many of which were employed in the public service of the newly founded state. See MARKIDES, The Rise and Fall, pp. 76–78.

of the Eastern Mediterranean at that time, could only come from the Western alliance – all the more given that all three guarantor powers of Cyprus were NATO members[43].

Makarios tried to keep Cyprus out of NATO's influence at any cost, a policy which was obviously determined much less by reason of state than by ideology. This is not, however, to be seen in the context of the contemporary system-clash of the Cold War, for Makarios was, in spite of occasional characterizatios as the »Castro of the Mediterranean«, definitely unsuspicious sharing leftist or even communist beliefs. A much more plausible interpretation is profound anti-Western resentment, which probably to some degree drew from ideological currents immanent to traditionalist (not traditional) Orthodoxy, but apart from that was undoubtedly based on opposition to colonialism, of which his homeland had experienced quite a harsh form since the 1930s. In this respect, Makarios' concept of ethnarchy was at the same time conservative, in holding on the Ottoman legacy of an Orthodox *millet* led by the church, as well as modern, in embracing the nationalist ideology of ethnic exclusiveness in room combination with a rhetoric of contemporary anti-colonialism.

This concept was doomed to founder upon reality, all the more so because Makarios' room for political manoeuvre constantly narrowed – especially since the establishment of the military dictatorship in Greece in 1967, which eventually also dealt the fatal blow to undivided Cyprus by launching a *coup d'état* against him in July 1974, in turn opening the gates for the subsequent Turkish invasion. With the military occupation of the northern part of the island by Turkish forces, the call for *Enosis* lost its function, almost a century after its appearance, and was replaced by a new goal, which was to overcome the factual partition of the island. With *Enosis*, however, also disappeared the Cypriot-Orthodox ethnarchy, which had been dependent on it. Deprived of charismatic leadership after the death of Makarios in 1977, it soon became reduced to anachronistic political folklore[44].

---

43 Consider, for example, the immediate rejection of the Sandys-Ball plan of January 1964, providing for the stationing of NATO troops as a peace-keeping force, by Makarios, who would only accept UN Blue Helmets, which remain in Cyprus to this day. One may ask whether NATO forces would really have done a worse job and, no less important, how likely a Turkish invasion ten years later would have been with the Green Line in Nicosia, guarded not by Blue Helmets, but by American GIs.

44 On the successor to Makarios III, see Andrekos Varnava, Chrysostomos I. 1977–2006: Makarios III was »a difficult act to follow«, in: Varnava/Michael (eds.), The Archbishops, pp. 293–310.

Conclusion

In order to describe Cypriot Orthodoxy in terms of political theology, it is important first of all to emphasise the procedural character of this phenomenon, something that contradicts imaginations of unbroken continuities reaching back to Antiquity or even »natural« self-evidence. The present analysis argues that it was inextricably linked to the concept of ethnarchy, which, however, underwent fundamental transformations from the early modern period until the twentieth century. Ethnarchy was initially a specific form of political representation with administrative competencies, which gradually emerged since the second half of seventeenth century in the context of Ottoman rule and was formally institutionalised in mid-nineteenth century during the era of Tanzimat reforms. British rule after 1878 marks a fundamental break in this development because it destroyed the legal basis of Orthodox ethnarchy in favour of secular principles of administration, taking over from the Ottomans only the separation of the population into religiously defined communities, which facilitated their policy of colonial domination. Lacking any formal institutional base, ethnarchy now became a term of more or less symbolic meaning, which, however, required ideological reinforcement in order to successfully claim moral authority.

This reinforcement was provided by Greek nationalism under the slogan of *Enosis*, which, after a deep internal crisis at the beginning of the twentieth century, was firmly integrated into the agenda of the church and from then on functioned as central lever for its claim to political leadership of the Orthodox Cypriots. It was, however, a form of nationalism that did not feature liberal currents of civic emancipation, instead proclaiming religious notions of salvation. Furthermore, it transcended the political goal of *Enosis* into an eschatology, which was propagated even more radically, the less reference it had to political pragmatism. This specific ideological construct can be justifiably characterised as a political theology, although less in the sense of a theory than with respect to its function as cornerstone of a meanwhile mystified concept of ethnarchy. Under the charismatic Archbishop Makarios III, this concept reached its peak but also its decline because, as a genuine by-product of colonial rule, it provided no sufficient foundation for meeting the challenges of political leadership and state-building under the conditions of twentieth-century modernity.

Marian Pătru

Religion, Politics, and Social Change

An Overview of the Intellectual History of Orthodox Political Theology in Romania in the Short Twentieth Century

Introductory Remarks

The analysis of theological-political discourse in a historical context as complex as the short Romanian twentieth century (1918–1989) inevitably involves the selection of concepts, thematic constellations, and authors with a high level of relevance for the given topic. A mapping of the entire discursive »territory« determined by theological-political reflection in the intellectual history of Romania, from the establishment of the national state at the end of the First World War until the fall of the communist regime, certainly deserves to be the subject not only of a study, but also of an entire volume. In addition to the theological discourse of the Romanian Orthodox Church (ROC), such exhaustive research should consider the discourse of different cultural currents, or that of far-right political movements in the interwar period, which massively used the concepts of Orthodox theology to articulate their ideology of a Christian state and society.

The following pages dwell only on that type of theological-political reflection, which is closely related to the institutional authority of the Romanian Church: official newspapers of the dioceses, or those that appeared with the blessing of a bishop, reviews and journals of Orthodox theological educational institutions, or books published by diocesan publishing houses. The discourse generated by these media is obviously a situational one, i. e., it is constituted as reaction to a certain *Zeitgeist* and thus does not represent the normative opinion of the church in the question of the relation between the spheres of religion and politics. However, this type of discourse is relevant primarily because it reflects the theological-political potential of the church's conceptual imaginary. In other words, theological-political discourse sheds light on the church's ability in every context and epoch to use the concepts of its theological tradition in order to provide an explanation for the kind of relationship, which ought to or already does exist with the state and, in general, with the sphere of politics.

Political Theology and Social Change

Political theology, as theorised by Carl Schmitt in the first half of the twentieth century, is closely linked to the process of secularisation of politics, a process, which has marked the history of Western Europe since the dawn of the modern *Weltanschauung* in the sixteenth and seventeenth centuries[1]. Indeed, Schmitt's book *Politische Theologie. Vier Kapitel zur Lehre von der Souveränität*[2] (1922) was one of the reactions of the conservative Catholic environment in Germany to the structural changes that modernity has produced: the separation of political and religious spheres, the separation of state and church, on the one hand, and the progressive de-Christianisation of European society on the other[3]. So Schmitt's thesis that »all significant concepts of the modern theory of the state are secularised theological concepts«[4], is not merely a simple theoretical assertion about the history of political concepts, but also an implicit critique of the evolution of the relationship between the religious and the political order in the modern history of Europe. For Schmitt, the separation of the sphere of politics from that of religion marked the birth of the modern state. However, the state continued to function as a secular replica of the transcendent God of Christian theology: »The omnipotent God became the omnipotent lawgiver«, and »the exception in jurisprudence is analogous to the miracle in theology«[5]. Schmitt ultimately suggests that, despite a state that defines itself as secular, there is in fact no autonomy of politics from the theological. Moreover, as Jan Assmann puts it, behind these central theses of Schmitt's thinking lies the postulate that, since religion and politics originally formed a unit, the modern separation between church and state is an error and an illegitimate evolution of the relationship between the two institutions[6].

The very association of theology with politics within a single concept in the post-Enlightenment civilisational context highlights Schmitt's critical orientation and his intention to invalidate »the possibility of a pure secular-rational foundation of

---

1 For a presentation of this process see Charles TAYLOR, A Secular Age, Cambridge 2007; Jonathan ISRAEL, Radical Enlightenment. Philosophy and the Making of Modernity, 1650–1750, Oxford 2001; Owen CHADWICK, The Secularization of the European Mind in the Nineteenth Century, Cambridge 1975.
2 Carl SCHMITT, Politische Theologie. Vier Kapitel zur Lehre von der Souveränität, Munich 1922.
3 Ulriche BRÖCKLING, Katholische Intellektuelle in der Weimarer Republik. Zeitkritik und Gesellschaftstheorie bei Walter Dirks, Romano Guardini, Carl Schmitt, Ernst Michel und Heinrich Mertens, Munich 1993.
4 Carl SCHMITT, Political Theology. Four Chapters on the Concept of Sovereignty, Chicago 2005, p. 36.
5 Ibid.
6 Jan ASSMANN, Herrschaft und Heil. Politische Theologie in Altägypten, Israel und Europa, Frankfurt am Main 2002, p. 24.

the political order«[7]. Essentially Schmitt's political theology »stands and falls with faith in revelation«[8] and raises again the old question of the religious legitimacy of political power[9]. Therefore, a theology is political, Assmann points out, and a theory of the state is theological, when each postulates a non-secular foundation of political authority's legitimacy[10]. Schmittian political theology can thus be understood as a manifesto urging the mobilisation of resources for a Christian counter-revolution[11], one that would establish the theological as the principle legitimising the state's authority and the social order created by its decisions.

Being a theological-*political* discourse, it is generated by theologians in reaction to the dynamics of political events that determine the structural changes of institutions, practices, and mentalities that are associated with social change[12]. From a methodological point of view, there is a very close relationship between the concept of social change and that of intellectual history. Intellectual history tried to capture precisely the causal relationship between the social or cultural context in which an author lives and the way in which he problematises a certain idea[13]. Thus, even if it is not always specified explicitly, which event determines a certain theological-political reaction, any interpretation of the essence of politics/state and its relationship with religion/church and social order is more or less the answer to a *Zeitgeist* generating the discourse.

The Birth of Politics from the Orthodox Spirit of the Nation

The theological-political discourse in the twentieth-century ROC resulted from the interaction between a religious-political pattern specific to Eastern Christianity, the Byzantine Symphony, and the social, cultural, and political dynamics of Romania.

---

7 Ibid., p. 20.
8 Heinrich MEIER, The Lesson of Carl Schmitt. Four Chapters on the Distinction between Political Theology and Political Philosophy, Chicago 2011, p. 66.
9 Miguel VATTER, The Political Theology of Carl Schmitt, in: Jens MEIERHENRICH/Oliver SIMONS (eds.), The Oxford Handbook of Carl Schmitt, Oxford 2016, pp. 245–268, at p. 246.
10 ASSMANN, Herrschaft und Heil, pp. 20f.; Heinrich MEIER, Political Philosophy and the Challenge of Revealed Religion, Chicago 2017, pp. 12–14.
11 Reinhard MEHRING, Carl Schmitt: Denker im Widerstreit. Werk – Wirkung – Aktualität, Freiburg im Breisgau 2017, p. 365.
12 Regarding the concept of social change, see Nico WILTERDINK, Social Change. Sociology, in: Britannica.com, 11 April 2022, URL: <https://www.britannica.com/topic/social-change> (11-08-2023).
13 Cf. Peter E. GORDON, What is Intellectual History? A Frankly Partisan Introduction to a Frequently Misunderstood Field, projects Harvard, Spring 2012, URL: <https://projects.iq.harvard.edu/files/history/files/what_is_intell_history_pgordon_mar2012.pdf> (11-08-2023).

The Byzantine religious-political paradigm presupposes a complementary relationship between the activity of the state, which is responsible for the political sphere, and that of the church, which deals with the religious, spiritual sphere of society[14]. The state and the church were conceived as two ways of manifesting the same Christianity[15]. Although the two institutions were separate from an administrative point of view, the church was nonetheless subordinated to state authority, which was embodied by the emperor[16]. In the aftermath of the conquest of Constantinople by the Ottoman Turks (1453), the Byzantine civilisational pattern survived in its most authentic form in the Danubian Principalities of Wallachia and Moldavia[17]. Starting in the middle of the nineteenth century, the modern Romanian state increasingly strengthened its control over the church. With the exception of canonical and dogmatic issues, any decision of the Holy Synod, even the election of new bishops, had to be confirmed by the state[18]. During the same period, in Transylvania, Metropolitan Andrei Şaguna managed to give the Orthodox Church an organisation totally independent from the Austro-Hungarian state. In addition to autonomy from the state, Metropolitan Şaguna's church constitution (»The Organic Statute«) from 1868 provided another essential principle, »synodality«, meaning that the parochial, the archpriest, and the diocesan synods, which dealt with administrative, financial, educational, and cultural matters of the church, consisted of two thirds laymen and one third clerics[19].

The core event of modern Romanian history was the union of Bessarabia, Bucovina, and Transylvania with the Kingdom of Romania in 1918. In terms of political life, the 1920s and 30s were characterised by the transition from democracy to authoritarianism. During the government of the National Liberal Party (PNL) from 1922 to 1926, a series of laws was adopted that aimed at strengthening the unity of the national state: a new constitution (1923), the law of administrative unification (1925), the law and the statute for organising the Romanian Orthodox Church

---

14 John MEYENDORFF, Byzantine Theology. Historical Trends and Doctrinal Themes, New York 1979, p. 213; Vasilios N. MAKRIDES, Östliches orthodoxes Christentum und Säkularität. Ein Vergleich mit dem lateinischen Christentum, in: Transit. Europäische Revue 47 (2015), pp. 59–75, at p. 60.
15 Hans-Georg BECK, Kirche und theologische Literatur im byzantinischen Reich, Munich 1977, p. 36.
16 Franz TINNEFELD, Kirche und Staat im byzantinischen Reich, in: Ostkirchliche Studien 54/1 (2005), pp. 56–78, at p. 76; Mihai-D. GRIGORE, Der Mensch zwischen Gott und Staat. Überlegungen zu politischen Formen im Christentum, in: Studii Teologice 6/1 (2010), pp. 105–175, at p. 163.
17 Nicolae IORGA, Byzantium after Byzantium, Oxford 2000, pp. 129–154, 231–234.
18 Alan SCARFE, The Romanian Orthodox Church, in: Pedro RAMET (ed.), Eastern Christianity and Politics in the Twentieth Century, Durham, NC 1988, pp. 208–231, at p. 211; Lucian N. LEUŞTEAN, The Political Control of Orthodoxy in the Construction of the Romanian State 1859–1918, in: European History Quarterly 37/1 (2007), pp. 61–80, at pp. 61f.
19 Paul BRUSANOWSKI, The Principles of the Organic Statute of the Romanian Orthodox Church of Hungary and Transylvania (1868–1925), in: Ostkirchliche Studien 60/1 (2011), pp. 110–138.

(1925), the Concordat with the Vatican (1927), and the National Education laws of 1924, 1925, and 1928 – also adopted by a liberal government[20]. In the new political and ecclesiastical context after 1918, the Orthodox Church of Transylvania/ Transylvanian Orthodox Metropolis fought to impose its church constitution as the basis for a unitary organisation of the whole ROC. In this context, the Transylvanian Church generated a discourse on the basis of which a thoroughly articulated theological-political conception can be reconstructed. Compared to that of the other regional churches that formed the Romanian Patriarchate after 1925, it must be said that the discourse of the intellectual elites of the Transylvanian Church is by far the most consistent in its level of theoretical elaboration. That is why the present study will focus almost exclusively on the analysis of this discourse[21].

The confrontation of the Șagunian model of church-state relations with that in the Old Kingdom of Romania, led to the reinterpretation of the Byzantine religious-political paradigm from the perspective of the Organic Statute. The promoters of Șagunianism believed that the state and the Orthodox Church ought to preserve the relationship that obtained in the Old Kingdom before 1918. Which means that the church had to remain a state institution and that the state kept its Orthodox character furthermore[22]. However, the normative principle of the interaction between the two institutions must be that of autonomy. This, as Metropolitan Nicolae Bălan of Transylvania (1920–1955), emphasises, did not in any way mean the separation of church and state, but only that the church should have the freedom to deal with those issues that correspond to its origin, being, and purposes. A possible separation of church and state, Bălan points out, would be to the detriment of both institutions[23]. The very fact that the essence and social functionality of the church are totally different from those of the state is in itself an argument for claiming

---

20 See Hans Christian MANER, Parlamentarismus in Rumänien (1930–1940), Munich 1997, pp. 44–49; Ioan SCURTU (ed.), Istoria Românilor, vol. 8: România Întregită, Bucharest 2003, pp. 253–255; Paul BRUSANOWKI, Rumänisch-Orthodoxe Kirchenordnungen (1786–2008), Cologne 2011, pp. 318–375; Irina LIVEZEANU, Cultural Politics in Greater Romania. Regionalism, Nation Building and Ethnic Struggle 1918–1930, Ithaca, NY 1995, pp. 44f.

21 For the presentation of the political theology of the Orthodox Church in Transylvania between 1918 and 1940, I will synthesise some key passages from my doctoral thesis: Marian PĂTRU, Das Ordnungsdenken im christlich-orthodoxen Raum. Nation, Religion und Politik im öffentlichen Diskurs der Rumänisch-Orthodoxen Kirche Siebenbürgens in der Zwischenkriegszeit, 1918–1940, Frankfurt am Main 2022.

22 Gheorghe CIUHANDU, Împreunarea bisericilor ortodoxe de pe teritoriul României-mari într-o singură biserică ortodoxă-romană și raportul acestei biserici față de stat, in: Analele Asociației Andreiu Șaguna a clerului Mitropoliei ortodoxe române din Ardeal, Bănat, Crișana și Maramureș. I. Actele primului congres al preoțimei din Mitropolia românilor ortodocși din Bănat, Crișana și Maramureș. ținut în Sibiiu în zilele de 6/19–8/21 Martie 1919, Arad 1919, p. 86.

23 Nicolae BĂLAN, Interviu acordat de Nicolae Bălan, in: Telegraful Român 68/15 (1920), p. 2.

church autonomy[24]. On the other hand, if the modern state has excluded the influence of the church from the process of legislating the social order, the state should also recognise the church's right to issue laws for its own internal organisation[25].

It is obvious that this reaffirmation of the Byzantine Symphony from the perspective of Șagunian autonomy has as its implicit purpose the categorical rejection of French secularism and in general of the religious-political paradigm proposed by the Enlightenment. Indeed, as Gheorghe Ciuhandu, a Transylvanian archpriest, points out that, while until the middle of the nineteenth century there had been a harmonious collaboration between the political and religious order of the Romanian Provinces, from that moment on the state sought to subdue the church, namely through a policy »aligned to the Western, inter-confessional model brought from Paris«[26]. In this context, the term »inter-confessional« refers to the religious neutrality of the state and is used by Ciuhandu as an antonym for Orthodox. This means that the state no longer understood itself as being in a privileged relationship with the Orthodox Church, as in the pre-modern period, but tried to relate equidistantly to all religious organisations that existed within it. What Ciuhandu suggests is that, in the Old Kingdom, the policy of the state towards the Orthodox Church was a caricature of French secularism, because the church was denied influence over the state while at the same time being subordinated and controlled by it. In short, in the discourse of Transylvanian theologians, the principle of church autonomy has a double function: On the one hand, it acts as a corrective of the Byzantine model, namely as a form of resistance to the state's tendency to control the church, and on the other, it creates the necessary framework in which the church can act in accordance with its origins and purpose.

From this perspective, autonomy is understood not only as a right of the church, but also as an obligation to act »so that the Kingdom of God may take refuge and flourish in the souls of believers and flow into public life«[27]. The canons that regulate the internal life of the church and the laws that specify the type of relationship between church and state must be designed to serve this religious-political purpose[28]. The crucial problem, therefore, consists in the relationship that must be established

---

24 Gheorghe CIUHANDU, Câteva cuvinte la reorganizarea unitară a Bisericii Ortodoxe Române, in: Telegraful Român 68/22 (1920), p. 2.
25 Id., Câteva cuvinte la reorganizarea unitară a Bisericii Ortodoxe Române, in: Telegraful Român 68/16 (1920), pp. 1f.
26 Id., Împreunarea, p. 97.
27 Id., Câteva cuvinte la reorganizarea unitară a Bisericii Ortodoxe Române, in: Telegraful Român 68/18 (1920), p. 1; Bisericanul [sic!], Autonomie și autocefalie bisericească, in: Revista Teologică 11/1–3 (1921), pp. 33–50, at p. 39; Ilarion V. FELEA, Împărăția lui Dumnezeu, in: Revista Teologică 21/3 (March 1931), pp. 73–78, at p. 76.
28 CIUHANDU, Câteva, p. 2.

between the church, the national state, and the legal system that it generates in order to regulate interaction between social actors and society as a whole. In this argumentative context, the state is not conceived by Transylvanian theologians as a simple external actor to the religious-spiritual activity of the church. The role of the state is not only to give the church the freedom necessary for its religious mission, but also to partner with the church and become an agent of the realisation of the God's Kingdom in the life of society.

The premise of this collaboration consists in the ontological relationship postulated by Transylvanian theologians between Orthodoxy, the Romanian nation, and the state. In different ways and from different perspectives, they conclude that »our Orthodoxy, intertwined with all our past, lies at the basis of the existence and unity of the Romanian nation and builds the fundament of the independent and free life of this nation in its national state«[29]. Just as the »Romanian soul« cannot be divided, so it is not possible to introduce a separation between »its manifestations, which are the state and the church«[30]. It must be emphasised that for the Transylvanian theologians, Orthodoxy represents the fundamental element in the »architecture of the Romanian soul«, the element that determines »*what* the Romanian nation is and *how* it is«[31], in other words, Orthodoxy fundamentally marks both the ontological structure of the nation and its specific manifestation in history. In this sense, interpersonal relations and, therefore, individual and group ethics, are nothing more than an extension of the ecclesial interpersonal ethos at the level of the entire national community[32].

This discourse is based on one of the central ideas of modern national mythology, namely that in the case of the Romanians, unlike other peoples, ethnogenesis and Christianisation were concomitant phenomena. Moreover, there is a causal relationship between Christianisation and ethnogenesis, Christianity being the existential framework that allowed the Romanian people to coalesce into a nation with its own identity[33]. Therefore, if Christianisation is a *Urphänomen* in the existence of

---

29 [N.N.], Patriarhia românească, in: Telegraful Român 73/82–83 (1925), p. 1; Ion MATEIU, Mirenii și drepturile lor în biserică, in: Renașterea 16/21 (1938), pp. 2–3, at p. 3.
30 Un preot [sic!], În apărare, in: Telegraful Român 73/87 (1930), p. 1.
31 Dumitru STĂNILOAE, Între românism și catolicism, in: Telegraful Român 78/29 (1930), p. 2. See Pr. S [sic!], Biserica ortodoxă trebuie să fie dominantă în statul român, in: Foaia Diecezană 38/10 (1923), p. 1; N. [Nicolae Colan], Ortodoxia și renașterea națională, in: Viața Ilustrată 3 (1939), p. 3; Traian MOSIC, Ortodoxia noastră, in: Telegraful Român 84/10 (1936), p. 2; Grigorie COMȘA, Ortodoxia și românismul în trecutul nostru, in: Biserica și Școala 57/17 (1933), pp. 1–3, on p. 2; [N.N.], Ce este legea românească, in: Legea românească 1 (1924), p. 1; Isidor TODORAN, Creștinism și națiune, in: Legea Românească 2 (1937), p. 21.
32 Dumitru STĂNILOAE, Ortodoxie și Românism, Sibiu 1939, pp. 79f.
33 Gheorghe CIUHANDU, Ortodoxia românească, in: Revista Teologică 25/7–8 (1935), pp. 288–304, at p. 289; Griogorie COMȘA, Ortodoxia și românismul în trecutul nostru, in: Biserica și Școala 57/18

the nation, then the political body is identical to the confessional-national one. Given this implicit syllogism of nationalist discourse, the conclusion can only be that through the nation Orthodoxy »forms the soul and intimate structure of the state«, which means that any transformation of the religious order has an effect on the political one, »influencing the general development of the country«[34]. This conception of the causal relationship between Orthodoxy, nation, and state can be summarised in the formula »the Orthodox are the nation that makes up the Romanian national and unitary state«[35].

The state and the church have in common the fact that each of them imprints on the nation a certain political and moral order. Given the relationship between Orthodoxy, nation, and state, Transylvanian theologians emphasise the need for a very close relationship between the two types of order. Gheorghe Ciuhandu points out that the transfer of the moral order, specific to the church, into the life of society and the state takes place through the human person, who fulfils a double social role, being at the same time citizen of the state and member of the church[36]. Considering that the vast majority of citizens are also members of the Orthodox Church, Pompei Moruşca emphasises that the state »cannot oppose the reality that the church [...] has dominion over all state institutions, allowing it to imprint on them the character of Orthodox Christianity and to breathe on them its spirit, to give the state and the life of society the direction of their future development«[37]. Thus, if the Romanian state is a national state and if Orthodoxy is the existential basis of the nation, then the state must be a form of political manifestation of the Romanian-Orthodox nation.

This type of discourse obviously addresses the state, which is implicitly urged to return to what it was in the pre-modern period. Indeed, Ion Mateiu emphasises that, throughout history, the political doctrine of the Romanian state towards the church was based on an awareness of the need for unity of the two national institutions. The idea of this unity did not originate in any philosophical system, but was the result of the people's instinct for conservation[38]. Romanian statehood, as Ion Mateiu points out, has its very beginnings in the Orthodox Church, because the church is what

---

(1933), pp. 3–5, at p. 2; Vasile IANCU, Tradiționalismul și ortodoxia, in: Telegraful Român 76/72 (1928), p. 2; A.G. MIHAILOVICIU, Ortodoxia națională, in: Foaia Diecezană 53/18 (1938), pp. 2f., at p. 2.

34 Ion MATEIU, Valoarea concordatului cu Vaticanul, in: Telegraful Român 77/68 (1929), p. 1.

35 [N.N], Catolicizarea României IV, in: Legea Românească 16 (1932), p. 3; [N.N.], Gazeta noastră, in: Renașterea 1/1 (1923), p. 1.

36 CIUHANDU, Împreunarea, p. 85; see Lucian BORCIA, Tendințe primejdioase, in: Telegraful Român 68/2 (1920), p. 1.

37 Pompei MORUȘCA, Organizarea Bisericii Ortodoxe Române, in: Revista Teologică 13/11 (1923), pp. 329–341, at p. 333.

38 Ion MATEIU, Statul și Biserica Ortodoxă, in: Telegraful Român 79/62–63 (1931), p. 1.

generated the first political organisation of the Romanians. Having generated the state, the church identified with it in all its actions[39]. In this unity between state and church, Mateiu identifies on the one hand the old pattern of the Byzantine Symphony, on the other a religious-political model superior to the Byzantine one because »here, unlike in Byzantium, the state and the church were creations and life forms of the same national soul. Therefore, we have an Orthodox Church, not only *of* the state, but also national, perfectly able to identify with the state in all its ideal concerns and aspirations«[40].

The discourse is thus not limited to identifying forms of perpetuation of the Byzantine Symphony; it also highlights the limits of this religious-political pattern and its subsequent metamorphoses in the national context. Starting from the idea of the relationship between church, nation, and state, the discourse postulates not only the necessity of the church's autonomy from the state, but also the fact that the national state is not autonomous from the church. This dependence or lack of autonomy of the state *vis-à-vis* the church is not of institutional but of axiological nature. The policy of the state must be in accordance with the moral values that the church imposes on its believers. The idea that Romanian statehood was institutionally articulated after the Christianisation of the people, already implies a form of symbolic superiority of the religious over the political.

This idea will become clearer if we analyse the concept of the relationship between the state, politics, and the law by which the state regulates the life of society. In the article *Cele două împărății* (*The two kingdoms*), originally published in the review *Gândirea*[41] and republished in the volume *Ortodoxie și Românism* (*Orthodoxy and Romanianhood*) in 1939, Dumitru Stăniloae sees in politics a practical concretisation of the normative principles of law, i. e., the means by which the state opposes evil and social disorder[42]. For Stăniloae, the problem of the law and implicitly of the state consists in the fact that they do not act positively, they do not create individual morality, but only prevent the multiplication of evil through coercion. However, this coercion determines in its turn people's resistance to the law, which leads to the multiplication of evil[43]. The tension between law and morality is not experienced by those »who work for order and according to the indications of the law«, but only by those whose personal morality contradicts the legal social order. In the

---

39 Ibid.; see also Emilian STOICA, Statul român și biserica neamului, in: Analele Asociației »Andrei Șaguna« a Clerului Mitropoliei Ortodoxe Române din Ardeal, Bănat, Crișana și Maramurăs. Actele congresului al X-lea cu caracter cultural al asociației clerului »Andrei Șaguna« ținut în Brașov în zilele de 11 și 12 noemvrie 1930, Arad 1931, p. 56.
40 MATEIU, Statul, p. 1.
41 See Dumitru STĂNILOAE, Cele două împărății, in: Gândirea 16/1 (1937), pp. 26–35.
42 Id., Ortodoxie și Românism, p. 237.
43 Ibid., p. 238.

case of moral people there is a »full conformity between their way of thinking and acting and order«, so that for them the law no longer exists from a »subjective or actual« point of view. The law is thus transformed »into an autonomous norm, into a norm given to himself by the voluntary subject, and it is not imposed on him from outside«[44]. This idea can be formulated in the form of the following principle: the more morality the less law, and the more a society exists according to the Christian moral code, the less relevant the existence of the state.

Therefore, the subjective annulment of the law does not mean a denial of the state's importance. »The kingdoms of the law would have been abolished by themselves«, Stăniloae points out, »if the Kingdom of Christ had been fully and universally imposed«, or when this finally happens at the end of history[45]. The dialectic between law and morality is thus specific to the historical existence of man, and its overcoming takes place only at the eschatological level. Until then, the existence of the state is justified, but on the condition that it is just and aware that it is not autonomous from God but must, on the contrary, remain at his service[46]. The only valid criterion by which the church evaluates the state is whether or not its actions serve the »righteous order of God«[47], in other words, if the legal/political order of the state is in accordance with the morality of the church, and thus the divine revelation codified by the church in the Christian moral order.

The subordination of the state's action to the divine moral order does not in any way deny the state's autonomy towards the church[48]. Yet if the two institutions are mutually autonomous, what in fact does it mean that the church has the right to ask the state not to forget that it is in the service of God? This type of oscillation of the discourse between the assertion of the mutual autonomy of the state and church and the need for the state to obey God presupposes that the state and the church are institutionally and administratively autonomous but at the same time that the state is morally and axiologically dependent on the church. This type of paradoxical relationship is the logical result of the idea that the state and the church are two ways of manifesting the nation. It is obvious that, in his article, Stăniloae considers the Romanian national state and its existential premise, namely the ontological relationship between nation and Orthodoxy. The fact that this article was selected by the Romanian theologian to be part of a collection of studies dedicated to Orthodox nationalism clearly indicates that, for him, this is the key to understanding his reflections on the relationship between church and state or law.

---

44 Ibid., pp. 239f.
45 Ibid., p. 248.
46 Ibid., p. 260.
47 Ibid., p. 245.
48 Ibid., p. 261.

If in Stăniloae the idea of a causal relationship between the Christian-Orthodox morality of the nation and the laws of the state is suggested rather than developed, in other authors this relation is theorised in an elaborated theological conception of law and state. In a speech delivered in the Romanian Parliament in 1924, Bishop Roman Ciorogariu (1852–1936) stated the basic principle of this theory of law when he declared that any law issued by the state »must be an evolution in the life of our people«[49]. The state's law-giving process, emphasises the theologian I.N. Lungulescu, should consist in extracting from the moral code of society those principles fit to become laws[50]. If social morality is the premise of the law, it means that in a Christian society the law issued by the state must be the normative objectification of the divine moral order, which in turn is synthesised in the biblical idea of justice[51]. In this sense, the moral order can be defined as »the holy will of God, manifested in the natural law and in the positive divine laws, entrusted to revealed religion for preaching and safeguarding«[52]. Both its legitimacy as state and the obligation of its laws for society stand or fall with how the state relates to the divine will[53]. Consequently, the law must remain the »faithful disciple of morality« because both have the same purpose, namely the salvation of people[54].

By subordinating the law to Christian morals, the state creates a soteriological framework complementary to that offered by the church. In this sense, the church has the mission to work »for the moral regeneration of the citizens«, while that of the state is »to watch over and control the public order among the citizens«[55]. The state and the church thus have their own way of action: The state acts on man from the outside, by law or coercion, while the church transforms man from within, by love and grace[56]. The church's and the state's respective fields of activity can be defined and delimited with reference to ontology and phenomenology: Through grace and love the church effects an ontological transformation, one taking place within the human being, while the state has access only to its manifest actions. Therefore, the state, by law and coercion, can order only the phenomenological

---

49 [N.N.], Discursul PSS Ep. Roman în ședința Senatului din 10 iunie, in: Legea Românească 25 (1924), p. 1.
50 I.N. LUNGULESCU, Concepția creștină a dreptului, in: Revista Teologică 25/3-4 (1935), pp. 159–166, at p. 160.
51 Ibid., p. 162.
52 O. BUCEVSCHI, Biserica și politica, in: Renașterea 10/28-29 (1932), pp. 1–3, at p. 2.
53 Ibid., p. 1.
54 LUNGULESCU, Concepția creștină, p. 166.
55 Ioan EVUȚIAN, Regenerarea morală și ordinea publică, in: Biserica și Școala 46/31 (1922), pp. 2f., at p. 2; Isaia SURU, Necesitatea relațiunilor dintre Biserică și Stat, in: Foaia Diecezană 45/7 (1930), pp. 2f., at p. 2.
56 STĂNILOAE, Ortodoxie și Românism, p. 248.

level of the human person and of society. What Transylvanian theologians implicitly state is that the policy of the national state is authentic only if it is based on laws that codify the moral order of the Orthodox nation. In other words, if it wants to be a national state, the Romanian state must assume a political praxis in accordance with the moral values that the church has imposed on the nation since its formation.

Thus, according to the above analysis, the church must be autonomous from the state, but from the point of view of the ultimate goal – the community of Orthodox citizens – the state cannot be autonomous from the church. What logically results from this syllogism is that the ultimate authority in the society does not belong to the state but to God, who exercises it through the revelation codified in the set of norms and moral-religious values. Therefore, within this common project of organising society as a kingdom of God, the political activity of the state no longer has a rational-immanent premise, but a revelational-transcendent one. The functionality of the state is thus part of the process of achieving the kingdom of God and is also subordinated to it.

The subordination of the political order to that of Orthodox Christian morality is a direct consequence of the ontological relationship between Orthodoxy and the nation. The divine revelation settled in the Bible and in the tradition of the church is not the only instrument with which Transylvanian theologians approached the essence and functionality of the state and of the social order. There is also the ethno-theological narrative presented above[57]. In this context, ethno-theology implies that the moral order of the Romanian-Orthodox nation ought to be the criterion of state policy, revealing this type of discourse to be political and ethno-theological. From this perspective, the relationship between Orthodoxy and the nation creates a problem of legitimacy for the national, secular state, one that the discourse does not explicitly indicate but which can be logically derived from its argumentation. This problem of legitimacy could be formulated as follows: Unlike the church, which is an *Urphänomen* in the life of the nation, the state is a late and artificial invention; the state politically organises from the outside a nation already morally organised from within by the church. The church thus appears as a precondition of the state and morality as a precondition of politics. As we have already indicated, this is why the discourse of the Transylvanian theologians oscillates between postulating the necessity of the church's autonomy from the state and affirming the impossibility of the axiological and moral autonomy of the state from the church.

---

57 For the concept of »ethno-theology«, see Roland CLARK, Nationalism, Ethnotheology, and Mysticism in Interwar Romania, in: The Carl Beck Papers in Russian & East European Studies 2002 (2009), pp. 1–47.

Nichifor Crainic and the »Christian Political Catechism«

The theologising of nationalist discourse – and, consequently, the political ethno-theology resulting from it – is specific to an interwar cultural current called Orthodoxism. The Romanian Orthodox Church contributed to it primarily through the theological discourse of the Transylvanian Church. Orthodoxism addressed not only the field of theology, but also that of politics and consequently rejected a clear separation of the religious sphere from the secular one[58]. Among the lay intellectuals and theologians who were part of this movement, the most important was Nichifor Crainic (1889–1972), professor of Orthodox theology at the University of Bucharest[59]. Compared to the methodological framework outlined at the beginning of this study, Crainic is an exception because he did not express his central ideas in newspapers, reviews, or books closely related to the institutional authority of the ROC. The intellectual core of Orthodoxism was the review *Gândirea* (1921–1944)[60], whose editor he had been since 1926.

Crainic's theological-political conception is based, on the one hand, on the idea of ontological relationship between Orthodoxy and the Romanian ethnic community and, on the other, on the concept of theandry, i. e., the union of God and man in the person of Jesus Christ. Crainic emphasises that, through this union, the whole of existence is included in Jesus Christ, so that neither »the Christian faith occupies a discrete compartment neither in the existence of the individual nor in that of the community; it is not a private affair, as the secular mentality would have it«[61]. Based on this theandric paradigm, Crainic concludes that »the Christian vision of the world is holistic«, because »there is not a truth of faith and another truth of science; there is not a good of Christian morality and another good of philosophical ethics; there is not a beauty of the church and another beauty of art. There is only one truth, which takes on the aspect of good in the practice of love and the aspect

---

58 Nicolai STAAB, Rumänische Kultur, Orthodoxie und die Westen. Der Diskurs um die nationale Identität in Rumänien aus der Zwischenkriegszeit, Frankfurt am Main 2011, p. 23; see also Keith HITCHINS, Orthodoxism. Polemics over Ethnicity and Religion in Interwar Romania, in: Ivo BANAC/ Katherine VERDERY (eds.), National Character and National Ideology in Interwar Eastern Europe, New Haven, CT 1995, pp. 135–180.
59 For a presentation of Crainic's theology, see Christine HALL, Pancosmic Church – Specific românesc. Ecclesiological Themes in Nichifor Crainic's Writings between 1922 and 1944, Uppsala 2008; Roland CLARK, Nationalism and Orthodoxy. Nichifor Crainic and the Political Culture of the Extreme Right in 1930s Romania, in: Nationalities Papers 40/1 (2012), pp. 107–126; id., Orthodoxy and Nation-building. Nichifor Crainic and Religious Nationalism in 1920s Romania, in: Nationalities Papers 40/4 (2012), pp. 525–543.
60 Keith HITCHINS, Gândirea – Nationalism in a Spiritual Guise, in: Kenneth JOWITT (ed.), Social Change in Romania. A Debate on Development in a European Nation, Berkeley 1978, pp. 140–173.
61 Nichifor CRAINIC, Modelul teandric, in: Gândirea 19/1 (1940), pp. 1–7, at p. 3.

of beauty in the creations of art«[62]. Ethics, aesthetics and, as I shall show below, politics are manifestations of the Logos, of the divine truth embodied in the person of Jesus Christ.

In 1937, Crainic published the study *Programul statului etnocratic* (*Programme of the Ethnocratic State*), in which he synthesised the basic principles of Orthodoxism in the form of a »Christian political catechism«[63], as which the work was welcomed in the public discourse of the Transylvanian Church. The premise of his study consists in a semantic preference, namely in rejecting the concept of *demos* and implicitly of democracy and replacing it with *ethnos*. The demos, i. e., »the people regardless of race and religion«, is the antonym of ethnos, which refers to a nation »with historical identity, biological and psychological homogeneity, spiritual unity, with its own will to power«[64]. This opposition between ethnos and demos originates in the opposition between the ethno-nationalism of Johann Gottfried Herder (1744–1803), which massively influenced Orthodoxism[65], and the civic nationalism of Jean-Jacques Rousseau (1712–1778)[66]. Essentially, for Herder, the state must be made up of members of a certain ethnic group[67], while in Rousseau's view, the state is constituted by the community of citizens, regardless of their ethnicity, through their free decision objectified in a social contract concluded between them and the state[68].

Consequently, Crainic explicitly rejects Ernest Renan's notion, influenced by Rousseau, that the nation is a daily plebiscite[69] and states that not the demos but the ethnos »creates its own political expression in the national state«[70]. As the form of

---

62 Ibid.
63 Ion Beju, Etnocrație și Creștinism, in: Telegraful Român 85/45 (1937), p. 4. Crainic's study was enthusiastically received by Transylvanian theologians and presented as one that expresses the true conception of how the Romanian state should be organised. See, for example, Dumitru Stăniloae, Ortodoxie și etnocrație, in: Telegraful Român 86/24 (1938), p. 1; Grigorie T. Marcu, Naționalismul lui Nichifor Crainic, in: Telegraful Român 87/7 (1940), pp. 1f.; D. Tudor, Ortodoxie și Etnocrație, in: Biserica și Școala 68/38 (1938), pp. 322–325.
64 Nichifor Crainic, Programul statului etnocratic, in: Id., Ortodoxie și Etnocrație, Bucharest 1997, pp. 239–272, at pp. 241f.
65 See Victor Neumann, Neam, Popor sau Națiune. Despre identitățile politice europene, Bucharest 2015, pp. 141–174.
66 For a comparative analysis of the two types of nationalism see, for example, Brigit Nübel, Zum Verhältnis von Kultur und Nation bei Rousseau und Herder, in: Regine Otto (ed.), Nationen und Kulturen. Zum 250. Geburtstag Johann Gottfried Herders, Würzburg 1996, pp. 97–111.
67 »[…] the most natural state [Staat] is […] one people [Volk], with one national character«, Johann Gottfried Herder, Outlines of a Philosophy of the History of Man, New York 1966, p. 249.
68 See Jean-Jacques Rousseau, The Social Contract, in: Id., The Social Contract and The First and Second Discourses, New Haven, CT 2002, pp. 149–254.
69 Crainic, Programul, p. 242.
70 Ibid., p. 241.

organising the ethnic community, the state is the institutional concretisation of the features of the respective community, namely biological and psychological homogeneity, homogeneity of faith, and territorial unity[71]. The power of the ethnocratic state consists in the unique spirit that imprints on its subjects »a unitary style of national life: in morals, in culture, in laws, in economics [...]«. This conception of the spiritual life of the state, continues Crainic, is expressed through the Orthodox Church, which is the church of the Romanian nation. As such, the ethnocratic state accepts its doctrine without reservation[72]. Since the ethnocratic state is a moral state and since »there is no other criterion of good than the Christian one«, the state imagined by Crainic is necessarily a Christian state. »His morals are expressed in the formula: The law of Christ is the law of the state«. Consequently, democratic laws that are not in accordance with Christian morality should be repealed[73].

Given this definition of the state in ethnic and Orthodox-Christian terms, the otherness par excellence to which the ethnocratic state refers and by which ultimately defines itself is represented in Crainic's conception by the Jews. They are perceived as a constant threat not only to the Romanian state but also to *any* national state[74]. Members of ethnic minorities within the ethnocratic state who were proved to be its enemies were to lose their citizenship and to be expelled[75]. Crainic does not specify the criteria according to which a person or a group is defined as enemy of the ethnocratic state; it is certain that, according to the ideas in his *Programme*, anyone who was not ethnically Romanian and confessionally Orthodox was a possible enemy of the state. Since its pattern is influenced by Herder, the nationalist Orthodoxism operates more or less explicitly with the distinction between ethnos and demos, i. e., between nation and society. In other words, from the perspective of Orthodoxism, the state manages the whole of society within a unitary territory (i. e., the demos), but only the nation (i. e., the ethnos) builds the state and determines its functioning.

It should be emphasised that the *Programme of the Ethnocratic State* appeared in the context of the strengthening of the extreme right in the political life of Romania in the second half of the 1930s. In 1935, *Liga Apărării Național-Creștine* (LANC; National Christian Defence League) and *Partidul Național Agrar* (National Agrarian Party) merged and formed *Partidul Național-Creștin* (PNC; National Christian Party), whose emblem, like that of the German Nazi party, was the swastika. During this period, Romania's principal fascist organisation, the so-called »Legion Archangel Michael« or »Iron Guard«, founded by Corneliu Zelea Codreanu

---

71 Ibid., p. 242, 246.
72 Ibid., p. 252.
73 Ibid., p. 270.
74 Ibid., p. 246.
75 Ibid., p. 247.

in 1927, became a mass political movement[76]. These political organisations had in common several main ideas: ethnic nationalism, antisemitism, and the intention to transform the Romanian state into a Christian one[77]. The consolidation of far-right political forces was largely the effect of the dissatisfaction among important segments of the Romanian society, especially young people[78], with the policy of the impotent major parties of the time, *Partidul Național Liberal* (PNL; National Liberal Party) and *Partidul Național Țărănesc* (PNȚ; National Peasant Party). Both the Iron Guard and the PNC promised a radical break with the way of doing politics, which was specific to the old parties. When Crainic wrote that »the law of Christ is the law of the state«, he was in fact denying the entire political tradition of modern Romania's separation of religion and politics. It should be emphasised that Crainic was one of the main ideologues of the Iron Guard until 1935, when he joined the PNC. The *Programme of the Ethnocratic State* was initially written to serve as the party's manifesto[79].

Realisation of the Political Ideal Type: The National-Christian State

In this political context, the idea that the Romanian state must be a Christian one appears more and more explicitly in the discourse of the Transylvanian theologians. It is not just a matter of speculation on the relationship between nation, Orthodoxy, and state, but a discourse of immense urgency, demanding immediate practical measures. Paradigmatic in this sense is Stăniloae's article *Spre statul român creștin* (*Towards the Romanian Christian State*), published in April 1936. Stăniloae builds his argument on the dialectics between reason and faith, which he transfers to the field of politics in order to identify the causes of the Romanian political and moral crisis in the mid-1930s[80] and to propose a remedy. That crisis, Stăniloae points

---

76 Armin HEINEN, Legiunea »Arhanghelul Mihail«. Mișcare socială și organizație politică. O contribuție la problema Fascismului internațional, Bucharest 2006, pp. 237f.

77 Keith HITCHINS, A Concise History of Romania, New York 2014, pp. 172–174; Ion MEZARESCU, Partidul Național Creștin 1935–1938, Bucharest 2018; Corneliu Zelea CODREANU, For My Legionaries: The Iron Guard, Madrid 1976.

78 Leon VOLOVICI, Nationalist Ideology and Antisemitism. The Case of Romanian Intellectuals in the 1930s, Oxford 1991; Roland CLARK, Holy Legionary Youth. Fascist Activism in Interwar Romania. Ithaca, NY 2015.

79 CLARK, Nationalism and Orthodoxy, p. 116.

80 The critique of the immorality and corruption of the Romanian politics was a central theme in the discourse of the Transylvanian theologians in the interwar period and especially in the 1930s. See Petru TOMA, Între progres și regres, in: Foaia Diecezană 48/39 (1933), pp. 5f., at p. 5; A.U. DOLOVEANU, Psihologia vremii, in: Foaia Diecezană 47/35 (1932), p. 4; Petru TOMA, Criză materială sau spirituală, in: Foaia Diecezană 48/42 (1933), p. 5.

out, was a sign that the road travelled so far had been wrong. The cause of the mistaken evolution was the fact that state policy lacked »the central element for the consolidation of the country: religious faith«. In order to get people to work for the common good of the nation, Stăniloae continues, »purely rational political and economic programmes« are not enough, but it is necessary that »at the helm of the Romanian state [...] the assistance of Christ be felt. [...] Politics based on faith is the best politics«[81]. Both Stăniloae and Crainic thus rejected a politics which, like the liberal political order, was based on rationalism and economics in favour of a new kind of politics based on religion and ethnicity.

The theological-political discourse of Orthodoxism thus constructs an ideal type that acts as an implicit critique of the state, which was far from functioning according to the principles stated above. Stăniloae's article marks a new stage in the theological-political discourse of Transylvanian theologians, namely the transition from the implicit theorising of the Orthodox state to its explicit assertion. This shift in discourse was obviously a reaction to the radical political change in the second half of the 1930s. In short, Transylvanian theologians have identified the signs of the concretisation of the religious-political ideal type they have built at a discursive level in the period after 1918. One of the most important signs in this regard were the parliamentary elections of December 1937, through which the political wing of the Legion »Archangel Michael«, the so-called party *Totul pentru Țară* (Everything for the Fatherland) became the third political force in Parliament with 15.58%, behind the PNL (35.92%) and PNȚ (20.40%), PNC came fourth with 9.15% of the votes[82]. These elections marked the beginning of a trend towards increasingly undemocratic and authoritarian regimes in Romania, an evolution culminating in the imposition of the communist dictatorship in the second half of the 1940s.

On 29 December 1937 King Carol II called on Octavian Goga, the leader of the PNC, to form the government. The new government took harsh antisemitic measures, such as beginning the process of withdrawing Romanian citizenship from Jews[83]. On 10/11 February 1938 King Carol II replaced the Goga government with a new government led by the Patriarch of the Romanian Orthodox Church, Miron Cristea, who was to be prime minister in three successive governments between 11 February 1938 and 6 March 1939. In this context, the king imposed his own authoritarian regime. The constitution of 1923 was replaced by an anti-democratic constitution that concentrated power in the hands of the king, the separation of powers in the state was annulled, and political parties were abolished[84]. In

---

81 Dumitru STĂNILOAE, Spre statul român creștin, in: Telegraful Român 84/18 (1936), pp. 1f., at p. 1.
82 Mircea MUȘAT/Ion ARDELEANU, România după marea unire. Volumul II, Partea II: Noiembrie 1933–Septembrie 1940, Bucharest 1988, pp. 735f.
83 International Commission on the Holocaust in Romania, Final Report, Jassy 2004, p. 41.
84 Lucian BOIA, Romania, Borderland of Europe, London 2006, p. 104.

September 1940 King Carol II abdicated in the favour of his son, Michael. The new king confirmed the full powers his father had given to the Prime Minister, General Ion Antonescu[85]. Between September 1940 and February 1941 Romania was ruled by a government led by General Antonescu and the leader of the Iron Guard, Horia Sima, under the so-called »National Legionary State«.

The nationalist and Christian rhetoric of the political regimes after 1938 was applauded by the Transylvanian theologians. Octavian Goga's government was hailed as »a government of integral nationalism« that initiated a »new era of historical reparation« in which »the new life of the state is built on the teachings of Christ«[86]. The fact that the new government chose the words »Christ, King, Nation« as its slogan was seen as a guarantee that the transformation of the Romanian state and society would be based on Christian truths[87]. In a representative article for the way in which the Transylvanian theologians positioned themselves towards this political change, it is stated that »Christian law and love of nation« were an integral part of the being of the Romanian soul. Therefore, Goga's government was doing nothing, but to reintegrate people's life into an authentic Christian framework[88].

The fact that Christianity was the solution to the problems of the Romanian state and society was confirmed in the eyes of Transylvanian theologians by the fact that, in order to alleviate political and social tensions, it was necessary for Patriarch Miron Cristea to be appointed prime minister[89]. Again, the political change was interpreted as a break with the wrong evolution of the political life of the state and as a return to a desired genuine Orthodox »authenticity«. By appointing the Patriarch of the Romanian Orthodox Church as head of the government, Carol II intended »to follow the same healthy path of our voivodal tradition« and to show that the most appropriate political reforms for the Romanian people are those designed »in the spirit of justice, order, and Christian wisdom«[90]. The new order imposed by Carol II thus marked a radical separation from the »old state based on an ideology that only poorly suited our souls«[91]. For Stăniloae, political change during the royal dictatorship and implicitly the change of historical epoch consists essentially in the transition »from the individualistic, liberal, rationalist, democratic form of social

---

85 Dennis DELETANT, Hitler's Forgotten Ally. Ion Antonescu and his Regime. Romania 1940–44, New York 2006, p. 50, 53.
86 Renașterea [The Redaktion], Guvernul Octavian Goga, in: Renașterea 16/2 (1938), p. 1.
87 L.G. MUNTEANU, Creștinismul ca temelie a vieții sociale, in: Renașterea 16/4 (1938), pp. 2f., at p. 2.
88 R., Orientarea noului guvern, in: Legea Românească 3 (1 Februarie 1938), p. 1.
89 [N.N.], Acțiunea IPS Patriarh Miron pentru purificarea morală, in: Renașterea 16/44 (1938), on p. 1.
90 R., Noua constituție sub bolta bisericii, in: Legea Românească 5 (1 Martie 1938), p. 1.
91 D.I. BELU, Spre depășirea individualismului, in: Legea Românească 12 (15 Iunie 1939), pp. 158f.

life to one of national-solidarity, sustained, as is natural, not by the reason that separates, but by the religious faith that unites«[92].

Stăniloae sees in this type of national community a reflection of the community and communion between the three persons of the Holy Trinity, which represents the model »for the only right and natural organisation of social life«[93]. In addition to this trinitarian-transcendent criterion for the rightness of the social order, Stăniloae also introduces an immanent criterion of the internal organisation of the church. For him, the synodal organisation of the church is a reflection of the relations between the persons of the Holy Trinity and acts »as an example for the state and for the people, as an ideal and as a rebuke«. Both state and society discover in the church the example for their own being, so that the church exerts by its very existence a continuous »transfiguring« influence on them[94]. These words reaffirm the superiority of the religious over the political and of the church over the state in terms of its capacity to organise the social body.

Shortly after the proclamation of the National Legionary State, Stăniloae published an article whose title – *Restaurarea românismului în destinul său istoric* (*The Restoration of Romanianhood in its Historical Destiny*) – summarises the way in which the Transylvanian theologian perceived the new state order. Essentially, for Stăniloae, the Romanian people finds itself in a process of national resurrection[95]. The new policy of the Romanian state is a manifestation of »desires starting from the authenticity of the Romanian being« and the Romanian nation becomes, in the international political circumstances at the beginning of the 1940s, a »defender of Christianity against the Slavic and Bolshevik invasion«[96]. The role of the state as defender of the West is deduced by Stăniloae from the postulate of a typological relationship between the Romanian state, which goes through the »revolution [...] of its transformation into a national-legionary state«, and the Archangel Michael, who, as soldier of God, fights against evil[97]. The Romanian state is thus a political personification of the Archangel Michael. But the most important function of the Legionary National State is that it manages to »save us from disintegration and elevate us to the uplifting state of a nation«, »because it operates with the religious element«[98].

---

92 Dumitru Stăniloae, Principii de renaștere națională, in: Telegraful Român 88/3 (1940), p. 1.
93 Id., Sfânta Treime și viața socială, in: Telegraful Român 88/8 (1940), p. 2.
94 Id., Ortodoxia și viața socială, in: Telegraful Român 88/10 (1940), p. 1.
95 D.S. [Dumitru Stăniloae], Restaurarea românismului în destinul său istoric, in: Telegraful Român 88/39 (1940), p. 1.
96 Ibid.
97 Ibid.
98 Id., Creștinism și naționalism, in: Telegraful Român 88/40 (1940), p. 2.

It is interesting to emphasise in this context that, as previously stated, in the discourse of the Transylvanian theologians of the 1920s and 30s, Orthodoxy was the only force capable of creating a Romanian national community. If the National Legionary State is also the creator of the nation, along with Orthodoxy, does this mean that the National Legionary State is seen as the most authentic form of nation's political organisation? Stăniloae's argument obviously goes in this direction without explicitly stating this idea. The only explicit statement in this regard belongs to an anonymous author who approvingly cites Corneliu Zelea Codreanu's statement that the »Legion Archangel Michael« »is the political expression of Orthodoxy«[99]. It is obvious that for Stăniloae the Legionary National State represented the apogee of the process started in 1938, a process that led to the political objectification of the ontological relationship between the Romanian nation and Orthodoxy.

Totalitarian Framework and Conceptual Turn: From Ethnic to Social

In January 1941, General Antonescu removed the members of the Iron Guard from power and established a military dictatorship under his command. On 22 June 1941, Romania entered the war as an ally of Nazi Germany, hoping to retake north-eastern Transylvania, occupied by Hungary, and Bessarabia, which had been occupied by the Soviet Union in June and July 1940. Through a coup organised by King Mihai on 23 August 1944, General Antonescu was removed from power and Romania broke with Germany to join the Allies. On 31 August of the same year, the Red Army, now an ally of Romania, entered Bucharest. This event marked the beginning of the country's Sovietisation[100].

After August 1944, fewer and fewer articles appeared in the Transylvanian Church to debate on the issue of the religion and church's relation to politics and state. The hostile attitude towards communism gradually changed. If in the 1920es and 1930es communism and its Russian version – Bolshevism – were seen as a means by which the Antichrist acts in history[101], from August 1944 onwards, the same church newspapers and reviews began to identify common elements between Orthodox Christianity and communism. The new evolution of the discourse essentially intended to shift the emphasis from the »ethnic« to the »social« as a central operational

---

99 [N.N.], Solidari la muncă și uniți în cugetare, in: Biserica și Școala 64/48 (1940), p. 393.
100 DELETANT, Hitler's Forgotten Ally, pp. 69f.; Mihai BĂRBULESCU et al., Istoria României, Bucharest 2002, p. 366.
101 Coriolan BĂRBAT, Religia, biserica și marxismul, in: Telegraful Român 76/87 (1928), p. 1; Nic. TERCHILĂ, În țara lui Antichrist, in: Telegraful Român 78/62 (1930), p. 2; [N.N.], Pastorala episcopatului din Ardeal împotriva comunismului, in: Biserica și Școala 60/42 (1936), pp. 1–5; Dumitru STĂNILOAE, Biserica împotriva comunismului, in: Telegraful Român 60/42 (1936), p. 1.

concept, through which the state and the political order were approached. Thus, central concepts of Marxist ideology – such as social class, social equality and the proletariat – were increasingly used in the public discourse of the Transylvanian Church and interpreted from a Christian point of view[102].

In this context, Stăniloae's article *Social și etnic* (*Social and Ethnic*) is exemplary for this transition from anti- to pro-communist discourse. Stăniloae points out that Christianity has never endorsed racist theory, but merely stated that each people have own specific characteristics, which distinguishes it from other ethnic groups[103]. The conceptual dissociation between race and ethnicity seeks both the rejection of racism and the implicit rejection of German National Socialism, i. e., of the ideological adversary of communism. Through this dissociation, Stăniloae creates the possibility of harmonising the concept of the ethnic with that of the social, i. e., ethno-nationalism with communism. »Even Russian Communism, which put the social problem in the most radical form, recognised the ethnic factor and counts on it. The Russian state is a federation of national republics«. Therefore, »it is necessary for us that the tendencies after the realisation of the much-desired social justice and brotherhood be not to despise the ethnic factor, but [...] to associate it with the social element«[104]. The Transylvanian theologians generally accepted very quickly the fact that the new socio-political order of Romania must be approached from the perspective of the presence of Red Army on Romanian territory. But there were also theologians who, in this transitional phase, built their discourse independently of the evolution in the ideological climate, namely by affirming the central ideas of theological-political interwar discourse.

Nicolae Gorun, for example, points out that Christianity appeared and existed in history independently of the socio-political factor, and this because its essence is spiritual. Therefore, Christianity is primarily interested in man's relationship with God, more precisely in the »salvation in Christ, which transcends the politico-economical-social framework«[105]. However, this dichotomy between history and transcendence/eternity, or between material and spiritual, does not mean that there is no connection between Christianity and politics. Gorun makes this case with reference to anthropology. Man, he affirms, is »a bio-spiritual unit, in which the

---

102 See, for example, id., Biserica în vremurile noi, in: Telegraful Român 68/41 (1944), p. 1; id., Proprietatea, funcție socială, in: Telegraful Român 68/72 (1944), p. 1; id., Sufletul muncitorului, in: Telegraful Român 68/76 (1944), p. 1; id., Biserica în noul orizont socială, in: Telegraful Român 68/97 (1944), p. 1; id., Creștinismul și viața social, in: Telegraful Român 68/102 (1944), p. 1; Coman, Problema spirituală a muncitorului, in: Telegraful Român 68/112 (1944), p. 1; Vasilescu, Evoluția vieții sociale, in: Telegraful Român 114 (1944), p. 1.
103 Dumitru Stăniloae, Social și etnic, in: Telegraful Român 105 (1944), p. 1.
104 Ibid.
105 Nicolae Gorun, Creștinismul și formele politice, in: Telegraful Român 89 (1944), p. 1.

two domains meet and influence each other. So, if purely religious concern can take one out of politics, so purely political-economic concern can atrophy the religious element in man«[106]. The solution to these extreme tendencies is to delimit the spheres of competence, so that »politics recognises the essential-spiritual function of Christianity and grants it freedom of action, without tending to replace it. Politics can never replace the religious function, which is of a different nature«[107]. Based on the same anthropological perspective, Gorun emphasises that, if the spiritual is the responsibility of Christianity and the biological is the responsibility of politics, and if the spiritual in man influences the biological, then »any political form must feed on the sources of life that Christianity offers«. Moreover, »a political form has as much good, as much perfection in it as it materialises from Christian spiritual imperatives«[108]. In other words, politics in itself cannot do the good; if it wants to do the good, politics must transform the Christian moral/spiritual order into a social order.

Gorun thus reaffirms the superiority of the religious over the political. He also takes up the idea of the interdependence between the authentic Christianising of society and the necessity of politics, an idea stated by Stăniloae in his study *Cele două împărății* (*The Two Kingdoms*). Indeed, Gorun states that »if all the individuals of a society were truly Christians, if all lived under the power of love for God and neighbour, the politico-socio-economic problem would solve itself. Political turmoil testifies to a lack of Christian life«[109]. Therefore, the criterion according to which political forms must be evaluated is how much Christian love, how much love of the neighbour there is in the decisions they make[110]. Gorun thus affirms two central principles of the theological-political discourse of the interwar period: the one according to which the more Christian a society is, the less necessary are the politics, and the principle according to which the state must collaborate with the church to achieve the spiritual goal of a Christian society, namely salvation in the love of Christ. Gorun's conclusion is that the church supports any form of politics, which in turn supports the realisation of the commandment of Christian love in society, but this does not mean that the church identifies with any political form. The church »does not belong to any party, social class, or historical epoch […]. It is independent. Political forms change over time; the church remains the same and lasts over time«. The influence of the church on politics is only an indirect consequence of its spiritual mission and consists in Christianising politics by »intensifying the Christian life to

---

106 Ibid.
107 Ibid.
108 Ibid.
109 Ibid.
110 Ibid.

such an extent that the political forms also feel its influence«[111]. Gorun's reflections or those of Emilian Vasilescu, for example, who postulated the idea of a Christian state as an institutional objectification of the people's religiosity[112], are the last, increasingly pale echoes of the theological-political discourse specific to interwar Orthodoxism.

With the imposition by Moscow of Petru Groza government (6 March 1945–30 December 1947), a government in which the communists held important positions[113], it became clear that Romania was turning into a satellite of the Soviet Union. The parliamentary elections of 19 November 1946 were massively rigged to make the communists the main political force in parliament[114]. The next steps towards dictatorship were the dissolution of the PNL and the PNȚ in August 1947 and the forced abdication of King Michael, who left the country on 30 December of that year. On the same day, the creation of the Romanian People's Republic was announced[115]. The proclamation of the republic practically meant the last essential step by which the Romanian state was transformed into a totalitarian communist state, inaugurating a form of political organisation that would be maintained until the revolution in 1989.

In the Romanian communist state, the social actors were, as in any totalitarian state, allowed to produce only that type of discourse, which confirmed the official ideology. Indeed, totalitarianism is characterised by the monopoly of a single party over political activity and over the ideology that becomes the official truth of the state. In order to impose this unique truth, the state owns and uses a monopoly on the means of persuasion (e. g., press, radio) and coercion[116]. The attitude of the Romanian communist state towards religious organisations materialised in the law of Cults adopted on 4 August 1948, a law that took over forms and concepts from the similar law in the Soviet Union[117]. Article 6 specified that religious cults may function freely if their practices and rituals are not contrary to the constitution, security, or public order of the country. Priests who acted against the communist public order were suspended or removed from office[118]. The effects of the religious policy of the communist state were dramatic. For instance, between 1945 and

---

111 Ibid.
112 Emilian VASILESCU, Stat creștin, in: Telegraful Român 68/86 (1944), p. 1.
113 Vladimir TISMANEANU, Stalinism for All Seasons. A Political History of Romanian Communism, Berkeley 2003, p. 90; Dennis DELETANT, Romania under Communism. Paradox and Degeneration, New York 2019.
114 TISMANEANU, Stalinism, p. 92.
115 Ibid., p. 94.
116 Raymond ARON, Democracy and Totalitarianism, London 1968, pp. 193f.; see also Hannah ARENDT, The Origins of Totalitarianism, New York 1951, pp. 392f.
117 Cristian VASILE, Biserica Ortodoxă Română în primul deceniu comunist, Bucharest 2005, p. 209.
118 Ibid., pp. 209f.

1964 alone, the state sent 1,725 Orthodox priests to prison[119]. The Greek Catholic Church (the largest church in Romania after the Romanian Orthodox Church) was dissolved by a state decree on 1 December 1948 and all its bishops together with numerous priests were sent to prison[120].

It is symptomatic of the political monopoly and censorship imposed by the state after 1948 that until 1989 the ROC's theological discourse produced only one truly important study on the relationship between religion/church and politics/state: Liviu Stan's *Relațiile dintre biserică și stat. Studiu istorico-juridic* (*The Relations Between Church and State. A Historical-Legal Study*) that was published in *Ortodoxia. Revista Patriarhiei Române* (*Orthodoxy. Review of the Romanian Patriarchate*) in 1952. Stan's personal attitude toward the radical political changes since the late 1930s fits perfectly with his view of the church's relationship with various political forms. In the 1930s and 1940s, Stan was one of the most important members of the intellectual elite of the Transylvanian Church and a supporter of the Romanian extreme right (between 1937 and 1938, he was a member of the Iron Guard). Under the National Legionary State, he became the head of the Department for Religious Denominations[121]. From 1941 to 1948, he was professor of canon law at the Theological Academy in Sibiu and after that, until 1972, at the Orthodox Theological Institute in Bucharest. For a while he worked as an adviser in the Ministry of Cults[122]. Given his ability to function equally well in radically opposed political systems, it is not surprising that his 1952 study is built on the principle of church's adaptability to any of the political forms with which it interacts.

Stan's study has as its premise the historicity of the church and the methodological principle of the dissociation between the two aspects of its identity: the church as a visible society and an expression of divine grace[123]. As part of society, Stan points out, the church fulfils its mission in time so that it cannot ignore the continually transforming conditions, in which human life occurs. »Neither believers nor the church can work for salvation detached from the material basis of life, detached from the earth and time«[124]. Existing »in the flow of time and in its conditions«, the church »did not link its nature or its mission« to any particular historical epoch. For church mission, the most important condition of man's historical existence is

---

119 Ibid., p. 12.
120 See id., Între Vatican și Kremlin. Biserica Greco-Catolică în timpul regimului comunist, Bucharest 2003.
121 Ionuț Biliuță, Fascism, Race, and Religion in Interwar Transylvania. The Case of Father Liviu Stan (1910–1973), in: Church History 89/1 (2020), pp. 101–124.
122 Mircea Păcurariu, Dicționarul Teologilor Români, Bucharest 1996, p. 412.
123 Liviu Stan, Relațiile dintre biserică și stat. Studiu istorico-juridic, in: Ortodoxia. Revista Patriarhiei Române 3–4 (1952), pp. 353–456, on p. 353.
124 Ibid.

the »condition of the state«[125]. Stan highlights that the church relates to the state in the same way as it relates to the other historical conditions that constitute the specificity of a certain epoch. Thus, in the case of its relationship with the state, »the church does not have a dogmatic axiom, but in fact is guided only by certain principles which derive from its situation and work in time«[126]. Stan's argument is thus based on a theory of the historicity of anything human and implicitly of any institutional action, which allows him to state the central principle of the church-state relationship, namely adaptability. It must be emphasised that this is a one-way adaptability, namely of the church to the state conditions, which excludes any claim of the church to influence the decisions of the state and thus the social order. The difference between this theological-political conception and the interwar one is thus radical.

For Stan, the adaptability of the church is based, on the one side, on the lack of a normative outlook on its relationship with the state and, on the other, on the method in which the church sees itself within this relationship. In this sense, Stan defines the church not from the perspective of theology, but from that of social sciences[127]. Thus, for the Romanian theologian, the church is a »kind of society at the base of which lies, as the determining element, the Christian religious faith, which unites all those who share it [...]. Therefore, in relation to the state, the church must be seen just as it presents itself, as a visible society [...]«[128]. Stan points out that, although the purpose of religious associations is transcendent, it can only be achieved through efforts in the immanent conditions of earthly life. That is why religious associations can ignore »neither the purpose nor the means of the state«[129]. Stan emphasises that no religious organisation can identify with the political organisation of the state because their nature, purpose, and means are different[130]. The church demands from the state only freedom of faith and freedom of religious expression[131].

If the definition of the church proposed by Stan belongs to the general field of social sciences and does not reflect any ideological option of the author, the definition he gives to the state is communist[132]. Thus the state is presented as a political organisation that emerged from society's division into social classes, in

---

125 Ibid., pp. 354f.
126 Ibid., p. 355.
127 Ibid., p. 356.
128 Ibid.
129 Ibid., p. 357.
130 Ibid., p. 358.
131 Ibid., p. 366.
132 On the communist conception of the state, see John F. HENRY, The Theory of the State. The Position of Marx and Engels, in: Forum for Social Economics 37/1 (2008), pp. 13–25.

other words, to represent and enforce the power of the ruling class. Being result of divided society into classes, it means that the state will disappear when society is no longer divided into classes[133]. Again, the difference between this conception and interwar political theology is obvious: The principle »the more Christian a society is, the less politics (and therefore the state) is needed« is replaced by the principle »the more socialism the less state«. Moreover, Stan indicates that the Bolshevik revolution of 1917 inaugurated a socialist order that was eventually accepted by the church, which understood both that the socialist state respected its religious freedom and that the church should not interfere in state politics[134]. Thus, Stan concludes, »only in the socialist order was the church's field of activity precisely delimited from that of the state«[135]. The difference between the theological-political conception of the pre-communist period and this one is radical. Stan affirms the state's monopoly over politics and explicitly denies the church any political role. Both in Stan's conclusion and in the pre-communist discourse of the Transylvanian theologians, the idea of religious-political authenticity can be identified; in Stan's case, however, it is not about recovering a practical model from the past, but about the concretisation, *hic et nunc*, of a theoretical religious-political one. It is very likely that, in the words quoted above, Stan refers to the religious-political model of Enlightenment which promoted a strict separation between church and state.

Conclusions

Stan's discourse is not that of a political theologian (for him there is no relationship between divine revelation and politics, or between divine authority and that of the state), but of someone who supports the normative opinion of the secular state towards the church. It is no coincidence that Stan's study appeared in the same year that a new constitution of the Romanian communist state was promulgated[136] (the first was issued in 1948), a constitution which, for the first time in the history of Romanian constitutionalism, did not refer to the Romanian Orthodox Church by name. This did not, however, mean that the model of the Byzantine symphony had been abandoned. Although there was no discourse on the theological legitimation of the political order, on a practical level the relations between the ROC and the communist state were very tight, as they had been with the previous political regimes. The Byzantine symphony never ceased to be the frame of reference for

---

133 STAN, Relațiile, p. 361.
134 Ibid., p. 447.
135 Ibid.
136 See Constituția Republicii Populare Române din 1952, published by Camera Deputaților (cdep), URL: <http://www.cdep.ro/pls/legis/legis_pck.htp_act_text?idt=1454> (10-11-2023).

the relationship between the two institutions. The strict separation between church and state, which Stan sees materialised in communism, meant the annulment of any political role of the church and, at the same time, a strict control of its activity by the communist regime. In these circumstances, the church supported the official ideological discourse of the state and its political actions, implicitly legitimising them in front of the believers[137]. Thus it was inevitable that the totalitarian state would control the public activities of the church, just as it controlled every social actor. At the same time, it was inevitable that, based on the Byzantine symphony pattern assumed by the church, the church would find ways to reach a *modus vivendi* with the communist state.

After 1989, the Romanian Church leaders justified their collaboration with the communist regime, claiming that it was the only way that the church could survive and continue its activity and thus be able to take care of the spiritual needs of the believers[138]. The premise on which the church bases this attitude is an anthropological-social one and it is the implicit premise of the Byzantine symphony: The church must be on good terms with the state because only in this way can the believer maintain a balance between his roles as member of the church and member of the state; a direct conflict between church and state would have the effect of a conflict between the believer's two social roles, and such a conflict would harm him and the church community as a whole.

Whether what is being interpreted is the relationship between church/religion and state/politics from the perspective of ethno-theology and the principle of church autonomy, or the far-right and authoritarian regimes of 1938–1944, or the relationship between church and communist state: All these are forms of what Hans Blumenberg calls »work on myth«. In Blumenberg's conception, myths are narratives that were created by man out of the need to explain and thus control »the conditions of his existence«[139]. Myths »are distinguished by a high degree of constancy in their narrative core and by an equally pronounced capacity for marginal variation. These two characteristics make myths transmissible by tradition«[140]. Each new generation reinterprets the myths – works on them – in order to find ways to orient itself in the existential conditions of each new age. In the three types of reinterpreting the Byzantine symphony, the idea of a close relationship between church and state plays the role of a constant narrative core, and the

---

137 Lucian N. LEUȘTEAN, Orthodoxy and the Cold War. Religion and Political Power in Romania, 1947–1965, London 2008; Olivier GILLET, Religie și naționalism. Ideologia Bisericii Ortodoxe Române sub regimul comunist, Bucharest 2001.
138 See Lavinia STAN/Lucian TURCESCU, Religion and Politics in Post-Communist Romania, New York 2007, pp. 65–89.
139 Hans BLUMENBERG, Work on Myth, Cambridge, MA 1985, p. 4.
140 Ibid., p. 34.

marginal variations are, in this case, the contextual interpretations and justifications of how the interaction between the two institutions takes place. This discursive pattern is not only to the intellectual history of the Orthodox political theology in Romania in the short twentieth century, but can be identified more generally in the theological-political discourses of the national Orthodox Churches in the post-Byzantine period.

Regula M. Zwahlen

Towards a Negative Orthodox Political Theology?

The Russian Orthodox Diaspora in Western Contexts

Introduction

After the fall of communism, it was lamented that traditional Orthodox countries showed »an ambivalence and incoherence when encountering the possibility of […] becoming liberal democracies«[1], and there is no doubt that an elaborate Orthodox political theology »in the liberating and radical sense of the term« does not exist[2]. There are many, mainly historical reasons for this. However, Paul Ladouceur observed that

> the dilemma facing Orthodox in liberal democracies at the beginning of the twenty-first century was not dissimilar to that facing Christian thinkers in late imperial Russia: How to support commendable social programmes and goals, and the noble ideas […] of democratic states without approving the secular philosophies which lay behind them[3]?

Indeed, this question was of major concern for »progressive« religious intellectuals in the first half of the twentieth century, like Semën Frank, Nikolai Berdiaev and Sergii Bulgakov, who also were rather »ambivalent and incoherent« towards the concept of democracy as such[4]. Nevertheless, it has been argued that in response to the »theocratic« imperial state tutelage of the church in Russia, these thinkers developed a Russian version of a »new political theology« that avoided the instrumentalisation of religion for political purposes[5]. In order to qualify this statement, we need to take a closer look at their work in the post-revolutionary decades of the

---

1 Aristotle Papanikolaou, The Mystical as Political. Democracy and Non-Radical Orthodoxy, Notre Dame, IN 2012, p. 5.
2 Pantelis Kalaitzidis, Orthodoxy and Political Theology, Geneva 2012, p. 9, 53, 65f.
3 Paul Ladouceur, Modern Orthodox Theology. Behold, I Make All Things New, London 2019, pp. 346f.
4 See Regula M. Zwahlen, Sergii Bulgakov's Reinvention of Theocracy for a Democratic Age, in: Journal of Orthodox Christian Studies 3/2 (2020), pp. 175–194.
5 Randall A. Poole, Russian Political Theology in an Age of Revolution, in: Robin Aizlewood/Ruth Coates (eds.), Landmarks Revisited. The Vekhi Symposium One Hundred Years On, Brighton, MA 2013, pp. 146–168, at p. 146.

1920s and 1930s, especially considering the overall »pro-Hitlerian spirit [...] amid the majority of the [Russian] emigration«[6].

I will argue that the Russian philosophers in exile developed a »Negative Political Theology«. They excelled in discerning the sore spots of existing political systems and church-state relations but were reluctant to articulate positive visions of an ideal Christian society. Nevertheless, their spiritual ideas were »full of political import«[7] and rather clear about what a Christian social alternative to existing political systems was *not*. Therefore, they can be likened to a »new political theology« that appealed to traditions of negative theological thinking[8]. Facing the consolidation of the Communist system and the rise of National Socialism in the 1930s, some Russian thinkers kept developing concepts of individuality and freedom despite the strongly anti-individualistic character of Slavophile or Orthodox discourse that usually contrasts the person to the individual as well as communion to individuality[9]. It is important to stress that they criticised the political concept of democracy not so much because of its inherent individualism but from their fear of the »tyranny of the faceless majority«[10], and because they refused to worship democracy as a pseudo-religion aiming to solve all human moral problems[11].

Evert van der Zweerde has clarified that most Russian thinkers did not think in terms of autocracy vs. democracy (or communism vs. capitalism), but in terms of anthropocracy vs. theocracy, and that their sense of theocracy did not exclude a positive attitude towards democracy[12]. In addition, I suggest that – taking into account Berdiaev's, Bulgakov's, and Frank's main theological paradigm of man-Godhood (*chelovekobozhie*) vs. God-manhood (*bogochelovechestvo*) – the opposite of anthropocracy is not theocracy, but in their case »theanthropocracy«. Instead

---

6 Catherine BAIRD, The »Third Way«: Russia's Religious Philosophers in the West, 1917–1996, PhD thesis, McGill University, 1997, p. 432.

7 See Christopher STROOP, »A Christian Solution to International Tension«: Nikolai Berdyaev, the American YMCA, and Russian Orthodox influence on Western Christian Anti-communism, c. 1905–1960«, in: Journal of Global History 13/2 (2018), pp. 188–208, at p. 207.

8 Bernd WACKER/Jürgen MANEMANN, Political Theology. History of a Concept, in: John K. DOWNEY et al. (eds.), Missing God? Cultural Amnesia and Political Theology, Berlin 2006, pp. 170–181, at p. 178.

9 Vasilios N. MAKRIDES, Orthodox Personalism. In Favor of or Against Human Rights?, in: Elisabeth-Alexandra DIAMANTOPOULOU/Louis-Léon CHRISTIANS (eds.), Orthodox Christianity and Human Rights in Europe, Brussels 2018, pp. 239–272, at p. 241.

10 BAIRD, The »Third Way«, p. 398.

11 See Novgorodtsev's review of F.J.C. Hearnshaw's »Democracy at the Crossways« (1918): Pavel I. NOVGORODTSEV, Demokratiia na rasput'e, in: Sofia 1 (1923), p. 102, 104.

12 Evert van der ZWEERDE, Theocracy, Sobornost', and Democracy. Reflections on Vladimir Putin's Philosophers, in: Christoph SCHNEIDER (ed.), Theology and Philosophy in Eastern Orthodoxy, Eugene, OR 2019, pp. 11–31, at pp. 24f.

of emphasising the opposition between God and the human being (or the world), they drew on the concept of human beings built in God's image and likeness substantiating a universal ontological potential for creative, Chalcedonian synergy[13]. In this view, even secular »anthropocracy« need not necessarily be fought as long as humans do not claim to be God themselves and fight religion. They tried to »hold on to the good« (1 Thessalonians 5:21) of any modern secular thought – be it the Enlightenment, humanism, socialism, or democracy – and to integrate it in their concepts of »theanthropocracy«.

For this contribution, I picked out some writings from a huge pile of debates and texts written in the 1920s and 1930s and ready to be examined by those who seek to learn from these Orthodox thinkers' encounter with Western modernity. I will trace the intellectual development of the »progressive« Russian Orthodox thinkers in exile by highlighting some of their debates on monarchy, socialism, and fascism.

The Post-Revolutionary Tasks of the Russian Diaspora

Lively debates about theocracy and church-state relations took place in Russia long before 1917[14]. Eventually, the February Revolution heralded the post-Constantinian era: the abdication of the tsar, the organisation of elections to the Russian Constituent Assembly by the Provisional Government, the All-Russian Council of the Orthodox Church in 1917, and the liberation of the church from state tutelage was endorsed by a large part of the Russian society, including many Orthodox theologians and priests who conceived of Easter 1917 as Russia's resurrection as a republic[15]. The All-Russian Council almost enthusiastically developed new church-state relations. The statement on »The relation of the church to the state« was the only document the Council was able to publish on 2 December 1917[16], and reflects that the majority of the clergy and liberal politicians did not seek a complete separation of church and state. They advocated the »primacy« (*pervenstvuiushchaia Tserkov'*) of the Orthodox Church in Russia instead of its former »dominance«

---

13 Regula M. ZWAHLEN, Das revolutionäre Ebenbild Gottes. Anthropologien der Menschenwürde bei Nikolaj A. Berdjaev und Sergej N. Bulgakov, Münster 2010, p. 357.
14 See ZWAHLEN, Bulgakov's Reinvention.
15 Pavel ROGOSNYJ, Die »Kirchenrevolution« von März bis August 1917, in: Religion & Gesellschaft in Ost und West 45/4–5 (2017), pp. 27–29, at pp. 27f.
16 Aleksei BEGLOV, Das Landeskonzil der Russischen Kirche und die Revolution, in: Religion & Gesellschaft in Ost und West 45/4–5 (2017), pp. 30–33, at p. 32.

(*gospodstvuiushchaia*), but were determined not to violate the religious conscience of adherents to different faiths[17].

Given the frontal attack on religion after the Bolshevist October Revolution, which drove both »democrats« and »monarchists« into exile, the debates about how to relate to the political sphere were to be continued by the Russian Orthodox diaspora. As many put it, in Russia, theocracy was not replaced by democracy, but by a »reversed theocracy«, according to Sergii Bulgakov[18], or even by a »satanocracy«, according to Berdiaev and Frank[19]. Anton Kartashëv, for a short period Ober-Procurator of the Holy Synod under the provisional government in 1917, seemingly coined »the formula that the Russian Church, after the council and the revolution, had ›come out of the Constantinian phase of its history‹« in 1923[20].

In the 1920s, several movements tried to attract the younger generation of the Russian emigration, including the Russian Student Christian Movement (RSCM), the Eurasian Movement, the fascist movement of Young Russians (*Mladorossy*), and the movement of the National Bolsheviks. Apart from the RSCM, they all shared a »strong nationalism, presented a program of social reforms, and claimed to be of Orthodox inspiration«[21]. In this context, the authors of »The Way«, a review strongly associated with the RSCM, Berdiaev's Academy of Religious Philosophy, and the St Serge Institute of Orthodox Theology in Paris, advocated the »primacy of the spiritual principle«, but agreed on three rather political points: »Criticism of the bourgeois spirit, rejection of both communism and capitalism, and rejection of nationalism«[22].

Despite such rejection of nationalism, *Put'* (*The Way*) was also keen to prevent »denationalisation« and to bridge the gap between the Russian emigration and religious people in Soviet Russia with the help of the Orthodox Church. That was the first of the »post-revolutionary and not pre-revolutionary« spiritual tasks of the Russian emigration listed in the very first issue of *The Way* in 1925[23]. The second task consisted in establishing a community with Christians of all confessions in

---

17 See Konstantin KOVYRZIN, Pomestnyi sobor 1917–1918 godov i poiski printsipov tserkovno-gosudarstvennykh otnoshenii posle Fevral'skoi revoliutsii, in: Otechestvennaia istoriia 4 (2008), pp. 88–97.
18 Sergei N. BULGAKOV, U sten Khersonisa, St Petersburg 1993, p. 149.
19 Nikolai A. BERDIAEV, Novoe srednevekov'e. Razmyshlenie o sud'be Rossii i Evropy [1924], in: Id. (ed.), Smysl tvorchestva, Moscow 2004, pp. 545–628, at p. 572; Semën L. FRANK, Religioznye osnovy obshchestvennosti, in: Put' 1 (1925), pp. 9–30, at p. 28.
20 Antoine ARJAKOVSKY, The Way. Religious Thinkers of the Russian Emigration in Paris and their Journal 1925–1940, Notre Dame, IN 2013, p. 243.
21 Ibid., p. 121.
22 Ibid., p. 248.
23 Nikolai A. BERDIAEV et al., Dukhovnye zadachi russkoi ėmigratsii, in: Put' 1 (1925), pp. 3–8, at p. 5. A youth movement called the »Post-Revolutionaries« was created by Iurii Shirinskii-Shikhmatov,

the West. However, the West was considered to be exhausted, and the East was expected to »gain more world importance than before«. The Russian diaspora's closer contact with the Western world was thus still conceived as a part of God's providence with regard to the »Russian mission« to guide humanity[24]. With regard to the Russian diaspora, the review was supposed to fight on two fronts: against secularist tendencies that wanted to engage in spiritual creativity outside and beyond the Orthodox Church, and against ecclesial tendencies against any kind of new creativity within the Orthodox Church[25].

In the 1920s, the East-West divide still dominated the idea of preserving spiritual Russian culture until the Soviet nightmare would be over, which was expected to happen soon[26]. The Russian emigration even compared itself to the Jewish diaspora[27], having taken from its morally tainted homeland the elements of moral renewal[28]. Despite their strong emphasis on the *spiritual* dimension of their new social, cultural, and historical activities, the editors of *The Way* were certainly well aware of the political implications. So was their principal opposition, the monarchist synod of the Russian Orthodox Church Abroad in Sremski Karlovtsi, which according to Bulgakov had remained »true to pre-revolutionary routine«[29], and the »Eurasians«, who contrasted »Russia-Eurasia« to Western European culture. However, the monarchist and Eurasian debates faded when the consolidation of Stalin's power in 1928 shattered anybody's plans to return to their homeland[30]. Shortly afterwards, the »debate on the limits of East and West disappeared from the pages of the review«[31].

In the 1930s, *The Way* became a kind of »nonconformist workshop trying to elaborate a third way« in search »for political alternatives to democracies that were

---

who believed in turning the dynamic spirit of the Soviet Union towards »genuine Russian humanism« and published a journal called *Utverzhdenie (Affirmation)*. See BAIRD, The »Third Way«, pp. 346f.

24 See Ana SILJAK, Nikolai Berdiaev and the Origin of Russian Messianism, in: The Journal of Modern History 88 (2016), pp. 737–763, at p. 737.

25 BERDIAEV et al., Dukhovnye zadachi, p. 7.

26 Marc RAEFF, Russia Abroad. A Cultural History of the Russian Emigration 1919–1939, New York 1990, p. 61.

27 BERDIAEV et al., Dukhovnye zadachi, p. 3.

28 ARJAKOVSKY, The Way, p. 6.

29 Nikita A. STRUVE, Bratstvo Sviatoi Sofii. Materialy i Dokumenty 1923–1939, Moscow 2000, p. 511.

30 ARJAKOVSKY, The Way, p. 34, 133, 192, 198f.; Paul L. GAVRILYUK, Georges Florovsky and the Russian Religious Renaissance, Oxford 2013, p. 77. In 1929, the Eurasian movement split because of ideological differences over how to deal with consolidated Soviet power. See Stefan WIEDERKEHR, Die eurasische Bewegung. Wissenschaft und Politik in der russischen Emigration der Zwischenkriegszeit und im postsowjetischen Russland, Cologne 2006, pp. 58–60; Marlène LARUELLE, Les idéologies de la »troisième voie« dans les années 1920. Le mouvement eurasiste russe, in: Vingtième Siècle. Revue d'histoire 70/2 (2001), pp. 31–46.

31 ARJAKOVSKY, The Way, p. 188, 200.

neither fascist nor communist«³², as well as economic alternatives to capitalism and socialism. According to its editors, the old Russian imperial order had been sinful and pagan rather than Christian, having permitted capitalist exploitation and hence caused the rise of Bolshevism. For them, both systems were evil, and »on their ruins« they wanted to build a Christian society³³. Intellectuals like Berdiaev and Frank identified not only a crisis of monarchy, but a »worldwide crisis of all social-political ideologies and forms«³⁴, since no-one could wholeheartedly believe in socialism or democracy anymore³⁵. According to Berdiaev, this crisis could only be overcome by the »real realisation of true theocracy«, which would not be a »simulation of a ›Christian state‹«³⁶, but the overcoming of the social-political chaos by the creation of a new spiritual cosmos similar to the »complex and rich« spiritual universe of the Middle Ages, but based on freedom instead of violence³⁷. However, Berdiaev never elaborated on how his vision of a »foundation and consolidation of state and society in religion« (instead of their separation) and »overcoming of democracy« would actually work³⁸. Instead, he expressed a rather prophetic view of the rise of »strong powers, often dictatorial«, which »popular sovereignty« will equip with »sacral attributes of power«³⁹. In his view, Italian Fascism was a creative phenomenon in contemporary political life which, like communism, embodied a »will to life and will to power, an uncovering of biological force instead of law«⁴⁰, a »transit from juridical forms to life itself«⁴¹. Berdiaev considered this to be a positive, but chaotic dynamic, which only a Christian society could transform into a spiritual cosmos that guaranteed human freedom⁴². Catherine Baird summarised the vision of the »Third Way« thus:

---

32 Ibid., p. 199.
33 BERDIAEV et al., Dukhovnye zadachi, p. 8.
34 BERDIAEV, Novoe srednevekov'e, p. 624.
35 FRANK, Religioznye osnovy, p. 10.
36 BERDIAEV, Novoe srednevekov'e, p. 623.
37 Ibid., p. 557, 561, 567.
38 Ibid., p. 569, 625. With Berdiaev's help and YMCA funding, Ilya Bunakov-Fondaminskii founded the review *Novyi Grad* (*New City*) addressing the young emigres in order to discuss concrete economic, political, and social issues (1931–1939), BAIRD, The »Third Way«, pp. 348f. See also Marc RAEFF, L'émigration et la »Cité nouvelle«, in: Cahiers du monde russe et soviétique 29/3-4 (1988), pp. 543–552; and Andrei SHISHKOV, »Novii Grad« kak Politiko-Teologicheskii Proekt, in: Trudy Kyiivs'koii Dukhovnoii Akademii 36 (2022), pp. 159–168. Novyi Grad became the organ of the »Orthodox Action« in Paris, a group devoted to the practical support of refugees, migrant workers, and the unemployed.
39 BERDIAEV, Novoe srednevekov'e, p. 575.
40 Ibid., p. 560.
41 In contrast, Bulgakov emphasised the importance of the rule of law and the separation of church and state. See ZWAHLEN, Bulgakov's Reinvention.
42 BERDIAEV, Novoe srednevekov'e, p. 561, 567.

The transformation [...] incorporated a spiritual conception of the divine worth of each human being. A society must be created in which work had a creative purpose and was not simply drudgery. Politics had to cease being the purview of elites, and instead take into account the unique abilities and needs of each citizen in the land. The »third way« embraced decentralization of powers in order that those most affected could make decisions about their economy and their governance. It envisioned a Christian socialism or humanism which would be more righteous, but also more uplifting to personal pride[43].

Hence, the contributors to *The Way* did not initially develop a concept of democracy because for them the church's spiritual independence with respect to all types of power was crucial.

Monarchism and Theocracy

The »theocratic« question – whether or not Orthodoxy was deeply related to monarchy – was widely debated in the 1920s[44]. According to Marc Raeff, »most émigrés were monarchists in a vague, sentimental way«, but were »split in several ways – from radical reactionaries to moderate liberal constitutionalists«[45]. One of the debates revolved around a book by the monarchist Mikhail Zyzykin defending *Tsarskaia vlast' i zakon o prestolonasliedii v Rossii* (*Tsarist Power and the law of Succession to the Throne in Russia*) (Sofia 1924) within the »Brotherhood of St Sophia«. This group of exiled Russian professors and priests from Berlin, Prague, and Paris stood in close contact with the RSCM, united by a concern for the preservation of Orthodox theology, but was not politically homogeneous at all. They agreed that they did not endorse the idea of legitimism[46], but Pëtr Struve still defended the institution of monarchy, while Vasilii Zen'kovskii argued that the promotion of a Christian culture was more important than the restoration of the monarchy. Georgii Florovskii highlighted the tsar's potential for corruption by »hard power«, and Nikolai Losskii denied an existential relationship between Orthodoxy and monarchism and later wrote about the kinship of *sobornost'* and democracy[47]. Bulgakov con-

---

43 BAIRD, The »Third Way«, p. 366.
44 ARJAKOVSKY, The Way, p. 104.
45 RAEFF, Russia Abroad, p. 8.
46 STRUVE, Bratstvo, p. 63.
47 Nikolai O. LOSSKII, Organicheskoe stroenie obshchestva i demokratiia, in: Sovremennye zapiski 25 (1925), pp. 343–355.

cluded that the church must detach the principles of theocracy »from absolutism, and somehow reconcile them with the principles of Popular Government«[48].

But not all Russian thinkers endorsed the political system of democracy in the same way. In the very first issue of *The Way*, Frank and Berdiaev declared that all known political systems had failed[49]. In *The Kingdom of God and the Kingdom of Caesar*, Berdiaev drew on the distinction between God and Caesar (Matthew 22:21) to explain that Christianity accepted the kingdom of Caesar – be it monarchy, a democratic, or a socialist republic – as a necessity in order to pursue its goals within the order of sinful nature[50]. The confusion of both kingdoms took place in the Old Testament[51] and in the emergence of Christian statehood – be it caesaropapism or papocaesarism: But theocracy is a universal, spiritual category, while monarchy is a relative, natural category. However, Berdiaev considered the establishment of a Christian statehood by Constantine not a misfortune, as »rationalist and Protestant sources« would have it, but an inevitable providential second step in the destiny of Christianity, which was now followed by a third period, namely secularisation. In this new period, Christians should not try to regain Christian statehood, because »power in the hands of Christians is more than problematic«[52]. In order to keep the concept of theocracy free from political instrumentalisation, Berdiaev suggested treating it in the light of negative theology[53], so that from now on, one could only say what theocracy *was not*.

Hence, in his view, first, theocracy was not a violent force calling for violent changes, but changed the »internal order of the world«. Berdiaev drew on the example of the pre-Constantinian Christians who accepted »power established by God« (Rom 13:1), even if they suffered persecution. The subversive overcoming of slavery by the early Christian idea of human brotherhood instead of upheaval served

---

48 Sergius BULGAKOV, The Old and the New. A Study in Russian Religion, in: The Slavonic Review 2/6 (1924), pp. 487–513, at pp. 511f.
49 FRANK, Religioznye osnovy, p. 10. Frank elaborated on the universal principles of a Christian society: solidarity, freedom, service (asceticism), tradition, theocracy (vs. democracy), authority (vs. democracy, forced power), hierarchy (qualitative multiplicity), aristocracy (rule of the worthiest), equality, and biunity.
50 Nikolai A. BERDIAEV, Tsarstvo Bozhie i tsarstvo kesaria, in: Put' 1 (1925), pp. 31–52, at p. 33.
51 In contrast to Grigorii Trubetskoi's account that there is a biblical foundation of monarchy, Berdiaev observed a conflict between theocratic and monarchist concepts. Despite the theocratic vocation of the Jewish people, they had succumbed to the temptation of deification of a king (1 Samuel 12:19); Grigorii TRUBETSKOI, Spor o monarkhii, in: Put' 4 (1926), pp. 172–175, at p. 172; Nikolai A. BERDIAEV, Dnevnik filosofa (Spor o monarkhii, o burzhuaznosti i o svobode mysli), in: Put' 6 (1926), pp. 176–182, at p. 178.
52 BERDIAEV, Tsarstvo Bozhie, pp. 37–39, 48.
53 Ibid., p. 42.

as an example[54]. For them, theocracy had been a synonym for the kingdom of God in its eschatological sense. Therefore, there was neither a Christian justification of the Russian Revolution nor of restoration by force by emigrant right-wing monarchist circles. In Berdiaev's view, the monarchists dreamt about revenge, violence, and bloodshed just like the German right-wing nationalists and the French nationalist group *Action française*, although the former at least hated Christianity, while the latter instrumentalised the Catholic Church[55].

Second, theocracy was not a political system. In theory, Berdiaev appreciated Lev Tikhomirov's book on *Monarkhicheskaia gosudarstvennost'* (*Monarchist Statehood*) from 1905, which was very popular at the time[56], because of its »democratic character with regard to social matters«. But he considered it as much a utopia as papal theocracy and an ideal socialist structure. In practice, all monarchies became tyrannies by using force. The state's submission to natural law and divine justice in the Middle Ages was replaced by pagan or »unlimited humanist absolutism«, and the universal idea of theocracy was replaced by nationalism[57]. In Russia, Peter I had created a pseudo-Christian autocratic state, and the church hierarchy and the passivity of the people were to be blamed for letting it happen. The corruption of such »theocracy« became most visible when the last tsar put his trust in a man like Rasputin instead of the church[58].

Third, the concept of theocracy did not justify a church »sacrament of holy royal power«[59]. The ecclesial anointing of the Russian Tsars as a »gift of the Holy Spirit« introduced the kingdom of Caesar into the kingdom of God. It happened because the church could not refrain from sanctifying the whole of human life, including state power, but at a certain point it succumbed to the »great historic temptation« of equating the kingdom of God with human power[60]. In Berdiaev's view, the anointing of the tsar corresponded to the same heresy of man-Godhood as any other absolutisation of man in radical humanism and socialism.

---

54 See Sergij BULGAKOV, Die zwei Städte. Studien zur Natur gesellschaftlicher Ideale, Münster 2020, pp. 211f.
55 BERDIAEV, Dnevnik filosofa, p. 180. Berdiaev criticised Jacques Maritain's early sympathy for the movement and advocated the spiritual liberalism in the church. See Nikolai A. BERDIAEV, Katolichestvo i Action Française, in: Put' 10 (1928), pp. 115–123, at pp. 122f.
56 Tikhomirov was a former revolutionary terrorist who – in search for social justice – became a supporter of official Orthodoxy. See Anatoly KORCHINSKY/Oxana ZAMOLODSKY, The Terrorist »Tigrykh« vs. the Monarchist Leo Tikhomirov. Why Tikhomirov »Stopped Being a Revolutionary?«, in: Jens HERLTH/Christian ZEHNDER (eds.), Models of Personal Conversion in Russian Cultural History of the 19th and 20th Centuries, Bern 2015, pp. 95–104.
57 BERDIAEV, Tsarstvo Bozhie, p. 42, 44f.
58 Id., Dnevnik filosofa, p. 178.
59 Id., Tsarstvo Bozhie, pp. 34–36.
60 Ibid., p. 41, 43.

And, fourth, theocracy did not correspond to a »godless democracy«, for which Berdiaev had »no sympathy whatsoever« because of »its faceless, anonymous formalism«[61], which has nothing in common with Christian society. Nevertheless, Berdiaev came to rather surprising conclusions: In the new epoch, Christian society must accept the truthfulness (*pravdivost'*) of secularisation and democracy in the name of freedom[62]. No violent political system could claim to be Christian and therefore any state system must be secularised. In this way, Berdiaev turned upside down the monarchists' claim that men need monarchy because of their sinful human nature: Sin was the very reason why all human utopias fail, and since democrats believed neither in primordial sin nor in the perfection of human nature, democracy »is created for an imperfect and sinful condition«[63], making it quite an appropriate system in this world. In short, Christians of the new post-Constantinian period should accept secularisation and democracy as context, even if they cannot strive for them as spiritual goals, because Christianity strives for the transformation of the whole life.

Berdiaev's second and third points triggered fierce opposition. In his *Letter of a Monarchist*, A. Petrov deplored Berdiaev's (as well as Bulgakov's and Kartashëv's) unjust condemnation of »Russian monarchist ideology«. For example, the »Highest Monarchist Council«, founded in 1921 in Bad Reichenhall and led by Nikolai E. Markov and Nikolai D. Tal'berg, could not be accused of supporting the old synodal structure and of »religious nationalism«. Furthermore, the negation of the special providential mission of Russian Orthodox Tsardom, likened to the »New Israel« in many a church hymn, was a monstrosity in Petrov's view, and the anointing of the tsar belonged to the understanding of all Eastern churches. By no means could the concept of tsarist autocracy in Russia be compared to the utopia of socialism. The concept of a pious tsar as a servant of the Heavenly Father illustrates that there is an eschatological, mystical meaning of monarchy: »The meaning of monarchy lies in the constant personification of the religious-moral ideal that lives in the people by the person of the monarch, in the personification of God's justice«[64]. Furthermore, in contemporary Russia, the simple Russian people now resisted the satanic power largely by gathering around the church, while the Russian people abroad were losing

---

61 Id., Dnevnik filosofa, p. 179.
62 Id., Tsarstvo Bozhie, p. 39. This is reminiscent of the words of the German constitutional judge Ernst-Wolfgang Böckenförde, who explained the positive meaning of the secular state to conservative Catholics in 1967 thus: »The liberal (*freiheitlich*) secularised state depends on premises which it cannot guarantee itself. *This is the great adventure it has undertaken for freedom's sake*« (emphasis added); Ernst-Wolfgang BÖCKENFÖRDE, Der säkularisierte Staat. Sein Charakter, seine Rechtfertigung und seine Probleme im 21. Jahrhundert, Munich 2007, p. 71.
63 BERDIAEV, Tsarstvo Bozhie, p. 45.
64 A. PETROV, Pis'mo monarkhista v redaktsiiu zhurnala »Put«, in: Put' 3 (1926), pp. 134–139, at p. 137.

faith quickly. Therefore, the power of the Russian people nourished the faith in the reconstruction of Russian Tsardom.

Berdiaev did not doubt the sincere religiosity of the Russian monarchists, but thought that the monarchists in emigration hindered the overcoming of Bolshevism in Russia. Especially the right-wing monarchists obviously did not accept the separation of church and state endorsed by the All-Russian Church Council and did everything to separate the Orthodox Church in Russia and abroad. Furthermore, he did not find any foundation of a religious-mystical concept of autocratic monarchy in Holy Scripture, least of all in the New Testament, where God reveals himself as a father not as a monarch[65].

In his remarks on the debate between Berdiaev and Petrov, Grigorii Trubetskoi insisted that a monarch – as a human being – would always need to be sanctioned by the church and preferred this kind of religious sanction to the will of the people, the only source of power in democracy[66]. Berdiaev agreed that the Orthodox Church should care for the realisation of God's justice in the life of society and the state, but he found little evidence that autocratic monarchy did a lot in this regard. On the contrary, a lot of hate against Jews, leftists, members of the intelligentsia, and adherents of other faiths could be found in right-wing monarchist sermons and circles. Religious monarchism was not grounded on justice, but on lies and insincerity, and hence caused secularisation[67]. By supporting the political concept of monarchy, the church succumbed to the temptation of Dostoevsky's Grand Inquisitor: It charged one person with the whole burden of freedom and responsibility and took it away from the Christian people. But the time had come for each Christian to take the whole amount of freedom and responsibility on himself[68], since the kingdom of God was the Kingdom of Christ and general royal priesthood[69]. However, Berdiaev still insisted that he was not a democrat and on the relativity of each political system. In his view, after »pre-revolutionary« pseudo-Christian statehood, a »post-revolutionary« Christian society must get rid of juridical and political forms and focus on its pre-Constantinian situation[70]. Future church-state relations were thinkable only as an external concordat, not as an internal goal of Christianity. Christians should realise the kingdom of God eschatologically in each moment of their lives as a transformation of the world into a new heaven and a new earth, and »the Christian Church should finally stop relying on state power

---

65 Nikolai A. Berdiaev, Otvet na pis'mo monarkhista, in: Put' 3 (1926), pp. 140–144, at p. 141.
66 Trubetskoi, Spor, p. 172.
67 Berdiaev, Otvet, pp. 141–143.
68 Id., Dnevnik filosofa, p. 178.
69 Id., Tsarstvo Bozhie, p. 50. On »royal priesthood« in Bulgakov, see Zwahlen, Bulgakov's Reinvention, p. 185.
70 Berdiaev, Dnevnik filosofa, p. 177.

and develop its own energy from within. [...] People will gather around religious, inner spiritual indicators, and not outer, political ones«[71].

Berdiaev believed in the coming of totally new forms of spiritual and social life. Apart from temporarily accepting secularisation and democracy, his only practical advice consisted in supporting unions of Orthodox workers instead of Orthodox monarchy, because the new epoch would overcome capitalism by establishing a new appreciation of the concept of »labour«[72].

Socialism and Social Christianity

The concept of work was closely related to Berdiaev's and Bulgakov's past as »Christian socialists«. New debates on socialism evolved after the »World Conference of Life and Work« (1925) in Stockholm, which aimed, after the experience of the First World War, at the social renewal of society through a common Christian conscience[73]. Among the Russian emigrants, the topic enjoyed a revival by the end of the 1920s, when Bulgakov held lectures on »Christian sociology« (1927–1928) at the St Serge Institute in Paris[74]. Nikolai Klepinin taught a course on »The Social Problems of the Contemporary World and Christianity«, Boris Vysheslavtsev gave a lecture on »Socialism and Christianity« at the Academy of Religious Philosophy in 1929[75], and in 1931, Fëdor Stepun discussed the German theologian Paul Tillich's »Baselines of Religious Socialism« of 1923[76].

In the following, I shall present only a brief insight in these debates. In 1929, the Soviet monthly journal *Antireligioznik* published unknown sources by the »Higher Church Board in the South of Russia« from September 1920 in Crimea, just before the last units of the White Army were defeated by the Red Army. In the journal, Boris Kandidov, a specialist for the collaboration of the Orthodox Church with

---

71 Id., Tsarstvo Bozhie, pp. 51f.
72 Id., Dnevnik filosofa, p. 182.
73 ARJAKOVSKY, The Way, p. 169.
74 Sergei N. BULGAKOV, Khristianskaia sotsiologiia [1928], in: Vadim V. SAPOV (ed.), S.N. Bulgakov. Trudy po sotsiologii i teologii, Moscow 1997, pp. 528–565.
75 ARJAKOVSKY, The Way, p. 129.
76 See Fëdor A. STEPUN, Religioznyi sotsializm i khristianstvo, in: Put' 29 (1931), pp. 20–48. In the West, »Religious Socialism« emerged in Switzerland at the beginning of the twentieth century and even became a political party (*Bund der Religiösen Sozialisten Deutschlands*) from 1926 to 1933 among evangelical Christians in Germany. The »Tillich Circle« published the *Blätter für Religiösen Sozialismus* between 1920 and 1927 and the *Neue Blätter für den Sozialismus. Zeitschrift für geistige und politische Gestaltung* between 1930 and 1933. Already in 1905, Bulgakov compared the social demands by Swiss pastor Hermann Kutter and Vladimir Solov'ëv. See Sergei N. BULGAKOV, Bez plana, in: Igor I. EVLAMPIEV (ed.), S.N. Bulgakov. Pro et contra, St Petersburg 2003, pp. 245–249.

conservative forces, wrote about the »charlatan« Bulgakov's task of formulating an official church statement on the nature of socialism[77]. Bulgakov, a former professor of political economy, immediately commented on this in the *Messenger of the RSCM*. He confirmed that he had been commissioned to draft such a statement, because a priest called Vladimir Vostokov had called for socialism to be anathemised, which Bulgakov strongly rejected. However, the statement had never been discussed or adopted[78]. Bulgakov's comment received three public reactions, among them one from Frank, which allow some conclusions to be drawn about the Russian thinkers' new approaches to the old social question in an »apophatic« key.

First, socialism was not primarily an atheistic religion, but a socio-economic system expressing a certain »truth«[79] with regard to social justice, which now took centre stage in the ecumenical Life-and-Work-movement of »social Christianity«[80]. In reply to a former member of the St Petersburg Christian Student Movement, Baron Stackelberg, who insisted that social Christianity had nothing in common with atheist socialism[81], Bulgakov suggested that an anathema on socialism would do harm to the social gospel of the church. The church should fight socialism not by negating atheism and socialism in the same breath, but by positively acknowledging the latter's practical, ethical importance[82]. However, by its former indifference with regard to social questions, the church had caused socialism's close relation to militant atheism.

Second, »social Christianity« did not promote a certain economic system. The complexity of various forms of socialism and capitalism must be considered, and, in Bulgakov's view, the institutions of economic liberty and private property seemed more suitable for social development than socialist state slavery. By citing a British liberal's words, »we all are now socialists«, Bulgakov supported »social regulations of capitalistic industry« because capitalist exploitation was unacceptable for the church[83]. When Mr. Khilkov, a Tolstoian, accused him of a »soft« reconciliation with capitalism that was not in line with the Sermon on the Mount[84],

---

77 Boris Kandidov, »Dni pokaianiia« v Krymu v sentiabre 1920 goda (Istoricheskaia spravka po neopublikovannym materialam), in: Antireligioznik 7 (1929), pp. 69–75, at p. 70.
78 Sergii Bulgakov, Pravoslavie i sotsializm (Pis'mo v redaktsiiu), in: Vestnik RSKhD 1 (1930), pp. 7–9, at p. 7.
79 On »the truth of socialism« in Solov̌ev, see Vladimir Solovyov, Lectures on Divine Humanity, Hudson, NY 1995, p. 3.
80 Bulgakov, Pravoslavie i sotsializm, p. 9. Bulgakov explicitly mentioned his early works from 1903 to 1917.
81 A. Shtakel'berg, Otvet professoru prot. S. Bulgakovu, in: Vestnik RSKhD 7 (1930), pp. 29f., at p. 30.
82 Sergii Bulgakov, Po povodu dvukh pisem, in: Vestnik RSKhD 7 (1930), pp. 25–27, at p. 26.
83 Id., Pravoslavie i sotsializm, p. 8.
84 A. Khilkov, Otkrytoe pis'mo v redaktsiiu »Vestnika«, in: Vestnik RSKhD 7 (1930), pp. 30–32, at p. 32.

Bulgakov criticised Khilkov's radical utopian claims and polemically reminded him of having sent his letter »by state post, written on a typewriter from capitalist production for publication in a journal that is issued under the technical and social conditions of the printing business etc. etc«[85]. In the same vein, Frank criticised all concepts of utopia, revolution, and class struggle, while the two most important principles of a Christian society were »personal freedom« and »social solidarity«. In their name, both state-coerced socialism and capitalist economic exploitation must be denied. The church's task was to guarantee the balance of freedom and solidarity, and economists and statemen should do empirical research in this regard[86].

Third, »social Christianity« does not deny historical institutions, least of all the church. In response to Khilkov's remark that Bulgakov should have stressed the church's responsibility for socialist atheism much stronger[87], Bulgakov criticised Tolstoi's »pious nihilism« that considered the church's entire history to be antichristian. The church, despite its social sins, was not the only reason for socialism's nexus with atheism, because the very source of atheism was the dialectic of the human spirit between good and evil at work in any historical institution. In Bulgakov's view, instead of negating all cooperation, everybody should participate in the »common work of spirit and conscience, especially in the realm of social Christianity« within existing institutions according to the possibilities and limits of one's epoch[88]. Emphasis on the historical relativity of all human institutions had always been of great importance for Bulgakov. In another essay on *The Soul of Socialism* (1931), Bulgakov referred to his book *Two Cities* (1911), in which, referring to Augustine, he discussed the difficulty of distinguishing the *civitas Dei* from the *civitas diabolica*, even within the (visible) church[89], as well as the relativity of the church's tasks in this world: »The Christian ideal of the Kingdom of God is realised historically in a whole series of alternating historical tasks: at the present time, one of these is the attainment of social justice along with personal liberty«[90]. Once that balance was attained, the church would move on. Therefore, Bulgakov criticised Paul Tillich's appraisal of socialism as a »divine fact« (*kairos*) and called for a »careful and patient examination of a situation as it has concretely developed before one makes a final judgement«[91]. In short, everyone is called to seek social justice for one's age in

---

85 BULGAKOV, Po povodu, p. 27.
86 Semën FRANK, Khristianstvo i sotsializm, in: Vestnik RSKhD 4 (1940), pp. 15–19, at p. 18.
87 KHILKOV, Otkrytoe pis'mo, p. 31.
88 BULGAKOV, Po povodu, pp. 26f.
89 Id., Die zwei Städte, p. 8.
90 Id., The Soul of Socialism, in: Rowan WILLIAMS (ed.), Sergii Bulgakov. Towards a Russian Political Theology, Edinburgh 1999, pp. 229–268, at p. 248.
91 Ibid., pp. 250f.

a dynamic way, condemning neither socialism nor church history out of hand. Because of the historical relativity of human institutions, Bulgakov would never again link Christianity to a certain political or economic system, nor would he condemn a »just cause« only because of its atheist or secular outlook.

Fourth, »social Christianity« was not based on a socialist, but on a Christian anthropology. This important point was made by Frank in reply to Bulgakov, who had not mentioned it in his response to *Antireligioznik*. In Frank's view, socialism was not only an economic system, but an anthropology that traced any human evil back to social injustice, while in Christian social philosophy, social injustice was only a part of the general evil in human relations in consequence of sin. From a Christian point of view, no secular social order would prevent men from doing evil. Therefore, a Christian rejects not only socialism's »open« atheism as denial of religion, but also its »hidden« atheism as denial of personal morality and social responsibility of the human person, who in the famous Marxist view »is not creator of social life [...] but the irresponsible ›product‹ of his ›milieu‹«[92]. Like Frank, Bulgakov had always criticised socialist anthropology for being based on sociologism and economism that deny human liberty. In this regard he rejected not only communist »compulsory collectivism« but also the capitalist »standardisation of human life«. The latter, on the one hand, atomises society and leads to greater individualism, while, on the other hand, it forcibly unites

> these human atoms in the process of economic and national life – in the factory (industrialisation), in cities (urbanisation), in national institutions (state centralism), and in general the collectivisation of human life on the basis of the »general good«. This is what can be designated as the socialism of concrete life, independently of its economic form (so that in this sense the supremely rationalized society is perhaps no less »socialistic« than the coercive regime of communism)[93].

Bulgakov feared that atomised individuals would socialise anew around conflicting interests and saw the only way to overcome such tensions »in ecclesial life«. A Christian society should creatively tackle these challenges by searching for new answers to the questions raised by

> this hopeless conflict between the egocentricity of individualism and the sadism of communism, between the soullessness of statism and the snarling of racism [...]. Yet it is only the church that possesses the principle of true social order, in which the personal and the

---

92 Frank, Khristianstvo i sotsializm, p. 16.
93 Bulgakov, The Soul of Socialism, pp. 261f.

collective, freedom and social service can be given equal weight and unified harmoniously. It is itself this very principle, living sobornost'[94].

Fifth, the church as *principle* of social order must remain independent from any political social order. In Bulgakov's view, the church

> *is* in fact apolitical – in the sense, that it can never identify its eternal values with any relative or contingent task, or any historical institutions (as was once the case in Russia […]). The church cannot be a party: it must be *the conscience of a* society, never using humility as an excuse for compromise or indifferentism. But it cannot go along with the secularist disintegration of social order; rather must its spiritual domination struggle towards victory from within[95].

By the church's »struggle for spiritual domination from within« Bulgakov meant its mode of action under democratic circumstances: »The church's methods of influence change; the work is no longer done outside, from above, but from within, from below, from the people and by the people […] so that the church influences the state in a democratic way«[96]. It is true that in Bulgakov's »apocalyptic« mindset, a secular democratic system was not a goal to be achieved, but a temporary period to be overcome. In his view, there was no neutral zone between atheist (or »pagan«) and religious worldviews[97] – everything would sooner or later be qualified by the »human dialectic«, but this did not mean that anything »secular« automatically belonged to the kingdom of evil. In the end, the »truth« of any just cause like human liberty and social justice would find its roots in the church even if it was first promoted by secular forces[98]. These ideals would thrive if the church met them with constructive criticism, but they might be distorted by the church's indifference or if they were forced to seek realisation outside the church[99].

Fascism and Christian Universalism

Admittedly, Bulgakov's, Berdiaev's, and Frank's positive statements about democracy and secular culture were rather scarce. Therefore, their search for a »Third Way« or »personalism« was sometimes perceived as »anti-liberal, anti-capitalist, and in a

---

94 Ibid., p. 264.
95 Ibid., pp. 256f.
96 BULGAKOV, The Orthodox Church, pp. 163f.
97 Id., The Soul of Socialism, p. 233.
98 ZWAHLEN, Bulgakov's Reinvention, p. 181.
99 See the chapter on »Church and culture« in BULGAKOV, Die zwei Städte, pp. 561–570.

certain manner anti-democratic«[100]. Several historians even believed to have found fascist impulses in their ideas, because in their view, »any condemnation of ›liberal values‹ or ›democracy‹« was among the »clear signs of nascent fascism«[101]. Indeed, the journals *The Way* and *The New City* declared outright opposition to fascism only by the end of 1935, when the Russian thinkers in exile identified the common threat of communism and National Socialism by using the same term for both: totalitarianism[102].

In order to get a broader picture of how the Russian thinkers in exile dealt with fascism, it is revealing to look at some debates and publications of the year 1934. After the victory of the Nazi Party and the appointment of Hitler as chancellor in Germany, the overall sense of political crisis was prominently addressed at the Eighth International Congress of Philosophy on »Philosophy and Life«, which was held in Prague in September 1934 and attended by Semën Frank. Five of the twenty-eight panels were dedicated to »The Crisis of Democracy«[103]. Commenting on the Congress, Frank discerned two ways of dealing with the problem of uniting life and philosophy: either to »secularise« philosophy by adapting it to practical necessities of life, or to »deepen« it by rising it to »the concrete religious wholeness of life«[104]. The split between »deep« and »secular« philosophy was represented by two greeting addresses, one by Edmund Husserl, who in view of the impossibility of philosophical unanimity called for independent free inner contemplation of thought, the other by Ferdinand Tönnies, who considered »liberal principles« and positivism the only way to counter »Caesarist autocracy« (à la Hitler) and *spiritual* chaos. According to Frank, the congress' focus on »the crisis of democracy« was too political, and he even agreed with the Italian Fascist Giovanni Bodrero that this crisis corresponded to the crisis of the Enlightenment with its optimistic belief in humanity. He also

---

100 BAIRD, The »Third Way«, p. 399.
101 Ibid., p. 398.
102 Ibid., pp. 401f. In his autobiographical notes from 1939, Bulgakov proclaimed his »progressive« principles of freedom and human dignity, and their irreconcilability with any kind of »totalitarianism«. See Sergij BULGAKOV, Aus meinem Leben. Autobiographische Zeugnisse, Münster 2017, p. 23.
103 Lutz GELDSETZER, Bibliography of the International Congresses of Philosophy. Proceedings 1900–1978, Munich 1981, pp. 33–36. Other Russian participants were Nikolai Lossky (»Die christliche Weltauffassung als allseitige Synthese«), Sergius Hessen (»Das Prinzip der Totalität [tsel'nost'] in der Pädagogik«) and Georg Katkov (»Zur Widerlegung des Pessimismus auf metaphysischem Gebiete«). There were no participants from the Soviet Union. According to Frank, Soviet philosophy manifested its bankruptcy by its absence, while the participating Russians surprisingly shared the same idea »of truth as universal plenitude and absolute unity« without prior consultation among themselves. See ARJAKOVSKY, The Way, p. 349.
104 Semën FRANK, Filosofiia i zhizn' (Mezhdunarodnyi filosofskii s"ezd v Prage), in: Put' 45 (1934), pp. 70f.

criticised the French supporters of democracy for still adhering to their naive belief in reason[105]. Indeed, Bodrero's diagnosis of a »crisis of the human soul« was close to the diagnoses of the Russian thinkers[106]. In Frank's view, the strongest »democrat« at the congress was not a philosopher, but the Czech minister for foreign affairs, Edvard Beneš, who emphasised spiritual freedom as the foundation of any social life[107]. In his conclusion Frank stated a clash of the utilitarian-humanist and the religious-philosophical philosophical tendencies, but appreciated at the same time that at least among each of them national and confessional boundaries had been overcome. Amid the Russian religious philosophers, the Catholics, especially Erich Przywara, made the greatest impression[108]. In short, the positivism and negative attitude towards religion by the French defenders of democracy was the main reason why the Russian philosophers seemed to have more in common with Italian fascists. However, Frank's emphasis on spiritual freedom indicates that there were quite crucial differences as well. In his conference paper, Frank highlighted the feeble persuasiveness of all contemporary social outlooks (*Anschauungen*) in comparison with Christian faith, the Renaissance, and the Enlightenment. Modern thought should, in his opinion, escape from the »web of inadequate concepts« by bravely facing the mystery of reality (in God). An adequate modern philosophy would start from a »knowing state of not knowing« (*wissendes Nichtwissen*) and he suggested Nicholas of Cusa' *docta ignorantia* and »negative theology« as guiding principles for a

> philosophy of tolerance, not in the sense of *formal* toleration of misconceptions, but in the sense of a *factual* (*sachlich*) recognition of the many-sidedness of truth, thus of the relative justification of a variety of principles, hence in the sense of a conscious affirmation of the *coincidentia oppositorum*. It is a philosophy of respect and love, in contrast to the dominant tendency to despise and hate, to annihilate the enemy[109].

Indeed, fascism's hatred of communism was appealing to the »White« elements of the diaspora who were committed to overthrow communism in Russia by any means. Already in 1936, former White Army officers recruited emigres for a new army allied with the Nazis and negotiated Hitler's promise to restore the Russian

---

105 Ibid., pp. 71f.
106 Anatolii I. MAILOV, Russkaia religioznaia filosofiia v »Puti« (Vypusk 1). V protivostoianii k fashizmu i paganizatsii, St Petersburg 1992, p. 15.
107 FRANK, Filosofiia i zhizn', p. 72.
108 Ibid., pp. 74–76.
109 Simon FRANK, Die gegenwärtige geistige Lage und die Idee der negativen Theologie, in: Actes du huitième congrès international de philosophie à Prague 2–7 sept., 1934, ed. by the organising committee, Nendeln 1968, pp. 445–448.

monarchy. In 1941, the Paris police intercepted pamphlets of the Karlovtsi Synod to »incite Russian refugees to join the ranks of the German army by fighting the Soviets«[110]. In that year, 35,000 people called themselves »Russian fascists« and distinguished themselves from Italian and German paganism by their »Christian fascism«[111]. In this light, maintaining a »third way« position became more and more difficult. In the eyes of the majority of Russian emigration in France, the »third way« philosophers were in fact »allied with the franco-masons of the Jew world, and in the counter-espionage service of countries hostile to Germany«[112]. The fact that Berdiaev's Religious-Philosophical Academy, the St Serge Institute, and *The Way* were mainly sponsored by the American YMCA as well as the Church of England and Episcopal Church of the United States added to these suspicions[113].

Other developments indicate that the Russian philosophers nuanced their »antiliberal« positions with regard to notions like »nation« and »people«[114]. First of all, they followed the developments in Germany closely and considered the movement of »German Christians«, who tried to align German Protestantism with Nazism, to be a consequence of the religious crisis of Protestantism[115]. However, Semën Frank (anonymously, because he lived in Berlin[116]), commented on »the voices of conscience in Germany« as a proof of Protestantism's spiritual strength. He praised Karl Barth's open condemnation of the new perversions of Christianity in his »strict

---

110 BAIRD, The »Third Way«, p. 403, 413f., 430–438. On the ambivalent attitude of the Russian Orthodox Church Abroad toward Nazi Germany, see Michael SHKAROVSKY, The Russian Orthodox Church Outside of Russia and the Holocaust, published by the Historical Studies of the Russian Church Abroad (ROCOR), 2016, URL: <https://www.rocorstudies.org/2019/12/07/the-russian-orthodox-church-outside-of-russia-and-the-holocaust> (11-09-2023); Michail SHKAROVSKIJ, Die Kirchenpolitik des Dritten Reiches gegenüber den orthodoxen Kirchen in Osteuropa (1939–1945), Münster 2004.
111 John J. STEPHAN, The Russian Fascists. Tragedy and Farce in Exile 1925–1945, London 1978, p. 57; Denis JDANOFF, »Russische Faschisten«. Der nationalsozialistische Flügel der russischen Emigration im Dritten Reich. Das Forschungsportal zu Ost-, Ostmittel- und Südosteuropa [Digitale Osteuropa-Bibliothek: Geschichte 3], Berlin 2003, p. 27, URL: <https://www.doi.org/10.5282/ubm/epub.548>. See also Mikhail AGURSKY, The Jewish Problem in the Russian Religious Radical Right. The Case of Metropolitan Antonii (Khrapovitskii), in: Ostkirchliche Studien 36/1 (1987), pp. 39–44.
112 BAIRD, The »Third Way«, p. 439.
113 By the same token, some YMCA leaders were accused of socialist beliefs by American anti-Bolshevik groups. Matthew MILLER, The American YMCA and Russian Culture. The Preservation and Expansion of Orthodox Christianity, 1900–1940, Plymouth 2013, p. 19.
114 See Sergei N. BULGAKOV, Natsiia i chelovechestvo, in: Id. (ed.), Sochineniia v 2 tomakh, vol. 2, Moscow 1993, pp. 644–653; Nikolai A. BERDIAEV, Mnogobozhie i natsionalizm, in: Put' 43 (1934), pp. 3–16.
115 Vasilii ZEN'KOVSKII, Krizis protestantisma v Germanii, in: Put' 42 (1934), pp. 56–67, at p. 56.
116 Aleksandr S. TSYGANKOV/Teresa OBOLEVITCH, Nemetskii period filosofskoi biografii S.L. Franka (novye materialy), Moscow 2019, pp. 64–74.

sermon about the absolute otherness of God with regard to the world and culture« and any particular ethnicity. But in Frank's view, Barth was too unforgiving with regard to Christians ready for compromise in order to save the church – which reminded him of accusations against the Russian church in its tragic situation. Criticising Barth's disinterest for religious problems of historic life[117], Frank praised Friedrich Heiler's sensitivity to such problems – especially for the Jewish question, which made the »German Christians« invent fairy tales about Christ's »northern spirit«. As leader of the »High Church« movement (*Hochkirchliche Bewegung*) and editor of *Eine heilige Kirche* (later: *Una sancta*), Heiler reminded the Protestants of the distinction between God and Caesar and of the early Christians' loyal citizenship of Rome – with one exception: The refusal to worship the emperor should be the only reason to become a martyr. If possible, Christians should concentrate on deeds of universal love, especially »for those whom the world deprives of love, for the persecuted and defamed of any sort, for those socially treated like outcasts«[118].

In his journal, Heiler published several articles about Jewish-Christian relations (one of them by Frank[119]), and among them an article about the *Ostkirche und Judentum* (*Eastern Church and Jewry*) by the German Orthodox convert Paul Hoecke, who praised the strong condemnation of the Jews in the Orthodox liturgy[120]. By this publication, Heiler wanted to throw light on »the loveless non-spirit« of certain Christians, and it provoked a sharp protest by the team of the St Serge Institute in Paris against the »unsatisfactory presentation« of the Eastern Churches' view of Judaism. In an open letter, they condemned Hoecke's »anti-Judaism and even antisemitism on a cultural-national basis« by highlighting the antiquated character of the quoted passages in the liturgy and emphasising a spiritual perspective on Jewish-Christian relations[121].

A further important development was that, in the wake of the *World Conference of Life and Work* from 1925 in Stockholm, some Orthodox thinkers quite enthusiastically received Karl Barth's dialectical theology as a »German theological renewal« in contrast to the liberal Protestantism of the nineteenth century[122]. In its very first issue in 1925, *The Way* published an article by the German theologian Paul Tillich about Karl Barth's rejection of Christoph Blumhardt's religious socialism

---

117 Semën FRANK [S.], Golosa khristianskoi sovesti v Germanii, in: Put' 43 (1934), pp. 62–71, at pp. 64–67.
118 Ibid., pp. 69–71.
119 [N.N.], Die Tragödie des Judentums, in: Eine heilige Kirche 4/6 (1934), pp. 128–133, published anonymously »von einem Judenchristen«.
120 Paul HOECKE, Ostkirche und Judentum, in: Eine heilige Kirche 4/6 (1934), pp. 168–173, at p. 173.
121 Sergius BULGAKOFF, Östliche Orthodoxie und Judentum, in: Eine heilige Kirche 7/9 (1934), pp. 266f., at pp. 266f.
122 ARJAKOVSKY, The Way, pp. 169f.

aiming at realising the kingdom of God on earth at the price of transcendence[123]. That was a well-known subject among Russian thinkers. Like Frank, Berdiaev welcomed Barth's project, but criticised its secularised perception of God's creation (*Entgottung der kreatürlichen Welt*), its humiliation of the human person, and its emphasis on God's word instead of God's incarnation[124]. In the same vain, Vasilii Zen'kovskii considered that Barth's emphasis on the freedom of the church went too far by negating any role of the church in history[125]. All in all, the Russian thinkers were impressed by Barth's approach but raised objections against his devaluation of culture, history, and social life.

In addition, the Russian thinkers restated their emphasis on Christian universalism. With regard to church-state relations, Frank expressed a clear sympathy for the supranational universality of the Catholic Church. In a state, freedom of confession should not only be formally acknowledged – as in Soviet Russia – but the state should create conditions for freedom of confession to thrive. He considered a multiplicity of national churches normal because of the church's involvement in human history, but in order to bridge all these worldly separations and diversities, the church must never forget its »supranational unity«. In Frank's view, it was the only and indispensable condition in order to guarantee the freedom of the church, and, in the context of an increasingly pagan world, it should enhance ecumenical cooperation[126].

In the context of the 1930s the notion of »paganisation« was used mainly to describe the spiritual impact of the Nazi regime and as a synonym of »modern zoological antireligious nationalism« and »secularisation«[127]. If earlier, the religious philosophers had defended the value of the nation as a principle of variety against socialist cosmopolitism and the class principle, they now emphasised the church's universality[128]. Berdiaev highlighted this in his review of *Kirche, Volk und Staat*, a volume by some German Protestants who did not participate in the Oxford »World Conference on Church, Community, and State« in 1937 and bluntly negated Christian universalism. In this context, Berdiaev also praised Catholic universalism

---

123 Paul TILLICH, Dialekticheskaia teologiia, in: Put' 1 (1925), pp. 148–154, at p. 148.
124 Nikolaj BERDJAJEW, Die Krisis des Protestantismus und die russische Orthodoxie. Eine Auseinandersetzung mit der dialektischen Theologie, in: Orient und Occident 1 (1929), pp. 11–25, at pp. 16f. See Andreas PANGRITZ, Die Rezeption Karl Barths und der dialektischen Theologie in der russischen Religionsphilosophie, in: Susanne HENNECKE (ed.), Karl Barth und die Religion(en), Göttingen 2018, pp. 247–253.
125 ZEN'KOVSKII, Krizis protestantisma, p. 67.
126 Semën FRANK, Staat und Kirche in der östlichen Orthodoxie, in: Eine heilige Kirche 7/9 (1934), pp. 244–250, at pp. 245–247, 250.
127 STROOP, A Christian Solution, p. 193.
128 MAILOV, Russkaia filosofiia, pp. 51f.

and humanism, as well as the work of Christian conscience done by those German Protestants who »are capable of sacrifice and struggle«[129].

All in all, the Russian philosophers' engagement with European Christian thought led them to overcome their own stereotyped visions of nations and confessions and their own somewhat arrogant Russian Messianism, which was still on display in the 1920s. Their constant struggle against Eurasianist and Russian nationalist and fascist views, but especially their insights with regard to the »German Christians« and the French *Action française* enhanced their awareness of the problem of nationalism within the church[130], and, at least in Bulgakov's case, of the importance of the rule of law[131].

Berdiaev's Religious-Philosophical Academy closed in 1939 and the journals *The Way* and *The New City* ceased publication while the St Serge Institute and the RSCM survived and operated under harsh conditions of isolation. Certain people linked to it were members of the *Action Orthodoxe* following the Nazi occupation, some of whom died as martyrs in German concentration camps[132]. Despite all of their efforts to overcome the concept of restoration by a spiritual revolution, they remained a minority within the Russian emigration[133].

Conclusion

The »ambivalence and incoherence« with regard to the political system of liberal democracy of those Russian Orthodox thinkers mainly considered to be the »progressive« ones, cannot be argued away. But it can be better understood by contextualisation and analysis of their argumentation. With regard to historical context, one has to bear in mind that their main works were written *before* the Second World War. For example, the current debate about the compatibility of the Orthodox tradition and human rights discourse is often held without considering that today's human rights discourse is not a logical consequence of centuries of (Western) intellectual history, but rather an unprecedented historical consequence

---

129 Nikolai A. BERDIAEV, Kirche, Volk und Staat. Stimmen aus der Deutschen Evangelischen Kirche zur Oxforder Konferenz, Berlin 1937 [Review] in: Put' 54 (1937), pp. 74–76, at p. 74, 76. See also Forschungsabteilung des Ökumenischen Rates für Praktisches Christentum (ed.), Kirche, Staat und Mensch. Russisch-orthodoxe Studien, Genf 1937, with contributions by Berdiaev, Bulgakov and others.

130 MAILOV, Russkaia filosofiia, p. 49, 55.

131 ZWAHLEN, Bulgakov's Reinvention, pp. 192f.

132 ARJAKOVSKY, The Way, pp. 521f; see Maria SKOBTSOVA, Pravoslavnoe delo, in: Novyi Grad 10 (1935), pp. 111–115.

133 BAIRD, The »Third Way«, p. 399, 415f., 425.

of (not only Western) common political decisions *after* the devastating war experiences in the twentieth century[134]. Moreover, it is well known that many Western Christians and Churches developed strong statements about the Christian foundations of human rights only after the Second World War. Therefore, especially in Berdiaev's, Frank's, and Bulgakov's case, I suggest their intellectual development might be compared with that of their Catholic friend Jacques Maritain. He underwent a development from a rather anti-liberal personalism in the 1930s to a quite new conjunction of the concepts of human dignity and individual rights after the Second World War and became a founding father of the »Universal Declaration of Human Rights« in 1948[135] and of the declaration of *Dignitatis humanae* by the Second Vatican Council in 1965[136].

These Russian thinkers in exile took both the problem of *sobornost'* – the social challenge of a »healthy« balance between the person, the individual, and community – and the »post-secular« problem of the place of religion and the church in modern secular societies seriously. As mentioned earlier, they did not elaborate positive, easily applicable visions of a Christian society. After all, they knew their own arguments against utopian visions of building a (socialist) kingdom on earth and against »theocratic« systems like Russian autocracy, the aspirations of power-hungry church hierarchs and other totalitarian temptations far too well. In view of the monarchist tendencies among the majority of the Russian emigration and the rise of Communist and Nazi rule, they rather developed aspects of a »negative political theology« in order to avoid the church's political instrumentalisation in the future. In their view, »theocracy« neither uses violence, nor is it a political or an economic system. They insisted on the meaning of history and culture, historical relativity of institutions, Christian universalism and the personal responsibility of humankind to stand up for individual freedom and social justice using the political instruments of their time. They mainly drew on theological concepts of humans created in the image and likeness of God, the royal priesthood of all Christians, the distinction between God and Caesar, and advocated for the freedom of the church within the framework of freedom of conscience and religion.

---

134 Linde LINDKVIST, Religious Freedom and the Universal Declaration of Human Rights, Cambridge 2017, p. x.

135 Samuel MOYN, Personalism, Community, and the Origins of Human Rights, in: Stefan-Ludwig HOFFMANN (ed.), Human Rights in the Twentieth Century, Cambridge 2010, pp. 85–106, at pp. 85–87; MAKRIDES, Orthodox Personalism, p. 244, 270. Actually, »The Universal Declaration of Human Rights« is a good example for »negative political theology«, because for the sake of international recognition, the UN Commission on Human Rights deliberately, and after many debates, abstained from metaphysical justifications. See Regula M. ZWAHLEN, Christliche Akteure und Menschenrechte, in: Religion & Gesellschaft in Ost und West 46/12 (2018), pp. 8–10.

136 On Berdiaev's role, see Gianmaria ZAMAGNI, Das »Ende des konstantinischen Zeitalters« und die Modelle aus der Geschichte für eine »neue Christenheit«, Freiburg im Breisgau 2018.

As for Berdiaev, seemingly the least »democratic« and most ambivalent thinker of the Russian diaspora, he considered freedom of thought the emigration's main task[137]. In his writings explored above, he only mentioned in passing that in the new post-revolutionary period, secularisation and democracy provided the best political conditions for such freedom. By claiming that secularisation was a sad consequence of the religious autocracies' failure[138], Berdiaev was inconsistent with regard to his own logic of providential historical development. If Constantine's confusion of God's and Caesar's kingdoms by introducing Christian statehood was part of God's providence, so was secularisation. Such ambivalence with regard to secular politics, greeted in the name of freedom, but negated in the name of a »real Christian society«, caused many further inconsistencies in Berdiaev's and other emigrants' »political theologies«.

However, I suggest that if we take into account their theological works, their main intellectual framework does not establish an opposition between theocracy and democracy, but between anthropocracy and »theanthropocracy«. They redefined »theocracy« in a way that any modern secular thought that stands up for universal human dignity and social justice finds even stronger justification in their concept of God-Manhood in the sense of God-human synergy, as long as it does not bluntly deny or fight the concept of religion. On this basis, their »negative political theology« contributed to what contemporary Orthodox theologians under new historical circumstances are developing as a positive Orthodox political theology in terms of »Chalcedonian politics«[139] or of an »Eastern Orthodox Christian Theology of Secularism«[140].

---

137 BERDIAEV, Dnevnik filosofa, p. 176.
138 Id., Tsarstvo Bozhie, p. 39.
139 Aristotle PAPANIKOLAOU, Overcoming Political Nestorianism. Towards a Chalcedonian Politics, in: Martin G. POULSOM et al. (eds.), Grace, Governance and Globalization, London 2017, pp. 114–124, at pp. 120f.; Nathaniel WOOD, »I Have Overcome the World«. The Church, the Liberal State, and Christ's Two Natures in the Russian Politics of Theosis, in: George E. DEMACOPOULOS/Aristotle PAPANIKOLAOU (eds.), Christianity, Democracy, and the Shadow of Constantine, New York 2017, pp. 155–171, at p. 167.
140 Brandon GALLAHER, A Secularism of the Royal Doors. Toward and Eastern Orthodox Christian Theology of Secularism, in: Aristotle PAPANIKOLAOU/George DEMACOPOULOS (eds.), Fundamentalism or Tradition. Christianity after Secularism, New York 2019, pp. 108–130.

Kristina Stoeckl

The Origins, Development and Diffusion of »Political Hesychasm«

Introduction

Hesychasm is a meditative prayer tradition practiced by Orthodox monks since early Christian times. The practice was conceptualised theologically in the fourteenth century by Gregory Palamas (1296/97–1359). Since then, Hesychasm has become the object of numerous theological and philosophical treatments, in particular during the »Silver Age« of Russian religious philosophy. But only in the mid-twentieth century, under the unlikely conditions of Soviet communism and the Cold War, do we find two distinctively political interpretations of Hesychasm by the Russian philologist Gelian Prokhorov (1936–2017) and the Russian second-generation émigré theologian John Meyendorff (1926–1992). This chapter outlines the origins of »Political Hesychasm« in the treatments of Meyendorff and Prokhorov and then traces the influence of this concept in contemporary Russian philosophy and Orthodox theology. The focus lies on recent treatments of political Hesychasm by Orthodox authors who have made the concept the ground for political arguments about Christian Orthodox uniqueness and anti-Westernism. The chapter closes with a discussion of contemporary treatments of political Hesychasm that resist the trend of Orthodox anti-Westernism.

The Neo-patristic turn in Orthodox theology in the twentieth century has frequently been criticised for ignoring the real social and political problems in contemporary societies and for failing, therefore, to develop an Orthodox social ethics and a political theology that is up to the challenges of the modern world. The sharp distinction made by Paul Valliere and Robert Bird between the Neo-patristic school and the »modern theology« of the »Russian School« is a case in point for this judgment[1]. This assessment overlooks, however, that the Neo-patristic turn has also produced its own political theology: the theology of political Hesychasm.

Political Hesychasm is a topic that cannot be omitted from a publication about »Orthodox Christian Political Theologies«. It represents one piece in of the puzzle

---

1 Paul VALLIERE, Modern Russian Theology. Bukharev, Soloviev, Bulgakov. Orthodox Theology in a New Key, Edinburgh 2000; Robert BIRD, The Tragedy of Russian Religious Philosophy. Sergei Bulgakov and the Future of Orthodox Theology, in: Jonathan SUTTON/Wil van den BERCKEN (eds.), Orthodox Christianity and Contemporary Europe, Leuven 2003, pp. 211–228.

that is the contemporary panorama of political theologies in the Orthodox context. The study of its history, development, and present-day usage illuminates important facets of contemporary Orthodox theological thought. As I set out to offer, in this chapter, a critical analysis of political Hesychasm, I can draw on several studies that make my task easier. These are, first, the essay »*Der Nördliche Katechon*« by Michael Hagemeister, who offers a broad contextualisation of political Hesychasm in Russian Eurasian and Slavophile thought from the beginning of the nineteenth to the twenty-first century[2]; second, a book chapter by Andrey Shishkov that contains a critical appraisal of Hesychasm and Neo-Palamism in the context of contemporary Orthodox theology[3]; and third, the book-length study by Daniel Payne of political Hesychasm in contemporary Greek-Orthodox thought[4]. I also draw on a few short texts and book reviews written by myself in the past and on first-hand debates with two contemporary representatives of Hesychast studies, namely Sergei S. Horujy (Khoruzhii) and Vladimir Petrunin[5]. This chapter does not present a completely new argument with respect to any of these texts. Instead, it draws together the different interpretations and debates elaborated in various languages (German, Russian, English) and disciplines (history, theology, philosophy) in order to answer the question where political Hesychasm as a concept comes from, where it stands today and what practical implications it has for the self-understanding of Orthodox Christians. With the exception of my references to Payne and Yannaras, who discuss political Hesychasm in the Greek-Orthodox context, my focus in this chapter is on Russia.

---

2 Michael HAGEMEISTER, Der »Nördliche Katechon« – »Neobyzantismus« und »Politischer Hesychasmus« im postsowjetischen Russland, Erfurt 2016.
3 Andrey SHISHKOV, Eastern Orthodoxy, Conservatism, and (Neo)Palamite Tradition in Post-Soviet Russia, in: Mikhail SUSLOV/Dmitry UZLANER (eds.), Contemporary Russian Conservatism. Problems, Paradoxes, and Perspectives, Leiden 2019 pp. 321–346.
4 Daniel PAYNE, The Revival of Political Hesychasm in Contemporary Orthodox Thought. The Political Hesychasm of John Romanides and Christos Yannaras, Lanham, MD 2011.
5 Kristina STOECKL, Political Hesychasm? Vladimir Petrunin's Neo-Byzantine Interpretation of the Social Doctrine of the Russian Orthodox Church, in: Studies in East European Thought 62/1 (2010), pp. 125–133; ead., Book Review: The Revival of Political Hesychasm in Contemporary Orthodox Thought. The Political Hesychasm of John Romanides and Christos Yannaras, by Daniel P. PAYNE; Vladimir PETRUNIN, Politicheskii Isikhazm i ego traditsii v sotsial'noi kontseptsii Moskovskogo Patriarkhata, in: Journal of Contemporary Religion 26/3 (2011), pp. 499–502; Kristina STOECKL, Book Review: The Globalization of Hesychasm and the Jesus Prayer. Contesting Contemplation, in: Journal of Contemporary Religion 27/1 (2012), pp. 166f. Information about a seminar-discussion with S. Horujy and V. Petrunin (in Russian): Заседание семинара. В.В. Петрунин, published by the Institute of Synergetic Anthropology, URL: <http://synergia-isa.ru/?p=8604> (11-13-2023).

I. What is Hesychasm?

For a start and especially for readers who are new to the term »Hesychasm«, a clarification is necessary. Hesychasm (from Greek *hesychia*, »stillness«) describes the tradition of contemplative prayer in Eastern Orthodox Christianity. Hesychasm is generally used as a shorthand for Orthodox asceticism, but more precisely it refers to the practice of the »Jesus Prayer«. The Jesus Prayer is a psychosomatic prayer and meditation technique, the origins of which go back to the desert fathers of the first centuries of Christianity[6]. Through the incessant, concentrated repetition of the name of Jesus Christ that follows the rhythm of the heart's beating, the ascetic is said to reach inner peace (*hesychia*) and freedom from all passions (*apatheia*), and to experience an ecstatic vision of God (*theoria*). In the fourteenth century, the question whether the sensual experiences that practitioners reported to have gone through during prayer, like the vision of light or the perception of pleasant smell, should be considered a true experience of divine reality or purely subjective imagination, led to a divisive theological dispute. One the one side stood those who insisted on the divine reality of the visions experienced during ascetic practices, on the other side stood the sceptics, who considered the divine to be unknowable and intangible. The first group was led by Gregory Palamas, a monk, theologian and Archbishop of Thessaloniki in the late Byzantine period; the second by the theologian Barlaam of Calabria (ca. 1290–1348). It was in the context of this conceptual struggle that Palamas developed his theological justification of Hesychasm. This justification rested on the distinction between the divine essence, which is unknowable, and divine energies, which emanate from the divine essence like rays of light from the sun and which are accessible to human experience. Palamas' teaching of divine energies was rejected as heretic by scholastic theologians in Rome, but was recognised as a dogma by the Byzantine Orthodox Church in 1341, 1347, and 1351. Since then, Hesychasm has been considered a specific feature distinguishing Orthodox theology from Western Christianity[7].

In the popular book *Why Angels Fall. A Journey through Orthodox Europe from Byzantium to Kosovo*, Victoria Clark documents the lived experience of Hesychasm in Orthodox monasteries in Southeastern Europe[8]. Furthermore, in *The Globalization of the Jesus Prayer*, Christopher Johnson studies Hesychasm outside the

---

6 Christopher D. L. JOHNSON, The Globalization of Hesychasm and the Jesus Prayer. Contesting Contemplation, London 2010, pp. 16f.
7 The description of the hesychast controversy in this paragraph is summarised from HAGEMEISTER, »Der Nördliche Katechon«, pp. 18–20.
8 Victoria CLARK, Why Angels Fall. A Journey through Orthodox Europe from Byzantium to Kosovo, London 2001.

Eastern Christian context, as one popular spiritual exercise among others that is finding followers among urban spiritual seekers across the Western world[9].

Whereas Hesychasm and the Jesus Prayer denote a religious practice, it is really their doctrinal justification, Palamism, that assumes a political character. Political Hesychasm interprets the theological struggle of the past between hesychasts and scholastics as the intellectual backdrop to a confrontation between East and West that is defined chiefly in political and cultural terms. The outcome of this struggle is said to determine the history of Orthodox civilisation all the way from Byzantium to contemporary Russia. I will discuss this interpretation of political Hesychasm, the main focus of my contribution, in sections II and III. There also exists, however, an alternative interpretation of Hesychasm and Palamism, which draws theological conclusions from Palamism that are at odds with the prevalent anti-modern and anti-Western political and cultural interpretation. I will call this approach »ethical Hesychasm« and discuss it in section IV.

II. Political Hesychasm in Byzantine and Russian Studies in the Twentieth Century

The term »Political Hesychasm« was coined and explored in the 1960s and 1970s by the Orthodox second-generation émigré theologian John Meyendorff (1926–1992) and by the Soviet historian Gelian Prokhorov (1936–2017)[10]. Meyendorff and Prokhorov spoke of political Hesychasm in the historical context of political struggles in Byzantium in the middle of the fourteenth century. From their theological and historical perspective, political Hesychasm was the main answer to a historical-political puzzle, namely to the question how the Orthodox Church survived the fall of the Byzantine Empire.

After centuries of almost complete scholarly neglect, the study of Gregory Palamas and his theology of Hesychasm was revived by Meyendorff, who wrote a path-breaking dissertation about him[11]. Meyendorff was a student of Georges Florovsky,

---

9 JOHNSON, The Globalization of Hesychasm.
10 Daniel Payne gives a good overview of the early study of Palamism in the twentieth century. Among the first scholars to study Palamas systematically were the Russian Bishop Basil Krivocheine, who wrote the first major work on Palamas, published in Prague in 1936, and the Romanian theologian Dumitru Stăniloae, who in 1938 published *The Life and Teaching of St Gregory Palamas*, a work that remained largely unknown due to a lack of translations from Romanian. Archimandrite Cyprian Kern wrote in 1947 *Elements of the Theology of Gregory Palamas*. This was the literature on Palamas available to the two students of Georges Florovsky, Vladimir Lossky and John Meyendorff, whose major works have shaped Orthodox theology in the twentieth century in a Palamist key. See PAYNE, The Revival, pp. 126–128.
11 John MEYENDORFF, St Grégoire Palamas et la mystique orthodoxe, Paris 1959.

the father of the Neo-patristic turn in twentieth century Orthodox theology; and from the perspective of patristic theology, it was only to be expected that Palamas and his teaching would also come under new scrutiny. In the panorama of over a millennium of patristic literature, Palamas comes rather late – long after the Orthodox Church defined its relationship to the Byzantine state and almost three centuries after the culmination of dogmatic differences between Orthodox and Latin Christianity in the schism of 1054. And yet, hardly any other theologian from late antiquity to the end of the Middle Ages has inspired so many commentators in the twentieth and even the twenty-first century. This is doubtlessly due to the pivotal role he played in distinguishing Orthodox teaching from Latin scholasticism in the crucial period of the fourteenth century, his influence on monasticism, and the impact of his teaching on the religious and political life of late Byzantium.

Meyendorff uses the term »Political Hesychasm« to refer to a social, cultural, and political programme carried out in the fourteenth century by prominent Byzantine leaders, which had widespread influence in Slavic countries[12]. According to Meyendorff, the hesychast monks from Mount Athos promoted »new forms of Orthodox universalism«[13] that allowed Orthodoxy to survive even after the fall of the empire.

The [hesychast] revival was linked with catastrophic events [...]: the empire and the cultural pride of Byzantium had been shattered by Latin conquests and the Turkish challenge. There was no reliable anchor of salvation left except the Orthodox Church. But the church's strength was not seen in structures contingent to the empire, but rather in its eschatological, mystical and ascetical traditions, maintained by monks[14].

Meyendorff credits the theology and practice of Hesychasm with preserving the Orthodox Church at a time when its institutional structure, previously supported by the Byzantine state, had been almost shattered.

This interpretation is echoed by the Soviet Byzantinist Gelian Prokhorov, who first proposed the term »Political Hesychasm« in the mid-1960s[15]. He distinguished three periods of Hesychasm in Byzantine history: a »private [*keleinyi*] period«, during which Hesychasm was practiced by monks, but did not have a larger societal

---

12 Id., Byzantine Hesychasm, London 1974.
13 Id., Rome, Constantinople, Moscow. Historical and Theological Studies, New York 1996, p. 43.
14 Ibid., pp. 41f.
15 Gelian Prokhorov, Isikhazm i obshchestvennaia mysl' v vostochnoi Evrope v XIV v., in: Literaturnye sviazi drevnikh slavian (Trudy otdela drevnerusskoi literatury) 23 (1968), pp. 86–108. See also id., Ètnicheskaia integratsiia v vostochnoi Evrope v XIV veke. Ot isikhastskikh sporov do Kulikovskoi bitvy, in: Doklady otdeleniia etnografii 65/2 (1966), pp. 81–100; id., Kul'turnoe Svoeobrazie Epochi Kulikovskoj Bitvy, in: Kulikovskaia bitva i pod'em natsional'nogo samopoznaniia (Trudy otdela drevnerusskoi literatury) 34 (1979), pp. 3–17.

impact; a »monastic [*kinovial'nyi*] period«, in the mid-fourteenth century, which saw the theological elaboration of Hesychasm in the dispute between Gregory Palamas and Barlaam of Calabria; and a third period of »political [*politicheskii*] Hesychasm«, from the mid-fourteenth century until the fall of Constantinople in 1453, during which Hesychasm left the monasteries and became a social phenomenon[16]. At the end of a period of civil war in Byzantium, in 1347, all important positions in the Orthodox Church of Constantinople were occupied by hesychasts, i. e., followers of Palamas who had stood on the side of the winning party in the civil war. In this period, Hesychasm became, in the words of Prokhorov's student Vladimir Petrunin, a »political factor of East European dimensions«[17]. During the first half of the fifteenth century, the Orthodox Church faced the option of union with the Roman Catholic Church, under preparation at the Councils of Basel and Ferrara-Florence. The union was supported by the last Byzantine rulers, in particular by Constantine XI Palaiologos, but it was fiercely opposed by the hesychast clerics. Ultimately, this disagreement led to a break between the religious and secular leadership of Constantinople, which contributed to its fall to the Ottomans in 1453. The following quotes from Petrunin's book are indicative of this interpretation:

> The Orthodox Church preserved the purity of its teaching by burying the Byzantine Empire, or rather, that what remained of it. The church preferred Turkish domination over union [with the Roman Catholic Church][18].

> We see that the church did not ally itself passively with the politics of the emperor's court [...] it did not sacrifice the purity of its faith in a closer religious and political alliance with the Catholic West[19].

> In the last hundred years of existence of the Byzantine Empire, the church was the custodian of the imperial idea, not the imperial court of Palaiologos[20].

Both Prokhorov and Meyendorff concur that Hesychasm spread from Mount Athos to the Balkans and Russia through the work of travelling monks and translations of hesychast literature in Slavic languages. »Perhaps the most spectacular development connected with the hesychast revival«, Meyendorff writes, »was the spread of

---

16 Vladimir PETRUNIN, Politicheskii Isikhazm i ego traditsii v sotsialnoi kontseptsii Moskovskogo Patriarkhata, St Petersburg 2009, p. 31 (all translations from Russian are my own).
17 Ibid., p. 66.
18 Ibid.
19 Ibid., p. 69.
20 Ibid., p. 70.

monasticism in northern Russia. St Sergius of Radonezh (ca. 1314–1392) was the acknowledged father of this Northern Thebaid, as it began to be called«[21]. Also in the Russian context, Meyendorff writes, the hesychasts took on a political role:

> In the spirit of the Byzantine hesychasts, his contemporaries, Sergius became involved in the social and political life of the times. […] He supported the unity of the Church of Russia – whose dioceses were located throughout the bitterly feuding Principalities of Moscow and Lithuania – and blessed Moscovite troops before their first victorious battle against the Mongols (1380)[22].

For both Meyendorff and Prokhorov, therefore, political Hesychasm was a theological and a political programme, something that involved a specific religious practice and determinate political action[23]. It is important to stress that for both the main puzzle was the survival of the church in times of political breakdown, namely, the endurance of a living practice and faith when the institutional structures that supported the church were shattered both by attacks from outside as well as by a perceived internal weakness. The political Hesychasm of Meyendorff and Prokhorov must, I believe, be read as much as a judgment on Orthodoxy in late Byzantium and as a comment on the Orthodox Churches under communism during the Cold War. For both scholars it seems to have been evident that, through the teachings of Palamism, the Orthodox faith would resist communist atheism in the monasteries and in theology.

Michael Hagemeister points to an important additional source for the study of Hesychasm, in particular for Prokhorov. This is the philosophy of names (*imyaslavie*), connected with the names of Pavel Florensky and Aleksei Losev[24]. Prokhorov repeats an idea already developed by Florensky, namely that of a »new Middle Ages« as an alternative to the Western Renaissance. The teachings of Palamas are interpreted by Prokhorov as a »pre-Renaissance counter-Reformation« or a specifically »Orthodox Renaissance«, one which does not emulate the return to pagan antiquity of which the Western Renaissance is declared »guilty«. Palamism, Hagemeister summarises, is understood to prepare the conditions for a mystical-contemplative equivalent to rationalist, secular humanism[25].

---

21 MEYENDORFF, Rome, Constantinople, Moscow, p. 44.
22 Ibid., p. 44.
23 Kallistos WARE, Act out of Stillness. The Influence of Fourteenth-Century Hesychasm on Byzantine and Slav Civilization, Toronto 1995, p. 4.
24 Michael HAGEMEISTER, Imjaslavie – Imjadejstvie. Namensmystik und Namensmagie in Russland (1900–1930), in: Tatjana PATZER (ed.), Namen: Benennung – Verehrung – Wirkung. Positionen der europäischen Moderne, Berlin 2009, pp. 77–98.
25 HAGEMEISTER, Der »Nördliche Katechon«, pp. 20–22.

III. Political Hesychasm in Twenty-First Century Russia

In twenty-first century Russia, after the end of the USSR, political Hesychasm has received renewed attention. Proponents of political Hesychasm see the church in a struggle with Western influences and with a Russian state and society that are not sufficiently »resilient« in their Orthodoxy and liable to »succumb« to Western influences. The main interpretative lines have not changed from the 1960s and 1970s, when Meyendorff and Prokhorov popularised the concept. Despite the changed historical circumstances, the »lesson« of Palamism continues to appear persuasive, at least to the contemporary interpreters of political Hesychasm I will introduce below.

Vladimir Petrunin, a student of Prokhorov's, has produced an updated version of political Hesychasm for the twenty-first century. In *Politicheskii Isikhazm i ego traditsii v sotsial'noi kontseptsii Moskovskogo Patriarkhata*, published by the Aleteiia publishing house in St Petersburg in 2009, he argues that in the year 2000, more than 500 years after the fall of Byzantium, the ideas of political Hesychasm had found a new embodiment in the official document of the Russian Orthodox Church *The Bases of the Social Concept of the Russian Orthodox Church* (hereafter referred to as »Social Doctrine«), especially in the exposition of the principles that guide the relationship with the state[26]. For Petrunin, the Russian Orthodox Church is again facing the challenge of fighting off Western influence, and political Hesychasm is the intellectual armour to this effect. Disobedience to the state might be the only means to achieve this goal. Prokhorov wrote the foreword to Petrunin's study. The frontispiece carries a blessing of the Metropolitan Ilarion (Alfeev), then still Bishop of Vienna and Austria[27].

In his study, the author Petrunin draws a parallel between the late Byzantine and the post-Soviet period. He demonstrates that the former was characterised by the elaboration of the theology of Hesychasm in response to the influence of Western scholasticism and humanism, while the latter, in Russia today, is characterised by the formulation of an Orthodox social teaching in response to Western secularism, liberalism, and capitalism. Petrunin explains in the introduction that the book is a comment on the definition of church independence (the principle of non-subordination, *nepovinovenie*) in the »Social Doctrine«. The »Social Doctrine« was adopted by the Russian Orthodox Church in the year 2000 and was generally perceived as an important step towards the church's renewal and self-positioning after the fall of communism. Church-independence was one important principle

---

26 PETRUNIN, Politicheskij Isikhazm, p 80.
27 The summary of Petrunin on the next three pages follows my previous exposition in STOECKL, Political Hesychasm.

enshrined in the »Social Doctrine«. The precise definition can be found in section III.5, which I quote according to the official English translation on the website of the Moscow Patriarchate:

> The church remains loyal to the state, but God's commandment to fulfil the task of salvation in any situation and under any circumstances is above this loyalty. If the authority forces Orthodox believers to apostatise from Christ and His church and to commit sinful and spiritually harmful actions, the church should refuse to obey the state[28].

Orthodoxy derives its authority from two sources, theology and tradition (*predanie*). Petrunin explains the principle of non-subordination not on grounds of theology, but on grounds of tradition, i. e., he looks for historical precedents of non-subordination of the church *vis-à-vis* the state. He finds such precedents during the last century of the Byzantine Empire: In that period, he argues, the Orthodox Church developed an autonomous political standpoint and strategy *vis-à-vis* the Byzantine rulers, whom it reproached for their collaboration with Western powers and the Roman Catholic Church. The fact that the Patriarchate of Constantinople did not go along with the emperors' policy of rapprochement is interpreted by Petrunin as a manifestation of the principle of non-subordination and political Hesychasm.

In the second half of the book, Petrunin presents the Russian Orthodox Church as the stronghold of Russian identity in the post-Soviet transition. The following quotes amply exemplify this argument:

> The end of the twentieth century saw the attempt to construct a new statehood of Russia on liberal values, elaborated in the framework of Western European culture. Russia proclaimed itself part of the Western world, which led to the *de facto* denial of the independent existence of an Orthodox civilisation, the centre of which was, after the fall of the Byzantine Empire, Russia[29].

---

28 »The Bases of the Social Concept of the Russian Orthodox Church (Official Translation)«, Official Website of the Department for External Church Relations of the Moscow Patriarchate, URL: <https://www.mospat.ru/en/documents/social-concepts/>. Because of access restrictions imposed in the European Union on Russian propagandistic websites, the official page of the Russian Orthodox Patriarchate was on 16 November 16 2023 inaccessible; see alternative on the website of the Russian Orthodox Church in Diaspora, URL: <https://russianorthodoxchurch.ca/en/the-basis-of-the-social-concept-of-the-russian-orthodox-church/2408> (11-16-2023).

29 PETRUNIN, Politicheskii Isikhazm, p. 81.

In exchange for Russian (*russkii*) Orthodox and Soviet communist universalism, there arrived a Russian (*rossiiskii*) liberal globalism, which looked at Russia not as independent centre in the world, but included it in the orbit of the Western civilisation[30].

It is entirely clear that only Orthodoxy is the guarantee for the independent existence of Russia in the contemporary world. Today the Moscow Patriarchate is the one and only organisation that has maintained millenary continuity over the entire course of Russian history[31].

In his foreword, Gelian Prokhorov writes that this book is »a warning« to the government and to secular society. The warning consists in the fact that the Russian Orthodox Church might deny – and may exhort its members to deny – support to the Russian government in case this government should leave the path of truth as defined by the Orthodox Church.

Today in Russia, just like 600 years ago in the Byzantine Empire, the Orthodox Church is the only serious and organised opponent to the West and its secular values. […] The further movement of Russia down the road of secularisation could constitute a dangerous precedent for the church to make use of its right to call the people to civil disobedience[32].

Prokhorov even goes one step further, calling Russia »doomed« were it to forfeit the church's support. He writes that in periods where the state and the church were in harmony – such as the period of Constantine the Great, that of Prince Vladimir in the Kievan Rus' and of Dmitrij Donskoj – »miracles could happen«, meaning »the birth of a people« (*etnogenez*). The example of the fall of Byzantium showed, in his view, just like the fall of the Romanov Empire and of the Communist Regime, that when the church denied the state its support, this state was doomed[33]. »The author sees and shows«, Gelian Prokhorov writes about his student Petrunin,

the remarkable similarity between the situation of post-communist contemporary Russia, having surrendered to the pressures of liberalism and globalisation, and the late Byzantine period, re-established after overcoming sixteen hundred years of exploitation by the Latin Empire. In the difficult political circumstances of the fourteenth and fifteenth century, the Byzantine rulers and humanists gave in to the pressures from the West. Only the

---

30 Ibid.
31 Ibid., p. 82.
32 Ibid., pp. 122f.
33 Ibid., pp. 7f.

Orthodox Church proved to be, then as now, the fortress that withstood this contaminating influence[34].

With this book, Petrunin interpreted the political theology of the »Social Doctrine« in a very different key from most other commentators. Several readers (including myself[35]) saw in the »Social Doctrine«, when it was approved by the Holy Synod in 2000, a first step towards a genuine Orthodox social ethics in a modern key. Rudolf Uertz, for example, wrote that »the document contains important impulses for a constructive confrontation with the modern order«[36], and Konstantin Kostjuk interpreted the »Social Doctrine« as an important step towards becoming more modern and as a self-ascribed challenge for the church[37]. Alexander Agadjanian, more cautiously, emphasised the ambivalence of the document between a pragmatic social and a conservative political agenda[38]. Upon reading Petrunin's interpretation of the »Social Doctrine«, this conservative political agenda stands out very clearly. In his reading, the »Social Doctrine« manifests the opposition of the Russian Orthodox Church to the liberalisation, democratisation, and secularisation of the Russian state. With the hindsight of almost twenty years since the publication of the »Social Doctrine«, we can say that the anti-Western, anti-democratic Orthodox political theology detected by Petrunin appears to have caught the gist of this document more authentically than the optimistic, almost enthusiastic comments of observers who saw in it, like Uertz, »a constructive confrontation with the modern order«.

Petrunin's treatment of the »Social Doctrine« is couched in an interpretative context not immediately associated with the politically pragmatic leaders of the Moscow Patriarchate, but instead with the most conservative intellectual and fundamentalist clerical circles. The argument that the history of Byzantium presents a »lesson« to the contemporary Russian state is commonly heard among conservatives in Russia. The most prominent example of this narrative was a tele-

---

34 Ibid., p. 5.
35 STOECKL, Political Hesychasm.
36 Rudolf UERTZ/Lars Peter SCHMIDT (eds.), Beginn einer neuen Ära? Die Sozialdoktrin der Russisch-Orthodoxen Kirche vom August 2000 im interkulturellen Dialog, Moscow 2004, p. 95.
37 Konstantin KOSTJUK, Die Sozialdoktrin der Russisch-Orthodoxen Kirche. Schritt zur Zivilgesellschaft oder Manifest des Orthodoxen Konservatismus?, in: Rudolf UERTZ/Josef THESING (eds.), Die Grundlagen der Sozialdoktrin der Russisch-Orthodoxen Kirche. Deutsche Übersetzung mit Einführung und Kommentar, St Ottilien 2001, pp. 174–196; Konstantin KOSTJUK, Die Sozialdoktrin. Herausforderung für die Tradition und die Theologie der Orthodoxie, in: UERTZ/SCHMIDT (eds.), Beginn einer neuen Ära?, pp. 67–74; Konstantin KOSTJUK, Der Begriff des Politischen in der Russisch-Orthodoxen Tradition, Paderborn 2005.
38 Alexander AGADJANIAN, Breakthrough to Modernity. Apologia for Traditionalism: The Russian Orthodox View of Society and Culture in Comparative Perspective, in: Religion, State & Society 31/4 (2003), pp. 327–346.

vision documentary, produced in 2008, which presented the history of the fall of Byzantium in such terms. In this documentary, entitled *Gibel' imperii. Vizantiiskii urok*, Archimandrite Tikhon (Shevkunov) explains the fall of the Byzantine Empire as a consequence of »inner weakness« and Western harmful influence and indirectly recommends a series of steps in order to prevent a repetition of history, for example the nationalisation of natural resources, the suppression of oligarchs, the safeguarding of the Orthodox faith against sects and proselytism[39].

To be precise, the term »Political Hesychasm« is not always used by authors representative of this position, such as Alexander Dugin or Arkadii Maler. Even though Dugin is the more well-known of the two, both have developed an ideology of »Neo-Byzantism« according to which Russia is the »withstander« (*katechon*) to *Western* expansion[40]. Their interpretation of Palamism, Orthodox mysticism, and the Byzantine legacy connects seamlessly to the views by Prokhorov and Petrunin outlined above. The ideology finds a concrete application in the interpretation of Crimea annexation by Russia[41]. Maler wrote on his blog:

> When the hesychast doctrine was established, Byzantium experienced the era of its decline, and Moscow Rus', on the other hand, began to rise. [...] At the same time, St Sergius of Radonezh founded the Trinity Monastery near Moscow, and the Kiev Metropolis finally ceased to have the name of the Kiev and became the Moscow Metropolis, in the time of Metropolitan Alexy (1354–1378). The triumph of Hesychasm occurred in the rise of Moscow Rus', the last stronghold of independent Orthodoxy. And today, the return of Tavria to Russia frees her from all the threats to canonical Orthodoxy in Ukraine – both

---

39 The website of the film, including an English version of the complete text, can be found at URL: <http://vizantia.info> (11-13-2023).
40 See references in Hagemeister, Der »Nördliche Katechon« as well as Marlene Laruelle, Aleksandr Dugin. A Russian Version of the European Radical Right?, in: Woodrow Wilson International Center for Scholars and Kennan Institute Occasional Papers Series 294 (2006), Single Issue; Anton Shekhovtsov/Andreas Umland, Is Aleksandr Dugin a Traditionalist? »Neo-Eurasianism« and Perennial Philosophy, in: The Russian Review 68/4 (2009), pp. 662–678; Anton Barbashin/Hannah Thoburn, Putin's Brain. Alexander Dugin and the Philosophy Behind Putin's Invasion of Crimea, in: Foreign Affairs, p. 31 March 2014, URL: <https://www.foreignaffairs.com/articles/russia-fsu/2014-03-31/putins-brain> (11-13-2023); Mikhail Sokolov, New Right-Wing Intellectuals in Russia. Strategies of Legitimization, in: Russian Politics & Law 47/1 (2009), pp. 47–75; Maria Engström, Contemporary Russian Messianism and New Russian Foreign Policy, in: Contemporary Security Policy 35/3 (2014), pp. 356–379.
41 I summarise this discussion of »Political Hesychasm« and the Crimea question from Shishkov, Eastern Orthodoxy.

Uniate influence and autocephalist schism. For those who care about which church they join and which priest they confess to, this liberation is of absolute importance[42].

In this view, the annexing of Crimea to Russia becomes a symbolic restoration of the succession of Byzantium to Russia in modern times. Thus, Ukraine becomes the territory where the clash between the New Byzantium and the West occurs. For this reason, political Hesychasm also appeals to Russian nationalists. Egor Kholmogorov lays bare the theologian-hesychasts' idea of nation:

> Did the hesychasts have, at the same time, their own idea of nation, which could be opposed to pagan nationalism? Without a doubt, they did. It was the conception of the »holy nation« [*narod*], animated by zeal for Orthodoxy, whose members arranged their lives according to God's Law, and in return, received God's special blessing and special powers of grace in all their being[43].

The role of the »holy nation« is, of course, assigned to the Russians:

> The greatest of the hesychast Patriarchs, Philotheos Kokkinos, the disciple of Palamas, saw in the role of such a holy nation […] Russians. […] The Byzantine hesychasts quite consciously singled out the Russians for their outstanding spiritual qualities, for the unusual intensity of their spiritual life […][44].

In this way, political Hesychasm becomes the basis for a nationalist ideology of the chosenness of the Russian people. In the ideological cauldron of the Russian extreme right, political Hesychasm is one influential ingredient.

IV. Ethical Hesychasm

Throughout this chapter, I have used the term »political theology« in the sense of a theological approach to the political. It makes sense to speak about political theologies in the plural as »the ways in which theology conceives of the relationship of the church and of her mission to bring about salvation in relation to the political

---

42 Arkadii MALER, Palamizm i vovzrashchenie Tavrii, Personal blog of Arkadii Maler, 16 March 2014, URL: <https://arkadiy-maler.livejournal.com/2014/03/16/> (11-20-2023).
43 Egor KHOLMOGOROV, Vizantizm kak Ideia [Byzantism as Idea], in: APN-Agenstvo Politicheskikh Novostei Nizhnii Novgorod, 13 February 2008, URL: <http://apn-nn.com/113888-538205.html> (11-13-2023), please note: the website ist insecure.
44 Ibid.

sphere as a system of power and institutions«⁴⁵. Once we understand political theologies as a variety or a range of stances which a religious tradition can take *vis-à-vis* the »challenges of political modernity«⁴⁶, political Hesychasm stands out as a conservative, anti-democratic, and anti-liberal Orthodox political theology; it defines the radical right of the politico-theological spectrum in the Orthodox context. The question that I want to consider in this last section is whether this radical right politico-theological legacy is the only one possible from the starting point of Hesychasm and Palamism? Or, to put the question differently, is the politico-theological vision to come out of the Neo-patristic theology of Florovsky, Lossky, and Meyendorff – or even Losev, for that matter – necessarily conservative, anti-democratic, and anti-liberal?

A few Orthodox theologians have made Hesychasm and Palamism fruitful for a different type of Orthodox political theology. Their works and contexts could not be more different, they come from different churches and also belong to different generations, but they both offer a critical approach to political Hesychasm. These are, for the purposes of this chapter and without any claim to exhaustiveness, the Russian Orthodox philosopher and theologian Sergei Horujy and the Greek American Orthodox theologian Aristotle Papanikolaou.

Sergei Sergeevich Horujy (1941–2020) is a Russian theologian, philosopher, and mathematician who has dedicated most of his intellectual career to the exploration of Hesychasm⁴⁷. With the inevitable background in pre-revolutionary Russian religious philosophy, Horujy, influenced by Meyendorff's books, soon began to elaborate Palamism in his original philosophical-anthropological key, which differed significantly from the debates about *imiaslavie* still *en vogue* in the Moscow circle of religious intellectuals around Losev⁴⁸. As already stated in the introduction, Orthodox theology has often been criticised for lacking systematic social teaching⁴⁹, leading some scholars to argue that we can speak of an Orthodox social ethics only from the turn of the nineteenth to the twentieth century onwards, reaching its

---

45 Ingeborg GABRIEL et al., Introduction, in: Kristina STOECKL et al. (eds.), Political Theologies in Orthodox Christianity. Common Challenges – Divergent Positions, London 2017, pp. 1–11.
46 These three challenges are: the religious-cultural disconnection (rupture), religious freedom (liberty), and an anthropocentric public morality (mastery). See Kristina STOECKL, Political Theologies and Modernity, in: Ead. et al. (eds.), Political Theologies, pp. 15–24.
47 The following two paragraphs follow my exposition in ead., New Frontiers in Russian Religious Philosophy. The Philosophical Anthropology of Sergey S. Horujy, in: Russian Studies in Philosophy 57/1 (2019), pp. 3–16.
48 Sergey S. HORUJY, The Idea of Energy in the »Moscow School of Christian Neoplatonism«, in: Norbert FRANZET al. (eds.), Pavel Florenskij. Tradition und Moderne, Frankfurt am Main 2001, pp. 69–81.
49 Vasilios MAKRIDES, Why Does the Orthodox Church Lack Systematic Social Teaching?, in: Skepsis. A Journal for Philopsophy and Interdisciplinary Research 23 (2013), pp. 281–312.

first culmination in the works of Bulgakov[50]. The strong ascetic tradition within Orthodoxy has been singled out as the culprit for this »otherworldly focus« of Orthodoxy, which prevented, as expressed Vasilios N. Makrides has put it, the modern »ontological upgrading of this world at the expense of the otherworld«[51]. In the first two sections of this article, I have demonstrated that the ascetic tradition has also given rise to a politically conservative formulation of political theology, namely political Hesychasm. In this chasm between a lack of political theology and a radical right political theology, Horujy's work traces an alternative trajectory.

In one of his many articles, entitled *Dve formatsii isikhastskoi ėtiki* (*Two formations of hesychast ethics*), he addresses the question of social ethics from the perspective of Hesychasm[52]. His main point is that Orthodox theology is able to elaborate a social ethics, even if considered within a strictly ascetic framework. Horujy distinguishes two formations of hesychast (i. e., ascetic) ethics. These two formations correspond to two stages of ascetic practice. The first consists of withdrawal from the world; it is guided by »a pull to the desert« (*poryv v pustyne*) and is therefore anti-social. The goal of the solitary life chosen by the hermit was not, however, mere individual salvation. Hesychast practice included a second stage of ascetic practice, which assumed a return of the experienced ascetic to the world.

Up to this point, Horujy's analysis of hesychast practice does not differ much from the standard account given by Meyendorff or Prokhorov, who also make a distinction between the individual and the social phase of Hesychasm. Where Horujy sharply differs from his two predecessors, however, is in his conceptualisation of the »return« of the hesychast to the social world. Whereas in particular for Prokhorov and for other contemporary enthusiasts of political Hesychasm this return corresponds to a programme that is defined first and foremost theologically (against Western theology and humanism in general) and geopolitically (against the West), Horujy elaborates the ethical aspects of this return. He associates the stage of return in hesychast practice with an »ethics of burden sharing« exemplified by the tradition of Russian eldership (*starchestvo*). Horujy takes this tradition at face value and turns to original material and documentary accounts, in order to deduce from these texts a concrete existential practice. Horujy writes that the communication put in place by the elders anticipated modern day findings in psychology and psychoanalysis, but the way the elders enacted these practices was sharply different from today's forms of counselling. In modern-day counselling the psychologist, psychoanalyst, or counsellor remains detached from the patient and helps the patient to confront his or her grievances autonomously. Horujy, by contrast, describes the elders as

---

50 VALLIERE, Modern Russian Theology.
51 MAKRIDES, Why Does the Orthodox Church, p. 292.
52 Sergei S. HORUJY, Dve Formatsii Isikhastskoi Ėtiki, in: Id. (ed.), Issledovaniia po Isikhastskoi Traditsii, St Peterburg 2012, pp. 4–25.

taking upon themselves the others' grievances, literally at the expense of their own personal health and well-being. He finds affinities between this idea of social ethics and the ethics of responsibility of the French philosopher Emmanuel Levinas.

Horujy is highly critical of the concept of political Hesychasm, as evidenced in a published exchange with Petrunin[53]. There, Horujy states that political Hesychasm contradicts Hesychasm as a spiritual-anthropological phenomenon and calls »completely unacceptable« the erasure of the dividing line between the spiritual and the political. While he does not use the term himself, I would argue that we could describe his position as an »Ethical Hesychasm«. The political implications of this ethical Hesychasm are not spelled out in his works, but his personal distance from the intellectual circles cited in section III gives evidence of the conclusions he has drawn from his philosophy for his own personal political position[54].

One theologian who has, by contrast, made the political implications of an ethical Hesychasm explicit is Aristotle Papanikolaou. In his book *The Mystical as Political*[55], Papanikolaou develops an Orthodox political theology on the basis of Palamism that extends beyond a reflexive opposition to the West and a nostalgic return to a Byzantine-like unified political-religious culture. The central element of Palamism, in his reading, is the principle of divine-human communion. Papanikolaou concludes that the ascetics of divine-human communion cannot be confined either to the monastery or to the church, but that the whole world is the field where divine-human communion and its imperative of love must be played out. »The political community is not the antithesis to the desert«, he writes, »but one of the many deserts in which the Christian must combat the demons that attempt to block the learning of love«[56]. Shishkov interprets Papanikolau's project as showing »that a critically reinterpreted tradition of Palamism could be the groundwork for protecting democracy and human rights from theological positions«[57].

---

53 See the protocol of a debate held in 2012, published by the Institute of Synergetic Anthropology, URL: <http://synergia-isa.ru/?p=8604> (11-13-2023).
54 The Greek theologian and philosopher Christos Yannaras would agree with Horujy judgment that political Hesychasm is a *contradictio in terminis*. Yannaras disagrees with the treatment of his work offered by Daniel Payne in his book, which is subtitled *The Political Hesychasm of John Romanides and Christos Yannaras*; see Norman RUSSEL, Metaphysics as a Personal Adventure. Christos Yannaras in Conversation with Norman Russel, ed. by Christos YANNARAS, Yonkers, NY 2017, p. 79.
55 This is an argument first made by Andrey Shishkov, who has called the political Hesychasm outlined in sections II and III »romantic political Hesychasm« and what I call ethical Hesychasm in section II »critical political Hesychasm«.
56 Aristotle PAPANIKOLAOU, The Mystical as Political. Democracy and Non-Radical Orthodoxy, Notre Dame, IN 2012, p. 4.
57 SHISHKOV, Eastern Orthodoxy.

Papanikolaou wholeheartedly endorses the attribute »political« for his interpretation of divine-human communion – in fact, for him »the mystical is the political«[58]. In light of the complex history of political Hesychasm outlined in this essay, it should be clear that his »mystical as political« differs profoundly from and indeed directly challenges the »Hesychasm as political« of Russian conservatives. Papanikolaou does not discuss the political Hesychasm of Meyendorff, Prokhorov, or their contemporary interpreters in his book, even though he is no doubt aware of them and of the ways in which the historical dispute between Palamas and Barlaam, between Orthodox mysticism and Neo-scholasticism has been interpreted in ways that fuel, to this day, Orthodox anti-Westernism and anti-liberalism. Papanikolaou's political theology of divine-human communion directly challenges this trend.

Conclusion

Political Hesychasm represents one piece in the puzzle that is the contemporary panorama of political theologies in the Orthodox context. The study of its history, development, and present-day usage illuminates important facets of contemporary Orthodox theological thought. In sections II and III, I showed that political Hesychasm in the Russian context today is confined to a conservative, far-right intellectual sphere in which it is used as a justification for anti-Westernism, anti-Liberalism, and even military aggression in eastern Ukraine. In section IV, I made the argument that this political Hesychasm is not the only political theology possible to emerge from an intellectual engagement with Palamism, citing two contemporary authors and their works – Sergey Horujy and Aristotle Papanikolaou – in evidence. I have discussed their approach under the heading of »ethical Hesychasm«. In the introduction, I started from the observation that the Neo-patristic turn in Orthodox theology in the twentieth century has frequently been criticised for ignoring the real social and political problems in contemporary societies and for failing, therefore, to develop an Orthodox social ethics and a political theology that is up to the challenges of the modern world. I argued that such an assessment overlooks that the Neo-patristic turn has indeed produced its own political theology: the theology of political Hesychasm. The aim of this chapter was to outline the meaning of political Hesychasm, its contemporary uses, pitfalls, and alternatives.

---

58 Papanikolaou, The Mystical, p. 1.

Sebastian Rimestad

In the Shadow of a »Big Brother«

Political Theology in the Orthodox Minority Churches from Finland to Poland

Political theology exists wherever people think about the relationship between the religious and the secular world. The peculiar Christian Orthodox version of such thinking is most apparent in contexts where the Orthodox Church traditionally commands a majority of the population. Nevertheless, there is political theology also in the minority Orthodox Churches of the borderland between Russia and Western Christianity. This contribution aims to show how the political theology that develops in these contexts is influenced by the proximity to heterodox Christian communities and the Orthodox minority's situation. It does so in four steps. The first section defines political theology for the purpose of this chapter and highlights some important preliminary factors for the further analysis of political theology in this context. Second, the official birth of the minority Orthodox Churches and their growth in the first half of the twentieth century is analysed, before the third section examines mostly successful attempts by the Soviet-controlled Orthodox Church to bring them back in its fold. The final section looks at the post-Soviet developments, which saw the rebirth of independent minority churches and the diversification of political theology.

Political Theology

Political theology is, as already stated, theological thinking that considers the relationship between the religious and the secular world. In principle, then, political theology is supposed to be the backbone of church politics. However, in the Orthodox world, much more so than among the Western confessions, church politics is often characterised by pragmatism and geopolitical considerations, which are then justified in hindsight with reference to theological thinking. This has not always been the case, however. In the run-up to the Union of Brest of 1596, for example, theological reflection preceded political action. The union – between the Eastern Orthodox and Roman Catholics in the territory of Poland-Lithuania – was prepared in long theological discussions. These talks were initiated by the Orthodox bishops, who argued that a) union was always desirable, b) it was their duty as shepherds to make sure the flock was not discriminated, and that c) a union would help ward off the »threat« posed by the Reformation. Moreover, d) they were dissatisfied with recent developments in the relationship with the Patriarch of Constantinople[1]. It is not always easy to distinguish church politics and political theology in this case, but it is possible to trace the link between theological reasoning and subsequent political action.

The retraction of this church union in those areas that belonged to the Russian Empire more than two centuries later, in 1839, was much less clearly accompanied by theological reasoning[2]. On the contrary, the Most Holy Synod of the Russian Orthodox Church, together with the imperial administration, administratively re-joined the Greek-Catholic dioceses to the Orthodox Church. They had the help of local bishops, who had prepared the move through liturgical and educational reforms, but the process was not really accompanied by theological argumentation, other than the idea that the integrity of the Orthodox Church had been restored after an aberrant development. The move was clearly a political project, which did not even need to be justified theologically. The difference between the two events was the political environment in which they occurred. Whereas the Union of Brest took place within the multi-confessional Commonwealth of Poland-Lithuania before it had consolidated to a modern bureaucratic political system, the 1839 *vozsoedinenie* happened within the modernised Russian Empire, where the Orthodox Church was the ruling confession[3].

In fact, the Russian Empire's attitude to religion in general was characterised by politicising Orthodox Christianity and delegitimising any other religious community as foreign to the empire[4].

New Independent Churches

All along the western border of the former Russian Empire, new states appeared after World War I and the Bolshevik Revolution, which threw their Orthodox communities into turmoil, with all but the Lithuanian Orthodox Church leaving the jurisdiction of the Moscow Patriarchate by the outbreak of World War II. Developments in Finland, Estonia, and Poland were similar, whereas Latvia and Lithuania

---

1 Christoph SUTTNER, Die Anfänge der Brester Union, in: Id./Wolfgang Nikolaus RAPPERT (eds.), Kirche in einer zueinander rückenden Welt, Würzburg 2003, pp. 339–370, at pp. 345f.
2 Barbara SKINNER, Conversion and Culture in Russia's Western Borderlands, 1800–1855, in: Yoko AOSHIMA (ed.), Entangled Interactions between Religion and National Consciousness in Central and Eastern Europe, Brookline, MA 2020, pp. 29–49.
3 See also the contribution by Evert van der Zweerde in this volume.
4 See Cyril HOVORUN, Political Orthodoxies. The Unorthodoxies of the Church Coerced, Minneapolis 2018, pp. 66–73.

went their own ways. Nevertheless, there are important differences between all the cases, needing a closer look.

Especially in the case of Finland, the decision to leave the jurisdiction of the Moscow Patriarchate and embark on the road to autocephaly was clearly a political project. Just as in the Balkans, where the secular governments had demanded new autocephalous churches in the previous century, the Finns wanted a national Orthodox Church, a second state church to stand alongside the Lutheran one. In contrast to the Orthodox governments in the Balkans, however, the political establishment in Finland was predominantly Lutheran. Nevertheless, it was eager to limit the influence of its former masters (i. e., Russia) and thus took the initiative to achieve church independence. Moreover, the relationship of the Finnish Orthodox community to the new state had to be defined, especially as its funding from Moscow suddenly broke away in the spring of 1918.

The government issued new statutes for the Orthodox Church in November 1918, loudly protested by the only Orthodox bishop in Finland, Seraphim (Luk'ianov) and the pro-Russian faction of the Finnish Church. The statutes proclaimed that the Finnish government had the right to interfere in the organisation of the church and its internal affairs[5]. As Russian protests did not die down and Archbishop Seraphim refused to cooperate with the government and the Finnish faction of the church, a government-sponsored delegation was dispatched to the Patriarch of Constantinople. The Patriarch was considered the preeminent bishop of the Orthodox Church and the only decisional factor capable to reorder church matters in Finland, especially since official communication with the Moscow Patriarchate was impossible. The delegation consisted of the Lutheran diplomat Emil N. Setälä as well as the archpriests Sergei Solntsev and Herman Aav. The latter was an Estonian designated to replace Archbishop Seraphim as the new head of the Finnish Church.

It is difficult to say whether the struggle between Finnish nationalists and Russians in the Finnish Orthodox Church, which has been termed a »spiritual civil war«[6], contains much political theology. The parties certainly tried to argue theologically, but they did not develop a full theology on this basis. Archpriest Mikael Michailov argued in 1919 that the government had acted like Jesus, hurrying across water to help his disciples in need[7], and Seraphim argued that he was canonically bound to his superior, the Church of Russia.

The Russian tradition of politicising the Orthodox Church was still strongly resonant with Archbishop Seraphim, who was eventually expelled for not satisfying the requirement for Finnish civil servants to learn the Finnish language. He moved

---

5 Mika NOKELAINEN, Vähemmistövaltiokirkon synty [The Birth of a Minority State Church], Helsinki 2010.
6 Ibid., p. 279.
7 Ibid., p. 196.

on to the Russian Orthodox Church Outside Russia (ROCOR) in Serbia, which in many ways is the paramount example of politicised Russian Orthodoxy. During World War II, he returned to the Moscow Patriarchate and became Exarch for Western Europe after the death of Metropolitan Evlogii. There certainly is an element of political theology in this path, but that is outside the scope of this chapter. As long as he was still in Finland, his argumentation was less theological than nationalist and conservative.

The Finnish delegation to Constantinople – which was in turmoil at that time (1923) – argued politically once it got there. The Finnish Church needed independence because it had matured enough and because the troubles in the Russian Church made it impossible to stay in contact with it[8]. The delegation did not mention the differences of opinion with Bishop Seraphim. When the Patriarch required an episcopal mandate, Setälä argued that the Finnish Church statutes gave the supreme power to the church assembly, not to the head bishop. Patriarch Meletios IV answered that he was not really responsible for the Finnish Church, but until normal relations with the Russian Church could resume, he was willing to take the community under his protection. The goal of autocephaly was not attained, but the autonomy that Patriarch Tikhon of Moscow had granted in February 1921 was replaced by a wider autonomy under Constantinople. Back in Finland, the synod proceeded to write a letter to Moscow, explaining that they were now an autonomous church, regarding Constantinople as their honorary head, which elicited a brisk reply from Moscow. The Finnish eparchy was ordered to return to Moscow jurisdiction, a threat that was followed by action only after World War II[9].

In the Polish case, the point of departure was different, as the episcopate was divided. The bishops all argued that the new political situation – independence from Russia – required a new ecclesiastical basis – independence from the Russian Church. However, while some of them (Elevferii [Bogoiavlenskii] of Vilnius, Panteleimon [Rozhnovskii] of Pinsk-Novogrudek and Vladimir [Tikhonitskii] of Grodno) wanted strictly to follow canonical regulations, waiting for a Russian local council to award them independence, others (Jerzy [Jaroszewski] of Minsk, and Dionisii [Waledynski] of Kremenec) were more self-assertive and wanted to proclaim autocephaly without waiting for a Russian decision.

At the same time, the secular government was also interested in a quick settlement regarding the status of the Orthodox Church in independent Poland, and

---

[8] Setälä's report of the journey is found in the Archive of the Finnish Ministry of Foreign Affairs, Helsinki, 44, J. See also Sebastian RIMESTAD, The Challenges of Modernity to the Orthodox Church in Estonia and Latvia (1917–1940), Frankfurt am Main 2012, pp. 90–92.

[9] U.V.J. SETÄLÄ, Kansallisen ortodoksisenm kirkkokunnan perustamiskysysmys Suomen politiikassa, 1917–1925 [The Question of Establishing a National Orthodox Church in Finnish Politics, 1917–1925], Helsinki 1966, pp. 178f. See also RIMESTAD, The Challenges, pp. 94f.

naturally supported the latter[10]. Moreover, diplomatic talks between the Polish representative in Constantinople and the Patriarchate were conducted from 1920. At the behest of the Polish government, Metropolitan Jerzy was offered the vacant see of Warsaw in 1921, the most important one in the country, and in June 1922 the Polish bishops' synod decided by three votes to two to break ties with Moscow and to turn to Constantinople for autocephaly[11]. The dissenting bishops were confined to monasteries for alleged canonical transgressions. Elevferii of Vilnius later became the metropolitan of independent Lithuania, the only country arising from the former Russian Empire where the Orthodox Church did not leave the jurisdiction of the Moscow Patriarchate. Elevferii was also Moscow's Exarch for Western Europe after 1934.

Later in 1922, Metropolitan Jerzy was assassinated by a fanatical pro-Russian monk. His place was taken by Dionisii, while the government conducted talks with Constantinople to achieve Polish autocephaly. Together with the other newly consecrated government-friendly bishops, the nationalistic Metropolitan Dionisii pushed ahead with efforts to establish autocephaly. However, due to the quick succession of Patriarchs in Constantinople at the time (Meletios IV [1922–1923], Gregorios VII [1923–1924], and Constantine VI [1924–1925]), the solemn declaration of Polish Orthodox autocephaly came only in 1925[12]. Dionisii argued that the Russian Church would have accepted Polish autocephaly if it had had a legitimate Patriarch. Here too the forceful reaction from the Russian Church came only after World War II.

The Estonian Church was an intermediate case. The first ever ethnic Estonian Bishop Platon (Kulbusch) had been murdered by retreating Bolsheviks in January 1919, after only one year in office[13]. The Estonian Orthodox representatives were eager to avoid being orphaned again. When Patriarch Tikhon was imprisoned in 1922, the Estonian Orthodox Church, with its newly consecrated Archbishop

---

10 Andrzej Borkowski, Pertraktacje rządu polskiego z patriarchatem ekumenicznym w sprawie przyznania autokefalii Kościołowi prawosławnemu w Polsce w latach, 1920–1923 [The Discussions of the Polish Government with the Ecumenical Patriarchate Regarding the Autocephaly of the Polish Orthodox Church, 1920–1923], in: Antoni Mironowicz et al. (eds.), Autokefalie Kościoła prawosławnego w Polsce [The Autocephaly of the Orthodox Church in Poland], Bialystok 2005, pp. 123–138.

11 The third vote in favour of the decision came from Bishop Aleksander (Inozemtsov), who had been controversially consecrated Bishop of Lublin earlier that year. Archbishop Elevferii boycotted the meeting. See Mirosława Papierzyńska-Turek, Między tradycją a rzeczywistością. Państwo wobec prawosławia, 1918–1939 [Between Tradition and Reality. The State and Orthodoxy, 1918–1939], Warsaw 1989, p. 111; see also Borkowski, Pertraktacje, pp. 129f.; Edward D. Wynot Jr., The Polish Orthodox Church in the Twentieth Century and Beyond, Lanham, MD 2015, p. 32.

12 Papierzyńska-Turek, Między tradycją, pp. 120–125.

13 Rimestad, The Challenges, pp. 81–86.

Aleksander (Paulus) of Tallinn at its head, decided to ask for ecclesiastical independence in Constantinople. Aleksander joined the Finnish delegation mentioned above and received a *tomos* almost identical to the one for the Finnish Church – autonomy within the jurisdiction of Constantinople[14]. Unlike Finland, however, the Estonian letter of explanation sent to Moscow never received an official reply, and the Russian Church only reacted to Estonia's jurisdictional switch at the outbreak of World War II.

In all three cases, there is little political theology going on, the arguments tending to be geopolitical and having little to do with theology. Occasional attempts were made somehow to ground the argument on theological foundations, but these were mostly ad hoc and commonplace statements, such as the imperative to keep the church united, the Patriarch of Constantinople being the final arbiter in the Orthodox Church, and appeals to his solidarity with the errant flock. There definitely was no full-scale political theology developed in these communities at this juncture.

The Latvian case is also interesting, although on a different level. Archbishop Jānis of Latvia never officially left the jurisdiction of Moscow, as he claimed to possess a document from Patriarch Tikhon granting the Latvian Church full ecclesiastical autonomy[15]. It is not clear what document he referred to, since no such document has survived in any archive. Jānis managed to direct all energy within the Latvian Orthodox community towards fighting the strong communist tendencies in Latvian society instead of the canonical link with the Patriarchate of Moscow and its association with the Soviet Union. He used the church as a political platform to rally against socialist ideas.

Archbishop Jānis remained a political figure throughout the 1920s and was elected to the Latvian parliament for three consecutive sessions. He fought against the communists in the Latvian Social Democratic Party and for the rights of the Orthodox Church on every occasion. However, there is little political theology to be found in this context either, but rather political rhetoric with an Orthodox Christian foundation[16]. Jānis was murdered in 1934 and has since been canonised as a martyr, although it was most likely his political activities and not his faith that had him killed. The Latvian Church also switched to the Patriarchate of Constantinople in 1936, but this was an entirely secular political project with little theological backing. The discussion leading up to the switch emphasised canon law issues of hierarchies and the need to have a bishop to trust. However, the most decisive role in the decision was played by the new quasi-authoritarian regime in Latvia[17].

---

14 Ibid., pp. 91–96.
15 Ibid., p. 127.
16 Ibid., pp. 127–129.
17 Ibid., pp. 159–175.

Most of the developments within these »fringe churches« in the 1920s and 1930s followed a similar pattern. There was much politics in the church and the church was politically active, but there was little theological reasoning behind this activity. At least not systematically written down by anyone. The Orthodox communities were too concerned with reappraising their history in light of current political circumstances or justifying their existence among other Christians to develop any stringent and profound political theology.

The closest approximation to political theology may perhaps be found in the nationalisation efforts of all of these churches. These included government-supported measures to ensure linguistic and cultural conformity to the dominant national community. The Fennicisation efforts in Finland were the most thorough ones, including liturgy, church music, the calendar question, and the official language[18]. The Russian element was to be completely eradicated. In Poland, the same strategy was attempted, but it was met with staunch resistance from the Ukrainian Orthodox, who opposed Polonisation, instead demanding Ukrainisation[19]. Because of generous rules of cultural autonomy in Estonia, there were distinct Estonian and Russian communities within the Estonian Orthodox Church, each with their own bishop. The two occasionally clashed, but mostly kept their distance, and most Estonisation efforts were only applied to the Estonian community[20]. The Latvian case again differed, since Archbishop Jānis was able to stifle all internal conflicts within the Orthodox community and focus on external enemies. Nationalisation efforts were low-key in Latvia and did not generate conflicts until the end of the 1930s, when the situation was rather different.

The Post-War Era

World War II changed the entire picture. First, Moscow's attempts to regain jurisdiction over these churches[21] stimulated a debate within them about ecclesiology. In most cases, this debate was brief. In Estonia and Latvia, for example, the Moscow

---

18 Timo FRILANDER, Valtiovalta, venäläiset ja kalenterikysymys, 1917–1923 [The Government, the Russians, and the Calendar Question, 1917-1923], in: Ortodoksia 44 (1995), pp. 56–84; id., Ajanlaskukysymys ja Suomen kansallistuva ortodoksinen kirkko, 1923–1927 [The Calendar Question and the Nationalising Finnish Orthodox Church, 1923–1927], in: Ortodoksia 46 (1997), pp. 80–103; Maria TAKALA-ROSZCZENKO, The Nationalization of Liturgy in the Orthodox Church of Finland in the 1920s–30s, in: Review of Ecumenical Studies Sibiu 9/2 (2017), pp. 154–172.
19 WYNOT, The Polish Orthodox Church, pp. 26–29.
20 RIMESTAD, The Challenges, pp. 181–199.
21 Daniela KALKANDJIEVA, The Russian Orthodox Church, 1917–1948. From Decline to Resurrection, London 2015.

takeover followed swiftly once the states had been incorporated by the Soviet Union in the summer of 1940. The heads of the local Orthodox Church were invited to Moscow in March 1941, where they publicly repented the »schism« they had caused[22]. It is difficult to say to what extent those statements were voluntary, for as soon as the Germans drove the Soviets out of Estonia and Latvia later that year, both church leaders retracted their repentance[23].

During the German occupation, which lasted for three years, there were different priorities, but Metropolitan Sergii (Voskresenskii), the Moscow appointee as exarch for all three Baltic republics, tried to endear himself to the occupation authorities by feigning distance from Soviet ideology. He wrote a long memorandum to the German occupation authorities, in which he proposed an independent Orthodox Church for the occupied areas, accusing the heads of the former Estonian and Latvian Churches of political and nationalist motives, which he did not share[24]. Moreover, Sergii initiated the so-called Pskov Mission, an Orthodox missionary endeavour in the German-occupied areas of the Soviet Union, which portrayed the Nazis as religious saviours from the atheist Soviet regime[25]. The underlying theology, however, was less political than missionary and opportunistic.

Also, further south, as Edward Wynot notes, »the actions of the Polish Orthodox leadership during World War II did nothing to endear itself either to the Poles or Soviets«[26]. Instead, the Orthodox Church played an important role in the Germans' strategy to conquer Eastern Europe. After the war, with Poland in the Soviet orbit, the Moscow Patriarchate put pressure on the bishops to renounce their autocephaly, as had happened in Estonia and Latvia. The long discussion ended in 1948, when the Polish bishops publicly repented having turned to Constantinople two decades earlier and were promptly granted autocephaly by Patriarch Aleksii I of Moscow in return[27]. In all these discussions, however, there was more concern with procedure and formal lines of authority than with political theology.

The Finnish case was different, prompting Daniela Kalkandjieva to call the corresponding chapter in her book »The Finnish failure«[28]. Discussions between the

---

22 Id., pp. 76–78; Andrei Sõtšov, Achievement of and Fight for Independence of the Orthodox Church of Estonia in 1940–1945, in: Grigorios D. Papathomas/Matthias H. Palli (eds.), The Autonomous Church of Estonia/L'Église Autonome Orthodoxe d'Estonie, Katérini 2002, pp. 285–305, at pp. 290–295.
23 Sõtšov, Achievement, pp. 297f.
24 Kalkandjieva, The Russian Orthodox Church, pp. 122f.
25 К.П. Обозный, История Псковской Православной Миссии, 1941–1944 гг. [The Pskov Orthodox Mission, 1941–1944], Moscow 2008; Kalkandjieva, The Russian Orthodox Church, p. 124.
26 Wynot, The Polish Orthodox Church, p. 58.
27 Ibid., pp. 62–64; Kalkandjieva, The Russian Orthodox Church, pp. 226–231.
28 Kalkandjieva, The Russian Orthodox Church, pp. 231–233; Juha Riikonen, Kirkko politiikan syleilyssä [Church in the Embrace with Politics], Joensuu 2007.

Finnish Orthodox Church and the Moscow Patriarchate after the war went on for twelve years, but in the end, Moscow was not able to regain jurisdiction in Finland. This was largely due to the Finns insisting on the need to confirm every move in advance by a local church council. Unlike in Poland, the Soviet authorities were not able to infiltrate and influence the proceedings of these councils. In 1957, Moscow finally recognised Finnish autonomy under Constantinople as legitimate, and this has been the status quo ever since.

It seems that the Finnish Church had, in the course of the inter-war period, become accustomed to the Constantinople way of solving political questions, which was less hierarchical than that of Moscow. The political culture in the respective Patriarchates differed, and the Finns preferred the Constantinople way. Again, this is not systematically expounded, but there are elements of a political theology here, which have been touched upon by Finnish Orthodox theologians since then. However, because of the linguistic barrier, not much of this is accessible to the non-Finnish reader. Moreover, the political theology that has emanated from the Orthodox Church of Finland has primarily been about national identity.

The best-known Finnish Orthodox theologians are the two archbishops that followed Hermann Aav in the post-war period. First, there is Archbishop Paavali (Yrjö Omari, 1914–1988), who was archbishop from 1960 to 1987. Even though he had Russian roots, he was a strong advocate for an independent Finnish Church. He was among the main negotiators in the struggle with Moscow following World War II, arguing that the Finnish Church had been *de facto* autocephalous since 1923 and relations with the Russian Church would be better if it stayed that way[29]. During his episcopate, he delivered on this promise by pursuing a close relationship with the Moscow Patriarchate and refusing to condemn the Soviet Union politically – in keeping with the Finnish foreign policy of non-alignment. This role between the ideological camps came to fruition during the Pan-Orthodox talks in Rhodes in 1964, where Paavali acted as a mediator between positions. In the 1970s, the archbishop wanted to push for formal autocephaly, after some disappointing experiences with interference from Constantinople, but the project did not bear fruit[30].

---

29 See id., Arkkipiispa Paavali – esipaimen ja jälleenrakentaja [Archbishop Paavali – Head, Shepherd and Reconstructor], published by ortodoksi.net, URL: <https://www.ortodoksi.net/index.php/Arkkipiispa_Paavali_%E2%80%93_esipaimen_ja_j%C3%A4lleenrakentaja> (11-20-2023).
30 Paavali wished to take up friendly relations with the Orthodox Church in America (OCA) that had been declared autocephalous by the Russian Orthodox Church in 1970, but this wish was vehemently blocked by Constantinople, revealing the flawed Finnish self-conception of being *de facto* autocephalous.

His successor from 1987, Archbishop Johannes (Rinne, 1923–2010), was the first convert leader of an autonomous Orthodox Church[31]. He had studied Lutheran theology and converted only after completing his doctoral studies in 1966. He was strongly influenced by Byzantine thought and reversed the policies of his predecessor in relation to Constantinople. For Johannes, Constantinople was the norm, not the Russian Church. As a result, discussions of autocephaly were toned down and the relationship with Greek traditions grew. Since most of Johannes' activities belong to the post-Soviet era, they will be discussed later on.

In the other churches, there was hardly any possibility of developing this kind of independent political theology. In the Estonian and Latvian case, the reunion with the Russian Church stifled everything that had flourished during the inter-war period. Especially in Estonia, a similar preference for the political culture of the Patriarchate of Constantinople had arisen – as in Finland –, but it had no chance of survival within the Soviet Union. When the second Soviet invasion loomed in 1944. There was a mass exodus of Estonians and Latvians, including Orthodox clergy and faithful, who settled in Germany, Sweden, and the Americas. While the local Orthodox Church was fully subordinated to the Moscow Patriarchate, ecclesiological thinking continued in exile, then often with a decidedly anti-Soviet stance[32]. In Poland, the marginalisation of the Orthodox Church and the socialist suppression of church independence ensured a similar fate. The Orthodox Church found an arena in the official socialist ideology of international peace but could not develop any original theology[33]. It was only after the end of the Cold War that new possibilities arose.

Political Theology in the Post-Soviet World

The collapse of Soviet socialism enabled the churches around the Baltic Sea to regain their independence. In the case of Latvia (and Lithuania), this meant becom-

---

31 Archbishop Johannes was awarded the honorary title of Metropolitan of Nicaea following his retirement in 2001. See Johannes Nikean metropoliitta [Metropolitan Johannes of Nicaea], published by ortodoksi.net, URL: <https://www.ortodoksi.net/index.php/Johannes_Nikean_metropoliitta> (11-20-2023).

32 Andrei Sõtšov, Eesti apostlik-õigeusu pagulaskiriku vaimulike kirjavahetus kodumaaga ja selle kajastumine EAÕK häälekandjas Jumala Abiga 1950. aastatel [The Correspondence between Clergy of the Estonian Orthodox Exile Church and the Homeland and its Reflection in the Journal Jumala Abiga in the 1950s], in: Acta Historica Tallinnensia 10 (2006), pp. 178–192; Martin Juhkam (ed.), Eesti Apostlik Ortodoksne Kirik Eksiilis, 1944–1960 [The Estonian Apostolic Orthodox Church in Exile, 1944–1960], Stockholm 1961; Alexander Cherney, The Latvian Orthodox Church, Welshpool 1985.

33 Wynot, The Polish Orthodox Church, pp. 69f.

ing autonomous parts of the Moscow Patriarchate. Theological thinking in these two churches remained intimately linked to that of the Russian Church, with one exception. The Latvian Orthodox priest Jānis Kalniņš, who was charged with investigating the case of his namesake, the interwar Archbishop Jānis, in order to prepare his canonisation, started to question the legitimacy of the Moscow Patriarchate's jurisdiction in Latvia[34]. His books are a mixture of autobiography, anti-Russian polemic, and historical investigation. As such, they are probably the approximation to political theology in the Latvian case. For Kalniņš it is bad theological practice to have foreigners leading the local Orthodox Church, and he underlines the benign beginnings of Orthodox Christianity in mediaeval and then nineteenth century Latvia[35] while condemning the political machinations of the Moscow Patriarchate[36]. He refers to archimandrite Antonin Kapustin, who claimed that »we [Russians] consider ourselves politically strong, thereby distancing ourselves from the ecumenical church«[37]. His outspokenness led to Kalniņš being silenced and defrocked by the Latvian Orthodox Church – even with the involvement Patriarch Aleksii II of Moscow[38] –, but he continues to speak and write publicly[39]. He claims to have episcopal blessing, although it is not clear from whom.

In Poland, the post-Soviet era has not produced many famous Orthodox theologians. In relation to the national question, the Orthodox Poles are happy to be able to celebrate both 1924 and 1948 as their date of birth, according to the narrative needed at the moment. In their relations to Constantinople, the earlier date is important, whereas for visitors from Russia, the church dates back to 1948. Such a pragmatic stance cannot be attributed to a set political theology, however, but rather to strategic considerations. However, in terms of national politics, the Polish Orthodox Church pursues a strategic rather than theological path: The restitution of previously confiscated property, minority politics, and religious instruction are all issues, in which the Orthodox have a stake and for which they have fought persistently throughout the 1990s and early 2000s[40]. In terms of political theology, the Orthodox Church of Poland is clearly oriented towards its »Big Brother«, the Catholic Church in Poland. In the Polish context, it is the Catholic Church that

---

34 Jānis KALNIŅŠ, Process, Riga 2015; Oļegs PEĻEVINS, Ieskats Latvijas Pareizticīgās Baznīcas vēsturē [Outline of the History of the Latvian Orthodox Church], in: Latvijas Pareizticīgā Baznīca, 1988.–2008. gads [The Latvian Orthodox Church, 1988–2008], Riga 2009, pp. 46–51.
35 Jānis KALNIŅŠ, Latvju krusta ceļš [Latvia's Way of the Cross], Riga 2012.
36 Id., Latvijas Pareizticīgā Baznīca. Vēstures komentārs [The Latvian Orthodox Church. A Commentary on History], Riga 2007.
37 Id., Process, p. 99, quoting Kiprian Kern's biography of Kapustin from 1997.
38 Ibid., p. 96; PEĻEVINS, Ieskats, p. 50.
39 His autobiography appeared in the fourth edition in 2017. He has since then published several biographies of nationalistic Latvian Orthodox clergy.
40 WYNOT, The Polish Orthodox Church, pp. 83–107.

sets the agenda theologically, and the Orthodox Church largely follows it while occasionally criticising the Catholic standpoint. At the same time, the question of the Ukrainian and Belarusian minorities figures prominently in the publications of the Polish Orthodox theologians, but with no distinct Polish political theology discernible.

Following the autocephaly of the Orthodox Church of Ukraine in January 2019, the Polish Orthodox Church reacted by not recognising the new church. It still officially does not recognise it, remaining loyal to the Russian Orthodox Church. However, according to commentators, this position is not widely shared in the clergy and even among the bishops. Moreover, the wording of the official statements is vague and leaves the door open to *de facto* recognition and subsequent reassessment[41]. A vague letter of support from Polish first-hierarch Metropolitan Sawa to Metropolitan Onufrii, head of the Ukrainian Orthodox Church, in mid-December 2020 fuelled speculations that the Polish Church remained undecided, which it officially denied[42]. Anyway, there is more strategic calculus than political theology in this line of action.

The Finnish Church is a different case. The political theology emanating from this church, when it is not concerned with nation and Orthodox ecclesiology, is aligned to the political theology of the Finnish Lutheran Church. This can, for example, be observed in relation to gender questions and sexual minorities. Finland is a rather liberal society, and the Finnish Lutheran Church is open to female priesthood and same-sex relations. The local Orthodox Church also displays a different attitude to these questions than that which is commonplace in countries with an Orthodox majority. A public outcry was heard from across the Orthodox world after metropolitan Ambrosius of Helsinki, another former Lutheran, invited the female head bishop of the Finnish Lutheran Church to enter the altar of his cathedral in 2015 and ordered deacons to pray for her. Ambrosius was later reprimanded by Patriarch Bartholomew of Constantinople, but replied calmly that:

> I consider this to be not a warning but taking of a stand. It is quite clear that the Patriarch of Constantinople lives in a different phase of church development compared to us. People in Eastern Europe have not really learned about ecumenism, because they have lived so long in an Orthodox monoculture. – I invited her there myself. She was in the altar room

---

41 Artur Deska, Polski Autokefaliczny Kościół Prawosławny a Ukraina [The Polish Autocephalous Orthodox Church and Ukraine], published by Kresy24.pl, 02-18-2019, URL: <https://kresy24.pl/polski-autokefaliczny-kosciol-prawoslawny-a-ukraina> (11-20-2023).

42 For the letter, see Митрополит Польский Савва заговорил »византийским языком, published by Русская Линия, 12-15-2020, URL: <https://rusk.ru/newsdata.php?idar=88629> (11-20-2023). The repudiation was reported by RIA Novosti on 17 December 2020, URL: <https://ria.ru/20201217/pravoslavie-1589800786.html> (11-20-2023).

to see how a priest is ordained in our church. She did not participate in the rituals. For me, this is important interaction, and in our Finnish context this something completely normal. – This is not a disagreement on the doctrine. This is about the openness of the Orthodox Church, about whether we want to live in a ghetto or orient ourselves toward the future. – The Orthodox Church has a fine relationship with the Lutheran Church. It is important to maintain this relationship. – One can see a kind of phobia against feminism in the Orthodox world. Women priesthood is something people are afraid of, although this is an open question in the Orthodox Church. We have never taken a stand on women priesthood, deciding that it will never happen[43].

Whether this really is political theology or rather lived ecumenism is debatable, but it shows how the context shapes the way theologians frame their views.

The issue of same-sex relationships is also discussed in far more liberal terms in the Finnish Orthodox Church than elsewhere in the Orthodox world. A report from the conservatively-minded Finnish brotherhood of Saint Kosmas of Aitolia on this issue maintains that this debate within the Finnish Church since the early 1990s has lacked theological grounding in Orthodox tradition, instead going along with developments in secularised society[44]. According to the report, homosexuality in the Finnish Church is not discussed on a free theological basis, but is accompanied by threats, public denunciations, and dishonest use of mass media on both sides. The report concludes with the warning that »a deep-going change of the way of thinking is going on in the Orthodox Church of Finland, in which catholic truth is being replaced by Protestant individualistic thinking anchored to the spirit of the world«[45].

The above mentioned Metropolitan Ambrosius is singled out as the main proponent of this change. At a gathering of the Finnish Council of Churches, he argued that

> Finland is a model country in inter-church cooperation. If the Finnish Orthodox Church would have not been so much bound by international praxis, cooperation might be even closer in Finland. We are the receptive part in the process; we follow the discussion going on in the Lutheran Church. And it has had an effect on us, for instance, in regard with

---

43 This translation of Ambrosius' explanation to a Finnish newspaper as well as a balanced analysis of the event can be found in the article: Ambrosius, Metropolitan of Helsinki, published by Wikipedia, URL: <https://en.wikipedia.org/wiki/Ambrosius,_Metropolitan_of_Helsinki> (11-20-2023).
44 The Brotherhood of Saint Kosmas of Aitolia, A Report on the Homosexuality Debate in the Orthodox Church of Finland, Joensuu 2010, URL: <http://www.kosmas.fi/PDF-files-veljeston%20paasivu/Finn_Ort_Probl_2009_Autumn.pdf> (11-20-2023).
45 Ibid., p. 36.

ordination of women; in this matter, we certainly are on a wave completely different from the rest of the Orthodox world[46].

His official biography on the church's website on the occasion of his retirement early 2018 characterises his eposcopate as beset by reproaches, while he was only trying to break the boundaries that hindered church growth[47].

The Estonian context, finally, is also interesting, since there emerged two parallel Orthodox churches after the end of the Soviet Union[48]. One was a continuation of the Soviet-era Moscow Patriarchate Orthodox Church, whereas the other was a revived Estonian Orthodox Church under the jurisdiction of Constantinople. While these two churches were roughly (but not completely) divided along ethnic lines, they were adamant not to refer to ethnicity in official theological statements. Instead, the conflict centred on legal, pastoral, and historical arguments. As the home diocese of Patriarch Aleksii II, the Estonian diocese of the Moscow Patriarchate had a special place within the Russian Orthodox Church. It was also headed by Aleksii's long-time colleague, Metropolitan Kornilii (Jakobs) of Tallinn, who was the longest-serving bishop of the Russian Church when he died in 2018, aged 92[49]. The Patriarchate spared no effort trying to justify the legitimacy of Moscow's jurisdiction in Estonia. Then again, the arguments were mostly legal and historical, and there was little political theology as such behind these efforts, except for the general Moscow line of thought[50].

The other church, reporting to Constantinople, was more permeated with its own political theology. Like Kalniņš in Latvia, this theology tried to build on the developments of the Estonian interwar years, but also on the experience of the Estonian Orthodox Church in exile, which had survived in Sweden[51]. The idea was to create a version of Orthodox Christianity that was aligned with Estonian national consciousness. Just as the main thrust of the argument for the Moscow Church emanated from Moscow, so the Constantinople Church received significant help from foreign sources. The Greek canon law specialist Grigorios Papathomas, a long-time teacher at the Institut St Serge in Paris as well as professor at the University of

---

46 Quoted ibid., p. 32.
47 Maria HATTUNEN, Metropoliitta Ambrosius cläkkeelle [Metropolitan Ambrosius Enters Retirement], published by ort.fi, 12-28-2017, URL: <https://www.ort.fi/uutishuone/2017-12-27/metropoliitta-ambrosius-elakkeelle> (11-20-2023).
48 Sebastian RIMESTAD, Orthodox Churches in Estonia, in: Lucian LEUSTEAN (ed.), Eastern Christianity and Politics in the Twenty-First Century, London 2014, pp. 295–311.
49 See his autobiography Митрополит Корнилий, О моем пути [About my Journey], Tallinn 2009.
50 See Православие в Эстонии [The Orthodox in Estonia], vols. 1 and 2, ed. by протоиер. Н. Балашов/С.Л. Кравец, Moscow 2010.
51 See PAPATHOMAS/PALLI (eds.), The Autonomous Church.

Athens, was charged with canonically justifying Constantinople's efforts in Estonia. He published several works in different languages to further its cause. This includes a small theological treatise published in Estonian and Russian purporting to tell the theological truth about the situation in Estonia[52].

At the same time, the first post-Soviet head of this church was Archbishop John of Finland (1996–1999), as *locum tenens*. For him and his assistant, priest Heikki Huttunen, being in charge of the Estonian Church was an opportunity to rebuild it on the basis of the Finnish experience with Byzantine roots[53]. The theological foundations of this endeavour were less pronounced, though. It was more an exercise of rebuilding broken relationships and a lost sense of ecclesial community in the face of a partially hostile and ethnically charged political environment.

In 1999, Metropolitan Stephanos (Charalambidis) took over, a Cypriot who had previously been Bishop of Nice in France. He continued to keep up with developments on the Côte d'Azur and his experience in the French diaspora also enabled him to come to terms with Estonian conditions. Under his leadership, the project of creating an »Estonian« Church has been somewhat toned down. Stephanos' theology is much less nationalistic and historically charged than what some of the church members would like to see[54]. For Stephanos, unity with Constantinople is of utmost importance, which is why he also sharply criticises Moscow's refusal to accept Constantinople as canonical arbiter. Due to Ukrainian autocephaly, the prospect of the two Estonian churches reconciling is as far away as ever.

Conclusion

The case of metropolitan Stephanos neatly shows that political theology is something that arises out of a particular context. However, for a well-formulated, comprehensive political theology to appear, this context needs a certain stability. In the area covered in this chapter, only the Finnish Church can be said to have achieved this kind of stability, meaning that it generated a shared political theology – even if it might be occasionally overstretched. The other contexts have all been too unstable over the last century. This obviously does not mean that there cannot be individual

---

52 Grigorios D. PAPATHOMAS, Õnnetus olla väike kirik väikesel maal / Несчастье быть маленькой церковью в маленькой стране [The Misfortune of Being a Small Church in a Small Country], Tallinn 2007.
53 METROPOLITAN JOHN OF NICAEA, Involved in the Life of the Orthodox Church of Estonia (1996–1999), in: PAPATHOMAS/PALLI (eds.), The Autonomous Church, pp. 307–320; Heikki HUTTUNEN, The Resurrection of a Church, in: Ibid., pp. 399–416.
54 See MÉTROPOLITE STEPHANOS DE TALLINN ET DE TOUTE L'ESTONIE/Jean-François JOLIVALT, La véritable histoire des Orthodoxes d'Estonie, Paris 2012, pp. 299–316.

theologians in these contexts, who develop coherent systems of political theology. However, until these political theologies are shared by a majority in the church, the context needs to stabilise. In Poland and in Estonia, this is happening at the moment. The context in Latvia and Lithuania is not the local one, but that of the Church of Russia. In addition, the small size of these communities impairs their ability to foster a distinctive political theology.

The case of Jānis Kalniņš in Latvia is one of opposition to the church leadership, which therefore cannot become common theology. There are also such cases of opposition within the Russian Church – Sergei Chapnin and Cyril Hovorun, for example. Political theology that arises out of opposition to the ideological underpinnings of the official church represent interesting cases, even though they seldom fall on fertile ground. In diasporic Orthodoxy, such theological thinking against the mainstream is much more likely to appear and flourish. This was the case with the interwar Russian theological renaissance in Paris as well as later with Alexander Schmemann and Olivier Clément. Similarly, in recent years, it is the diaspora context that has given rise to the most interesting new approaches to political theology, such as Aristotle Papanikolaou and George Demacopoulos at Fordham University in New York.

Moreover, in times of instant communication, profound thinking is much less dependent on geographical context than it was a century ago. In the Orthodox Church, too, political theology has diversified globally and is no longer bound to the specific location and ecclesiastical context in which it is elaborated. While it mostly emanates from a specific ecclesial context, it is not limited to that, as long as it is articulated in a major language. However, some forms of adversity, be they political or confessional, seem to provide an impetus for theological thinking, as the churches on the fringes of the former Russian Empire testify.

Sophie Zviadadze

State, Church, and the Post-Soviet Political Theology of the Georgian Orthodox Church[1]

Introduction

The influence of the Georgian Orthodox Church (GOC) on public and political affairs and the rapprochement between the state and the GOC are significant characteristics of post-Soviet Georgian society. This trend is shaped, among other factors, by specifics of religious culture, the intersection of religion and nationalism, and historical and political settings. This chapter looks at the evolution of the relationship between the state and the Georgian Orthodox Church and political theology in the practice of the post-Soviet Georgian Orthodox Church. The new coronavirus has profoundly changed the world as we knew it. Death, with its accompanying rituals, its visual manifestations, and the discussions revolving around it, once seemingly banished from modern society, has made a remarkable comeback as a hot topic for wide discussions. The pandemic has been an eye-opener at many levels by uncovering flaws within economic policies, the crisis of the democratic nation-state, the urgency of revising value systems, and other domains. As Carl Schmitt once said, the rule proves nothing, the exception proves everything[2].

In an utterly new formation of political and societal crisis, many intellectuals were reminded of Carl Schmitt and his famous book *Political Theology*. This period saw many articles dedicated to the new reality. Some commentators, especially those who are hopeful of human prudence (e. g., Alain Badiou, Judith Butler), believe that the crisis provides a window of opportunity for positive changes while others fear that the new global order provides legitimacy to authoritarianism[3].

---

1 The Georgian texts referred to in the footnotes are cited with English titles. The author has translated the titles and quotations.
2 Carl SCHMITT, Political Theology. Four Chapters on the Concept of Sovereignty, Chicago 2005, p. 15.
3 For example, Agamben argues that the coronavirus and the fear it has instilled, a desire to protect »naked life«, have forced human beings to reject everything that makes them human. See Giorgio AGAMBEN, The Invention of an Epidemic, 26 February 2020, in: European Journal of Psychoanalysis. Coronavirus and Philosophers: A Tribune, February–May 2020, published by European Journal of Psychoanalysis, URL: <https://www.journal-psychoanalysis.eu/articles/coronavirus-and-philosophers/> (11-20-2023).

In this regard, Georgian debates revealed another aspect. The role played by the GOC in the state of emergency has sparked a series of discussions around political theology. Amidst the spread of the new Covid-19 virus, many countries declared states of emergency. Serbia and Romania put religious services on hold in the period before Easter, while the Holy Synod of the Orthodox Church of Greece postponed the Easter service[4]. The same period saw debates over religion and science unfolding among Orthodox theologians. Discussions of the ritual of Holy Communion and its theological implications entered the public domain[5]. In Georgia, these debates were rather superficial, with proponents of the unchanged rite of Holy Communion, more likely than providing theological arguments as justification for their position, depicting bloodcurdling consequences of the End Times that would follow the »closure« of churches. The situation gave rise not so much to conceptual debates about religion and medicine, tradition and modernity than to a rivalry between church and the state. A challenge faced by religion soon became the challenge of the state: Who has greater legitimacy – secular or religious authorities? This very question is the core of the present chapter, which looks into the specifics of the relationship between church and the state, the political role of the church, and its stance on the »political« in post-Soviet Georgia.

The concept of »political theology« has a binary meaning for the purpose of this chapter. The first is its wider meaning, i. e., the relationship between theology and the »political« in general, including political power and institutions[6]. This meaning combines the participation of a church in the field of politics, its attitude towards political order, democracy, human rights, secular statehood, and their theological interpretation. At the same time, the concept of »political theology« will be used as it was in the famous work of Carl Schmitt, who believed that theological concepts stand behind political authority, political systems, and political theory in general. His key claim is that all modern political concepts – notably that of sovereignty – are in fact secularised notions of Christian theology. Since it is a Schmittian sovereign that is uncovered in Georgia amidst the Covid-19 pandemic, we cannot bypass Schmitt's semantics of political theology.

---

[4] The Ukrainian Church has returned to the tradition of handing wine and bread to communicants, while in Russia, the world's largest Orthodox Church, started disinfecting communion spoons.

[5] Fr. Nicholas Dassouras, From one Spoon to Many, published by Public Orthodoxy, 08-04-2020, URL: <https://publicorthodoxy.org/2020/08/04/from-one-spoon-to-many/> (11-20-2023); Panagiotis G. Pavlos, Why should Orthodoxy Remain Public in Coronavirus times?, published by Public Orthodoxy, 05-25-2020, URL: <https://publicorthodoxy.org/2020/05/25/why-should-orthodoxy-remain-public-in-coronavirus-times/> (11-20-2023).

[6] Vasilios N. Makrides, Political Theology in Orthodox Christian Contexts. Specificities and Particularities in Comparison with Western Latin Christianity, in: Kristina Stoeckl et al. (eds.), Political Theologies in Orthodox Christianity. Common Challenges and Divergent Positions, London 2017, pp. 25–54.

The question of Orthodox political theology arrived hand in hand with the question of secularism in Georgia's academic and public debates[7], while the renaissance of this concept in the West coincides with the revision and critique of theories of secularism. In general, matters pertaining to Eastern Christianity and modernity, Orthodox Christianity and secularism, including political theology, remain poorly researched[8]. It was not until later that they drew academic attention. This happened when the political role and public representation of Orthodox Churches came to the fore amidst the radical social and political transformation of the twentieth century. Delayed reflection on political theology and secularism had its objective reasons: the experience of diverse modernisation processes, the process of differentiation of social spheres at various times, or living under dictatorships and totalitarian regimes for long periods. This experience has left imprints not only on the shaping of the church's structure and role within the modern political system, but also on the theological reflection.

As a rule, unique characteristics pertaining to the relationship between religion and politics are viewed in the context of wider developments in Orthodox countries. Factors often used to explain unique religious transformation patterns include shared experience of totalitarian systems and religious policies, the interrelation of nationalism and religiosity, and delayed processes of development

---

7 A spark of interest in political theology in Georgia followed academic research and debates around secularism – was a response to political reality and the church's political influence. When a collection of analytical articles was published in Georgian in 2009, the topic was still tabooed. However, the same period saw issues pertaining to political theology gaining a foothold in Georgia's academic circles and publications. A conceptual framework was built on the analysis of an early stage in the development of the GOC, as well as the analysis of the religious-mythological narrative about the origins of the Bagrationi dynasty, cases of historical and modern relationships between the GOC and secular powers. For instance, in his article, Kakhaber Kurtanidze highlights the differences between the political theologies of the Western and Eastern Churches and promotes the ideas of Christos Yannaras. See also Giorgi MAISURADZE, Der heilige Georg – ein Held christlicher politischer Theologie, in: Sigrid WEIGEL (ed.), Märtyrer-Porträts. Von Opfertod, Blutzeugen und heiligen Kriegern, Munich 2007, pp. 95–99; Giga ZEDANIA/Merab GHAGHANIDZE, Secularisation. Concepts and Contexts, Tbilisi 2009; Zaal ANDRONIKASHVILI, Glory of Fatigue. Martyrological Paradigm of Georgian Political Theology, in: Giga ZEDANIA (ed.), Political Theology. Before and After Modernity, Tbilisi 2012, pp. 5–22; Sergo RATIANI, Political Theologies across Epochs, in: Ibid., pp. 113–150.

8 Elizabeth PRODROMOU, Christianity and Democracy. The Ambivalent Orthodox in: Journal of Democracy 15/2 (2004), pp. 62–75; STOECKL et al. (eds.) Political Theologies in Orthodox Christianity; ead., The Russian Orthodox Church as Moral Norm Entrepreneur, in: Religion, State & Society 44/2 (2016), pp. 132–151.

into a national state[9]. Because of these factors, the significance attached to religion and the church varies across contexts (e. g., rising in Poland while it dwindled in other countries)[10]. The extent to which the process of secularisation is foreseeable beyond the West remains an open question[11]. A classical secularisation theorist, David Martin, argues that secularism may well be a phenomenon that is typical only of Western societies[12]. Other sociologists assume that a wave of secularisation awaits post-communist countries and is likely to leave behind a religious situation resembling that of Western countries[13]. The argument advanced by proponents of this view is based on the specifics of Eastern and Southeastern Europe's religious culture. A paradigm of classical secularism links the process not only to that of modernisation, but also to the experiences of Enlightenment and Reformation. Therefore, scholars view the process of secularisation in Orthodox countries with a certain scepticism. Orthodox Christianity is generally cited as the reason for this scepticism. Peter Berger doubts the »compatibility« of Orthodox Christianity (as compared to Catholicism and Protestantism) with secularism and pluralism[14]. While it is true that the history of the Orthodox Church and the presence of a strong national church constitute significant factors, Orthodox Churches, regardless of shared cultural characteristics, demonstrate dissenting forms of religious transformation. Orthodox countries have developed a shared and at the same time unique political theology which represents a blend of singular characteristics of religion, politics, history, and culture. This area requires deeper research, bringing together contextual, historical, and social perspectives. The present chapter reviews the main trends within the political theology of the GOC in the post-Soviet period.

---

9 Willfried SPOHN, Europeanisation, Multiple Modernities and Religion – The Reconstruction of Collective Identities in Post-Communist Central and Eastern Europe, in: Gerd PICKEL/Kristina SAMMET (eds.), Transformations of Religiosity. Religion and Religiosity in Eastern Europe, 1989–2010, Wiesbaden 2012, pp. 29–50, at p. 30.
10 Olaf MÜLLER et al., Wandel religiös-kirchlicher Orientierungsmuster und Verhaltensweisen in Osteuropa, in: Manfred BROCKER (ed.), Religion, Staat, Politik. Zur Rolle der Religion in der nationalen und internationalen Politik, Wiesbaden 2003, pp. 99–126.
11 PICKEL/SAMMET (eds.), Transformation of Religiosity.
12 David MARTIN, Europa und Amerika. Säkularisierung oder Vervielfältigung der Christenheit – Zwei Ausnahmen und keine Regel, in: Otto KALLSCHEUER (ed.), Europa der Religionen. Ein Kontinent zwischen Säkularisierung und Fundamentalismus, Frankfurt am Main 1996, pp. 161–180.
13 Steve BRUCE, Modernisation and Religion. Sociologists and Historians Discuss the Secularisation Thesis, Oxford 1992; Detlef POLLACK, Religiousness Inside and Outside the Church in Selected Post-Communist Countries of Central and Eastern Europe, in: Social Compass 50/3 (2003), pp. 321–334.
14 Peter L. BERGER, Christianity and Democracy. The Global Picture, in: Journal of Democracy 15/2 (2004), pp. 76–80.

Some Historical and Political Features of the Development of the Georgian Orthodox Church

This section provides an overview of just one period in the history of the GOC, covering the period between the annulment of its autocephaly in 1811 to the dissolution of the Soviet Union in 1990. A foundation of the GOC's modern political theology lies in the recent past, the time that shaped the modern image of the church. Modern society is the condition, in which church's authority is challenged, the social significance of religion is diminished, and we are faced with the »modernisation of religious consciousness«[15]. Therefore, the historical context given here is meant only to illustrate the extent to which theological thinking was disrupted and what political events may have influenced the development of the GOC in recent times.

The annexation of Kingdom of Kartl-Katheti by Tsarist Russia in 1801 led to the annulment of autocephaly of the GOC in 1811. The Georgian Church was ruled as an Exarchate by the Synod of the Russian Orthodox Church, which, in turn, reported to an Ober-Procurator, a civil official of the Russian Empire. As part of the Empire's Russification policy, Russian became the language of instruction in religious schools and of the liturgy. This led to an estrangement between church and parish communities[16]. The prominent Georgian theologian and priest Grigol Peradze (1899–1942) believed that the Russian rule degraded the importance of Christianity in Georgia and that the annulment of autocephaly had resulted in the »dominance of the Orthodox Russia, the use of the church as a political weapon [...], and our religious abandonment«[17].

The beginning of the nineteenth century saw the transition from a traditional agrarian society to a modern one accompanied by the spread of political ideologies, party activities, and the diversification of societal spheres. From a sociological perspective, these developments constitute the process of modernisation. In Georgia, modernisation was marked by specific features such as a resurgence of nationalist ideas articulated by Georgian enlighteners promoting the idea of a modern nation-state. In times of epic change, Georgian ecclesiastical and theological thought had already been weakened and influenced heavily by the Russian Orthodox school, with Russian spiritual seminaries and academies running across the country and

---

15 Jürgen HABERMAS, Religion in the Public Sphere, in: European Journal of Philosophy 14/1 (2006), pp. 1–25, at p. 13.
16 Erich BRYNER, Die Ostkirchen vom 18. bis zum 20. Jahrhundert [Kirchengeschichte in Einzeldarstellungen III/10], Leipzig 1996, p. 67.
17 Grigol PERADZE, Sermon delivered at an Orthodox service in Paris on 31 May 1931, in: Id., Commentaries to Our Lord. Sermons, Essays, Tbilisi 2001, pp. 7–12.

leaving their unfavourable marks on the development of the GOC[18]. In the first half of the nineteenth century, some Georgians saw a divinely blessed sovereign in the newly enthroned emperor and found an alternative idea of statehood to be almost inconceivable. This disposition may account for the passivity demonstrated by both secular and spiritual leaders[19]. The lack of initiative had hampered the national awakening in the church. A parallel rise of nationalism and liberation movements was noticeable since the 1860s among the prominent thinkers known as the »Georgian Enlighteners«[20].

In the second half of the nineteenth and at the onset of the twentieth century, Georgian writers and public figures made great efforts to draw the attention of the public to the importance of education, national aspiration, and liberal or socialist ideas. Readers of newspapers (*Droeba, Iveria, Tsnobis Purtseli, Kvali*) would follow the radical political and social changes taking place across Europe with great interest. Developments unfolding in France, especially the adoption of *laïcité* law in 1905, turned out to be of particular interest for the Georgian public, sparking a series of open debates between representatives of the church and those promoting »progressive« ideas[21].

Ioane Gomarteli, for instance, did not shy away from criticising clerics and the »red tape in the church«[22]. In response, an influential member of the clergy, the Rev. David Ghambashidze, criticised Gomarteli for supporting proletarians and atheists and for imitating French anticlericalism[23]. Even though the church felt threatened by the uncertainties of the new time and the rise of liberal, socialist, and other ideas, Rev. Ghambashidze nevertheless held up the Western model of liberal government:

---

18 In seminaries operating under the Russian Empire, Russian was the language of instruction. These establishments were among the most powerful instruments of Russification. Many of the students in spiritual academies (often previously expelled) would become leaders of anti-tsarist and revolutionary movements.

19 Levan GIGINEISHVILI, Foreword: Catholicos-Patriarchs of All Georgia: 1917–1927. Letters, in: Ilia University Library 3 (2010), pp. 7–18, at p. 12.

20 Ilia Chavchavadze (1837–1907) was the leader of the self-determination movement. He completely separated religion from the Russian Orthodox Church. His narrative focused on a secular concept of *patria* – homeland –, while he deemed religion a part of culture and traditions.

21 The Bishop of Imereti, Gabriel Kikodze (1825–1896), was one of the founders of the Society for the Spreading of Literacy among Georgians. He opened several secular and parish schools with his own money. Kikodze was among the clergymen who fiercely protested in 1886 against the removal of Georgian as language of instruction from schools.

22 In his article Gabriel KIKODZE, What Should the Georgian Clergy Do?, in: Mtskhemsi 17 (1905).

23 Davit Ghambashidze was the editor-in-chief of the *Mtskemsi Magazine*.

We openly admit that we have no belief in people's happy life where representatives of these very people have no control over the disposal of the state's revenues and expenditures. We do not believe that people can live decent and successful lives where there is no freedom of the individual, of the press, or of faith[24].

It is the time when Georgian clergymen entered the public sphere, criticising or defending actual societal changes. In 1905, the religious magazine *Mtskemsi* wrote that »never ever before has our clergy been discussed as much as for the past two years«[25]. The same year, the priest Ilarion Jashi argued that the church had

started condemning European education from altars and declared secular arts and sciences harmful. The intelligentsia protested. The clergy were soon convinced that they would not do much on their own against an intelligentsia with European education and started to butter up and pander to the government to claim their loyalty. The government extended its patronage to the clergy[26].

Such articles were not uncommon. Articles published in religious magazines (*Mtskemsi, Shinauri Sakmeebi, Jvari Vazisa*) highlighted such issues of interest as religion and science, religious and spiritual education, and the urgency of restoring the autocephaly of the GOC. The period between 1905 and 1907 saw the emergence of the »autocephalist movement«, whose members would publish religious, informational, and political magazines and newspapers[27]. The common tenor of these articles was that the bridge between people and the clergy has been broken and that the church needed to be reformed.

It is evident that »successful European countries« were deemed an alternative to the Russian monarchy. Along with the growing resentment at tsarism, the idea of monarchy started to diminish in the ecclesiastical narrative, too. The rise of the pro-autocephaly and nationalist ideas somehow »protected« Georgian clergy from a monarchy-based political theology. The campaign took off in 1905 with materials appearing in the press, discussions, organised gatherings and published

---

24 Deacon Davit GHAMBASHIDZE, On the article of Dr. Ioane Gomarteli »What should the Georgian Clergy Do?«, Mtskemsi 19 (1905), pp. 1–5, at p. 4.
25 [N.N.], What they say about our clergymen, in: Mtskemsi 21 (1905), p. 4.
26 Ilarion JASHI, Why the priest and parishioners have distanced from each other?, available in Georgian published by Orthodox Theology, URL: <http://orthodox-theology.blogspot.com/2011/08/blog-post.html> (11-20-2023).
27 Simon Mchedlidze was the editor-in-chief of the *Shinauri Sakmeebi* magazine, the priest Ioseb Jichavadze was the editor-in-chief of the newspapers *Sitkva* and *Svetitskhoveli*.

manifestos[28]. The same year saw the establishment of the Brotherhood for the Autocephaly of the Georgian Church, whose members called on the clergy to not mention the name of the Exarch during services and to cut all ties with his chancellery[29]. In December 1905, delegates of all the clergy of Georgia prepared a draft declaration of autocephaly. The authors were adamant that state and church should be separated. »It is critical [...] that not only must the church be liberated from the state, but the state must also be freed from the church: The two must stay away from each other«[30].

However, the 1905–1907 liberation movement failed to achieve the restoration of autocephaly, while its members fell victims to repression. The February Revolution of 1917 triggered a series of developments leading to the decentralisation and ultimately to the dissolution of the Russian Empire. The Georgian Church seized the opportunity provided by the issuance of decrees on the freedom of the Synod and the right of nations to self-determination and, on 12 March 1917, the Synod of the GOC declared independence. The Synod also elected a »Catholicos-Patriarch of all Georgia«. On 26 May 1918, Georgia declared its independence.

The socialist (*Menshevik*) government of the First Georgian Republic took a rather secular approach to religion. As a result of the *Law on the Separation of the State and the Church* adopted on 16 November 1918, religious classes in schools were removed from curricula, some of the lands and property belonging to the church were seized, and state budgetary support was revoked – from the adoption of the law onward, the whole body of churches had to support itself[31]. In his letter, Bishop Leonide Okropidirdze denounced the state's course of action, but without praising the past:

> The church must be liberated from political tasks and duties and should only provide such services, which aim at spiritual and moral upbringing as well as the purification of the society. The church must not interfere in political affairs of the state, nor must the state

---

28 Khatuna Kokrashvili, The Question of the Restoration of Autocephaly of the Georgian Church and the Georgian Clergy (1905–1913), in: Issues of Modern Georgian History 7 (2004), pp. 109–131; Gvantsa Burduli, A Draft Plan for the Reorganisation of the Georgian Orthodox Church (18 December 1905), in: Works of Humanitarian and Law Studies 3 (2015), pp. 42–52.

29 Shorena Japaridze, Georgian clergy for the restoration of autocephaly of the Georgian Church (1905–1907), published by church.ge, 08-27-2011, URL: <http://library.church.ge/index.php?option=com_content&view=article&id=404%3A-1905-1907-&catid=47%3A2010-03-11-12-05-46&Itemid=67&lang=ka> (11-20-2023).

30 Ibid.

31 Sergo Vardosanidze, The Georgian Orthodox Church from 1917 to 1927, Tbilisi 2000, p. 25; id., Collection of Legal Acts of the Georgian Democratic Republic, Tbilisi 1990, p. 10.

be responsible for ecclesiastic and religious functions or extend its patronage upon the church in the same way that it was done in the Byzantine and the later Russian Empire[32].

This period was marked by heated debates about a myriad of theological and ecclesiastical issues including church reform, the relationship between state and church, the administrative reorganisation of the church, the freedom of the individual, and religion. The priest Epiphane Chkhaidze, who was executed during the »Red Terror« in 1937, was one of the Georgian clergymen who, faced with the new political and social reality, recognised the insufficient and unsuccessful nature of reforms within the church. While reflecting on the church during the time of the First Democratic Republic, he concluded that even though the church accommodated itself to democratic rules, it did not meet the increased ideological and spiritual demands[33]. One of the reasons lay in the detrimental alliance between church and state: »The church has lost its primal image. After associating itself with the state, it became a bad servant of the state. It was used as a tool to serve people's harmful intentions and aspirations«[34].

At that time, the last public and political statement made by the church was a memorandum condemning the Russian occupation submitted to Genoa Conference by Patriarch Ambrosi Khelaia. Later, when he was arrested for this act of bravery, he addressed the court with the following words: »My letter was a true ecclesiastical act and if it acquired a political character, it is a sign that it was meant to be this way [...] if people were unhappy losing their freedom. I thought, too, that the deprivation of political liberty would be followed by the oppression of the church«[35].

The aforementioned Grigol Peradze, a theologian, archimandrite, and scholar of Oriental Studies, is a prominent representative of this new Christian outlook[36]. Peradze resorted to science, education, and »sober wisdom« to find a new language intended to bring religion and modernity closer to each other:

---

32 Catholicos-Patriarch Leonide Okropiridze, A Letter on the Separation of the Church from the State, in: Catholicos-Patriarchs of All Georgia: 1917–1927. Letters, in: Ilia University Library 3 (2010), pp. 36–40, at p. 37.
33 Newspaper *Sakhalho Sakme*, No. 860, 26 June (1920), pp. 2f.
34 Ibid.
35 Gigineishvili, Foreword, p. 7.
36 Grigol Peradze was educated at the universities of Bonn and Berlin. He was ordained in 1931. Peradze founded the St Nino Georgian Orthodox Church in Paris. Later he became a director of an Orthodox religious school in Warsaw. In 1927, Grigol Peradze attended an international conference, *Faith and Social System*, held in Lausanne. During World War II, he would routinely shelter victims of Nazi oppression, especially Jews, for which he was captured and sent to Auschwitz. He died in the gas chamber on 6 December 1942. In 1995 Grigol Peradze was canonised by the Georgian and Polish Orthodox Churches.

> Citizenship is the battle that every citizen has to wage within his own circle, time, and self. Citizenship requires consciousness, integrity, thinking, reflection, wit, soundness; citizenship requires looking at things with an open mind, prudence, deliberation, modesty, which is not that of slavery but rather of an educated person, listening to others, looking for, finding and recognising a human being in another human being [...]. Citizenship is sacrifice, setting oneself on fire in order to enlighten others[37].

After the annexation of Georgia by Russian troops in 1921 and later establishing the Soviet rule of governance, an anti-religion policy was introduced by authorities. The initial phase had been particularly brutal. Property was seized from all religious associations in the country, and places of worship were shut down or modified to serve secular purposes. State authorities launched a hunt against clergy, and those who, despite the prohibition, dared to participate in religious ceremonies, faced a series of negative repercussions[38]. From being an object of oppression, the GOC eventually became an institution subjected to the state. Some Georgian Orthodox believers chose to move to a pro-communist platform. The participants of an ecclesiastical convention held in Kutaisi on 26–27 December 1926 publicly expressed their loyalty to the state. Soviet authorities established a tradition of bringing the church closer to the state. The year 1924 saw an end to reformist or anti-occupation tendencies with traces in Christian thought, the idea of the rebirth of the church being erased from institutional memory.

In the wake of the World War II, Stalin chose to switch tactics and »allowed« the functioning of religious organisations[39]. Under Soviet rule, the GOC was fully controlled by the state. All statements made during those times were made in fear of the Soviet regime. On 21 July 1948, Patriarch Kalistrate (1932–1952) released an appeal to Stalin:

> The finest of all men! It was my dream as an old man to see the pride of our people and the greatest man the world has ever seen with my own eyes. Alas, fate decided otherwise. Perhaps I did not deserve this. Dear Joseph, please accept the sincerest gratitude of the Georgian Church and its leader for enlisting the mother-church as a faith-based organisation of the Soviet Union[40].

---

37 PERADZE, Commentaries to Our Lord, p. 54.
38 In 1923, the fight against religion reached its peak with »unions of godless fighters« being established across the entire Soviet Union, including Georgia. These groups fought against every manifestation and sign of religiosity in society.
39 The Russian Orthodox Church recognised the autocephaly of the GOC in 1943.
40 As early as 1922, while serving as a deacon, Kalistrate was arrested and sentenced to three years of imprisonment in Metekhi prison for his anti-Soviet activities.

The 1960s and 1970s saw the GOC's absorption into state structures as control eventually grew into collaboration. In a report concerning the church, a department for propaganda at the Central Committee of the Communist Party of Georgia underlined that »the church is no longer against science and modernisation. It has come to terms [with them]«[41]. As proof, the same report included an excerpt from a sermon delivered by Catholicos-Patriarch Ephrem II praising the Soviet Union's role as peacemaker throughout the world and the programme of the Communist Party, thanks to which »in just few decades people will live as it was promised by Christ«[42]. The 1980s saw a rise of interest in religion[43]. The national awakening brought along a religious transformation with the public image of the institutional church gradually changing and the religious publishing increasing in the country. By 1980, 15 eparchies of the GOC had been restored, and a seminary opened in 1988. The Georgian liturgy returned, and the tradition of old Georgian liturgical chant experienced a strong revival[44].

Political Theology in Practice – The Pragmatic and Uneasy »Symphony« of Two Powers

The post-Soviet Georgian Church was built on the Soviet heritage of the alliance with the state. Despite that, during the crisis of the post-Soviet transition, the church appeared in the people's eyes as a counterweight to an unreliable political space. Lived memory of repressions coupled with the religious awakening in the 1980s laid the foundation for the church's new authority. The national-cultural significance of religion contributed to a stronger linkage between ethnoreligious nationalism and the GOC. In the new political and social reality, the church managed to be the »defender« of nationalism[45].

In the 1990s, the GOC's authority and reputation were a far cry from what it managed to acquire in the years to follow. For instance, an appeal of Patriarch Ilia II, in the night of 9 April 1989 tragedy, urging the anti-Soviet, pro-independence people, to move into the forecourt of Kashueti Cathedral for prayer was rejected.

---

41 Archives of the Department of Propaganda at the Central Committee of the Communist Party. Archives of the Ministry of Internal Affairs, Fond 14, Opis' 50, Delo 199, List 38–51, 1975.
42 Ibid.
43 Temur PANJIKIDZE, Religious Life in Georgia (Past and Present), Tbilisi 2006.
44 The long road to the restoration of the GOC's autocephaly came to an end on 3 March 1990, when the Ecumenical Patriarch of Constantinople finally recognised it.
45 Giga ZEDANIA, Nationalismus und Religion in Georgien, in: Religion und Gesellschaft in Ost und West 6 (2011), pp. 16–20; Silvia SERRANO, De-secularising National Space in Georgia, in: Identity Studies 2 (2010), pp. 37–58.

People decided to remain in front of the government palace on that fateful night[46]. During the President Gamsakhurdia's first term in office, the church did not enjoy much influence as a public actor, having not yet shaken off the controversial Soviet legacy. During the government of Eduard Shevardnadze (1992–2003), the GOC managed to become a powerful source of political legitimation. This period saw an informal yet politically cemented »rapprochement«, with both powers relying on this alliance as an instrument to reciprocally reinforce their respective authority. The public perceived the church as a factor of balance against the backdrop of civil war and of political and social crises.

This alliance had created a situation whereby the Patriarch and the church were »supra-political« yet present in the political arena. Moreover, as a result of this alliance, the Patriarch stood beside the authorities – to be precise, besides President Shevardnadze – when political crises were looming[47]. The Patriarch would attend every significant political or public event, whether it was the signing of the new constitution (1995), the celebration of the construction of the Baku-Tbilisi-Ceyhan pipeline (2003), or some other important event. He performed important »political rituals«, such as the baptism of Shevardnadze and other former high-ranking Soviet officials, and the president's oath ceremony at the Svetitskhoveli Cathedral. The political alliance was climaxed in 2002 by a constitutional agreement, which granted the GOC the status of public law and entitled it to various privileges[48]. The terms and conditions of the agreement were rather controversial, and heated debates continued around issues pertaining to the funding of the GOC in the form of »compensation for the damage endured by the church during Soviet rule«, even though the extent of this damage has never been calculated[49]. In reality, the funding

---

46 The »April 9 tragedy« (also known as »Tbilisi massacre« or »Tbilisi tragedy«) refers to the events in Tbilisi, Georgian Soviet Socialist Republic, on 9 April 1989, when an anti-Soviet demonstration was brutally crushed by the Soviet Army.

47 Eva FUCHSLOCHER, Vaterland, Sprache, Glaube. Orthodoxie und Nationenbildung am Beispiel Georgiens, Stuttgart 2010, p. 158; Sopiko ZVIADADZE, Religion und Politik in Georgien. Die Beziehungen von Staat und Kirche und die Säkularisierungsproblematik im postkommunistischen Georgien, Hamburg 2014, p. 70.

48 Constitutional Agreement between the Georgian State and the Georgian Orthodox Church, published by The Legislative Herald of Georgia, 10-22-2002, URL: <https://matsne.gov.ge/ka/document/view/41626> (11-20-2023). Pursuant to the resolution of the Georgian government of 20 April 2015 [§10], high-ranking clergymen and officials of the Patriarchate's administration are entitled to a diplomatic passport [§11].

49 The state recognises Orthodox church-buildings, monasteries (both functional and non-functional), their ruins, as well as the land on which they stand as property of the church (§7.1); the state acknowledges the material and moral loss sustained by the church during the Soviet occupation (between 1921 and 1990); the church is owner *de facto* of part of the seized property; the state takes the responsibility to partially compensate such loss (§11.1 of the Resolution of the Council of Ministers of the Georgian Soviet Socialist Republic No 183 from 12 April 1990). This

provided to the church represents a fee paid to a »strategic partner« for the support it has routinely provided[50].

In the period following the Rose Revolution of 2003, the relationship between church and state moved to a new stage. The new political team brought to power by the revolution vowed to introduce a secular and liberal-democratic form of governance. It was for the first time that the state had made some steps towards eliminating discrimination by means of religion. Freedom of religion and the integration of ethnic and religious minorities were for the first time priorities on the state's agenda. However, the separation of church and state turned out to be a far more complicated project. It did not take long for the church to feel the »modernisation effect«. The period between 2004 and 2007 was marked by a lingering tension between church and state, with the former managing to maintain its power and further reinforce its authority against the backdrop of »accelerated modernisation«. The church continued to exert its influence over certain political decisions.

Moreover, like Shevardnadze, Saakashvili had to resort to the church's support when political crises seemed imminent. In 2004, the Gelati Cathedral hosted an inaugural ceremony for the newly-elected President Saakashvili. This may have resonated with Saakashvili's desire to imprint his presidency on Georgian history in the manner of David the Builder (r. 1089–1125), the greatest and most successful Georgian ruler in history and the original architect of the so-called »Georgian Golden Age«. Holding an inaugural ceremony in 2008, however, was rather a demonstration of the willingness of Saakashvili, now elected for a second term, to have the church as a political supporter. At that time, the country had already entered a period of political crisis, which led to the church's budget being supported from the presidential reserve. For instance, donations were made through the Ministry of Internal Affairs to provide luxurious cars for high-ranking members of the clergy[51]. Such practices were maintained even after the major political changes of 2012. In fact, the elections of 2012 were marked by the unprecedented involvement of the

---

article continues to cause controversy since no commission has ever been convened and therefore there has been no estimation of the damage endured by the Orthodox Church. In addition, Soviet persecution and oppression affected all religious associations and organisations, not only the GOC.

50 Eka CHITANAVA/Giorgi NONIASHVILI, Funding of religious organisations by Georgian central and local authorities (review of the situation in the end of 2013 and the beginning of 2014 and a state policy after the change of the government), published by Tolerance and Diversity Institute (TDI) / Human Rights Education and Monitoring Center (EMC) [now Social Justice Center], Tbilisi 2014, URL: <https://tdi.ge/sites/default/files/religiuri_organizaciebis_dapinansebis_kvleva_tdi.pdf> (11-07-2023).

51 Ibid.

clergy in the electoral campaign[52]. High rank members of the clergy openly called on their parishioners to support the »Georgian Dream«, the main opposition party, which would allow more privileges and act more »nationally« – according to the church's expectations. Even though the GOC officially denies alliance with any political party, »political sermons« in the run-up to elections were and remain a common practice[53].

There are the fields where the state and the GOC tried to reinforce and back up each other's authority. There have been quite a few precedents for such practices. The first such case occurred in 2011 when the state, despite the church's protest, managed to enact amendments to the Civil Code, thus allowing religious groups and organisations to register as statutory bodies under public law. As a rule, the church supports a government-nominated candidate, but this does not imply the state's supremacy over the church. Rather, it means that the latter will be eligible for more privileges and financial support. The state struggles to become a sovereign in politics and is engaged in constant negotiations with the Patriarchate. However, legal initiatives, perceived by the church as threatening its institutional and moral monopoly, broke this »symphonic« relationship. The second such incident took place in 2014 when the parliament passed a law on the elimination of all forms of discrimination, against which the church vehemently protested. However, the Patriarchate, the representatives of which were very active in debates and discussions, still managed to have a say in shaping the final version of this law[54]. As a rule, not only does the church set the tone of public sentiment; it also directly influences decision-making processes, claiming that this interference has no religious goals and rather serves the preservation of national and traditional values. In 2013, while the Self-Governance Code was being drawn up, the Patriarch argued that the draft law would trigger segregation in Georgia and vowed that the church would never accept it. After this statement, representatives of the authorities consulted with the Patriarchate, so that in the end the draft was revised in a form acceptable to the church[55]. Despite some ambiguities, the mutual agreement on »moral issues« between the GOC, ruling party politicians and newly emerged far-right populist groups became evident[56].

---

52 Kristina MARGVELASHVILI, The Influence of the Orthodox Church. Political Processes and Elections in Georgia, in: Nino GHAMBASHIDZE (ed.), Religion, Society and Politics in Georgia, Tbilisi 2016, pp. 4–14, at p. 11.
53 Ibid.
54 The problem of the separation of state and church in Georgia, published by the Tolerance and Diversity Institute (TDI), URL: <https://www.tdi.ge/ge/page/saxelmciposa-da-eklesiis-urtiertgamijvnis-problema-sakartveloshi> (11-20-2023).
55 Ibid.
56 The groups such as »Georgian March«, »Conservative Movement«, »Georgian Idea« are labelled differently by scholars: ultra-nationalist, anti-liberal, ultra-conservative, radical far-right. I will use

The 17th May of 2013 could be marked as a focal point for the »value struggle« and the start of the GOC's effort to become a public moral authority. On 17 May 2013, around twenty civil activists announced that they were going to celebrate the international day against homophobia. In response, their opponents including the Orthodox clergy mobilised a massive rally of people. An official statement made by the church, expressing its dislike for the event, encouraged thousands of youth people to publicly protest against the 17 May event[57]. The following year, the church responded by declaring 17 May as a day of »family holiness« in an attempt to counter the IDAHO (International Day Against Homophobia).

This topic has once again become the subject of debates and protest rallies. On 17 May 2014, when the Parliament of Georgia adopted a law against the elimination of all forms of discrimination, the GOC was officially against adopting the law and labelled it as »propaganda of homosexuality«. Various far-right and radical religious groups demanded that the words »gender« and »sexual orientation« should be omitted from the text. One of the leaders of these groups was Levan Vasadze[58], who founded the public movement »Unity, Essence, Hope« in 2021.

The emergence of such radical far-right populist groups and the mutual loyalty between the church and these groups challenges the current political and social order. They are notorious for their hard-line anti-liberal, anti-LGBT, anti-Muslim, and pro-Russian stance. Some of these groups founded political parties (»Georgian March«, »Conservative Movement«) and own private Media (e. g., TV Alt–Info). On 5 July 2021, they contributed to mobilising the participants from different regions of Georgia in the violent demonstration against the »March of Dignity« planned within the Tbilisi Pride Week. Participants predominantly consisted of the supporters of Levan Vasadze's movement »Unity, Essence, Hope« and the »Georgian

---

»far-right populist groups« emphasising their common populist discourse. Their main narratives are anti-liberal, anti-LGBT, anti-Muslim, xenophobic, anti-feminist, and nativist.

57 The opponents did not limit themselves to slogans (»Stop Homosexual Propaganda in Georgia«), but also used physical force.

58 Levan Vasadze is co-founder of the Georgian Demographic Society XXI and representative of the World Congress of Families in Georgia. On 15–17 May 2016, Tbilisi hosted the tenth anniversary congress organised by Vasadze. He consequently released video podcasts with homophobic, anti-Western, and ultra-conservative content. For instance, his influence had been instrumental in the church's fierce resistance to the introduction of *Me and Society*, a textbook designed for civil education in schools. Since 2015, Vasadze has been busy organising demos and proposing legislative changes. The Georgian Demographic Society has lodged two initiatives in the Parliament demanding that notions such as »sexual orientation« and »gender« should be removed from the anti-discrimination law. He is also adamant that the »defamation of religious feelings« should be sanctioned by the Administrative Offence Code of Georgia. Vasadze is a close friend of Shio Mujiri, the Patriarch's *locum tenens*, while the head of the Patriarchate's press office, Andria Jaghmaidze, is on the teaching staff of Vasadze's private school. Vasadze's friendship and ideological alliance with the Russian ideologue of Eurasianism and new conservatism, Alexander Dugin, is the subject of criticism in society.

March«. The mobbing of LGBT Pride in Tbilisi on 5 July left over 50 journalists injured, among them one cameraman, who died a few days after the assault[59]. The violent event had several actors and predictors. Hence, this subject united the far-right populist movement, the controversial pro-Russian party, ultra-conservative and religious fundamentalist groups as well as an ordinary parish of GOC. The GOC as an institution with high public authority played a significant role in the unfolding of the event. On 29 June, the GOC accused the organisers of the nearing Tbilisi Pride of »propagating a non-traditional way of life under the guise of protecting human rights«. The GOC urged that the government must prevent »the destabilization of the country and of public life«[60]. In their sermons and statements, the Patriarchate of the GOC and the clergy openly called for a counter-demonstration. The Patriarchate announced two paraclesis (supplication services) and called on the parishioners to gather at the Kashveti Church on Rustaveli Avenue (at the same time and place the Tbilisi Pride March was announced): »[…] let's show the world that we protect our dignity«[61].

In May, the annual Easter Encyclical also thematised the gender issue. Patriarch Ilia II stated that »there is a period when national feelings disappeared, love, kindness, and justice […] are falsified […] traditional identities defining the human being – ›man‹ and ›woman‹, ›family values‹ have been erased«[62]. On the same day, a massive iron cross was erected in front of the Parliament by groups opposing the »Tbilisi Pride«. Civil society members are still demanding the removal of the cross, which in their opinion is a symbol of the 5 July violence, and not a religious symbol[63]. In their view, the illegally erected cross in front of the parliament symbolises the profanation of the Christianity and the politisation of religion in modern Georgian society.

---

59 In fact, Tbilisi Pride cancelled LGBTQ March for Dignity, citing a lack of safety guarantees by the Georgian Dream Government.
60 The Patriarchate publishes a statement against the »March of Dignity«, published by Radio Free Europe/Radio Liberty, 06-29-2021, URL: <https://www.radiotavisupleba.ge/a/31332214.html> (11-21-2023).
61 The Patriarchate openly attacks the Western countries' ambassadors and announces the contravention of the March of Dignity, published by Formula News, 07-03-2021, URL: <https://formulanews.ge/News/52943> (10-31-2023).
62 In his Easter Encyclical, Patriarch Lambasts »Post-humanism«, published by Civil Georgia, 05-03-2021, URL: <https://civil.ge/archives/417429> (11-21-2023).
63 What does the state intend to do with the cross erected near the parliament?, published by Netgazeti, 07-08-2021, URL: <https://netgazeti.ge/news/553174/> (11-21-2023).

The Evolution of the »Political« Point of View of the Patriarch and the Church

The political theology of the GOC in post-Soviet times has evolved around particular interpretations of historical and theological issues in response to actual challenges. Looking into the Patriarch's encyclicals and sermons is one of the way of understanding the church's narrative. Not only do these exercises considerable influence over Orthodox parishioners; they also serve as a concealed message to politicians. The analysis of Christmas and Easter Encyclicals issued from 1978 through 2021 reveals changes in the use of language, content, and undertone set by the Patriarch. They reflect transformations within society and politics. At times, the encyclicals echo current developments (i. e., ethnic conflicts and political confrontations), while at other times they attempt to bring certain issues (i. e., surrogacy and abortion) to the fore[64]. Gospel commentaries and general admonitions prevail in the letters issued from 1978 to 1989. The topics of the sermons and encyclicals are religious to the extent that it is difficult to tell from their content when and under what conditions they were composed. The Russian theologians Vladimir Solovëv and Vladimir Lossky are the most frequently cited authors in this period. The following years saw a slight, but still discernible emphasis on nationalist features reflecting the growing patriotic sentiments of the people: »As of today, the Georgian soil is sacred as it embraces the robe of Christ, Iveria is a land allotted to Virgin Mary, and Andrew, the First Called, and Simon, the Canaanite, preached here«[65].

Along with the systemic transformation, the encyclicals started to approach political issues. In the Encyclical of 1990, the collapse of the Soviet Union and changes in ideology were only a marginal presence (»ideals that we had believed to be perpetual are now gone because of their fragile foundations«). The 1991 Encyclical, however, refers to the new reality in clear images:

> We happen to be living in a very trying time full of political tensions and the imminent threat of destructive violence. Young people, being engrossed in politics, are deprived of the zeal to study and have turned their backs on hard work. Instead, a great many political parties, associations, and other public organisations have emerged[66].

---

64 They always »coincide« in time and content with stances of the Russian Orthodox Church.
65 Christmas 1978–1979, published by Orthodoxy, URL: <http://www.orthodoxy.ge/patriarqi/epistoleebi/sashobao1979.htm> (11-21-2023).
66 Christmas Encyclicals 1990 and 1991, published by Orthodoxy, URL: <http://www.orthodoxy.ge/patriarqi/epistoleebi/sashobao1990.htm> (11-21-2023).

Without knowledge of the political context (e. g., civil war and political chaos), it is difficult to fully grasp the meaning of the words used in the 1992 Christmas Encyclical:

> Part of the population seems to be annoyed with the church. Instead of protecting the church from politics and saying a heartfelt prayer for the unity of the nation, peace, and welfare, they have demanded that the church pick a side between the opposing parties. […] Should it be permitted that the church stands with one of the parties and, by doing so, grant moral support for one to slay the other[67]?

It is unlikely that such words belong to an institution distanced from politics. At the time, the church had no authority or reputation among political groups yet, while its role as mediator was only gradually beginning to reach certain societal circles. The rise of the church's influence and authority would come a little later.

The post-Soviet church experienced the effects of modernity with all their impact on religious pluralism. The Jehovah's Witnesses and other »suspicious«, »foreign-funded religious organisations«, particularly Protestant denominations, perceived as a threat, were a recurrent theme in the Patriarch's encyclicals and sermons of the 1990s:

> The time has come for all of us to recognise the threat posed by the unleashed rampage of foreign religious and totalitarian sects. The experience of the past few years has revealed that they reject and defame our national feelings, our past, history, and sacred values, and keep thousands of us away from the true path[68].

In the 1990s, the church officially denounced religious radicalism. However, clergy with fundamentalist sentiments continued to provide liturgical service in the parishes. The Union of Orthodox Parents, established in 1995 and bringing together both priests and parishioners, is among the most popular radical organisations. They fiercely fought against the missionary work of Jehovah's Witnesses, against Halloween celebrations, against Protestant religious groups, and against secular measures (i. e., the removal of religion classes from the national school curricula following the educational reform of 2005).

---

67 Christmas Encyclical 1992, published by Orthodoxy, URL: <http://www.orthodoxy.ge/patriarqi/epistoleebi/sashobao1992.htm> (11-21-2023).
68 Christmas Encyclical 1998, published by Orthodoxy, URL: <https://www.orthodoxy.ge/patriarqi/epistoleebi/saagdgomo1998.htm> (11-21-2023).

Religious radicalism and xenophobic sentiments were at their worst in both the church and public sphere[69]. The post-1995 period, which saw the church and the state serving as reciprocal sources of legitimation, might be taken to exemplify the Orthodox model of »symphony«. This rapprochement is well illustrated by the following statement made by the Patriarch:

> An opinion according to which the state ought to be separated from the church has gained prevalence in our public. This does not mean that the church must distance itself from public life and the social and cultural existence of the people. At the same time, it is of capital importance that Georgia, as an ancient Christian state, is guided by Christian ethics and builds a nation-state based on our traditions and Orthodox faith. The relationship between state and church is similar to that of soul and flesh whereby each has its own place and their harmonious existence is led by benevolence and intelligence[70].

If in Byzantium this model was in most cases concretised in Caesaropapism, in the case of Georgia the balance of power seemed tilted towards the church. The so-called symphony relies on mutual pragmatic benefits rather than theological doctrines underpinning the relationship between the two powers. The Patriarch openly supported political personalities (e. g., Eduard Shevardnadze) during the 1995 elections and expected the state to return the favour:

> It is true that every individual has the right to make free choices, but the state has the responsibility to protect its citizens from spiritual aggression, even more so when the actions of sects have already acquired anti-national and anti-statehood nature[71].

In the wake of the Rose Revolution of 2003, state policy went through a drastic change, which also affected religious matters, top priorities being the fight against religious radicalism and the protection of religious freedom. The same period saw ambiguity dominating the ecclesiastical narrative. Patriarch and other members of clergy referred to Europe and liberalism and stressed their ambivalence. By doing so, the church stood up to the new political agenda, unfortunately without much

---

69 From the political perspective, the concerns of the church manifested themselves in several instances. The 1995 Constitution highlights the special role played by the GOC in Georgian history; in 1997, the GOC left the World Council of Churches; in 2002, a constitutional agreement was concluded between state and church.
70 Christmas Encyclical 1998. All encyclicals are available at URL: <http://www.orthodoxy.ge/patriarqi/sarchevi.htm> (11-21-2023).
71 Ibid.

theological reflexion. The pragmatic ecclesiastical discourse had embraced such new concepts as technological progress, individual freedom, or liberalism:

> Even though the church is based on a hierarchy, it never restricts the freedom of the individual [...]. Sadly, we have all seen so-called reformers, both pseudo-liberals and pseudo-conservatives [...]. The past few years have witnessed the strengthening of both directions in Georgia. They have targeted the church and led to inappropriate, often defamatory and insulting, discussions[72].

On the one hand, the church managed to pragmatically assess the new political reality and avoid open confrontation with the new secular and liberal political elite. The GOC officially welcomed the introduction of visa-free travel for Georgian citizens endorsed by the EU[73]. This position was the result of the political affinity and of negotiations between state and the church. The GOC has often displayed a deep gap between official statements and everyday politico-theological discourse. On the other hand, it also managed to tackle radical societal transformations and »accelerated modernisation«, which threatened to undermine its authority. The church successfully imposed a taboo on critical voices against itself and adopted a nationalistic discourse stressing the function of the church as the authentic bearer of traditions and national identity.

In 2014, the Patriarch's Encyclical introduced a series of new topics. The encyclical, in its entirety, was dedicated to the definition and criticism of postmodernism and unlimited freedom:

> Every epoch has brought new challenges to Christianity. However, the postmodern era is striking with its mega-challenges. [...] We all know that the earth and the universe in general have their own laws, and this is the reality. However, modern thinking tells us that there is no general reality and that we have invented this reality. Therefore, one can, at one's own discretion, recognise certain occurrences as existent or reject them as non-existent. [...] All taboos must vanish! We must dismiss all restrictions of the past! Everything that I desire and that pleases me is good! However, there is the only rule that

---

72 Christmas Encyclical 2005, published by Orthodoxy, URL: <https://www.orthodoxy.ge/patriarqi/epistoleebi/saagdgomo2005.htm> (11-21-2023).
73 Patriarch – we think not only about what Europe will bring us, we think about what we will bring to Europe, published by Interpressnews, 12-19-2015, URL: <https://www.interpressnews.ge/ka/article/359220-patriarki-chven-vpikrobt-ara-marto-imaze-evropa-ras-mogvitans-chven-vpikrobt-imis-shesaxeb-chven-ras-shevitant-evropashi/> (11-23-2023).

must be followed: We must not violate the rights of others, especially those of minorities. This is the law⁷⁴!

In this context, the »rights of others« are meant in a negative sense, as the product of postmodernism and a sign of the decline of traditional values. The same Christmas Encyclical of 2014 further states: »Freedom of choice is one of the divine graces bestowed upon men by God, however, there is a fundamental difference between the teaching of Christ and the concept of ›liberty‹ propounded by pseudo-liberals«⁷⁵. In addition to labelling minority rights and freedom of choice as postmodern distortions of reality and denouncing them from the pulpits, the church has also established other ways to channel its anger and resentment. It resisted, for instance, the adoption of anti-discrimination laws and allied itself with ultra-nationalist groups to demonstrate every year against the »International Day Against Homophobia«, as showed above⁷⁶.

Topical »moral issues« such as the definition of marriage and the family or LGBTQ+ rights became a dominant theme in sermons and the church's official statements. The GOC has become an active promoter of »traditional values«. Alongside a global resurgence of »new conservativism« and far-right populism, a factor to be reckoned with is the suspected and controversial influence of the Russian Orthodox Church (ROC) on the GOC's positions towards gender issues. The GOC and Georgian society as a whole are the targets of the ROC's »norm entrepreneurship«, the concept used by Kristina Stoeckl while analysing the activity of the ROC in international morality politics. When the ROC acts as a moral norm entrepreneur, promoting traditional values and its own interpretation of human rights, it inevitably – directly or indirectly – affects the GOC⁷⁷.

The Pluralisation of Religious Reflections through Internet

In general, the church's political and secular role became far more controversial. Confrontations within the church and scandals around church personalities have

---

74 Christmas Encyclical 2014, published by Orthodoxy, URL: <https://www.orthodoxy.ge/patriarqi/epistoleebi/saagdgomo2014.htm> (11-21-2023).
75 Ibid.
76 These groups include, for example, the »Georgian March«, an active proponent of a homophobic, neo-Nazi, and ultra-radical agenda. Its suspicious ties with Russian foundations have often been in the focus of public debates. A visit paid by »Georgian March« leaders to the Patriarch triggered a particularly harsh reaction.
77 Kristina STOECKL, The Russian Orthodox Church as a Moral Norm Entrepreneur, in: Religion, State & Society 44/2 (2016), pp. 132–151.

made media headlines since religion ceased to be a taboo topic in public discourse. The pronouncements of the GOC and influential members of the clergy receive much public attention. Print media, blogs, social media, television, and radio have contributed to a greater visibility of the church and the spread of its narrative into the public sphere, while making discussions around religious issues more pluralistic and open to secular arguments. The internet, particularly, has offered a space both for strengthening traditional religious discourse and for alternative ideas. If the public sphere has moved, in however small a way, towards liberal or secular ways of thinking about religion or the church, the relationship between state and church, or at least its political performance, still remains the same[78].

The stance and the narrative of the church have evolved along with societal transformation into a harsh reaction to religious pluralism manifested in the Last Judgement discourse. The period following Georgia's independence saw the rise of quasi-religious beliefs in the Last Judgement, especially among marginal and fundamentalist groups with unconventional religiosity. The Last Judgement theme would become a main issue of popular belief when it came to technological innovations such as the internet or electronic ID cards. The sermons of Elder Gabriel (Urgebadze), Elder Paisios of Mount Athos, Seraphim Rose, and Justin Popović focusing on the Last Judgement gained popularity after 1990[79]. Especially Elder Paisios and Elder Gabriel enjoy immense popularity, first among the consumers of religious literature and more recently among the users of religious websites.

Elder Gabriel represents an example of non-traditional religiosity in contemporary Georgia. Even before he was canonised by the Georgian Church in December 2012, his gravesite near Tbilisi was a popular pilgrimage destination, and he is now much-quoted on the internet. Most of his sermons concern the Last Judgement and criticise modernity. Such topics are popular among the clergy favouring an »eschatological language«. The dream of patriarch Ilia II about the End Times is also very popular, and Ilia is often mentioned in sermons as the »Patriarch of End Times«. The analysis of the discourse of the post-Soviet GOC reveals that nowadays the church usually invokes eschatology as an instrument for strengthening its power. It is important to note that while the official statements of the Patriarch and other high-ranking clergy have always been conservative and anti-modernist, eschatological allusions were rather rare. Confrontations within the church, scandals around the candidacy of a future Patriarch, the rise of anticlericalism, and the church's

---

78 The nomination ceremony for the ruling party's candidates in the 2020 parliamentary elections was also attended by high-ranking members of the church, while candidates' campaign photos included the unavoidable shots in the church.

79 A Georgian-language website that focuses exclusively on the End Times and uses exclusively sources in Russian is available in Georgian at apocalypse.ge, URL: <http://www.apocalypse.ge/publikaciebi_ioane_gvtismetyvelis_saidumlo.html> (11-21-2023).

waning authority during the Covid-19 crisis have created the favourable circumstances for bells tolling the End Times from the country's main cathedral. In July 2020, Archbishop Daniel drew parallels between Ilia II and Elijah of Tishbite, the preacher of the End Times. Archbishop Daniel was sure that it was no coincidence that the two share the same name:

> We have been witnessing the End Times approaching. There have been many signs. However, the most important omen, as the Lord says in the Gospel, is the multiplication of false teachings and false prophets in the form and on a scale that even chosen people and chosen Christian countries are easily tempted. This is truly the time preceding the advent of Antichrist[80].

We may argue that in an Orthodox-secular order fear is not induced by the End Times, but rather it is fear that creates eschatology. In January 2020, Patriarch Ilia II affirmed: »We must do everything to get ourselves prepared for the End Times. They are close. […] I have heard some believers saying that the End Times are close, but I tell you that they may as well be just few days away«[81]. Such a sermon from a high-ranking clergyman could not go unnoticed. The sermon was strongly frowned upon, with critics asking »why does the church try to intimidate parishioners?«, which eventually put the Patriarchate under pressure to react with a special communiqué.

Today, the church incorporates a wide spectrum of clergymen with dissenting views and values. Among them are the Russophiles, those with ultra-radical views, as well as pro-Western actors. Priest David Isakadze, the head of the ultra-radical Union of Orthodox Parents, labels democratic discourse and human rights activism as tools of a »Brussels dictatorship«. He argues that

> [Georgia] has been under pressure to let in migrants and refugees from other countries. It seems that the only reason Europe has allowed visa liberalisation is to lead thousands of foreigners to our country and degrade us physically! In no time, Georgians will constitute a minority of this country's population[82]!

It should be noted that the Patriarch had for many years been the only voice of the church. However, in recent years more and more members of the clergy have started

---

80 The Patriarch's Sunday sermon, published by Ambioni, 07-26-2020, URL: <http://www.ambioni.ge/sakvirao-qadageba-26-07-2020> (11-21-2023).
81 Ilia II. The Last Judgement is close, published by Radiotavisupleba, 01-12-2020, URL: <https://tinyurl.com/2pj2xx5n> (11-21-2023).
82 Available in Georgian at URL: <https://qartuliazri.reportiori.ge/inside.php?menuid=68&id=5317> (11-23-2023).

to reach out to the public. Although most of the clergy's public statements are in accordance with the official state policy, there still are some voices, which have been calling out Russia as an occupant while others make an appeal to the »communion« of faith when it comes to Russo-Georgian relations. The church's regularly expressed support for monarchy is a political manoeuvre rather than a representation of the institution's political theology. The Patriarch asserted that constitutional monarchy is the source of peace in any country and the people of Georgia, the country with a most ancient culture, may in future consider restoring the monarchy, since, in his eyes, Georgia *was* an ancient monarchy whose kings reigned in God's grace. This sermon hit media headlines and caught the attention of social media users. In contrast to the previous years, the idea of monarchy received stronger criticism. Even though the mainstream clergy still supported it, there were few priests who did not share the belief that monarchy is the best form of governance and that the ultimate obligation of a nation would be to »reinstate monarchy«. Deacon Ilia Chighladze of the Western European Diocese of the GOC in London compared absolute monarchy with dictatorship, saying it had no place in the twenty-first century[83].

Tapping into the advance in information technologies and the growth of the online community, the clergy have actively been involved in shaping the ecclesiastical discourse. Even though credit cannot be given solely to the advanced technologies, the internet has become a platform where people feel comfortable to voice and disseminate dissenting views. This has made discussions around religion more pluralistic. Signs of change in the discourse can be observed in the Western European Diocese of the GOC and among young Georgian theologians living abroad. Tamaz Lomidze, a deacon in Munich, highlights the crisis existing in the relationship between state and church and argues that

> there is only one way out of this crisis: The free state must progressively gain strength with its inviolable laws and structures and, at the same time, the church must irreversibly get weaker materially and allow its worldly influence to wither. We must not try to correct Christ's deeds. The Lord is not mistaken when he says, »My kingdom is not of this world«. It is a simple truth that the weaker the church is in this world, the stronger it is spiritually. The more the church shakes off its material obligations, the more it will have been bestowed grace to preach Christ's teaching and give a way to state authorities to build a free country. This is the only way out of the crisis for both the state and the church[84].

---

83 Deacon of GOC in the diocese of UK and Ireland, Ilia Chighladze on Monarchy, published by Tabula, 06-19-2017, URL: <http://tbl.ge/2deo> (11-21-2023).

84 Deacon Tamaz Lomidze. The more material duties the church removes, the more spiritual grace it will receive to preach the doctrine, published by Intepressnews, 03-10-2017, URL: <https://tinyurl.com/msck3y4d> (11-21-2023).

Similar views are rarely voiced by clergy serving in Georgia. A possible explanation may lie in the fact that, unlike most dioceses, Lomidze's diocese in Munich operates in a pluralistic and multicultural environment. In addition, the Patriarchate's ability to exert control over all its dependencies abroad seems to have declined.

The State, the Church, and Theological Debates in a Time of State Emergency

On 21 March 2020, the President of Georgia declared a state of emergency for the purpose of preventing the spread of Covid-19. The same day, Prime Minister Gakharia told the public that in the state of emergency no more than ten people could be gathered and drew everyone's attention, including that of the media, to the church: What would the church's response be to this restriction? The faithful wanted to know whether they would be able to attend next Sunday's service, and, most importantly, if they would be able to participate in the Easter liturgy. Another important question posed by restrictions under the state of emergency was whether the state would be able to stand by its commitment and not make an exception for the church. Unsurprisingly, the first question that the prime minister had to answer after making the announcement was whether the restrictions would be applied to the GOC. »The main goal and objective of the Government of Georgia is to take care of the health of our citizens regardless of their religious belief«, Gakharia said[85]. However, it did not take long before he had to water down and revise his response. The day before, on 20 March 2020, the Holy Synod ruled that regardless of a high risk of Covid-19, all churches would resume their services, nor would the rule for the holy sacrament be revised: »Questioning the essence of the holy sacrament and expressing this doubt by refusing to use the spoon as the alleged spreader of infection is utterly unacceptable«[86]. Any discussion around even a temporary closure of churches would be perceived as a battle against the church and a sign of the End Times, whereas the use of disposable spoons for Holy Communion was tantamount to blasphemy.

The developments brought about by the new coronavirus posed serious challenges to the church. The church had to come up with a theological response, which had never been discussed before. Over the course of many years, the church had closed itself off to any discussion, which would contain even a slightest attempt

---

85 Freedom of faith shall not be restricted by a decree – Talakvadze attends morning service, published by Netgazeti, 03-21-2020, URL: <https://netgazeti.ge/news/436389/> (11-21-2023).
86 Synod – Refusing to share a common spoon as a source of infection is totally unacceptable, published by Georgian Public Broadcaster, 03-20-2020, URL: <https://1tv.ge/news/sinodi-saziarebel-saertokovzze-uaris-tqma-rogorc-infeqciis-gadamtan-wyaroze-yovlad-miughebelia/> (11-21-2023).

to offer a new reading of the ecclesiastical tradition in a changing context, even though this would not mean a radical revision, but rather an effort to establish a connection between the tradition and the challenges of modernity. In the pandemic, the church's response looked more like of a competition with the state than a step towards finding common ground with the public. »The practice of using the spoon for the holy sacrament goes back thousands of years […]. By taking the holy sacrament, the faithful takes the holy Body and Blood of Christ as purification and treatment of body and soul«, read the statement of the Synod[87].

The general discourse created by bishops and popular clergymen was hardly a confrontation between secular and religious thinking, religious and medical opinions. It was more of a revival of conspiracy theories and existing fundamentalist trends. For instance, Bishop Job argued that the virus and the developments around it were the creation of unbelievers and »Freemasons«: »What should be important are the Patriarch's appeals rather than those of unbelieving governments and doctors«[88]. The second trend within the ecclesiastical discourse was the claim to »being a better Orthodox Christian«[89]. The bottom line in the sermons of high-ranking clergy in Georgia was that attending Sunday services was an act of bravery. They would draw comparisons between the bravery demonstrated by such congregations and that of Christian martyrs and national heroes. »Some people tell us to shut down our churches like Catholics, Muslims, and other religions. I am sure there will be no humankind on earth in 2 or 3 years«, said Bishop Job[90].

The statements of the Patriarchate of the GOC triggered greater criticism because of the church's controversial reputation. The GOC encouraged people to come to church, even though it might have been dangerous: »[In the past] not only did the faithful remain untroubled by the alleged dangers of taking Holy Communion, they would do so with increasing frequency«[91]. Some members of the clergy went so far as calling out the congregation to go to church on Easter eve as an existential matter for the church and the faith. »May you seek death and sacrifice for Christ« – a catch-line running through the sermons of many priests that triggered criticism and heated public debates. The church's call to come to service during the quarantine,

---

87 In such times the faithful were not afraid to take communion with a shared spoon – on the contrary – the Patriarchate, published by Publika, 02-29-2020, URL: <https://publika.ge/aset-periodebshi-morwmuneni-ar-ushindebodnen-saerto-kovzit-ziarebas-piriqit-sapatriarqo/> (11-21-2023).
88 Father Job calls on the congregation to not listen to doctors and encourages them to endanger their lives, published by News ON, 04-15-2020, URL: <http://go.on.ge/1j93> (11-21-2023).
89 Services in churches were put on hold by Greek, Romanian, and other Christian Orthodox Churches.
90 Bishop Job: If we close churches, there will be no humankind, published by Newshub, 03-29-2020, URL: <https://newshub.ge/news/sazogadoeba/meuphe-iosebi-tadzrebs-tu-davketavt-katsobrioba-aghar-iarsebebs> (11-23-2023).
91 Ibid.

it was argued, was »a symptom of theological and moral depravity, which has resurfaced in all its severity amid the pandemic. It appears that all theological knowledge of the Patriarchate and its faith boils down to the spoon«[92]. Former deacon Basil Kobakhidze believed that this is »false mystical ecstasy and fetishist attitude towards God as well as to rituals and the Holy Communion«[93].

The sermons preached at that time by the Patriarch and influential clergy were dominated by the themes of a looming Armageddon. The pandemic and changed reality provided a new momentum for controversial, if not entirely marginal, ideas and notions promoted by members of the clergy: visions of the Patriarch, watering streets with Holy Water, Georgians as a chosen people, protecting the church from the Freemasons, and so on. Such statements would be followed by widely shared political, public, and theological criticism. More importantly, the voices of theologians when it comes to matters of religion and the church were almost never heard in Georgia. Those with views dissenting from the Patriarchate's official stance were too few in number to create an alternative discourse. Yet, this feeble voice rang lounder amidst the state of emergency.

Zurab Jashi is one of the theologians, who never let the church's statements go unnoticed and often voiced criticism from a theological perspective:

> Not only has [the church's decision] failed to bolster the faith of the congregation, but it also contains a threat of displaying the Christian faith as superstition attributed to magical rituals, which does not require a free and conscious response from an individual to the divine will. Moreover, it is bound to subvert the free will and thinking, precious graces that make us an image of God. On the other hand, no less danger comes from unrestricted gatherings during services, which is conducive to the spread of the disease and contradicts the sacred Testament calling us to love our neighbours[94].

The return of Basil Kobakhidze – once an outstanding member of the Orthodox Church, a fierce opponent of religious fanaticism and outspoken critic of flaws within the church, who left the church as a sign of protest – to the public sphere signalled the gravity of the situation. After having remained in the shadow for a while, Kobakhidze started making video appeals during the pandemic, in which he criticised the church's stance as non-Christian:

---

92 Giorgi MAISURADZE, The Church, the Virus and Logos, published by Radio Free Europe/RFE, 05-04-2020, URL: <https://tinyurl.com/5dkury4n> (11-21-2023).
93 Is the God great and the virus small? – an interview with former deacon Basil Kobakhidze, published by Radio Free Europe/RFE, 04-17-2020, URL: <https://www.radiotavisupleba.ge/a/30540114.html> (11-21-2023).
94 Zurab JASHI, The Pandemic and the Church, published by Social Justice Center, 04-14-2020, URL: <https://socialjustice.org.ge/ka/products/pandemia-da-eklesia-zurab-jashi> (11-23-2023).

We are talking about closing churches for a month, a quarantine. We are not talking about blasphemy or people being deprived of their right to participate in ceremonies [...] the worst thing is that members of the clergy – for instance, Father Nikoloz – challenge the faithful by saying that if you are afraid, stay at home. And the congregation thinks that even though the church has told me to stay home, am I not betraying God if I do so? With this disposition, the congregation demonstrates religious audacity[95].

Deacon Irakli Jinjolava was also among the few, who argued that temporarily refraining from attending liturgy during the pandemic does not imply a rejection of God: »Today is the time, when we can experience the presence of Jesus, become the true Body, Church and Eucharist of Christ while remaining in our homes«[96]. Furthermore, Zaza Tevzadze belonged to a rather small group of the clergy who would openly criticise the lack of spiritual education among the members of the clergy, religious radicalism, and institutional closure[97]. He argued that

> when the whole world struggles to cope with unprecedented danger, when a war is being waged between soundness and massive psychosis, between healthy religiosity and apocalyptic hysteria, and the balance of powers, as one would expect from the world, sways towards death with such indifference towards life [...], in this time, we join in God – in supreme love and the all-encompassing secret of eternity – by necessary isolation commensurable to the current situation[98]!

When it comes to the Patriarchate adamantly holding on to the usual liturgical practice, participants in public discussions believed that secular rather than religious motives were at stake. Basil Kobakhidze argued that »the church is the state within the state. If the Patriarch says that these are satanic authorities who threaten us, he is well capable of causing uprisings of people, police, and the army even in the hard times of the pandemics«[99].

The month between the declaration of the state of emergency and the Easter liturgy was a marathon of sorts: Who was going to rise victorious – the church or the state? Who will win the battle over managing the extraordinary? A few days before Easter, the prime minister was »invited« to the Patriarchate to »explain«

---

95 RFE, Is God great and the virus small?
96 The Pandemic and the idea of solidarity: what clergymen and theologians say, published by Social Justice, 04-16-2020, URL: <https://socialjustice.org.ge/ka/products/pandemia-da-solidarobis-idea-ras-fikroben-sasuliero-pirebi> (11-23-2023).
97 In response, the Patriarchate would »repress« the priest for his audacious, non-conformist, and liberal views.
98 The Pandemic and the idea of solidarity: what clergymen and theologians say.
99 RFE, »Is the God great and the virus small?«.

rules and measures applicable during the state of emergency and that a »ten-person rule« would not apply to the church. As a result, the Patriarchate issued a rather ambivalent statement declaring that there would be a liturgy in accordance with state regulations. In his turn, the prime minister also made a cleverly ambiguous statement. The language and the spirit of this statement were far from the previous one. For instance, in the statement made on 21 March, he unequivocally declared that »the rule applies to all, including the church«. Later, the prime minister offered the following opening line: »We are an Orthodox Christian state with a thousand years of cooperation between church and state. Keeping churches open is an existential matter for many of our esteemed believers«. In addition to buttering up the church, the state shifted the whole burden of decision-making to disoriented citizens, who had to abide by demands that the state had failed to make of the church: »A wise and intelligent citizen knows that they must not put the responsibility on the church and not wait for the latter's appeal to go to church. Nor should they wait for the state's green light to break the law«[100].

In 2020, the Patriarch's Easter Encyclical explicitly mentioned the contributions of doctors, the »actions of the government and the responsibility of the population«. The encyclical stressed that »by the grace of God, services have been held with the faithful in Georgian churches, including on Easter night«[101]. Many suspected that »keeping churches open« was nothing more than an expression of rivalry between the state and the church. The 2020 Easter was the culmination not so much of a forty-day fasting period than of the state of emergency. The church managed to assume control over each and every restriction imposed by the state, including the right to assembly, the number of people gathered, the distancing measures, and the breaking of the curfew. The pandemic revealed the real sovereign to be the church, the true authority in charge of the state of exception.

Conclusion

The Georgian Orthodox Church in post-Soviet times could be perceived as the main winner of system transformation. Since the 1990s, the Church gained the public trust and became a source for legitimation for political power. Considering the political and historical contexts, the GOC has »different political theologies pertaining to various epochs«[102]. Today the church »creates« its own political theology and

---

100 Prime Minister's Briefing, 04-14-2020, original at 1TV-First Channel, published by YouTube, URL: <https://www.youtube.com/watch?v=SYOVxd5hqoQ> (11-21-2023).
101 Patriarch Ilia, The Easter Message of the Catholicos-Patriarch of All Georgia, published by Patriarchate, 04-19-2020, URL: <https://patriarchate.ge/news/2605> (11-21-2023).
102 See Ratiani, Political Theologies across Epochs.

»invents Orthodox tradition«[103]. There is a body of evidence confirming that the environment, in which the church had to operate in the past was not conducive to the development of continuous theological thought. The process of the church defining its own place in the modern and secular era started in the early twentieth century and ceased fairly soon. The Soviet regime left an indelible mark on the church under its control and turned it into a secular institution of some sort. The GOC of post-Soviet Georgia is heir to this very distorted church. Instead of performing a theological reorientation and rethinking, the GOC decided to use its symbolic capital to express loyalty to ruling governments or to cement its authority in power games with the state. The church's response to drastic societal changes in post-Soviet society often fits political agendas rather than representing an attempt at a theological and ecclesiological rethinking of the new social reality. The church's dominant discourse is saturated by nationalist narratives, coupled with growing eschatological and populist ones. In a society where religion is the most important measure of national identity, the church is perceived to be the protector of this identity[104]. Besides that, any crisis and mistrust towards political institutions gives more legitimation to the »sacred dome«. During the crisis of the post-Soviet transition, the church appeared in the people's eyes as a counterweight to an unreliable political space. The tactical »political neutrality« of the Patriarch of the GOC turned out to be the desired mode for society. The church managed to create a »secular order« of its own and remained impenetrable during the chaos of the Covid-19 pandemic. The time for a state of emergency in Georgia confirmed that the GOC is the true sovereign in the country, the one ruling the state of emergency, as Schmitt would put it[105].

As mentioned above, the church's response to the challenges of the new reality consists mainly in religious thought confronting secular ideas. The response is, in most cases, limited to a church wrestling with the state, so that the latter can acknowledge its power. Giga Zedania argues that modern political theology is the response to differentiation processes and will exist as long as the church keeps rejecting modernity and points to its own tradition[106]. The GOC has been building its own political theology in response of pluralisation and secularisation processes. The question remains whether it is a truly Orthodox political theology, situational politics, or an invented *Kulturkampf* of the post-truth era.

---

103 Zurab JASHI, Inventing the Orthodox Tradition in the Post-Soviet Georgia, Tbilisi 2020.
104 Alexander UNSER et al., Predictors of Attitudes Towards the Right to Work: An Empirical Analysis Among Young People in Moldova and Georgia, in: Hans-Georg ZIEBERTZ (ed.), International Empirical Studies on Religion and Socioeconomic Human Rights, Wiesbaden 2020, pp. 129–168.
105 SCHMITT, Political Theology, p. 5.
106 ZEDANIA, Political Theology, p. 20.

Alexander Ponomariov

Orthodox Theopolitical Philosophies in post-2014 Ukraine

»Political Orthodoxy«

In the case of modern Ukraine, one can speak of Orthodox »political theolog*ies*«, whose breakout point was the bloody Maidan coup d'état of 2014. The invasion of Ukraine by the Russian Federation in 2022 has only exacerbated this phenomenon. Ukrainian Orthodox protagonists tend to separate »political theology« from »public theology«, seeing the former in terms of relations between church and state, and the latter in terms of relations between church and society. In so doing, they prioritise »public theology« over »political theology«, which distinguishes the Ukrainian approach from contemporary Russian Orthodoxy. At the same time, the Ukrainian authors (with the exception of the Ukrainian Orthodox Church under the Moscow Patriarchate) idealise Maidan so much that they present it both as a *Messiah* for the decolonisation of Ukraine from Russian »imperial« and »barbarian« culture and the cornerstone for building Ukrainian civil society.

It has been noted that, »while Orthodox theology is gaining a more prominent place in western scholarship, political theology remains overwhelmingly Catholic and Protestant«[1]. Besides, it is argued, »public ecclesiology depends on the particular public of which one speaks«[2]. Furthermore, in the Orthodox milieu, one can speak mostly of individual attempts at theological reflection, attempts »which did not enjoy an official endorsement«[3]. In post-2014 Ukraine, individual reflections are clearly the case; and the so-called »political theology« is developed by a few persons (one of whom lives and works abroad) for a specific public, and is based on established Protestant and Roman Catholic doctrines.

It should be noted that there were a few and rather weak institutional church attempts to formulate some aspects of Ukrainian »political theology«. One of them

---

[1] Nathaniel WOOD/Aristotle PAPANIKOLAOU, Orthodox Christianity and Political Theology, in: Ruben RODRIGUEZ (ed.), T&T Clark Handbook of Political Theology, London 2020, pp. 337–351, at p. 337.
[2] Aristotle PAPANIKOLAOU, Whose Public? Which Ecclesiology?, in: Kristina STOECKL et al. (eds.), Political Theologies in Orthodox Christianity. Common Challenges – Divergent Positions, London 2017, pp. 229–242, at p. 242.
[3] Vasilios N. MAKRIDES, Political Theology in Orthodox Christian Contexts. Specificities and Particularities in Comparison with Western Latin Christianity, in: STOECKL et al. (eds.), Political Theologies, pp. 25–54, at p. 27.

was a joint »Address of the Traditional Ukrainian Churches on the Twentieth Anniversary of the Referendum to Confirm the Act of Independence of Ukraine«, issued in 2011[4]. In it, the Ukrainian Orthodox Church under the Moscow Patriarchate (UOC MP), the Ukrainian Orthodox Church of the Kiev Patriarchate (UOC KP), and the Ukrainian Greek Catholic Church proclaimed on the twentieth anniversary of the separatist declaration of Ukraine's independence from the USSR that was adopted in August 1991 by the parliament of this then-Soviet republic and reconfirmed at a referendum in December that year. The address of the three churches was written quite cautiously. For one, it admitted that, 20 years after the fall of the Soviet Union, a new generation of Ukrainians had come of age whose members were not »burdened by the defects of the Soviet past«. The question the churches asked was how to organise a decent life for Ukrainian society. The answer to this question was traditional: The unity of society can only be based on Christian spiritual ideals, social self-organisation, and mutual support. Given the ostensible triviality of its content, the address went largely unnoticed.

A more visible and widely debated (yet not systematic) institutional attempt was an ad-hoc condemnation by the UOC MP of the fundamentalist Orthodox grassroots movements in the 2000s, such as the Union of Orthodox Brotherhoods of Ukraine, the Orthodox Society of Odessa, the Spiritual and Patriotic Union, and others. In December 2007, the UOC MP explicitly condemned the politicisation of these organisations, calling it »political Orthodoxy«: »We also condemn the so-called ›political Orthodoxy‹, which implies the introduction of political slogans into the church pale, because it does not correspond to the spirit of Christ's kerygma«[5]. A year later, the UOC MP reiterated the subject calling it the »promotion of ideas

---

4 Ukrainian Orthodox Church (MP), Ukrainian Orthodox Church (KP), and Ukrainian Greek Catholic Church Published Joint Address to Ukrainian People Calling to »Use God's Gifts« for Affirmation of Ukraine's Independence (УПЦ МП, УПЦ КП та УГКЦ оприлюднили спільне Звернення до українського народу із закликом »використовувати Божі дари« в утвердженні незалежності України), published by Religion in Ukraine, 12-01-2011, URL: <https://www.religion.in.ua/news/vazhlivo/13362-upc-mp-upc-kp-ta-ugkc-oprilyudnili-spilne-zvernennya-do-ukrayinskogo-narodu-iz-zaklikom-vikoristovuvati-bozhi-dari-v-utverdzhenni-nezalezhnosti-ukrayini-fotoreportazh.html> (11-23-2023).

5 »Ми також засуджуємо так зване ›політичне православ'я‹, яке передбачає внесення в церковну огорожу політичних гасел, оскільки це не відповідає духу Христової проповіді«, see Bishops' Council of the Ukrainian Orthodox Church of 2007. Minutes No 2 of the Session of the Council (Архієрейський Собор УПЦ 2007 року. Протокол No. 2 засідання Собору єпископів Української Православної Церкви), published by Синодальний інформаційно-просвітницький відділ УПЦ, 12-21-2007, URL: <http://web.archive.org/web/20220419154327/http://orthodox.org.ua/article/protokol-%E2%84%962-zas%D1%96dannya-soboru-%D1%94piskop%D1%96v-ukra%D1%97nsko%D1%97-pravoslavno%D1%97-tserkvi-1> (11-28-2023).

and liturgical rites that contradict the rules and teaching of the Orthodox Church«[6]. In particular, the UOC MP pointed out, said organisations had promoted the idea of the canonisation of the controversial Tsar Ivan IV (also known in the West as »Ivan the Terrible«), and another person with a controversial reputation, Grigorii Rasputin. Besides, the movements demanded so-called »national repentance« for the murder of the last Russian Tsar, Nicholas II, who had been »insufficiently glorified« by the Moscow Patriarchate in 2000. Other demands included the spreading of eschatological fears, urging Orthodox believers to repent for the acceptance of the taxpayer identification number, new digital IDs, and similar electronic data. Although the locution »political Orthodoxy« gained currency and a certain popularity, it has not resulted in any full-scale theopolitical philosophy of the UOC MP outside the official »Bases of the Social Concept« (adopted in 2000).

After the event in Ukraine known as the Maidan Revolution in 2013/2014, the UOC MP as the largest Orthodox community released a series of addresses to the nation. When on 24 February 2014 it became clear that the Maidan protesters had prevailed, the UOC MP addressed the nation with a reminder that the separation of the church from the state does not imply its separation from Ukrainian society, and warned the new revolutionary authorities against interfering in internal church affairs, specifically regarding the top-down creation of one local Orthodox Church in Ukraine[7]. Following the outbreak of war in the east of the country, the UOC MP expressed its – traditionally inclusive – approach concerning all those who suffer because of the combat actions and emphasised the impossibility for the clergy to partake in civil standoffs or use the church pulpit for preaching political ideas[8]. This motion underlined once again that the UOC MP, as an institution, attempted to

---

6 »[Р]озповсюджуються ідеї та літургійні обряди, які суперечать правилам і вченню Православної Церкви«, see Meeting of 11 November 2008. Journal No. 93 (Засідання 11 листопада 2008 року. Журнал No. 93), published by Священний Синод УПЦ, 11-11-2008, URL: <https://sinod.church.ua/2014/01/15/zasidannya-11-listopada-2008-roku/> (11-23-2023).

7 »Відділення Церкви від держави не означає її відокремлення від українського суспільства«, see Address of the Holy Synod of the Ukrainian Orthodox Church to State Authorities (Звернення Священного Синоду Української Православної Церкви до державної влади), published by Українська Православна Церква, 02-24-2014, URL: <https://news.church.ua/2014/02/24/zvernennya-svyashhennogo-sinodu-ukrajinskoji-pravoslavnoji-cerkvi-do-derzhavnoji-vladi/> (11-07-2023).

8 »Ми ще і ще раз нагадуємо, що участь духовенства в акціях громадянської непокори є неприпустимою. Також є неприйнятними використання церковного амвону для пропаганди будь-яких політичних ідей«, see Address of the Holy Synod to Bishops, Clergy, Monks, and Laymen Regarding the Latest Developments in Ukraine (Звернення Священного Синоду до єпископату, духовенства, ченців та мирян у зв'язку з останніми подіями в Україні), published by Українська Православна Церква, 07-06-2014, URL: <https://news.church.ua/2014/06/19/zvernennya-svyashhennogo-sinodu-do-jepiskopatu-duxovenstva-chenciv-ta-miryan-u-zvyazku-z-ostannimi-podiyami-v-ukrajini/> (11-23-2023).

stay above politics. However, the tectonic fissure, which brought about the outbreak of Ukrainian theopolitical discourse known as »political theologies«, had already taken place.

»Political Theology« or Theopolitical Philosophy?

Vasilios N. Makrides points out a few aspects of the topic. First, he believes that it would be more productive to talk about the notion of »political theology« in the plural, an argument that certainly applies to the Ukrainian case. Second, although the term »political theology« is used to describe the overall relationship between Christian communities and political power, other definitions can be considered, too – for instance, »political philosophy«[9]. The latter is closer to my approach to the issue: For example, I opted elsewhere for alternative definitions because »Orthodox theology« is different from the mentioned terminology used in connection with politics. In particular, Orthodoxy early enough developed a narrow understanding of theology – i. e., Trinitology, Christology, and Pneumatology – as specific and concrete teaching about God in Himself (i. e., the Trinity) and about His general *oikonomia* with regard to the universe and humans. As it is reflected, for instance, in the rare titles of John the Theologian, Gregory the Theologian, and Symeon the New Theologian, Orthodox theology is about mystical knowledge of God, deification, and the like. From this narrow perspective, the popular label »political theology« would arguably be overstretched. That an organised religion like a Christian Church must interact with state and secular society does not mean, in my opinion, that the way this interaction is designed should be called theology only because this or that religion is prone to speak on behalf of God or gods. Hence, one can distinguish between Orthodox theology *per se* and theopolitical philosophies such as »political theology« and »public theology«[10]. That said, here I nevertheless use the terms »political theology« and »public theology« in quotation marks – not because I find them correct or felicitous, but because they pertain to the Ukrainian authors whose theopolitical philosophies I analyse.

---

9 MAKRIDES, Political Theology, p. 26.
10 Cf. Alexander PONOMARIOV, The Visible Religion. The Russian Orthodox Church and her Relations with State and Society in Post-Soviet Canon Law (1992–2015), Frankfurt am Main 2017, p. 52.

A Future Vector for Ukrainian »Political Theologies«?

Another term in circulation is »theopolitics«, that is, an interconnection between religion and political actions. However, it rather emphasises a practical aspect, i. e., the way politics *is done* with the help of religion, although the doing of politics goes hand in hand with its theorisation. I want to address here the example of the new Global Exchange on Religion in Society initiative of the High Representative of the European Union for Foreign Affairs and Security Policy, slated to begin in the first half of 2020[11]. On 3 June 2020, the Ukraine-based Foreign Policy Research Institute announced the receipt of an EU grant for theopolitical research into the question of church unification: According to the information published on its website, it was tasked with creating a roadmap for the »ecumenical reunification and return« of the Greek Catholic Churches of the Byzantine rite in Ukraine and elsewhere to the Ecumenical Patriarchate. The Ukrainian and the Ruthenian Greek-Catholic Church would thus join the newly created Orthodox Church of Ukraine under the Ecumenical Patriarchate.

Until recently, such projects seemed anything but realistic. Indeed, a day after the announcement was published, the Institute deleted the information from its website, stating that it had been a hacker intrusion[12]. At the time of writing, however, the information can still be found in Google's web cache. Yet the European Commission's programme is real, and the announced funding looks realistic (145,000 Euros, initially for 2020–2021). Besides, the Foreign Policy Research Institute is not known in the country for being prone to hackers. It is quite plausible that the Institute deleted the sensitive announcement for fear of a lasting scandal that might disrupt the

---

11 Federica Mogherini to Host a Conference towards Global Exchange on Religion in Society, published by European External Action Service, 09-05-2019, URL: <https://eeas.europa.eu/headquarters/headquarters-homepage/66973/federica-mogherini-host-conference-towards-global-exchange-religion-society_en> (11-23-2023).

12 Studying the Public Opinion and Securing the Most Effective Ways for the Ukrainian and Rusyn Greek Catholic Churches to Join the Orthodox Church of Ukraine, as well as Creating a Roadmap of Applying the Ukrainian Experience to Achieve the Ecumenical Reunification of the Orthodox and Greek Catholic Churches of the Byzantine Rite (Вивчення громадської думки громадян та забезпечення найбільш ефективних шляхів приєднання Української та Русинської греко-католицьких церков до Православної церкви України, а також створення дорожньої карти використання українського досвіду для екуменічного возз'єднання православних та греко-католицьких церков візантійського обряду), published by Foreign Policy Research Institute, 06-03-2020. See about the hacker intrusion and the deletion of the link URL: <https://www.fpri.kiev.ua/news_view/shanovni-chitachi/> (11-28-2023).

intended research, which was to be carried out of the public gaze (i. e., closed-door research)[13].

Since Maidan, Ukraine has been through a number of previously *unimaginable* transformations, so the unification of the churches in the country is not in principle impossible. In particular, the deleted project aimed at the development of amendments to Ukrainian and European legislation to ensure the norms and rules of the process of transfer of state-owned real estate assets in temporary or permanent possession to churches and religious organisations and/or transfer of state-owned real estate from one church to another, including churches in other jurisdictions. This implies the creation of a single register of church assets to ensure the transparency of the unification process.

The would-be EU grant postulated Russian »hybression«, a neologism implying »hybrid aggression«, a definition popular in Ukraine. This »hybression« is directly linked to social institutions such as religion. It was underlined that Moscow continued to destabilise the situation in Ukraine by provoking inter-confessional conflicts and that only a united church could resist this aggression. The unification of the Ukrainian Churches was to help strengthen Ukrainian society. The united Ukrainian Church is seen here as the second step after the creation of the Orthodox Church of Ukraine (OCU). The next steps should be a roadmap for the comprehensive »return« to the jurisdiction of the Ecumenical Patriarchate of the Catholic churches of the Byzantine rite. If true, it reveals in finer detail the strategic thinking of the Ecumenical Patriarchate to expand its influence.

Furthermore, the odds for unification shorten during times of social and political breakdowns, such as the Covid-19 pandemic or the war with Russia. It should be pointed out in this connection that the Ukrainian Greek Catholic Church has already proposed the OCU to jointly move toward unity, stressing »the foundation of the future Patriarchate of the united Kyiv Church«[14]. In a commentary to a leading Ukrainian news outlet concerning the deleted announcement, the press service of the Ukrainian Greek Catholic Church pointed out that the churches were exchanging declarations on their readiness to work out the roadmap[15]. The initiative

---

13 Исследование об объединении грекокатоликов и ПЦУ объявили фейком и списали на атаку хакеров (Research on Unification of Greek Catholics and OCU Declared Fake due to Hackers), published by Страна.ua, 06-04-2020, URL: <https://ctrana.news/news/271201-uhkts-ne-dumaet-pro-obedinenie-s-ptsu-.html> (11-28-2023).

14 [Ф]ундамент майбутнього патріархату об'єднаної Київської Церкви, see His Beatitude Sviatoslav Congratulated His Beatitude Epiphany (Блаженніший Святослав привітав Блаженнішого Епіфанія), published by Офіційний інформаційний ресурс Української Греко-Католицької Церкви, 12-18-2018, URL: <http://news.ugcc.ua/documents/blazhenn%D1%96shiy_svyatoslav_priv%D1%96tav_blazhenn%D1%96shogo_ep%D1%96fan%D1%96ya_84815.html> (11-23-2023).

15 »Между нами есть пока обмен декларациями о готовности обрабатывать дорожную карту«, see Греко-католики заявили, что не начинали процесс объединения с ПЦУ (Greek Catholics Say

could thus have chances of becoming a game-changer in Ukraine and the Orthodox world, which would inevitably affect Ukrainian theopolitical philosophies. So far, however, the process of theopolitical philosophising in Ukraine is informed by the country's revolution of 2014, including the takeover of Crimea, the armed conflict in Donbass that followed it, and, of course, the war with the Russian Federation.

Maidan: A New Paradigm for Ukraine

Ukrainian Orthodox theopolitical philosophies are developing fast, the strongest incentive being the disruptive events of late 2013/early 2014 known as »Maidan« after the central square in Kiev that was their focal point[16]. Some call the events at Maidan a »revolution of dignity« (Револющія гідності), while others view them as a coup d'état that violently overthrew the country's disliked yet legitimate president Viktor Yanukovich, which eventually resulted in the loss of Crimea, the protracted war in Donbass, and the Russian military invasion of 24 February 2022.

Maidan, as a base (*Basis*) in Marxist philosophy, became a game-changer in many respects (although not Ukraine's notorious corruption), including the religious landscape and the outbreak of political theologising, religion being part of the Marxist superstructure (*Überbau*). In fact, the Maidan coup involved only 20 percent of Ukraine's population[17]. Moreover, a driving force of the Maidan unrest was western Ukrainians who, largely, are not Orthodox, whereas the largely (nominally)

They Have Not Started Unification with the Orthodox Church of Ukraine), published by Страна.ua, 06-03-2020, URL: <https://ctrana.news/news/271094-v-uhkts-prokommentirovali-vozmozhnoe-obedinenie-s-ptsu.html> (11-28-2023).

16 See the selected publications on Maidan and the Churches in Ukraine Andrii KRAWCHUK/Thomas BREMER (eds.), Churches in the Ukrainian Crisis, London 2016; Cyril HOVORUN, Українська публічна теологія [Ukrainian Public Theology], Kiev 2017; Yurii PODOROZHNII, Українська православна політична теологія Г. Коваленка і Б. Огульчанського [The Ukrainian Orthodox Political Theology of Heorhii Kovalenko and Bohdan Ohul'chans'kii], in: Філософія і політологія в контексті сучасної культури 6/21 (2017), pp. 76–85; Yurii PODOROZHNII, Діалог Церкви і суспільства в сучасній українській теології [Dialogue between Church and Society in Contemporary Ukrainian Theology], PhD thesis, Kiev 2018, URL: <https://npu.edu.ua/images/file/vidil_aspirant/dicer/D_26.053.21/Podorozhniy1.pdf> (11-23-2023); Elizabeth A. CLARK/Dmytro VOVK (eds.), Religion during the Russian-Ukrainian Conflict, London/New York 2020.

17 Irina BEKESHKINA, During the Euromaidan, 20 percent of Ukraine's Population Took Part. A Poll by »The Democratic Initiatives« (В Евромайдане приняли участие 20 % населения Украины – опрос »Деминициатив«), published by Интерфакс-Украина, 11-19-2016, URL: <http://interfax.com.ua/news/general/235218.html> (11-07-2023).

Orthodox southeasterners were in the absolute majority as passive observers until late February 2014[18].

At the same time, it is characteristic of Ukrainian theologians – either those of the UOC MP or, especially, the protagonists of Maidan – never to speak up about the local Ukrainian *holocaust* in Odessa on 2 May 2014 (after the Ancient Greek ὁλόκαυτος, i. e., »completely burned«), when dozens of people were burned to a cinder by Ukrainian neo-Nazis. By May 2019, according to the United Nations Human Rights Monitoring Mission in Ukraine, »no one has been held responsible for the acts that led to the killings and violent deaths of 48 people and injuries to an estimated 247 people« (§50), which »suggests a lack of genuine interest from the authorities to ensure justice for victims and accountability for perpetrators« (§5)[19]. By May 2020, »neither the investigations nor trials have progressed«[20]. In this connection it is not surprising that the post-Maidan authorities are not interested in investigating their own crimes against humanity, which might result in disruptive revelations not only concerning the incumbent Ukrainian powers that be, but also the role of the Western governments and/or leaders who publicly supported that transformation.

The horrific murder of dozens of political opponents in the name of the »Maidan values« became a vicious portent of things to come. It also demonstrates the cowardice and hypocrisy of the Orthodox communities in Ukraine. The UOC MP, at least, does not preach Maidan and its »ideals« (outlined below), whereas other authors do elevate the Maidan Revolution as a pattern for Ukrainian civil society. Moreover, for instance, the leading protagonist of »Maidan theology«, Cyril Hovorun, writes freely about how the Jewish Holocaust, also known as Ha-Shoah in Hebrew (השואה, i. e., »*the* destruction«), changed the relationship between church, state, and society in the West[21]. Yet he is not willing to theologise about the Maidan-related horrible incident of Odessa.

---

18 Alexander Ponomariov, Religion. Culture. Civilization: Models for Understanding the Ukraine-Russian Crisis of 2014 (Религия. Культура. Цивилизация: модели для понимания украинско-российского кризиса 2014 г.), in: Проблемы национальной стратегии 2 (2017), pp. 55–75, at pp. 64–67.

19 Briefing Note. Accountability for Killings and Violent Deaths on 2 May 2014 in Odessa, published by United Nations Human Rights Monitoring Mission in Ukraine / United Nations Human Rights Office of the High Commissioner, 05-02-2019, URL: <https://reliefweb.int/report/ukraine/united-nations-human-rights-monitoring-mission-ukraine-briefing-note-accountability-0> (11-28-2023).

20 Accountability for Killings and Violent Deaths on 2 May 2014 in Odessa, published by: United Nations Human Rights Monitoring Mission in Ukraine / United Nations Human Rights Office of the High Commissioner, 05-02-2020, URL: <https://reliefweb.int/report/ukraine/accountability-killings-and-violent-deaths-2-may-2014-odesa-enuk> (11-23-2023).

21 »В Європі нацизм і Голокост змусили Церкви докорінно переоцінити свої стосунки із державою та суспільством«, see Hovorun, Ukrainian Public Theology, p. 107.

Indeed, these events have brought about a »new paradigm for Orthodoxy in post-Maidan Ukraine«[22] although, in my view, this paradigm owes little the »society of dignity« at Maidan. Rather, what Maidan theologians portray as their ideal society was a disparate crowd who helped deconstruct their own country. Many participants have been disappointed by the outcome of events and dismayed at the immense bloodshed that followed.

In his collection of essays on Ukrainian »public theology«, published in 2017 in Ukrainian, Hovorun argues that theology, despite being metaphysical, demonstrates an inclination for »the political«[23]. Given that Hovorun glorifies and elevates Maidan as being Messianic for Ukrainian society, and that Western »political theology« knows little about what happened in Ukraine during Maidan, the political base of the Maidan coup first needs to be approached honestly and soberly, before turning to the superstructure of the respective theopolitical philosophies.

Recent data show that it was the rebel street fighters who started the shootout at Maidan and killed the SWAT officers before the latter opened fire in return[24]. It is highly noteworthy that the first step the revolutionary authorities made after seizing power was the law of 21 February 2014, which pardoned Maidan-related crimes across the board[25]. As the United Nations Human Rights Monitoring Mission in Ukraine pointed out, this immunity law »provides that all people who participated in mass protests and are suspected or accused of crimes, including violence or killing of a law enforcement officer, between 21 November 2013 and 28 February 2014 are exempted from criminal responsibility«[26]. Besides, under this law, state prosecution offices were obliged to destroy the then-existing case files. It is also

---

22 Andrii Krawchuk, Redefining Orthodox Identity in Ukraine after the Euromaidan, in: Krawchuk/Bremer (eds.), Churches, pp. 175–202, at p. 192.
23 Hovorun, Ukrainian Public Theology, p. 31.
24 Who Began the Manslaughter at Maidan: »Strana.ua« publishes the Name-by-Name List of the »Parasiuk [A Leader of the Rebel Fighters at Maidan] Team« (Кто начал бойню на Майдане. »Страна« публикует пофамильный список 34 членов »группы Парасюка«), published by Страна.ua, 02-18-2020, URL: <https://ctrana.news/news/250376-kto-ubival-ljudej-na-majdane-20-fevralja-2014-hoda-dokumenty-sledstvija.html> (11-28-2023).
25 Law of Ukraine »On Prevention of Persecution and Punishment of Individuals with Regard to the Events, which Took Place during the Peaceful Assemblies, and on Recognition of Certain Laws of Ukraine as Repealed« (Закон України »Про недопущення переслідування та покарання осіб з приводу подій, які мали місце під час проведення мирних зібрань, та визнання такими, що втратили чинність, деяких законів України« [Відомості Верховної Ради (ВВР), 2014, No. 12, ст. 186]), published by Верховна Рада України, URL: <https://zakon.rada.gov.ua/laws/show/743-18> (11-23-2023).
26 Accountability for killings in Ukraine from January 2014 to May 2016, published by Office of the United Nations High Commissioner for Human Rights, 07-14-2016, URL: <http://www.ohchr.org/Documents/Countries/UA/OHCHRThematicReportUkraineJan2014-May2016_EN.pdf> (11-23-2023).

telling that the first item repealed with regard to the Maidan protesters by the immunity law was Article 109 of the Criminal Code of Ukraine on the »actions aimed at a forceful change or overthrow of the constitutional order or seizure of state power«[27]. According to the law, »the participation of individuals in the mass protests shall be confirmed by their application submitted to the relevant office or official«[28].

This Maidan justice is surrealistic because any stranger or even gangster could file such an application; and many people unrelated to Maidan indeed did so in order to claim damages from the state out of thin air. In other words, by exempting themselves and their accomplices from criminal responsibility for the killings of police officers, the seizure of governmental buildings, and other penal acts during the Maidan standoff, the coup authorities confessed exactly those crimes that they had listed as amnestied in their hasty legislation. On 20 February 2020, the United Nations Human Rights Monitoring Mission in Ukraine had to admit that this immunity law »prevents the investigations into the killings of the law enforcement officers«, and recommended repealing it altogether[29].

Maidan Revolutionaries came to power by way of lawlessness because the applicable laws of Ukraine that stood in Maidan's way when it came to seizing political power in the country were declared inapplicable to its street fighters. Yet, these illegitimate authorities were immediately recognised as legitimate by Western governments. In the meantime, the Russian Federation took advantage of the legal vacuum in order to take over Crimea. Nevertheless, a few months later, Moscow recognised the new authorities in Ukraine, too. The window of opportunity to change Ukraine was shut, and the fully-fledged war in the east (hypocritically called an Anti-Terror Operation) began – with tanks, aircraft, heavy artillery, and missiles. The current tragedy of Ukraine – the years of nightmare in Donbass, the loss of Crimea, and the invasion by the Russian Federation in 2022 – are direct consequences of the bloody Maidan coup.

---

27 »Стаття 109. Дії, спрямовані на насильницьку зміну чи повалення конституційного ладу або на захоплення державної влади«, see The Criminal Code of Ukraine (Кримінальний кодекс України), published by Верховна Рада України, URL: <https://zakon.rada.gov.ua/laws/show/2341-14> (11-23-2023).

28 »Для цього Закону участь особи у масових акціях протесту підтверджується її заявою відповідному органу чи посадовій особі«, see Law of Ukraine »On Prevention of Persecution and Punishment of Individuals with Regard to the Events, which Took Place during the Peaceful Assemblies, and on Recognition of Certain Laws of Ukraine as Repealed« (Ibid.).

29 Accountability for Killings and Violent Deaths During the Maidan Protests, published by United Nations Human Rights Monitoring Mission in Ukraine, 02-20-2020, URL: <https://ukraine.un.org/sites/default/files/2021-01/Briefing%20note%20on%20Maidan%20investigations%20ENG%20final.pdf> (11-28-2023).

»Political Theology« and Theopolitical Propaganda

Depending on the attitude to Maidan, the war in Donbass of 2014–2022 was seen either as a war between Ukraine and Russia or as a civil war. Theopolitical philosophies reflect this polarisation. A kind of quintessence of this polarisation concerning the churches can be exemplified by the position, according to which Ukraine began its transition from the USSR toward the EU only in 2014, after the Maidan standoff, whereas the UOC MP is a remnant of the »Russian world« in the country[30].

In particular, the UOC MP celebrates the »Russian« 9 May as the Victory Day in World War II, instead of the European 8 May. In the Russian Federation, 9 May has indeed become a civil-political religion. Through its involvement in the identity politics of 9 May, emphasises the protagonist of this position Dmytro Horevoy, the UOC MP legitimises and sanctifies Russia's political religion. For Horevoy, it means a foreign politics of memory, as if millions of Ukrainians had never fought in the Red Army against the Third Reich: »After removing [German] Nazism from Ukrainian soil, the Soviet Union did not bring freedom but took over this territory. In western Ukraine, the resistance lasted a decade after the war«[31]. According to his logic, however, the Ukrainians took over their own Ukraine for the most part. Moreover, he goes on to state that the UOC MP and historical truth are opposite each other, which, in his opinion, should justify the change of the UOC MP title to »The ROC in Ukraine« in the eyes of Ukrainian society.

In light of this, Horevoy connects 9 May to the public gesture of the UOC MP Primate, Metropolitan Onufrii. In particular, on 8 May 2015, Onufrii, together with two other UOC MP leaders, remained seated in the parliament during a commemoration of the Ukrainian Army fighting in Donbass, when President Poroshenko combined the commemoration of World War II according to the Western tradition (i. e., on 8 May) with the »Russian-Ukrainian« war in Donbass. »That time, they were the only ones who did not stand up. This time, they were the only ones [among the churches] who took to the streets to celebrate 9 May. It shows whom they consider [their] heroes and what their ›Great Patriotic [War]‹ implies«[32]. This position is not so much about »political theology« but flat-out theopolitical propaganda.

---

30 Dmytro Horevoy, Агенти політичної релігії Росії. УПЦ (МП) просуває в Україні чужу політику пам'яті [Agents of Russia's Political Religion: The Ukrainian Orthodox Church (MP) Promotes in Ukraine Someone Else's Memory Politics], published by Радіо Свобода, 05-13-2020, URL: <https://www.radiosvoboda.org/a/30609043.html> (11-23-2023).

31 »Радянській Союз, потиснувши нацизм із українських земель, не надав свободу, а захопив ці території. Опір цьому на Західній Україні тривав із десяток післявоєнних років« (Ibid.).

32 »Тоді вони єдині не встали, а зараз вони єдині у карантин вийшли на відзначення 9 травня. Це свідчить про те, кого вони вважають героями і де є їхня ›Велика вітчизняна‹« (Ibid.).

Given that it was published by the U.S.-sponsored Radio Liberty, it is no surprise that its discourse is radically anti-Russian.

Horevoy is quite a popular Ukrainian commentator on the subject of Orthodox Churches, and his invectives are similar to the fringe statements of the ex-president of Ukraine, Peter Poroshenko (in office 2014–2019), who is famous for equating Ukrainian autocephaly with Ukraine's independence, national security, and even Ukrainian statehood *per se*[33]. Moreover, autocephaly in Poroshenko's representation is a question of the whole world's geopolitics[34]. Poroshenko's »political theology« culminated on 20 September 2018, when he proclaimed that Ukrainian Church independence implied a second declaration of Ukrainian independence and the fall of the Third Rome[35], i. e., the Russian Federation and the Russian Orthodox Church. Hovorun also fell into this category when he called for the liberation of the Ukrainian Church from the captivity of the »Russian world«[36].

The Rise of »Maidan Theology«

Today, the best-known Ukrainian theologian internationally is Cyril Hovorun[37], who currently lives and teaches in Sweden. Other Maidan protagonists admit that they learned about »political theology« in the academic sense from Hovorun[38]. Originally from Central Ukraine, Hovorun began his clerical career under the

---

33 Alexander Ponomariov, Ukrainian Church Autocephaly. The Redrawing of the Religious Borders and Political Identities in the Conflict between Ukraine and Russia, in: Russian Analytical Digest 231 (2019), pp. 2–9, at p. 3.

34 Виступ Президента України під час участі у »молитовному заході за Україну« [Address of the President of Ukraine [Poroshenko] at »The Prayer for Ukraine«], published by President of Ukraine, 10-14-2018, URL: <https://www.vinrda.gov.ua/news/top-novyny/vystup-prezydenta-ukrainy-pid-chas-uchasti-u-molytovnomu-zakhodi-za-ukrainu> (11-28-2023).

35 Head of State: Tomos is actually another Act of Declaration of Ukraine's Independence, published by President of Ukraine, 09-20-2018, URL: <https://www.president.gov.ua/en/videos/glava-derzhavi-tomos-ce-faktichno-she-odin-akt-progoloshenny-994> (11-28-2023).

36 Нам треба звільнити українську церкву з полону »руського миру« – архімандрит Кирило Говорун [We Must Liberate the Ukrainian Church from the Captivity of the »Russian World«, says Cyril Hovorun], published by Theological Club in the Name of St Maximus the Confessor, 06-05-2017, URL: <https://tinyurl.com/47nscfnv> (11-28-2023).

37 Yurii Chornomorets, Перспективи богослов'я в Україні [The Prospects of Theology in Ukraine], published by RISU (Релігійно-інформаційна служба України), 09-03-2019, URL: <https://risu.org.ua/ua/index/blog/~chernomorets/77038/> (11-23-2023).

38 Georgii Kovalenko, Публічна теологія або Богословствування онлайн [Public Theology or Online Theologising], published by Orthodoxy in Ukraine, 02-12-2015, URL: <https://www.religion.in.ua/main/bogoslovya/28248-publichna-teologiya-abo-bogoslovstvuvannya-v-konteksti-yevromajdanu-ta-revolyuciyi-gidnosti-v-ukrayini.html> (11-28-2023).

auspices of the incumbent Patriarch Kirill, who ordained him as a deacon in 2005 and as a priest in 2006. Later, their ways parted, and two Kirills (Cyril being the anglicised version of Kirill) found themselves on opposite sides of the barricades.

When Maidan broke out in late 2013, Hovorun praised it as an extraordinary event. In particular, he posted a text in December 2013 (reworked in his book *Ukrainian Public Theology* in 2017) that became the manifesto of Ukrainian »Maidan theology«. At Maidan, he wrote, »a community is being born or has already been born, which is a textbook-like example of civil society and its almost pure substratum. This community identifies itself based on the common values of dignity, honesty, non-violence, mutual assistance, and readiness for self-sacrifice«[39]. Moreover, he opined, the phenomenon of Maidan makes the churches replace the two-dimensional church-state relation with the three-dimensional church-state-society, whose precise order should be »church-society-state«, in which constellation the state fades into the background.

This approach, however, was criticised by other Ukrainian authors for idealising Maidan and attributing to it the features of the church and even closer proximity to the Kingdom of God than the Ukrainian churches could ever have[40]. At the same time, both the criticised and the critic agree that the church is the largest institution of Ukrainian civil society[41]. The latter opinion was also developed by Podorozhnii (see below), who goes beyond the triangle of church-society-state and suggests a more complex relationship of four actors: church, state, Christian civil society, and secular civil society[42] – which, in my opinion, is a theological exaggeration because there is no Christian civil society in Ukraine or, for that matter, in Russia.

A few other priests from Ukraine followed Hovorun's path. One of them was Andrii Dudchenko, who put forward his list of church reforms in early 2014 to help

---

39 »На Майдане рождается или уже родилось сообщество, которое является хрестоматийным примером гражданского общества – его почти чистый субстрат. Это сообщество идентифицирует себя на основе общих ценностей: достоинства, честности, ненасилия, взаимопомощи, готовности к самопожертвованию«, see Cyril Hovorun, Богословие Майдана (Theology of Maidan), published by Киевская Русь, 12-12-2013, URL: <www.kiev-orthodox.org/site/churchlife/4975/> (11-23-2023).

40 »Ця книга занадто ідеалізує соціальність майдану, приписуючи їй риси церкви та більшу подібність до ідеалу Царства Божого, ніж то є у сучасних церквах України«, see Chornomorets, Перспективи.

41 »В украинских условиях Церковь – наибольший институт гражданского общества«, see Yurii Chornomorets, Украинское и российское православие: необходимость »перезагрузки« [Ukrainian and Russian Orthodoxy: The Need for »Reload«], published by RISU (Релігійно-інформаційна служба України), 11-15-2011, URL: <https://risu.org.ua/article_print.php?id=45421&name=open_theme&_lang=ru&> (11-28-2023).

42 »Де-факто, існує не трикутник ›церкви-суспільство-держава‹, а значно більш складні відносини чотирьох акторів: церкви, християнське громадянське суспільство, держава, світське громадянське суспільство«, see Podorozhnii, Діалог Церкви і суспільства, p. 131.

the UOC become Ukrainian society's »own« church⁴³. The first reform on the list was the liturgical commemoration of the Ukrainian nation-state. In the liturgical books used by the UOC MP, he stressed, the prayers for the state read »For *our* God-protected state, its authorities, and army«. At the same time, in Russia, as well as in ROC parishes abroad, prayers are said for »our God-protected Russian state«. Dudchenko thus demanded that the liturgical commemoration in the Ukrainian Orthodox Church included references to the Ukrainian nation-state. This is an interesting detail because the UOC MP is portrayed as a copy of the ROC with an inferiority complex.

The same pertains to the commemoration of the Ukrainian saints against that of »purely Russian« saints such as the Russian Royals, Matrona of Moscow, Ksenia of St Petersburg, Aleksei of Moscow, and some Moscow bishops. Dudchenko demands that the UOC should mention more Ukrainian saints, including Crimean saints, as a means of anti-Russian propaganda. Further, on the second Sunday after the Pentecost, the UOC MP commemorates »all the Saints in the Russian state«. Although the calendars published by the Kiev Metropolis of the UOC MP mention »the Saints of [Kievan] Rus'«, the Church Slavonic text still mentions »Russian« saints. This is a standard word in the paradigm of Church Slavonic, yet, for modern Ukrainians, it evokes the current geopolitical standoff. The adjective »Russian« is also used in other services. According to Dudchenko, it is necessary to replace »Russian« with »[the Saints] of Rus'« and the »Russian state« with »our state«.

»Ten Bullet Points« for the Orthodox Church of Ukraine (2019)

In early 2019, a group of Ukrainian Orthodox parish clergy and laymen published a similar list called »Ten Bullet Points« about the reforms of which, in their opinion, Ukrainian Orthodoxy was badly in need⁴⁴. It is noteworthy that among the signatories were both Hovorun and Dudchenko. The initiative followed the declaration of Ukrainian autocephaly issued by the Ecumenical Patriarchate in January 2019. As such, it represents the second stage of Maidan-related theopolitical philosophising connected with the appearance of the Orthodox Church of Ukraine. Although

---

43 Andrei DUDCHENKO, Life in the Church. The Ukrainian Orthodox Church in Search for Ukrainian Identity (Жизнь в Церкви. Украинская Православная Церковь в поисках украинской идентичности), published by Киевская Русь, 05-11-2014, URL: <http://www.kiev-orthodox.org/site/churchlife/5189> (11-27-2023).

44 10 тез для Православної Церкви України (Ten Bullet Points for the Orthodox Church of Ukraine), published by RISU (Релігійно-інформаційна служба України), 01-31-2019, URL: <https://risu.ua/10-tez-dlya-pcu-viryani-opublikuvali-propoziciji-do-planu-diy-novoji-pomisnoji-cerkvi_n96159> (11-27-2023).

its Primate Metropolitan Epiphanii met with the authors of »Ten Bullets« shortly after the publication and the parties discussed the idea of creating a permanent expert council for the »effective collaboration« of his church and the public sector[45], the »Ten Bullet Points« rather confirm the thesis about the individual nature of Orthodox theopolitical philosophies and their lack of institutional endorsement, since no bishop signed up to the initiative[46].

First, the authors express the need for a »true« *sobornost'*. In theory, they say, all churchgoers form one Body of Christ, whereas in practice, laymen are excluded from most aspects of church life, relations between clergy and laity being rigidly hierarchical. In this regard, they demand a renewal of parish life and a eucharistic revival because parish life is shaped by the priest and normally ends with the end of the divine service. The church must reinvent the concept of church membership and Ukrainian liturgical traditions. It is noted that 85 percent of nominal Orthodox Christians have never read the Bible, nor can they explain the Gospels, suggesting the need for a new Evangelisation of Ukrainians.

The rejection of the paradigm of church-state relations and any kind of *symphonia* of the Byzantine or Western type constitutes the core of the »Ten Bullet Points«[47]. Besides, the Orthodox Church as a community of citizens of Ukraine should play an active role in social processes and discussions on all levels. Church members must learn to take an active position during social transformations. A priority should be not the church-state relationship but relations between church and society[48].

Concerning the state, the church must return to its capacity as a mediator in the dialogue between state and society and protect the citizens from state violence. The

---

45 »Обговорювалася також ідея створення постійної експертної ради при Предстоятелю задля налагодження ефективної взаємодії між Церквою та громадським сектором«, see Metropolitan Epiphany Met with Co-authors of »Ten Bullet Points for the Orthodox Church of Ukraine« (Митрополит Епіфаній зустрівся зі співавторами »'10 тез для Православної Церкви України«), published by Православна Церква України, 03-08-2019, URL: <https://www.pomisna.info/uk/vsi-novyny/mytropolyt-epifanij-zustrivsya-zi-spivavtoramy-10-tez-dlya-pravoslavnoyi-tserkvy-ukrayiny/> (11-27-2023).

46 »However, so far, no bishop has signed the ›Ten Bullet Points‹, which fact is already interpreted as reluctance to radically change something in the Church« (»Проте досі жоден з єпископів не підписав ›10 тез‹, і це вже витлумачують, як небажання змінювати кардинально щось у Церкві«), see Volodymyr Volkovskii, Ten Bullets for the OCU. Outcomes of the First Year [of the New Church] (Володимир Волковський, Десять тез для ПЦУ. підсумки першого року), published by RISU (Релігійно-інформаційна служба України), 03-03-2020, URL: <https://risu.org.ua/ua/index/blog/~ww/79125/> (11-27-2023).

47 »[Українська Церква потребує] відмови від парадигми ›церковно-державні стосунки‹, будь-якої 'симфонії' візантійського чи західного типу, відмови від політизації Церкви«, see 10 тез для Православної Церкви України (Ten Bullet Points for the Orthodox Church of Ukraine).

48 »Пріоритетними мають бути стосунки Церкви і громадянського суспільства, а не Церкви та держави«, ibid.

church as a public institution needs checks and balances as a protection from the notorious abuse of episcopal power; it also needs elected clergy and fair ecclesiastical justice. It is not surprising that the authors see the ideal and »intrinsically Ukrainian« example of such a community in Maidan[49].

Theopolitical Reforms within the UOC MP

After the coup of 2014, the UOC MP found itself in the difficult situation of being accused of anti-Ukrainian actions. In this connection, the church appealed to horizontal precedence, to borrow a term from common law. In late December 2015 its primate, Metropolitan Onufrii, allowed individual parishes to omit the commemoration of Patriarch Kirill if this would ease theopolitical tensions. Reference was made to the practice of the Romanian Orthodox Church: Onufii pointed out that priests in Romania commemorate only their diocesan bishop, and the bishop commemorates the Patriarch. He noted that, given the circumstances, it should be possible for priests in Ukraine also to refrain from commemorating the Patriarch of Moscow, which could be justified by church *oikonomia*[50]. Moreover, speaking about the liturgical prayers for the state, Onufrii agreed to replace the words »for the Russian state« with »the state of Rus'« or »our state«[51]. Interestingly, this is in line with the above-discussed proposition of Dudchenko.

The UOC MP has had parishes that would not commemorate the Moscow Patriarch since the 1990s, especially in the west of the country. The late Patriarch of Moscow Aleksii II permitted this practice. Traditionally, however, the Patriarch of Moscow and All Rus' is commemorated throughout the UOC MP, whereas in the other LOCs, the local or relevant Patriarch is commemorated by the bishops and by not regular priests. Metropolitan Anthony of the UOC MP underlined in this respect:

---

49 »Властиво український ідеальний приклад такої позиції – становище Церкви на Майдані«, ibid.

50 »Митрополит Онуфрій згадав про те, що в Румунії за службою священик поминає тільки свого єпископа, а вже єпископ – Патріарха. ›Якщо десь сьогодні гостро стоїть питання, то можна й утриматися від поминання Патріарха‹, – зазначив він, бо це ›буде виправдано ікономією‹«, see »When God's Gift is Confused with Scrambled Eggs«. Impressions of Eyewitnesses of the Assembly of the Kyiv Eparchy of the Ukrainian Orthodox Church (»Божий дар з яєчнею«. Враження очевидців від єпархіальних зборів Київської єпархії УПЦ), published by Релігія в Україні, 12-29-2015, URL: <https://www.religion.in.ua/main/31430-bozhij-dar-z-yayechneyu-vrazhennya-ochevidciv-vid-yeparxialnix-zboriv-kiyivskoyi-yeparxiyi-upc.html> (11-27-2023).

51 »Щодо зміни у богослужбових текстах слів про ›Російську державу‹ на ›державу українську‹ або ›нашу‹ висловився позитивно, і порадив замінювати на ›державу Руську‹ чи ›нашу‹«, ibid.

Peace is above all, […] this is what is most important. For in our church people have different preferences, but if this issue is currently problematic for someone […] who cannot separate politics from religious life, then for a while it can be allowed to deviate from the norm. We need to give such people time[52].

However, the invasion of Ukraine by the Russian Federation on 24 February 2022 brought about historic changes both for Ukraine and the world, religion included. Among other things, the political position of Patriarch Kirill, who provided a religious justification for Russian aggression, made the UOC MP convene a local church council on 27 May 2022[53], which approved a range of resolutions on its *de facto* autocephaly[54]. Kirill's loyalty to the Kremlin culminated in September 2022, when he preached *ex cathedra* a flat-out Orthodox heresy that the fulfilment of one's military duty warrants an absolution of all sins of fighters if they die on the battlefield, with an implicit reference to the Ukrainian situation[55]. This

---

52 »Мир понад усе, […] це найголовніше. Тому, що у нашій церкві є люди різних вподобань, але якщо це питання на даний момент для когось є проблемним, […] не можуть відокремити політику від релігійного життя, тоді на якийсь час дозволяється відхилення від норм. Треба дати таким людям час«, see Metropolitan Anthony, Head of Affairs of the UOC-MP. After the Change of Political Power, it has Become Less Stringent (Керуючий справами УПЦ МП митрополит Антоній. Після зміни влади стало легше), published by Главком, 12-23-2019, URL: <https://glavcom.ua/interviews/keruyuchiy-spravami-upc-mp-brmitropolit-antoniy-pislya-zmini-vladi-stalo-legshe-648317.html> (11-27-2023).

53 Resolution of the Council of the Ukrainian Orthodox Church of 27 May 2022 (Постанова Собору Української Православної Церкви від 27 травня 2022 року), published by Українська Православна Церква, 05-27-2022, URL: <https://news.church.ua/2022/05/27/postanova-soboru-ukrajinskoji-pravoslavnoji-cerkvi-vid-27-travnya-2022-roku/> (11-27-2023).

54 Alexander Ponomariov, Cuius Regio, Eius Religio? The Theopolitics of Ukrainian Autocephalies, in: Russian Analytical Digest 286 (2022), pp. 5–10.

55 »We know that today many are dying in the fields of the internecine battle. The church prays that this battle may end as quickly as possible, that as few brothers as possible may kill each other in this fratricidal war. And at the same time, the church is aware that if someone, moved by a sense of duty, by the need to fulfill his oath, remains faithful to his calling and dies in the performance of his military duty, he undoubtedly commits an act tantamount to sacrifice. He sacrifices himself for others. And so, we do believe that this sacrifice washes away all the sins one has committed« (»Мы знаем, что сегодня многие погибают на полях междоусобной брани. Церковь молится о том, чтобы брань сия закончилась как можно быстрее, чтобы как можно меньше братьев убили друг друга в этой братоубийственной войне. И одновременно Церковь осознает, что если кто-то, движимый чувством долга, необходимостью исполнить присягу, остается верным своему призванию и погибает при исполнении воинского долга, то он, несомненно, совершает деяние, равносильное жертве. Он себя приносит в жертву за других. И потому верим, что эта жертва смывает все грехи, которые человек совершил«), see Patriarchal Sermon on the 15th Week after Pentecost after the Liturgy in the Alexander Nevsky Retreat (Патриаршая проповедь в Неделю 15-ю по Пятидесятнице после Литургии в Александро-Невском скиту), published by Русская

heretical development marks a new chapter in the modern »political theology« of the Moscow Patriarchate, making Kirill potentially liable to an ecclesiastical trial should it ever take place. The year 2022 thus put an end to the UOC MP as it existed between 1990 and 2022. The future fate of this church, even in independence from Moscow, remains unpredictable given the witch-hunts under the conditions of war.

A Dissertation on »Public Theologies« (2018)

In 2018, a PhD dissertation on public theologies in Ukraine, albeit not only Orthodox ones, was submitted in Kiev. Among the Orthodox developments, the author focused on Hovorun and briefly mentioned two other individuals[56]. He noted that, since late 2007, Ukrainian Orthodoxy had actively emphasised its *apolitical* nature and condemned »pro-Russian« »political Orthodoxy«. Even long before 2022, Ukrainian researchers were prone to using the »pro-Russian« label if they struggled to find a better argument and had reason to believe it would stick. For instance, the Holy Synod of the UOC MP condemned »political Orthodoxy« based on the resolutions of the ROC issued in 2004 and 2008, and of Patriarch Aleksii's resolution of 2007. Ostensibly, at that point, these ROC documents defined the discussed theopolitical grassroots movements as something »anti-Russian« in the Russian Federation itself[57].

Summing up the Ukrainian status quo in his dissertation, Podorozhnii argues that the Maidan Revolution had resulted in the emergence of Ukrainian Orthodox »political and public theologies«, with the former focusing on the relationship between church and state, and the latter tackling church and civil society. The leading figure here is Hovorun, in whose view Maidan expressed itself through religious symbols and terms. However, Hovorun personally did not take part in Maidan, observing it from a considerable distance, and therefore idealised it[58]. The picture of the social at Maidan, as imagined by the Ukrainian theologian, is far from reality; and even if Maidan had been the embodiment of ideal relations, it would be a clear exaggeration to portray it as a bearer of ecclesiastical qualities[59].

Православная Церковь, 09-28-2022, URL: <http://www.patriarchia.ru/db/text/5962628.html> (11-27-2023).
56 Podorozhnii, Діалог Церкви і суспільства, pp. 120–148.
57 Meeting of 11 November 2008: Journal No. 93.
58 Podorozhnii, Діалог Церкви і суспільства, p. 124.
59 »Уявлювана українським богословом картина соціального на Майдані далека від реальності. Але навіть якби Євромайдан був втіленням ідеальних відносин, зображувати його як носія церковних якостей було б явним перебільшенням«, ibid., p. 137.

According to Podorozhnii, nationalist ideas were much more visible at Maidan than Christian ones[60]. Only a significant idealisation of both the church environment and civil society could lead Hovorun to his unconditionally optimistic conclusions about the *symphonia* of church and society in Ukraine. In reality, the phenomenon of Maidan became possible because skills of solidarity had been instilled in western Ukraine through Greek Catholic social doctrine[61]. This observation about the leading role of the Ukrainian Greek Catholic community in shaping the Maidan protests and, eventually, »Maidan theology« is very important and is confirmed by polls conducted *during* the Maidan standoff[62].

Podorozhnii concludes that the »political theology« of Hovorun is a much-simplified theory compared to Roman Catholic and Protestant theologies, as it contains numerous gaps, assumptions, and simplifications, which makes it a failed project[63]. Even more simplified are the projects of Heorhy (Georgii) Kovalenko and Bohdan (Bogdan) Ohul'chans'kii, who also idealise Maidan, propose a theology of direct action, and view Ukrainian Orthodoxy as a special type of civil society[64]. Specifically, in Ohul'chans'kii's model, the source of political power and the personification of this power is society, whereas the political elites are only employees hired to perform a limited number of tasks. Accordingly, the main and the only partner in the dialogue with the church should be civil society[65].

---

60 Ibid., p. 125.
61 »Між тим, сам феномен Майдану став можливим завдяки тому, що навички солідарності були прищеплені на Західній Україні через свідому реалізацію УГКЦ настанов соціальної доктрини церкви«, ibid., p. 136.
62 »[В] начале февраля 2014 г. 55% протестующих на Майдане являлись выходцами с Западной Украины, а […] 12 декабря 2013 г. униатский епископ и ›апостольский экзарх‹ Борис Гудзяк признал, что, по его оценкам, *щодня до половини людей на Майдані – це є члени нашої церкви*, что вполне коррелирует с социологией жителей западных областей на Майдане« [»At the beginning of February 2014, 55 percent of the Maidan protesters were from western Ukraine, and […] on 12 December 2013, the Uniate Bishop and ›Apostolic Exarch‹ Boris Hudziak admitted that, according to his estimates, *daily up to 50 percent of Maidan protesters are members of our church*, which correlates well with the sociology of western Ukrainians at Maidan«], see PONOMARIOV, Religion. Culture. Civilization, p. 64, 67.
63 »В цілому, політична теологія архімандрита Кирила (Говоруна) є значно спрощеною теорією порівняно із католицькими і протестантськими аналогічними богословськими побудовами. Також у роздумах українського богослова наявні численні проблеми, припущення, спрощення. Все це робить українську православну політичну теологію архімандрита Кирила невдалим проектом«, see PODOROZHNII, Діалог Церкви і суспільства, p. 140.
64 Id., Українська православна політична теологія.
65 »У цій моделі джерелом політичної влади та уособленням влади взагалі є народ, суспільство. Політикум, політична еліта – лише найняті службовці для виконання обмеженого числа завдань. Відповідно, головним і практично єдиним діалогічним партнером церкви має бути лише суспільство«, ibid., p. 78.

This mindset distinguishes Ukrainian Orthodox theopolitical philosophies from Russian ones, which focus on church and state; in particular, on relations between the Patriarch and the Kremlin, whose new symbol became the heresy concerning salvation on the battlefield professed by Patriarch Kirill with regard to Ukraine.

Conclusion: »Maidan Theology« and the Mental Warp, 1204 vs. 2014

Along with the radical changes in the country, the Maidan coup of 2014 and its consequences brought about a tectonic fissure in Ukrainian Orthodoxy commensurate with the shock of 1204 for Byzantium. The invasion of Ukraine by the Russian Federation in 2022 only exacerbated the phenomenon of 2014.

Although the UOC MP as the largest Orthodox Church in Ukraine maintained explicit canonical unity with Moscow until mid-2022, the most vocal theopolitical discourse in the country was nevertheless the breaking away from Russian-style Orthodoxy. This was so under President Poroshenko (in office 2014–2019) and it quickly became the norm under Vladimir Zelensky (in office since June 2019).

The famous »Babylonian captivity« of Russian Orthodoxy by Western Christianity, pointed out by the Russian theologian Georges Florovsky back in 1937, is paralleled in post-2014 Ukraine by the idea of the »Moscow captivity« of Orthodoxy in this country[66]. Despite the hopes in 2019 that the then-new Zelensky administration would act rather neutrally toward the churches[67], the patterns established under Poroshenko began to prevail early enough and became utterly militant in 2022.

Besides the Orientalism that is applied, even within Ukraine, to its southeastern provinces on the one hand and to the UOC MP on the other, a »neo-post-Byzantine« frame has come to the fore: The takeover of Crimea by the Russian Federation in 2014 can be considered through the 1204 model, when Constantinople was conquered by Western crusaders, in which the roles of East and West are reversed (i.e., 1204 vs. 2014)[68]. I interpret the takeover of Crimea by the Russian Federation in light of this reversed model, in which Ukraine is now »the civilised West« under attack from »the barbarian East«. After 2014, Ukraine as a nation-state is standing under a big postcolonial sign with the need to demolish Russian »colonial« culture, including Russian-style Orthodoxy represented by the UOC MP. It is noteworthy

---

66 Ponomariov, Ukrainian Church Autocephaly, p. 2.
67 Cf. the cautious optimism regarding the presidency of Zelensky back in 2019: Alexander Ponomariov, Theopolitische Entwicklungen in der Ukraine 2019, in: Religion & Gesellschaft in Ost und West 1 (2020), pp. 13–15.
68 Ponomariov, Ukrainian Church Autocephaly, p. 5.

that the allusion to the Fourth Crusade and the sacking of Constantinople was also used in Ukraine by the UOC KP against the new OCU.

Orthodox anti-Westernism is a well-known feature. Although Orthodoxy is usually considered to represent »the East« in contrast to Roman Catholicism and Protestantism (»the West«), the latter »has functioned as an absolute marker of difference from what is considered to be the essence of Orthodoxy, and, thus, ironically, has become constitutive of the modern Orthodox self«[69]. The famous Greek thinker Christos Yannaras with his »anti-Western obsession« – specifically, his notion of »the barbarian West«[70] – is a case in point. Scholars see the historical roots of this anti-Westernism in the estrangement between the western and eastern parts of the Roman Empire, although the impact of 476 is seen by some as less disruptive than previously thought[71]. In this regard, one of the first instances of high-profile scorn for the Latin West comes from the ninth century, when the Byzantine Emperor Michael III (842–867) insulted Pope Nicholas I (858–867) by referring to the Latin language as »barbaric« and »Scythic«[72]. By 800, one Roman imperial tradition had become *two* traditions[73], and, with the crowning of Charlemagne in that year, Constantinople faced a conceptual rival to its claim to embody the Roman Empire and idea[74]. However, even the so-called Great Schism of 1054 was not perceived by contemporaries as a »permanent separation« of East and West[75]. The radical change came in 1204 with the »barbaric actions against Greeks«[76] and the colonisation of »the beautiful city of Constantine« (ἡ Κωνσταν-

---

69 George DEMACOPOULOS/Aristotle PAPANIKOLAOU, Orthodox Naming of the Other. A Postcolonial Approach, in: Ibid. (eds.), Orthodox Constructions of the West, New York 2013, pp. 1–22, at p. 2.
70 Vasilios N. MAKRIDES, »The Barbarian West«. A Form of Orthodox Christian Anti-Western Critique, in: Andrii KRAWCHUK/Thomas BREMER (eds.), Eastern Orthodox Encounters of Identity and Otherness. Values, Self-Reflection, Dialogue, New York 2014, pp. 141–158.
71 Jonathan ARNOLD, Theoderic and the Roman Imperial Restoration, New York 2014.
72 Tia KOLBABA, Theological Debates with the West. 1054–1300, in: Anthony KALDELLIS/Niketas SINIOSSOGLOU (eds.), The Cambridge Intellectual History of Byzantium, Cambridge 2017, pp. 479–493, at p. 481.
73 Michael MCCORMICK, Western Approaches (700–900), in: Jonathan SHEPARD (ed.), The Cambridge History of the Byzantine Empire, c. 500–1492, New York 2008, pp. 395–432, at p. 432.
74 Peter SCHREINER, Byzanz, 565–1453, Munich ⁴2011, p. 21.
75 Vasilios N. MAKRIDES/Dirk UFFELMANN, Studying Eastern Orthodox Anti-Westernism. The Need for a Comparative Research Agenda, in: Jonathan SUTTON/Wil van den BERCKEN (eds.), Orthodox Christianity and Contemporary Europe, Leuven 2003, pp. 87–120, at p. 91.
76 »How would I dedicate history, this most excellent thing and most wonderful invention of Greeks, to barbaric actions against Greeks« (»[π]ῶς ἂν ἔγωγε εἴην τὸ βέλτιστον χρῆμα, τὴν ἱστορίαν, καὶ κάλλιστον εὕρημα τῶν Ἑλλήνων βαρβαρικαῖς καθ᾿ Ἑλλήνων πράξεσι χαριζόμενος«), see Ioannes Aloysius van DIETEN (ed.), Nicetae Choniatae Historia. Pars Prior Praefationem et textum continens [Corpus Fontium Historiae Byzantinae: Vol. 11, 1: Ser. Berolinensis], Berlin 1975, p. 580.

τίνου καλλίπολις) by the »scattered Western people« (*παρὰ γενῶν ἑσπερίων σποραδικῶν*)⁷⁷.

Given that there are currently two competing Orthodox communities in Ukraine, the UOC MP and the OCU, it is possible to speak about Ukrainian Orthodox theologies. The starting point for the active development of Ukrainian »political theologies« is unanimously recognised to be the bloody Maidan Revolution of 2014. Ukrainian authors tend to separate »political theology« from »public theology«, seeing the former in terms of relations between church and state, and the latter in terms of relations between church and society. At the same time, the ideal Ukrainian society is imagined as the crowd at Maidan. In so doing, the public aspect (i. e., civil society) is prioritised over the political aspect, which distinguishes the Ukrainian approach from contemporary Russian Orthodoxy. For the ROC establishment, it is vital to be constantly connected to the Kremlin, whose possible disfavour would be interpreted as a failure of the whole post-Soviet Orthodox project.

In Ukraine, state, church, and society form a theological triangle, and some add a fourth element by dividing »society« into civil and ecclesiastical – which, however, is wishful thinking. Furthermore, Ukrainian authors idealise Maidan so much that they present it as both a *Messiah* for the decolonisation of Ukraine from Russian »imperial« and »barbarian« culture and the cornerstone for building Ukrainian society.

---

77 Ibid., p. 585.

Efstathios Kessareas

The »Gordian Knot« of Ethnocentrism and Universality

Comparing the Political Theologies of the Church of Greece and the Ecumenical Patriarchate of Constantinople

Introduction

The Orthodox Church is neither homogeneous nor monolithic, despite the existence of common dogmatic beliefs and common ritual practices. Clerical and lay actors occupy different positions in the ecclesiastical field and have different or even contrasting visions for the church's place and role in the contemporary world. These visions take on more concrete form as political theologies – that is, broadly speaking, theoretical formulations *and* proposals about the appropriate relationship between religion and politics, and more generally between the church and the secular world. In so doing, the institutional churches and individual actors attempt to respond to the challenges posed by modernity[1], as well as to urgent contemporary sociopolitical issues. But in their attempt to legitimise particular visions for the church in the modern world and de-legitimise antagonistic ones, they also (de)justify particular versions of social, political, and economic reality. Seen in this light, political theologies are »instrument[s] of action and power«, to use Bourdieu's definition of language[2]. This action can go in different directions: transformation, reform or, most usually in the case of Orthodoxy, maintenance of the existing relations.

We are thus dealing with a »struggle«, in the Weberian sense of the term, which is not independent from the broader one that takes place among contrasting secular ideologies (e. g., liberalism vs. conservatism). This struggle has been intensified under the conditions of multiple and continuous crises of our epoch (e. g., environmental, financial and migration crises, coronavirus pandemic, war in Ukraine), leading to a renewed interest in the subject of political theology in Orthodoxy. Monographs, collective volumes, and papers written mostly by the-

---

1 Kristina Stoeckl views political theologies as elaborated responses to three major challenges of modernity: the rupture between religious and cultural identity, religious freedom, and anthropocentric morality. See Kristina STOECKL, Modernity and Political Theologies, in: Ead. et al. (eds.), Political Theologies in Orthodox Christianity: Common Challenges and Divergent Positions, London 2017, pp. 15–24.
2 Pierre BOURDIEU, Language and Symbolic Power, Cambridge 1991, p. 37.

ologians³; official statements and documents produced directly by or under the auspices of the official churches⁴; workshops and conferences⁵; and a variety of religious discourses illustrate this interest. My argument is that this interest is not merely a theoretical one, for instance, an examination of why political theology has been less developed in Eastern Orthodoxy compared to Western Christianity⁶. Rather, it is the natural outcome and at the same time the »locomotive engine« of the struggle between actors with different visions of the church's position *vis-à-vis* politics, culture, and society.

This chapter is dedicated to demonstrating this symbolic struggle by examining two kinds of political theology in contemporary Greek Orthodoxy: a more ethnocentric one that defends the unity between the church and the nation-state as a necessary presupposition for the preservation of the Greek ethno-cultural identity in an age of globalisation, and a more globally oriented one, which promotes the ecumenical character of the Orthodox Church, supporting Western modernity and its core liberal values, albeit critically. Previous research has shown that the Orthodox Church of Greece adopts a defensive attitude towards globalisation as it attempts to preserve the nineteenth-century fusion of Orthodoxy with modern nationalism, whereas the Ecumenical Patriarchate of Constantinople favours a more open perspective that actually corresponds to its self-understanding as a supra-

---

3 For example, Aristotle PAPANIKOLAOU, The Mystical as Political: Democracy and Non-Radical Orthodoxy, Notre Dame, IN 2012; Pantelis KALAITZIDIS, Orthodoxy and Political Theology, Geneva 2012; STOECKL et al. (eds.), Political Theologies in Orthodox Christianity.

4 For example, David Bentley HART/John CHRYSSAVGIS (eds.), For the Life of the World: Toward a Social Ethos of the Orthodox Church, Brookline, MA 2020; The Coordinators on Behalf of the Drafting Committee Revd. Dr Brandon Gallaher and Dr Pantelis Kalaitzidis, A Declaration on the »Russian World« (Russkii mir) Teaching, in: Public Orthodoxy, 13 March 2022, URL: <https://publicorthodoxy.org/2022/03/13/a-declaration-on-the-russian-world-russkii-mir-teaching/> (all websites cited were accessed on 03-23-2023).

5 The fact that the International Theological Association (IOTA) has created, among many other groups, a Political Theology Group, which recently organised the sessions »Religious Nationalism and the Politics of Identity« and »The Place of Religion in the Public Sphere« at the IOTA international conference in Volos (11–15 January 2023), illustrates the great interest in this field. Other examples are the international conference »Orthodox Christian Political Theologies: History, Development, Specificities, Contextualisation« (The Leibniz Institute of European History (IEG), Mainz, 26–28 April 2018), which led to the present collective volume, and the workshop »Political Modernity and the Responses of Contemporary Orthodox Theology« (Institute for Human Sciences, Vienna, 16–17 January 2014), which led to the publication of STOECKL et al. (eds.), Political Theologies in Orthodox Christianity.

6 For an analytical presentation of the role of both socio-political and religious factors in the underdevelopment of political theology in Orthodoxy compared to Western Christianity, see Vasilios N. MAKRIDES, Political Theology in Orthodox Christian Contexts: Specificities and Particularities in Comparison with Western Latin Christianity, in: STOECKL et al. (eds.), Political Theologies in Orthodox Christianity, pp. 25–54.

territorial religious institution[7]. I will follow this line of study, examining on the one hand discourses produced by the Church of Greece and by ultra-conservative individual clerical and lay actors, and on the other hand, discourses produced by the Ecumenical Patriarchate of Constantinople and open-minded clerics and lay theologians, irrespective of the ecclesiastical jurisdiction to which they belong.

My intention here is neither to offer a historical analysis (though I will provide some basic information) nor to analyse the complex structure of the religious field in Bourdieu's sense of the term[8]. I shall only compare, in a quasi-ideal typical manner, the divergent ethnocentric and globalist *mentalities* that exist in the Orthodox Church. In so doing, I do not imply that the official churches and the individual actors examined here do not accept the ecumenical values of Christianity (e. g., ethic of brotherliness) or the historical reality and importance of the nation-state, respectively. However, as I will show by examples, all these common elements are arranged in a different hierarchical order according to the idea-value (Orthodox nation or Ecumenical Church) at the centre of each political theology and which is depicted as an earthly manifestation of the category of totality (God), or at least as a necessary means towards the ultimate religious goal of salvation[9].

Methodologically, I adopt an interpretative approach. For the systematic comparison of indicative discourses, I investigate the stance of their producers towards controversial issues like church and nation, church-state relations, religion and secularity. I also explore how they perceive and evaluate the so-called fundamental categories of thought, and specifically the categories of person, time, and space. Since, according to Émile Durkheim, these principal categories are the »skeleton of thought«[10], we expect to find them in political theologies, too. An investigation of the exact interpretation of these categories will reveal the specific character and orientation of each political theology. Last but not least, I draw on the framing perspective[11], pointing out core strategies of legitimation of specific visions for the church.

---

7 See Victor ROUDOMETOF, Greek Orthodoxy, Territoriality, and Globality: Religious Responses and Institutional Disputes, in: Sociology of Religion 69/1 (2008), pp. 67–91; id., The Evolution of Greek Orthodoxy in the Context of World Historical Globalization, in: Victor ROUDOMETOF/Vasilios N. MAKRIDES (eds.), Orthodox Christianity in the 21st Century Greece: The Role of Religion in Culture, Ethnicity and Politics, Farnham 2010, pp. 21–38.

8 See Pierre BOURDIEU, Genesis and Structure of the Religious Field, in: Comparative Social Research 13 (1991), pp. 1–44.

9 My understanding of the concept of »hierarchy« is influenced here by the work of Dumont. See Louis DUMONT, Postface: Toward a Theory of Hierarchy, in: id., Homo Hierarchicus: The Caste System and its Implications, Chicago 1980, pp. 239–245.

10 Émile DURKHEIM, The Elementary Forms of Religious Life, New York 1995, p. 9.

11 See Robert D. BENFORD/David A. SNOW, Framing Processes and Social Movements: An Overview and Assessment, in: Annual Review of Sociology 26/1 (2000), pp. 611–639; David A. SNOW, Framing

Ethnocentric Political Theology: The Church as Soul of the Nation

Ethnocentric political theology attributes great value to the Greek nation, defending the national role of the church. The latter is perceived as the »ark« not only of the Orthodox faith, but also of Greek linguistic and ethno-cultural identity. The producers of this political theology occupy different positions within the religious field, and this is reflected in their rhetoric and behaviour. Put in rather schematic terms, this category ranges from the so-called religious fundamentalists (also known as »ultra-traditionalists« or »rigorists«)[12], who perceive the relation between the church and the nation as an organic unity and themselves as »guardians of Thermopylae«[13], to the hierarchy of the Church of Greece (referred to in this section as »the Church«), which also defends the nation-state-church link, but does not reach the level of rigorism of the fundamentalists, except perhaps in individual hierarchs known for their ultra-conservative rhetoric. Despite the significant differences between (but also within) these groups, with each side apt to accuse the other of heresy or compromise, what they share is a common interest in maintaining the national role of the church and close church-state relations. This common substratum, which manifests on the surface either in the form of nationalism (in the case of the fundamentalists) or in the form of ethnocentrism (in the case of the official church), differentiates this kind of political theology from the globally oriented one that we will examine in the next section.

The explanation for the church's orientation towards the nation, which in some cases verges on adoration, is to be sought in history. Without going into detail, it is important to keep in mind that the Church of Greece was established as independent (autocephalous, in ecclesiastical terminology) from the Ecumenical Patriarchate by the newly independent Greek state in 1830. Its autocephaly was recognised by the Patriarchate in 1850. In fact, the Church of Greece functioned as a national and state church in the sense that it became part of the state administration

---

Processes, Ideology, and Discursive Fields, in: Id. et al. (eds.), The Blackwell Companion to Social Movements, Malden, MA 2004, pp. 380–412.

12 For the phenomenon of religious fundamentalism in Orthodoxy, see, for example, Efstathios Kessareas, The Greek Debt Crisis as Theodicy: Religious Fundamentalism and Socio-political Conservatism, in: The Sociological Review 66/1 (2018), pp. 122–137; id., Εκκλησία, ιδεολογία και πολιτική στην Ελλάδα της Μεταπολίτευσης. Κοινωνιολογική προσέγγιση, Athens 2022, pp. 137–144; Vasilios N. Makrides, Orthodox Christian Rigorism: Attempting to Delineate a Multifaceted Phenomenon, in: Interdisciplinary Journal for Religion and Transformation in Contemporary Society 2/2 (2016), pp. 216–252; Davor Džalto/George E. Demacopoulos (eds.), Orthodoxy and Fundamentalism: Contemporary Perspectives, Lanham, MD 2022.

13 This self-understanding belongs to the former editor-in-chief of the ultra-conservative religious newspaper *Orthodoxos Typos*, see Giorgos Zervos, Πού βαδίζει η ελληνόφωνος Ορθοδοξία, in: Orthodoxos Typos 1865 (2011), p. 6.

and overwhelmingly embraced and served national ideals and aims; for instance, Greek irredentism in the form known as the *Megali Idea* (Great Idea)[14]. Even when this ceased to be a national policy after the Asia Minor Catastrophe in 1922, it still survived as an ideology within religious circles, especially monastic ones. However, in the context of modern democracy, clerical intellectuals attempted to transform it into the »contemporary Megali Idea«, namely the transfer of Orthodoxy's spiritual tradition to Western Europe and the whole world[15]. Even though this »contemporary Megali Idea« renounces territorial expansionism, it nevertheless retains feelings of superiority and historical mission. As I have argued elsewhere, the church became a kind of legitimate medium not only between the faithful and God, but also between the people and the nation, and this in turn has made the nation and the church to be perceived as conjoined twins sharing the same sacred, national blood[16]. Roudometof has rightly argued that »Orthodoxy was equally absorbed into modern Greek national identity, paving the way for the ›nationalization of Orthodoxy‹«[17].

It is not accidental that in cases of church-state conflict (e. g., over the ecclesiastical property issue in 1987 and the exclusion of religious affiliation from ID cards in 2000)[18], the ecclesiastical hierarchy depicted the church as soul of the nation in order to secure its interests and de-legitimise the initiators of secularising policies by portraying them as traitors who turn against their own Mother, the saviour of the nation:

Oh, if the great heroes [παλληκάρια, brave men] of our nation came out of their graves [...], who founded, supported and praised the spiritual essence of this nation, what would have said if they had seen the demolition of the Greek Orthodox presence in society, which is

---

14 For the *Megali Idea*, see Elli Skopetea, Το »Πρότυπο Βασίλειο« και η Μεγάλη Ιδέα: Όψεις του εθνικού προβλήματος στην Ελλάδα (1830–1880), Athens 1988; Vasilis Kremmydas, Η Μεγάλη Ιδέα. Μεταμορφώσεις ενός εθνικού ιδεολογήματος, Athens 2010; Vasiliki Karafoulidou, »... της μεγάλης ταύτης ιδέας...«. Όψεις της εθνικής ιδεολογίας 1770–1854, Athens 2018.
15 See Kessareas, The Greek Debt Crisis, p. 257.
16 See id., The Orthodox Church of Greece and Civic Activism in the Context of the Financial Crisis, in: Rupert Graf Strachwitz (ed.), Religious Communities and Civil Society in Europe. Analyses and Perspectives on a Complex Interplay, Berlin 2019, pp. 61–118, at p. 72; id., Εκκλησία, ιδεολογία και πολιτική στην Ελλάδα, p. 38.
17 Roudometof, The Evolution of Greek Orthodoxy, p. 27. For an explanation of the nationalisation of Orthodoxy, see Vasilios N. Makrides, Why are Orthodox Churches Particularly Prone to Nationalization and even to Nationalism?, in: St Vladimir's Theological Quarterly 54/3-4 (2013), pp. 325–352.
18 For a detailed analysis of these two church-state conflicts, see Kessareas, Εκκλησία, ιδεολογία και πολιτική στην Ελλάδα, pp. 157–260.

attempted by some of their children, and the blows they strike against their own mother, the church[19]?

The church's freedom guarantees the freedom of the people, of the whole Nation[20].

This church that has fought and was sacrificed [...] for the freedom of the Greek Nation, it is now again fighting for its own freedom. In other words, it is fighting for the freedom of the believing people[21].

It is clear from the above that the ethnocentric political theology does not distinguish the church from Greek society and the Greek nation. They form an inseparable unity depicted as a precondition for freedom and for the existence of the nation itself. This ideology of unity also has implications for church-state relations, as we will shortly see. It might be objected that these passages come from periods of church-state conflict and when the church was under the leadership of dynamic archbishops like the late Christodoulos, who developed a strong nationalist and anti-globalisation rhetoric. The answer is that in periods of conflict we find in exaggerated discursive form what is the basic self-understanding of the church, namely as the ark of the Greek nation. It is not just individual hierarchs, but the church as an institution that sets great value upon the nation. This can also be easily observed during the tenure of the current Archbishop Ieronymos, even though he adopts a more moderate ecclesiastical policy than his predecessor. The following excerpt from a speech that Archbishop Ieronymos delivered in the context of the ecclesiastical celebrations of the 200th anniversary of the beginning of the War of Independence illustrates this point:

> Other peoples rebelled against their church. But we, the Greeks, fought in 1821 together with our Orthodox Church, which nourished us with the desire for liberation. The ground

---

19 ARCHBISHOP CHRISTODOULOS, Ομιλία του Μακαριωτάτου Αρχιεπισκόπου Αθηνών και Πάσης Ελλάδος κ.κ. ΧΡΙΣΤΟΔΟΥΛΟΥ στη Λαοσύναξη της Θεσσαλονίκης, in: Holy Synod of the Church of Greece (ed.), Εκκλησία και ταυτότητες: Θεολογική και νομική θεώρηση του ζητήματος των ταυτοτήτων, Athens 2000, pp. 289–308, at p. 295 (all English translations from the sources are mine).
20 Holy Synod, Ανοιχτή Επιστολή προς τον Πρόεδρο της Δημοκρατίας, τον Πρωθυπουργό, τον Αρχηγό της Αξιωμ. Αντιπολιτεύσεως, τους Αρχηγούς των Κομμάτων της Βουλής, τους Προέδρους των Δικαστηρίων, τον Πρόεδρον της Ακαδημίας Αθηνών, τους Πρυτάνεις των Πανεπιστημίων, in: Ekklisia 12 (1/15 December 1987), pp. 465–470, at p. 466.
21 Holy Synod, Ποιμαντορική Εγκύκλιος 2446 της Ιεραρχίας της Εκκλησίας της Ελλάδος προς τον ελληνικό λαό, in: Ekklisia 6 (1/15 June 1987), pp. 225–228, at p. 227.

we walk on is watered with blood from fustanellas[22] and rassa[23]! Our Nation rebelled »for the Holy Faith of Christ and for the Freedom of the Fatherland«, as the Samiot revolutionary and scholar Georgios Kleanthis wrote[24].

Apart from history itself, the church-nation link needs sacred legitimation. In the encyclical *To the People: The Orthodox Church and the Value of Homeland* published in 2006, when the church was under the leadership of Christodoulos, the Holy Synod extols all earthly homelands and nations, and their boundaries, attributing them to »God's creative will«[25]. It also justifies them through various quotes from the Bible and from the church fathers. But how can the ecumenicity of the church be reconciled with the particularity of the nation-state? The hierarchy attempts to resolve this contradiction with the following simile: Like the infinite Christ took the finite human nature to save the latter, so the Ecumenical Church took on in critical times the »ethnarchic« role »in order to save the Genos of the Greeks, and through the latter to bring Christianity and Civilisation to other peoples«[26]. A sense of mission and superiority is evident here. The ethnocentric orientation of the church is not perceived as a contradiction, but is fully legitimised through the construction of the following hierarchy of values: »Homeland is a value, which in the hierarchical order of values holds the second place after God, who not only is the highest Being, but also the absolute ›Value of [all] Values‹«[27]. In an attempt to dispel any accusation of nationalism, the hierarchy places itself in the category of »healthy patriotism«, stressing that it condemns ethnophyletism and racism[28].

Likewise, the current Archbishop Ieronymos highlighted that »our church wants historical memory and national identity to be maintained«, and that it plays a crucial role in reminding and honouring the »Hellenic and Christian roots of the civilisation of the Unforgotten Homelands«[29]. To avoid accusations of irredentism,

---

22 *Fustanella*, a type of traditional garment, is the national costume of Greece associated in the collective imaginary with the fighters of the Greek War of Independence.
23 The *rasson* (cassock) is a long robe worn by Orthodox clerics.
24 ARCHBISHOP IERONYMOS, Το Έθνος μας εξεγέρθηκε »για του Χριστού την Πίστη την Αγία και της Πατρίδος την Ελευθερία«, in: OrthodoxTimes, 1 October 2020, URL: <https://www.orthodoxtimes.gr/tis-draseis-tis-ekklisias-tis-ellados/>.
25 Holy Synod of the Church of Greece, Προς το Λαό: Η Ορθόδοξη Εκκλησία και η αξία της πατρίδος, in: Ecclesia.gr 41 (2006), pp. 1–4, at p. 2, URL: <https://www.ecclesia.gr/greek/holysynod/prostolao/41.pdf>.
26 Ibid., p. 1.
27 Ibid., p. 3.
28 Ibid.
29 ARCHBISHOP IERONYMOS, Χαιρετισμός του Αρχιεπισκόπου για την έναρξη του Α΄ Επιστημονικού Συνεδρίου Μνήμης Μικρασιατικού Ελληνισμού της Εκκλησίας της Ελλάδος, in: Ecclesia.gr (10-14-

he clarified that »this in no way entails a mood of revenge or fanaticism«[30]. It is obvious that the church sets great value upon the past not only as valuable source of its religious tradition, but also because of its self-understanding as an ark preserving the historical memory of the nation and thereby the nation itself. The church, the archbishop continues, is highly interested in the »deep and unbiased knowledge of history and in the safeguarding of historical memory, for these elements connect us with our past and our roots, and at the same time they give meaning to the future«[31]. The organisation of public feasts and activities by the church to honour the great national accomplishments and traumas of the past, such as the Greek Revolution of 1821 and the »Asia Minor Catastrophe« of 1922 (following the Greek-Turkish War, 1919–1922), testify to its interest in preserving national memory. This collective memory is considered absolutely necessary for the maintenance of the »diachronic consciousness of the nation« against a contemporary »movement of modern atheism«, which is accused of questioning the national role of the church and aiming to destroy the »Greek Orthodox Identity of the Genos«[32]. But for the church hierarchy, the cause of national freedom was the Orthodox faith rather than the Enlightenment: »Those men who did not think with rational arguments gave us our freedom because, with their great faith, they had God's protection«[33]. It should not come as a surprise, therefore, that the hierarchy calls Orthodoxy »the ark that saves the Greek people and the Genos, a precious component of their consciousness and identity«, quoting the words of the Orthodox writer and icon painter Photis Kontoglou: »In this land, Orthodoxy and Greece go together«[34].

Let us now see how this overemphasis on the nation affects the perception of the fundamental category of the person. As everyone knows, Orthodox theology conceptualises both the Trinity and human beings as relational entities (*prosopon*). In the case of ethnocentric political theology, this perception is used as a spearhead against the West as a type of civilisation that gave birth to a totally different anthropological type, the rational individual. More specifically, »Orthodox man«, who is allegedly distinguished by such unique qualities as »›humaneness‹ and ›philotimo‹«[35], is diametrically juxtaposed to the »good citizen« and »wise

---

2022), URL: <https://www.ecclesia.gr/greek/archbishop/default.asp?cat_id=&id=1086&what_main =1&what_sub=22&lang=gr&archbishop_who=2&archbishop_heading=Κείμενα%20-%20Ομιλίες>.

30 Ibid.
31 Ibid.
32 Holy Synod of the Church of Greece, Προς το Λαό: Η Ορθόδοξη Εκκλησία και η Επανάσταση του 1821, in: Ecclesia.gr 46 (2011), pp. 1–4, at p. 1, URL: <https://www.ecclesia.gr/greek/holysynod/ prostolao/46.pdf>.
33 Ibid., p. 4.
34 Ibid.
35 Georgios METALLINOS, Σχέσεις και Αντιθέσεις: Ανατολή και Δύση στην πορεία του Νέου Ελληνισμού, Athens 1998, p. 167. The untranslatable term *philotimo* (*φιλότιμο*) is formed by the root words

man« of Ancient Greek and modern humanism, as well as to the »good Christian« of pietism[36]. The exemplar is the »God-man«, namely the saint who has attained deification, and not the »intellectual man«[37]. In short, Orthodox Christianity is contrasted with both secularity and Western Christianity, for the latter is considered to be the womb of the first.

Religious actors extol the importance of such charismatic figures as the saint and the national hero. They connect or even conflate the figures of Neomartyrs (those executed for their faith by the Ottomans) and Ethnomartyrs (martyrs for the nation), promoting them as exemplars of sacrifice for both the Orthodox faith and the nation. Elsewhere I have given many examples of such discourses[38]. For instance, the official publishing house of the church advertised an anniversary book entitled *The Neomartyrs of the Genos* as follows:

> The struggle of the Greeks was conducted for »Christ's holy faith and for the freedom of the fatherland«, as the fighters of 1821 were confessing. It is thus not only about a national anniversary, but about the conjunction, interpenetration, the common route and undisturbed unity between Hellenism and Orthodoxy. The holy Neomartyrs, who were the soul of the [national] struggle, express this truth[39].

I will mention a new example that comes from the same period of the celebrations of the 200th anniversary of the Greek War of Independence. The church created a special commemorative medal to offer it to persons for their services to the nation. In his speech on the occasion of the presentation of the medal, Archbishop Ieronymos extolled the services of the Neomartyrs and Ethnomartyrs to the nation as follows:

> This commemorative year was dedicated by our church to the Holy Neomartyrs, those holy figures who died for the Cross and our land, for the blue-white [national flag] and for our Panagia [All-Holy Mother of God], for the Holy Faith of Christ and for the Freedom

---

philos (friend) and *timi* (honour). A person has *philotimo* when he or she does the »right thing«. Put differently, when her or his conduct does not violate the core value system of her or his personality and of the broader community where she or he belongs.

36 Id., Ορθοδοξία και Ελληνικότητα: Προσεγγίσεις στη Νεοελληνική Ταυτότητα, Athens 1992, p. 65, 81; id., Σχέσεις και Αντιθέσεις, p. 19; id., Παράδοση και Αλλοτρίωση: Τομές στην Πνευματική Πορεία του Νεωτέρου Ελληνισμού κατά τη Μεταβυζαντινή Περίοδο, Athens 1986, p. 39, 40.

37 Id., Ορθοδοξία και Ελληνικότητα, p. 68; id., Σχέσεις και Αντιθέσεις, p. 167.

38 See Efstathios KESSAREAS, Saints, Heroes, and the »Other«: Value Orientations of Contemporary Greek Orthodoxy, in: Religions 13/4 (2022), 360, pp. 1–17.

39 Apostoliki Diakonia, 1821–2021. Οι Νεομάρτυρες του Γένους, in: apostoliki-diakonia.gr, URL: <http://www.apostoliki-diakonia.gr/diakonia/NewEdition/ekdoseis.asp?file=neomartyres.htm>.

of the Fatherland […]. We will honour with this symbolic and laudatory manner the Orthodox, Christian heritage of the Holy Neomartyrs and Ethnomartyrs, and those who hold high the flag of our Fatherland in dangerous times. We forge with this wonderful work of art the ore of reverence for those who confessed Christ, and the ore of honour for those who continue today to glorify Hellenism and to represent it with brilliance in the oikumene[40].

The perception of the church as the ark of the nation does not remain at an abstract level, but seeks to preserve and even reinforce the existing close church-state relations. Since the church is perceived as the »soul of the nation« and as having »watered the roots of our Nation«, as Metropolitan Seraphim of Piraeus emphatically stated[41], it is expected that the political authority recognises and protects the church's privileged position in the state and society. Their argument is that both institutions serve the same collectivity, the Greek people. To legitimise the existing system of church-state relations as relations of mutual cooperation, the ecclesiastical hierarchy appeals to the past, invoking the Byzantine model of *symphonia*. This system is considered to be appropriate even within the completely different historical context of secular modernity. For instance, in a recent address to the Prime Minister of Greece, Kyriakos Mitsotakis, who was visiting the Holy Synod, Archbishop Ieronymos extolled »the spirit of *synallilia* [mutual reciprocity]«, which springs from the fact that »we are all members of one great nation and serve a great people, which never ›goes unnoticed‹«[42]. Moreover, he underlined that the »Church of Greece has been the unsleeping helper of the State's social welfare work since the creation of the Greek State«. The archbishop further requested the state's legislative support for its »innovative development goals« (e. g., the issue of the church's property), which would have a positive impact on society in general[43]. The particular interests of the institutional church and of its dominant stratum of hierarchy are equated with the interests of the whole society on the grounds that there is no difference between the church and society, but rather indissoluble maternal blood ties:

---

40 ARCHBISHOP IERONYMOS, Ομιλία Μακαριωτάτου την ημέρα παρουσίασης μεταλλίου, in: Ecclesia.gr (02-01-2021), URL: <https://www.ecclesia.gr/greek/archbishop/default.asp?cat_id=&id=913&what_main=1&what_sub=22&lang=gr&archbishop_who=2&archbishop_heading=Κείμενα%20-%20Ομιλίες>.

41 METROPOLITAN SERAPHIM OF PIRAEUS, Το προεκλογικόν αίτημα κεντροαριστερών κομμάτων δια τον διαχωρισμόν Κράτους-Εκκλησίας, in: Orthodoxos Typos 1931 (2012), p. 1, 7.

42 ARCHBISHOP IERONYMOS, Προσφώνησις επί τη επισκέψει του Πρωθυπουργού κ. Κυριάκου Μητσοτάκη εις την Ι. Σύνοδο, in: Ecclesia.gr (12-13-2021), URL: <https://www.ecclesia.gr/greek/archbishop/default.asp?cat_id=&id=1070&what_main=1&what_sub=22&lang=gr&archbishop_who=2&archbishop_heading=Κείμενα%20-%20Ομιλίες>.

43 Ibid.

The destiny of our homeland and of the Greek people is also the destiny of the Church of Greece. The mother cannot afford to be complacent and ask things for herself when her children need her. Whatever belongs to the Church of Greece in the last analysis belongs to Greek society and its people[44].

Close church-state relations undoubtedly offer symbolic and material advantages to both authorities. It is not accidental that the church offers support and legitimacy to the political system, for instance during the period of the financial crisis, when Greece's position in the Eurozone and in the European Union was at stake[45]. It does not follow from this that the church does not oppose state's initiatives that promote secularisation. Any policy that challenges its primacy in Greek society and its influence on politics is de-legitimised as a great danger to the nation itself. The same applies to globalisation: its economic benefits are welcomed, but its negative impact on the alleged homogeneity of society is rejected:

> We are not against development and progress [...]. The globalisation as an economic and developmental pursuit is something we approve of. But as a levelling of cultures is dangerous and must be rejected. What do we have to gain from globalisation, if we lose the wealth of our tradition, if we are transformed into a people without self-consciousness and without culture[46]?

The difficulty for the church is to find a functional balance between tradition and modernity. One can easily observe that it attempts to combine its conservative beliefs on moral and social issues with administrative, technological, and economic modernisation (e. g., investments, religious tourism)[47]. This policy of »conservative liberalism«[48] may function at the level of economy, but it produces intense contradictions at the level of values, for the demand for a privileged position on the grounds of its national role cannot be easily reconciled with the context of multiculturalism and pluralism. The immanent framework of modernity poses a serious challenge to the church, for the functional differentiation of society means that the various subsystems of the latter do not need legitimation from a supra-empirical reality or an all-encompassing meaning[49]. In Orthodox-majority countries like Greece, which lie halfway between the West and the non-Western world in terms

---

44 Ibid.
45 See Kessareas, The Orthodox Church of Greece and Civic Activism.
46 Archbishop Christodoulos, Ομιλία, p. 297.
47 For its activity in the field of religious tourism, see Efstathios Kessareas, Faith, Economy, and Politics: Religious Tourism in Contemporary Greece, Erfurt 2022.
48 Id., Εκκλησία, ιδεολογία και πολιτική στην Ελλάδα, p. 254.
49 Charles Taylor, A Secular Age, Cambridge, MA 2007.

of their secularity[50], the secularisation process generates intense tensions. The lack of an ultimate meaning that is taken for granted and the rapid socio-political, economic, and technological changes are perceived by the hierarchy as a chaotic condition that threatens the church's presence and role in society, culture, and politics. The *symphonia* model is promoted as a solution on the grounds that it provides meaning and order to this chaotic reality. Of course, it also secures the interests of the church. In a speech delivered in 2021, Archbishop Ieronymos outlined the challenges of secular society and the crucial role of the church as a shield against chaos:

> Society is not the same as that of earlier times. The technological developments with the issues arising in the field of bioethics, the environmental issue, and the secularisation of society create a new type of human being. The paradigm of the world changes. There is the opinion that even the question of the meaning of life is unnecessary, because life does not need meaning. A life, however, without the coherence that the meaning of purpose offers is a chaotic life. We as a church are often called to deal with the chaos. Our relations with the state also very often go through fluctuations, too […] The economic hardship and others social parameters make difficult both our work and our presence in our homeland[51].

Turning our attention to individual clerical and lay actors, who have a more conservative and traditionalist profile, we can observe that all the previous viewpoints are expressed in a more overt and more intense form. The following passage illustrates the idolisation of the *symphonia* model:

> The Orthodox principle of mutual reciprocity [συναλληλία] of the two ministries [διακονίες] of human life [are] the spiritual (priesthood) and the political (kingship or state). Spiritual and political leaders are servants and ministers of the »self-ruling« (dominant) people, according to the great Rigas [Velestinlis]. Both these ministries in the Greek Orthodox tradition have a common aim, according to Basil the Great: »the salvation of the people« (namely, theosis) […] The ecclesiastical realm (clergy and people) preserves the purer and more realistic patriotism. But this extremely disturbs those who have re-

---

50 Vasilios N. MAKRIDES, Secularity and Christianity: Comparing Orthodox with Western Perspectives, in: The Greek Orthodox Theological Review 63/3–4 (2018), pp. 49–107.
51 ARCHBISHOP IERONYMOS, Προσφώνηση τοῦ Μακαριωτάτου Ἀρχιεπισκόπου Ἀθηνῶν καί πάσης Ἑλλάδος κ. ΙΕΡΩΝΥΜΟΥ στήν τακτική σύγκληση τῆς Ἱερᾶς Συνόδου τῆς Ἱεραρχίας τῆς Ἐκκλησίας τῆς Ἑλλάδος, in: Ecclesia.gr (10-04-2021), URL: <https://www.ecclesia.gr/greek/archbishop/default.asp?cat_id=&id=1066&what_main=1&what_sub=22&lang=gr&archbishop_who=2&archbishop_heading=Κείμενα%20-%20Ομιλίες>.

jected the concepts of »fatherland« and »nation« in the name of a destructive ideological globalisation that threatens humankind in its entirety[52].

The ideal of a symphonic complementarity between the two authorities, as Makrides rightly observes, holds a special position in the Orthodox collective imaginary[53]. We can also add that the *symphonia* discourse is not politically neutral, but it is crucial part of the polemic these actors hold against those whom they derogatively call atheist secularists and forces of the »New World Order«, who are allegedly planning the complete separation of church and state in Greece. Again, such a development is perceived both as a *contradictio in terminis* and as a great national danger:

> Thus, any concept of a (harsh) »separation« of the two ministries (namely, *the total break of the relations of cooperation and joint-diakonia between them*) is unthinkable in the Orthodox tradition, because it presupposes a religiously discoloured, autonomous and absolute state, which devours the whole organism of Genos/Nation and subjugates everything, without recognising as *legally equivalent* and *equal* to the priestly *diakonia* and, therefore, is in an open or disguised manner hostile towards the Orthodox faith[54].

A more careful look at the proposed model of *symphonia* reveals that it is in fact a hierarchical relationship, in which the »church-soul« has primacy over the »state-body« in the sense that the latter becomes a kind of zombie without the life-giving spirit of the first. It is strongly believed that behind state neutrality is hidden the ultimate goal of anti-Christian forces: to separate the church from the nation. But this means death, since, as we have said, for this mode of thought, the church is the soul of the Greek nation:

> A church-state separation that might happen is in fact separation between the church and the nation […]. The relations of mutual reciprocity between the church and the authority of the state transfuses in a mystical manner a portion of God's blessing and grace from the ecclesiastical organisation to the institution of the state through the church's prayer. In a sense, this relationship is parallel to the relationship between the body and the soul. So, imagine the state-body estranged from its natural unity with its church-soul to walk

---

52 Georgios METALLINOS, Ποιμαντικός λόγος και κοινωνικά δρώμενα, in: Orthodoxos Typos 1900 (2011), p. 5.
53 MAKRIDES, Political Theology in Orthodox Christian Contexts, p. 29.
54 Georgios METALLINOS, Εκκλησία και Πολιτεία στην Ορθόδοξη Παράδοση, Athens 2000, p. 29 (emphasis in original).

around inanimate, lacking liveliness, walking dead. Then whatever new it produces, this will exude stench, corruption (decay), greater perishability, and finally death[55].

These religious actors claim that they do not wish the church to take over or replace the state, but for the two authorities to work closely together in serving society. However, in their discourse, this relationship becomes so close that it leaves no room for real differentiation in the modern sense. On the contrary, state, church, and society become united by the common glue of Orthodoxy. Without the latter, in their eyes, chaos emerges. To prevent this catastrophic outcome, they demand a state that will legislate according to the moral values and principles of the Orthodox Church, securing the interests of the latter against the proponents of secularism and multiculturalism:

> The history of our nation is kneaded with our belief in God. In this way, a sacred tradition was created, we call it the »Greek Orthodox« tradition [...]. [There is] a treacherous effort to adulterate and abolish the Greek Orthodox tradition so that our country would cease to be an Orthodox country. No, we will not allow this to happen! We the clergy and especially the bishops, who have sworn to be guardians of the sacred traditions, no, I repeat, we will not allow atheism in our land [...] [Let us make] a contract that we as a nation will legislate and guide our lives according to the commandments of the Son of Theotokos, of our Lord Jesus Christ, whom we want, and we demand that our current and future leaders and governors of our land believe in him[56].

To put it plainly, the vision is for a »Christian-state«, as we can also see in the following wish: »May all of our Greece become a Christian state, a state of the Panagia [All-Holy Mother of God], a nation of Christ, a nation of the Panagia through secret mystical prayers«[57]. This state undertakes the role of safeguarding Helleno-Christian morality against ideological opponents like advocates of left atheism: »Only immoralists and atheists write ›Hatred for the Nation and the bosses‹! Christians love their Nation (Genos), and their homeland and all people, even their enemies. Only ›if there is no God is everything permitted‹«[58]. This enemy construction is a classic method of de-legitimising opposing ideologies. The enemy is both internal and external: the secular state, the bishops who are

---

[55] METROPOLITAN SERAPHIM OF PIRAEUS, Ο χωρισμός Κράτους – Εκκλησίας αποτελεί εις την ουσίαν χωρισμόν Εκκλησίας – Έθνους, in: Orthodoxos Typos 2010 (2014), p. 6.

[56] METROPOLITAN IEREMIAS OF GORTYNA AND MEGALOUPOLIS, Όχι άθεη η πατρίδα μας Ελλάδα, in: Orthodoxos Typos 2009 (2014), p. 4.

[57] Sarantis SARANTOS, Τραγικότης…εν Χριστώ ελπίδες…, in: Orthodoxos Typos 1994 (2013), p. 7.

[58] Michail E. MICHAILIDIS, Μίσος για το Έθνος και τα αφεντικά, in: Orthodoxos Typos 1992 (2013), p. 1.

being stigmatised as ecumenists, and the global powers – all presented as forces of de-Christianisation:

> Our people will remain entirely unprotected, because, on the one hand, their true spiritual shepherds, the priests, will be marginalised or even persecuted by unworthy bishops, and on the other hand, the state authorities will be left unchecked to hasten, together with the assistance of foreign powers, the complete de-Christianisation of our Fatherland[59].

For the ultra-conservatives, the *Metapolitefsi* period, which began after the fall of the military dictatorship in 1974, is perceived as apostasy, namely as a falling away from the Greek Orthodox faith and tradition. The actual reason why they condemn or at least feel uneasy with the liberal values and the pluralistic character of secular democracy is that the latter undermines the monopoly of faith that the church used to enjoy in Greek society with the help of authoritarian regimes. Their fear is justified: Their right-wing ambition of a »Greece of Greek Christians« cannot be realised in conditions of free antagonism among beliefs, ideas, and cultures that a democratic society presupposes and favours.

In the case of the ultra-conservatives, the vision for a Christian state is clothed in the guise of the Byzantine *synallilia* model. Therefore, what these actors actually aspire to is the »Orthodoxisation« of all spheres of human life, for they perceive the church as the most fundamental pillar of the nation-state that encompasses and determines all other particular identities and domains of life. The functional differentiation of modern society is accepted only on the assumption that the various spheres of life are in line with what in their eyes is most important, Greek Orthodox values and principles. They strongly believe that the institutional church should always submit to its sacred tradition and by no means adapt them to the ephemeral needs of the surrounding environment. Secular society is viewed as a kind of fallen state that has deviated from the salvific embrace of the Orthodox Church (perceived as mother of the nation) and from its historical mission given by God. The accomplishments and pleasures of the secular mode of life are perceived as a diabolical temptation and obstacle to the ultimate goal of salvation. Likewise, the creation of a global and multicultural society is perceived as a ticking bomb that will destroy the very foundations of the Orthodox nation. In the ethno-religious ideology, it is the nation-state that represents the category of space *par excellence*. The latter is perceived in the form of a closed and secluded territory, where a homogeneous community worships and defends the »unchanging situations« of religion and nation against the evil forces of atheist secularism, multiculturalism,

---

59 Vasilios E. Voloudakis, Οι επίσκοποι θα χωρίσουν την Πολιτείαν από την Εκκλησίαν ερήμην των πρεσβυτερων, in: Orthodoxos Typos 1901 (2011), p. 5.

globalisation, and what they derogatively call the »American way of life«[60]. As one might expect, the advocates of »ethnodoxy«[61] extol the importance of physical and symbolic borders, for the latter establish a clear boundary that separates the (allegedly) homogeneous Greek ethno-religious identity from those who (allegedly) threaten to adulterate it.

A sense of superiority and mission is a common *topos* in ecclesiastical and especially monastic milieus, of course with different emphases. A single example is enough: »The Greek [nation] was born by the favour of divine providence to become the teacher for humankind; this task was assigned to it; this was its mission; this was its calling among the nations«, a Greek archimandrite emphatically stated[62]. It is important to note that these religious actors, who reject globalisation as hegemony of Western modernity, counter-propose another kind of »globalisation«: the grandeur of the Byzantine Empire. This has also implications for the evaluation of the modern Greek state which, in their eyes, is suffocated in a limited geographical space and therefore is too small and weak to encompass the ecumenicity of the national soul. Feelings and attitudes associated with the irredentist Great Idea, namely the goal of rebuilding the Byzantine Empire, spring from here, finding best expression in contemporary prophetic discourses, as I have recently shown elsewhere[63]. It is worth quoting at length a passage that reveals the core framing strategies of diagnosis (problem identification and attribution of blame), prognosis (proposal for a solution to the problem), and motivation (vocabularies of action):

> [Due to] the regeneration of 1821 [...] the Genos was healed; it found its health. The historical Fall [of Constantinople] did not end up in a real conquest. I am afraid that we experience this real conquest for many decades now. The symptoms are clearly evident. We have sold out and selling out everything for a mess of pottage, for the glittering euro-silver coins. We blaspheme and offend the holy and the sacred [...] we legitimate moral deviance and promote immoral and debauched persons as spiritual exemplars. Our politicians are proud of turning the ecumenical Hellenism of Alexander the Great and of Constantine the Great into a poor province of Europe, a small Frankish state, again [leaving it] without any substantial help against the Turks. Many of the ecclesiastical leaders accept that Orthodoxy is no longer the One, Holy, Catholic, and Apostolic Church, but churches, and what is more sister and equal churches, the schisms and heresies [...]. Let us hope that the Genos,

---

60 Georgios ZERVOS, Η διοικούσα Εκκλησία συμπορεύεται μετά των Ελλήνων οπαδών της παγκοσμιοποιήσεως, in: Orthodoxos Typos 1867 (2011), p. 1, 7.
61 For the term, see Vyacheslav KARPOV et al., Ethnodoxy: How Popular Ideologies Fuse Religious and Ethnic Identities, in: Journal for the Scientific Study of Religion 51/4 (2012), pp. 638–655.
62 SARANTOS, Τραγικότης...εν Χριστώ ελπίδες..., p. 7.
63 Efstathios KESSAREAS, »Signs of the Times«: Prophecy Belief in Contemporary Greek Orthodox Contexts, in: Social Compass 70/1 (2023), pp. 73–90.

instead of the impious laws and ungodly education, will return to the laws of »divine cybernetics«, so we can avoid divine abandonment and not – this time voluntarily – suffer the true, final conquest[64].

It can immediately be seen that for these ultra-conservative religious actors the »real conquest« is secular modernity and not the Fall of Constantinople, because it created an atheistic and immoral society that worships Mammon instead of God, whereas after the Fall the Genos may have lost its political independence but due to the church retained, as they stress, its Orthodox soul. Responsibility for this alleged decay is attributed to everyone who adopts this mode of life, but the more blame is assigned to those in power, specifically to church leaders and politicians, who transformed the ecumenical and glorious Hellenic and Byzantine world into a poor and insignificant region of today's Europe. In such a framing, the return to the »laws« of God and values of Greek Orthodoxy is promoted as the only real solution to the conditions of the multiple crisis of our era. The nation can secure its existence and brilliant future only by becoming again the broader category of Genos. This presupposes a reconnection of people to their true identity, which, the argument runs, has been distorted by the destructive influences from the »barbarian« West[65]. But this small modern nation-state is fiercely defended by the same actors against its arch-enemies, particularly Turkey. In their nationalist mode of thought, there is no contradiction in so far as the modern nation-state continues to carry the essential elements of the Byzantine Empire – like the central place of the church in culture and society and the intertwining of church and state. Put another way, in their eyes, the modern nation-state is fully legitimised as a small empire, which, despite its dramatic territorial shrinkage, carries the same grand national soul that was clearly manifested during the Byzantine era.

In their case, too, the past is the prevailing frame of temporal reference. But here the past is more clearly an ideal (Byzantium) that aims to encompass every level of human experience, because it is identified with holy truth itself. This mechanistic attachment to a glorified past gives rise to attitudes of traditionalism or even fundamentalism, since any proposed change is perceived as a threat to an allegedly unchangeable tradition. As it is emphatically stated, »the dogmas, the holy canons and traditions of the church […] by no means change with the passing

---

64 Theodoros Zisis, Η άλωση της Πόλης κατά τον Γεννάδιο Σχολάριο, in: Τα πνευματικά αίτια της άλωσης της Πόλης και η ηθικοοικονομική κρίση της εποχής μας, Thessaloniki 2011, pp. 83–112, at pp. 111f.
65 For the »Barbarian West« as an ideological scheme promoted by some Orthodox intellectuals, see Vasilios N. Makrides, »The Barbarian West«: A Form of Orthodox Christian Anti-Western Critique, in: Andrii Krawchuk/Thomas Bremer (eds.), Eastern Orthodox Encounters of Identity and Otherness: Values, Self-Reflection, Dialogue, New York 2014, pp. 141–158.

of time, but they remain valid and unchanged until the end of the ages«[66]. For those reformists »who despise, change, and abolish the laws of God«, the wrath of God is coming[67]. The golden motto here is: »full steam backwards«[68]. By this they mean a »quick-as-possible return to the graceful roots of our (pure) Orthodoxy, to orthopraxy, which is taught by the spirit of *Romiosini*«[69]. This return is celebrated as a »real revolution for the Genos«[70]. Thus, it is not democracy or science, not to mention socio-political revolution, that will provide the solution to the problems of contemporary society (e. g., the financial crisis, the coronavirus pandemic), but the »return to the life-giving roots of our race, to the Helleno-Orthodox civilisation that teaches ideals, virtues and unsurpassed orthodox values«[71].

To sum up: The Church of Greece produces an ethnocentric political theology by which it aims to legitimise its close relationship with the state and secure its symbolic and material interests. Understanding itself as soul of the nation, it becomes vocal in highlighting the need for the maintenance of ethno-religious identity in the age of globalisation. Of course, as an institution that is fully involved in the modern world, it expresses this political theology in a more moderate, »lighter« – one could say, politically correct – form, compared to individual ultra-conservative clerical and lay actors who produce a more intense and aggressive discourse. In their case, the *symphonia* model corresponds to a Christian state which, in practice, abolishes the functional differentiation of modern society. Likewise, globalisation becomes an instrument of atheist forces to de-Orthodoxise the Greek nation.

The Political Theology of Universality: The Church as a Civil Society and Global Actor

The political theology of universality, as the term itself suggests, has a global orientation and an open attitude towards religious and cultural diversity. It strongly criticises ethnocentrism as a betrayal of the ecumenical values of Christianity and

---

[66] Heiliger Agathangelos Esphimenites [Ἅγιος Ἀγαθάγγελος Ἐσφιγμενίτης], Μαρτυρία Ἀγωνιζόμενης Ὀρθοδοξίας Ἁγιορειτῶν Μοναχῶν 196 (2003), p. 4.
[67] Christos K. Livanos, Τα αίτια των δεινών μας, in: Orthodoxos Typos 2005 (2014), p. 5.
[68] Michail E. Michailidis, Ὀπισθεν ολοταχώς, in: Orthodoxos Typos 2011 (2014), p. 1.
[69] Ioannis N. Markas, Το ασυμβίβαστον δυτικής ζωής και ανατολικής πίστεως, in: Orthodoxos Typos 1906 (2011), p. 6.
[70] Ibid.
[71] Alexandros Mygdanalevros, Μετάνοια: Ορθόδοξος πνευματική πορεία Ελληνικού Έθνους, in: Orthodoxos Typos 2011 (2014), p. 3.

for impeding the constructive engagement of the church with the condition of (post)modernity. The Ecumenical Patriarchate of Constantinople and the churches under its jurisdiction, the *International Orthodox Theological Association* (IOTA), the Theological Academy of Volos in Greece, theologians who write in the *Public Orthodoxy* blog of the *Orthodox Christian Studies Center* of Fordham University are representative examples of such a globally oriented and pro-multicultural trend within Orthodoxy. It is again important to keep in mind that the ethnocentrism/universality distinction should be perceived in hierarchical terms. But now, as I will show by examples, the hierarchy of values is reversed: The Ecumenical Church is the manifestation of the category of totality that encompasses the partial nation-state. This reversal produces contrasting attitudes towards secular modernity compared to the ones that we saw in the previous section. More specifically, the call for returning to traditional values is transformed into a call for opening the church to the modern world.

On the institutional level, the Ecumenical Patriarchate of Constantinople is one of the strongest advocates and promoters of the church's global orientation. Some basic background information can shed light on the reasons for this. With regard to history and the memories and predispositions that it generates, the Patriarchate, as everyone knows, was the religious centre of the Byzantine Empire, where Orthodox Christianity was developed and flourished. After the Fall of Constantinople in 1453, it functioned as a religious and political authority representing before the Sultan the so-called *Rum millet*, that is the Orthodox faithful irrespective of ethnic, linguistic or other cultural differences. However, the term »Romioi« (Ρωμαίοι, Ρωμιοί) became in the end intertwined with a Greek identity, although initially the term did not denote such a narrow ethnic identity. We could thereby say that the Patriarchate acquired from the very beginning an ecumenical identity and orientation, but we should not forget that this stemmed from and corresponded to the imperial structures of the time. In the epoch of the modern nation-state, the establishment of independent churches challenged both the ecumenical ideology as well as the material interests of the Patriarchate. The latter condemned the emerging identification of Orthodoxy with nationalism, so-called ethnophyletism, but finally could not but accept the new historical reality of the nation-state: It recognised and granted autocephaly to the newly established churches, which remained spiritually connected with the Patriarchate as their mother church.

The high spiritual status of the Patriarchate as *primus inter pares* among the other Orthodox churches reinforces its ecumenical image, although in practice there is intense internal antagonism in the Orthodox world, especially between the Patriarchate and the Russian Orthodox Church, which promotes its own global or transnational image based on the ideology of the »Third Rome« and more recently on the ideology of a transnational Russian Orthodox civilisation, the so-called

»Russian world«[72]. Another reason for the global orientation of the Patriarchate lies in its structural position as a minority religion in Muslim-majority Turkey and with the majority of its main flock outside that state's borders; for instance in the USA, Canada, and Australia. Due to the international immigration that led to the formation of a large Greek Orthodox diaspora, the Patriarchate functions as a transnational church[73]. But, »while, as a practical matter, the Patriarchate operates as a *transnational* institution for ethnic Greeks *alone*, its own self-image is that of a *global* institution«, Roudometof observes[74]. Indeed, the Patriarchate undertakes initiatives of global importance that transcend territorial or religio-cultural boundaries, but at the same time aims to preserve the particular religio-cultural heritage of *Romiosini*, as we will see below.

John Chryssavgis, a well-known theologian and archdeacon of the Patriarchate, calls Ecumenical Patriarch Bartholomew a »transnational figure of global significance«[75] who undertakes a »leadership role on broader social and global matters«[76]. Indeed, the Patriarch pursues initiatives on critical issues like climate change, peace, poverty, justice, economy, and interfaith dialogue and, by so doing, promotes the Patriarchate's status as a global actor. His speeches and messages to powerful organisations and international conferences such as the World Economic Forum, the European Parliament, UNESCO, the United States Congress, the G8, and the World Conference on Religion and Peace are particularly revealing in this regard. In a word, globality stands at the heart of the Patriarchate's political theology.

---

72 The political theology of the Russian Orthodox Church is outside the scope of this chapter. For a recent critique on the »Russian world« ideology from the standpoint of the liberal Orthodox political theology, see *A Declaration on the »Russian World« (Russkii mir) Teaching*.

73 According to Roudometof, in the epoch of the modern nation-state the Greek-Orthodox (Rum) diasporic communities have been transformed into communities of transnational Hellenism, see Victor ROUDOMETOF, From Greek-Orthodox to Transnational Hellenism: Greek Nationalism and the Identities of the Diaspora, in: Allon GAL et al. (eds.), The Call of the Homeland: Diaspora Nationalisms, Past and Present, Leiden 2010, pp. 139–166; id., Transnationalism and Globalization: The Greek Orthodox Diaspora between Orthodox Universalism and Transnational Nationalism, in: Diaspora 9/3 (2000), pp. 361–397; id., Orthodox Christianity as a Transnational Religion: Theoretical, Historical and Comparative Considerations, in: Religion, State & Society 43/3 (2015), pp. 211–227. As regards the Ecumenical Patriarchate, see also id., Greek Orthodoxy, Territoriality, and Globality; Ciprian BURLACIOIU, Migration und Diasporabildung in der östlichen Orthodoxie des 20. Jahrhunderts. Zwei Fallbeispiele: Das Ökumenische Patriarchat in Konstantinopel und die russische Orthodoxie, in: Id. (ed.), Migration and Diaspora Formation: New Perspectives on a Global History of Christianity, Berlin 2022, pp. 273–291.

74 ROUDOMETOF, Greek Orthodoxy, Territoriality, and Globality, p. 77.

75 John CHRYSSAVGIS, Introduction: Ecumenical Patriarch Bartholomew, in: Id. (ed.), In the World, Yet not of the World: Social and Global Initiatives of Ecumenical Patriarch Bartholomew, New York 2010, pp. 1–14, at p. 9.

76 Ibid., p. 1.

Bartholomew himself characterises the Patriarchate a »transnational and spiritual force«[77], »dedicated to encouraging order, providing meaning and promoting justice in the international arena«[78]. Likewise, he stressed that the Patriarchate »must help bring the spiritual principles of ecumenism, brotherhood, and peace to the fore«[79], »serving global ideals, civilising and preaching love in every direction«[80]. Of course, it does not follow from this that a critique of globalisation is absent. On the contrary, »as a means of making humanity homogeneous«, it is rejected, and its negative consequences on economy and environment are highlighted[81]. But this critique does not lead to a defensive attitude. Rather it aims at fostering active participation in the global scene towards humanising globalisation. It is believed that this can happen through the church's »spiritual ecumenicity«, namely a »form of globalization that proclaims that all human beings of every race and language and of all cultures should be united by bonds of love, brotherhood, and cooperation«[82]. This is, of course, a common religious scheme of thought, but here it is invoked not in juxtaposition to the modern world, but as a kind of corrective.

Still the tension between the particular Greek identity and the vision for universality remains. An identification of the Patriarchate exclusively with the former endangers its ecumenical image. To avert this danger, Patriarch Bartholomew depicts the Patriarchate as representing the category of totality, which encompasses and transcends partial historical categories like ethnic or linguistic identities. The following passage illustrates this point:

> our Patriarchate is not a »national« church but rather the fundamental canonical expression both of the ecumenical dimensions of the gospel message and of its analogous responsibility within the life of the church. This is the deeper reason that the church fathers and the councils have given this Patriarchate the name *Ecumenical*. The loving care of the Church of Constantinople exceeds any linguistic, cultural, ethnic, or even religious definition, as it seeks to serve all peoples. Although firmly rooted in particular history, as any institution is, the Ecumenical Patriarchate transcends historical categories in its perennial mission of service[83].

---

77 Ibid., p. 56.
78 Ibid., p. 27.
79 Ibid., p. 151.
80 Ibid., p. 52.
81 Ibid., p. 129.
82 Ibid., p. 126.
83 Ibid., p. 165.

Although the Patriarchate perceives itself as guardian of the »spiritual legacy« of the Byzantine Empire[84], it simultaneously attempts to connect itself with broader categories like the »suffering humankind«[85]. The »reality of the nation-state«[86] and the importance of »our own national identity«[87] are accepted (accompanied with a strong condemnation of »parochial nationalism, fragmenting communalism, and aggressive expansionism«)[88], but the centre of gravity is clearly shifted towards the global scene and towards broader formations like the European Union. Here, the Orthodox Church is transformed from the soul of the Greek nation (an image that we saw in the previous section) to the »soul« (together with the other churches) of the European Union[89]. According to the Patriarch, the church has to »fulfil its role not only in individual nations but on a European level, with the shared aim to construct civil society«[90]. »Protection of human rights, quality of life [...] strong civil society«[91], and »pluralist democracy«[92] are core values and ideas for this kind of political theology. The Patriarchate seeks a greater mission than that of an ark that saves the traditions of a specific nation. It aspires to a leadership role by acting as a crucial civil society and global actor:

> The church, together with the political world, sees the urgent need to form a leadership that understands both modern pluralist democracy, especially in such a multicultural mosaic as the European Union, and the spiritual dimension of society at large, about which the church cares deeply[93].

> We believe that our participation in building up the common European *oikos* (home) will substantially contribute to the enrichment of the European peoples through the pure evangelical truths as they are experienced in the Orthodox world. And so European civilization will rediscover the nuances of the Christian ethos, which are still being preserved in Orthodoxy, and be grounded in our ancient Christian tradition. The participation of our Orthodox peoples in building up the Europe of tomorrow will not render us spiritually *negligible*, but it will indeed signify for Europe a new period[94].

---

84   Ibid., p. 48.
85   Ibid., p. 189.
86   Ibid., p. 26.
87   Ibid., p. 110.
88   Ibid., p. 26.
89   Ibid., p. 182.
90   Ibid., p. 177.
91   Ibid., p. 176.
92   Ibid., p. 175.
93   Ibid.
94   Ibid., p. 181.

The subtitle »Beyond Borders: Global Responsibility«[95] illustrates the »spirit« and orientation of this political theology. However, this »spirit« can on other occasions be expressed in a contradictory form, for instance, when the discourse is addressed to different audiences. This is because the Patriarchate, apart from its aspiration to act as a global actor, understands itself as the ark of *Romiosini*. In such cases, globality recedes in favor of the local on the grounds that Constantinople is, according to Patriarch Bartholomew, »the most sacred Center of Orthodoxy«:

> We remain on the »holy ground«, because here is the Polis [city, Constantinople] of Panagia Pammakaristos, the Polis of our Fathers, the most sacred centre of Orthodoxy. We continue here, because here we were born, here is our homeland, here everything is known and familiar to us. We love everything because we know it, and we know it because we love it. We persevere, because here is our history, our present and our future, the traces and the aroma of our culture, because here we are not strangers, and nothing is foreign and alien to us. We stay and fight, because this is our irrevocable decision, because we want to guard Thermopylae, »never betraying what is right«. We remain in our Polis, because we believe in the providence of the benevolent God. This is where the Lord commanded us [...]. We continue to be »confident at all times«, and we call on the expatriates who live abroad, not only not to forget their Polis, but to return to their homeland, where their lives will gain immeasurable meaning, and new horizons of existential fullness will open for them[96].

An excellent example of theological extroversion and a positive attitude towards modernity is the document entitled *For the Life of the World: Towards a Social Ethos of the Orthodox Church*, drafted by an international (mostly US-based) committee of theologians and clergymen under the auspices of the Patriarchate. As I have argued elsewhere, the document reflects the progressive values of Orthodox actors who possess high intellectual capital and mainly operate in international multicultural and multi-ethnic environments[97]. There is neither sufficient space nor any need to provide a detailed analysis of this document[98], which addresses a variety of subjects, many of which continue to produce heated debates and polarisations in

---

95 Ibid., p. 67.
96 Marina Zioziou, Βαρθολομαίος: Παραμένουμε στα άγια χώματα – Εδώ είναι το Κέντρο της Ορθοδοξίας, in: ethnos.gr (11-22-2019), URL: <https://www.ethnos.gr/ekklisia/article/73510/bartholomaiosparamenoymestaagiaxomataedoeinaitokentrothsorthodoxias>.
97 Efstathios Kessareas, The Church in Times of Crises: A Refuge or a Driver for Change?, in: The Wheel Journal 28/29 (2022), pp. 66–71.
98 This has been done by many experts on Orthodoxy. See, for example, Vasilios N. Makrides, Le nouveau document social de l'Église orthodoxe. Son orientation, son élaboration, son contexte et son importance, in: Istina 65/4 (2020), pp. 387–413.

Orthodoxy; for instance, church-state relations, ecumenical relations, nationalism, democracy, pluralism, secularism, science, sexuality, human rights, and women. What is important for our purposes is to highlight that this document attempts to offer a kind of reconciliation between tradition and modernity by setting out what we may call a path of double acceptance/rejection: on the one hand, acceptance of the great value of the Orthodox tradition, but rejection of a mechanistic attachment to an idealised past that fosters attitudes of fundamentalism; on the other hand, acceptance of the condition of modernity but rejection of its negative aspects and consequences, which are in sharp contrast to the principles and values of Christianity. Let me give a few examples[99].

As one might expect from a theological document, it makes extensive use of religious concepts and ideas, such as *theosis*, communion, the world as fallen order, the eucharist, monasticism, and so on. The salvific importance of all these elements is recognised, but these are interpreted and evaluated in an extrovert way that makes possible the constructive engagement of the church with the modern world. For instance, the ultimate religious goal of *theosis* (deification), from a world-rejecting and contemplative stance performed by few bearers of charisma, acquires a social dimension, becoming a multifaceted inner-worldly activity that aims to bring the whole of creation into communion with God:

> The ultimate destiny [...] is nothing less than our *theosis*: our deification and transformation by the Holy Spirit into members of the body of Christ [...]. *But,* then, this must be a *corporate* destiny, as it is only through our *participation* in the community of Christ's body that *any of us* [...] can enter into full union with God. Our spiritual lives, therefore, cannot fail also to be *social lives*. Our piety cannot fail also to be an *ethos*[100].

The spiritual legacy of Byzantium is much appreciated, but any idolisation of the imperial structures of that historical era is rejected. As it is stated, there is a »dangerous temptation among Orthodox Christians to surrender to a debilitating and in many respects fantastical nostalgia for some long-vanished golden era, and to imagine that it constituted something like the sole ideal Orthodox polity«[101]. On the contrary, it is the »democratic genius of the modern age« that is highly praised as a »very rare blessing indeed«. Christians are urged to »actively support [democratic values] and work for the preservation and extension of democratic institutions and

---

99 I use here the text that is available on the website of the Greek Orthodox Archdiocese of America: David Bentley Hart/John Chryssavgis (eds.), For the Life of the World: Toward a Social Ethos of the Orthodox Church (2020), URL: <https://www.goarch.org/social-ethos>. For excerpts from the document, I give the relevant paragraph number.
100 Ibid., § 3 (emphasis added).
101 Ibid., § 10.

customs«[102], rejecting »belligerent forms of nationalism and blasphemous philosophies of race«[103]. The same positive attitude exists towards the issue, controversial in Orthodoxy, of human rights. It is clearly stated that believers »should support the language of human rights« not because the latter are identical with the Orthodox perception of the human being as a person, namely as a relational being, but because a »common social accord, one that insists upon the inviolability of human dignity and freedom, is needed for the preservation and promotion of a just society«[104]. The following excerpt also illustrates well this point:

> The language of human rights is, in many ways, a minimal language. It is also, however, a usefully concise language that can help to shape and secure rules of charity, mercy, and justice that the church regards as the very least that should be required of every society; and so, it is a language that must be unfailingly affirmed and supported by all Christians in the modern world[105].

Therefore, the legal framework of human rights is supported on the grounds that it offers in the modern world possibilities for the protection of every human being as an image of God. That is why, cultural and social pluralism is not regarded as a threat to Orthodoxy, but as a »blessing« and »gracious gift«, which the church must actively support[106]. As it is stressed, »the church must in fact support those government policies and laws that best promote such pluralism«[107]. As regards the church-state relations, the »dissolution of the ancient compact between state and church – or throne and altar« is also perceived as a »great blessing«, because it is believed that it gives to the church the opportunity to dedicate itself to its core salvific mission, »uncompromised by alliance with worldly ambitions«[108]. Thus, *symphonia* here is understood and promoted as a form of cooperation between the church and the political authority »toward the common good and [...] against injustice«, and not as a »justification for the imposition of religious Orthodoxy on society at large, or for promotion of the church as a political power«[109]. This »common good« is considered to be the »true essence of a democratic political order«, to which the church can greatly contribute, for it can protect society from degenerative phenomena like »pure individualism, free market absolutism, and a spiritually

---

102 Ibid.
103 Ibid., § 11.
104 Ibid., § 12; see also § 61.
105 Ibid., § 63.
106 Ibid., § 12.
107 Ibid.
108 Ibid., § 13.
109 Ibid., § 14.

corrosive consumerism«[110]. There are many similar phrases in the document that point out the negative consequences of market capitalism and particularly of what is referred to as »capitalist culture«; for instance, »promotion of unremitting material acquisition«, »fleeting materialist fascinations and trivial material appetites«[111], »sexuality [...] colonized by the logic of consumerism and the dynamics of the market«[112], »›wage slavery‹«[113], »inordinate debt«, »unscrupulous and rapacious creditors«[114], »deification of profit, [the] pervasive modern ethos of consumerism, and [the] base impulses of racism, sexism, and egocentrism«[115].

This kind of political theology accepts the functional differentiation of secular society, but opposes secularism as an ideology that aims to impose the privatisation of faith and the exclusion of the church from the public sphere:

> Religion, moreover, is understood in such societies as essentially a private pursuit, which must not intrude upon public discussions of the common good. But this is false in principle and, almost invariably, oppressive in practice. For one thing, secularism itself is a form of modern ideology, invested with its own implicit concept of the good and the just; and, if it is imposed too imperiously upon a truly diverse society, it becomes just another authoritarian creed [...] every ideology can become oppressive when it is given unchallenged power to dictate the terms of public life. While a *modest secular order* that does not impose a religion on its citizens is a perfectly good and honourable ideal, a government that restricts even ordinary expressions of religious identity and belief all too easily becomes a soft tyranny that will, in the end, create more division than unity[116].

Although it is emphatically stated that the Orthodox Church »is not *a* church, but *the* Church«[117], an attitude of »openness« is promoted[118], as believers are urged to »meet together in love and work together for the transformation of the world«[119] without any hidden agenda to »convert them to some cultural ›Byzantinism‹«[120]. The great enemy for this political theology is fundamentalism, for the partiality of

---

110 Ibid.
111 Ibid., § 17.
112 Ibid., § 18.
113 Ibid., § 36.
114 Ibid., § 39.
115 Ibid., § 65.
116 Ibid., § 80 (emphasis added).
117 Ibid., § 50.
118 Ibid., § 54.
119 Ibid., § 52.
120 Ibid., § 51.

the latter is considered to cancel in practice the »church's whole cosmic vision«[121], which, the argument goes, can only be fulfilled through dialogue and love. We can thus say that the producers of this political theology attempt to forge a middle way between, on the one hand, the extreme secularists who aspire to the privatisation of faith and the exclusion of religion from the public sphere, and on the other hand the religious fundamentalists who desire the »Orthodoxisation« of all spheres of life with the assistance of the state. An ethnocentric political theology is accused of betraying the church's ecumenical identity, even when ethnocentrism is not expressed with rigorism. It is worth quoting at length an extract from the speech delivered by the Metropolitan Ambrosios of Korea at the Opening Ceremony of the 2nd International Conference of the International Orthodox Theological Association (IOTA) in Volos, because it clearly demonstrates this critique and the open-minded mentality from which it stems:

> We Orthodox believers around the world are not actually the body of Christ. We feel that we are not brothers in Christ, but strangers. […] In practice our national identity has priority and our Orthodox faith comes second; first, we are Russians, Serbs, Bulgarians, Greeks, Romanians, Arabs, etc. and second comes our Orthodox identity. Thus, there is no deep desire to address ethnophyletism in the diaspora, since it would require a spiritual revolution within our identities. It is absolutely necessary for us to understand that the nation which is a worldly reality that will be abolished at the last days (eschata) should not for any reason be converted into an ecclesiastical criterion that destroys the unity of the church […] Instead of standing each other as brothers and sisters, our ethnophyletism separates us into opposing groups ready for war. […] Our ethnophyletism makes us heretics because we do not place Christ and his church above everything […] what Cyril of Jerusalem calls »the body and fellowship of Christ« is for us inferior to our national or ethnic DNA, the language of love is of lower value than our national language and our cultural heritage […] our own church […] in the final analysis looks more like an ethnic ghetto than a church in the foreign country where we live as an Orthodox diaspora […] ethnophyletism is diametrically opposed to the work of proclaiming the gospel because it is based exclusively on the blood of the ancestors, while the church is based on the blood of Christ[122].

Therefore, this political theology clearly distinguishes the blood and holy sacrifice of Christ from the blood and worldly sacrifice of national heroes. The first

---

121 Ibid., § 73.
122 METROPOLITAN AMBROSIOS OF KOREA, The Heresy of Ethnophyletism (Keynote Address & Florovsky Lecture), published by YouTube (03-03-2023), URL: <https://www.youtube.com/watch?v=-Jp_LAu1Flo>.

constitutes the ultimate value that leads to universal unity and peace, whereas the second, though important in its own worldly terms, remains nevertheless a worldly value that leads to fragmentation and conflict. Since ethnocentrism obscures or even reverses the ecclesiastical hierarchy of values, it is rejected as a heresy.

I would now like to briefly discuss political theologies produced by individual lay theologians, which are marked by the same spirit of openness to alterity and rejection of ethnocentrism. As these actors do not hold an ecclesiastical position, they are, at least theoretically, in a better position to express without contradictions the »spirit« of this political theology than the institutional church, which must also deal directly with matters of ecclesiastical diplomacy and strategy. The ecclesiastical discourse enjoys recognition as a form of »legitimate language« and the bishop's sceptre (σκῆπτρον), a ceremonial staff, symbolises the position of authority of these high-ranking hierarchs – to recall Bourdieu's analysis of authorised language[123]. In the case of lay theologians, their own »sceptre« is their academic credentials and the high prestige they enjoy as religious intellectuals.

The work of the Orthodox theologian Aristotle Papanikolaou is an excellent example of a pro-modern and anti-rigorist political theology. As he states in his book *The Mystical as Political: Democracy and Non-Radical Orthodoxy*, he attempts to »forge a (non-radical) Orthodox political theology that goes beyond a reflexive opposition to the West or a nostalgic return to a Byzantine-like, unified, political-religious culture«[124]. The main reason behind this attempt is the urgent need for a constructive engagement of the church and its theology with the modern world due to the new context of pluralism and multiculturalism. Likewise, in the introduction to the book *Political Theologies in Orthodox Christianity*, it is underlined that the »task for Christian theologians is to formulate a normative and theologically grounded vision of how the church is to relate to the political sphere in a situation characterised by growing religious pluralism worldwide«[125]. The secular world, for Papanikolaou and like-minded theologians, is not a demonic place, against which the church must raise impassable walls so as to defend its own religious truth, or a place that the church must conquer in order to impose its own moral values and attitudes. Rather, it is another arena of ascetical struggle, where the church and the faithful should proclaim and live the gospel message without attempting to impose it on the basis of any religious, cultural or historical privileges:

---

123 BOURDIEU, Language and Symbolic Power, p. 109, 113.
124 PAPANIKOLAOU, The Mystical as Political, p. 11.
125 Ingeborg GABRIEL et al., Introduction, in: STOECKL et al. (eds.), Political Theologies in Orthodox Christianity, pp. 1–11, at p. 3.

It is not secular in the sense of being antireligion, nor in the sense of the complete privatization of religion; it is secular only in the sense that a common theological perspective does not justify the form and movement of the political, cultural, or economic spheres of a political community. The rejection of a common theological perspective also does not mean that religion has no voice within public deliberations; religion simply cannot be the dominant voice[126].

To articulate such a political theology, Papanikolaou gives an activist meaning to »traditional« categories and practices of Orthodoxy such as *theosis* and *ascesis*. As we have already mentioned for the Patriarchate's document above, in his work too these categories do not refer to a world-escaping attitude that leads to union with God, but to a multifaceted inner-worldly activity that aims to bring both society and nature into communion with God. He strongly believes that this kind of practice can foster active civil and social engagement under conditions of equality and dialogue, which can be the basis of »the common good« that transforms the different actors into members of a pluralistic society. The great impediment to his »politics-as-asceticism« praxis is what he calls »politics of bullying«[127], namely rigorist attitudes that are in striking contrast to such core modern and Christian values as equality and freedom. Thus, the separation of church and state and the existence of a political space distinct from the church are perceived not as a »betrayal«[128], but as a »liberation«[129], for they will give the church the opportunity to stand on its own feet without expecting the state or any other authority to secure its »cultural hegemony«[130]. The following passages make clear this viewpoint:

> In a context in which the conditions for the possibility of rejecting God are maximized, it is more likely to be the case that existing as a Christian has little to do with cultural, social, or political expectations; that existing as a Christian is less about ethnic identity and more about an actual relation with God structured through a particular tradition[131].

> The challenge for the Orthodox Churches is to discern their limits in the public realm and to resist the temptation to appeal to history for privileging the morality of the Orthodox tradition within the public sphere[132].

---

126 PAPANIKOLAOU, The Mystical as Political, p. 144.
127 Ibid., p. 198.
128 Ibid., p. 76.
129 Ibid., p. 56.
130 Ibid., p. 51.
131 Ibid., p. 143.
132 Ibid., p. 12; see also id., Whose Public? Whose Ecclesiology?, in: STOECKL et al. (eds.), Political Theologies in Orthodox Christianity, pp. 229–242.

This kind of political theology sets great value upon Western liberal democracy, despite a critique of its hyper-individualistic and consumerist aspects. Although Papanikolaou is careful enough to avoid a simplistic identification of Orthodoxy with modern liberalism, stressing for instance that the implementation of »politics-as-asceticism« will lead to a political community that »looks something like a liberal democracy«[133] and that »such a community is one that looks like a liberal democracy, minus the anthropological baggage of modern liberalism«[134], his support for liberal democracy is more than evident. It is not accidental that his book ends with the following words: »An ascetics of divine-human communion shapes a political space that is liberal democratic«[135].

Another example in this category of political theology is the work of the Greek theologian Pantelis Kalaitzidis, who is director of the Volos Academy for Theological Studies in Volos (Greece). This case shows that the religious field in Greece is not comprised only of the ethnocentric and ultra-conservative currents that we examined in the previous section[136]. Kalaitzidis strongly criticises ethnocentric religious discourse as a »theology of authority and heteronomy« that serves relations of power instead the spirit of love and communion of the gospel[137]. He speaks of the »temptation of Judas« in Orthodoxy, by which he means the replacement of the mission of salvation by such worldly interests as the destiny of the nation[138]. He, too, strongly urges the church to develop a constructive relationship with the pluralistic and open environment of the globalised world, which, as he argues, cannot happen without abandoning the anachronistic vision for an »authoritarian and state-subsidized« church that draws legitimacy from its national role[139]. In the context of (post)modernity, the ethnarchic role of the church not only is considered to be unrealisable, but, more importantly, undesirable because it adulterates the salvific message of the church. On the contrary, Western modernity and multiculturalism are accepted because they are associated with the modern value of freedom, which also stands at the heart of Orthodoxy:

---

133 Papanikolaou, The Mystical as Political, p. 198.
134 Ibid., p. 86.
135 Ibid., p. 200.
136 For a detailed analysis of various currents of thought that exist in the ecclesiastical field in Greece, see Kessareas, Εκκλησία, ιδεολογία και πολιτική στην Ελλάδα, pp. 59–153; id., Orthodox Theological Currents in Modern Greece after 1974: Ongoing Tensions between Reform and Conservatism, in: Journal of Modern Greek Studies 33/2 (2015), pp. 241–268.
137 Kalaitzidis, Orthodoxy and Political Theology, p. 36.
138 Id., The Temptation of Judas: Church and National Identities, in: Greek Orthodox Theological Review 47/1-4 (2002), pp. 357–379.
139 Id., Orthodoxy and Political Theology, p. 90.

Perhaps the synthesis we seek in today's period of late modernity, with its tendency to escape into post-modernity and its desecularization, might be a discourse from the church and theology that relates to the community of citizens, that new element and new achievement of our times – a discourse that must speak to a society and a public space that are less and less likely to be identified with the state and civil power; a discourse that will respect all the positive achievements of modernity and secularization, that will not forget the nature of religious associations, a nature profoundly voluntary and grounded in free will, not connected with the state or the powers that be. This public discourse of the church and of theology cannot, however, reproduce the forms and prototypes of medieval »Christendom« or Byzantine theocracy. Nor can it have tendencies toward domination or ambitions in the world, nor again be possessed by neo-romantic dreams of returning to some sort of pre-modern »Christian« society or »Christian« Empire (whether it be the Byzantine/Roman, or Tsarist Russia, or indeed the modern Balkan monarchies)[140].

It is more urgent now than ever that it [the church] move beyond its ethnocentric discourse, that it abandon any illusion of returning to Byzantine theocracy, or any other romantic, anti-modern idea of »Christian society«, like »Holy Russia«, the sacralized Balkan monarchies, etc. Theocracy and neo-nationalism, which are simply secularized forms of eschatology, can no longer be the church's vision for politics. [...] All of this, of course, will be just hollow words and wishful thinking if it is not accompanied by our acknowledgment and acceptance, finally, of the achievements of western modernity and the reality of multi-cultural societies[141].

What the above passages clearly show is that we have a temporal and special shift from the imperial past of the Byzantine theocracy to the contemporary democratic context of civil society, which is perceived as an open space for communication, reflection, and dialogue where the faithful can freely develop missionary activity with the aim of transforming the world according to Christian values. As is stated, the »life of the church is marked by dynamic process of becoming, a continuous transformation, and in this way it gradually *becomes* the kingdom of God«[142]. Thus, the emphasis is placed upon the present activity of believers who always keep an eye on the future, and this activity is juxtaposed to an attitude of idolisation of the past and of passive expectation of the eschaton. The latter is conceptualised as »something active, not passive; it is transformative, not an escape from the world; it is located in worship and prayer, but also in action«[143]. The category of the future

---

140 Ibid., pp. 83f.
141 Ibid., p. 136.
142 Ibid., pp. 107f.
143 Ibid., p. 113.

is highlighted, for it functions as a crucial safety net to prevent the identification of the church with any existing socio-political reality:

> Christians do not worship the past, because they are turned toward the future, the *eschaton*, from which they await the fulfillment of their existence. This, however, is not a denial of the present, because the *eschaton* does not destroy but rather transforms history, turning it into eschatological history and imbuing it with meaning and purpose[144].

> The key [...] is to be found in eschatology, which is related to the dialectic between the present and the future, the »already« and the »not yet«, which pervades the church's sojourn in the world. Eschatology introduces, furthermore, an attitude toward life that maintains a distance from the structures of the world, a refusal to settle down and identify oneself with the world and history, without however any trace of disdain for the world and history or any flight from them. For eschatology also entails repentance for the past, as well as faith in and openness toward the future and the final outcome of history, while at the same time pointing to a permanent suspension of any final and established meaning within history, to constant doubt and radical criticism of the meaning of all institutions, and implying instead the notion of movement without end, unceasingly and constantly gaining in richness[145].

The adoption of an open perspective is also reflected in the interpretation of the fundamental category of the person. No doubt this political theology, too, understands the category of the person as a relational being and not as an individual. But this common Orthodox perception does not serve here as ideological cover for confrontation with Western modernity. The role of the Ethnomartyrs and Neomartyrs is recognised and honoured, but it is also contextualised. What is more, a new emphasis is placed upon the devotion of the bearers of charisma to the needs of the ordinary people, and especially to those in extreme need. As I have elsewhere demonstrated in detail, at the heart of this political theology stands the category of the »Other« and not the church as a form of institutional authority[146]. The concept of the »Other«, which has been particularly highlighted by postmodernism, is legitimised through its association with the traditional religious concern for the poor and the oppressed and is used as a spearhead against the political theology of ethnocentrism, which views the church through the lens of state authority and nation. Thus, for the political theology of universality, the crucial agent of history is not a charismatic figure (e. g., a prophet or a saint), but the church understood

---

144 Ibid., p. 110.
145 Ibid., pp. 85f.
146 See Kessareas, Saints, Heroes, and the »Other«.

as a community of believers who undertake activities that benefit society and its most vulnerable members without any desire for domination. As is emphatically stated:

> The public ecclesiastical role should embody the Cross-centered ethos of Christ. It should be a witness to the new reality which the church lives, and a protest against social and institutional evil, as well as the violation of human dignity and freedom; it should be a voice defending the »other«, the »foreigner«, the least of our brothers, the needy, the weak, and the victims of history, who are all icons of »the Other« *par excellence*, the »foreigner« *par excellence*[147].

In sum, the quest is for creative syntheses, which will draw from the rich tradition of Orthodoxy and at the same time will foster an open attitude and interaction with the modern world. A »spirit of the middle way« that detests all forms of absolutism, be it militant secularism or religious fundamentalism, marks this political theology. This »middle way« mentality can be illustrated by taking a closer look at the preferred church-state relations in Greece: Neither the creation of an authoritative Christian-state nor the French *laïcité* are considered appropriate models for the Greek case. The first is rejected on the grounds that it violates the essence of religion; the second, because it does not take into consideration the historical presence and role of Orthodoxy in Greece plus because it may open the bag of Aeolus, throwing the church into the arms of the fundamentalists. What is proposed is a clearer »institutionalization of their distinct roles« that will take into account the character of Greek society and the values and procedures of the democratic state (e. g., transparency, accountability)[148]. This middle way mentality appeals particularly to believers who belong to the new and well-educated middle classes, which, as regards Greece, have grown rapidly during the *Metapolitefsi* period following the restoration of democracy in 1974.

I will end this section with another case, which also demonstrates very clearly the attempted reconciliation between tradition and modernity. Brandon Gallaher, Orthodox theologian and deacon, who »served as a Theological Subject Expert in the Press Office of the Ecumenical Patriarchate during the Holy and Great Council of Crete in June 2016«[149], attempts to articulate an »Eastern Orthodox

---

147 KALAITZIDIS, Orthodoxy and Political Theology, p. 84.
148 See An Interview with Dr. Pantelis Kalaitzidis, in: Kulturgeschichte des Orthodoxen Christentums (11-02-2022), URL: <https://www.uni-erfurt.de/fileadmin/fakultaet/philosophische/Seminar_Religionswissenschaft/Orthodoxes_Christentum/The_Challenge_of_Worldliness_to_Contemporary_Christianity_Projektseite/Interviews/Interview_with_Dr._Kalaitzidis.pdf>.
149 See Theology and Religion, Staff Profiles, Professor Brandon Gallaher, published by University of Exeter, URL: <https://theology.exeter.ac.uk/staff/gallaher/>.

Christian theology of secularism«, as he puts it¹⁵⁰. He strongly believes that this kind of theology is absolutely necessary in order for the Orthodox Church to overcome deeply embedded anti-Western and anti-secularist feelings that impede its constructive encounter with the modern world:

> It is time to balance antinomically Orthodox anti-secularism with a positive Eastern Orthodox Christian theology of secularism. Such a new experimental theology tries to see how Orthodoxy might boldly bear witness to Christ in the modern pluralistic and secular West, to respond to the contemporary challenges the West presents to Eastern Orthodoxy¹⁵¹.

The proposed »positive theological vision of the secular«¹⁵² is constructed from both traditional Orthodox categories and modern secular ones. Actually, the context, values and concepts of Western (post)modernity (e. g., pluralism, human rights, sexual diversity, the Other, civil society, choice, freedom, multiple modernities, secular hybridity) are justified with reference to such Orthodox concepts as *kenosis*, *ascesis, crucifixion, sacrifice*, and *self-sacrificial love*. To cite a characteristic example:

> When it is said that *secularization* is a form of *kenosis*, I mean that in Christ we see the culmination of a divine-human movement of God's complete self-gift to creation and then to *civil* society where he relativizes himself, emptying himself of all claims to centrality, to being the foundation of truth and morality. He withdraws to illumine so that his creatures can freely choose to follow him or not, organize their communities in light of him or not, choosing to do so not because it is natural and the end of their nature but merely as they are struck by the witness of his *love*, his coaxing them forward through the persuasion of *the Spirit* who ever turns them more deeply to his weakening grace on the *cross*¹⁵³.

This understanding of secularisation in religious terms allows the latter to appear not as a threat to religion, but as a golden opportunity for the emergence of the real essence of Orthodoxy. As it is stated, it is a »holy withdrawal of the sacred to make room for the secular – the human in the image of God – to be itself«, and thereby constitutes a »gift of God«¹⁵⁴. This theological configuration has, according

---

150 Brandon GALLAHER, A Secularism of the Royal Doors: Toward an Eastern Orthodox Christian Theology of Secularism, in: Aristotle PAPANIKOLAOU/George E. DEMACOPOULOS (eds.), Fundamentalism or Tradition: Christianity after Secularism, New York 2020, pp. 108–130, at p. 110.
151 Ibid., p. 124.
152 Ibid., p. 110.
153 Ibid., p. 120 (emphasis added).
154 Ibid.

to Gallaher, positive practical consequences, for it enables the church to abandon world-escaping or authoritative attitudes and thereby actively, but critically participate in civil society:

> The church does have a space in creation and, within creation itself, a space and voice in civil society. I am not advocating political quietism. Yet its space is a space to witness, reaching out beyond itself, and, therefore, is not a platform to lecture or tell the different parts of society, the different portions of the human organizations that make up a political commonwealth; they should not be in and of the world, although it can and should at times critique aspects of civil society that are counter to the gospel ethic[155].

In sum, these theologians have high intellectual capital that enables them to move easily between Orthodox theology and modern secular thought. Their aim is to bring Orthodox theology and the church into a constructive relationship with the context of secular modernity. Overcoming the polarisation between the nationalisation and the privatisation of the Orthodox faith is, from their standpoint, the royal road to this goal.

Concluding Remarks

Orthodox Churches oscillate between the universalist values of Christianity and their institutional position and role within the nation-state. This oscillation between universality and particularity becomes evident at the level of political theology, which provides theoretical legitimation of the church's relationship with politics, culture, and society. Speaking in ideal-typical terms, one can discern, on the one hand, an ethnocentric political theology which defends the national role of the church, close church-state relations, and the primacy of the church in society and culture, and, on the other hand, a more globally-oriented political theology, which attempts to adjust the church to the conditions of pluralism and multiculturalism of (post)modernity. But a preference for particularity does not exclude universality – and vice versa. This is because we are not dealing with a Manichaean, but with a hierarchical antithesis: Common concepts are arranged in a different order according to the medium (e. g., the Orthodox nation with its national church or transnational church) that expresses more in history the category of totality (God) and can lead the world to the latter.

On the institutional level, the church of Greece and the Ecumenical Patriarchate of Constantinople respectively are characteristic producers of these two ideal-types

---

155 Ibid., p. 123.

of political theology. Of course, this does not mean that the real attitude of the two churches is in absolute accordance with these political theologies. For instance, the Church of Greece, despite its ethnocentric rhetoric, engages in financial and other collaborations at the European and international level (e. g., in the field of religious tourism) and strongly supports Greece's European orientation, despite the rise of strong nationalist sentiments in large segments of Greek society, especially during the financial crisis. The Patriarchate of Constantinople, despite its transnational self-understanding and universalist orientation, is closely associated with the identity of Christian Hellenism and at times favours particularity; for instance, it intervenes for the creation of autocephalous churches (e. g., in Ukraine), which actually function as national churches.

The political theologies of ethnocentrism and universality are more clearly articulated by individual clerical and lay theologians. In the case of ultra-conservative actors, the ethnocentric political theology takes the form of nationalism that is directed against what they perceive as atheist forces of globalisation and as the »barbarian West«. Their vision is the establishment of a Christian state that will propagate Helleno-Christian/Helleno-Orthodox values and impose the church's hegemonic place in society. In the case of anti-fundamentalist theologians, Western liberal democracy becomes a kind of secular equivalent of universality in the sense that it is perceived as an ideal context for the development of free and energetic activity in accordance with the universal values of Christianity. But even here, one can find variations and contradictions, especially during critical times. For instance, during the 2015 Greek bailout referendum, religious ultra-conservatives, who traditionally perceive the European Union as a kind of monster that threatens the existence of the Greek nation, either toned down their rhetoric or even supported Greec's participation in the »heretical« European Union[156].

Irrespective of their different orientation, what these political theologies have in common is that they are all used as instruments of action: Their producers formulate a specific vision for the church's place and role in modernity and, in so doing, attempt to mobilise the institutional church and the faithful to undertake corresponding actions that will fulfil these visions. Therefore, political theologies are neither purely theoretical contemplations nor politically neutral. In an attempt to address the challenges of modernity and contemporary issues in light of what they consider genuine Orthodox ethos, the producers of these political theologies necessarily end up siding with particular ideological, political, and economic perspectives, be it nationalism or liberalism, or national or supranational capitalism. In that sense, Orthodox political theologies can be viewed as »translations« of broader secular

---

156 See Efstathios Kessareas, Οικονομική κρίση, ευρωπαϊκός προσανατολισμός και ελληνορθόδοξη ιδεολογία, in: Το Βήμα των Κοινωνικών Επιστημών/Social Science Tribune 20/76 (2023), pp. 28–63.

ideologies to the religious field – of course not mechanically, but in dialogue with the rich Orthodox theological tradition.

What is certain is that political theologies are not independent of their historical context. Religious intellectuals play an important role in the formulation and dissemination of schemes of thought that will enable the church to adjust to changing historical conditions. Thus, the political theology of ethnocentrism cannot be understood outside the context of the modern nation-state, whereas the need for the articulation of a political theology of universality is reinforced under the structural and ideological changes of globalisation and multiculturalism.

Index[1]

A

Adam and Eve   39, 44, 45
Adamaioi   44, 47
administration   35, 64, 77, 78, 117, 119, 120, 123, 127, 129, 130, 136, 137, 227, 234, 236, 308, 334, 372, 378
Adrianople   77, 172
Africa   25, 26, 28, 181, 185, 187, 188, 193, 201, 231
Agapetos Diakonos   104
Akropolites, George   63
Aleksander Paulus of Tallinn, Archbishop   312
Aleksei/Aleksey, Tsar   96–99, 106, 107, 110, 112, 314, 366
Aleksei/Aleksii II, Patriarch   317, 320, 368
Alexander II, Tsar   173, 174
Alexandria   14, 29, 31, 93
Ambrosius of Helsinki, Metropolitan   318, 319
Ambrosius of Korea, Metropolitan   401
anarchy   41, 123, 127, 128, 154
Anglicans   113, 127, 227
Antichrist   166, 167, 256, 345
Antioch   14, 29, 65, 93, 147, 223
Antiquity   11, 26, 32, 37, 44, 47, 55, 57, 65, 129, 131, 153, 155, 171, 222, 224, 236, 293, 295
anti-Semitism   156, 252, 284
Antonescu, Ion   254, 256
apostolicity   216, 217
Arendt, Hannah   12
aristocracy   49, 78, 79, 122, 272
Armenia   129, 225
Armenian Church   129
asceticism   66, 211, 272, 291, 403, 404
Asia   212
Asia Minor   24, 129, 137, 177, 229, 379, 382
Assmann, Jan   153, 238, 239
Athanasius, Bishop of Alexandria   14, 29
atheism   153, 156, 218, 277–279, 295, 382, 388
Augustine/Augustinus, Aurelius   16, 119, 167, 278
Australia   394
Austria   171, 205, 206
authorities   79, 89, 111, 121, 134, 136, 138, 139, 141, 142, 167, 173, 206, 229, 314, 315, 324, 332, 334, 336, 346, 350, 355, 360–362, 366, 385, 387–389
authority   12, 34, 59, 64, 65, 67, 74, 75, 78, 81, 85, 87, 98, 110, 120, 121, 123–125, 127, 130, 132, 133, 135, 141, 145–148, 150, 161–164, 200, 206, 222, 224–226, 228, 233, 234, 236, 237, 239, 240, 248, 249, 262, 272, 297, 314, 324, 327, 333–338, 340, 342, 345, 351, 352, 384, 387, 393, 399, 402–404, 406
autocephaly   20, 64, 118, 221, 223, 309–311, 314–316, 318, 321, 327, 329, 330, 332, 333, 364, 366, 369, 378, 393
Autocracy   83
autocracy   19, 20, 85, 86, 88, 89, 96, 100, 154, 160, 166, 172, 266, 274, 281, 287

---

1 The lemmas »Church« and »Orthodoxy (general)« were not included in this section due to their high frequency throughout the volume.

B

Bakunin, Mikhail   131, 152, 156–159, 166, 167
Bălan, Nicolae, Metropolitan   241
Balkans   24, 65, 118, 133, 134, 136, 171, 175, 206, 210, 294, 309
baptism   24, 25, 30, 77, 122, 334
Barth, Karl   283–285
Bartholomew I, Patriarch   318, 394, 395
Beck, Hans-Georg   36, 103
Bela IV, King   72
Benjamin, Walter   153
Berdiaev/Berdyaev, Nikolai   156, 164, 165, 265, 266, 268, 270, 272–276, 280, 283, 285–288
Berger, Peter   326
Bezold, Carl   200
Bible   39, 40, 51, 146, 189, 190, 199, 248, 367, 381
Bismarck, Otto von   187
Blachernitissa, Icon   109, 177
Blumenberg, Hans   101, 263
bolshevism   165, 256, 270, 275
Boris III, Tsar   139
Boris-Michael, Tsar   56
Bosnia   205, 206, 219
Bourdieu, Pierre   375, 377, 402
Bremer, Thomas   203
Brest, Union of   307, 308
Britain   24, 175, 176, 179, 180, 185, 188, 229, 233
Bucharest   23, 80, 136, 249, 256, 260
Buchenau, Klaus   203
Bulgakov, Sergii/Sergei/Sergey   154, 155, 164, 167, 265, 266, 268–271, 274–281, 286, 287, 303
Bulgaria   20, 53, 54, 56, 62, 64, 67, 73, 132, 134–138, 141–144, 149, 150, 169
Bulgarian Orthodox Church   132–143, 145, 147–150
Burckhardt, Jacob   24

Byzantium   15, 18, 36, 37, 48, 50, 79, 83, 86, 93, 96, 103, 117, 124, 176, 224, 245, 291–296, 298–301, 341, 372, 391, 398

C

Caecilian, Bishop   25, 28
Caesar   164, 166–168, 272, 273, 281, 284, 287, 288
Cain and Abel   39, 45
Calvinists   113, 127
Canada   394
capitalism   205, 266, 268, 270, 276, 277, 296, 400, 410
Carol II, King   253, 254
Catherine II, Empress   170, 171
Catholics   123, 178, 210, 225, 274, 282, 307, 348
ceremony   58, 193, 334, 335, 344, 401
Christianity   11, 12, 14, 18, 23–25, 28, 29, 32, 36, 37, 40, 43, 46, 52, 54, 67, 89, 94, 124, 126, 132, 133, 151–153, 157, 159, 160, 162, 170, 181, 188, 203, 204, 207, 208, 213, 218, 221, 239, 240, 243, 244, 254–258, 272–279, 283, 291, 293, 307, 308, 317, 320, 325–327, 338, 342, 372, 376, 377, 381, 383, 392, 393, 398, 402, 409, 410
Chrysanthos of Cyprus, Archbishop   223, 225, 226
Chrysostom, John   16, 113
Church of Cyprus   221–226, 228, 230, 231
citizen   12, 31, 36, 61, 62, 66, 130, 135, 195, 244, 247, 248, 250, 271, 332, 341, 342, 347, 351, 367, 382, 400, 405
class   116, 158, 168, 181, 194, 211, 257, 258, 261, 262, 278, 285, 407
Clément, Olivier   322
Clergy   65
clergy   25, 26, 35, 61, 75, 81, 87, 88, 98, 99, 116–118, 120–122, 124, 128–130, 132, 136, 138, 139, 142, 146, 150, 178, 184,

192, 206, 212, 223, 224, 226–228, 267, 316–318, 328–330, 332, 335–338, 340, 341, 344–350, 355, 366–368, 386, 388
Codreanu, Corneliu Zelea   251, 256
Cold War   235, 289, 295, 316
colonialism   185, 235
Communism   15, 165, 180, 205, 256, 257, 263, 265, 266, 268, 270, 279, 281, 282, 289, 295, 296
community   12, 13, 33, 37, 59, 62, 66, 67, 75, 95, 101, 105, 108, 112, 122, 129, 138, 160, 190, 191, 207, 218, 222, 226, 228, 230, 231, 233, 243, 248–251, 255, 256, 263, 268, 285, 287, 304, 308–310, 312, 313, 321, 346, 355, 365, 367, 368, 371, 383, 389, 398, 403–405, 407
conciliarity   138
confession   31, 34, 37, 69, 126, 127, 268, 285, 286, 307, 308
conservatism   337, 375
Constantine I, Emperor   14, 23–32, 34, 35, 37, 87, 88, 102–104, 106, 109, 191, 272, 288, 298, 390
Constantine IX Monomachos, Emperor   94
Constantine VII, Emperor   85
Constantinople   20, 31–33, 50, 56, 60, 62–65, 69–71, 73–78, 86, 88, 90, 93–95, 105, 107, 109, 111, 112, 115, 120, 123, 125, 127, 130, 133–135, 144–147, 150, 169–177, 179, 188, 205, 206, 210, 212, 216, 223–225, 240, 294, 297, 308–312, 314–318, 320, 321, 333, 372, 373, 376, 377, 390, 391, 393, 395, 397, 409, 410
Cossacks   106, 112
Covid-19   323, 324, 345, 347, 352, 358, 375, 392
Crainic, Nichifor   249–253
Crimean War   134, 171–173, 300, 301, 359, 362, 372
Croatia   209

crusades   155
Curtea de Argeș   73
Cyprus   20, 221–226, 228–235
Cyril and Methodius, Saints   215, 216
Cyril/Kirill, Patriarch of Moscow   19, 95, 127, 365, 368–370, 372

D

Dagron, Gilbert   102
Danilo II, Archbishop   58, 59, 64
Danubian Principalities   20, 21, 62, 78, 79, 105, 111, 171, 240
David the Builder, King   335
David, King   95, 96
death   19, 24, 30, 32, 54, 55, 58, 74, 76, 88, 89, 93, 97, 98, 137, 143, 155, 159, 171, 192, 212, 213, 228, 230, 235, 310, 323, 348, 350, 360, 387, 388
democracy   124, 132, 155, 163, 240, 250, 265–268, 270–272, 274–276, 280–282, 286, 288, 304, 324, 379, 389, 392, 396, 398, 402, 404, 407, 410
dialectics   21, 33, 69, 70, 246, 252, 278, 280, 284, 406
dictatorship   235, 253, 254, 256, 259, 325, 345, 346, 389
divinity   26, 64, 153, 157
Dmitrii Donskoi, Prince   84, 90
dogma   17, 31, 33, 75, 123, 124, 135, 146–149, 206, 211, 216, 223, 240, 261, 291, 293, 375, 391
Dominicans   71, 72
Dositheos, Patriarch   108, 111
Dostoevsky, Fëdor/Fyodor   153, 156, 159, 160, 167, 208, 211, 275
Dugin, Alexander   300, 337
Dušan, Stefan, Tsar   59, 60, 75
Dyophysitism   34

E

Easter   26, 87, 191, 267, 324, 338, 339, 347, 348, 350, 351
ecclesiology   150, 204, 208, 215, 216, 218, 219, 313, 316, 318, 352, 353
economy   215–217, 271, 277, 385, 394, 395
ecumenical councils   34, 75, 140, 147, 148, 207, 221, 223
Ecumenical Patriarchate   20, 73, 75, 79, 115, 118, 123, 147, 177, 205, 357, 358, 366, 376–378, 393–395, 407, 409
ecumenism   318, 319, 395
Edict of Milan   23, 25
education   35, 51, 113, 125, 149, 213, 217, 237, 240, 241, 308, 328, 329, 331, 337, 340, 350, 391
emperor   14, 15, 18, 23–37, 41–44, 48, 50–53, 60, 63, 65, 78, 79, 81, 85, 86, 88, 89, 91–94, 102–106, 109–111, 141, 171, 175, 182, 184, 186, 187, 189–193, 197–199, 206, 223, 224, 240, 284, 294, 297, 328, 373
Empire   14, 25–27, 29, 32–37, 47, 48, 53, 59–61, 63, 65, 71, 80, 85, 88, 89, 92, 93, 95, 107, 110, 111, 116–118, 121–123, 128–130, 133, 135, 136, 160, 164, 170, 171, 173, 175, 177, 180, 181, 185, 187, 188, 191–194, 197, 199, 205, 223, 224, 228, 230, 233, 234, 292–294, 297, 298, 300, 308, 311, 322, 327, 328, 330, 331, 373, 390, 391, 393, 396, 405
endowment   55
Enlightenment   103, 157, 206, 209, 211, 238, 242, 262, 267, 281, 282, 326, 382
Enosis   s. unity
equality   122, 142, 225, 257, 272, 403
eschatology   135, 151, 188, 215, 230, 233, 236, 344, 345, 405, 406
Estonia   308, 309, 311–314, 316, 320–322
ethics   s. morality
Ethiopia   19, 181–200

ethnophyletism   144, 381, 393, 401
eucharist   s. Holy Communion
European Union/EU   37, 297, 342, 357, 358, 363, 385, 396, 410
Eusebius, Bishop of Caesarea   14, 27, 28, 78, 102
Eustathios, Bishop of Thessaloniki   40, 44–47, 51, 52
Exarchate   115, 116, 125, 133–139, 141, 143–145, 149, 150, 327

F

faith   13, 24, 25, 31, 33, 34, 36, 37, 44, 55, 61, 66, 67, 72, 74, 81, 83, 84, 90, 92, 94, 95, 98–100, 113, 122, 123, 130, 135, 148, 154, 169, 183, 186, 188, 209, 212, 213, 218, 239, 249, 251–253, 255, 261, 275, 282, 294, 295, 300, 312, 329, 332, 341, 346, 348, 349, 378, 382, 383, 387, 389, 400, 401, 406, 409
fascism   205, 267, 270, 281–283
Filofei of Pskov, Monk   89, 95, 96, 169
Filotheos of Cyprus, Archbishop   225
Finland   308–310, 312, 313, 315, 316, 318, 319, 321
Florensky/Florenskii, Pavel   164, 295
Florovsky/Florovskii, Georges/Georgii   15, 35, 156, 271, 292, 302, 372
France   103, 174, 176, 179, 185, 188, 195, 283, 321, 328
Frank, Semën/Semyon   164, 165, 265, 266, 268, 270, 272, 277–285, 287
freedom   24–26, 32, 36, 37, 55, 107, 159, 162, 163, 165, 167, 241, 243, 258, 261, 262, 266, 270, 272, 274, 275, 278, 280–282, 285, 287, 288, 291, 302, 329–331, 335, 341–343, 363, 375, 380–383, 399, 403, 404, 407, 408

G

gender   318, 337, 338, 343
geopolitics   89, 100, 364
Georgia   324, 325, 327, 330, 332, 333, 336, 337, 341, 342, 344–349, 352
Georgian Orthodox Church   323–339, 341–344, 346–348, 351, 352
Germany   172, 174, 186, 187, 189, 190, 193, 195, 205, 238, 256, 276, 281, 283, 316
Gerontism   120, 122
globalization   291, 395
God   12, 14, 20, 21, 24–29, 31, 34–36, 40, 41, 43, 45–49, 52, 53, 58, 62, 65, 66, 69, 80, 81, 84, 85, 87, 89, 92, 96, 100, 106, 108, 111, 112, 119, 125, 126, 128, 140, 146, 152, 154–160, 162–168, 182, 183, 187, 207, 209–213, 215, 217, 230, 238, 242, 243, 246–249, 255, 257, 258, 266, 267, 269, 272–275, 278, 282, 284, 285, 287, 288, 291, 297, 301, 343, 346, 349–351, 356, 365, 366, 377, 379, 381–383, 387–389, 391, 392, 397–399, 403, 405, 408, 409
God-Man   156, 159, 211–213, 288
governance   41, 45, 131, 135–138, 141, 146, 150, 234, 271, 332, 335, 336, 346
Gratian, Emperor   30
Great Powers   137, 172, 175
Great Schism   373
Greece   20, 63, 115, 118, 133, 134, 136, 171, 175, 228–230, 232–235, 324, 376–378, 381, 382, 384, 385, 387–389, 392, 393, 404, 407, 409, 410
Greek Catholic Church   260, 354, 357, 358
Greek Orthodox Church   149, 348
Greek Project   171
Greek-Catholics   *s. Greek Catholic Church*
Gregory of Nazianz   113
Gregory IX   72

H

Habsburg   91, 92
Habsburg Empire   91
Hagia Sophia   33, 169–171, 176, 177
hagiography   65
harmony   27, 35, 64, 79, 96, 98, 123, 298
Ḫaylä Śǝllase, Emperor   182, 185, 192, 196–198
Herder, Johann Gottfried   250, 251
heresy   29, 30, 75, 76, 87, 89, 273, 369, 372, 378, 402
Herzegovina   59, 205, 219
Hesychasm   *s. Palamism*
Hesychasm, political   16, 20, 289, 290, 292–297, 300–305
historiosophy   20
Hitler, Adolf   195, 266, 281, 282
Holy Communion   97, 135, 324, 347–350, 398
Holy Cross   23, 29, 30, 55, 63, 84, 94, 176, 383, 407, 408
Holy Lance   60
Holy Land   90, 177–179
Holy Spirit   31, 53, 216, 273, 398
Holy Trinity   31, 34, 91, 162, 255
homoiosis   *s. likeness*
homophobia   337, 343
homosexuality   319, 337
Hovorun, Cyril   27, 322, 360, 361, 364–366, 370, 371
human rights   286, 287, 304, 324, 338, 343, 345, 360–362, 396, 398, 399, 408, 431
humanism   156, 207, 208, 211, 215, 217, 267, 269, 271, 273, 286, 295, 296, 303, 383
Hungary   74, 205, 256
Hungro-Wallachia, Metropolis   21, 73, 74, 77
Husserl, Edmund   281

I

icons   55, 63, 106, 109, 170, 177, 382, 407
idealism   69
ideology   30, 52, 84, 92, 119, 126–128, 130, 155, 158, 170, 172, 174, 184, 194, 204, 218, 235, 237, 254, 257, 259, 274, 300, 301, 314, 316, 339, 379, 380, 389, 393, 394, 400
Ignatius, Bishop of Antioch   14
Ilarion Alfeev, Metropolitan   296
Ilia II, Patriarch   333, 338, 344, 345
imperialism   175, 185, 207, 209, 210, 218, 219
individualism   207, 208, 211, 217, 266, 279, 399
industrialisation   279
internet   344, 346
Iona of Muscovy/Moscow, Metropolitan   83, 86
Islam   17, 130, 155, 187, 192
Islamic State   155
Israel   35, 90, 95, 96, 112, 155, 162, 181, 183, 184, 194, 274
Istanbul   117, 129, 135, 137, 143, 145
Italy   24, 185, 188
Ivan III, Grand Prince   85–88, 90, 91, 94, 96, 100, 107
Ivan IV, Tsar   85, 91–97, 99, 105, 355

J

Japan   185, 197–199
Jerusalem   19, 90, 91, 93, 96, 98, 108, 110, 169, 170, 172, 175, 178, 179, 182, 190, 191, 197, 401
Jesus Christ (the Lord, the Savior)   41, 42, 44, 50, 52, 55, 137, 140, 154, 167, 217, 249, 250, 291, 292, 309, 345, 346, 350, 388, 397
John of Polyvotos, Saint   61, 62, 66
John of Rila, monk   61, 62
Judaism   12, 87, 284

Julian, Emperor/Julian the Apostate   41–44, 51
jurisdiction   20, 35, 71, 73, 75, 115, 116, 120–122, 125, 134–138, 144, 145, 147, 149, 205, 206, 224, 225, 308–313, 315, 317, 320, 358, 377, 393
justice   19, 41, 78, 155, 230, 247, 254, 257, 273–275, 277, 278, 280, 287, 288, 338, 360, 362, 368, 394, 395, 399
justification   12, 64, 153, 193, 196, 264, 273, 282, 287, 288, 291, 292, 305, 324, 369, 399
Justinian I, Emperor   18, 29, 33–37, 106

K

Kallistos I, Patriarch   63, 73
Kant, Immanuel   42
Karatheodoris, Stephanos   120, 121, 126, 128
Katechon   156, 166, 290, 300
Khomiakov, Aleksey   211
Kiev/Kyiv   84, 91, 104, 176, 298, 300, 354, 359, 366, 370
Kingdom of God/Christ   100, 154, 156, 157, 165, 166, 176, 242, 246, 248, 272, 273, 275, 278, 285, 365, 405
kingship   41, 95, 183, 198, 386
Kosovo   208, 291
Kremlin   86, 369, 372, 374
Kusber, Jan   19, 105
Kyprianos of Cyprus, Archbishop   226
Kyrillos II of Cyprus, Archbishop   228

L

Lampardis, Paisios, Patriarch   108, 111
Latins   62, 75
Latvia   308, 312–314, 316, 317, 320, 322
Lausanne, Treaty of   229
law   12, 26, 31–34, 37, 39, 41, 43–47, 65, 78, 85, 99, 110, 116, 125, 130, 133, 137, 139–142, 145–147, 177, 183, 196, 198,

227, 229–231, 238, 240–242, 245–248, 251, 252, 254, 259, 260, 270, 271, 273, 286, 301, 312, 320, 328, 330, 336, 337, 342, 343, 346, 351, 361, 362, 368, 391, 392, 399
laymen   75, 120, 129, 134, 135, 138–140, 145–148, 150, 240, 366, 367
Lazar Hrebeljanović, Prince   62, 75, 208
Legion Archangel Michael   251, 253, 256
LGBT/LGBTQ/LGBTQ+   337, 338, 343
Liberalism   273, 296, 298, 305, 341, 342, 375, 385, 404, 410
Licinius, Emperor   25
likeness   80, 81, 213, 217, 267, 287
Lithuania   87, 92, 295, 307, 308, 311, 316, 322
liturgy   35, 55, 97, 146, 177, 178, 284, 313, 327, 333, 347, 350, 351
Losev, Aleksei   295, 302
Lossky, Vladimir   281, 292, 302, 339
Loucaris, Cyril, Patriarch   127
Lutherans   113, 309, 318

M

Macarius of Egypt, Saint   211
Macedonia   61, 65, 115, 134, 136, 137, 205
Maidan Revolution   353, 355, 358–363, 365, 368, 370–372, 374
Makarios III of Cyprus, Archbishop   221, 222, 229, 231–236
Man-God   156, 159, 266, 273
Maritain, Jacques   273, 287
Marxism   157
Mary, the Mother of God   339
Maximilian I, Emperor   91
Maximos/Maximus/Maxim the Confessor/Homologetes   40, 41
media   70, 232, 237, 319, 337, 344, 346, 347
Megali Idea   174, 379
Mehmed II, Sultan   117, 225, 232

Meiji Constitution   197, 198
Meletios IV, Patriarch   310, 311
Messianism   20, 95, 286
Metz, Johann Baptist   13, 204
Meyendorff, John   289, 292–296, 302, 303, 305
miaphysitism   34, 35
Milbank, John   155
millet   20, 115–119, 121, 125, 127–130, 134, 225, 235, 393
minorities   31, 130, 251, 318, 335, 343
Mircea I, Prince   74
Miron Cristea, Patriarch   253, 254
Mitsotakis, Kyriakos   384
modernity   18, 20, 184, 189, 236, 238, 267, 302, 324, 325, 331, 340, 344, 348, 352, 375, 376, 384, 385, 390, 391, 393, 397, 398, 404–410
Moldavia   s. Danubian Principalities
monarchy   49, 101, 102, 104, 107, 119, 124–126, 128, 130, 160, 181, 196, 199, 208, 267, 270–272, 274–276, 283, 329, 346
monasticism   45, 67, 213, 215–217, 293, 295, 398
morality   21, 46, 47, 75, 230, 243, 245–251, 279, 289, 299, 302–305, 341, 343, 375, 388, 403, 408
Moscow Patriarchate   21, 83, 112, 297–299, 308–311, 314–317, 320, 353–355, 368, 370
Moscow/Muscovy   19–21, 80, 83–98, 104–107, 109, 110, 112, 113, 118, 169, 170, 173, 176, 177, 259, 295, 297–300, 302, 308–317, 320, 321, 353–355, 358, 362, 366, 368, 370, 372
Moses   44, 106, 183
Mount Athos   59, 64, 74, 76, 77, 173, 293, 294, 344
Mənilək II, Emperor   185, 187–192, 195, 196, 199

N

National Socialism   257, 266, 281
nationalism   126–128, 132–134, 149, 150, 174, 204, 207, 209–212, 216, 227, 228, 236, 246, 250, 252, 254, 257, 268, 273, 274, 285, 286, 301, 323, 325, 328, 333, 376, 378, 381, 393, 396, 398, 399, 405, 410
Neagoe Basarab, Prince   69, 79–81
Nemanja, Stefan, Prince   54, 59, 60, 64
Nemanja, Stefan-Simeon, Prince   53, 58
Neo-Orthodoxism   156, 165, 205, 218, 289, 290, 293, 302, 305
Nephon/Niphon II, Patriarch   69, 76–79
Neuilly, Treaty of   136–138, 143, 145, 149, 150
Nevsky, Alexander   175
New Israel   90, 96, 112, 274
Nicene-Constantinopolitan Creed   207, 217
Nicholas Alexander, Prince   73
Nicholas II, Pope   56, 355
Nicholas of Cusa   282
Nietzsche, Friedrich   156, 208
Nikodemos/Nicodim of Tismana, Monk   69, 73–76
Nikon, Patriarch   90, 95, 97, 106, 110, 112, 169
Nil Sorskii, Monk   88

O

Old Believers   95, 98
Onufrii, Metropolitan   318, 363, 368
Orthodox Church of Finland   315, 319
Orthodox Church of Ukraine   357, 358, 366, 367, 373, 374
Orthodoxy, Baltic   21
Orthodoxy, Bulgarian   s. a. Bulgarian Orthodox Church, 132, 401
Orthodoxy, Cyprus   s. a. Church of Cyprus, 221, 222, 236
Orthodoxy, Finnish   s. Orthodox Church of Finland
Orthodoxy, Georgian   s. a. Georgian Orthodox Church, 21, 323
Orthodoxy, Greek   s. a. Greek Orthodox Church, 107, 116, 122, 129, 149, 227, 230, 231, 234, 376, 378, 379, 382, 383, 386, 388, 389, 391, 394, 397, 401, 407
Orthodoxy, Polish   s. a. Polish Orthodox Churches, 21, 311, 314, 317, 318
Orthodoxy, political   19, 33, 37, 40, 103, 354, 355, 370
Orthodoxy, Romanian   s. a. Romanian Orthodox Church, 243, 244, 246, 248, 249, 252, 256, 348, 401
Orthodoxy, Russian   s. a. Russian Orthodox Church, 95, 98, 100, 112, 132, 157, 174, 180, 296, 310, 353, 372, 374, 401
Orthodoxy, Serbian   s. a. Serbian Orthodox Church, 53, 64, 401
Orthodoxy, Ukrainian   s. a. Orthodox Church of Ukraine, 366, 370–372
Ottoman Empire   116–118, 121, 129, 130, 133, 135, 136, 170, 171, 175, 191, 193, 205, 233

P

Palamism   16, 20, 217, 289–297, 300–305
Palestine   14, 172, 174, 177–180
Pan-Orthodoxism   20, 315
Pan-Slavism   20, 173–175, 179, 204, 208, 217
papacy   56, 72, 78, 92, 93, 160, 192, 210, 224, 373
Parliament   102, 118, 130, 163, 228, 247, 253, 259, 312, 336–338, 354, 363, 394
Patriarchate (as an institution)   20, 21, 65, 73, 75, 77, 79, 83, 93, 99, 112, 115–118, 120–126, 129, 133–136, 144, 147, 150, 176, 177, 205, 210, 212, 223–225, 241, 260, 297–299, 308–312, 314–317, 320,

336, 338, 345, 347–351, 353–355, 357, 358, 366, 370, 376–378, 393–397, 403, 407, 409, 410
Paul, Apostle   30, 40, 148, 152, 166
Pavlidis, Gregorios/Grigorios   123, 124, 127, 128
Pentarchy   225
Peter I, Tsar   83, 96, 98–100, 108, 118, 120, 170, 173, 273
Peter, Apostle   31
Petrunin, Vladimir   290, 294, 296–300, 304
Photios I, Patriarch of Constantinople   20, 40–45, 50–52, 174
Plato/Platon   11, 40, 164
Poland   92, 108, 307, 308, 310, 313–317, 322, 326
Poland-Lithuania   92, 307, 308
Polish Orthodox Churches   317, 318, 331
politics   11–16, 19–21, 24, 28, 43, 50, 69, 70, 85, 86, 101, 131, 132, 152, 153, 155, 156, 159, 161, 165, 167, 168, 180, 185, 204, 224, 234, 237–239, 245, 248–250, 252, 253, 256–258, 260, 262, 263, 271, 288, 294, 307, 308, 313, 317, 324–326, 336, 339, 340, 343, 352, 356, 357, 363, 369, 375, 376, 385, 386, 403–405, 409
polytheism   11, 153
Pope (as an office)   30, 56, 72, 78, 92, 93, 160, 192, 210, 224, 373
Popović, Justin   204, 210–214, 216–218, 344
Poroshenko, Peter   363, 364, 372
Possevino, Antonio   84, 93, 94
power   11, 18–20, 24, 27, 32, 33, 35–37, 40, 53, 55, 57, 58, 60, 61, 63, 64, 66, 67, 70, 78, 79, 82, 83, 85–88, 91, 92, 96, 98, 100–103, 106, 109, 116, 118, 120, 122, 123, 127, 128, 130, 139, 142, 146–150, 155, 158, 161–163, 167, 169, 174, 176, 180, 185, 187, 188, 193, 195, 197, 198, 205, 206, 210, 221, 223–228, 231, 235, 239, 250, 251, 253, 254, 256, 258, 262, 269–275, 287, 297, 301, 302, 310, 324, 325, 334, 335, 341, 344, 350–352, 356, 360–362, 368, 371, 375, 389, 391, 399, 400, 404, 405
Prokopovich, Feofan, Archbishop   99
protest   87, 123, 139, 167, 284, 309, 336, 337, 349, 361, 362, 371, 407
Protestant   12, 16, 103, 104, 119, 124, 127, 129, 191, 208, 272, 284–286, 319, 340, 353, 371
Protestantism   123, 126–128, 283, 284, 326, 373

Q

Queen of Sheba   181–183, 189–191, 193–197, 200, 201

R

racism   257, 279, 381, 400
Radu the Great, Prince   74, 77–79
rationalism   207, 208, 211, 217, 253
referendum   134, 354, 410
reform   14, 51, 73, 75, 76, 79, 98, 99, 106, 117, 118, 120, 122–130, 145, 148, 150, 167, 225, 226, 236, 254, 268, 308, 331, 340, 365, 366, 375
Reformation   55, 101, 119, 127, 295, 308, 326
Rehberg, Karl-Siegbert   69
Reinhard, Wolfgang   129
relics   20, 53–65, 67, 97, 106, 112, 113, 170
religion   11–14, 24, 26, 31, 32, 36, 45, 92, 101, 115, 117, 119, 122, 131, 134, 152, 153, 155, 157, 161, 167, 168, 181, 204, 207, 210, 222, 237–239, 247, 250, 252, 253, 256, 260, 263, 265–268, 270, 277, 279, 282, 287, 288, 308, 323–333, 335, 338, 340, 344, 346, 348, 349, 352,

356–359, 363, 369, 375–377, 389, 394, 400, 401, 403, 407, 408
republicanism 206
revolution 136, 141, 153, 166, 167, 175, 176, 206, 239, 255, 259, 262, 267, 268, 273, 278, 286, 308, 330, 335, 341, 355, 359, 360, 370, 374, 382, 392, 401
ritual 27, 57, 101, 184, 259, 319, 323, 324, 334, 349, 375
Roman Empire 14, 25, 27, 35–37, 47, 85, 92, 373
Romania 20, 133, 134, 136, 237, 239–241, 251–254, 256, 257, 259, 260, 264, 324, 368
Romanian Orthodox Church 144, 149, 237, 239–241, 249, 253, 254, 260, 262, 263, 343, 363, 366, 368, 370, 374
Romanides, John 217, 304
Rome 20, 40, 73, 88–95, 99, 107, 126, 127, 169, 174, 210, 212, 216, 284, 291, 364, 393
Rousseau, Jean-Jacques 153, 250
rule 14, 20, 24, 27, 31, 32, 37, 41, 46, 50, 66, 76, 78, 81, 83, 85, 86, 90, 92, 94–96, 98, 102, 105, 108, 111, 112, 122, 124, 135, 139, 146, 150, 177, 182, 196, 205, 206, 209, 210, 222–234, 236, 270, 272, 286, 287, 313, 323, 325, 327, 331, 332, 334, 336, 342, 347, 351, 355, 358, 399
Rus 84, 91, 298, 300, 366, 368
Russia 83–85, 91–95, 97, 99, 106, 113, 118, 152, 153, 156, 157, 159–161, 163, 164, 170–173, 175–179, 188, 265, 267–269, 271, 273–276, 280, 282, 285, 290, 292, 294–301, 307, 309, 310, 317, 322, 327, 346, 358, 363, 365, 366, 405
Russian Orthodox Church 16, 21, 86, 95–97, 132, 141, 152, 269, 283, 296–299, 308, 310, 315, 318, 320, 327, 328, 332, 339, 343, 364, 393, 394

S

Saakashvili, Mikheil 335
sacerdotium 19, 28, 34, 35, 64, 111
Şaguna, Andrei, Metropolitan 240
Saint-Savahood 20, 203
salvation 33, 35, 43, 44, 51, 55, 70, 89, 108, 112, 133, 159, 207, 215, 217, 230, 236, 247, 257, 258, 260, 293, 297, 301, 303, 372, 377, 386, 389, 404
Samuel, Tsar 61, 95, 96
San Stefano, Treaty of 137
Schilling, Heinz 104, 129
Schmemann, Alexander 24, 27, 30, 32, 36, 322
Schmitt, Carl 13, 101, 131, 152, 156, 158, 166, 204, 221, 238, 239, 323, 324, 352
secularism 119, 227, 242, 288, 296, 325, 326, 388, 389, 398, 400, 407, 408
Serbia 21, 53, 54, 64, 67, 73, 75, 115, 133, 134, 136, 137, 205, 209, 210, 213, 217, 310, 324
Serbian Orthodox Church 53, 60, 75, 136, 149, 203, 205, 206, 209, 210, 216, 218, 219
Sergei/Sergius of Radonezh, Saint 84, 295, 300
Sèvres, Treaty of 143
Shevardnadze, Eduard 334, 335, 341
sin 50, 160, 274, 278, 279, 369
Skylitzes, George 61
Slavs 170, 173, 175, 216, 218
sobornost 156, 165, 208, 211, 217, 271, 280, 287, 367
Socialism 164, 165, 257, 262, 266, 267, 270, 271, 273, 274, 276–279, 281, 284, 316
society 12, 13, 32, 35, 42–45, 48, 51, 52, 87, 116, 119, 128, 130, 131, 134, 140, 152, 153, 157–166, 168, 172, 174, 178, 179, 212, 213, 216–218, 228, 237, 238, 240, 243–248, 251, 252, 254, 255, 258, 260–262, 266, 267, 270–272, 274–276,

278–280, 287–289, 296, 298, 305, 312, 318, 319, 323, 326–328, 330, 332, 337–339, 343, 352–358, 360, 361, 363, 365–367, 370, 371, 374, 376, 379, 380, 384–386, 388, 389, 391, 392, 396, 399, 400, 403, 405, 407–410, 431
Solomon, King   106, 110, 181–184, 190, 191, 194, 195, 197, 201
Solovëv/Solovyov/Solovyev, Vladimir   151–153, 155–157, 159–165, 167, 168, 276, 277, 339
sophiology   20, 167
soteriology   215, 247
soul   35, 43, 111, 161, 212, 242–245, 254, 278, 282, 341, 348, 379, 383, 384, 387, 390–392, 396
Soviet Union/USSR   164, 256, 259, 269, 281, 296, 312, 314–316, 320, 327, 332, 333, 339, 354, 363
Spain   24
Stăniloae, Dumitru   245–247, 252–258, 292
state   12–16, 18–20, 25, 27, 28, 32, 33, 35–37, 39, 48, 50, 52, 60, 69–71, 83, 84, 86, 88, 92, 93, 95, 98, 99, 104, 109, 111, 115–119, 121–125, 128–130, 132–146, 149, 150, 152, 155, 157, 158, 160–163, 165–168, 171, 172, 174, 176, 178–181, 183, 185, 188, 194, 199, 205, 206, 209, 213, 216–219, 221, 226, 231, 233–248, 250–263, 265–267, 270, 273–275, 277–280, 282, 283, 285, 293, 296–299, 304, 308, 309, 314, 323, 324, 326, 327, 329–336, 341–344, 346–353, 355, 356, 358, 360–363, 365–368, 370, 372, 374, 376–381, 384–394, 396, 398, 399, 401–407, 409–411
St Petersburg   174, 176, 178, 277, 296, 366
Sultan (as an office)   77, 118, 120, 130, 132–134, 143, 145, 177, 225, 232, 233, 393

Svetosavlje   s. Saint-Savahood
Sweden   85, 92, 316, 320, 364
symphony   18, 19, 27, 33, 34, 36, 60, 64, 65, 67, 109, 161, 167, 176, 239, 242, 245, 262, 263, 341
Syria   65, 73, 172, 179, 199, 211, 233

T

Tanzimat   116, 117, 120, 122, 129, 226, 236
Taylor, Charles   154
Tertullian, Quintus Septimius Florens   16
theanthropy   s. a. God-Man, 156
theocracy   32, 33, 155, 160, 164, 165, 266–268, 270, 272–274, 287, 288, 405
Theodosius I, Emperor   29–34, 37, 80, 81, 104
theology   11–21, 27–29, 34–36, 55, 67, 69, 70, 78, 80–85, 89, 99, 101, 102, 109, 110, 117, 131–135, 140, 142, 145, 147, 149, 150, 152–160, 165–168, 181–188, 190, 191, 193, 194, 196–200, 203–205, 210, 212, 214–216, 218, 221, 222, 236–239, 241, 248, 249, 261–266, 268, 271, 272, 282, 284, 287–293, 295–297, 299, 301–305, 307–310, 312–327, 329, 339, 346, 351–353, 356, 360, 361, 363–365, 370, 371, 374–378, 380, 382, 392, 394, 396, 397, 400–411, 425, 428, 429, 431
theosis   386, 398, 403
Thessaloniki/Thessalonike   30, 40, 44, 51, 53, 63, 77, 291
Third Rome   20, 88–95, 99, 169, 174, 364, 393
Tillich, Paul   276, 278, 284
totalitarianism   259, 281
tradition/Holy Tradition   11, 18, 29, 31, 40, 51, 54, 55, 58, 60, 63, 64, 73, 83, 89, 94, 96, 102, 103, 109, 110, 121, 123, 127, 131, 140, 152, 155, 161, 166, 181, 182, 184, 188, 191, 193, 195, 196, 198, 206, 209, 211, 215–217, 222, 224, 232, 237, 248,

252, 254, 263, 266, 272, 286, 289, 291, 293, 297, 302–304, 309, 316, 319, 324, 328, 332, 333, 341, 342, 348, 352, 363, 367, 373, 379, 382, 385–389, 391, 396, 398, 403, 407, 411
transcendence 257, 285
translatio imperii 19, 84, 87, 89, 106, 112, 170, 181, 194
Transylvania s. a. Danubian Principalities, 71, 72, 240, 241, 256
Trnovo/Tarnovo 53, 54, 56, 59, 61–65, 67, 75
Turkey 122, 143, 170, 171, 175, 176, 233, 234, 391, 394
Tyranny 123, 124, 211, 266, 400

U

Ukraine 19, 300, 301, 305, 353–355, 357–375, 410
United States of America/USA 188, 205, 283, 315, 316, 394, 398
unity 26–28, 63, 65, 87, 102, 105, 120, 121, 135, 138, 145, 155, 164, 207–209, 211–213, 218, 227–231, 233–236, 240, 243–245, 250, 251, 281, 285, 295, 321, 337, 340, 354, 358, 372, 376, 378, 380, 383, 387, 400–402
Uspenskii, Porfirii, Archimandrite 172, 173

V

Valens, Emperor 30
values 18, 30, 36, 40, 43, 66, 69, 70, 102, 103, 184, 213, 217, 245, 248, 280, 281, 285, 297, 298, 303, 323, 336–338, 340, 343, 345, 360, 365, 376–378, 380–383, 385, 388, 389, 391–393, 396–398, 401–405, 407–410

Varro, Marcus Terentius 11, 221
Victoria, Queen 193, 194, 196
Vladimir Monomakh, Grand Prince 91, 94
Vladimirskaia, Icon 109
Vladislav Vlaicu I, Prince 74
Voegelin, Eric 13

W

Wallachia s. a. Danubian Principalities, 21, 69, 70, 73–80, 105, 240
Weber, Max 375
Wilhelm I, Emperor 186
Wilhelm II, Emperor 175, 187–191
Wilson, Woodrow 137
World War 1/World War I/First World War/WW1 132, 136, 150, 169, 171, 175, 178, 179, 193, 194, 204, 207, 209, 210, 228, 234, 237, 276, 308
World War 2/World War II/Second World War/WW2 195, 204, 205, 210, 211, 218, 231, 286, 287, 308, 310–315, 331, 332, 363

Y

Yannaras, Christos 17, 214, 217, 290, 304, 325, 373
Yoḥannǝs IV, Emperor 184, 186, 187, 192, 194
Yǝkunno Amlak, Emperor 182
Yugoslavia 136, 175, 204, 205, 210, 218

Z

Zäwditu, Empress 185, 192–196, 199
Zizioulas, John N. 214, 216
Zoe Sophia Palaiologos/Palaiologina, Princess 86, 88, 91, 107

Notes on Contributors

Daniel Benga has been professor for liturgics, patristics and church history at the Institute of Orthodox Theology of the Ludwig-Maximilian University of Munich since 2017. He wrote two PhD theses, one on the relations between the Lutheran Reformers and the Orthodox Church in the sixteenth century (Bucharest 2000), and the other on the Lutheran theologian and reformer David Chytraeus and his knowledge of Orthodox Christianity (Erlangen 2001). Another field he works in concerns the ethos of ancient Christianity and the history of the Nicene-Constantinopolitan Creed. His publications include *David Chytraeus (1530–1600) als Erforscher und Wiederentdecker der Ostkirchen. Seine Beziehungen zu orthodoxen Theologen, seine Erforschungen der Ostkirchen und seine ostkirchlichen Kenntnisse* (Wittenberg 2006); *Metodologia cercetării științifice în teologia istorică* (Bucharest 2005); *Identități creștine europene în dialog. De la mișcarea husită la ecumenismul contemporan* (Sibiu 2010); *Cred, mărturisesc și aștept viața veșnică. O istorie teologică a Simbolului Niceo-Constantinopolitan* (Bucharest 2013).

Vladimir Cvetković is a senior research associate at the Institute of Philosophy and Social Theory of the University of Belgrade. He holds an MA in theology from Durham University (UK) and a PhD in philosophy from the University of Belgrade. He had been a research and teaching fellow at the universities of Los Andes (Colombia), Princeton (USA), Aarhus (Denmark), St Andrews (UK), Oslo (Norway), and Niš (Serbia). His research interests include patristics, ancient and Byzantine philosophy and Orthodox theology. He is the editor (with Alex Leonas) of the Brepols series *Subsidia Maximiana*, dedicated to Maximus the Confessor. Among his recent publications are *Justin Popović: A Synthesis of Tradition and Innovation* (in Serbian, Belgrade 2021); with Dragan Bakić (eds.), *Bishop Nikolaj Velimirović: Old Controversies in Historical and Theological Context* (Los Angeles 2022); with Alex Leonas (eds.), *Studies in St Maximus the Confessor's Opuscula Theologica et Polemica* (Turnhout 2023).

Lora Gerd has been chief researcher at the Russian Academy of Sciences (St Petersburg Institute of History) as well as lecturer at St Petersburg State University and Theological Academy. Her research focuses on the Russian policy in the Christian East, church influence in the Ottoman Empire, and the role of Russia in the Eastern Question. She has edited a number of primary archival sources, such as the correspondence of George Begleri, 1878–1898 (2003), the journals and reports of Antonin Kapustin, priest of the Russian Church in Athens and Constantinople, 1850–1865 (4 vols., 2015–2017), and archives on the history of St Panteleimon Monastery on Mount Athos (2015). She has written a monograph on *Russian Policy in the Orthodox East: The Patriarchate of Constantinople (1878–1914)* (Warsaw 2014).

Mihai-D. Grigore was Stanley S. Seeger Research Fellow at the Center for Hellenic Studies of Princeton University from January to May 2012. From November 2012 to June 2022, he was Senior Fellow at Leibniz Institute of European History in Mainz. Since 2022, he has been working with a research scholarship from the Gerda Henkel Foundation on a project concerning the mobility of monks and the creation of polycentric orders in the Orthodox world. His research interests include historical and political anthropology in the Middle Ages and pre-modern Europe, inter-confessional dynamics, Byzantine and Southeast European intellectual history, political philosophy, and institutional history before the Enlightenment. His most recent publications are *Neagoe Basarab – Princeps Christianus. The Semantics of Christianitas in Comparison with Erasmus, Luther, and Machiavelli (1513–1523)* (Oxford 2021); with Florian KÜHRER-WIELACH (eds.), *Orthodoxa Confessio? Konfessionsbildung, Konfessionalisierung und ihre Folgen in der östlichen Christenheit Europas* (Göttingen 2018 [VIEG Beiheft 114]).

Anthony Kaldellis is a professor of Classics at the University of Chicago. He has published many books and articles on the history, culture, and literature of Byzantium, ranging from the fourth to the fifteenth centuries. A number of his publications focused on the reception of the classical tradition, including *Hellenism in Byzantium* (2007) and *The Christian Parthenon* (2009). He subsequently turned to the Roman aspects of Byzantine society, writing *The Byzantine Republic* (2015) and *Romanland: Ethnicity and Empire in Byzantium* (2019). He published a new, comprehensive history of the Eastern Empire with Oxford University Press: *The New Roman Empire: A History of Byzantium* (2024). Kaldellis has translated many Byzantine texts into English, including historians such as Genesios, Attaleiates, and Laonikos Chalkokondyles. He is also the host of the academic podcast *Byzantium & Friends*.

Daniela Kalkandjieva holds a PhD from Central European University and is a project leader at Sofia University St Kliment Ohridski. Her primary research focuses on the interaction of Orthodox Churches with domestic and international politics. She is the author of the monographs *The Bulgarian Orthodox Church and the State, 1944–1953* (1997) and *The Russian Orthodox Church, 1917–1948: From Decline to Resurrection* (2015). Her recent publications include »Religion and Forced Displacement in Modern Bulgaria«, in: L.N. LEUSTEAN/V. HUDSON (eds.), *Religion* *and Forced Displacement in Eastern Europe, the Caucasus, and Central Asia* (London 2022); »Caesar and God in the Public Sphere: Religious and Secular Discourse in Post-Atheist Bulgaria«, in: D.F. EICKELMAN/S. EVSTATIEV (eds.), *Christians and Muslims in Balkan Public Space* (Leiden 2022).

Efstathios Kessareas is a postdoctoral research fellow at the Faculty of Philosophy (Department of Religious Studies) of the University of Erfurt, Germany. He previously conducted postdoctoral research at the Centre for Social Theory of Ghent University, Belgium. He holds a PhD in sociology and an MA in religious studies. He studied Greek philology and sociology. He is author of the book *Church, Ideology, and Politics in Post-dictatorial Greece. A Sociological Approach* (Athens 2022) (in Greek). His articles have been published in journals including *The Sociological Review, Social Compass, Journal of Modern Greek Studies, Byzantine and Modern Greek Studies, and Religions*. His publications include »›Signs of the Times‹: Prophecy Belief in Contemporary Greek Orthodox Contexts«, in: *Social Compass* (2023); »Economic Crisis, European Orientation, and Greek Orthodox Ideology« (in Greek), in: *Social Science Tribune* (2023); »Faith, Economy, and Politics: Religious Tourism in Contemporary Greece«, in: *Erfurter Vorträge zur Kulturgeschichte des Orthodoxen Christentums 21* (2022).

Jan Kusber has held the chair in Eastern European History at the Johannes Gutenberg University of Mainz since 2003. Between 2009 and 2015 he was chairman of the Association of Eastern European Historians in Germany (VOH), and since 2015 he has been vice-president of the German Society for Eastern European Studies. In research and teaching, he deals with the history of the Russian Empire, the history of Poland and the Baltic States, as well as the cultures of remembrance and history politics in Eastern Europe. Monographs: *Krieg und Revolution in Russland, 1904–1906* (Stuttgart 1997); *Eliten- und Volksbildung im Zarenreich während des 18. und in der ersten Hälfte des 19. Jahrhunderts* (Stuttgart 2004; in Russian: Moscow 2018); *Kleine Geschichte St. Petersburgs* (Regensburg 2009); *Katharina die Große. Legitimation durch Reform und Expansion* (Stuttgart 2022).

Vasilios N. Makrides has been Professor of Religious Studies (specialising in Orthodox Christianity) at the Faculty of Philosophy of the University of Erfurt since 1999. His research interests include comparative religious and cultural history as well as the sociology of Orthodox Christianity; religious and cultural relations between Eastern and Western Europe; Orthodox Christianity, modernity, and science; and Greek Orthodox diasporic communities. His latest book publications include: with Gayle E. WOLOSCHAK (eds.), *Orthodox Christianity and Modern Science: Tensions, Ambiguities, Potential* (Turnhout 2019); with Sebastian RIMESTAD (eds.), *Coping with Change: Orthodox Christian Dynamics between Tradition, Innovation,* *and Realpolitik* (Berlin 2020); with Sebastian RIMESTAD (eds.), *The Pan-Orthodox Council of 2016 – A New Era for the Orthodox Church? Interdisciplinary Perspectives* (Berlin 2021).

Stanislau Paulau is junior professor of Global History of Christianity and Orthodox Christian Studies at the Faculty of Theology of the Martin Luther University of Halle-Wittenberg, Germany. He studied Theology and Religious Studies in Minsk, Berlin, Göttingen, Geneva, and Addis Abeba, and has been a Senior Fellow at the Leibniz Institute of European History in Mainz. His research interests include the theology and history of the Eastern and Oriental Orthodox Churches in modern era (Eastern Europe, Northeast Africa, and the Middle East); entangled and global history of Christianity; history of the Ecumenical Movement; inter-confessionality and trans-confessionality. His latest publications include *Das andere Christentum. Zur transkonfessionellen Verflechtungsgeschichte von äthiopischer Orthodoxie und europäischem Protestantismus* [VIEG Bd. 262] (Göttingen 2021); with Martin TAMCKE (eds.), *Ethiopian Orthodox Christianity in a Global Context: Entanglements and Disconnections* (Leiden 2022).

Nikolas Pissis studied history and archaeology at the University of Athens and history of Eastern and Southeastern Europe at Ludwig Maximilian University of Munich. In 2017, he received his PhD from the Free University of Berlin with a dissertation on *Russia in the political imagination of the Greek World (1645–1725)*, which was published (in German) in 2020 by Vandenhoeck & Ruprecht. He has taught courses on Modern Greek history at the Free University of Berlin since 2008. From 2012 to 2022, he was research associate at the interdisciplinary collaborative research centre of the same university »Episteme in Motion. Transfer of Knowledge from the Ancient World to the Early Modern Period«. Since October 2022, he has been assistant professor for the history of Eastern and Southeastern Europe at the Department of History, Ionian University.

Alexander Ponomariov grew up in Ukraine, studied Orthodox theology at St Tikhon Orthodox University in Moscow, and received both his MA and PhD from the University of Passau in Germany. His research focuses primarily on Orthodox canon law and the interplay between politics and religion in Russia and Ukraine. He is the author of *The Visible Religion: The Russian Orthodox Church and her Relations with State and Society in Post-Soviet Canon law (1992–2015)* (Frankfurt am Main 2017). He is currently working on a book tackling the theopolitics of Ukrainian autocephaly and its impact on canon law and ecclesiology.

Marian Pătru holds a PhD in historical theology from the Ludwig Maximilian University of Munich. Since 2019 he has been scientific director of the Foundation »Reconciliation in Southeast Europe« in Sibiu, Romania. Recent publications: *Das Ordnungsdenken im christlich-orthodoxen Raum. Nation, Religion und Politik im öffentlichen Diskurs der Rumänisch-Orthodoxen Kirche Siebenbürgens in der Zwischenkriegszeit (1918–1940)* (Berlin 2022); »The ›poporală‹ Sheet Libertatea and the Shaping of the Anti-Semitic and Extreme Right Peasant Mind in Greater Romania (1919–1925)«, in: *Slavonic and East European Review*, vol. 101, No. 1, January (2023), pp. 91–113. He has published extensively on the intellectual history of Orthodox Christianity, dealing with topics such as political theology, theology of religions, and the connections between the Romanian Orthodox Church and the political far right.

Sebastian Rimestad is senior research fellow in the Heisenberg Programme of the German Research Foundation (DFG) at the University of Leipzig. He completed his PhD in 2011 at the University of Erfurt with a thesis on *The Challenges of Modernity to the Orthodox Church in Estonia and Latvia (1917–1940)* (Frankfurt am Main 2012). His research interests are religion and politics, Eastern Orthodoxy, religion in the Baltic States, and religious conversions. His latest publications include *Orthodox Christian Identity in Western Europe: Contesting Religious Authority* (London 2021); with Vasilios N. MAKRIDES (eds.), *The Pan-Orthodox Council of 2016 – A New Era for the Orthodox Church? Interdisciplinary Perspectives* (Berlin 2021); and with Emil B. HILTON SAGGAU et al., *Moderne ortodokse kirker* (Frederiksberg 2021).

Dimitris Stamatopoulos is professor of Balkan and Late Ottoman History at the University of Macedonia, Thessaloniki. He has been a member of the Institute for Advanced Study (Princeton) and a visiting professor at the École des Hautes Études en Sciences Sociales (Paris). He has held Senior Fellowships at Princeton University, the Leibniz Institute of European History (Mainz), at the Freiburg Institute for Advanced Studies, and at the University of California, Berkeley. He is the author of many books and articles on nationalism in the Balkans and the history of the Orthodox Christian populations in the late Ottoman Empire. His books include *The Eastern Question or Balkan Nationalisms: Balkan History Reconsidered* (Göttingen 2018); (ed.), *European Revolutions and the Ottoman Balkans: Nationalism, Violence and Empire in the Long Nineteenth Century* (London 2019); and *Byzantium after the Nation: The Problem of Continuity in Balkan Historiographies* (Budapest 2022).

Kristina Stoeckl has been professor of sociology at LUISS Rome since March 2023. From 2015 to 2023 she worked at the Department of Sociology of the University of Innsbruck and was principal investigator of the European Research Council-funded project *Postsecular Conflicts*. She holds a PhD from the European University Institute (Florence) and has held research and teaching positions at the University of Rome Tor Vergata, the University of Vienna, Central European University, the

Robert Schumann Center for Advanced Studies, and the Institute for Human Sciences/IWM (Vienna). Her research areas are the sociology of religion and social and political theory, Orthodox Christianity, religion-state relations in Russia, and problems of political liberalism and religion. She has published *The Russian Orthodox Church and Human Rights* (London 2014); *Russian Orthodoxy and Secularism* (Leiden 2020); and with Dmitry Uzlaner, *The Moralist International: Russia in the Global Culture Wars* (New York 2022).

Boris A. Todorov holds a PhD in Mediaeval History from the University of California, Los Angeles (2007). His research has focused on memory, hagiography and political discourse among the South Slavs, from the ninth to the fourteenth century. His publications include: »Hagiography as Political Theology: A Mid-Fourteenth-Century Case from Bulgaria«, in: Courtney M. Booker/Hans Hummer/Dana Polanichka (eds.), *Visions of Medieval History in North America and Europe* (Turnhout 2022); »Trnovo«, in: David Wallace (ed.), *Europe: A Literary History, 1348–1418*, vol. 2 (Oxford 2016); and »The Value of Empire: Tenth-Century Bulgaria between Magyars, Pechenegs and Byzantium«, in: *Journal of Medieval History* 36:4 (2010). He is currently the Deputy Head of the Zlatarski International IB World School, Sofia.

Ioannis Zelepos is Associated Professor at the University of Ioannina, Department of History and Archaeology, with *venia docendi* for Southeast European History and Modern Greek Studies from the University of Vienna. His research interests include early modern religious cultures, Enlightenment, identity discourses, nationalism in Southeastern Europe, and modern Greek migration. His publications include »The Historical Background of the Cyprus Problem – just a Conflict of Ethnic Nationalism?«, in: *Austrian Review of International and European law* 19 (2014); »A Comparative View on Confessionalization in Ottoman Orthodoxy: The Publishing Program of the Kollyvades-Movement and Jewish Ladino Musar Literature in the ›long‹ 18th century«, in: Kostas Sarris et al. (eds.), *Confessionalization and/as Knowledge Transfer in Greek-Orthodox Church* (Wiesbaden 2021); »Inter-religious Contact and Interaction in Ottoman Cyprus: Orthodox, Muslims, Catholics, Armenians and Jews in European Travelogues from the 15th to the 18th Century«, in: Julia Chatzipanagioti et al. (eds.), *Textualising the Experience – Digitalising the Text: Cyprus through Travel Literature (15th–18th Centuries)* (Athens 2023).

Sophie Zviadadze is a sociologist and scholar of religious studies. She is an associate professor at Ilia State University in Tbilisi, Georgia, where she holds the chair of the Master's programme in religious studies. Her main research interests are secularism, politics and religion, lived religion, religion and collective memory, and religious transformation, particularly in the post-Soviet South Caucasus. Her latest publications include: »The Many Faces of Islam in Post-Soviet Georgia – Faith, Identity, and Politics«, in: Egdūnas Račius/Galina M. Yemelianova (eds.), *Muslims of Post-Communist Eurasia* (London 2022), pp. 246–266; »Religion in the South Caucasus: Tradition, Ambiguity, and Transformation – Editorial«, in: *Journal of Religion in Europe* 14:3-4 (2021), pp. 1–17; »Church as a Homeland and Home as a Place of Worship – Transformation of Religiosity among Georgian Migrants in Paris«, in: Jayeel Serrano Cornelio et al. (eds.), *Routledge International Handbook of Religion in Global Society* (London 2021), pp. 292–302.

Regula M. Zwahlen has been Scientific Director of the Sergii Bulgakov Research Center at the Department of Faith and Religious Studies and Philosophy, University of Fribourg, Switzerland, since 2011. As well as co-editing the German edition of the Russian theologian Sergii Bulgakov's works, her research interests include the intellectual history of the Russian and Soviet Empires, concepts of personality, human rights discourses, and political theology. Her most recent publications include »Sergii Bulgakov's Reinvention of Theocracy for a Democratic Age«, in: *Journal of Orthodox Christian Studies* 3:2 (2020), pp. 175–194; »Sergei Bulgakov's Intellectual Journey (1900–1922)«, in: *Oxford Handbook of Russian Religious Thought* (Oxford 2020), pp. 277–292; »Freedom«, in: *The Edinburgh Critical History of Nineteenth-Century Christian Theology* (Edinburgh 2018), pp. 85–104. In addition, she co-edits the journal *Religion & Gesellschaft in Ost und West*.

Evert van der Zweerde has been professor of Social and Political Philosophy at the Faculty of Philosophy, Theology and Religious Studies at Radboud University, Nijmegen, since 2010. Among his research interests are the philosophical theory of democracy, civil society, ideology, Soviet philosophy, Orthodox Christianity, and Russian philosophy. Recent publications include: Alfons Brüning/Evert van der Zweerde (eds.), *Orthodox Christianity and Human Rights* (Leuven 2012); Bas Leijssenaar/Judith Martens/Evert van der Zweerde (eds.), *Futures of Democracy* (Eindhoven 2014); Alexander Agadjanian/Ansgar Jödicke/Evert van der Zweerde (eds.), *Religion, Nation and Democracy in the South Caucasus* (London 2015); Взгляд со стороны на историю русской и советской философии; сборник статей (St Petersburg 2017) (collected articles in Russian translation); Η φιλοσοφία στη Ρωσία απο τον Σολοβιόφ στην Περεστρόικα και μετά (Thessaloniki 2022) (collected articles in Greek translation); and *Russian Political Philosophy: Anarchy, Authority, Autocracy* (Edinburgh 2022).